Charles Seale-Hayne Library

University of Plymouth

(01752) 588 588

LibraryandITenquiries@plymouth.ac.uk

The Science of Reason

This volume is a state-of-the-art survey of the psychology of reasoning, based around, and in tribute to, one of the field's most eminent figures: Jonathan St B. T. Evans.

In this collection of cutting edge research, Evans' collaborators and colleagues review a wide range of important and developing areas of inquiry. These include biases in thinking, probabilistic and causal reasoning, people's use of "if" sentences in arguments, the dual-process theory of thought, and the nature of human rationality. These foundational issues are examined from various angles and finally integrated in a concluding panoramic chapter written by Evans himself.

The nineteen chapters, all written by leading international researchers, combine state-of-the-art research with investigation into the most fundamental questions surrounding human mental life, such as:

- What is the architecture of the human mind?
- Are humans rational, and what is the nature of this rationality?
- How do we think hypothetically?

The Science of Reason offers a unique combination of breadth, depth and integrative vision, making it an indispensable resource for researchers and students of human reason.

Ken Manktelow is Professor of Psychology at the University of Wolverhampton. He was an undergraduate at Plymouth when Jonathan Evans joined the Psychology department, and became Evans' first research student. Part of his PhD was published in a paper with Evans in 1979. His main interests are in the psychology of deontic reasoning and rationality, and his work is reported in several books (two with David Over) and research papers.

David Over is a Professor of Psychology at Durham University. He has collaborated with Jonathan Evans, publishing numerous articles and two books with him, on dual-process theory and the new, probabilistic paradigm in the psychology of reasoning.

Shira Elqayam is a senior lecturer in psychology at De Montfort University. She was a postdoctoral fellow at the University of Plymouth where Jonathan Evans was her supervisor. Since then she has collaborated with Evans on several topics, as well as with David Over. Her main interests are in the psychology of disjunctive reasoning, meta-deduction, and rationality.

The Science of Reason

A Festschrift for Jonathan St B. T. Evans

**Edited by Ken Manktelow, David Over,
and Shira Elqayam**

Psychology Press
Taylor & Francis Group
HOVE AND NEW YORK

First published 2011
by Psychology Press
27 Church Road, Hove, East Sussex BN3 2FA

Simultaneously published in the USA and Canada
by Psychology Press
270 Madison Avenue, New York, NY 10016

*Psychology Press is an imprint of the Taylor & Francis Group, an
Informa business*

Copyright © 2011 Psychology Press

Typeset in Times by RefineCatch Limited, Bungay, Suffolk
Printed and bound in Great Britain by
TJ International Ltd, Padstow, Cornwall
Cover design by Andrew Ward

British Library Cataloguing in Publication Data
A catalogue record for this book is available from the British Library

Library of Congress Cataloging-in-Publication Data
  The science of reason : a Festschrift for Jonathan St. B. T. Evans /
    edited by Ken Manktelow, David Over, and Shira Elqayam.
    p. cm.
  Includes bibliographical references and index.
  1. Reasoning (Psychology).   2. Thought and thinking.   3. Problem
    solving.   I. Evans, Jonathan St. B. T., 1948–.   II. Manktelow,
    K. I., 1952–.   III. Over, D. E., 1946–.   IV. Elqayam, Shira.
  BF442.S25 2010
  153.4′3–dc22
                                                            2010002556

ISBN: 978-1-84872-015-2 (hbk)

Contents

Figures

Tables

Contributors

Linden J. Ball is at the Department of Psychology, Lancaster University, Lancaster, UK. Email: l.ball@lancaster.ac.uk

Pierre Barrouillet is at the Faculty of Psychology and Educational Sciences, Geneva University, Geneva, Switzerland. Email: Pierre.Barrouillet@pse.unige.ch

Nick Chater is at the Department of Psychology, University College London, London, UK. Email: n.chater@ucl.ac.uk

Aimée Crisp is at the Department of Psychology, Durham University, Durham, UK. Email: a.k.crisp@durham.ac.uk

Shira Elqayam is at the School of Applied Social Sciences, De Montfort University, Leicester, UK. Email: selqayam@dmu.ac.uk

Jonathan St B. T. Evans is at the School of Psychology, University of Plymouth, Plymouth, UK. Email: j.evans@plymouth.ac.uk

Aidan Feeney is at the Department of Applied Psychology, University of Durham, Stockton-on-Tees, UK. Email: aidan.feeney@durham.ac.uk

Katrin Fischer is at the School of Applied Psychology, University of Applied Sciences Northwestern Switzerland, Osten, Switzerland. Email: Katrin.Fischer@fhnw.ch

Keith Frankish is at the Department of Philosophy, Open University, Milton Keynes, UK. Email: k.frankish@open.ac.uk

Caroline Gauffroy is at the Faculty of Psychology and Educational Sciences, Geneva University, Geneva, Switzerland. Email: Caroline.Gauffroy@unige.ch

Sonja Geiger is at the School of Psychology, University of Western Australia, Crawley, Australia. Email: geiger@cyllene.uwa.edu.au

Vittorio Girotto is at the Faculty of Arts and Design, University Iuav of Venice, Venice, Italy. Email: vgirotto@iuav.it

Michel Gonzalez is at the Laboratory of Cognitive Psychology, CNRS, University of Provence, Marseilles, France. Email: Michel.gonzalez@univ-provence.fr

David W. Green is at the Department of Psychology, University College London, London, UK. Email: d.w.green@ucl.ac.uk

Richard A. Griggs is at the Department of Psychology, University of Florida, Gainesville FL, USA. Email: rgriggs@ufl.edu

Simon J. Handley is at the School of Psychology, University of Plymouth, Plymouth, UK. Email: s.handley@plymouth.ac.uk

Philip N. Johnson-Laird is at the Department of Psychology, Princeton University, Princeton NJ, USA. Email: phil@princeton.edu

Maria Kasmirli Department of Philosophy, University of Sheffield, Sheffield, UK Email: m.kasmirli@sheffield.ac.uk

Gernot D. Kleiter is at the Faculty of Psychology, University of Salzburg, Salzburg, Austria. Email: gernot.kleiter@sbg.ac.at

Cynthia S. Koenig is at the Department of Psychology, St Mary's College of Maryland, St Mary's City MD, USA. Email: cskoenig@smcm.edu

Paolo Legrenzi is at the Faculty of Arts and Design of the University Iuav of Venice, Venice, Italy. Email: plegrenzi@iuav.it

Ken Manktelow is at the Department of Psychology, University of Wolverhampton, UK. Email: k.i.manktelow@wlv.ac.uk

Nicola J. Morley is at Unilever Research & Development Port Sunlight, Wirral, Merseyside, UK. Email: Nicki.Morley@unilever.com

Helen Neilens is at the Department of Psychology, University of Plymouth, Plymouth, UK. Email: h.neilens@plymouth.ac.uk

Stephen E. Newstead is at the School of Psychology, University of Plymouth, Plymouth, UK. Email: s.newstead@plymouth.ac.uk

Mike Oaksford is at the Department of Psychology, Birkbeck College, University of London, London, UK. Email: m.oaksford@bbk.ac.uk

Klaus Oberauer is at the Department of Experimental Psychology, University of Bristol, Bristol, UK. Email: k.oberauer@bristol.ac.uk

David Over is at the Department of Psychology, University of Durham, Durham, UK. Email: david.over@durham.ac.uk

Niki Pfeifer is at the Faculty of Psychology, University of Salzburg, Salzburg, Austria. Email: niki.pfeifer@sbg.ac.at

Guy Politzer is at CNRS/University of Paris, Paris, France. Email: politzer@univ-paris8.fr

Keith E. Stanovich is at the Department of Human Development and Applied Psychology, University of Toronto, Toronto, Canada. Email: kstanovich:oise.utoronto.ca

Valerie A. Thompson is at the Department of Psychology, University of Saskatchewan, Saskatoon, Canada. Email: valerie.thompson@usask.ca

Maggie E. Toplak is at the Department of Psychology, York University, Toronto, Canada. Email: mtoplak@yorku.ca

Richard F. West is at the School of Psychology, James Madison University, Harrisonburg VA, USA. Email: westrf@jmu.edu

1 Paradigms shift

Jonathan Evans and the science of reason

Ken Manktelow

University of Wolverhampton

David Over

University of Durham

Shira Elqayam

De Montfort University

This book has been compiled as a tribute to one of the most influential figures in the psychology of human reasoning: **Jonathan St B. T. Evans**. It also happens to be an apposite moment to compile this volume, since the scientific study of reasoning has undergone a theoretical and methodological revolution in recent times. Even a decade ago, a volume such as this would have looked quite different. The developments in the field are paralleled by those in Jonathan's own intellectual history. This is, of course, no accident: there has been a deep mutual influence between the Evans view of reasoning and the broader field. In this opening chapter, we shall offer an outline of the wider paradigm shift and also of Jonathan's scientific biography. This will enable us to situate the 18 chapters contributed by researchers who have all worked either with Jonathan or in areas that he has been closely associated with or, in some cases, initiated.

The systematic study of human reasoning began with the classical philosophers (Kneale & Kneale, 1962). Their interests were primarily normative. They wanted to know how people ought to reason, and laid the foundation for normative systems of logic. They did sometimes try to make empirical points about people's actual reasoning, and as well as so much else, we owe to them the first studies of common biases and fallacies. The first scientific psychologists of reasoning took from the classical philosophers what we can call the *binary* or *deductive paradigm*. In this paradigm, human reasoning is binary and dichotomous. Propositions used in reasoning are either true or false and either consistent or inconsistent with each other. An inference has a conclusion that either does or does not follow necessarily and deductively, from premises assumed to be true. No account is taken in the binary paradigm of the fact that premises can be believed with varying degrees of confidence.

If the conclusion follows necessarily, the inference is valid; if the conclusion does not follow necessarily, the inference is invalid and a fallacy. Until quite recently, almost all research in the psychology of reasoning was in this old paradigm (the mental models theory of Johnson-Laird & Byrne, 1991, is a good example.)

There is, however, a *new paradigm* in the psychology of reasoning, which can be described in a number of ways. In terms of *what* it is that is being computed – the computational-level analysis – the new paradigm can be described as the *decision-theoretic, epistemic, probabilistic,* or *Bayesian paradigm*. In this sense it is more general than the old binary paradigm and encompasses it as a special case, when propositions are either completely accepted, or assumed, or completely rejected. The new paradigm is much more general in being about all degrees of subjective probability and utility. People have varying degrees of confidence in the propositions that they use in reasoning, which is aimed at goals desired to a greater or lesser extent. These subjective degrees of belief affect the different degrees of confidence that people have in their conclusions. Some inferences that were dismissed as fallacies in the binary paradigm can be seen as well justified probabilistic inferences in the new paradigm. In this paradigm, people make inferences primarily from their actual beliefs, held with more or less confidence, and not from premises they simply assume to be true. Jonathan's recent book *Hypothetical Thinking* (Evans, 2007) shows this aspect of the new paradigm in action. See Oaksford and Chater (2007, 2009) for another leading version of the new paradigm, and also Over (2009), and Chater and Oaksford (2009).

Jonathan Evans has been a psychologist of reasoning for four decades and has recently been a driving force behind the development of the new decision-theoretic, probabilistic paradigm. He has made many contributions to both the older paradigm and the more general newer paradigm. He has, for example, published more than fifty papers on the conditional "if – then" and conditional reasoning. The study of conditionals is yet another subject that goes back to classical philosophers, but Jonathan became dissatisfied with the treatment of conditionals in the old paradigm. He and his collaborator **David Over** (names in bold are those who have contributed to the present volume) argued for a new view that would take proper account of subjective probability (Evans & Over, 2004; Over & Evans, 2003). Theories of conditionals have technical aspects that we will discuss briefly below in a technical afterword to this introduction.

Jonathan has long taken an interest in decision making as well as reasoning and the biases and fallacies that people are prone to in both activities (Evans, 1989). More recently, he has started to combine these interests in the development of the new paradigm within a dual-process account of the mind, much of it also in collaboration with David Over, from Evans and Over (1996) and Evans and Over (2004), to Evans (2007).

The growing emphasis on dual processing and the centralization of dual-process theories can be seen as the algorithmic-level aspect of the new paradigm – that is, the underlying psychological processes it is committed to. In Jonathan's approach, normative analyses have always taken second seat to psychological hypotheses about actual processes. In his framework, there are two systems or processes in the mind, which he calls System 1 and System 2 or Type 1 and Type 2. System 1 is "lower" level, rapid, automatic, of high capacity, and independent of working memory. System 2 is "higher" level, slow, deliberate, of more limited capacity, and "conscious" in the sense of being dependent on working memory. It works by hypothetical thinking: mental simulation of epistemic possibilities. People can employ System 2 in explicit, step-by-step reasoning in working memory, but many of the relevant beliefs they use as premises will be supplied by System 1. The degrees of confidence with which beliefs are held can be the result of rapid and automatic judgement in System 1, as when we think we see a bear in the bushes, or the result of a System 2 inference, as when we go on to use our scientific knowledge and explicitly infer that the "bear" is probably an optical illusion. This approach has inspired other major theoretical contributions to the new paradigm that emphasize dual processing, most notably that of **Keith Stanovich** and **Richard West** (e.g., Stanovich, 1999, 2009; Stanovich & West, 2000).

Jonathan's angle on cognitive architecture, reflected in the way he combines his dual-process theory with the probabilistic aspect of the new paradigm, is one way in which his approach differs from others, such as that of Oaksford and Chater (2007) on the one hand, and Stanovich and West on the other. Jonathan's combination of both aspects of the new paradigm, dual-process theory with the probabilistic approach, raises many questions that are explored and debated in the chapters that follow.

Jonathan Evans: An outline biography and an outline of this book

The earliest reference we can find to what would now be recognized as an experiment on reasoning is to one by Störring in 1908 on the classical topic of syllogisms. **Guy Politzer** (2004) discusses this study and tells us more about syllogistic reasoning, in both its formal and less formal guises, in his chapter here (Chapter 2); as we shall see, syllogistic reasoning is an area where Jonathan occupies a crucial role in research. Störring's paper did not exactly open the floodgates, however. There were intermittent appearances of studies, almost always on Aristotelian syllogisms, over the next half century (the paper by Wilkins, 1928, is still widely cited). One has to remember that for much of this period, psychology was subject to the behaviourist hegemony, and that the study of all mental processes was severely hampered. The grip of behaviourism started to slacken in the 1960s: the cognitive revolution was taking its first steps. That, not entirely coincidentally, was the period where we can find the beginnings of the modern science of reason.

For us, its true begetter was Peter Wason, who set in train a series of ground-breaking studies at University College London (UCL), starting around the year 1960. He had the Midas touch when it came to devising experimental paradigms, having produced the verification task, the 2 4 6 task, the THOG problem and, of course, the selection task. He was helped by a group of extraordinarily talented people who converged on UCL in the 1960s. Many went on to become eminent in the field, and several are in this book. One of them was Jonathan Evans.

As we hinted above, Jonathan's intellectual biography reads like a brief history of the whole domain, something that can be readily appreciated from his chapter in the current volume. One of the striking aspects of his work is its extraordinary versatility, from fine-tuned, rigorous experimental research to broad-brush synthesis and meta-theoretical analysis. Like Wason, Jonathan introduced and refined experimental paradigms, as we shall see with the negations paradigm and belief bias. He is also an educator, having to his name two advanced textbooks on reasoning, Evans (1982) and Evans, Newstead and Byrne (1993), and a book on research strategy (Evans, 2005). Perhaps most importantly, however, Jonathan has led theoretical and meta-theoretical work in several areas: dual processing, rationality, conditionals, and the intersection of reasoning with judgement and decision making. We can trace the development of these ideas through the time course of his work.

Jonathan went to UCL as an undergraduate psychology student in 1966. This, of course, was the year of the first published account of the Wason selection task (Wason, 1966). He graduated in 1969 with first class honours, and began his PhD under Wason's supervision (Wason was assisted by **Phil Johnson-Laird**) that same year. His PhD was awarded in 1972. Its subject matter reflected Wason's own prior interests, in that it was concerned with the effects of syntactic variables, especially negation, on human inference. Wason (1972) gives an account of his own work in this area, and this year turned out to be something of an *annus mirabilis* for the science of reason. Wason and Johnson-Laird (1972) published their classic book, the first book on the psychology of reasoning in the modern era. It was the year of Jonathan's twenty-fourth birthday and his first three published papers on reasoning, and this work is mentioned by Wason and Johnson-Laird. All these papers were on conditionals and two of them concerned a statistical tendency, matching bias, which opened the door to much of his later theorizing and experimentation. It remains a topic of interest today, as you can see in Chapter 9 by **Simon Handley** and colleagues, which appears in a section devoted to conditionals (see below). The third addresses a theoretical problem, interpretation, which was later to feed into another major theme of Jonathan's work, human rationality.

However, even before that, in 1971, he had published his first paper of all: an account of a statistical software program for transforming data so that they could be subjected to parametric statistical techniques. This was remarkable in the pre-personal computer age: in those days, computers were the size of houses, attended by a cabal of white-coated drones, in (usually) the only air-conditioned rooms in the building. This paper was itself a forerunner of a continuing interest: Jonathan has published a large number of articles in the computing press, and is a skilled programmer in a number of different languages. In 1971, programming meant hours hunched over a keyboard, typing thousands of lines of code into a machine that punched holes into hundreds of cards the size of airline tickets. One space or symbol wrong and the program failed.

As we mentioned, several of Jonathan's colleagues from his UCL days are present in this volume. Phil Johnson-Laird contributes Chapter 7 in the conditionals section in which he pits the claims of his theory of mental models against one of its most serious rivals, the suppositional theory developed by Jonathan in collaboration with Over and Handley (Evans & Over, 2004; Evans, Handley, & Over, 2003; Over, Hadjichristidis, Evans, Handley, & Sloman, 2007). **David Green** presents a review of his work on reasoning as argumentation (Chapter 4), in which he offers an extension of Jonathan's dual-process theory, of which more shortly. Reasoning as argumentation has also figured in Jonathan's recent research (see Thompson, Evans, & Handley, 2005).

Following his doctoral work, Jonathan spent 3 years at what is now part of London Metropolitan University, before, in 1974, making the move to Plymouth, which has been his academic home ever since, and where he retains a position as an emeritus professor. This was in the very early days of the psychology department there: its degree programme was starting only its second year. One of those first undergraduate students was one of the editors of this book, **Ken Manktelow**, who remembers only dimly Jonathan's course on mathematical psychology, but recalls very clearly the impression made by a lecturer who used his own papers as teaching materials. A member of the academic staff, having been appointed the year before, was **Steve Newstead**, and the two began to work together, publishing their first joint paper in 1977. They edited a festschrift for Wason (Newstead & Evans, 1995) and wrote, with Ruth Byrne, their bestselling textbook (Evans et al., 1993). Newstead appears as the co-author of two chapters here. In the first (Chapter 9), by Handley, Newstead and **Helen Neilens** (Handley was appointed lecturer at Plymouth in the early 1990s; Neilens was Simon and Steve's PhD student), the authors return to that earliest empirical pattern reported in 1972: matching bias, and its appearance in the Wason selection task (Evans & Lynch, 1973). They depart somewhat from Jonathan's original (but not current) take on this phenomenon, which was that selection task responses were entirely determined by relevance cues: they contend that real reasoning is involved after all.

In his second contribution (Chapter 15), Newstead is a co-author with **Valerie Thompson** and **Nicki Morley**. Thompson has been a regular visiting scholar at Plymouth, having spent sabbaticals there, while Morley, as Nicki Lambell, was Jonathan's PhD student in the 1990s. In their chapter, they address the subject matter of her thesis, belief bias in syllogistic reasoning. Jonathan can be credited with reopening this area of research with his now classic paper (Evans, Barston, & Pollard, 1983), in which the authors put into place, for the first time, the necessary methodological controls, found the belief by logic interaction which is the source of all current theorizing about belief bias, and advanced possible explanations which are still being debated today. Thompson et al. in their chapter pick up on the central role of belief bias in dual-process theorizing, and raise questions for current versions of the theory.

Both Steve and Jonathan spent sabbatical periods at the University of Florida, hosted by **Richard Griggs**, during this early Plymouth period. Also during this period, in 1976, Manktelow joined Jonathan's research team as a PhD student, at the same time as Paul Pollard who, with another Evans PhD student, Julie Allen (Barston), was the co-author of the classic belief-bias paper just cited. Also joining the research group in the 1970s was Phil Brooks. He has, like all these other former students, published significant papers with Jonathan, but has the unique distinction of also having published with Wason: theirs was the first full research paper on Wason's devilish THOG problem (Wason & Brooks, 1979). Griggs has returned to that problem in Chapter 5 (co-authored by **Cynthia Koenig**) here; they refer in their account, as do the majority of our contributors, to the dual-process theory.

Linden Ball and **Aidan Feeney** also joined Jonathan's band of successful PhDs, in the 1980s and 1990s respectively. Ball's chapter (Chapter 14) forms a pair with that of Thompson et al., in that he also concerns himself with belief bias and the dual-process theory and, like them, puts response time analysis centre stage. Chronometric measurement featured in the early paper by Evans and Newstead (1977), and Ball follows their lead in using these data to unpack the components of reasoning. His results, like those of Thompson et al., raise important questions about, and puncture some of the assumptions of, dual-process theory. Feeney, writing with **Aimée Crisp** (Chapter 12), ventures into an area unexplored by Jonathan himself, for once: the conjunction fallacy, in its causal guise. Once again, they use dual-process ideas in explaining their results, particularly in the form that appears in Jonathan's recent book on hypothetical thinking (Evans, 2007).

All this talk about dual processes takes us back to those mid-1970s days, and to the only two papers that Evans and Wason ever wrote together (Evans & Wason, 1976; Wason & Evans, 1975). These pioneered the study of dual processes in reasoning – indeed, they introduced the term – in work on the selection task, employing the method of permuting negative components in the target conditional (the "negations paradigm"), which Jonathan had invented during his doctoral work. Jonathan has written relatively few papers that feature the selection task, but dual-process theorizing and research have figured in his work ever since, and in fact are now his main interest. This is reflected in the proportion of contributions to this book: the dual-process section is the largest, and even two of the chapters on conditionals have dual-process concerns. The dual-process section opens with a chapter by **Paolo Legrenzi** (Chapter 11). Legrenzi is the final UCL associate to appear here: he spent some time there around the year 1970, when Jonathan was a PhD student. Legrenzi reaches back to dual-process studies of the selection task, and further still: he has found that Jerome Bruner, in 1960, was addressing dual-process concerns, in the very early days of cognitive psychology. He reaches out more widely too, into the pedagogy of reasoning, a long-standing interest of his, and invokes THOG along the way.

A sometimes overlooked feature of Jonathan's work in the 1970s was the appearance of a paper on statistical judgement (Evans & Dusoir, 1977). This foretold another area in which he has been active in subsequent years, and also reflects, as he relates in his own chapter, an awareness of the issues raised by Kahneman and Tversky's "heuristics and biases" programme of research into probability judgement and, later, decision making. Indeed, the original form of the Evans dual-process theory of reasoning (Evans, 1984) was couched in the terms *heuristic–analytic* (see Evans, 2006 for a revision of this approach), and its components bear some resemblance to those in Kahneman and Tversky's (1979) prospect theory: framing (heuristic) and valuation (analytic). This interest in probabilistic thinking is represented here not only by Feeney and Crisp's Chapter 12 (see above; and that of Stanovich et al., see below), but also in Chapter 3 by one of Legrenzi's long-standing colleagues, **Vittorio Girotto**, written with **Michel Gonzalez**. They look directly at the ways in which people think about probability and expectation, and how this feeds into decision processes.

A similar distinction, between initial representation and the fleshing-out process required for skilled deduction, was later introduced in Johnson-Laird's mental model theory, as **Pierre Barrouillet** and **Caroline Gauffroy** point out in Chapter 10, and as Johnson-Laird himself acknowledges in Chapter 7. During the 1990s Jonathan attempted, as he narrates in his chapter, to reconcile his earlier dual-process theorizing with the mental model theory. However, Jonathan's later thinking has moved away again from this framework, as you can see in his chapter and in the others in the dual-process section. His early book chapter on statistical inference with Pollard (Pollard & Evans, 1983), incidentally, introduces a frequentist interpretation of Kahneman and Tversky's tasks years before it became the main arm of the alternative approach of cognitive–ecological theorists such as Gigerenzer (see Gigerenzer, Todd, & the ABC Group, 1999).

Jonathan was appointed to a professorship at Plymouth in 1985. In 1988, he played a leading role in setting up the first International Conference on Thinking, held at the University of Aberdeen, Scotland. It has taken place every Olympic year ever since, most recently in Venice, Italy, and Jonathan has often been on its organizing committee. The second was held at Plymouth, and featured a symposium convened by Evans and Newstead in honour of, and attended by, Peter Wason (from which derived the festschrift mentioned earlier). The "Wason symposium" was an extraordinary event that will live long in the memories of all who were present. The earlier Aberdeen conference had one unforeseen but highly significant byproduct: it was where Manktelow introduced Jonathan to the second of this book's editors, David Over. Shortly thereafter, at Johnson-Laird's instigation, the three produced a joint paper (Evans, Over, & Manktelow, 1993) and then there followed a series of major Evans–Over publications, among them two books (Evans & Over 1996, 2004). The first of these is an influential dual-process account of rationality and reasoning. The second sets out in detail their suppositional theory of conditionals, a major alternative to the hitherto dominant mental models account (Johnson-Laird & Byrne, 1991, 2002).

The suppositional theory is one of Jonathan's major current research streams, along with further developments of the dual-process theory. It is at heart both an epistemic theory, emphasizing the role of supposition and belief, and a probabilistic theory, in that one of its main implications is that belief in a conditional assertion is equivalent to the conditional probability of the "then" clause given the supposition of the "if" clause. As a probabilistic theory, it has been influenced by the approach to conditionals pioneered by **Mike Oaksford** and **Nick Chater**, for instance in their radical reappraisal of the Wason selection task (Oaksford & Chater, 1994). In Chapter 16, Oaksford and Chater address for the first time the relation between their Bayesian framework and dual processes, and aspects of the suppositional theory are also addressed there. In Chapter 8 **Niki Pfeifer** and **Gernot Kleiter** concentrate on an issue that has occupied Jonathan and his suppositional colleagues, Over and Handley: the psychological status of the paradoxes of the material conditional (see "Technical afterword on conditionals" below). These are truly paradoxical in some applications of mental models theory (see Johnson-Laird's chapter), but are circumvented by suppositional theory. Pfeifer and Kleiter present the first experimental data on the paradoxes. They offer an analysis in terms of probability logic. Both Oaksford and Chater and Pfeifer and Kleiter confront the question of appropriate norms for the dual processes.

Klaus Oberauer, **Sonia Geiger**, and **Katrin Fischer** in Chapter 6 also address the suppositional theory, and also take a probabilistic approach; Oberauer was one of the first researchers, along with Jonathan and his colleagues, to conduct empirical tests of the probability of the conditional (e.g., Oberauer & Wilhelm, 2003). Oberauer et al. report experiments using a novel technique, and these raise questions about both the suppositional theory and the mental model theory. The tension between these approaches is a feature of a number of the contributions here, but it is a healthy tension, as the chapter by Barrouillet and Gauffroy sets out most clearly. They consider conditionals and the dual process, suppositional and mental model theories, and argue, using developmental data, that the differences between them may be more apparent than real. They put forward a new integrative account in support of their case.

Many of the people whose names appear in this text have attended the workshops on reasoning that Jonathan has organized at Plymouth in recent years, and in some cases, as we have seen, this has led to more enduring scientific collaborations. **Shira Elqayam**, the third of this volume's editors, came to Plymouth in 2004 to work with Jonathan as a postdoctoral researcher. Jonathan introduced her to David Over at the 5th International Conference on Thinking, at Leuven, Belgium, in 2004, and she was soon collaborating with both of them, resulting in several joint publications. In Chapter 18 of this volume, she considers, as many contributors do, the question of norms for rational thinking, and sets out her new relativist view, extending work she has done with Jonathan. Keith Stanovich, Rich West, previous visitors to Plymouth, and **Maggie Toplak** (Chapter 17) also look closely at the normative question, following Stanovich's detailed consideration of it in a book (Stanovich, 1999), which was both greatly influenced by Jonathan's thinking, as they relate in their chapter, and has greatly influenced Jonathan's, as he has often acknowledged. They consider belief bias and heuristics from a dual-process point of view and ground debates about them firmly in data on individual differences, leading to a reconsideration of the nature of the processes, especially System 2.

Jonathan's most recent book was published in 2009, and is an edited volume deriving from the conference he convened in 2006, called *In Two Minds* (itself the title of a famous paper summarizing the Evans dual-process theory: Evans, 2003). The co-convener of the conference, and co-editor of the book, was **Keith Frankish**. Here in Chapter 13, along with **Maria Kasmirli**, Frankish considers an aspect of thinking that, as they point out, has not loomed large in the reasoning literature, scalar implicature, and they do so from a dual-process perspective. They raise an issue that is also addressed by Stanovich et al., and is the subject of Jonathan's current research: the need to supplement dual-process theory with a "Type 3" control process.

So here we are, at the present day, and Jonathan's books total is now in double figures, while his journal article total passed the hundred mark some years ago. It is therefore not surprising that Jonathan has also been much involved in editorial activity. He has served on the board or as an associate editor of several of the leading international journals in psychology, and in 1995 became the founder and editor-in-chief of the only dedicated journal in the field, *Thinking and Reasoning*. He has occupied the post ever since. This is not only a testament to Jonathan's stamina, but also represents in itself a major contribution to the science of reason. Indeed, this contribution extends even further: he has distilled his experience of writing, reviewing, and editing research papers, supervising PhD students and devising and conducting experiments into an engaging how-to book (Evans, 2005). With the present volume, his contribution to the progress of the science of reason as well as its practice should now be perfectly clear. All three of us owe him a lot, and we are proud to have been able to put this tribute together. We thank everyone who has contributed, and most of all, we thank Jonathan himself.

Technical afterword on conditionals

We will here make some brief points about conditionals in the old and new paradigms, with the object of giving the background to some of the more technical debates in the book, especially in Part II: If. In the older, binary paradigm, a natural language indicative conditional, "if p then q", was held to be equivalent to the material conditional of elementary logic, which is itself equivalent to "not-p or q" (Johnson-Laird & Byrne, 1991, pp. 73–75). One reason the old paradigm is called "binary" is its limitation to truth (T) and falsity (F), rather than subjective probabilities, in truth tables. Here is the truth table for the material conditional:

p	q	if p then q
T	T	T
T	F	F
F	T	T
F	F	T

We can use a *truth table task* to see how far people conform to the above table in their evaluations of conditionals (Evans & Over, 2004, pp. 34–44). Consider a pack of cards with a letter written on the left and a number on the right and a conditional about a card drawn from this pack, "If there is a B written on the left then there is a 5 written on the right." By the above table, participants who are shown a card with a B on the left and a 5 on the right, a "B & 5" card, should say the conditional is "true". If they see a card with a B on the left and not a five on the right, like a "B & 9" card, they should say the conditional is "false". Finally, if they are presented with any card not having a B on it, like a "D & 5" or a "D & 7" card, they should again say the conditional is "true".

Actual experiments of the type we have just described reveal that people do not comply with the above material conditional table. They agree with the first two lines, but if they are shown a card without a B on it, they tend to judge the card "irrelevant" (I) to deciding whether "if p then q" is T or F. Most produce what is usually called the "defective" truth table (Wason, 1966):

p	q	if p then q
T	T	T
T	F	F
F	T	I
F	F	I

This "defective" pattern of response is one prima facie problem for the binary paradigm. Others are the "paradoxes" of holding that the natural language indicative conditional is the material conditional. Since the material conditional is equivalent to "not-p or q", it validly follows from "not-p" and "q". However, we would not have confidence in a natural language conditional merely because we believed "not-p" or believed "q". For example, we believe that Obama has not given up smoking since becoming President, but we would not infer from that, if he has given up smoking, then he has damaged his health. Another such paradox, much less discussed by psychologists, is that "p & not-q" and so p, validly follows from the negation or denial of a material conditional. The denial of "not-p or q" is equivalent to the assertion of "p & not-q". But although we would deny that, if Obama has given up smoking, then he has damaged his health, we would not infer from that that Obama has given up smoking. That would be absurd, when we believe that he has not done so.

The new probabilistic paradigm has prima facie solutions to the problems we have listed, but to explain what these are, we must first explain more about it. This paradigm looks beyond truth and falsity to people's subjective probability judgements. In particular, it takes account of the fact that people have more or less confidence in natural language conditionals, and these degrees of belief affect their conditional reasoning. In Jonathan's influential version of the new paradigm, people evaluate a conditional "if p then q" with the *Ramsey test* (Ramsey, 1931/1990; Evans & Over, 2004; Over & Evans, 2003), which is very similar to the simulation heuristic (Kahneman & Tversky, 1982; Evans, 2007). They suppose, or simulate, p, and then assess to what extent q follows from p. The result should be that they judge the probability of the conditional, P(if p then q), to be the conditional probability of q given p, P(q|p). There is considerable experimental evidence (see Evans, 2007, for a review) in support of the *conditional probability hypothesis* that people judge P(if p then q) to be P(q|p).

It is important to be quite precise about this hypothesis. Suppose we say, "If p then our confidence in q is high"; this statement contains what logicians call a scope ambiguity. The use of "confidence" in it could have narrow scope, making it "If p then (our confidence in q is high)", or the use could have wide scope, meaning "Our confidence is high that (if p then q)". It is the wide scope reading that is the same as the conditional probability in people's judgements, by the conditional probability hypothesis. The point should be made perfectly clear by considering an instance of the conditional, "if p then p". We would be claiming to be omniscient if we said that "If p then (our confidence in p is absolutely high)" for arbitrary p. But we would simply be expressing the trivial conviction that P(p|p) = 1 if we said, "Our confidence is absolutely high that (if p then p)". Using the Ramsey test, our confidence has to be wide, covering both p and q, to assess any evidential relation between p and q. To claim that the narrow scope reading is the conditional probability is to commit what logicians call the *modal fallacy* (Bradley & Swartz, 1979; Over et al., 2007).

Supporters of the conditional probability hypothesis should be dissatisfied with the term "defective" for the above truth table describing people's judgements about "if p then q". There is nothing wrong with these judgements given the hypothesis. It would be better, and more appropriate, to use the phrase the *de Finetti table*, after de Finetti (1937/1964), who proposed a table like it for normative reasons. Both de Finetti and Ramsey compared natural language indicative conditionals to conditional bets, "if p then I bet you q", which are void when "not-p" holds. Based on this comparison, a prediction is that people would also tend to lose interest in the indicative "if p then q" as they became more confident that "not-p" holds, although they might assert the counterfactual, "if p were the case then q would be". It is significant that the two founders of subjective probability theory thought of indicative conditionals as similar to conditional bets and associated both with conditional probability (see Oberauer & Wilhelm, 2003, and Politzer, Over, & Baratgin, 2010, on conditional bets and indicative conditionals).

Consider a truth table task and a new paradigm explanation of it. Assume people are presented with a "B & 5" card and asked to make a judgement about the indicative, "If there is a B written on the left then there is a 5 written on the right" (as applied to that card and not the whole pack – see Evans et al., 2003). They can see the card and that "B & 5" clearly holds, causing them to express the judgement with confidence that the conditional is "true". Going on in the table, they will be confident that the conditional is "false" or "not true" if they see a "B & 9" card. But in contrast with those two cases, they will be unable to make a judgement, about truth or probable truth, if they are simply presented with a "not-B" card, say a "D & 5" card. They respond with "irrelevant" – this corresponds to de Finetti's "void" cases (see also Ramsey, 1931/1990). When it is about a "not-B" card, the indicative is like a void bet, although it might be replaced with the counterfactual, "If there had been a B on the left then there would have been a 5 written on the right."

People's actual uses of "true" and cognate words are little investigated in the psychology of reasoning beyond experiments on truth tables. These words appear to be ambiguous or at least to have a range of uses in natural language, with one use being pleonastic and simply expressing a degree of confidence in or commitment to an assertion (Edgington, 2003; Over et al., 2007). For example, the word "true" applied to a matter of subjective taste may only mean an endorsement of a judgement, such as when someone says that a chosen wine goes well with a meal and another person replies, "True". To say with confidence that a conditional is "true" or "certainly true" may be to indicate that it is highly probable (Evans, 2007), with "true" pleonastic or pragmatic (see also Adams, 1998, on the pragmatic notion of truth). However, the development of the new paradigm should encourage the psychological study of the relation between people's uses of "true" and their probability judgements.

Supporters of the conditional probability hypothesis can also explain why the paradoxes of the material conditional are absurd inferences, by noting that, in a single premise inference, the probability of the conclusion of a valid inference cannot coherently be less than the probability of the premise

(Adams, 1998). Inferring "if p then q" from "not-p" is invalid given the conditional probability hypothesis, since people can coherently have high confidence in "not-p" when they have low confidence in q given not-p. Equally, they can coherently have high confidence in the negation of "if p then q", because the conditional probability of not-q given p is very high, when they have little confidence in p. A closely related inference to the paradoxes is inferring "if not-p then q" from "p or q". This is valid for the material conditional, but not under the conditional probability hypothesis. If this were a valid inference, then a denial of "p or q" would follow from a denial of "if not-p then q". And since an assertion of "not-p" follows validly from a denial of "p or q", "not-p" would have to follow from a denial of "if not-p then q". Thus "not-p" would follow from the denial or negation of a conditional, "if not-p then q", which produces absurd results. We would deny that, if Obama has not continued to smoke, then he has damaged his health, but we would not infer from that that Obama has not continued to smoke.

Part II: If illustrates how important the debate about conditionals has become in the psychology of reasoning. The conditional is fundamental to all reasoning, which consists of inferring what follows *if* certain premises hold or probably hold. Theories of human reasoning, in whatever paradigm, must explain conditional reasoning, and by publishing more papers than perhaps anyone else in human history on conditional reasoning, no one has done more than Jonathan to place it at the centre of contemporary research.

References

Adams, E. W. (1998). *A primer of probability logic*. Stanford: CLSI Publications.

Bradley, R., & Swartz, N. (1979). *Possible worlds: An introduction to logic and its philosophy*. Indianapolis, IN: Hackett.

Chater, N., & Oaksford, M. (2009). Local and global inferential relations: Response to Over (2009). *Thinking & Reasoning, 15*, 439–446.

de Finetti, B. (1964). Foresight: Its logical laws, its subjective sources. Translated in H. E. Kyburg & H. E. Smokier (Eds.), *Studies in subjective probability* (pp. 55–118). New York: Wiley. (Originally published 1937)

Edgington, D. (2003). What if? Questions about conditionals. *Mind and Language, 18*, 380–401.

Evans, J. St B. T. (1982). *The psychology of deductive reasoning*. London: Routledge & Kegan Paul.

Evans, J. St B. T. (1984). Heuristic and analytic processes in reasoning. *British Journal of Psychology, 75*, 451–468.

Evans, J. St B. T. (1989). *Bias in human reasoning: Causes and consequences*, Hove, UK: Lawrence Erlbaum Associates Ltd.

Evans, J. St B. T. (2003). In two minds: Dual process accounts of reasoning. *Trends in Cognitive Sciences, 7*, 454–459.

Evans, J. St B. T. (2005). *How to do research*, Hove, UK: Psychology Press.

Evans, J. St B. T. (2006). The heuristic–analytic theory of reasoning: Extension and evaluation. *Psychonomic Bulletin and Review, 13*, 378 395.

Evans, J. St B. T. (2007). *Hypothetical thinking: Dual processes in reasoning and judgement*. Hove, UK: Psychology Press.

Evans, J. St B. T., Barston, J. L., & Pollard, P. (1983). On the conflict between logic and belief in syllogistic reasoning. *Memory and Cognition, 11*, 295–306.

Evans, J. St B. T., & Dusoir, A. E. (1977). Proportionality and sample size as factors in intuitive statistical judgement. *Acta Psychologica, 41*, 129–137.

Evans, J. St B. T., & Frankish, K. (2009). *In two minds: Dual processes and beyond*. Oxford: Oxford University Press.

Evans, J. St B. T., Handley, S. J., & Over, D. E. (2003). Conditionals and conditional probability. *Journal of Experimental Psychology: Learning, Memory and Cognition, 29*, 321–335.

Evans, J. St B. T., & Lynch, J. S. (1973). Matching bias in the selection task. *British Journal of Psychology, 64*, 391–397.

Evans, J. St B. T., & Newstead, S. E. (1977). Language and reasoning: A study of temporal factors. *Cognition, 5*, 265–283.

Evans, J. St B. T., Newstead, S. E., & Byrne, R. M. J. (1993). *Human reasoning*. Hove, UK: Lawrence Erlbaum Associates Ltd.

Evans, J. St B. T., & Over, D. E. (1996). *Rationality and reasoning*. Hove, UK: Psychology Press.

Evans, J. St B. T., & Over, D. E. (2004). *If*. Oxford: Oxford University Press.

Evans, J. St B. T., Over, D. E., & Manktelow, K. I. (1993). Reasoning, decision making and rationality. *Cognition, 49*, 164–187.

Evans, J. St B. T., & Wason, P. C. (1976). Rationalisation in a reasoning task. *British Journal of Psychology, 63*, 205–212.

Gigerenzer, G., Todd, P. A., & the ABC Group (1999). *Simple heuristics that make us smart*. Oxford: Oxford University Press.

Johnson-Laird, P. N., & Byrne, R. M. J. (1991). *Deduction*. Hove, UK: Lawrence Erlbaum Associates Ltd.

Johnson-Laird, P. N., & Byrne, R. M. J. (2002). Conditionals: A theory of meaning, pragmatics, and inference. *Psychological Review, 109*, 646–678.

Kahneman, D., & Tversky, A. (1979). Prospect theory: An analysis of decision under risk. *Econometrica, 47*, 263–291.

Kahneman, D., & Tversky, A. (1982). The simulation heuristic. In D. Kahneman, P. Slovic, & A. Tversky (Eds.), *Judgment under uncertainty: Heuristics and biases* (pp. 201–210). Cambridge: Cambridge University Press.

Kneale, W., & Kneale, M. (1962). *The development of logic*. Oxford: Oxford University Press.

Newstead, S. E., & Evans, J. St B. T. (1995). *Perspectives on thinking and reasoning: Essays in honour of Peter Wason*. Hove, UK: Lawrence Erlbaum Associates Ltd.

Oaksford, M. R., & Chater, N. (1994). A rational analysis of the selection task as optimal data selection. *Psychological Review, 101*, 608–631.

Oaksford, M. R., & Chater, N. (2007). *Bayesian rationality*. Oxford: Oxford University Press.

Oakford, M., & Chater, N. (2009). Precis of Bayesian rationality: The probabilistic approach to human reasoning. *Behavioral and Brain Sciences, 32*, 69–84.

Oberauer, K., & Wilhelm, O. (2003). The meaning(s) of conditionals: Conditional probabilities, mental models, and personal utilities. *Journal of Experimental Psychology: Learning, Memory and Cognition*, *29*, 680–693.

Over, D. E. (2009). New paradigm psychology of reasoning. *Thinking & Reasoning*, *15*, 431–438.

Over, D. E., & Evans, J. St B. T. (2003). The probability of conditionals: The psychological evidence. *Mind & Language*, *18*, 340–358.

Over, D. E., Hadjichristidis, C., Evans, J. St B. T., Handley, S. J., & Sloman, S. A. (2007). The probability of causal conditionals. *Cognitive Psychology*, *54*, 62–97.

Politzer, G. (2004). Some precursors of current theories of syllogistic reasoning. In K. I. Manktelow & M. C. Chung (Eds.), *Psychology of reasoning: Theoretical and historical perspectives*. Hove, UK: Psychology Press.

Politzer G., Over, D. E., & Baratgin, J. (2010). Betting on conditionals. Manuscript submitted for publication.

Pollard, P., & Evans, J. St B. T. (1983). The role of representativeness in statistical inference: A critical appraisal. In J. St B. T. Evans (Ed.), *Thinking and reasoning: Psychological approaches*. London: Routledge & Kegan Paul.

Ramsey, F. P. (1990). *The foundations of mathematics and other logical essays*. London: Routledge and Kegan Paul. (Original work published 1931)

Stanovich, K. E. (1999). *Who is rational? Studies of individual differences in reasoning*. Mahwah, NJ: Lawrence Erlbaum Associates, Inc.

Stanovich, K. E. (2009). Distinguishing the reflective, algorithmic, and autonomous minds: Is it time for a tri-process theory? In J. St B. T. Evans & K. Frankish (Eds.), *In two minds: Dual processes and beyond*. Oxford: Oxford University Press.

Stanovich, K. E., & West, R. F. (2000). Individual differences in reasoning: Implications for the rationality debate. *Behavioral and Brain Sciences*, *23*, 645–726.

Störring, G. (1908). Experimentelle Untersuchungen über einfache Schlussprozesse [Experimental research on simple inferential processes]. *Archive Für Die Gesamte Psychologie*, *11*, 1–127.

Thompson, V. A., Evans, J. St B. T., & Handley, S. J. (2005). Persuading and dissuading by conditional argument. *Journal of Memory and Language*, *53*, 238–257.

Wason, P. C. (1966). Reasoning. In B. M. Foss (Ed.), *New horizons in psychology 1*. Harmondsworth, UK: Pelican.

Wason, P. C. (1972). In real life negatives are false. *Logique et analyse*, *57–58*, 17–38.

Wason, P. C., & Brooks, P. J. (1979). THOG: The anatomy of a problem. *Psychological Research*, *41*, 79–90.

Wason, P. C., & Evans, J. St B. T. (1975). Dual processes in reasoning? *Cognition*, *3*, 141–154.

Wason, P. C., & Johnson-Laird, P. N. (1972). *Psychology of reasoning: Structure and content*. London: Batsford.

Wilkins, M. C. (1928). The effect of changed material on ability to do formal syllogistic reasoning. *Archives of Psychology*, *102*.

Part I
Thinking and reasoning
Psychological approaches

2 Solving natural syllogisms

Guy Politzer

University of Paris

In an important review devoted to deductive reasoning, Jonathan Evans (2002) examined the use of the "deduction paradigm", that is, a type of laboratory task in which participants are presented with a set of premises assumed to be true, and asked to generate a conclusion that follows validly or to evaluate the validity of a conclusion. He argued that this paradigm turns out to be inappropriate to the objectives that have become the focus of researchers' interest, such as the study of pragmatic and probabilistic inferences which draw on world knowledge, and whose premises have various degrees of belief. He nevertheless suggested that it would be unwise to abandon this paradigm altogether as it remains the right tool to study formal deductive reasoning.

One of the main tasks pertaining to this paradigm, in fact the oldest ever studied by psychologists, is categorical syllogisms. One may question whether after a century of investigation there is still something to be learned about people's deductive competence from research on syllogistic reasoning. In this chapter this question will receive a double answer: a negative answer as far as the usual laboratory task is concerned, as it will be claimed that it has been deeply misused; but also an affirmative answer in the sense that previous research has ignored the ecological relevance of syllogisms: this has often been denied but it will be argued that this stems from a fallacious conception of the epistemological status of the formal arguments and from a subsequent bias in their instantiation. Finally, it will be shown that lay people are highly competent and successful in using syllogisms once a methodological precaution has been taken, which turns the arguments into *natural syllogisms* satisfying the demand of ecological validity.

Natural syllogisms and the status of formal syllogisms

Surprisingly, there seems to be little reflection in the psychological literature on the nature of the knowledge or competence that is revealed by participants' performance on the common syllogistic task. With the possible exception of the "rational analysis" (Anderson, 1990) based on the distinction between a computational level and an algorithmic level, researchers seem to be little concerned with the epistemological status of the formal arguments (or of their instantiations) presented to the participants. To illustrate what is meant, consider the following joke. Two persons come across a barking dog. One of them says: "Beware! This dog is barking." The other one replies: "Never mind, you know that when a dog is barking, it never bites." Then the first one says: "OK, I know this, but does the dog know it too?"

Asking participants to solve a formal syllogism amounts to asking them to access the formal language of the theoretical model and to draw inferences within this model, that is, to behave like logicians who have formal knowledge (like the character who *knows* that the dog does not bite). The treatment of the formal argument is situated at a level of cognition that differs from that of the individuals outside the laboratory who (like the dog *unaware* that it does not bite) draw a conclusion from the categorical relations that they currently entertain in working memory. The arguments that reasoners actually process are less constrained than those used in the laboratory, which are abstractions that underlie reasoners' actual arguments. Classical syllogisms constitute an idealization that goes beyond the arguments observable in daily life, which we will call *natural syllogisms*. The latter may differ from the former by a number of superficial features such as the order of the premises, the place of the conclusion, their insertion in a dialogue; more important, they differ by the existence of a premise that contains a relation of category inclusion retrieved from long-term memory (but is absent in their typical enthymematic realizations). This feature is crucial and will be considered in detail below.

To put it yet otherwise, solving syllogisms of the type used in the laboratory requires a level of abstraction that it would be necessary for the individuals to reach in order to formulate the *formal* argument that they would have to produce, should they be asked to justify their *informal* natural argument. To this extent, the laboratory task is a metacognitive task that tests participants' awareness of the rules that guide their own inferential production outside the laboratory.

From the foregoing considerations it follows that, for a century, research on syllogistic reasoning has been deeply misdirected: instead of considering natural arguments it has focused on formal artificial arguments that have no ecological validity. If the laboratory task is of any interest to the investigation of reasoning, this is only to the extent that it helps reveal the variety of strategies that people use to solve deductive arguments, the majority of which escape their knowledge and capabilities. In the present chapter, little reference will be made to the considerable literature and the main theories that concern the laboratory task. However, as an aside, it will be shown that one of the main strategies used by participants to solve the laboratory task is but an application of the way natural syllogisms are solved. A method of proof that dates back to Aristotle, called *ecthesis*, and a recent logical analysis of syllogisms will be brought together and shown to yield essentially the same procedure. Then, the bulk of the chapter will be devoted to showing that the procedure in question is automatically involved while processing natural syllogisms.

This leads one to the prediction that near perfect performance is to be expected on natural syllogisms, a prediction that will be shown to be experimentally supported.

Aristotle's proof by ecthesis

Two methods of proof used by Aristotle are well known. Four "perfect syllogisms" with a status akin to axioms of the system are first identified (namely, AAA-1, AII-1, EAE-1, and EIO-1; see the Appendix (p. 34) for the designation of the syllogisms). The first method is applicable to all the other syllogisms but two. It consists in turning the syllogism under consideration into a perfect one by the conversion of one or both premises, or by changing the order of the premises. The second method, which consists of a *reductio ad impossibile*, is applied to the remaining two syllogisms, after which there is no need for another kind of proof. However, Aristotle described another method, called *ecthesis* (or proof by exposition). Here is an example given by Aristotle in the *Analytica Priora* (6, 28a) to prove AAI-3 *(all M are P; all M are S/ some S are P*; the reader is reminded that a sentence such as *all M are P* is formulated as *P belongs to every M*): "if both P and S belong to every M, should one of the M, e.g., N, be taken, both P and S will belong to this, and thus P will belong to some S" (Barnes edition, 1984, Vol. 1, p. 46), a more common formulation of which would be "if all M are both P and S, should one of the M, e.g., N, be taken, this will be both P and S, and thus some S will be P." There have been discussions among logicians and historians of logic about the logical type of the exposed entity, N. Some (Lukasiewicz, 1957; Patzig, 1968) have proposed that it is a category common to the subject and the predicate (or to the subject and the negated predicate) of a particular sentence. This view has some technical difficulties and the more recent analyses offered by Lear (1980), Mignucci (1991), Smiley (1973), Smith (1982) and Thom (1976) concur in considering N as an individual variable, making ecthesis akin to existential instantiation in natural deduction. Whichever view is the correct interpretation, *the essence of an ecthetic proof consists in extracting an individual* (or a subcategory that can be treated as a whole) *with a double predication and then searching for a triple predication before dropping the middle term.*

We now illustrate this by giving two examples. First, take the valid syllogism EIO-3: *no M is P; some M is S/ some S are not P*. From the second premise extract one or several individuals that are both M and S; because these are M, having property P is precluded by the first premise; that is, there are individuals that are M and S but not P, hence *some S are not P*. Second, take the pair of premises OI-3: *some M are not P; some M are S*. Extract again an individual that is both M and S; but this time the first premise predicates not-P of some individual M without warrant that this coincides with the extracted individual, so that no conclusion follows: this example shows that the invalid syllogisms can also be identified by ecthesis.

The property of case identifiability

Interestingly, one approach to syllogistic reasoning, namely Stenning and Yule's (1997) which is both logical and psychological, turns out to capture essentially the same notion as ecthesis. They show that syllogisms exist and are soluble owing to one structural property which they call "identification of individual cases". An individual either possesses or does not possess each of the three properties that define the categories S, M, and P; this defines eight types of individuals: S+M+P+, S+M+P–, S+M–P+, S+M–P–, S–M+P+, S–M+P–, S–M–P+, S–M–P–. When the joint premises of a syllogism warrant the existence of such a type, the syllogism is valid. To identify the individual case that defines the conclusion the authors describe two algorithms: one, graphical, which will not concern us, and the other, sentential, which is relevant to our current purpose.

The premises of the syllogisms are first interpreted in propositional terms, which gives the following encoding:

$$\text{all} = X{\rightarrow}Y; \text{ some} = X\&Y; \text{ no} = X{\rightarrow}\neg Y; \text{ some not} = X\&\neg Y$$

The algorithm has three parts. The first part aims to identify a premise that provides the first two terms of the individual description, called the *source premise*. It is either a unique existential premise, or the unique universal premise that has an end-term subject. (Failure to find either indicates that there is no valid conclusion.) At this stage, one of the terms is necessarily M. The second part aims to complete the description with the second end term. To do this, the quality (polarity) of M in the incomplete description is compared with the quality of M in the non-source premise (which is always a conditional premise). There are three possibilities: (1) if the qualities match and M is the subject of the non-source premise, a modus ponens is applied and its conclusion (which is the predicate of the non-source premise) provides the third term of the description; (2) if the qualities do not match and M is the predicate of the non-source premise, a modus tollens is applied whose conclusion (the subject of the non-source premise) provides the third term of the description; (3) otherwise there is no conclusion. At this stage, either there is a complete description of an individual case, or there is no conclusion. The third part of the algorithm produces the final conclusion by deleting the middle term and introducing a quantifier (which is existential unless there are two universal premises and only one of them has an end-term subject).

We illustrate the algorithm with two examples. First, consider again EI-3 (*no M is P; some M is S*). It is rewritten as M→¬P; M&S. The source premise is the particular premise, which yields M+S+ as the first two terms of the description. As M+ matches the quality of M in the first premise, modus ponens applies as M→¬P; M, to yield ¬P and then the full description M+S+P–, hence the conclusion *some S are not P*. Second, consider AO-2 (*all P are M; some S are not M*). The source premise is the particular premise, which yields S+M– to start the description. Because in the first premise M is predicate and positive, there is a mismatch and modus tollens applies as P→M; ¬M, to yield ¬P and the full description S+M–P–, hence the conclusion *some S are not P*. In both examples, through this procedure an individual has received a double predication twice, viz. M+S+ and then M+P– in the first case, S+M– and then M–P– in the second case to produce the full description (a triple predication), hence the conclusion after abstraction of M. In brief, Stenning and Yule's verbal algorithm turns out to be a general procedure of application of ecthesis to all syllogisms.

Before turning to natural syllogisms, we will have a quick look at the laboratory task.

Evidence of the ecthetic strategy in the formal task

If, as will be claimed below, ecthesis is the mechanism that reasoners use to solve natural syllogisms, one can expect to find some trace of it in the formal task; that is, participants of higher cognitive abilities who have reached some critical level in their metacognitive development could apply ecthesis spontaneously. Indeed, the use of ecthesis can be inferred from studies where care was taken to exploit verbal protocols (for more details see Politzer, 2004).

In the first experimental investigation of syllogistic reasoning (and possibly also the very first experimental study of reasoning) Störring (1908) described two strategies, one visual corresponding to the use of diagrams, the other verbal which he called the process of *insertion*. This consists of selecting the end term of one premise and inserting it next to the middle term in the other premise. Then the conclusion is obtained by extraction from the composite expression. For example, given the IA-4 pair of premises, *some P are M; all M are S*, a participant said "all the M, including some P, are S" which by abstraction of M yields *some P are S*. Similarly Ford (1995) described a "substitution behaviour" that consists of replacing one term in a premise with another, as when solving an algebraic problem (which collapses Störring's insertion and abstraction). Keeping the IA-4 pair as an example, the second premise allows one to give the value of S to M and the value of S can be substituted for M in the first premise, hence the conclusion. According to Ford (1995), the premise that provides the replacement term plays the role of a rule relating membership of class M and property S (more generally, of class C and property X), while the premise that contains the term to be replaced provides specific objects whose status with regard to S (generally to C or X) is known. It is noteworthy that specific objects are considered. To produce a valid conclusion: the process of substitution is guided by two pairs of rules that are formally equivalent to modus ponens for one pair and modus tollens for the other.

In sum, these reports concur to emphasize the pivotal role played by the extraction of a subcategory or an individual from one premise and keeping its two-term characterization before inserting it in the other premise, in other words they describe the ecthetic strategy in their own way.

Given the evidence of the use of the ecthetic strategy in the laboratory task, one can expect that performance could be enhanced if this strategy could be primed. Indeed this prediction was supported. Politzer and Mercier (2008) used singular syllogisms, that is, syllogisms with one premise in which the classical sentence *some X are Y* is replaced with the definite singular *this X is a Y* or the indefinite singular *there is an X that is a Y*. There was a fourth condition using the definite plural *these X are Y*. As predicted, comparing the *some* condition and the *this* condition (which cumulates singularity and definiteness) performance increased sharply (globally by about 40%) for almost all syllogisms tested. Also, the singular conditions yielded higher performance than their plural counterparts and the same obtained for the definite versus indefinite comparisons. All this means that by referring to definite (rather than indefinite) or to singular (rather than plural) elements of a category, one can prime the exposition strategy among a sizeable proportion of individuals.

Finally, one can find a remarkable insight in Braine's (1998) theoretical approach. Although he did not develop a theory of syllogistic reasoning proper, he hypothesized that what characterizes good reasoners is the application of a specific strategy that he called the choice of a "secondary topic". The secondary topic is the subset of the subject category of which the middle term can or cannot be predicated ("the S that are, or are not, M, as determined by the premise relating S and M"). This clearly delivers a doubly predicated subset. Then the conclusion follows by application of a modus ponens or a modus tollens. One of Braine's examples is the AA-3 pair, *all M P; all M S*. Once the secondary topic *the S that are M* has been found, it follows from the first premise, and by application of the generalized modus ponens of his predicate-mental logic (generalizing *these S are M; if something is an M, it is a P; therefore these S are P*) that *some S are P*. In brief, one can interpret Braine's view by saying that good reasoners are those who can execute an ecthetic strategy.

A first step toward naturalizing the formal task: Using knowledge-based categorization

If, in order to prime ecthesis and subsequently solve the syllogism, it is crucial that a double predication should occur, then one can think of taking advantage of one of the most important features of categorization, namely the possibility for an entity to be referred to by the name of a category (the hyperonym) or by the name of a subcategory (the hyponym). In that case the double characterization will be realized automatically. Now, consider a quantified sentence F that relates the category *rose* with some other object category (e.g., *fragrant*) whether by quantifying the roses that are or are not fragrant, or quantifying the fragrant objects that are or are not roses. This quantified relationship in which the subcategory *rose* is involved may (or may not) entail another quantified relationship in which the category *flower* is involved. And similarly a quantified sentence G can relate the category *flower* with an object category such as *fragrant* and again there may or may not follow another quantified relationship in which the subcategory *rose* is involved. The entailed relationship is the conclusion of the syllogism whose major premise is one of the quantified sentences F or G, and whose minor premise is the quantified sentence expressing a very small part of the individual's knowledge about the inclusion of categories, namely that all roses are flowers. This analysis provides the rationale for the experiments that will be reported. In an instantiated formal syllogism of the type commonly used in which the minor premise is an A sentence, the relationship expressed is always new information given in a fictitious context (e.g., *all the foreigners are vegetarians* when one is instructed to consider different groups of people) whether or not such a context is explicitly provided. In this sense, the relationship is arbitrary and conventional (as opposed to knowledge based). It was hypothesized that for the 16 syllogisms with an A minor premise (viz. AA-1 to AA-4, EA-1 to EA-4, IA-1 to IA-4, and OA-1 to OA-4) performance on the formal task would be enhanced if the minor premise (A) contained a category inclusion relation. This is because the double predication of an individual by both terms of the sentence is automatically satisfied: an entity that is a rose is a flower *eo ipso*. In the first experiment it was hypothesized that merely naming a category (or a subcategory) would be sufficient to cue participants to exploit the category inclusion and prime the ecthetic process.

Experiment 1

Participants were high school students aged 16 to 18 untutored in logic. They were presented with booklets containing one problem with a different context on each page. For this and the next two experiments, there were 16 different contexts. Each context was introduced by just a few words. There was a control group that received a standard laboratory task and an experimental group that received a modified task in which no minor premise proper appeared but instead a single word appeared (a hyperonym or a hyponym). Each pair of premises (or major premise and single word) was introduced by a few words to set up the context. Participants had to decide whether or not a conclusion necessarily followed, and in the affirmative to choose the quantifier and fill in the blanks (in the SP or the PS order) using the categories underlined. Here is an example for the AA-3 syllogism:

    – control condition:

    At an international conference,
    all the Japanese are <u>jurists</u>
    all the Japanese are <u>organizers</u>

– experimental condition (one word replaced the minor premise):

At an international conference,
all the Japanese are jurists
            Asians

In both conditions this was followed by the following multiple choice:

Conclusion:
☐ *all the* _____   *are* _____
☐ *some* _____   *are* _____
☐ *some* _____   *are not* _____
☐ *no* _____   *is* _____
☐ *there is no conclusion that is necessarily true*

The correct answer for the control condition is *some organizers are jurists*, or *some jurists are organizers*, and for the experimental condition *some jurists are Asians* or *some Asians are jurists*; the latter is based on the implicit minor premise *all Japanese are Asians* cued by the hyperonym *Asians*.

Results and discussion

Collapsing across the 16 problems, the mean rates of correct response were 49.4% for the control condition and 63.2% for the experimental condition. This overall difference can be regarded as modest in terms of effect size, but there are three problems that gave rise to a ceiling effect with a success rate above 90% in the control condition; when these are removed, the rates of correct response were 39.2% and 56.8%, respectively.

This difference was not due to a few problems, but concerns the great majority of the problems: there was a significant increase for eight problems, a nonsignificant increase for three problems, no difference for one problem and a nonsignificant decrease for one problem. This difference was significant ($p < .01$, sign test) and we can conclude that the improvement in performance is robust.

In brief, the mere mention of the S term (which in the present example is a hyperonym, *Asian*) invites the category inclusion of M (*Japanese*) in S and the subsequent processing of individuals that are M and S (viewing a *Japanese* as an *Asian*). This generalizes to the eight problems in the third and fourth figure. The same obtains when the S term mentioned is a hyponym: this invites the category inclusion of S in M and the subsequent processing of individuals that are S and M, which corresponds to the eight problems in the first and second figures.

It might be objected that the cueing word does not necessarily operate by suggesting a category inclusion. For example, in the present example participants could formulate the missing minor premise as *some Asians are Japanese*, hence an easy syllogism (AII-4) that delivers the appropriate conclusion. However, a problem-by-problem examination shows that this is exceptional and that, if anything, such a formulation renders the problems more difficult overall. Nevertheless, the next experiment aimed to test that an inclusion relation between nonarbitrary categories explicitly expressed by the *all* minor premise would also result in an enhanced performance.

Experiment 2

Participants were second and third year psychology students untutored in logic. The procedure and materials were the same as in Experiment 1 except for the addition of a third condition in which the minor premise stated explicitly the inclusion relation so that, keeping the scenario and the same mood already used as an example, the pair of premises was:

> *At an international conference,*
> *all the Japanese are jurists*
> *all the Japanese are Asians*

The results confirmed the observations of the first experiment. Leaving out two syllogisms with a ceiling effect, the percentage of correct responses was 38.2% for the control condition, 54.0% and 51.0% for the cued and the explicit inclusion conditions, respectively. The improvement was significant in both experimental conditions (sign test, $p < .05$). Moreover, the effect of the manipulation was extremely close in the two experimental conditions: the trend in the change in performance (no increase, nonsignificant increase or significant increase) was identical on all problems but one and the same obtains for the rate of correct responses that did not differ significantly except for one problem. We can conclude that the existence of an inclusion relation between categories that is stored in long-term memory enhances performance, whether this relation is explicitly or implicitly present in the minor premise (when it is present, the task remains formally equivalent to a standard instantiated syllogism).

Even though the manipulation was successful in two experiments run with different populations, one might imagine alternative explanations for the gain in performance. A very simple explanation could be based on the most conspicuous feature of the categories in the minor premise, namely their high familiarity. Indeed, we have claimed that this is what primes the ecthetic process when there is an inclusion relation between categories. But it might be argued that familiarity is sufficient, possibly because familiar categories are less demanding for working memory than are the arbitrary categories commonly used. The third experiment aimed to rebut this objection. If familiarity alone is enough to facilitate the solution, then one should expect people to experience a similar facilitation with other syllogisms, especially with the eight valid syllogisms that have an E minor premise. In addition, the response format was changed to a three-option format in order to ascertain that the previous results were not linked to the five-option format.

Experiment 3

Participants were postgraduate students, mostly from arts and the social sciences, and they were untutored in logic. Like in the second experiment there were three conditions (control, cued, and explicit) but the 16 pairs already studied were supplemented with eight other pairs (AE-1 to AE-4 and IE-1 to IE-4). In addition, the response format was changed as shown in the following examples (still referring to the AA-3 problem)

– for the control condition:

☐ *there is a conclusion that is necessarily true*
_____ *jurist(s)* _____ *organizer(s)*
_____ *organizer(s)* _____*jurist(s)*
☐ *there is no conclusion that is necessarily true*

– for the two experimental conditions:

☐ *there is a conclusion that is necessarily true*
_____ *jurist(s)* _____ *Asian(s)*
_____ *Asian(s)* _____ *jurist(s)*
☐ *there is no conclusion that is necessarily true*

Results

Two important points deserve consideration. First, for the syllogisms with an A minor premise, the gain in performance was even stronger than it was in the two previous experiments. The same analysis (that excluded three problems with a ceiling effect) indicated an increase in performance on all problems for the cued condition ($p < .001$) and on all but one ($p < .01$) for the explicit inclusion condition. The rate of correct responses was 34.2% for the control condition and jumped to 48.8% and 54.2% for the cued and the explicit inclusion conditions, respectively. Second, for the eight problems with an E minor premise, as predicted no improvement was observed; discarding again two problems (AE-2 and AE-4) that have a rate of success above 85% in the control condition, there was in fact a decrease in performance ($p < .05$ for both conditions).

Discussion

In this experiment the manipulation that consists in priming ecthesis resulted in increasing the rate of correct responses by about one half. This greater facilitation can be attributed to the population or to the different response format, or both. However, the fact that across the three experiments the average rate of success in the experimental conditions does not exceed 60% suggests that the maximal facilitation has not been attained.

The other result may be more important, for it concerns the essence of the ecthetic process. It is based on the notion that whereas an inclusion premise can prime ecthesis, an exclusion premise cannot, and we can now examine more precisely why. To do so, we will contrast the AA-3 and AE-3 pairs of premises using the following instantiation concerning, say, a grocer's goods – AA-3:

> major premise: *all the apples are red*
> minor premise: *all apples are fruit*

AE-3:

> major premise: *all the apples are red*
> minor premise: *no apple is a pear*

Conceiving of an apple as a fruit is automatic and virtually irrepressible due to our knowledge of categories, so that the conclusion of AA-3 *some fruit are red* is compelling. In contrast, conceiving of an apple as a non-pear, however obvious and trivial this may be, is deeply arbitrary, even more so than conceiving of an apple as an object of which some property is predicated, precisely because the number of such properties is relatively limited whereas the categories or properties which contrast with *apple* are potentially infinite. Whereas one is automatically cued to think of an individual known to be a member of a category X (e.g., an apple) as an instance of its supercategory (fruit), there is no reason for being automatically cued to think of such an individual as a non-X (except for reasons specific to the context, or in the particular case where X and non-X are dichotomous or complementary in the context). In brief, whereas the inclusion premise primes ecthesis by suggesting a double predication for an individual such as being an apple and a fruit, the exclusion premise does not have this power. This explains the predicted failure in using common categories to improve performance with the AE and IE pairs of premises.

So far evidence has been presented that supports the claim that to prime ecthesis it is crucial that there exist a minor premise (explicit or implicit) containing a category inclusion relation retrieved from long-term memory. It was mentioned in the first section of this chapter that, in addition, natural syllogisms are typically inserted in a dialogue and that the order of the sentences that constitute the argument, including the conclusion, may differ from the textbook/laboratory presentation. We now adduce experimental evidence that when these requirements are satisfied – that is, when one is dealing with natural syllogisms – performance is close to the maximum.

Natural syllogisms: In dialogic situations shared background knowledge of categories prewires ecthesis

Experiment 4

Participants in the fourth experiment were readers in a public library who either were university students or already held a degree. The problems were again framed in various scenarios and presented in booklets. There were two experimental conditions defined by the materials. One control condition aimed to present a typical laboratory task. Here is an example, using again the AA-3 pair of premises:

> *In a park,*
> *all the roses are frozen*
> *all the roses are new varieties*

There were five options to conclude: four options with an A, I, O, or E sentence (*all the new varieties are frozen*, etc.) and a fifth option *one cannot logically conclude*, the meaning of which was carefully explained in the instructions.

In the experimental condition the context was introduced by a three-sentence scenario that presented two characters. The first character asked a question starting with "is it true that" followed by a sentence that was the conclusion of the syllogism. Then the second character uttered an answer starting with "I have seen that" followed by a sentence that was the major premise of the syllogism. No minor premise was stated: this was assumed to be background knowledge shared by the two interlocutors (and of course shared by the participants) so that, pragmatically, the minor premise can be given the status of an implicated premise. With the AA-3 example, one scenario introduces Mary and Peter who has just been in the park alone. Then the dialogue takes place as follows:

> *Mary asks: "Is it true that in the park some flowers are frozen?"*
> *Peter replies: "I have seen that in the park all the roses are frozen"*
> *Mary can conclude that the answer to her question is:*
> ☐ *it is true*   ☐ *it is false*   ☐ *it is possible*

The valid syllogisms appeared twice, once with a correct *true* answer, and once with a correct *false* answer. With the current example, the answer is *true*. In the *false* version Mary's question is *"Is it true that in the park no flower is frozen?"* For the invalid syllogisms, the question coincided with the erroneous conclusion that is the most frequent according to the reasoning literature on syllogisms. In all the cases, after answering the three-choice question, participants were asked to justify their choice in their own words.

Results

We apply the same analysis as earlier. The mean percentage of correct answers on the standard task was 47.4% after discarding four problems (AA-1, AA-4, EA-1, EA-4) for which performance was at a ceiling level (above 85%; the rate was 59.9% when these are included). These values are typical of what is reported for the laboratory task in the literature. In contrast, on the natural syllogism task, the rate of correct responses for the 12 problems without ceiling effect jumped to 78.9%. The improvement was general: there was no change for one problem and an increase for 11 problems ($p < .001$). Notice that this time the size of the gain is considerable as the rate of success passed from less than 50% to close to 80%.

The analysis of the justifications given in the implicit condition is very informative. For the valid syllogisms, about one half consisted of a demonstration that could be of two kinds: either the implicit premise was stated explicitly, or the whole formal syllogism was stated in full (including the implicit premise now spontaneously made explicit by the participant). This provides compelling evidence that these participants did solve the natural syllogisms with comprehension of their logical structure. Slightly less than one half of the justifications were fully consistent with the answer but not informative enough to constitute a full demonstration. The remaining justifications were either inconsistent with the answer or based on empirical considerations (a few per cent in each case).

For the invalid syllogisms the justifications that were compatible with the answer but underinformative constituted one quarter of the cases (and there were also a few per cent of incorrect justifications). More important, the justifications that constituted a demonstration that the conclusion was possible but not necessary amounted to 70% of the total. It is also remarkable that it is for these pairs that the greatest amelioration took place: the rate of correct answers shifted from 21%, that is no better than chance, to 85%, that is close to perfect performance. Of course, one must be cautious in interpreting participants' performance. In judging that a conclusion offered to them does not necessarily follow from the premises they are not, strictly speaking, proving that the syllogism is invalid. But they could do so by using the same type of proof applied to each of the quantified sentences (A, I, O, E) and show that none of these necessarily follows. Because the proof is similar in all these cases, there is reason to assume that participants would produce a similar proof, should they be required to do so. This is because the putative conclusion that was offered to them was the most frequent error, so that in all likelihood they could also resist other putative conclusions that are not so enticing. Considering that the subset of invalid syllogisms that have an A premise are notoriously difficult, it is worth examining why participants' performance was improved in all the experiments reported and more specifically in the last one.

For this purpose we take an IA-1 pair of premises followed by its modal erroneous conclusion which is a *some* sentence. We compare in turn a standard laboratory problem, its counterpart with a minor premise that has an explicit category inclusion (of the type used in Experiments 2 and 3) and then its dialogic presentation as used in the present experiment.

Consider first the following artificial syllogism:

> *some flowers (M) are frozen (P)*
> *all the new varieties (S) are flowers (M)*

To appreciate that it is invalid, one must understand that an individual characterized after the minor premise by S and M (flowers that are new varieties) need not be characterized by P (frozen) because this individual comes from a subset of M that may or may not coincide with the M-individuals referred to in the major premise. Few reasoners are aware of this. In contrast, given:

> *some flowers (M) are frozen (P)*
> *all roses (S) are flowers (M)*

or even better as in Experiment 4:

> *Mary asks: "Is it true that in the park some roses are frozen?"*
> *Peter replies: "I have seen that in the park some flowers are frozen"*

it is apparent from the categorization stored in long-term memory that a rose (S M) is a *particular* flower (a member of a subcategory) and as such need not coincide with any of the members of the flower category that are frozen (M P), which need not be roses: the non-necessary existence of an individual case is readily made available. In other words, knowledge of the categorization that obliges one to conceive of a rose as a flower also obliges one to conceive of a flower as possibly a rose or not a rose. This justification was expressed in various formulations that can be paraphrased by "there are flowers other than roses so that there may not be frozen roses". Of course, there is some artificiality in the task used in Experiments 2 and 3 due to the minor premise that is pragmatically anomalous (even though the instructions warned that one of the premises would state "an obvious truth"), so that performance was still far from perfect. But when presented as in Experiment 4, participants not only process a natural dialogue but, more important, focus on a specific statement (the conclusion) to evaluate, as they would in their daily life: then they can exhibit their full grasp of the syllogism.

Conclusion

For more than two millennia, since their description by Aristotle until the nineteenth century, logicians and philosophers used to consider syllogisms as the yardstick of rationality and human reasoning abilities. Then, after this view had been abandoned in the wake of the Fregean revolution, surprisingly enough psychologists took a strong interest in a task based on them, which they called *syllogistic reasoning*: it consists of solving instantiated exemplars of formal syllogisms, which amounts to investigating the extent to which people untutored in logic access the formalization made by classical logicians of a special set of deductive arguments. A century of research on this paradigm has yielded little more than the observation that people resort to various strategies and various heuristics to solve problems that, with a number of notable exceptions, are too hard for the majority of reasoners.

In this chapter a subtly, but radically different view on syllogisms is taken. They are regarded as formal descriptions of the underlying structure of enthymematic arguments that people spontaneously use in their daily argumentation. Their essential characteristic is that the implicit premise contains an inclusion relation between two categories that belong to a hierarchy stored in long-term memory. It has been argued that reasoners' competence in using these arguments is based on a mechanism that exploits a fundamental property of formal syllogisms described by Stenning and Yule (1997) as *case identifiability* and that this mechanism, which was outlined by Aristotle as a method of proof called *ecthesis*, turns out to be built in and executed by the category inclusion structure: this is why, contrary to the formal laboratory task, lay people are surprisingly highly proficient in their spontaneous natural syllogistic reasoning.

References

Anderson, J. R. (1990). *The adaptive character of thought*. Hillsdale, NJ: Lawrence Erlbaum Associates, Inc.

Aristotle. (1984) *Complete works. The revised Oxford translation*. J. Barnes (Ed.) Vol. 1. Princeton, NJ: Princeton University Press.

Braine, M. D. S. (1998). Steps toward a mental predicate logic. In M. D. S. Braine & D. P. O'Brien (Eds.), *Mental logic* (pp. 273–332). Hillsdale, NJ: Lawrence Erlbaum Associates, Inc.

Evans, J. St B. T. (2002). Logic and human reasoning: An assessment of the deduction paradigm. *Psychological Bulletin, 128*, 978–996.

Ford, M. (1995). Two modes of mental representation and problem solution in syllogistic reasoning. *Cognition, 54*, 1–71.

Lear, J. (1980) *Aristotle and logical theory*. Cambridge: Cambridge University Press.

Lukasiewicz, J. (1957). *Aristotle's syllogistic from the standpoint of modern formal logic*. Oxford: Clarendon Press.

Mignucci, M. (1991). Expository proofs in Aristotle's syllogistic. In H. Blumenthal & H. Robinson (Eds.), *Aristotle and the later tradition* (pp. 9–28). Oxford Studies in Ancient Philosophy. Oxford: Clarendon Press.

Patzig, G. (1968) *Aristotle's theory of the syllogism*. Dordrecht, Germany: Reidel. (Original German edition 1958)

Politzer, G. (2004). Some precursors of current theories of syllogistic reasoning. In K. Manktelow & M. C. Chung (Eds.), *Psychology of reasoning. Theoretical and historical perspectives* (pp. 214–240). Hove, UK: Psychology Press.

Politzer, G., & Mercier, H. (2008). Solving categorical syllogisms with singular premises. *Thinking and Reasoning, 14*, 434–453.

Smiley, T. J. (1973). What is a syllogism? *Journal of Philosophical Logic, 2*, 136–154.

Smith, R. (1982). What is Aristotelian ecthesis? *History and Philosophy of Logic, 3*, 113–127.

Stenning, K., & Yule, P. (1997). Image and language in human reasoning: A syllogistic illustration. *Cognitive Psychology, 34*, 109–159.

Störring, G. (1908). Experimentelle untersuchungen über einfache Schlussprozesse [Experimental research on simple inferential processes]. *Archiv für die Gesante Psychologie, 11*, 1–127.

Thom, P. (1976). Ecthesis. *Logique et Analyse, 74–75–76*, 299–310.

Appendix

The four classical quantified sentences

> A: *all X are Y* = universal affirmative
> E: *no X is Y* = universal negative
> I: *some X are Y* = particular affirmative
> O: *some X are not Y* = particular negative

The four figures (in the traditional logical numbering)

	1	2	3	4
major premise	M P	P M	M P	P M
minor premise	S M	S M	M S	M S

M is the middle term, P and S the end terms.

The designation of syllogisms

In a designation such as, e.g., EIO-1 the first three letters indicate the mood, that is, the first premise (the major premise) is an E sentence, the second premise (the minor premise) an I sentence and the conclusion an O sentence; the number indicates the figure.

An example of a formal syllogism (in the AAI-3 mood):

> *all M are P*
> *all M are S*
> ∴ *some S are P*

This formal syllogism instantiated:

> *all the roses are frozen*
> *all the roses are new varieties*
> ∴ *some new varieties are frozen*

The associated natural syllogism:

> *all the roses are frozen*
> *{all roses are flowers}*
> ∴ *some flowers are frozen*

3 Probability evaluations, expectations, and choices

Vittorio Girotto

University IUAV of Venice

Michel Gonzalez

University of Provence

Consider the following passages:

> Subjective probabilities play an important role in our lives. The decisions we make, the conclusions we reach, and the explanations we offer are usually based on our judgements of the likelihood of uncertain events such as success in a new job, the outcome of an election, or the state of the market.
>
> (Kahneman & Tversky, 1972, p. 430)

> Many decisions are based on beliefs concerning the likelihood of uncertain events such as the outcome of an election, the guilt of a defendant, or the future value of the dollar.
>
> (Tversky & Kahneman, 1974, p. 1124)

> Diagnosing whether a patient has a disease, predicting whether a defendant is guilty of a crime, and other everyday as well as life-changing decisions reflect, in part, the decision-maker's subjective degree of belief in uncertain events.
>
> (Barbey & Sloman, 2007, p. 241)

What these extracts have in common are two things. First, they are the opening sentences of papers devoted to the study of probabilistic reasoning. Second, they justify this study by stressing the importance of probabilistic judgements in decision making. The point is that in the almost 40 years of interval between the seminal papers of Kahneman and Tversky and the recent review by Barbey and Sloman, very few studies have actually investigated the relation between probabilistic judgements and choices. More importantly, virtually all studies on probabilistic reasoning have asked respondents to express their beliefs about uncertain events by assigning a number on the [0,1] probability scale. One implicit assumption seems to underlie all these studies: the standard numerical evaluations reveal the respondents' expectations. Suppose that respondents have to evaluate the chances of two complementary events, A and B. If they assign 90% chances to A and just 10% chances to B, it seems reasonable to conclude that they expect that A will occur and to predict that, if they have to make a bet, they will bet on A rather than on B. Are these predictions correct? In other words, does the standard way of expressing a probability evaluation by means of a fraction or a percentage actually reveal the respondents' expectations? Do they actually bet on the event to which they attribute the higher probability? In this chapter, we try to answer these questions by discussing a series of studies we have recently conducted on judging and deciding about uncertain events. The results we have obtained show that in some cases respondents make bets that disagree with their standard probability evaluations: They bet on A rather than on B, but attribute the lower probability to A.

The chapter proceeds as follows. It starts by comparing standard and non-standard forms of probability evaluations. Then, it presents and comments on the evidence of discrepancies between standard probability evaluations and bets, and compares these discrepancies to previously reported discrepancies between choices and nonprobabilistic judgements. Finally, it discusses these findings in the light of the current dual-process accounts of reasoning and judgement under uncertainty.

Standard and nonstandard probability evaluations

The almost universal use of standard numerical judgements in the literature on probabilistic reasoning has one curious implication. If assigning a number on the [0,1] probability scale is the usual way in which individuals express their expectations about uncertain events, it follows that individuals who are not able to compute a fraction or a percentage should not be able to express their expectations. In particular, individuals who are too young to know the symbolic numerical system (Barth, Le Mont, Lipton, & Spelke, 2005), or individuals who live in an innumerate culture, like those that count only "roughly one", "roughly two", and "many" (Gordon, 2004; Pica, Lerner, Izard, & Dehaene, 2004), should not be able to express their degree of belief in uncertain events. In fact, since the beginning of their research programme, Tversky and Kahneman have argued that naïve individuals typically express their expectations by means of non-numerical judgements:

> These beliefs [about the likelihood of uncertain events] are usually expressed in statements such as "I think that . . .," "chances are . . .," "it is unlikely that . . .," and so forth. Occasionally, beliefs concerning uncertain events are expressed in numerical form as odds or subjective probabilities.
>
> (Tversky & Kahneman, 1974, p. 1124)

Indeed, individuals who certainly are not able to make a standard probability judgement express their expectations by means of qualitative judgements. In particular, preschoolers succeed in problems asking for a posterior probability evaluation in which they have to indicate which of two events is more likely to occur. For example, starting from the age of about 5, children solve problems similar to the following one (adapted from Girotto & Gonzalez, 2008):

> This bag contains four round chips (all black) and four square chips (three white and one black). I draw one chip randomly from the bag. If, by touching it, I feel that it is square, is it more likely that I get a black chip or a white chip?

Even infants appear to have expectations about future events. Of course, they do not express them in a verbal way. For instance, given a transparent container in which three identical objects and one different in colour and shape rebound at random, 12-month-olds look longer at the display – normally a sign of an unexpected event – when the single object, rather than one of the three identical objects, exits from the hole at the base of the container (Teglas, Girotto, Gonzalez, & Bonatti, 2007). This finding implies that from their early stages of development individuals base their expectations on an assessment of possibilities. More generally, the results about infants' and young children's probabilistic intuitions support a general hypothesis about naïve probabilistic reasoning.

One common way to evaluate a probability is *nonextensional*: the evaluation relies on some heuristic as, for example, when individuals infer that because an exemplar is typical of a class, it has a high probability of being a member of the class (e.g., Kahneman & Tversky, 1972). Another common way is *extensional*: the probability of an event is evaluated from the different possible ways in which the event may or may not occur. Consider the above chip problem. In order to solve it, one may consider that there are three white chips and just one black chip in the set of square chips. Hence, under the assumption that each chip has the same chances to be drawn, one infers that, in the considered set, drawing one white chip is more likely than drawing one black chip. This way of solving the problem without using the probability calculus is an example of an *extensional* evaluation of chances, and the hypothesis that individuals represent the different possibilities in evaluating probabilities is part of a general theory of probabilistic reasoning based on mental models (Johnson-Laird, Legrenzi, Girotto, Sonino-Legrenzi, & Caverni, 1999). Results obtained with adult participants have corroborated the hypothesis. In particular, adults succeed in otherwise difficult probability problems provided that they can reason extensionally about sets of possibilities (e.g., Evans, Handley, Perham, Over, & Thompson, 2000; Girotto & Gonzalez, 2001, 2002).

Many researchers have taken for granted that assigning a number on the [0,1] interval is the *only* form of numerical probability evaluation (e.g., Gigerenzer & Hoffrage, 2007, p. 266). These researchers have neglected the alternative ways of evaluating probability. In particular, one can express a probability judgement in *odds* form. The judgement "the probability of A is 1/4" is formally equivalent to the judgement "the odds against A are 3 to 1". Assigning probability values in odds terms appears to be the earliest form of probability evaluation. As pointed out by Franklin (2001), one does not see numerical ratios like "40 per cent of all" or "one in five of all" before the beginning of the eighteenth century. The early works using numerical probability, like those of Pascal and Huygens, based the determination of the expected value of a risky prospect on odds values, rather than on standard probabilities. For instance, in his pioneering work on the calculus of the games of chance, Huygens (1657/1714, p. 5) wrote: "If the number of chances I have to gain *a*, be *p*, and the number of chances I have to gain *b*, be *q*. Supposing the chances equal; my expectation will then be worth (*pa* + *qb*) / (*p* + *q*)."

Moreover, there are written traces that, before the advent of the probability theory in the seventeenth century, individuals assigned numerical chances to alternative outcomes, like in odds evaluations. For example, Shakespeare provides several examples of numerical odds in the form "it is x to 1 that something will happen": "Twenty to one then he is shipped already" (Shakespeare 1590/2008, *The Two Gentlemen of Verona*, I.1) and "Your niece will not be seen; or if she be, it's four to one she'll none of me" (Shakespeare 1601/2008, *Twelfth Night*, I. 3).

In order to make a standard probability evaluation, one has to compute a normalized ratio (e.g., "1 out of 4"; "25%"). By contrast, in order to make a numerical odds evaluation, one has to assess the number of chances of an event A *and* those of the complementary event on the same scale (e.g., "1 vs. 3"). Given its less constrained nature, in some cases odds evaluations are easier to produce than the equivalent standard probability evaluations. In particular, Girotto and Gonzalez (2001) found that respondents solved posterior probability problems better when they had to make an odds judgement ("There are __ chances that hypothesis H is correct vs. __ chances that hypothesis not-H is correct"), rather than when they had to make a standard probability evaluation ("There are __ chances out of 100 that hypothesis H is correct").

Probability evaluations, expectations, and choices

What are the relations between probability judgements and choices under uncertainty? According to a normative viewpoint, choices reveal the expectations (i.e., beliefs) of rational agents (e.g., Ramsey, 1931/1964). According to a descriptive viewpoint, probability evaluations precede and determine choices (e.g., Tversky & Kahneman, 1974). Now, if assigning a number on the [0,1] interval is the natural way in which individuals express their expectancies about uncertain events, it follows that the standard probability evaluations should predict individuals' choices about the same events. Thus, if you assign 90% chances to event A and 10% to the complementary event B, one can predict that you will bet on A. Is this prediction correct? Our answer is negative: in some cases, individuals make bets that conflict with their probability evaluations.

Our starting point is that to make a choice one does not need to assess separately the probability of each outcome by means of a standard evaluation. On the one hand, individuals often make choices on the basis of a comparison of the reasons for and against the various alternatives, in which the estimation of probability values plays no role (Shafir, Simonson, & Tversky, 1993). On the other hand, individuals who certainly are not able to formulate a standard probability evaluation are nonetheless able to make bets that imply an implicit assessment of chances. Consider again the chip problem (Girotto & Gonzalez, 2008). Preschoolers solve it even when it asks not for a probability judgement, but for a bet:

> This bag contains four round chips (all black) and four square chips (three white and one black). I draw one chip randomly from the bag. If, by touching it, I feel that it is square, do you bet that I get a black chip or a white chip?

Of course, preschoolers do not evaluate the respective probabilities of the two possible outcomes before making their bet. To make it, they simply consider and compare the different ways in which the two outcomes can occur. In other words, they make a *comparison of chances*. It should be noted that individuals can make optimal choices even without making a complete comparison of chances. Suppose you roll three dice. Would you bet that the sum of the numbers turning up is 3 or 10? It is likely that you would bet on 10. It is unlikely, however, that you would try to determine the probabilities of the two outcomes considered. In fact, in order to make your bet you only need to enumerate the ways in which one can obtain the two outcomes. There is only one way to obtain 3 (1 + 1 + 1) and various ways to obtain 10 (e.g., 1 + 3 + 6, 1 + 4 + 5, 2 + 3 + 5). Actually, you do not even need to enumerate *all* the ways in which one can obtain 10. If you realize that there is just one way to obtain 3 and more than one way to obtain 10, you will conclude that 10 is more likely than 3 and bet on it. Indeed, individuals who do not know the probability calculus solve problems of this sort without assessing probabilities. Nine-year-olds do correctly choose the more likely outcome in a throw of two dice (Girotto & Gonzalez, 2005). Individuals playing games of chance, as early as in the thirteenth century, did the same (David, 1962; Girotto & Gonzalez, 2006). In sum, individuals make simple bets between two events without assessing separately the probability of each event. They base their choices on an extensional comparison of the respective chances of these events.

In their discussion of the model theory of probabilistic reasoning, Evans and Over (1996, p. 160) have questioned the assumption that decision making is based on numerical probability evaluation:

> We think that some decision making does take place through the explicit consideration of alternative possibilities, but we do not imagine that people make extensive use of numerals to express probabilities and utilities in their mental models [. . .] people often have [vague thoughts] of some states of affairs as more likely than others. One possibility is to treat "is more likely than" as a relation between models in the way that "is to the right of" is a relation between terms within mental models.

We concur with Evans and Over that individuals do not need to compute the probability of the various outcomes in order to make their choices. The reported findings show that even individuals, like young children, who are not able to make standard probability evaluations do make optimal bets about uncertain events. The same findings, however, show that these individuals' bets rest on a quantitative assessment of the various ways in which the events could occur. Young children are unable to express numerically the results of their assessment. But without the ability to make a correct comparison of quantities (of chances, cases, or frequencies) they could not make optimal bets.

When probability judgements and expectations disagree

The hypothesis that a simple choice, like a bet between two events, does not necessarily depend on a standard probability evaluation generates a counter-intuitive prediction. In some cases, individuals make bets that conflict with their standard probability evaluations. In other words, in some cases individuals attribute more than a 50% probability to event A but bet on the complementary event B. But how could an attentive individual ever produce conflicting answers of this sort? We posit that in some cases individuals make standard probability evaluations that disagree with their own chance comparisons and odds judgements. In particular, they may attribute more than a 50% probability to event A, but assign a greater numbers of chances to A than to B. Following our hypothesis that bets depend on chance comparisons or odds judgements, we predict that in these cases bets will be better aligned with nonstandard than with standard probability evaluations. In a series of recent studies, we have tested our hypothesis using a variety of posterior probability problems (Gonzalez & Girotto, 2010; Pighin, Girotto, Gonzalez, Savadori, & Barilli, 2005).

Naïve individuals' ability to evaluate a posterior probability is one of the most investigated topics of the entire literature on probabilistic reasoning (for a recent review, see Barbey & Sloman, 2007). Typically, respondents are provided with information about two competing hypotheses (H and not-H), which are differently associated to some evidence (E). Given information about one piece of evidence, respondents have to evaluate the probability of one hypothesis. Consider the following problem (adapted from Gonzalez & Girotto, 2010)

> Imagine a planet where there are only two kinds of creatures: the Plams and the Somos. You know that the colour of these creatures is variable. In particular, both kinds can be yellow coloured. Some studies have investigated this planet: if one detects the presence of one creature, there are 40 chances out of a total of 100 chances that it is a Plam and 60 chances that it is a Somo. Out of the 40 chances that it is a Plam, there are 20 chances that it is yellow coloured. Out of the 60 chances that it is a Somo, there are 5 chances that it is yellow coloured. A picture of this planet reveals the presence of a yellow coloured creature.
>
> You estimate that there is (are) ____ chance(s) out of 100 that the yellow coloured creature is a Plam rather than a Somo.

To produce the correct answer (i.e., 80%), one has to consider that the probability that a yellow creature is a Plam equals the quotient between the chances that a creature is a yellow Plam (20) and the chances that a creature is a yellow Plam or a yellow Somo (20 + 5). The problem provides all the numerical values necessary to evaluate the required probability. We found, however, that most respondents produced an erroneous evaluation. They tended to focus on the information concerning the focal hypothesis (Plam), and neglected the information concerning the alternative one (Somo). Their most frequent judgement was "20 out of 100". In other words, respondents answered by giving the probability that a creature is a yellow Plam, rather than the probability that a yellow creature is a Plam (i.e. "80 out of 100"). Most of the remaining judgements attributed less than a 50% probability to the Plam hypothesis. Notice that these erroneous evaluations went in the opposite direction compared with the correct one. Following the respondents' evaluations, one has to conclude that the Plam hypothesis is less likely than the Somo hypothesis. Following the correct evaluation, one has to conclude that the Plam hypothesis is more likely (80% chance) than the Somo hypothesis.

Consider now the following question:

> Evaluate the respective chances that the yellow coloured creature is a Plam or else a Somo, by completing the following expression: There is (are)____ chance(s) that it is a Plam versus ____ chance(s) that it is a Somo.

Unlike the previous question, which asked for a normalized evaluation, this question asks for an odds judgement. In order to answer correctly, respondents have simply to consider the chances that a creature is a yellow Plam (20) *and* the chances that a creature is a yellow Somo (5). As found by Girotto and

Gonzalez (2001/Study 4), most respondents answered correctly an odds judgement question of this sort. Notice that their correct evaluation went in the opposite direction compared with the erroneous evaluations elicited by the standard probability question. Unlike the latter, it implies that the Plam hypothesis is more likely than the Somo hypothesis.

Finally, consider the following question:

> Indicate which yellow coloured creature has the greatest chances of having been detected: a Plam or a Somo?

This question does not ask for a numerical evaluation, but simply for a *relative judgement*, which one can make on the basis of an assessment of the respective chances of the two hypotheses. Respondents did answer correctly ("Plam"). Notice that their judgement went in the same direction as their odds judgement, but contrasted with their standard probability evaluation.

Now, suppose we ask respondents to bet on one of the two hypotheses:

> You have to bet on the yellow coloured creature that has been detected: Plam or Somo?

How would they answer? Following the common assumption that standard probability evaluations express individuals' expectations and predict their choices, they should not bet on the Plam hypothesis because they tend to attribute less than a 50% probability to it. By contrast, if bets depend on chance comparisons and odds judgements, respondents should bet on the Plam hypothesis because they tend to attribute more chances to that hypothesis than to the alternative one. In agreement with our prediction, we have found that the large majority of participants betted on the Plam hypothesis. In sum, respondents betted on the hypothesis that they considered more likely than the alternative one, but to which they assigned less than a 50% probability.

We have replicated this finding in several other studies, in which we have varied the type and structure of information, using problems as different as the traditional posterior probability problems, some notorious probability teasers, like the three-card problems, and some new puzzles never tested before. We have also varied the type of respondents, by testing individuals personally concerned with the content of the problems. In particular, we have tested a large sample of pregnant women who had to make judgements and choices in posterior probability problems presenting realistic epidemiological information about some chromosomal anomaly (Pighin et al., 2005). Despite the differences in problem form and content and in respondents' involvement in the situation, we have obtained a strikingly similar pattern of answers: respondents make bets that are better aligned with odds judgements and chance comparisons than with standard probability evaluations. In some cases, they bet on the event favoured in their odds ratio or relative evaluation but to which they assign the lower probability. These findings support our hypothesis that in some cases standard evaluations do not reveal respondents' expectations.

Judgement and choice discrepancies: A vast phenomenon

Discrepancies between judgements and choices have been obtained in various studies. Tversky and Griffin (1991) pointed out that in decision theory the concept of utility has been used in two different senses: the contribution of a future outcome to the attractiveness of a choice (*decision value*, see Kahneman & Tversky, 1984/2000), and the degree of pleasure or pain associated with the actual experience of the consequences of a choice (*experience value*). The decision value is inferred from choices. The experience value is typically inferred from the judgements that individuals make about the consequences of their choices. The two values have been confused very often, given the common assumption that choices and judgements are consistent. In everyday life, however, the two values may differ. An obvious example is that sometimes individuals choose options that in the end make them unhappy. Choices and judgements may differ even when the judgement, like the choice, precedes the outcome. For example, Tversky and Griffin (1991) presented their participants with two job proposals, which differed in terms of absolute salary and relative position. One proposal offered a $35,000 salary to the candidate, but it offered a $38,000 salary to other workers with the same training and experience as the candidate. The other proposal offered a $33,000 salary to the candidate, but it offered a $30,000 salary to other workers with the same training and experience as the candidate. In sum, the first proposal offered a higher absolute salary, but a lower relative position than the second one. Some participants had to make a judgement: "At which job would you be happier?" They anticipated higher satisfaction in the job with the lower absolute salary and higher relative position. Other participants had to make a choice: "Which job would you choose to take?" They preferred the job with the higher absolute salary and lower relative position. Choices and judgements may differ even when the judgements, unlike well-being assessments, concern factual (e.g., quantitative) features of the options. For example, in some cases individuals prefer a gamble offering a greater probability to win and a lower pay-off to a gamble offering a smaller probability to win and a higher pay-off. However, if they have to set the selling price of each option, they attribute a lower price to the gamble they prefer (Lichtenstein & Slovic, 1971).

Our finding that choice and probability judgements may conflict should be distinguished from the previously reported evidence of judgement–choice discrepancies, for two reasons. First, in previous cases, the choices involved utility, that is, the options had different consequences (e.g., a high vs. a low salary), and the judgements concerned nonprobabilistic values (e.g., "Which option will make you happier?"). By contrast, in our case, the choices had to depend only on probabilities, and the judgements concerned probabilistic values. Second, in previous cases, the value judgements could not be measured relative to a normative standard (e.g., there is no yardstick to decide whether a given evaluation of a level of happiness is accurate or inaccurate). By contrast, in our case, the probability judgements could be considered accurate or inaccurate and the bets could be considered optimal or not optimal. To summarize, our finding extends previous evidence of judgement–choice discrepancies, by showing that these phenomena occur in a family of cases much larger than previously thought.

A dual-process phenomenon?

In the recent years, many researchers have defended the idea that there are two types of processes underlying human thinking and reasoning (e.g., Evans, 2003, 2008; Evans & Over, 1996; Kahneman & Frederick, 2002; Sloman, 1996; Stanovich & West, 2000). Some processes operate in a fast, automatic, and unconscious way. These processes are sometimes referred to as *System 1*. Some other processes operate in a slow, sequential, and effortful way. These processes are sometimes referred to as *System 2*, and are generally considered the basis of abstract thinking and hypothetical reasoning (Evans, 2003). One might argue that the reported discrepancies between various forms of probability evaluations and choices call for a dual-process explanation.

According to Barbey and Sloman (2007), respondents fail the typical posterior probability problems because these problems do not activate a nested set representation of possibilities. Thus, respondents produce erroneous evaluations based on associative principles, like similarity. For example, respondents often mistake the probability of one hypothesis, given one piece of evidence, for the apparently similar probability of that piece of evidence, given that hypothesis. By contrast, respondents succeed when the posterior probability problems activate an accurate representation of nested sets of possibilities. In this case, respondents make correct evaluations through deliberative processing consisting of applying elementary rules to an appropriate representation of sets and subsets:

> The dual-process model attributes (. . .) responses based on more deliberative processing that involves working memory, such as the elementary set operations that respect the logic of set inclusion and facilitate Bayesian inference, to a second rule-based system.
>
> (Barbey & Sloman, 2007, p. 244)

According to the dual-process account defended by Jonathans Evans and colleagues, respondents fail the typical posterior probability problems because the pieces of information used in these problems do not correspond to beliefs held by respondents:

The basic problem in the base-rate literature that we would like to stress is that the Bayesian priors used in the normative analyses are not prior beliefs [. . .] The mere presentation of these pieces of information in the wording of the instructions will not produce an internalized belief of the kind common to much real world reasoning, and so it is not surprising to us that the information is ignored in the absence of pragmatic cues as to its relevance.

(Evans & Over, 1996, pp. 101–102)

By contrast, respondents succeed when the problems activate the appropriate nested set representation. In these cases, respondents can use:

analytic procedures which involve constructing and manipulating mental models to represent the problem information. With standard presentations, it will appear to them that either base rate or else (more commonly) diagnostic information is relevant, but they will have no means of integrating the two. Only when problem design cues them to construct set-inclusive mental models will they succeed in computing the normatively correct solution.

(Evans & Elqayam, 2007, p. 262)

According to the dual-process account proposed by Kahneman and Frederick (2002), respondents solve posterior probability problems whose format:

makes it easier to visualize partitions of sets and detect that one set is contained in another [This sort of] format affects the corrective operations of System 2, not the intuitive operations of System 1; [it] improves respondents' ability to impose the logic of set inclusion on their considered judgements, but does not reduce the role of [heuristics] in their intuitions.

(Kahneman & Frederick, 2002, p. 69)

Despite the different factors to which they attribute the respondents' failures, all these accounts seem to converge on one point about respondents' successes. Respondents can apply their analytic procedures and produce correct evaluations only when the problems make the set relations transparent. We concur with the proponents of these accounts about the importance of activating an appropriate set representation. Their accounts, however, do not make it clear whether correct evaluations only depend on such a representation. In fact, we have used problems that did not differ in the information format: all our problems allowed the activation of the appropriate set representation. Yet, when respondents had to make a standard probability judgement, their evaluation was incorrect and conflicted with the correct evaluation they produced when they had to make an odds judgement, a chance comparison, or a bet. If the nested set representation leads to the application of the "deliberative processing", or the "analytical procedures", or the "corrective operations" of System 2, then problems that activate such a representation should elicit the same accurate responses regardless of whether they concern a standard or a nonstandard evaluation task or a bet task. It should be noted that we have used problems, like the above Plam–Somo one, that did not refer to respondents' actual beliefs. Now, following the specific dual-process account defended by Evans and colleagues (e.g., Evans, 2003; Evans & Elqayam, 2007; Evans & Over, 1996), problems of this sort are difficult to solve because they convey "statistical information requiring difficult System 2 reasoning to compute their effect on posterior probability" (Evans, 2003, p. 457). Yet, we found that most participants solve problems of this sort when they have to make an odds judgement or a chance comparison. If statistical information requires respondents to use difficult analytical procedures, then problems conveying this sort of information should be equally difficult to solve regardless of whether they ask for a standard probability evaluation or an odds judgement.

The current dual-process accounts could try to explain the reported findings by assuming that in some case the appropriate set representation is not sufficient to elicit accurate evaluations. Such an assumption, however, generates a further question: What are the factors that limit the appropriate application of the analytical procedures in conditions in which they should be activated by an appropriate set representation? The current dual-process accounts cannot easily answer this question. In our studies, respondents had to reason about nested sets of possibilities. Both odds and standard probability judgements required them to provide a numerical answer. Yet, in some cases, respondents provided odds judgements that conflicted with probability evaluations. Why do the analytical procedures activated by the nested set representation lead them to produce, say, the odds judgement "20 to 5 in favour of A" and the probability evaluation "20% chance in favour of A"?

In sum, it might be tempting to attribute the reported conflicts to the operation of two conflicting thinking processes, in the same way in which some authors have treated discrepancies between automatic and effortful inferences as implying "two minds in one brain" (Evans, 2003). The current dual-process accounts, however, do not seem to offer a convincing explanation for the reported conflicts. These accounts have correctly emphasized the importance of an appropriate representation to elicit accurate probability evaluations. However, they have failed to consider the importance of the *task demand* in determining the way in which naïve individuals reason and decide about uncertain events.

Conclusions

In this chapter, we have summarized a recent series of studies whose results show that formally equivalent ways to elicit probability evaluation may lead to conflicting answers. In some cases, respondents solve posterior probability problems by producing standard evaluations that conflict with nonstandard evaluations, like odds judgements and chance comparisons. In these cases, the respondents make bets that are better aligned with the nonstandard than with the standard probability evaluations. Taken together, these findings contravene the common assumption that the standard numerical evaluations of probability actually reveal respondents' expectations and predict their choices.

The reported discrepancies between different but formally equivalent probability evaluations, and between probability evaluations and choices, confirm the complexity of human thinking processes. But they also confirm the importance, suggested in many papers of Jonathan Evans, of relating reasoning and decision making.

References

Barbey, A. K., & Sloman, S.A. (2007). Base-rate respect: From ecological rationality to dual processes. *Behavioral and Brain Sciences, 30*, 241–254.

Barth, H., Le Mont, K., Lipton, J., & Spelke, E. S. (2005). Abstract number and arithmetic in preschool children. *Proceedings of the National Academy of Science, 102*, 14116–14121.

David, F. N. (1962). *Games, gods and gambling. A history of probability and statistical ideas.* London: Griffin.

Evans, J. St B. T. (2003). In two minds: Dual process accounts of reasoning. *Trends in Cognitive Sciences, 7*, 454–459.

Evans, J. St B. T. (2008). Dual process accounts of reasoning, judgments and social-cognition. *Annual Review of Psychology, 59*, 255–278

Evans, J. St B. T., & Elqayam, S. (2007). Dual-processing explains base-rate neglect, but which dual-process theory and how? *Behavioral and Brain Sciences, 30*, 261–262.

Evans, J. St B. T., Handley, S. J., Perham, N., Over, D. E., & Thompson, V. A. (2000). Frequency versus probability formats in statistical word problems. *Cognition, 77*, 197–213.

Evans, J. St B. T., & Over, D. E. (1996). *Rationality and reasoning.* Hove, UK: Psychology Press.

Franklin, J. (2001). *The science of conjecture. Evidence and probability before Pascal.* Baltimore, MD: Johns Hopkins University Press.

Gigerenzer, G., & Hoffrage, U. (2007). The role of representation in Bayesian reasoning: Correcting common misconceptions. *Behavioral and Brain Sciences, 30*, 264–267.

Girotto, V., & Gonzalez, M. (2001). Solving probabilistic and statistical problems: A matter of information structure and question form. *Cognition, 78*, 247–276.

Girotto, V., & Gonzalez, M. (2002). Chances and frequencies in probabilistic reasoning: Rejoinder to Hoffrage, Gigerenzer, Krauss, and Martignon. *Cognition, 84*, 353–359.

Girotto, V., & Gonzalez, M. (2005). Probabilistic reasoning and combinatorial analysis. In V. Girotto & P. N. Johnson-Laird (Eds.), *The shape of reason* (pp. 161–175). New York: Psychology Press.

Girotto, V., & Gonzalez, M. (2006). Norms and intuitions about chance. In L. Smith & J. Vonèche (Eds.), *Norms in human development* (pp. 220–236). Cambridge: Cambridge University Press.

Girotto, V., & Gonzalez, M. (2008). Children's understanding of posterior probability. *Cognition, 106*, 325–344.

Gonzalez, M., & Girotto, V. (2010). Eliciting probabilities: When choices and expectations disagree. Manuscript submitted for publication.

Gordon, P. (2004). Numerical cognition without words: Evidence from Amazonia. *Science, 306*, 496–499.

Huygens, C. (1714). *Libellus de ratiociniis in ludo aleae, or, The value of all chances in games of fortune* (W. Browne, Trans.). London: S. Keimer. (Original work published 1657) Retrieved February 5, 2010, from http://www.stat.ucla.edu/history/huygens.pdf

Johnson-Laird, P. N., Legrenzi, P., Girotto, V., Sonino-Legrenzi, M., & Caverni, J. P. (1999). Naive probability: A model theory of extensional reasoning. *Psychological Review, 106*, 62–88.

Kahneman, D., & Frederick S. (2002). Representativeness revisited: Attribute substitution in intuitive judgement. In T. Gilovich, D. Griffin, & D. Kahneman (Eds.), *Heuristics and biases: The psychology of intuitive judgment* (pp. 49–81). Cambridge: Cambridge University Press.

Kahneman, D., & Tversky, A. (1972) Subjective probability: A judgment of representativeness. *Cognitive Psychology, 3*, 430–454.

Kahneman, D., & Tversky, A. (2000). Choices, values and frames. In D. Kahneman & A. Tversky (Eds.), *Choice, values, and frames* (pp. 1–16). Cambridge: Cambridge University Press. (Reprinted from *American Psychologist*, 1984, *39*, 341–350)

Lichtenstein, S., & Slovic, P. (1971). Reversals of preference between bids and choices in gambling decisions. *Journal of Experimental Psychology, 89*, 46–55.

Pica, P., Lemer, C., Izard, V., & Dehaene, S. (2004). Exact and approximate arithmetic in an Amazonian indigene group. *Science, 306*, 499–503.

Pighin, S., Girotto, V., Gonzalez, M., Savadori, L., & Barilli, E., (2005). *How to achieve a better understanding of test accuracy in prenatal diagnosis.* Paper presented at the Society for Judgement and Decision-Making Annual Conference, Toronto, Canada, 12–14 November.

Ramsey, F. P. (1964). Truth and probability. In H. E. Kyburg Jr & H. E. Smokler (Eds.), *Studies in subjective probability* (pp. 61–92). New York: Wiley. (Original work published 1931)

Shafir, E., Simonson, I., & Tversky, A. (1993). Reason-based choices. *Cognition, 49*, 11–36.

Shakespeare, W. (2008). *The two gentlemen of Verona.* Oxford: Oxford University Press. (Originally published 1590)

Shakespeare, W. (2008). *Twelfth night.* Oxford: Oxford University Press. (Originally published 1601)

Sloman, S. A. (1996) The empirical case for two systems of reasoning. *Psychological Bulletin, 119*, 3–22.

Slovic, P. (1995). The construction of preference. *American Psychologist, 50*, 364–371.

Stanovich, K. E., & West, R. F. (2000). Individual differences in reasoning: Implications for the rationality debate. *Behavioral and Brain Sciences, 23*, 645–726.

Teglas, E., Girotto, V., Gonzalez, M., & Bonatti, L. L. (2007). Intuitions of probabilities shape expectations about the future at 12 months and beyond. *Proceedings of the National Academy of Science, 104,* 19156–19159.

Tversky, A., & Griffin, D. (1991). Endowment and contrast in judgments of well-being. In R. Zeckhauser (Ed.), *Strategy and choice* (pp. 297–318). Cambridge, MA: MIT Press.

Tversky, A., & Kahneman, D. (1974). Judgment under uncertainty: Heuristics and biases. *Science, 185,* 1124–1131.

4 Arguments in mind

David W. Green

University College London

Introduction

A general cognitive theory of human reasoning should cover the reasoning of individuals and of groups. We lack such a theory perhaps because reasoning theorists have until recently largely ignored the fundamental social character of the human mind. The first part of this chapter (The centrality of argument) presents the case for the central role of argument in coordinating action among social agents. It reinterprets experimental data suggesting that simple affective reactions to an issue are sufficient to explain opinion on an issue. Instead, it proposes that such reactions reflect complex mental representations that are better understood as argumentative in character.

The virtue of an argumentative approach is that it integrates rather than opposes affective and cognitive reactions. Such integration is clearly seen when individuals consider a future course of action. In thinking about future states of affairs and the desirability of one course of action over another we recruit past experience to simulate future possibilities and assess how we might feel. On the basis of such mental simulations we generate arguments to persuade or dissuade ourselves or others to or from a certain course of action. The second part of this chapter (Argument and mental simulation) elaborates on the idea that individuals construct an argument model: They mentally simulate a possible course of action and base their arguments on it. These arguments refer to causal paths in the simulation and can include affective reactions such as anticipatory regret to the outcome. The section reviews experimental data consistent with the predictions of the argument model. Current data leave open the psychological processes involved in the creation of an argument model and their neural basis.

The third part of this chapter (Argument and mental control) infers some of the processes and neural structures involved with reference to work on prospective memory. As might be expected, such research implicates regions associated with the retrieval of information from episodic memory. Regions active in theory of mind tasks are also recruited. This network of regions is also likely to be core to constructing an argument model because mental simulation is necessary to the formation of a mental causal model, and shifts in perspective are required to envisage a future possibility and to assess the persuasiveness of an argument. In groups, an agreement on a suitable course of action can emerge by different individuals contributing to the argumentative process until a shared argument model arises, but this entails the mobilization of attitudes of openness to the enquiry and trust in the possibility of resolution. The final part of this chapter (Conclusions and future directions) identifies the need to go beyond traditional dichotomies of thinking if the psychological and neural processes of the construction of argument models are to be understood.

The centrality of argument

Human beings are social animals and there are good reasons to believe that the need to interact with others was a significant driver in the evolution of the human brain and human mentality (Dunbar & Shultz, 2007). As social beings we need to coordinate with others in order to achieve our goals. Not all goals need to be discussed and not all means need to be considered. We live in cultural worlds where certain goals are presumed and the means of achieving them are habitual. But where circumstances provide new opportunities or new threats, how is such coordination normally achieved? Coercion is one way. But coercion however widespread has its limits as a means of building coalitions and achieving coordinated action. Another way is for individuals to agree through a process of argument in which the merits of possible courses of action are appraised. Individual, adult cognition reflects the fact that human beings are social agents engaged in argumentative transactions with others (Billig, 1987; Vygotsky, 1981).

At a minimum an argument comprises a claim and a reason for that claim (Voss & Means, 1991) and so allows for a range of different types of claim (e.g., about actions or future states of affairs) and types of reason (e.g., cognitive, affective, experiential). It therefore permits an integrative approach to the factors that weigh in decisions and overcomes the opposition between affect-based and reason-based approaches that has typified theoretical approaches.

For example, Slovic, Finucane, Peters, and MacGregor (2002, p. 415) write: ". . . using an overall, readily available affective impression can be far easier – more efficient – than weighing the pros and cons . . ." In contrast, Shafir, Simonson, and Tversky (1993, p. 34) observe that "Decisions . . . are often reached by focusing on the reasons that justify the selection of one option over another". Such opposition is not total; instead each group acknowledges a role for the other factor. Shafir et al. (1993, p. 32) suppose that ". . . choices may occasionally stem from affective judgments" and Finucane, Alhakami, Slovic, and Johnson (2000, p. 3, Note 2) note that ". . . many other cognitive operations have been shown to be important (. . .) and need to be integrated with our emerging understanding of the role of affect in judgments". But such work on integration remains to be done.

We can explore the issue concretely by considering the proposals of Slovic et al. (2002) in a little more detail. They propose that in reaching an opinion individuals access an "affect pool". This pool comprises a set of tags, either positive or negative in value, that has become associated with the mental representation of an issue. Their affective sum yields the decision or opinion. In a test of this notion, Slovic et al. presented participants with a topic and asked them to record in a word or a phrase any images, feelings and thoughts ("elicited thoughts" from now on) that came to mind. Participants rated each one on a 5-point affect scale running from −2 (very negative) to +2 (very positive) with 0 as the neutral point. They report that the summed affective value of these elicited thoughts is a good predictor of various kinds of preferences such as visiting different cities, adopting or maintaining different technologies (such as nuclear power), and purchasing stock in new companies.

But what is the nature of the representation that participants access to yield an elicited thought that they then rate? Is it distinct from the representation they access when they discuss their opinions? Green, Applebaum, and Tong (2006) asked participants to identify which, if any, of their elicited thoughts they would use as arguments in discussing the issue with a friend or colleague. Two experiments with two separate real-world controversial issues (electronic tagging of children; whether the UK should join the European Monetary Union) yielded an overlap of approximately 80% between elicited thoughts and endorsed arguments. Endorsement was more probable when the elicited thought had a nonzero affect rating. Participants also rated how strong an argument each endorsed thought would make. Summed argument strength correlated strongly with their summed absolute affective value with the number of arguments partialled out.

These results indicate that the method used by Slovic et al. (2002) does not simply elicit affective reactions as they supposed. Instead individuals are retrieving representations that are cognitively complex. But perhaps this should not be surprising. A single image can code a complex mental representation. For instance, an elicited thought about research into genetically modified crops such as "a corn cob with the head of a herring" symbolizes the unnatural consequences of such research. It yields cognitive–moral and affective arguments against it. But not only can a single elicited thought code a complex of ideas, a list of such thoughts may reflect complex relationships among them. One image may express an argument that undermines another. Such structure remains entirely implicit in their procedure. Of course, their procedure has the advantage that it does not induce structure where no prior structure exists. However, the strong relationship between thoughts, feelings and images and the representations that participants endorse as arguments suggest a richer structure undisclosed by the technique. The elicited representations may be better understood as primarily argumentative in form.

Argument and mental simulation

The concept of an argument does not deny the distinction between affective and cognitive reactions. On the contrary, it provides a way to integrate them as aspects of a person's thoughts about an issue. Consider the case of regret. Regret arises when a person perceives that an alternative course of action would have led to a better outcome – that is, an outcome with more pleasure or less pain. It is a cognitively based emotion. Individuals and groups may also prefer actions that minimize anticipatory regret (e.g., Loomes & Sugden, 1982). But how is such anticipatory regret ascertained? Mental simulation is key.

Mental simulation refers to the "imaginative constructions of hypothetical events or scenarios" (Schacter, Addis, & Buckner, 2008, p. 42). The critical point is that individuals imaginatively place themselves in a hypothetical scenario in order to explore possible solutions to a particular problem (see Schacter et al., 2008, p. 42). The adaptive value of mental simulation is that it allows individuals to judge outcomes without engaging in the actual behaviour. More precisely, the present proposal is that when individuals envisage a future possibility they construct a mental (i.e., qualitative) causal model (Craik, 1943; Johnson-Laird, 1983, Chapter 15; Sloman & Lagnado, 2005). Causal, rather than correlational, representations are well suited for reasoning about situations and for acting in the world because they indicate what is needed to change matters (see Pearl, 2000). They help identify suitable interventions that may lead to the desired goal. Individuals mentally run or simulate this causal model to examine its outcome (e.g., Kahneman & Tversky, 1982) and then examine their subjective response to such outcomes (e.g., Gilbert & Wilson, 2007). The neural basis of this process is a collaboration between cortical and subcortical systems (e.g., Coricelli, Dolan, & Sirigu, 2007). The former generate the imagined world and the latter generate an affective response to it. On the basis of the simulation and their subjective response to it individuals produce specific arguments. They create an argument model.

Arguments refer to the causal paths in the model and may issue as conditional statements. A persuasion is a conditional statement in favour of a course of action and comprises a consequent that refers to a desirable state of affairs (a benefit) and an antecedent that refers to a hypothetical course of action asserted to produce it (Thompson, Evans, & Handley, 2005). By contrast, a dissuasion is a conditional statement in which the consequent refers to an undesirable state of affairs. An argument based on anticipatory regret is one that focuses on the emotional cost of not carrying out the target action or of the cost of carrying out an alternative.

What is the evidence for the persuasive value of such arguments? Encouraging individuals to think along certain lines by a conditional statement is a common rhetorical device. Thompson et al. (2005) showed that participants can identify such arguments (e.g., "If the Kyoto accord is ratified there will be a downturn in the economy") and understand their import even if they do not agree with them as indicated by asking them to adopt their own perspective on the issue compared with the writer's perspective.

In an experimental context, participants may be encouraged to think along certain lines by a prompt. Extending earlier work by McCloy and Byrne (2002) to controversial policy issues (see above), Green et al. (2006) showed that opinions about a policy were significantly influenced by the nature of the prompt designed to elicit hypothetical thinking. Opinion became significantly more in favour of a policy given a counterfactual prompt such as "if only action X were to be taken" compared with a semifactual prompt such as "even if policy X were to be taken". In the case of a counterfactual prompt participants are led to identify a benefit associated with a policy. They generate conditional statements of the form, "If policy X were adopted there may be a benefit". In the case of a semifactual prompt, they are led to identify a cost associated with the policy; that is, a dissuasion. Here, the outcome of their mental simulation might be construed as a conditional statement of the form, "Even if policy X were adopted, there may be a cost". In this experimental context, the prompt is the antecedent and the listed thought the consequent. Further, consistent with a role for anticipatory regret, rated regret at the prospect of policy X not being adopted was significantly higher in those listing counterfactual thoughts.

Inviting participants to think about a possibility does not fully constrain how they do in fact think, any more than reading a conditional statement constrains them. The hypothesis that participants construct an argument model presumes that participants may envisage factors that could prevent the intended benefit (a disabling condition; Cummins, 1995) that would be expressed as a dissuasion. It predicts that the generation of an opposing argument (e.g., a dissuasion) will limit, perhaps block, the effect of a persuasive argument and this appears to be the case (Green, 2008, Experiment 1).

According to the hypothesis the precise impact of a dissuasive argument (i.e., a disabling factor) should depend on the structure of the causal model envisaged. In a test of this notion participants were invited to judge the relative persuasive power of two different cases for funding research into genetically modified (GM) crops (Green, 2008, Experiment 2). The first case (the independent argument case) proposed two independent benefits of GM crop research: (a) It would lead to new varieties of rice that grow in saltier conditions, overcoming the threat of less fresh water for farming and so ensuring supplies of rice; (b1) Such research will also create new varieties of vegetables resistant to damaging pests, thereby decreasing the use of harmful pesticides and so boosting resistance to disease in humans. The causal paths leading to these two benefits are independent. The second case (the dependent argument case) had the same first argument (a) but expanded the benefits associated with the new varieties of rice: (b2) Such varieties would mean that people on the coastal plains could continue to farm and live there and this would reduce the risk of war with nearby groups as they will not need to move in order to survive. The causal path yielding the benefits identified in the second argument (b2) also depended on the research producing new varieties of rice (a).

Initial preferences were equally divided between the two cases, suggesting different views of what makes an effective case (Weinstock, Neuman, & Tabak, 2004). However, when participants learned that the new varieties of rice would not be delivered within a government-imposed time limit of 5 years because of a problem with the technology, those who initially preferred the dependent argument case shifted their preference to the independent argument case. Its causal structure meant that undermining one causal path did not undermine the case as a whole. However, participants reinstated their initial preference when they learned that the relevant technology could be licensed from abroad. Such licensing meant that they could discount the earlier undermining argument. As predicted by the argument model hypothesis, the effects of undermining and discounting arguments depended on the structure of the causal model to which these refer.

Argument and mental control

What is involved in thinking about a future possibility and formulating an argument based on it; that is, creating an argument model? Work on prospective memory (e.g., Addis, Wong, & Schacter, 2008) indicates that envisaging an event in one's own future requires recollecting and adaptively recombining past experiences. Neuroimaging (fMRI) data support the idea that a common network of regions (including prefrontal and medial temporal lobe structures) mediates the recall of past episodes and the imagining of future ones (Schacter et al., 2008). Envisaging future events is more effortful than retrieving past episodes in that relevant details must recombine in order to create a coherent representation. Current evidence shows increased activation in a number of distinct regions including a hippocampal region implicated in the processing of relations among entities and in the right frontal pole involved in planning (Burgess, Quayle, & Frith, 2001).

Envisaging a future possibility also requires a shift in perspective. It requires a representation of a future world distinct from the current world. Interestingly, regions involved in theory of mind tasks (e.g., posterior cingulate/retrosplenial regions) that require individuals to adopt the perspective of another are also activated when individuals think about a future possibility involving the self.

Identifying a preferred course of action also requires assessing its subjective and affective value. In the case of cognitive-based emotion such as regret, orbital frontal regions interact with the amygdala. The literature suggests that the same interaction underlies the anticipation of regret (Coricelli et al., 2007).

The present proposal is that these regions are also likely to form a core network in the generation of an argument model. Encoding an argument will, in addition, strongly modulate components of the language network. Individuals may also consider the persuasiveness of a potential argument and so consider the likely reactions of the addressees. In some circumstances, this will require a shift in perspective between the self and a hypothetical or concretely imagined other in order to identify any flaws.

According to the argument model hypothesis a number of factors should affect the perceived persuasiveness of an argument. It will be affected by the nature of the mental simulation evoked by the argument and the affect associated with it. One specific factor may be the ease of simulating the future possibility. Ease may affect the perceived causal strength of the connection between the hypothetical action and its goal. If so, it should also be a factor in the assessment of the perceived strength of an argument and in the decision of whether to revise the argument or not. Interestingly, and consistent with this expectation, Heller (2006) proposed, in the context of accounting for differences in conviction rates between circumstantial and direct evidence, that it is the ease with which individuals can imagine the defendant guilty or not guilty that accounts for their verdicts. It is easier to mentally simulate direct evidence. Perhaps in general individuals prefer arguments based on ease to simulate scenarios. The precise form of the argument will also be important. So, for instance, if regret is a powerful motivator, then an argument based on anticipated regret may be more persuasive than one that simply emphasizes the benefit of a course of action while ignoring the affective cost of failing to adopt it.

These factors are ones that can apply to a wide range of different content but in many cases it is specific factors that need to be considered. For example, is it the case that the addressee is likely to have evidence that undermines a particular argument? In this case mental simulation of the reactions of a particular person may be required. The precise wording of the argument may also affect the nature of inferences that are invited and so the nature of the causal model that is constructed. A variety of considerations and reflective processes may then lead to the reconstruction of the initial argument model.

The need to engage in cycles of reflection and reformulation is not invariable. Coordination, the construction of a shared argument model, may arise through a distributed cognitive process in which argument and counterargument arise through the contributions of different members of the group. In such a process, individuals must respond to the declared positions of others and recognize when an argument undermines their position (Kuhn, 1991; Walton, 1989). In addition to these cognitive and communicative requirements coordination through argument requires the mobilization of certain personal attitudes and group practices. There must be trust that openness to the consideration of alternative courses of action can yield agreement. Further, where agreement cannot be reached through mutual conviction then other mechanisms are needed (e.g., voting on an issue) if action is to be taken rather than endlessly deferred.

Conclusions and future directions

I think it is apparent that a theory of argument generation whether within an individual or within a group requires theorists to go beyond traditional dichotomies of thinking such as the contrast between automatic and deliberative thinking (e.g., Evans, 2003; Sloman, 1996) and the idea of rationality as a conflict between emotion and reason (see Sanfey, Loewenstein, McClure, & Cohen, 2006). There are encouraging signs of a more integrative approach especially in the decision-making literature (Coricelli et al., 2007). Examining how individuals simulate possibilities, coordinate the shifts in perspective and evaluate the persuasive effectiveness of their arguments is very much a task for the future. The cognitive demands involved are high; which may explain why it is relatively rare for individuals to internalize what is required for effective argument (Kuhn, 1991). Distributed cognition can overcome such constraints but it still seems only too rare for groups to adopt norms that allow a shared argument model to develop and so resist the lure of coercion.

References

Addis, D. R., Wong, A. T., & Schacter, D. L. (2008). Age-related changes in the episodic simulation of future events. *Psychological Science, 19*, 33–41.

Billig, M. (1987). *Arguing and thinking: A rhetorical approach to social psychology.* Cambridge: Cambridge University Press.

Burgess, P. W., Quayle, A., & Frith, C. D. (2001). Brain regions involved in prospective memory as determined by positron emission tomography. *Neuropsychologia, 39*, 545–555.

Coricelli, G., Dolan, R. J., & Sirigu, A. (2007). Brain, emotion and decision making: The paradigmatic example of regret. *Trends in Cognitive Science, 11*, 258–265.

Craik, K. (1943). *The nature of explanation.* Cambridge: Cambridge University Press.

Cummins, D.D. (1995). Naïve theories and causal deduction. *Memory and Cognition, 23*, 646–658.

Dunbar, R. I. M., & Shultz, S. (2007). Evolution in the social brain. *Science, 317*, 1344–1347.

Evans, J. St B. T. (2003). In two minds. *Trends in Cognitive Sciences, 7*, 454–459.

Finucane, M. L., Alhakani, A., Slovic, P., and Johnson, S. M. (2002). The affect heuristic in judgments of risk and benefits. *Journal of Behavioural Decision Making, 13*, 1–7.

Gilbert, D. T., & Wilson, T. D. (2007). Prospection: experiencing the future. *Science, 317*, 1351–1354.

Green, D. W. (2008). Persuasion and the contexts of dissuasion: Causal models and informal arguments. *Thinking & Reasoning, 14*, 28–59.

Green, D. W., Applebaum, R., & Tong, S. (2006). Mental simulation and argument. *Thinking & Reasoning, 12*, 31–61.

Heller, K. J. (2006). The cognitive psychology of circumstantial evidence. *Michigan Law Review, 105*, 241–305.

Johnson-Laird, P. N. (1983). *Mental models: Towards a cognitive science of language, inference and consciousness.* Cambridge: Cambridge University Press.

Kahneman, D., & Tversky, A. (1982). The simulation heuristic. In D. Kahneman, P. Slovic, & A. Tversky (Eds.), *Judgment under uncertainty: Heuristics and biases* (pp. 201–208). New York: Cambridge University Press.

Kuhn, D. (1991). *The skills of argument*. Cambridge: Cambridge University Press.

Loomes, G., & Sugden, R. (1982). Regret theory: An alternative theory of rational choice under uncertainty. *Economic Journal, 92*, 805–824.

McCloy, R., & Byrne, R. M. J. (2002). Semifactual "even if" thinking. *Thinking & Reasoning, 8*, 41–67.

Pearl, J. (2000). *Causality: Models, reasoning and inference*. Cambridge: Cambridge University Press.

Sanfey, A. G., Loewenstein, G., McClure, S. M., & Cohen, J. D. (2006). Neuroeconomics: Cross-currents in research on decision-making. *Trends in Cognitive Science, 10*, 108–116.

Schacter, D. L., Addis, D. R., & Buckner, R. L. (2008). Episodic simulation of future events: Concepts, data and applications. *Annals of the New York Academy of Sciences, 1124*, 39–60.

Shafir, E., Simonson, I., & Tversky, A. (1993). Reason-based choice. *Cognition, 49*, 11–36.

Sloman, S. A. (1996). The empirical case for two systems of reasoning. *Psychological Bulletin, 119*, 3–22.

Sloman, S. A., & Lagnado, D. (2005). Do we "do"? *Cognitive Science, 29*, 5–39

Slovic, P., Finucane, M., Peters, E., & MacGregor, D. G. (2002). The affect heuristic. In T. Gilovich, D. Griffin, & D. Kahneman (Eds.), *Heuristics and biases: The psychology of intuitive judgment* (pp. 397–420). Cambridge: Cambridge University Press.

Thompson, V. A., Evans, J. St B. T., & Handley, S. J. (2005). Persuading and dissuading by conditional argument. *Journal of Memory and Language, 53*, 238–257.

Voss, J., & Means, M. (1991). Learning to reason via instruction in argumentation. *Learning and Instruction, 1*, 337–350.

Vygotsky, L. (1981). The genesis of higher mental functions. In J. Wertsch (Ed.), *The concept of activity in social psychology* (pp. 144–188). Armonk, NY: Sharpe.

Walton, D. N. (1989). Dialogue theory for critical thinking. *Argumentation, 3*, 169–184.

Weinstock, M., Neuman, Y., & Tabak, I. (2004). Missing the point or missing the norms? Epistemological norms as predictors of students' ability to identify fallacious arguments. *Contemporary Educational Psychology, 29*, 77–94.

5   Facilitation and analogical transfer on a hypothetico-deductive reasoning task

Cynthia S. Koenig
St Mary's College of Maryland

Richard A. Griggs
University of Florida

In this chapter, we describe how analogical transfer has been employed in our research on Wason's THOG problem (Wason, 1977, 1978; Wason & Brooks, 1979) to attain several goals. First, we wanted to determine if the improved performance on the Pythagoras (Needham & Amado, 1995), Blackboard (O'Brien, Noveck, Davidson, Fisch, Lea, & Freitag, 1990) and SARS (Girotto & Legrenzi, 1993) versions of the THOG problem could be replicated and better understood by examining the importance of various elements of these problems to achieving analogical transfer. Second, we wanted to determine if improved performance indicated participants had truly abstracted the solution principle of the standard THOG problem by exploring which components of the solution needed to be abstracted for facilitation and analogical transfer to occur. Finally, and perhaps most importantly, we wanted to explain why the THOG problem has been so difficult to solve and how a dual-processing theory of reasoning (Evans, 2003, 2007, 2008) enlightens our understanding of this difficulty. Before describing our research, an overview of the THOG problem, the basic empirical findings for it, and the most common explanations for performance are provided.

Wason's THOG problem

The THOG problem, a hypothetico-deductive reasoning task created by Peter Wason (Wason, 1977, 1978; Wason & Brooks, 1979), has generated substantial research interest for over three decades because most participants fail to solve it. The task entails the generation of hypotheses and a combinatorial analysis of their consequences within a state of uncertainty. Correct performance averages 12.32% and ranges between 0% and 29% (Koenig & Griggs, 2004a). Not only do most participants have difficulty solving the problem, but most experimental manipulations have failed to improve performance without making significant changes in underlying structural features (e.g., Griggs & Newstead, 1982) or problem presentation (e.g., Girotto & Legrenzi, 1989, 1993).

The THOG problem that Wason and Brooks (1979) developed has become known as the standard version of the task. It typically uses four geometric figures, such as a black square, a white square, a black circle, and a white circle. In the text of the problem, participants are told that the experimenter has written down one of two colours (e.g., black or white) and one of two shapes (e.g., square or circle). An exclusive disjunctive rule that relates the four figures to an arbitrary name, THOG, then follows. The rule is "If, and only if, one of the figures includes either the colour I have written down or the shape I have written down, but not both, then it is called a THOG." Participants are then told that one of the figures is a THOG (e.g., the black square) and they must decide whether or not each of the other figures is a THOG, is not a THOG, or that there is insufficient information to make a decision. A sample standard THOG problem is given in the Appendix to this chapter (p. 84).

To solve the problem, participants must first decide which colour–shape combinations could be written down. Given the exclusive disjunctive rule and the fact that the black square has been identified as a THOG, only white and square or black and circle could be written down. Irrespective of which combination is written down, the same solution follows. The white circle shares only one feature with each combination written down, and the white square and black circle share both or neither. Thus, both the white square and the black circle are definitely not THOGs and the white circle definitely is a THOG. Interestingly, participants often provide incorrect solutions that are mirror images of the correct solution – that is, stating that the white circle definitely is not a THOG and the white square and black circle either could be or definitely are THOGs. Wason and Brooks (1979, p. 84) labelled these "intuitive errors" because participants appear to select their responses based "on the designs rather than on the hypotheses".

Although correct performance on the THOG problem is typically low, research has demonstrated that the difficulty of the problem does not stem from participants' inability to understand the exclusive disjunctive rule (e.g., Wason & Brooks, 1979), generate hypotheses for the possible written-down combinations (e.g., Girotto & Legrenzi, 1989; Smyth & Clark, 1986), or test these hypotheses (Wason & Brooks, 1979). When these processes are examined individually, participants clearly demonstrate their ability to understand and execute them. The difficulty, however, seems to lie in the necessity of carrying out these processing steps in combination. As a consequence, participants get confused at some point and incorrectly simplify the task in ways that lead to the dominant intuitive errors first identified by Peter Wason (Newstead, Girotto, & Legrenzi, 1995). Many investigators of the THOG problem have subsequently tried to uncover which problem elements are responsible for these errors.

Girotto and Legrenzi (1989) proposed that intuitive errors occur because participants have difficulty separating the data (i.e., the values of the identified THOG) from the hypotheses to be generated (i.e., the possible written-down combinations). Extending this explanation, and labelling it "confusion theory," Newstead and Griggs (1992) suggested that working memory capacity might be surpassed when participants are challenged with the combined tasks of generating, holding in memory, and testing hypotheses. When participants are confused and uncertain about what could be written down, they simplify the task by reasoning that the values (i.e., colour and shape) of the exemplar (i.e., the identified THOG) are the values that have been written down or are the values critical for evaluating the other figures.

In the first case, participants reason that the white circle would not be a THOG and the other two designs would be. In the latter case, they use a perceptual matching strategy (i.e., matching each figure to the known exemplar and responding based upon the closeness of the match) and state that the white circle is not a THOG and the other two figures may or may not be THOGs because the black circle and white square each share one feature of the exemplar. The "confusion theory" explanation has garnered support because several empirical investigations have demonstrated that when a problem statement separates the values of the exemplar from those possibly written down, performance is improved (e.g., Girotto & Legrenzi, 1989, 1993; O'Brien et al., 1990).

Analogical transfer and the THOG problem

In most problem-solving tasks, a critical component is abstracting from a problem's surface features its underlying structure and the steps that must be executed to reach a solution, sometimes called the "solution principle" (e.g., Reeves & Weisberg, 1994). The importance of abstraction as a criterion for problem comprehension has been the basis of much of the research on analogical transfer. Specifically, the goal of problem solvers in an analogical transfer task is to use the strategy employed to solve a first problem (the source problem) when presented with a second problem (the target problem) that may differ in surface features but share common structural properties. If problem solvers are able to transfer learning from one problem to another, true abstraction of the solution principle is assumed. The empirical findings on analogical transfer reveal this rarely occurs without some type of "experimental" help (e.g., providing a hint to use the source problem when solving the target problem). Some researchers, however, have determined that a number of factors facilitate analogical transfer; these include providing two or more source problems (e.g., Gick & Holyoak, 1983), increasing surface and structural similarity between source and target problems (e.g., Holyoak & Koh, 1987), and presenting visual material that elucidates the underlying structure of the problem (e.g., Beveridge & Parkins, 1987). In all these experimental manipulations, problem solvers appeared to be assisted in abstracting the solution principle from a source problem and then applying it to solve the target problem.

In studies that have produced significant levels of facilitation on the THOG problem, it is not clear that successful participants have abstracted the task's underlying solution principle. We only know they answered correctly, not what led to that answer. One way in which researchers have indirectly approached this dilemma has been to see if participants' improved performance on facilitating versions of the THOG task helped them to solve the more difficult standard THOG problem (i.e., exhibit analogical transfer). However, almost all previous attempts to elicit analogical transfer have failed (see Griggs & Newstead, 1982, 1983; Smyth & Clark, 1986; Wason & Brooks, 1979).

Our recent studies have led us to question the validity of using facilitation as the criterion for inferring problem understanding and suggest that true understanding of this difficult task is best demonstrated by successful transfer to the standard abstract THOG problem (Koenig & Griggs, 2004a, 2004b; Koenig, Platt, & Griggs, 2007). In the remainder of the chapter, we describe our investigations of specific features in source THOG problems necessary for eliciting analogical transfer using thematic and abstract versions of the THOG task and conclude by explaining our findings in the context of dual-process theory (Evans, 2003, 2007, 2008). Because our research initially involved Needham and Amado's (1995) Pythagoras THOG problem, we describe it first.

Needham and Amado's Pythagoras THOG problem

The first successful attempt to achieve analogical transfer with the THOG task occurred with Needham and Amado's (1995) Pythagoras THOG problem. Even more impressive, Needham and Amado observed "spontaneous" transfer. Instructional training or performance feedback was not necessary as it usually is to obtain transfer. Needham and Amado's finding suggests that participants may have abstracted the solution principle from the Pythagoras problem and used this knowledge to solve the more difficult standard THOG problem.

The Pythagoras THOG problem includes geometric figures but uses a thematic narrative to separate the exemplar values from the possible hypotheses. One character (Professor Pythagoras) writes down the THOG-defining values and puts them in a location (on an index card taped over the assistant's desk) that is different from the location of the identified THOG (on the desk with the other to-be-classified figures). A different character (Professor Pythagoras's assistant) classifies the other figures. The problem statement includes a hypothesis generation request (i.e., asking participants to hypothesize the combinations of colour and shape that Professor Pythagoras might have written down) before asking participants to classify the remaining figures. The complete problem is given in the Appendix to this chapter (p. 84).

Needham and Amado (1995) argued that the narrative structure of the Pythagoras problem, in which one character writes down the defining properties for a specific purpose but another character uses those properties to apply the rule, was responsible for the observed facilitation (an average of 62% correct across two experiments) because the structure separates the properties of the positive exemplar from those possibly written down, leading to facilitation. They also argued that the hypothesis generation request is probably not necessary to produce facilitation because their Executioner THOG problem did so without this request. Their conclusion is supported by previous investigations of the THOG problem that have revealed that adding a hypothesis generation request to the problem does not improve performance (e.g., Girotto & Legrenzi, 1993; Newstead & Griggs, 1992; Smyth & Clark, 1986; Wason & Brooks, 1979). Needham and Amado, however, did not realize their Pythagoras THOG problem contained another feature that may have contributed to facilitation via separation. Specifically, in the problem statement each of the four geometric designs is referred to as a numbered figure (i.e., Figure 1, Figure 2, Figure 3, and Figure 4). The four figures are normally presented visually without any specific labels. In addition, instead of identifying the exemplar by colour and shape (e.g., the black square is a THOG), it is identified by a figure number (i.e., Figure 1 is a THOG).

To better understand why this labelling may be important, a proposal by O'Brien et al. (1990) concerning the source of THOG task difficulty needs to be considered. According to O'Brien et al., one explanation for poor performance on the THOG task is that participants experience difficulty separately encoding information concerning the written-down properties, the exclusive disjunctive rule, and the identified THOG because they all refer to the same colours (e.g., black or white) and shapes (e.g., square or circle). In response, participants conflate the problem information by assuming that "black and square" (the values of the identified exemplar) is the written-down combination used to classify THOGs, thus producing the intuitive errors described earlier. Girotto and Legrenzi (1989) suggested this conflation might be difficult to avoid because the two values of a THOG (colour and shape) have been shown in concept identification studies to be resistant to separation and conducive to inclusive disjunctive interpretations (Ketchum & Bourne, 1980). Thus, by labelling each design with this figural notation, the Pythagoras THOG problem may have facilitated separation by making it less likely that participants would conflate the values of the exemplar with the values of the written-down combinations.

Griggs, Koenig, and Alea (2001) investigated the importance of this labelling in three experiments by factorially combining the three features of the Pythagoras THOG problem – narrative structure, figural labelling, and hypothesis generation – to determine which were necessary for achieving significant facilitation. Although the narrative structure and figural labelling used in the Pythagoras problem independently led to significant facilitation (40–50% correct), pairing hypothesis generation with either factor or pairing the two factors together was necessary for producing substantial facilitation (>50% correct).

Testing the Pythagoras THOG transfer effect

Having identified the problem features responsible for facilitation on the Pythagoras THOG problem, we next decided to test the reliability of Needham and Amado's (1995) transfer effect for the Pythagoras THOG problem and then, if reliable, determine which problem features were necessary for eliciting transfer. According to Needham and Amado, the primary source of this transfer effect was the narrative structure, which facilitates separation through unique features of the Pythagoras "story". However, there is a plausible alternative explanation for the transfer. The same dimensions (shape and colour) and dimensional values (square and circle and black and white) were used in the source and target problems. In the Pythagoras THOG source problem, the black square was identified as a THOG, and in the target standard THOG problem, the black circle was identified as a THOG. Absent the context of an overlying theme in the standard THOG problem, participants may have relied upon a simple surface similarity heuristic. Specifically, participants may have noticed that the "to be classified" THOG (white circle) in the Pythagoras THOG problem had the "opposite" values of the exemplar (black square). Then, given the similarity between the two problems, participants could have merely chosen the white square as the THOG in the standard THOG problem because it had the "opposite" values of the exemplar (black circle). This seems plausible given that participants worked the standard THOG problem immediately after the Pythagoras THOG problem so their memory of selecting the white circle would have been easily accessible.

We designed several experiments (Koenig & Griggs, 2004a; Experiments 1–3) to determine whether or not Needham and Amado's (1995) transfer results for the Pythagoras problem were replicable and, if replicable, to introduce gradual changes in surface similarity to determine the strength of this transfer and the factors responsible for it. Participants were given 10 minutes for each problem, turned in the source problem before receiving the target problem, and were instructed that they could write on the problem sheet as they solved each problem. We replicated Needham and Amado's (1995) finding of substantial facilitation. Correct performance on the Pythagoras THOG (76%, 19/25) was significantly better than performance on the source standard THOG (12%, 3/25). We also replicated Needham and Amado's finding of analogical transfer; correct performance on the target standard THOG was significantly better when it followed the Pythagoras THOG (52%, 13/25) than when it followed the standard THOG (16%, 4/25).

We examined all problem sheets to determine if the notations participants made would provide evidence of solution principle abstraction. This analysis revealed that the Pythagoras THOG may have facilitated separation by making the necessity of reasoning about both possible written-down combinations more salient through hypothesis generation. In total 92% (12/13) of participants who achieved transfer in this condition provided this notation on both problem sheets, suggesting the solution principle was transferred to the target problem. In contrast to the Pythagoras THOG condition, very few participants in the standard THOG condition made additional notations on their problem sheets. It is noteworthy that participants in this condition who correctly solved the source, the target, or both standard THOG problems had made some type of additional notation. Fifty per cent (2/4) of participants who achieved transfer had written down both possible hypotheses.

These notational data and transfer results suggest that participants were likely abstracting the solution principle from the Pythagoras THOG problem and applying it to the target problem rather than adopting a simple perceptual matching strategy based on surface similarity between the source and target problems. To garner support for this hypothesis, we next reduced surface similarity between source and target problems by changing the values of the two dimensions (shape, colour) used in the target standard THOG problem. This change should have made it less likely that participants would adopt a perceptual matching strategy. Two new shapes (cross and heart) and patterns (stripes and dots) (e.g.,) replaced the shapes (square, circle) and colours (black, white) of the figures in the target standard THOG problem. We labelled this new target problem the Dotted Cross Standard THOG. The complete problem is given in the Appendix to this chapter (p. 85).

Correct performance on the source Pythagoras THOG (53%, 20/38) was significantly better than performance on the source standard THOG (21%, 8/38), and correct performance on the Dotted Cross Standard THOG was significantly better when it followed the Pythagoras THOG (45%, 17/38) than when it followed the Standard THOG (21%, 8/38). These results suggest that decreasing surface similarity between source and target problems did not impede the Pythagoras THOG problem's ability to elicit analogical transfer.

The notational data revealed that across both problem conditions, participants who achieved transfer (72%, 18/25) were more likely than participants who did not achieve transfer (33%, 17/51) to provide notations on source and target problem sheets. Not surprisingly, writing down the possible hypotheses for the source and/or target problems was the most common notation in the Pythagoras THOG condition. For those participants who made this notation on both problem sheets, 83% (15/18) achieved transfer. In contrast, of the 11 participants who provided this notation only on the source problem sheet, 4 achieved transfer.

These notational data suggest hypothesis generation may be an important structural feature that facilitates solution principle abstraction. Before examining this possibility, we introduced one further change in surface similarity to provide a stronger test of the perceptual matching strategy. We used a THOG problem introduced by Robert Cordell (1978), in which the dimensions in the THOG problem were letters (R and T) and numbers (6 and 8) and were presented as "cards". Four combinations of numbers and letters were presented in boxes and replaced the shapes/colours in the standard THOG problem, (e.g., | T   8 |). The rule was, "A card will be classified as a THOG if and only if it includes EITHER the letter written down, OR the number written down, BUT NOT BOTH." We labelled this new target problem the Letter/Number Standard THOG. The complete problem is provided in the Appendix to this chapter (p. 86).

Cordell observed no unique facilitating effects for this problem, and we replicated this in a pilot study. Using letters and numbers as the two dimensions in the THOG problem eliminated the internal/external surface similarity present in the source and target problems of our first two experiments. This provided a good test of the effects of surface similarity on transfer because it greatly lessened the probability that participants could use a perceptual matching strategy to solve the target problem. Thus, if transfer continued to be observed for this new target problem, it would likely be as a result of abstraction of the solution principle and not a consequence of surface similarity and perceptual matching.

Correct performance on the Pythagoras THOG (66%, 24/36) was significantly better than performance on the source standard THOG (19%, 7/36). More importantly, correct performance on the Letter/Number Standard THOG was significantly better when it followed the Pythagoras THOG (56%, 20/36) than when it followed the standard THOG (22%, 8/36). Among participants who solved the source, target, or both problems in the Pythagoras THOG condition, 85% (23/27) wrote down the correct hypotheses on the source and/or target problems. In total 92% (11/12) of participants who provided this notation on both problem sheets achieved transfer. In contrast, of the 14 who provided this notation only on the source problem, 4 achieved transfer. Interestingly, one participant who achieved transfer provided this only on the target problem.

The finding that the Pythagoras THOG continued to produce analogical transfer in the presence of significantly reduced surface similarity supports Gick and Holyoak's (1980, 1983) and Gentner's (1983) propositions that structural similarity is more critical than surface similarity to facilitating analogical transfer because it conveys the problem's underlying solution principle. Thus, if surface similarity is not necessary for eliciting transfer, which structural factors in the Pythagoras THOG are? The notations on the target problem sheets indicated that hypothesis generation might have facilitated abstraction of the THOG problem's solution principle.

Explaining the Pythagoras THOG transfer effect

Remember, the results of one of our earlier studies on the Pythagoras THOG problem (Griggs et al., 2001) revealed that the Pythagoras problem contains at least three facilitating factors – figural labelling, narrative structure, and hypothesis generation. Notably, substantial facilitation (>50% correct) was observed only when any two of these features were combined. Thus, we next explored whether or not Pythagoras THOG problems with only two of these features might also be capable of eliciting analogical transfer (Koenig & Griggs, 2004a; Experiment 4). Three versions of the Pythagoras problem (Narrative + Label THOG, Narrative + Hypothesis Generation THOG, and Label + Hypothesis Generation THOG) served as source problems. All three problems are given in the Appendix to this chapter (pp. 86–89). The Dotted Cross Standard THOG problem was maintained as the target problem because it seemed pragmatic to adopt a conservative approach. If too many changes were introduced (i.e., structural changes to the Pythagoras THOG and changes in both the dimensions and values of the figures in the target problem), it would have been difficult to ascertain which of these factors may have been responsible for either failed or successful analogical transfer.

The results replicated the combined facilitating effects of narrative structure, figural labelling, and hypothesis generation. Comparisons among source problems revealed that correct performance on the standard THOG (17%, 5/30) was significantly lower when compared with the Narrative + Label THOG (47%, 14/30), the Narrative + Hypothesis Generation THOG (57%, 17/30), and the Label + Hypothesis Generation THOG (73%, 22/30) problems. In addition, correct performance on the Label + Hypothesis Generation THOG was significantly better than the Narrative + Label THOG but not the Narrative + Hypothesis Generation THOG.

More importantly, a comparison among target problems revealed that performance on the Dotted Cross Standard THOG was significantly better when it followed the Narrative + Hypothesis Generation THOG (57%, 17/30) and the Label + Hypothesis Generation THOG (63%, 19/30) problems than when it followed the standard THOG (27%, 8/30). This facilitating effect was not observed with the Narrative + Label THOG. As in our first three experiments, the most frequent notation on all problem sheets was writing down the two possible hypotheses. In total 94% (30/32) of participants who wrote down the correct hypotheses on both problem sheets achieved transfer. The majority of these notations (21) occurred in those problem conditions that included a hypothesis generation request.

The results of this experiment helped to clarify the unique contributions that figural labelling, narrative structure, and hypothesis generation make to facilitation and analogical transfer. As in the Griggs et al. (2001) study, substantial facilitation was observed for any pairing of these factors. This was not, however, the case for analogical transfer. Specifically, it was only when either figural labelling or narrative structure was combined with a hypothesis generation request that significant analogical transfer was obtained. In contrast, when narrative structure was combined with figural labelling, analogical transfer failed to occur.

These results were surprising given that previous investigations of the

THOG task have convincingly demonstrated the nonfacilitating effect of adding a hypothesis generation request to the THOG problem (Girotto & Legrenzi, 1993; Newstead & Griggs, 1992; Smyth & Clark, 1986; Wason & Brooks, 1979). In addition, we had previously established that the Narrative + Label THOG could produce substantial facilitation even though it lacked this request. Why then did we find a different pattern for analogical transfer in this experiment?

One possible explanation involves the difference between explicit and implicit hypothesis generation requests. Girotto and Legrenzi (1989) suggested that facilitation on a THOG problem need not be a consequence of a direct hypothesis generation request but may occur when the problem statement includes a "plausible context for generating and testing hypotheses" (p. 134). For example, neither their Spy nor their Pub THOG problem included an explicit hypothesis generation request, but both problems produced substantial facilitation (75% and 89% correct, respectively). Thus, it is clear that an explicit request is not necessary if participants are persuaded by a problem's content to generate hypotheses as part of the problem-solving process. In the Pythagoras THOG problem and the two hypothesis generation problems, participants were explicitly asked to generate and test the possible written-down combinations. In contrast, the Narrative + Label THOG only implicitly made this request (i.e., participants played the role of generating and testing the combinations for Professor Pythagoras after learning that Figure 1 was a THOG).

Strong support for the importance of an explicit hypothesis generation request is derived from the notations participants made on their problem sheets. In the two hypothesis generation conditions, 76% of participants generated both correct hypotheses, whereas in the Label + Narrative THOG condition only 33% did so. Certainly participants in the Narrative + Label THOG condition were implicitly led to generate the hypotheses. It was simply much less likely than in those conditions in which the request was included explicitly within the problem statement. Although our results support Girotto and Legrenzi's (1989) findings of facilitation for problem versions that implicitly lead to hypothesis generation, they further indicate that an explicit request appears to be necessary for eliciting analogical transfer.

What role does hypothesis generation play in contributing to analogical transfer? Previous investigations of problem solving have demonstrated that some type of direct "help" is necessary for eliciting analogical transfer (Reeves & Weisberg, 1994). In the present study, this "help" was less direct than that normally used in studies of analogical transfer, which typically include training, specific instruction, and/or problem solutions. Rather, we provided indirect "help" by giving an explicit instruction to generate hypotheses only in the source problem, allowing participants to decide whether to use this step and the ensuing analysis with the target problem. We did not instruct them about the role of this step in the task's solution principle or directly instruct them to generate such hypotheses in the target problem.

Although this request is explicit in the source problem, it does not by itself provide a significant level of help because such a request does not produce facilitation or analogical transfer when no other facilitating problem features are present. Rather, our findings reveal that participants must be able to (1) separate the exemplar from the possible written-down combinations and (2) encode the "first step" of the THOG problem's solution principle – generating hypotheses for the two possible written-down combinations.

The generalizability of these findings (Koenig & Griggs, 2004a) concerning the necessity of an explicit hypothesis generation request for producing analogical transfer needs to be tested. Girotto and Legrenzi (1989) suggested that an explicit request for hypothesis generation was not necessary for producing facilitation if a problem included "a plausible context for generating and testing hypotheses" (p. 134). Girotto and Legrenzi clearly demonstrated this facilitation with their Two-level Spy problem as did Griggs et al. (2001) with their Narrative + Label problem. However, a problem that strongly implicitly leads participants to generate hypotheses and separates the data from the hypotheses may be capable of producing both facilitation and analogical transfer. O'Brien et al.'s (1990) Blackboard THOG may be such a problem. Next, we describe a study we conducted (Koenig & Griggs, 2004b) to investigate this possibility.

Generalizing the Pythagoras THOG transfer effect

The Blackboard THOG is an abstract version of the THOG task that facilitates performance quite differently from the Pythagoras THOG. In this version of the task, the participant is told that one of two colours and one of two shapes are written down on the left-hand side of the experimenter's blackboard and the other remaining colour and shape are written down on the right-hand side of the blackboard. The THOG rule then becomes, "A figure will be classified as a THOG, if, and only if, it includes either the colour written down on the left-hand side of the blackboard, or the shape written down on the left-hand side of the blackboard, but not both." Other than these changes, the problem statement is identical to the standard abstract version.

We (Koenig & Griggs, 2001) demonstrated that the Blackboard THOG leads to reliable facilitation (68% correct; 73% correct in a replication). We believe it does so by leading participants to construct a quasi-visual representation of the "binary, symmetric structure of the THOG problem because a blackboard is a stimulus onto which they can 'mentally' or 'physically' write both parts of the problem's structure" (p. 291). The Blackboard THOG educes separation of the data from the hypotheses by leading participants to consider both sides of the problem's structural tree (the combinations that could or could not be written down) and then to compare these with the exemplar provided. Participants' notations on their problem sheets supported this interpretation. In total 94% of participants drew a blackboard-type diagram, wrote "left" and "right" labels for colour–shape combinations, or wrote colour–shape combinations in a left–right fashion. The blackboard context appears to elicit a vivid spatial representation and facilitates performance by leading participants to spontaneously generate hypotheses.

Across three experiments (Koenig & Griggs, 2004b), using methodology developed for our Pythagoras THOG transfer research, we systematically reduced surface similarity between the source (Blackboard THOG) and target (standard abstract THOG) problems to determine the contributions of surface and structural features to analogical transfer. It was assumed that if significant transfer were achieved as surface similarity decreased, it would demonstrate that participants abstracted the task's underlying solution principle and provide evidence that a problem providing a context that strongly implicitly leads to separation and hypothesis generation may be just as successful in producing transfer as one that does this more explicitly.

In Experiment 1, correct performance on the Blackboard THOG (56%, 14/25) was significantly better than the source standard THOG (12%, 3/25) and transfer from the Blackboard THOG to the target standard THOG was observed. Correct performance on the target standard THOG was significantly better when it followed the Blackboard THOG (48% correct) than when it followed the source standard THOG (16% correct).

Notations on problem sheets suggested the Blackboard THOG was implicitly leading participants to consider both hypotheses by providing the quasi-visual context of a blackboard. This is nicely illustrated by the comments of one participant who achieved transfer: "The 'blackboard' example was better for me because it gave me the mental image I needed to construct the grid. I just made another grid for the second problem which met the criteria, and it was much easier." Specifically, 81% of participants who correctly solved either the Blackboard THOG, the target standard THOG that followed the Blackboard THOG, or both, had made additional notations that included (1) "left" or "right" labels; (2) blackboard-type drawings; and/or (3) labels of figures (e.g., "white square") written in a left–right orientation on the source or target problem sheet. In total 75% of those achieving transfer had written these types of notations on both problem sheets.

In Experiment 2, we decreased surface similarity by using the Dotted Cross Standard THOG as the target problem. Correct performance on the Blackboard THOG problem (50%, 19/38) was significantly better than the source standard THOG (21%, 8/38). However, correct performance on the Dotted Cross Standard THOG that followed the Blackboard THOG (37% correct) was not significantly better than performance on the Dotted Cross Standard THOG that followed the source standard THOG (21% correct).

These results support our assertion that a request for hypothesis generation must be made explicitly in combination with some separation feature in order to elicit significant levels of analogical transfer. The Blackboard THOG appears to achieve separation because facilitation was observed in Experiments 1 and 2. Even though the notational data again suggested that some participants were led to construct a problem structure that included both colour–shape combinations that could have been written down, the lack of surface similarity may have made it difficult for most participants to apply their source problem-solving strategy to the target problem. In other words, most participants needed to be explicitly instructed to generate these hypotheses.

In Experiment 3 we tested this possibility by creating two problems, the Blackboard THOG and the standard THOG, to which we added the hypothesis generation request stated as follows, "Given this piece of information about the Black Square, write down each of the possible things (each in the form: colour, shape) that I might have written down that would produce that result." The Dotted Cross Standard THOG problem was again the target problem.

Correct performance on the Blackboard + Hypothesis Generation THOG problem (70%, 21/30) was significantly better than the standard + Hypothesis Generation THOG problem (21%, 6/29) and the source standard THOG problem (10%, 3/29). More importantly, correct performance on the Dotted Cross Standard THOG that followed the Blackboard + Hypothesis Generation THOG (57% correct) was significantly better than performance on the Dotted Cross Standard THOG that followed the standard + Hypothesis Generation THOG (17% correct) and the source standard THOG (14% correct).

This experiment revealed that the Blackboard THOG was capable of producing facilitation and analogical transfer with reduced similarity between source and target problems if a hypothesis generation request was added to the problem statement. A significant proportion of participants (77%) who achieved transfer had correctly identified the two possible colour–shape combinations that could have been written down on both the source and target problems. In addition, the use of notations on both problem sheets indicating a reliance on the blackboard context to abstract the binary, symmetric structure (e.g., left–right labels and blackboard-type drawings) was more evident among those who achieved transfer (53%) than among those who failed to do so (15%).

These three experiments help to generalize and clarify our findings with the Pythagoras THOG by demonstrating that both separation and hypothesis generation are necessary for eliciting facilitation and analogical transfer for Wason's THOG task. They clearly support our proposal that an explicit hypothesis generation request is necessary for eliciting analogical transfer from most participants attempting to solve the THOG task.

In a final series of experiments (Koenig et al., 2007), we examined an abstract THOG task that leads to facilitation, Girotto and Legrenzi's (1993) SARS problem, to see if it would lead to analogical transfer to the standard THOG problem. The SARS problem serves as a good test for our proposal because it includes an explicit hypothesis generation request and, according to Girotto and Legrenzi, facilitates separation of the features of the exemplar from those written down. Before describing our transfer research with the SARS problem, we briefly summarize earlier research on it.

Girotto and Legrenzi's SARS problem

The SARS problem is essentially the standard THOG problem but with the following changes. Girotto and Legrenzi (1993) lexicalized the written-down combination by labelling it SARS, arguing this would allow participants to separate the features of the exemplar (a THOG) from the features written down (the SARS). Participants are told that one of the four designs (black diamond, white circle, black circle, and white diamond) has been defined as a SARS and that a design is a THOG if it has either the colour of the SARS or the shape of the SARS, but not both. In addition, the SARS problem included the following hypothesis generation instruction before the THOG identification task: "Knowing for sure that the black diamond is a THOG, you have to indicate which one or which ones, among the remaining designs, could be the SARS" (Girotto & Legrenzi, 1993, p. 705). Following this task, participants were given the THOG identification instruction, "Could you also indicate whether, in addition to the black diamond, there are other THOGs?" (p. 705). Correct performance (70%) on the SARS problem was very high. Girotto and Legrenzi attributed this facilitation to the problem's successful separation of the features of the THOG exemplar from those that were written down (those of the SARS) which led to problem understanding and the ensuing combinatorial analysis of the remaining design with respect to the hypothesized SARS combinations and the THOG rule.

Griggs, Platt, Newstead, and Jackson (1998) attempted to replicate the facilitation for the SARS problem but reached a different conclusion regarding the source of facilitation. In their first two experiments, they failed to find significant facilitation for the SARS problem when the standard three-choice THOG classification instruction (i.e., is a THOG, is not a THOG, or insufficient information) was used. In Experiment 3, however, when they used the classification instruction from the original SARS problem, significant facilitation was observed. Why the difference?

Griggs et al. (1998) concluded that an attentional heuristic explained this facilitation and that observed by Girotto and Legrenzi (1993). In the SARS problem statement, the black diamond is identified as a THOG, and this initially draws attention to the features "black" and "diamond". When instructed to determine which other designs might be the SARS, most participants correctly identified the black circle and white diamond as possibilities. Participants were then instructed to determine what they could say about "any other THOGs", which appeared to be interpreted as indicating there was "one other THOG". When faced with this atypical instruction, participants likely focused their attention on the one remaining figure, the white circle, and judged it to be the other THOG. Thus, according to this interpretation, the SARS problem produces facilitation because of an attentional heuristic and not because its structural features lead to problem understanding. Griggs et al. (1998, Experiment 4) found some support for this interpretation when they observed significant facilitation for an explicit one-other THOG instruction ("In addition to the Black Diamond, one other design is a THOG. Which other design is a THOG?").

Analogical transfer, dual-process theory, and the SARS problem

Based on the results of our analogical transfer research (Koenig & Griggs, 2004a, 2004b), we concluded that (1) a source problem entailing features that lead to separation or hypothesis generation may be sufficient to elicit facilitation, but (2) both are necessary to produce analogical transfer. These results not only demonstrate that analogical transfer may be a better criterion for judging problem understanding but they also support dual-process accounts of reasoning, which emphasize two distinct cognitive systems (Evans, 2003, 2007, 2008). In general, System 1 processes are rapid, parallel, and automatic in nature and are responsible for heuristical problem-solving strategies; and System 2, in contrast, is relatively slow, constrained by working memory capacity, and responsible for hypothetical thinking. Other differences between the two systems are that System 2 is volitional (rather than automatic), responds to verbal instructions, and is capable of overriding the default responses of System 1, such as those produced by attentional and matching heuristics, which may be involved in performance on the THOG problem. In our investigations of analogical transfer, the explicit instructions to generate hypotheses may have engaged System 2 processing, contributing to facilitation on the source problem and abstraction of the problem's solution principle.

By applying dual-process theory, two hypothesized outcomes for analogical transfer can be derived from the two competing explanations (described above) of the facilitation observed for the SARS problem. Girotto and Legrenzi (1993) would predict volitional System 2 reasoning (responsible for hypothetical thinking), which would lead participants to comprehend the solution principle of the THOG task and thus lead to analogical transfer. Griggs et al. (1998), in contrast, would predict more limited System 2 involvement. Whereas System 2 would probably be engaged during the hypothesis generation stage of the task, participants would probably default back to System 1 when given the "any other THOGs" instruction and respond via an attentional heuristic. In doing so, the solution principle of the THOG task would not be abstracted, resulting in no analogical transfer.

We (Koenig et al., 2007) tested these hypotheses using three source problems: (1) Standard THOG; (2) SARK; and (3) SARK + One Other THOG Instruction. The Dotted Cross Standard THOG problem was the target problem. All source problems entailed the same perceptual features (i.e., black square, white square, black circle, white circle). Except for using squares rather than diamonds, the SARK problem was the same as the SARS problem but with the name of the SARS changed to SARK. We made this change because the acronym "SARS" has been used since the Girotto and Legrenzi study to signify "sudden acute respiratory syndrome" and thus is no longer meaningless. A second version of the SARK problem incorporated the One Other THOG instruction to determine if results for it would mirror those for the SARS problem as they did in Griggs et al.'s (1998) earlier research.

Correct performance on the SARK problem (68%) and the SARK + One Other THOG instruction problem (82%) was significantly better than correct performance on the source standard THOG problem (14%). However, none of the source problems led to significant analogical transfer (per cent correct on the target problem was less than 20% in all three conditions). Although the vast majority of participants provided the correct hypotheses for both SARK problems, they failed to transfer the hypothesis generation strategy (as indicated by the lack of notations on the problem sheets) to the target problem. In studies of the Blackboard THOG and Pythagoras THOG, Koenig and Griggs (2004a, 2004b) noted high levels of notations on the source and target problems suggesting participants were abstracting elements of the solution principle from the source problem and transferring it to the target problem. Thus, these findings suggest the SARK problems did not lead to abstraction of the underlying solution principle of the THOG problem.

These results also support the attentional explanation of Griggs et al. (1998) for facilitation on the SARS problem. While most participants were able to correctly solve both versions of the SARK problem, transfer to the target problems did not follow. The difficulty emanating from the THOG problem seems to occur in response to working memory overload. When participants are tasked with generating hypotheses, holding them in memory, and testing the three possible THOGs, working memory capacity is exceeded and confusion results (Girotto & Legrenzi, 1989; Newstead & Griggs, 1992). In response to this confusion, participants may simplify the task by assuming the features of the identified THOG are the features that have been written down. When participants rely on these perceptual features to reason about the THOG problem (System 1 processes) rather than considering the logical structure of the problem (System 2 processes), they are more likely to make intuitive errors (labelling the white circle as Not a THOG, and the other two figures as THOGs or as indeterminate). As Griggs and Newstead (1983) noted, "perceptual matching is the better explanation of intuitive errors on this task . . . used only when subjects are confused by the logic of the problem and have recourse to no other basis for responding" (p. 451). Intuitive errors were the predominant error patterns in the standard THOG and target problems, suggesting that because System 2 processes are constrained by working memory capacity, participants reverted to System 1 processes to solve these problems.

So far we have argued that transfer did not occur because participants relied on System 1 processing in the source problem. However, transfer failure could occur either because the transfer of System 2 processing was either incorrect or incomplete or because the participant failed to recognize the analogy between the source and target problems and therefore did not transfer the relevant solution principle. We need to consider these alternatives in turn to rule out these possibilities.

If the solution principle was discovered in the source problem, we might still see transfer failure if the target problem involved a different application of the solution principle or if other System 2 processing was required in order to solve the target problem. This might be likely to happen in a reasoning setting where a solution principle is learned on one type of problem but the transfer problem differs substantially in the underlying structure or the type of task so that the application of the solution principle would differ enough to prevent successful and complete transfer. However, this scenario seems unlikely since the source and target problems in this study were isomorphs of one another and the types of decisions participants were making in both tasks were the same.

The other possibility is that the participants discovered the solution principle in the source problem but failed to see the analogy between the source and target problems. While the problems were isomorphs of one another, participants could have still failed to see the structural similarity if they focused instead on the superficial differences. For example, Gick and Holyoak (1980) found that most participants who discovered a solution schema in one problem-solving scenario failed to apply it to an isomorphic problem in a different scenario unless given a hint that the solution from the first problem might aid their search for a solution to the second problem. However, this explanation seems unlikely given that Koenig and Griggs (2004a, 2004b) have already demonstrated analogical transfer with other versions of the THOG (e.g., Blackboard and Pythagoras problems). Given that the source problem in the present study, which contained abstract content, in some ways has greater surface similarity to the target problem than the source problems in these previous studies, it is difficult to argue that the analogy would be noticed by participants in these past studies but not in this one.

What remains to be explained is why other THOG problems have produced transfer whereas the SARS problem does not. Koenig and Griggs (2004a) proposed that for analogical transfer to occur two conditions must be met: (1) the source problem must result in separation of the exemplar from the combinations that may be written down; and (2) the hypothesis generation strategy must be encoded. In the SARS problem, the labelling should fulfil the first of these requirements and hypothesis generation should be elicited when the participants generate the possible combinations for the SARS. Previous studies demonstrating transfer reveal that participants often transfer the hypothesis generation strategy as indicated by notations on target problems (Koenig & Griggs, 2004a, 2004b). That did not appear to be the case in our SARK study, which suggests that participants did not use a hypothesis generation strategy on the target problems even when they generated the possible combinations for the SARK in the source problem. Thus, participants did not abstract the problem's solution principle, and no transfer to the target problem was observed.

Dual-process theory provides an explanation for this transfer failure. Evans (2003) discusses the impact of competition between System 1 and System 2 processing. System 1 processes are believed to be automatic, occur without intention, and often involve the use of perceptual heuristics. Therefore, when a conflict occurs between the two systems, System 2 must "override or inhibit default responses emanating from System 1" (p. 456). However, Evans argues that suppression of System 1 is a high-effort process that only occurs when emphasis is placed on reasoning deductively, especially via verbal instructions. In the SARK study, participants were told they would be solving two deductive reasoning problems. Nevertheless, we do not believe this instruction caused participants to reason deductively and override System 1. The strongest evidence for this is derived from a comparison of correct performance on the source standard THOG (14%) and the two SARK source problem conditions (68% and 82%). If this instruction produced System 2 processing, performance should be significantly improved on the standard THOG problem. Further, in all of our previous transfer research (Koenig & Griggs, 2004a, 2004b), we used this instruction for all problem conditions and differences in performance were accounted for by other problem features.

Evans (2003) suggests that bias effects may reflect this sort of competition between System 1 and System 2 processes. In a situation closely analogous to the present problem, Platt and Griggs (1993) found that performance on Wason's four-card selection task (Wason, 1966, 1968) could be facilitated by introducing an explicit rule that blocked matching bias (a System 1 heuristic) and by directing participants to provide reasons for the selections they made (emphasizing System 2 processing). However, when an explicit rule allowing matching bias was introduced, facilitation was reduced (Platt & Griggs, 1995). This result suggests that participants reverted to the default System 1 strategy when it was possible. A similar process may be occurring in the SARS problem. Whereas the SARS problem may provide an opportunity for both separation and hypothesis generation, the System 1 attentional heuristic may be more likely to guide performance. Because those attentional cues are not present in the target problem, no transfer occurs.

If this analysis is correct, it suggests that participants give the right answer to the SARS problem but for the wrong reason. The problem instructions guide the participant to believe there is one other THOG, and since the other shape–colour combinations have already been identified, attention is drawn to the remaining figure. The SARK results also point out the importance of using the analogical transfer paradigm to determine whether participants abstract the underlying solution principle of a problem. Without using this procedure, it appears participants understand the solution principle of the SARS problem. They have a high rate of correct performance on it. However, the poor performance on the target problem in the transfer paradigm reveals that their correct selections are more likely attributed to System1 processing and not a true understanding of the logical structure of the task.

Summary

In this chapter, we have described our programmatic research (11 experiments and 790 participants) on facilitation and analogical transfer for Wason's THOG problem. Because this problem has proven to be so difficult to solve, we and others have tried to uncover exactly why this is so. Early investigations suggested that task demands overwhelm working memory and participants take mental shortcuts that lead to high failure rates. Thus, our goals have been to determine which components of the task lead to facilitation, to use analogical transfer as a more stringent criterion for problem comprehension, and to explain the difficulty of the task in the context of dual-process theory.

We began our research programme by examining which components of the THOG problem needed to be included in order for facilitation (Griggs et al., 2001; Koenig & Griggs, 2004a, 2004b) to occur on different versions of the THOG task. Our investigations of Needham and Amado's (1995) Pythagoras THOG, O'Brien et al.'s (1990) Blackboard THOG, and Girotto and Legrenzi's (1993) SARS problems clearly revealed that in order for substantial facilitation to occur, participants needed to be able to separate the data (i.e., the values of the identified THOG) from the hypotheses to be generated (i.e., the possible written-down combinations). Although the three problems we examined achieve this separation in distinctly different ways, they all produce substantial facilitation. Across all three problems, the per cent correct ranged between 68% and 76%.

We then decided to use a more stringent performance criterion – analogical transfer – to determine which components of the THOG problem's solution principle needed to be present in these three problems in order to facilitate problem comprehension. Previous research had primarily relied on facilitation as the criterion for deducing that participants had understood the THOG task. However, we believe this is a rather weak criterion, especially in the absence of protocol analysis, because it only indicates that participants produced the correct solution, not how or why. Our research clearly demonstrates that in order for participants to fully understand the THOG problem's underlying structure and transfer this knowledge to a target problem, the problem must: (1) entail features that lead to separation of the possible written-down combinations from the identified exemplar; and (2) explicitly request the hypothesis generation step.

Finally, our investigations of the THOG problem support a dual-processing theory of reasoning, which emphasizes two distinct cognitive systems. In the present context, it appears that explicit hypothesis generation instructions engage System 2 processing responsible for hypothetical thinking, leading to

82   *Koenig and Griggs*

abstraction of the THOG problem solution principle and successful analogical transfer. Dual-process theory, thus, explains why the Pythagoras THOG and Blackboard THOG problems that included explicit requests for hypothesis generation were successful in eliciting analogical transfer whereas the SARK (SARS) problem that only implicitly made this request was unsuccessful in doing so.

After re-examining the THOG problem using the analogical transfer research paradigm, it is evident that the solution principle of the task is not beyond the reasoning ability of most participants. We make this assertion despite the number of studies that have revealed very poor performance on this task. Dual-process theory has helped to clarify why successful performance on Wason's THOG task has been so elusive. Evans (2003) suggests that System 2 processing, which involves high effort, is a distinctly human capacity that evolved later than System 1 processing. As a consequence, a reliance on System 1 may be the default response in many problem-solving settings, especially those (like the THOG problem) that place high demands upon working memory. Our research supports dual-process accounts of reasoning and clarifies that the hypothetical-deductive reasoning required to solve Wason's THOG problem is possible when participants can be led to override System 1 processing and engage System 2 processing.

References

Beveridge, M., & Parkins, E. (1987). Visual representation in analogical problem solving. *Memory & Cognition, 15*, 230–237.

Cordell, R. (1978). *Mature reasoning and problem solving.* Unpublished dissertation. University of Nottingham.

Evans, J. St B. T. (2003). In two minds: Dual-process accounts of reasoning. *Trends in Cognitive Sciences, 7*, 454–459.

Evans, J. St B. T. (2007). *Hypothetical thinking: Dual processes in reasoning and judgement.* New York: Psychology Press.

Evans, J. St B. T. (2008). Dual processes accounts of reasoning, judgment, and social cognition. *Annual Review of Psychology, 59*, 255–278.

Gentner, D. (1983). Structure-mapping: A theoretical framework for analogy. *Cognitive Science, 7*, 155–170.

Gick, M. L., & Holyoak, K. J. (1980). Analogical problem solving. *Cognitive Psychology, 12*, 306–355.

Gick, M. L., & Holyoak, K. J. (1983). Schema induction in analogical transfer. *Cognitive Psychology, 15*, 1–38.

Girotto, V., & Legrenzi, P. (1989). Mental representation and hypothetico-deductive reasoning: The case of the THOG problem. *Psychological Research, 51*, 129–135.

Girotto, V., & Legrenzi, P. (1993). Naming the parents of the THOG: Mental representation and reasoning. *The Quarterly Journal of Experimental Psychology, 46A*, 701–713.

Griggs, R. A., Koenig, C. S., & Alea, N. L. (2001). De-confusing the THOG problem: The Pythagorean solution. *The Quarterly Journal of Experimental Psychology, 54A*, 921–933.

Griggs, R. A., & Newstead, S. E. (1982). The role of problem structure in a deductive reasoning task. *Journal of Experimental Psychology: Learning, Memory, and Cognition, 8*, 297–307.

Griggs, R. A., & Newstead, S. E. (1983). The source of intuitive errors in Wason's THOG problem. *British Journal of Psychology, 74*, 451–459.

Griggs, R. A., Platt, R. D., Newstead, S. E., & Jackson, S. L. (1998). Attentional factors in a disjunctive reasoning task. *Thinking and Reasoning, 4*, 1–14.

Holyoak, K. J., & Koh, K. (1987). Surface and structural similarity in analogical transfer. *Memory & Cognition, 15*, 332–340.

Ketchum, R. D., & Bourne, L. E. (1980). Stimulus–rule interactions in concept verification. *American Journal of Psychology, 93*, 5–23.

Koenig, C. S., & Griggs, R. A. (2001). Elementary, my dear Wason: The role of problem representation in the THOG task. *Psychological Research, 65*, 289–293.

Koenig, C. S., & Griggs, R. A. (2004a). Analogical transfer in the THOG task. *The Quarterly Journal of Experimental Psychology, 57A*, 557–570.

Koenig, C. S., & Griggs, R. A. (2004b). Facilitation and analogical transfer in the THOG task. *Thinking and Reasoning, 10*, 355–370.

Koenig, C. S., Platt, R. D., & Griggs, R. A. (2007). Using dual-process theory and analogical transfer to explain facilitation on a hypothetico-deductive reasoning task. *Psychological Research, 71*, 495–502.

Needham, W. P., & Amado, C. A. (1995). Facilitation and transfer with narrative thematic versions of the THOG task. *Psychological Research, 58*, 67–73.

Newstead, S. E., Girotto, V., & Legrenzi, P. (1995). The THOG problem and its implications for human reasoning. In S. E. Newstead & J. St B. T. Evans (Eds.), *Perspectives on thinking and reasoning* (pp. 261–285). Hove, UK: Lawrence Erlbaum Associates Ltd.

Newstead, S. E., & Griggs, R. A. (1992). Thinking about THOG: Sources of error in a deductive reasoning problem. *Psychological Research, 54*, 299–305.

O'Brien, D. P., Noveck, I. A., Davidson, G. M., Fisch, S. M., Lea, R. B., & Freitag, J. (1990). Sources of difficulty in deductive reasoning: The THOG task. *The Quarterly Journal of Experimental Psychology, 42A*, 329–351.

Platt, R. D., & Griggs, R. A. (1993). Facilitation in the abstract selection task: The effects of attentional and instructional factors. *The Quarterly Journal of Experimental Psychology, 46A*, 591–613.

Platt, R. D., & Griggs, R. A. (1995) Facilitation and matching bias in the abstract selection task. *Thinking and Reasoning, 1*, 55–70.

Reeves, L. M., & Weisberg, R. W. (1994). The role of content and abstract information in analogical transfer. *Psychological Bulletin, 115*, 381–400.

Smyth, M. M., & Clark, S. E. (1986). My half-sister is a THOG: Strategic processes in a reasoning task. *British Journal of Psychology, 77*, 275–287.

Wason, P. C. (1966). Reasoning. In B. M. Foss (Ed.), *New horizons in psychology*. Harmondsworth, UK: Penguin.

Wason, P. C. (1968). Reasoning about a rule. *The Quarterly Journal of Experimental Psychology, 20*, 273–281.

Wason, P. C. (1977). Self-contradictions. In P. N. Johnson-Laird & P. C. Wason (Eds.), *Thinking: Readings in cognitive science* (pp. 114–128). Cambridge: Cambridge University Press.

Wason, P. C. (1978). *Hypothesis testing and reasoning. Unit 25, Block 4, Cognitive psychology*. Milton Keynes, UK: Open University Press.

Wason, P. C., & Brooks, P. G. (1979). THOG: The anatomy of a problem. *Psychological Research, 41*, 79–90.

Appendix

Some variants of the THOG problem used in the analogical transfer research

Standard THOG problem

Below are four figures. Each figure is either black or white and square or circle. By writing down one of these colors (either black or white) and one of these shapes (either square or circle), I have developed a classification rule for the four figures.

The rule is: "A figure will be classified as a THOG if, and only if, it includes EITHER the color written down, OR the shape written down, BUT NOT BOTH." The figures are:

I will tell you that the Black Square is a THOG.

Using this piece of information and the classification rule given above, decide for each of the other figures whether or not it can be classified as a THOG.

For each figure, circle your choice:

White Square	IS a THOG	IS NOT a THOG	Can't tell
Black Circle	IS a THOG	IS NOT a THOG	Can't tell
White Circle	IS a THOG	IS NOT a THOG	Can't tell

Pythagoras THOG problem

Professor Pythagoras is a mathematician who works in the area of geometry. He is always coming up with various schemes for classifying different geometric figures. He works on both strange figures and simple ones. He leaves part of the job of classifying simple figures to his assistant.

For a while now, the professor has been working on schemes that classify various figures as to whether they are THOGs or not, depending on the color (black or white) and the shape (square or circle) of the figure. Each time the professor comes up with a new scheme, he gives his assistant an index card with information about the scheme, and the assistant tapes the card to the wall over his desk. On the card, the professor writes two things:

first, the name of one of the colors (either "black" or "white"), second, the name of one of the shapes (either "square" or "circle").

Below that card on the wall over the assistant's desk is posted the professor's permanent classification rule: "A figure will be classified as a THOG if, and only if, EITHER its color matches the color name on the card above, OR its shape matches the shape name on the card above, BUT NOT BOTH. If it matches BOTH the color and the shape names or NEITHER the color or shape name, then it is not a THOG."

On a certain day, the professor has given the assistant a new card to tape up, and the assistant is considering four figures he has on his desk. The figures are:

Figure 1   Figure 2   Figure 3   Figure 4

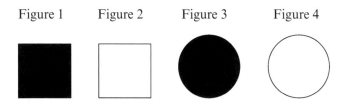

The assistant correctly classifies Figure 1 as being a THOG.

(1) Given this piece of information about Figure 1, write down each of the possible things (each in the form: color, shape) which Professor Pythagoras MIGHT have written on the new card that would produce that result.
(2) Using your answer to (1) and the classification rule given above, decide for each of the other figures, whether or not it can be classified as a THOG.

For each figure, circle your choice:

Figure 2	IS a THOG	IS NOT a THOG	Can't tell
Figure 3	IS a THOG	IS NOT a THOG	Can't tell
Figure 4	IS a THOG	IS NOT a THOG	Can't tell

Dotted Cross Standard THOG problem

Below are four figures. Each figure is either dotted or striped and cross or heart. By writing down one of these patterns (either dotted or striped) and one of these shapes (either cross or heart), I have developed a classification rule for the four figures.

The rule is: "A figure will be classified as a THOG if, and only if, it includes EITHER the pattern written down, OR the shape written down, BUT NOT BOTH." The figures are:

I will tell you that the Dotted Cross is a THOG.

Using this piece of information and the classification rule given above, decide for each of the other figures whether or not it can be classified as a THOG.

For each figure, circle your choice:

Dotted Heart	IS a THOG	IS NOT a THOG	Can't tell
Striped Heart	IS a THOG	IS NOT a THOG	Can't tell
Striped Cross	IS a THOG	IS NOT a THOG	Can't tell

Letter/Number Standard THOG problem

Below are four cards. Each card includes either an R or T and a 6 or 8. By writing down one of these letters (either R or T) and one of these numbers (either 6 or 8), I have developed a classification rule for the four cards.

The rule is: "A card will be classified as a THOG if, and only if, it includes EITHER the letter written down, OR the number written down, BUT NOT BOTH."

| R   8 | | T   8 | | R   6 | | T   6 |

I will tell you that | R   8 | is a THOG.

Using this piece of information and the classification rule given above, decide for each of the other cards whether or not it can be classified as a THOG. For each card, circle your choice:

| T   8 | IS a THOG | IS NOT a THOG | Can't Tell |

| R   6 | IS a THOG | IS NOT a THOG | Can't Tell |

| T   6 | IS a THOG | IS NOT a THOG | Can't Tell |

Narrative + Label THOG problem

Professor Pythagoras is a mathematician who works in the area of geometry. He is always coming up with various schemes for classifying different geometric figures. He works on both strange figures and simple ones. He leaves part of the job of classifying simple figures to his assistant.

For a while now, the professor has been working on schemes that classify various figures as to whether they are THOGs or not, depending on the color (black or white) and the shape (square or circle) of the figure. Each time the professor comes up with a new scheme, he gives his assistant an index card with information about the scheme, and the assistant tapes the card to the wall over his desk. On the card, the professor writes two things: first, the name of one of the colors (either "black" or "white"), second, the name of one of the shapes (either "square" or "circle"). Below that card on the wall over the assistant's desk is posted the professor's permanent classification rule: "A figure will be classified as a THOG if, and only if, EITHER its colour matches the color name on the card above, OR its shape matches the shape name on the card above, BUT NOT BOTH. If it matches BOTH the color and the shape names or NEITHER the colour or shape names, then it is not a THOG."

On a certain day, the professor has given the assistant a new card to tape up, and the assistant is considering four figures he has on his desk. The figures are:

Figure 1   Figure 2   Figure 3   Figure 4

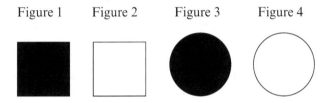

The assistant correctly classifies Figure 1 as being a THOG.

Using this piece of information and the classification rule given above, decide for each of the other figures, whether or not it can be classified as a THOG. For each figure, circle your choice:

Figure 2   IS a THOG   IS NOT a THOG   Can't tell
Figure 3   IS a THOG   IS NOT a THOG   Can't tell
Figure 4   IS a THOG   IS NOT a THOG   Can't tell

Narrative + Hypothesis Generation THOG problem

Professor Pythagoras is a mathematician who works in the area of geometry. He is always coming up with various schemes for classifying different geometric figures. He works on both strange figures and simple ones. He leaves part of the job of classifying simple figures to his assistant.

For a while now, the professor has been working on schemes that classify various figures as to whether they are THOGs or not, depending on the color (black or white) and the shape (square or circle) of the figure. Each time the professor comes up with a new scheme, he gives his assistant an index card with information about the scheme, and the assistant tapes the card to the wall over his desk. On the card, the professor writes two things:

first, one of the colors (either "black" or "white"), second, one of the shapes (either "square" or "circle"). Below that card on the wall over the assistant's desk is posted the professor's permanent classification rule: "A figure will be classified as a THOG if, and only if, EITHER its color matches the color on the card above, OR its shape matches the shape on the card above, BUT NOT BOTH. If it matches BOTH the color and the shape or NEITHER the color or shape, then it is not a THOG."

On a certain day, the professor has given the assistant a new card to tape up, and the assistant is considering four figures he has on his desk. The figures are:

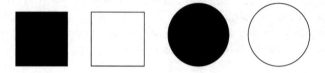

The assistant correctly classifies the Black Square as being a THOG.

(1) Given this piece of information about the black square, write down each of the possible things (each in the form: color, shape) which Professor Pythagoras MIGHT have written on the new card that would produce that result.

(2) Using your answer to (1) and the classification rule given above, decide for each of the other figures, whether or not it can be classified as a THOG.

For each figure, circle your choice:

White Square	IS a THOG	IS NOT a THOG	Can't tell
Black Circle	IS a THOG	IS NOT a THOG	Can't tell
White Circle	IS a THOG	IS NOT a THOG	Can't tell

Label + Hypothesis Generation THOG problem

Below are four figures. Each figure is either black or white and square or circle. By writing down one of these color names and one of these shape names, I have developed a classification rule for the four figures.

The rule is: "A figure will be classified as a THOG if, and only if, EITHER its colour matches the color name written down, OR its shape matches the shape name written down, BUT NOT BOTH. If it matches BOTH the color and shape names written down or NEITHER the color or shape names written down, then it is not a THOG." The figures are:

Figure 1   Figure 2   Figure 3   Figure 4

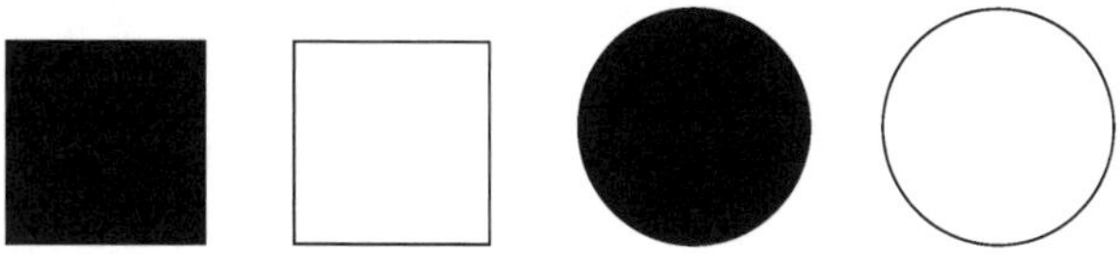

I can tell you that Figure 1 is a THOG.

(1) Given this piece of information about Figure 1, write down each of the possible things (each in the form: color, shape) which I MIGHT have written down that would produce that result.
(2) Using your answer to (1) and the classification rule given above, decide for each of the other figures, whether or not it can be classified as a THOG.

For each figure, circle your choice:

Figure 2	IS a THOG	IS NOT a THOG	Can't tell
Figure 3	IS a THOG	IS NOT a THOG	Can't tell
Figure 4	IS a THOG	IS NOT a THOG	Can't tell

Part II
If

6 Conditionals and disjunctions

Klaus Oberauer
University of Bristol

Sonja Geiger
University of Western Australia

Katrin Fischer
University of Applied Sciences
Northwestern Switzerland

Consider the following argument: "My keys are either in my pocket or on the shelf. Therefore, if my keys are not in my pocket, they are on the shelf". This argument sounds extremely compelling, but is it logically valid? For it to be logically valid, we would require that the conclusion (i.e., the conditional) follows necessarily from the premise (i.e., the disjunction) by virtue of its form, regardless of its content. Thus, for any propositions A and C, it cannot be the case that the premise "A or C" is true but the conclusion "if not A then C" is false. Whether or not the inference from a disjunction "A or C" to a corresponding conditional "if not A then C" is logically valid depends on how the conditional is understood.

Truth tables and mental models

One way of interpreting conditionals, which has been adopted by the theory of mental models (Johnson-Laird & Byrne, 1991, 2002), is as a *material conditional*. A material conditional is defined by its truth table, which lists all possible combinations of the truth or falsity of the antecedent and of the consequent (see Table 6.1). The material conditional is true for all cases except when the antecedent is true and the consequent is false. In the theory of mental models, a fully fleshed out representation of the conditional consists of the set of mental models for all truth-table cases that render the material conditional true. For the conditional "If A then C" these models are:

$$
\begin{array}{cc}
A & C \\
\neg A & C \\
\neg A & \neg C
\end{array}
$$

Table 6.1 Truth tables for inclusive disjunction and the corresponding material conditional, and for exclusive disjunction and the corresponding biconditional

	Negation at conditional			
	A or C (inclusive)	If not A then C (conditional)	A or C (exclusive)	If not A then C (biconditional)
A & C	T	T	F	F
A & ¬C	T	T	T	T
¬A & C	T	T	T	T
¬A & ¬C	F	F	F	F

	Negation at disjunction			
	Not A or C (inclusive)	If A then C (conditional)	Not A or C (exclusive)	If A then C (biconditional)
A & C	T	T	T	T
A & ¬C	F	F	F	F
¬A & C	T	T	F	F
¬A & ¬C	T	T	T	T

For a conditional with a negated antecedent, such as "If not A then C", the models are:

> A   C
> A   ¬C
> ¬A   C

Note that models can be arranged in any top-to-bottom order, and are presented here in the order of the truth tables (Table 6.1).

As Table 6.1 shows, the truth table of a conditional with a negated antecedent, "If not A then C" matches exactly the truth table of a disjunction "A or C". Likewise, the truth table of a conditional without negation, "If A then C", matches that of a disjunction with a negation at the first constituent, "Not A or C". (We will call these pairs of statements with matching truth tables *corresponding* pairs.) One complication in this analysis is that, according to truth-table semantics and according to the mental model theory, both conditionals and disjunctions can be interpreted in two different ways. Conditionals can be interpreted as material conditionals, which are true in three cases of the truth table, or as biconditionals (paraphrased as "if and only if A then C"), which are true only in two cases. Likewise, disjunctions can be interpreted as inclusive, such that they are true when both constituents are true, or as exclusive, such that they are false when both constituents are true. The truth tables of material conditionals match those of corresponding inclusive disjunctions, and the truth tables of biconditionals match those of corresponding exclusive disjunctions.

What can we predict from the mental model theory for how people judge inferences from a disjunction to a conditional? The model theory prescribes that people first build a set of mental models of the premise(s) and then formulate a conclusion that is true in all models of the premise(s). Depending on whether the disjunctive premise is understood exclusive or inclusive, people would build two or three mental models. For "A or C", these models would be:

Inclusive		Exclusive	
A	C		
A	¬C	A	¬C
¬A	C	¬A	C

The set of three models is compatible with a material conditional but not a biconditional. Therefore, reasoners should regard the conditional as a valid conclusion if they interpret it as a material conditional. The set of two models is compatible with both the material conditional and the biconditional. Therefore, people should regard the conditional as a valid conclusion regardless of whether they read it as a material conditional or a biconditional.

The reverse inference, from a conditional as premise to a disjunction as conclusion, can be analysed in a similar way. The conditional "If not A then C" can be fleshed out in two ways:

Material Conditional		Biconditional	
A	C		
A	¬C	A	¬C
¬A	C	¬A	C

The models of the material conditional are compatible with the conclusion "A or C" only if the latter is interpreted as inclusive – in that case, the sets of mental models of premise and conclusion are identical. When interpreted as exclusive, the disjunction is stronger than the conditional (i.e., it rules out more possibilities), so it does not follow from the conditional as a premise because the conclusion can be false while the premise is true (i.e., in the case of the conjunction A&C). The set of models of the biconditional is compatible with the conclusion "A or C" regardless of how the disjunction is interpreted. If interpreted as exclusive, the set of mental models of the disjunction is identical to that of the biconditional. If the disjunction is understood as inclusive, then its models are a superset of those of the biconditional, which means that whenever the biconditional is true, the inclusive disjunction is also true, so that it follows logically from the biconditional premise. (The predictions of the model theory are summarized in Table 6.5, p. 105, where those combinations for which the theory prescribes that the inference is logically valid are shaded in grey.)

The probabilistic view

The interpretation of natural-language conditionals as material conditionals or biconditionals has been critiqued both in philosophy (Bennett, 2003; Edgington, 1995) and psychology (Evans, Over, & Handley, 2005; Oaksford & Chater, 2001; Oberauer & Wilhelm, 2003). These critics hold that the conditional is not truth functional at all, that is, its truth value cannot be determined from the truth values of its constituents, as they are listed in a truth table. Rather, the conditional is understood as a *probability conditional*. A probability conditional is not a proposition that makes a claim about what is true or false, but rather expresses a high conditional probability of the consequent, given the antecedent. When understood as a probability conditional, "If A then C" is evaluated not as true or false but as more or less believable or probable, and its probability is defined as $P(C|A)$.

An expression with these features sits uncomfortably with propositional logic, which is based on truth-functional connectives and binary truth values. How can we evaluate whether "If not A then C", understood as a probability conditional, follows logically from "A or C"? Fortunately, Adams (1975) has worked out a logic for the probability conditional. The core axiom of this logic is that the *uncertainty* of a valid conclusion must not exceed the sum of the *uncertainties* of the premises, where *uncertainty* is defined as one minus the probability of a statement. For our case of an inference from a single premise, this means that the probability of the conclusion must not be smaller than that of the premise. In other words, if the premise "A or C" is accepted as true or at least highly probable, the conclusion "If not A then C" must be highly probable as well.

Over, Evans, and Elqayam (2010) discuss the implications of adopting the probability conditional for the validity of an inference from a disjunction to a conditional (see also Evans & Over, 2004). They distinguish between a constructive and a nonconstructive way of arriving at the disjunctive premise. A constructive way starts from knowing that one of the constituents is true, which implies that the disjunction must also be true. For example, when I feel that the key is in my pocket, I can state truthfully: "The key is either in my pocket or on the shelf", although this statement is pragmatically infelicitous because it conveys less relevant information than I have. My state of knowledge is different in the nonconstructive case, in which I don't know where the key is but can narrow it down to two possible locations, such that the most informative statement I can make is that "the key is either in my pocket or on the shelf".

In the nonconstructive case of saying "A or C", there are two possibilities, A and C, each with a probability > 0. The conditional "If not A then C" is to be evaluated by estimating $P(C|\neg A)$. Given our state of knowledge, the supposition of $\neg A$ narrows down the possibilities to one, namely C. Thus, assuming the disjunction is true, $P(C|\neg A) = 1$; more generally, our confidence that C is true once we suppose A to be false should depend strongly on our confidence in the disjunction. Therefore, we can regard the inference from "A or C" to "if not A then C" as very strong (it is nevertheless not logically valid, as demonstrated by Over et al., 2010, because one can construct cases in which the probability of the conclusion is smaller than that of the premise).

In the constructive case, there are two possibilities, A and C, with $P(A) = 1$ and $P(C) = 0$. Supposing $\neg A$ therefore forces us to leave behind our knowledge of reality, and to consider a counterfactual case: I know that the key is in my pocket, but what would be the case if it were not in my pocket? Moving into a counterfactual frame of reference (in possible-world semantics we might say: a counterfactual world) implies suspending some knowledge about the actual world, and this may include the knowledge on which our assertion of the disjunctive premise rests. I might know that the key is in my pocket because I feel it there, but when I imagine the counterfactual situation in which the key is not in my pocket, that knowledge would be suspended. Because that knowledge is the only reason why I stated the disjunction "the key is in my pocket or on the shelf", I should suspend that disjunction as well. Therefore, in the counterfactual situation in which the key is not in my pocket, there are no constraints on its whereabouts, and there is no reason to infer that it is on the shelf. In general, when our knowledge that $P(A) = 1$ is the only reason for believing "A or C", supposing $\neg A$ enforces a suspension of belief in "A or C", and thus, $P(C|\neg A)$ can have any value. Therefore, "If not A then C" does not follow from "A or C". The inference is not logically valid, and not even probabilistically strong.

What about the reverse inference from a conditional premise to a corresponding disjunction as conclusion? These inferences are logically valid according to Adams' probability logic as long as the disjunction is inclusive, because the probability of the conclusion is necessarily larger than (or equal to) the probability of the premise. The probability of the premise "If not A then C" equals $P(C|\neg A)$, which can be expanded to $P(A) \times P(C|\neg A) + P(\neg A) \times P(C|\neg A)$. The probability of the conclusion "A or C (or both)" equals $P(A) + P(\neg A) \times P(C|\neg A)$. The second addend in this equation is the same as in the expanded equation for the conditional, and the first addend, $P(A)$, can never be smaller than the first addend in the equation for the conditional, $P(A) \times P(C|\neg A)$. The inference from a conditional to an exclusive disjunction is not valid. The probability of an exclusive disjunction is $P(A) \times P(\neg C|A) + P(\neg A) \times P(C|\neg A)$. In this equation, the first addend can be smaller than the first addend in the equation for the conditional. To illustrate, it is easy to construct a counterexample, that is, an inference from a highly likely conditional to an unlikely exclusive disjunction: "If the CEO is not male then he is White" is highly likely for a typical company, but "The CEO is either male or White but not both" is unlikely to hold.

From this analysis we can predict on the basis of the probabilistic view that people should accept inferences from conditionals to the corresponding inclusive disjunctions, but not necessarily to exclusive disjunctions. They should not always accept the reverse inference from disjunctions to conditionals. Whether or not they do the latter should depend on whether the disjunctive premise has been introduced in a constructive or a nonconstructive way. Over et al. (2010) tested this latter prediction by an experiment comparing two groups of participants, one receiving a nonconstructive argument in which the disjunctive premise was simply stated as given, and a constructive argument with two steps, from "A" to "A or C", and from there to "if not A then C". Participants accepted the conditional as a conclusion more readily in the nonconstructive than the constructive group.

Experiments 1 and 2

In the remainder of this chapter we present a series of experiments investigating people's intuitions about the relation between conditionals and disjunctions, using the "direct inference" paradigm in which people are asked to evaluate conclusions from a single premise. This research has been motivated by the mental model view (for previous experiments applying the mental model theory to direct inferences see Ormerod & Richardson, 2003). We tested the prediction that people will endorse the inference from a disjunction to a corresponding conditional, or the reverse inference from a conditional as premise to a disjunction as conclusion, if they construct matching sets of mental models for the two statements. Specifically, they should infer a conditional from a disjunction if they understand the disjunction as inclusive and the conditional as material conditional (rather than biconditional). If they interpret the disjunction as exclusive, they should endorse the inference regardless of their interpretation of the conditional. For the reverse inferences – from conditionals as premises to disjunctions as conclusions – analogous predictions can be made. If the conditional is understood as a material conditional, people should accept a disjunctive conclusion as long as the disjunction is interpreted as inclusive. If people interpret the conditional as a biconditional, they should accept the disjunctive conclusion regardless of its interpretation.

Method

Participants

Both experiments were run through the internet. Responses were excluded if they were incomplete, if the same internet protocol address participated more than once, and if participants indicated in a post-experimental questionnaire that they had taken part in the same experiment before. A total of 564 participants in Experiment 1 delivered valid data and were on average 28 years old (ranging from 13 to 67); 40% were male. In Experiment 2, 270 participants delivered valid data; they were on average 26 years old (range 14 to 62), and 33% were male.

Design and materials

To assess people's interpretations of conditionals and disjunctions we asked them to complete one of two forms of a truth-table evaluation task (Johnson-Laird & Tagart, 1969). In this task participants are given a statement, such as "If A then C", and one of the four possible conjunctions of truth or falsity of each constituent (i.e., one of the four lines of the truth table). They are asked to judge whether the given conjunction renders the statement true, renders it false, or is irrelevant for its truth value. In our experiments we asked people to evaluate four kinds of statements, "if A then C", "if not A then C", "A or C", and "not A or C". Each statement was combined with four truth-table cases, for a total of 16 questions, presented in random order. Each statement was about a pair of letters, for example "If the pair contains a J then it contains a Z", followed by "NZ" (i.e., the false-antecedent, true-consequent case).

One common finding with this task when applied to conditionals is that people often judge the two false-antecedent cases as being irrelevant for the truth value of the conditional (Johnson-Laird & Tagart, 1969; Evans, Newstead, & Byrne, 1993). This is at odds with the material implication but is the normative answer under the probability conditional, because the probability conditional is evaluated on the basis of $P(C|A)$, for which the $\neg A$ cases are irrelevant. In more recent years some researchers have introduced variants of the truth-table task in which participants are asked whether the given truth-table case is compatible with the statement, rather than rendering it true (or false). With this instruction, a quite large proportion of adult participants judges the false-antecedent cases to be compatible with the conditional (Barrouillet, Grosset, & Lecas, 2000; Barrouillet & Lecas, 1999). This is again in line with the probabilistic view, because false-antecedent cases are compatible with the probability conditional. For instance, my conviction that "if it rains tomorrow, the temperature will drop" is fully compatible with the observation on the next day that it does not rain; my subjective conditional probability of a temperature drop, given rain, would still be very high.

The two versions of the truth-table evaluation task – asking whether a case renders the conditional true or false, versus asking whether a case is compatible or incompatible with the conditional – have never been directly compared in the same experiment, and this was one reason why we endeavoured in that comparison. Participants were allocated at random to one of two groups, one receiving "makes the statement true", "makes the statement false", and "is irrelevant for the truth or falsity of the statement" as response alternatives, the other receiving "is compatible with the statement", "contradicts the statement", and "is irrelevant for the statement". Another reason for introducing the compatibility version was more pragmatic: We were interested in testing whether people were more likely to accept inferences from disjunctions to conditionals (or in the reverse direction) when their truth-table evaluation patterns matched. When people give a large proportion of "irrelevant" judgements when evaluating the conditional, we cannot expect many matches with the truth-table patterns for the disjunction, because the latter rarely involve judgements of "irrelevant". We hoped that with the instruction to judge compatibility rather than truth, we would obtain a larger number of matching truth-table patterns.

The second part of each experiment consisted of six inferences with one premise above a line and one conclusion below the line. Four of them were the critical arguments:

Positive disjunction to negated conditional: "A or C"/"If not A then C"
Negated disjunction to positive conditional: "Not A or C"/"If A then C"
Positive conditional to negated disjunction: "If A then C"/"Not A or C"
Negated conditional to positive disjunction: "If not A then C"/"A or C"

The remaining two inferences were fillers:

Filler 1: "If A then not C"/"A or C"
Filler 2: "A or C"/"If A then not C"

The six inference tasks used again statements about pairs of letters. They were presented in a new random order for each participant. Participants judged whether or not the sentence below the line "follows logically" from the sentence above the line, that is, "whether the sentence below the line must be true if the sentence above is true".

Experiment 2 differed from Experiment 1 in two details. First, we dropped the compatibility condition. Second, we introduced a fourth response category, "don't know", because we speculated that some "irrelevant" judgements were reflections of indecision or confusion rather than confident judgements that the case is irrelevant for the statement. Giving participants an option to express their inability to make a confident judgement should render the judgements of "irrelevant" more valid.

Results

We first report results from the truth-table tasks, followed by results from the inference evaluation tasks, and finally the relations between the two tasks. In Experiment 2, only 25 of the 270 participants ever used the response category "don't know", so we excluded these 25 participants and treated the remaining 245 as an exact replication of the truth group of Experiment 1.

Truth-table tasks

Each participant evaluated the four cases of the truth table for each of the four statements. We classified the patterns of responses across the four truth-table cases for each statement. Three response options for four cases yield $3^4 = 81$ possible patterns. Patterns are referred to as four-letter codes for the truth values assigned to a statement, given the four cases in the truth table (Table 6.1) from top to bottom. Thus, the first letter stands for the statement's truth value when both constituents are true, the second letter stands for the statement's truth value when the first constituent is true and the second is false, and so on. This holds also for statements with negations, for example when the statement is "not A or C", the first letter codes the statement's truth value for the conjunction ¬A & C. As a consequence, corresponding pairs of disjunctions and conditionals, when interpreted truth functionally as in propositional logic or the theory of mental models, do not have the same truth-table patterns, because one statement in the pair always has a negated constituent whereas the other has not. For instance, the inclusive truth-table pattern for "A or C" is TTTF, whereas that for the corresponding conditional "If not A then C", interpreted as material conditional, is TFTT.

Table 6.2 lists the frequency of the most frequent patterns for the conditionals, and Table 6.3 lists the most frequent patterns for the disjunctions, separately for the two groups. A number of features in these data are noteworthy. Looking first at the conditionals, the pattern predicted by the probability conditional, and also reported in many previous studies, TFII (i.e., regarding the two false-antecedent cases as irrelevant) was clearly dominant for non-negated conditionals in the truth group. A second pattern that

Table 6.2 Frequencies of truth-table response patterns to conditionals, Experiments 1 and 2

Pattern	E1, Truth group		E1, Compatibility group		E2 (Truth)	
	If A then C	If not A then C	If A then C	If not A then C	If A then C	If not A then C
TFTT	8	6	32	30	7	3
TFFT	10	38	20	60	9	38
TFFF	17	15	14	12	20	10
TFII	117	46	83	20	109	37
TFFI	69	34	83	18	71	48
TFIT	7	7	11	15	9	12
TFTI	9	1	20	4	11	1
TFTF	0	8	2	0	4	2
TIFF	0	9	0	26	0	7
TIFI	0	20	3	21	0	20
TIFT	0	24	0	35	0	24
TIII	2	7	0	4	2	5
Others	28	52	29	52	3	38
Total	267	267	297	297	245	245

Notes
Patterns are given as four-letter codes for the truth values assigned to the statement for the four cases in the truth table (Table 6.1) from top to bottom (T = "true" or "consistent"; F = "false" or "contradicts"; I = "irrelevant"). See text for details.

Table 6.3 Frequencies of truth-table response patterns to disjunctions, Experiments 1 and 2

Pattern	E1, Truth group		E1, Compatibility group		E2 (Truth)	
	A or C	Not A or C	A or C	Not A or C	A or C	Not A or C
FTTF	94	10	102	17	100	9
TTTF	64	31	50	30	40	32
FTTI	34	0	53	0	40	1
ITTF	11	2	10	1	7	5
TTTI	9	0	30	0	8	1
TFFF	4	26	2	33	3	38
TIFF	0	18	0	32	1	24
TIFT	0	7	0	18	0	9
TTFF	2	21	3	19	1	14
TITF	0	10	0	15	0	8
TFFT	0	15	0	14	1	9
Others	49	127	47	118	44	95
Total	267	267	297	297	245	245

Notes
Patterns are given as four-letter codes for the truth values assigned to the statement for the four cases in the truth table (Table 6.1) from top to bottom (T = "true" or "consistent"; F = "false" or "contradicts"; I = "irrelevant"). See text for details.

has also been reported frequently before is TFFI; Evans and Over (2004) interpret it as the "defective biconditional" because it arises from the conjunction of two probability conditionals, the given conditional "if A then C" and its converse, "if C then A".

The prevalence of these two patterns was much reduced for the conditional with negated antecedent, which generated no clear modal pattern. Such a diffusion of response patterns when the antecedent is negated was not observed in a previous study in which we applied the truth-table evaluation task to a large sample (Oberauer, Geiger, Fischer, & Weidenfeld, 2007). Our previous study was laboratory based and involved psychology undergraduates, whereas the present study recruited a more heterogeneous sample. We speculate that the larger heterogeneity of educational background and cognitive ability, or less focused attention during the web experiment, led to more confusion by the negation and thereby to more erratic response patterns.

Comparing the truth group and the compatibility group in Experiment 1, we found that the TFII pattern was still dominant (for positive antecedents) in the compatibility group, although its frequency was reduced. No such reduction was found for the "defective biconditional", the TFFI pattern. An interesting observation regards the TFTT pattern, which is the normative pattern for the material conditional. Very few participants produced this pattern in the truth group, but its frequency increased markedly in the compatibility group. This is to be expected under the probabilistic view because the two false-antecedent cases, although not making the conditional true, are compatible with the conditional. What is more difficult to explain is the still high prevalence of the TFII pattern in the compatibility group. This pattern occurred mostly when the conditional's antecedent was positive, so that the false antecedent cases represented negative instances that mismatched the antecedent term in the conditional (e.g., "If the pair contains an A, then it contains a B" followed by XK). It seems that people often judged false-antecedent cases as irrelevant even in the compatibility group simply because they did not match the antecedent term in the conditional. We conclude that matching bias (Evans, 1972) is the most likely explanation for the occurrence of the TFII pattern in the compatibility group. Matching bias could also account for the TFFI pattern, and the fact that the prevalence of that pattern was not even reduced in the compatibility group relative to the truth group suggests that the "irrelevant" judgement in the TFFI pattern arose mainly due to a complete lack of matching between the false-antecedent, false-consequent case and the given conditional (see Oberauer et al., 2007).

Turning to the disjunctions, the two patterns corresponding to an exclusive interpretation (FTTF) and an inclusive interpretation (TTTF) were very prevalent for disjunctions without negation; the remaining frequent patterns were variants of these two in which one F was turned into an I. The response patterns given to disjunctions with negations were much more chaotic. Most patterns reflect no discernible rationale. Nevertheless, the patterns are not random – there is a preference, consistent across both groups, for patterns beginning with a T, which means that participants judge the case in which both constituents are true (i.e., the ¬A & C conjunction) to render "not A or C" true. It seems as if participants who were confused by the negation were assured that the disjunction is true only when they found that both constituents were true. In any case, the large amount of spread of responses across possible patterns suggests that people had difficulties understanding a disjunction with a negated constituent.

To formally evaluate the effect of response options (truth vs. compatibility) on the prevalence of "irrelevant" judgements for false-antecedent cases of conditionals, we computed for each participant the number of "irrelevant" judgements for a false-antecedent case of the two conditionals, and separately the number of "irrelevant" judgements for the corresponding false-first-disjunct cases of the two disjunctions (maximum four). An analysis of variance (ANOVA) with statement (conditional vs. disjunction) and group (truth vs. compatibility) showed that more "irrelevant" judgements were made for conditionals, and more were made in the truth group than the compatibility group. Of theoretical interest is the interaction, $F(1,562) = 27.2$. The mean number of "irrelevant" judgements for disjunctions was equally low in both groups (truth mean = 0.49, 95% CI = 0.41 to 0.58; compatibility mean = 0.55, 95% CI = 0.46 to 0.63). For the conditionals, more "irrelevant" judgements were made in the truth group (mean = 2.1, 95% CI = 1.97 to 2.27) than in the compatibility group (mean = 1.5, 95% CI = 1.37 to 1.66).

The reverse picture was obtained when we counted the number of "true" or "compatible" responses to false-antecedent and false-first-disjunct cases, respectively. For disjunctions, group made no difference (truth mean = 1.52, CI = 1.43 to 1.61; compatibility mean = 1.53, CI = 1.44 to 1.61), but for conditionals, false-antecedent cases were more often regarded as "compatible with the conditional" (mean 1.14, CI = 1.02 to 1.30), than they were regarded as "making the conditional true" (mean 0.59, CI = 0.46 to 0.71). Thus, as predicted by the probabilistic interpretation of the conditional, people were more inclined to think that the false-antecedent cases are compatible with the conditional than to think that they make the conditional true. This effect does not reflect a generally more lenient criterion for confirming compatibility than truth, because it arose only for conditionals, not for disjunctions.

Inferences from disjunctions to conditionals and vice versa

The proportion of participants accepting each inference is given in Table 6.4 for both experiments. No statistics are needed to see that inferences were accepted much more often when the conditional bore the negation than when the disjunction had a negated constituent. We believe that this reflects the fact that most participants had trouble understanding a disjunction with a negated constituent, as became evident in the truth-table task. In addition, there seems to be a more subtle trend for inferences from disjunctions to conditionals to be accepted more than the reverse inferences. This trend was significant in two of the six comparisons, for the inference from "A or C" to "If not A then C" in the compatibility group of Experiment 1 and in Experiment 2 (sign test, $Z = -2.8$, $p = .004$, and $Z = -2.6$, $p = .01$, respectively). The probabilistic view would predict, if anything, the opposite, because inferences from conditionals to disjunctions are logically valid as long as the disjunction is interpreted as inclusive, whereas inferences from disjunctions to conditionals are not valid at all.

Table 6.4 Proportion of participants accepting the inferences

	E1 truth	E1 compatibility	E2	E3 exclusive	E3 inclusive
"A or C" → "If not A then C"	.78	.84	.82	.86	.81
"If not A then C" → "A or C"	.72	.75	.72	.74	.71
"Not A or C" → "If A then C"	.25	.29	.30	.43	.38
"If A then C" → "Not A or C"	.24	.26	.27	.57	.57

Notes
E1 to E3 = Experiment 1 to 3; truth/compatibility designates the two groups in E1; exclusive/inclusive designates the instructions how to interpret the disjunction in E3. Only data from letter tasks are included from E3 for comparability with E1+2.

Relation between truth-table patterns and inferences

For testing the predictions of the mental model theory we focused on those truth-table patterns that could be categorized as reflecting an exclusive interpretation of the disjunction (FTTF, FTTI) or an inclusive interpretation (TTTF, TTTI); the pattern ITTF was ambiguous because declaring the case where both constituents are true as "irrelevant" means to remain undecided between the exclusive and the inclusive reading. For the conditionals we focused on patterns that could be interpreted as material conditional (TFTT), biconditional (TFFT, TFFI, TFIT, thus including "defective" biconditional patterns), and probabilistic (TFII). Participants who produced one of these relevant patterns in response to a conditional and its corresponding disjunction were cross-classified according to their two patterns. The proportion of participants in each cell of that cross-classification who accepted the inference from a conditional to a disjunction, or from a disjunction to a conditional, is listed in Table 6.5. The table lists only data for the inferences involving disjunctions without negation and conditionals with negated antecedent. When the negation was at the disjunction, people's truth-table patterns were so erratic that too few data points were left for the cross-classification.

In Table 6.5, those cells for which the mental model theory predicts that the inference should be accepted are shaded in grey. The table shows that there is no discernable systematic relation between the truth-table patterns

Table 6.5 Acceptance of inferences as a function of truth-table patterns, Experiments 1 and 2

	E1 truth		*E1 compatible*		*E2*	
	Acceptance of "A or C" → "If not A then C"					
	Exclusive	*Inclusive*	*Exclusive*	*Inclusive*	*Exclusive*	*Inclusive*
Material	0.33 (3)	1.0 (3)	1.0 (9)	0.88 (16)	1.0 (1)	0.50 (2)
Biconditional	0.91 (44)	0.75 (20)	0.94 (64)	0.87 (15)	0.86 (64)	0.85 (13)
Probabilistic	0.86 (22)	0.81 (21)	0.92 (12)	0.67 (6)	0.94 (17)	0.73 (15)
	Acceptance of "If not A then C" → "A or C"					
	Exclusive	*Inclusive*	*Exclusive*	*Inclusive*	*Exclusive*	*Inclusive*
Material	1.0 (3)	1.0 (3)	0.67 (9)	0.69 (16)	0 (1)	1.0 (2)
Biconditional	0.84 (44)	0.85 (20)	0.86 (64)	0.67 (15)	0.78 (64)	0.77 (13)
Probabilistic	0.64 (22)	0.76 (21)	0.75 (12)	0.67 (6)	0.65 (17)	0.80 (15)

Notes
Cell entries are proportions of participants in that cell who accepted the inference (total number of participant in the cell is given in parentheses). Cells shaded grey are those for which the mental model theory predicts high rates of inference acceptance. Inferences involving disjunctions with negations and conditionals without negations are not included because too few truth-table patterns fell in the relevant categories.

and whether or not an inference was accepted. We statistically evaluated the predictions of the mental model theory by computing a variable capturing its predictions for the acceptance of an inference – this variable was set to 1 for all participants in the grey cells of Table 6.5, and to 0 for all participants in the white cells. We correlated this predictor with the actual judgement on the inference, for the four inferences in each group (2 groups of Experiment 1 and one of Experiment 2). Only one of the twelve correlations was significant (predicted vs. observed acceptance of "not A or C/if A then C" in Experiment 2, $r = .22$, $p = .016$). Thus, these data lend little support to the predictions of the mental model theory. People's judgement of whether a conditional follows from a corresponding disjunction, or the other way round, cannot be predicted from their interpretations of these statements, as reflected in their truth-table patterns.

One potential limitation of this finding is that small or zero correlations can be obtained when one or both of the correlated variables have very poor reliability. Experiments 1 and 2 don't afford an estimate of reliability for the measurement of an individual's preferred truth-table pattern, or of their readiness to accept any of the inferences. Experiment 3 will address this problem.

Experiment 3

The third experiment was an attempt to improve people's understanding of disjunctions, in particular those with negations, by training with the truth-table task. We hoped to thereby obtain more interpretable truth-table patterns for the disjunctions, so that we could test their correspondence with truth-table patterns for conditionals on a more robust basis. Because we obtained multiple measurements of the truth-table task and the direct inferences, this experiment also served to assess the reliability of our measurements.

Method

Participants

Forty-two students from the University of Potsdam were enrolled in this laboratory-based experiment.

Design

The experiment consisted of a pretest, a training phase, and a posttest. In the pretest, participants' spontaneous truth-table evaluations for disjunctions and conditionals were assessed. In the training phase, they practised the truth-table task for disjunctions only. Different from the pretest, each disjunction was preceded by a cue clarifying whether the statement was to be interpreted as an exclusive or an inclusive disjunction (e.g., "Please interpret this statement as exclusive: There is a P or an M"). The difference between exclusive and inclusive disjunctions was explained at the beginning of training. Also different from the pretest, participants received feedback in the training phase. In the posttest, truth-table evaluations were again taken for both disjunctions and conditionals; this time the disjunctions were accompanied by the inclusive/exclusive cue as in the training phase, but no feedback was given. Finally, participants evaluated the direct inferences between conditionals and disjunctions, again with cues as to how the disjunctions were to be interpreted.

Materials

We constructed two sets of materials for the truth-table tasks. Both used the full negations paradigm (Evans, 1972), crossing negation of the first term (i.e., the antecedent in the conditionals) with negation of the second term (i.e., the consequent of the conditionals), resulting in four conditionals and four disjunctions. Each of these statements was combined with each of the four truth-table cases, for 32 tasks. One set of materials used letters, as in the preceding experiments. The other set used more concrete contents from one of four categories (vegetables, fruit, drinks, and animals), and pictures representing the truth-table cases (e.g., photos of vegetables on a board, or finger puppets representing animals).

We constructed three versions of the pictorial truth-table task. Version 1 presented one instance of each positive component in the conjunction, and none for each negated component. For example, the conditional "If there is no cucumber, then there is a tomato" would have to be evaluated for the true-antecedent, true-consequent case (a board with a tomato only), for the true-antecedent, false-consequent case (empty board), the false-antecedent, true-consequent case (board with cucumber and tomato), and the false-antecedent, false-consequent case (board with cucumber only). In Version 2, alternative exemplars are shown in place of negated components. For instance, the true-antecedent, true-consequent case for "If there is no banana, there is a pear" would show a basket with an orange and a pear. In Version 3, each picture contained four objects, of which at least two did not match a term in the statement to be evaluated. Negated components were also represented by alternative exemplars. For instance, the true-antecedent, true-consequent case for "There is no giraffe or there is an elephant" would be a set of four puppets: a rabbit, a mouse, a chicken, and an elephant. The purpose of the three versions was to introduce variety into the material to reduce boredom during the long training and testing sessions, and to explore whether negated components are represented by alternative objects or by voids. We did not find any systematic differences between people's responses to the three versions, however, so we aggregated across them for all reported analyses. Realizing the basic design of 32 tasks with three versions yields 96 tasks. These reduced to 88 tasks because the truth-table cases with non-negated components looked identical for Versions 1 and 2 (the versions differed only in how they depicted negated components).

The direct inferences were also tested with both kinds of contents, letters and concrete objects. We fully crossed content (letters vs. objects), interpretation of the disjunction (inclusive vs. exclusive), direction of inference (from disjunction to conditional vs. from conditional to disjunction), attachment of negation (to the conditional vs. to the disjunction), and location of the negation (on the first vs. the second term). The trials in which the negation was at the second term of a statement were regarded as fillers. The full design consisted of 32 direct inferences, 16 for each kind of content; they are summarized in Table 6.6.

Procedure

The experiment consisted of two sessions of approximately 1 hour. During the first session participants completed the pretest and the first part of the training phase. In the second session they continued with the training phase and completed the posttest. All tasks were presented via a computer program. In the pretest participants worked through the 32 trials of the letter-based truth-table task in random order, followed by 88 trials of the truth-table task with concrete objects from one of the categories, again in random order. The object category for the pretest was selected at random from the four categories; the remaining categories were assigned to training (2) and posttest (1).

In the training phase, only tasks with concrete objects were presented. They were selected at random without replacement from the 2 × 88 possible

Table 6.6 Direct inferences in Experiment 3

Direction	Attachment of negation	Inference (Negation at first term)	Excl.	Incl.	Inference (Negation at second term (filler))	Excl.	Incl.
Dis→C	Negation at conditional	p or q / if not p then q	V	mat	p or q / if p then not q	ex	N
	Negation at disjunction	not p or q / if p then q	V	mat	p or not q / if p then q	ex	N
C→Dis.	Negation at conditional	if not p then q / p or q	bic	V	if p then not q / p or q	ex + bic	N
	Negation at disjunction	if p then q / not p or q	bic	V	if p then q / p or not q	ex + bic	N

Notes
Entries in columns Excl. (for exclusive interpretation of the disjunction) and Incl. (for inclusive interpretation) show the validity of the inference, with V = unconditionally valid in propositional calculus; mat = valid if conditional is interpreted as material implication; bic = valid if conditional is interpreted as biconditional; ex = valid because of exclusivity of disjunction; N = not valid with any interpretation.

tasks; tasks solved correctly were removed from the pool, whereas tasks answered incorrectly could be selected again. In this way, training gradually focused on the difficult tasks. Each participant practised until reaching a criterion of 90% tasks solved correctly once. Feedback was given on each evaluation judgement. An evaluation was judged as correct if and only if it corresponded to the truth table for the appropriate disjunction (inclusive or exclusive according to the cue). Evaluations of cases as "irrelevant" were always regarded as errors. Feedback to errors was accompanied by the correct answer and a brief explanation presented by the computer.

The posttest began with testing truth-table evaluations of disjunctions and conditionals just as in the pretest (i.e., without feedback), with the only difference that now disjunctions were cued as being meant as inclusive or exclusive. Following this, participants completed the 32 direct inferences in random order.

Results

Truth-table evaluation tasks

Tables 6.7 and 6.8 present the frequencies of the theoretically most interesting patterns of truth-table responses to disjunctions and conditionals, separate for pretest and posttest. It is clear that the training had the desired effect on the patterns produced for disjunctions. The erratic patterns, summarized in the

Table 6.7 Frequencies of truth-table patterns for disjunctions, Experiment 3

	Pretest				*Posttest (Exclusive)*				*Posttest (Inclusive)*			
	PP	*PN*	*NP*	*NN*	*PP*	*PN*	*NP*	*NN*	*PP*	*PN*	*NP*	*NN*
	Letters											
FTTF	14	2	2	6	37	29	21	29	5	0	2	1
TTTF	7	3	4	8	4	1	8	4	32	28	27	32
Other	14	37	36	28	1	12	13	9	5	14	13	9
	Pictures											
FTTF	20	5	1	11	34	28	29	29	3	0	0	3
	18	2	1	14	34	24	24	29	4	1	1	3
	21	4	5	17	36	28	25	32	5	1	1	2
TTTF	16	7	5	12	4	1	5	6	35	32	35	33
	15	9	3	12	4	4	9	6	35	32	29	34
	17	10	6	14	54	5	6	5	35	30	33	36
Other	6	30	36	19	4	13	8	7	4	10	7	6
	9	31	38	16	4	14	9	7	3	9	12	5
	4	28	31	11	2	9	11	5	2	11	8	4

Table 6.8 Frequencies of truth-table patterns for conditionals, Experiment 3

	Pretest				Posttest			
	PP	PN	NP	NN	PP	PN	NP	NN
Letters								
TFTT	1	0	1	0	1	1	1	2
TFFT	1	0	4	3	2	5	4	8
TFII	17	20	8	6	22	22	15	17
TFFI	16	1	6	3	8	1	5	1
Other	7	21	23	30	9	13	17	14
Pictures								
TFTT	1	1	1	1	1	2	0	2
	1	1	1	1	1	1	1	3
	1	1	2	0	1	1	1	1
TFFT	2	0	3	2	3	4	4	2
	1	1	5	3	4	3	4	2
	1	2	2	3	3	3	4	4
TFII	19	28	15	18	22	26	20	20
	22	24	17	18	21	25	17	20
	17	26	18	17	21	22	18	19
TFFI	13	2	7	3	6	1	6	2
	9	3	5	2	8	1	5	2
	18	1	8	6	5	4	5	2
Other	7	11	16	18	10	9	12	16
	9	13	14	18	8	12	15	15
	5	12	12	16	12	12	14	16

category "others", became much less frequent, in particular for disjunctions with negations. Moreover, the majority of participants produced patterns that matched the prescribed interpretation of the disjunctions as inclusive or exclusive. It is noteworthy that, both before and after training, the frequency of "other" patterns, which reflect no coherent interpretation of "or", was higher for disjunctions with one negation (PN and NP in Table 6.7) than for disjunctions with two negations (NN in Table 6.7). This observation suggests that the difficulty people experience with disjunctions that have a negated term does not arise from their general difficulty with processing negations.

The truth-table patterns for conditionals were dominated by the TFII pattern, followed by the TFFI pattern. These two patterns are well explained by the probability conditional, as explained above. The two patterns that fit best with the mental model theory, TFTT (for the material conditional) and TFFT (for the biconditional) were hardly ever produced (a single participant very consistently produced the TFTT pattern).

During the pretest, we obtained three independent measures of the truth-table pattern of each conditional and each disjunction, the patterns generated with the letter task, and with Versions 1 and 3 of the picture task (patterns from Version 2 were not independent of Version 1 patterns because they shared the truth-table case without negated components). From these replications we estimated the reliability of our measures of people's interpretations of conditionals and disjunctions, as reflected in their truth-table patterns. We classified all patterns into the categories distinguished in Tables 6.7 and 6.8, for disjunctions and conditionals, respectively, and computed the contingency coefficient for membership in these categories. Contingency coefficients can be interpreted roughly like correlations for nominal data; a contingency of 0 means no relationship and a contingency of 1 means a perfect one-to-one correspondence between category membership according to two variables. For disjunctions, the contingency coefficients varied from .48 to .64 at pretest, and from .64 to .75 at posttest. For conditionals, they ranged from .67 to .80 at pretest, and from .60 to .83 at posttest. We conclude that the assignment of individuals to categories of truth-table patterns has moderate reliability. Oberauer et al. (2007) obtained even higher estimates of reliability for the crucial truth-table patterns of conditionals (i.e., TFTT, TFFT, and TFII). This should confer some retrospective confidence in the results of Experiments 1 and 2.

Inferences from disjunctions to conditionals and vice versa

Table 6.6 shows that the inferences can be classified into six categories. Among the inferences of interest, which represent the inferences from a disjunction to a corresponding conditional or vice versa, there are those that are valid according to propositional logic (and hence, according to the model theory) regardless of whether the conditional is interpreted as material or as biconditional ("unconditionally valid"), those valid if and only if the conditional is interpreted as material, marked "mat" in the table, and those valid if and only if the conditional is interpreted as biconditional, marked "bic" in the table. (Validity depends also on the interpretation of the disjunction, but this was fixed by the instructions on how to interpret each disjunction.) Among the filler inferences, there are two that are valid simply because the exclusive disjunction implies the conditional: if one conjunct is true, then the other is false (marked "ex" in the table). Two more fillers are valid if the conditional is interpreted as a biconditional, because then an exclusive disjunction follows from it (marked "ex + bic" in the table). The remaining fillers are invalid. We computed for each participant the proportion of inferences accepted in each of these categories, separately for letter and concrete object contents. These proportions were analysed by a 2 (content) × 6 (validity category) ANOVA. The main effect of validity was significant, $F(5,205) = 2.7$. The effect was decomposed by deviation contrasts that compare each category with the mean of all categories. This analysis showed that the invalid inferences were accepted less frequently (54%) than all others, which did not differ from each other (67%). Content had no effect. We can conclude that participants show some modest sensitivity to the logical validity of the inferences, although the acceptance rate for the definitely invalid fillers was still astonishingly high.

The factor that most affected the inference acceptance rate was, as in the first two experiments, whether the negation was attached to the conditional or to the disjunction. This effect is reflected in the two right-most columns of Table 6.4. These data present the acceptance rates for those four inferences that were already included in Experiments 1 and 2, thus allowing a direct comparison. For both inclusive and exclusive disjunctions, acceptance rates were high and roughly equivalent to those in the previous two experiments when the negation was attached to the conditional. When the negation was attached to the disjunction, acceptance rates were much lower – they were, however, higher than for the same inferences in the previous experiments. This latter finding probably reflects the effect of training, which improved participants' understanding of disjunctions with a negated term.

Relationship between truth-table patterns and inferences

The paucity of TFTT and TFFT patterns produced for conditionals in this experiment is unfortunate because we cannot look at participants who produced corresponding truth-table patterns for disjunctions and conditionals. The patterns for disjunctions hardly ever included an "irrelevant" judgement (7% at pretest, 0.4% at posttest), whereas most patterns for conditionals included at least one "irrelevant" judgement.

We took the alternative approach to count for each participant how often they produced each of the truth-table patterns of interest for a conditional. Each participant produced 4 patterns for conditionals with letters (one for each cell in the negation paradigm) and 12 patterns for the conditionals with pictures (3 replications of the negation paradigm for the 3 versions of pictures); therefore, each participant could produce each pattern up to 16 times. We designed four count variables to reflect, respectively, an individual's preference for interpreting the conditional as a material conditional (i.e., a high count for TFTT), as a biconditional (a high count for TFFT), as a probability conditional (a high count of TFII), or as a defective biconditional (a high count of TFFI). These variables were obtained from the posttest data.

The four variables reflecting truth-table patterns for conditionals were correlated with people's acceptance rates for the inferences in the six categories of validity. These correlations reflect whether a preference for one interpretation of the conditional is associated with a higher acceptance rate for inferences in one of the categories. According to the mental model theory, we should expect a correlation between the number of TFTT patterns and the acceptance of inferences in the categories "unconditionally valid" and "valid with material conditional". Likewise, we should expect a correlation between the number of TFFT patterns, and possibly the number of TFFI patterns (i.e., the defective biconditional), and the acceptance of inferences in the categories "unconditionally valid" and "valid with biconditional". Whereas the hypothesis about the TFTT pattern cannot be seriously tested with the present data because only one participant produced the TFTT pattern with an appreciable frequency, there was more variation between individuals in the number of TFFT and TFFI patterns, so the hypotheses concerning these patterns had a chance to be supported. Nevertheless, the Spearman rank correlations were all small and nonsignificant, with two exceptions: The acceptance rates for the valid fillers (category "ex" in Table 6.6) correlated positively with the TFII count and negatively with the TFFT count. None of these correlations lends any support to the hypothesis, outlined in the introduction, that inferences from "or" to "if" or vice versa are based on matching truth tables, or matching sets of mental models.

Again, these null correlations could be the result of a lack of reliability of the correlated variables. We have already shown that the truth-table patterns have reasonable reliability, especially at posttest. The reliability of the inference acceptance rates in the six categories was assessed by correlating acceptance rates for tasks with letters and tasks with concrete objects as contents. Across the six categories, these rank correlations ranged from .43 to .74. According to the Spearman–Brown prophecy formula, the correlation of .43 translates into a reliability of .60 for the composite of both variables, which was used in the correlations with the truth-table pattern counts above. Therefore, all variables involved in that analysis had at least moderate reliability.

Discussion and conclusions

Can "if" be translated into "or", and vice versa? For many pairs of corresponding conditionals and disjunctions there is a strong intuition that one implies the other. Propositional logic, as well as the theory of mental models, implies that "A or C" and "if not A then C" are equivalent when their interpretations are matched (i.e., inclusive disjunction with material conditional, and exclusive disjunction with biconditional). The probabilistic interpretation of conditionals, as incorporated, for instance, in the suppositional theory of Evans and Over (2004), denies this equivalence (Over et al., 2010). It holds that a conditional logically entails an inclusive disjunction but a disjunction does not logically entail a conditional, although the latter inference may be licensed pragmatically. The work presented in this chapter is an attempt to investigate people's intuitions about the relation between corresponding "if" and "or" statements.

One persistent new finding is that people endorse the inferences from conditionals to disjunctions and those from disjunctions to conditionals fairly strongly as long as the disjunction does not bear a negation of one of its terms. Endorsement rates plummet drastically when the disjunction includes a negation. This is probably due to people's difficulty with understanding such disjunctions. No comparable degree of difficulty was apparent when the antecedent or the consequent of the conditional was negated. Although with negated antecedents or consequents, the truth-table patterns of conditionals also became more erratic (as reflected, for instance, by the increased prevalence of the "other" category), the adverse effect of negations on conditionals was clearly more benign than that on disjunctions. This finding confirms the intuition of Evans and Over (2004) that we have relatively little difficulty understanding conditionals with negations. Disjunctions with negations, in contrast, remain difficult even after extended practice, although practice improves performance in the truth-table task. Even after practice with interpreting disjunctions, however, people hesitated accepting inferences from disjunctions to conditionals, or vice versa, when the disjunction had a negated term.

We found weak evidence for an asymmetry in the relation between disjunctions and conditionals. Conditionals were inferred from disjunctions slightly more often than the other way round. If people endorsed a probabilistic interpretation of the conditional, and if they were aware of its entailment that the inference from a conditional to a disjunction can be logically valid if the disjunction is interpreted as inclusive, but the reverse inference is not valid under any interpretation, they should make if-to-or inferences more readily than or-to-if inferences. The fact that we found, if anything, evidence for the opposite should be moderately worrying for the probabilistic theory. Theorists in this camp could argue that people don't make a sharp distinction between logically licensed inferences and pragmatically licensed inferences. According to Over et al. (2010), the inference from a disjunction to a conditional is pragmatically licensed when the disjunction expresses a state of ignorance about which of the two propositions in the disjunction is true. When a disjunction is just stated without discourse context, as in our experiments, interpreting them in this way conforms to the Gricean prescription for a speaker to be as informative as possible. Therefore, in the context of our experiments the or-to-if inference would be pragmatically licensed, and it is not surprising, from the point of view of the suppositional theory, that most people endorse it. Still, finding more inferences from "or" statements to corresponding "if" statements than the other way round is difficult to explain for the probabilistic theory (as well as for the mental model theory).

According to the mental model theory, the relationship between "if" and "or" is mediated by equivalent sets of mental models. The sets of mental models used to represent disjunctions and conditionals depend on an individual's interpretation of these statements. We attempted to measure people's preferred interpretations by truth-table evaluation tasks. We assumed that the pattern a person produced for a statement in the truth-table task represents their preferred set of mental models for representing that statement. On this assumption, we could derive predictions from the mental model theory about who should and who shouldn't be willing to accept the inference from a disjunction to a corresponding conditional, and vice versa. Across all three experiments, these predictions failed to be supported. This failure could in part be as a result of the small proportion of participants who produced matching truth-table patterns for corresponding conditionals and disjunctions. As in previous studies (reviewed by Evans & Over, 2004), people have a strong tendency to judge false-antecedent cases as irrelevant for the truth of a conditional, thus producing many TFII and TFFI patterns, which match none of the frequent patterns for disjunctions. This in itself can be taken as evidence in favour of the probabilistic interpretation of conditionals, which predicts the TFII pattern (and, less directly, the TFFI pattern).

Mental model theorists could argue that at least the TFII pattern is compatible with the model theory. One tenet of the mental model theory is that people often represent a conditional by only one explicit model of the true-antecedent, true-consequent case, together with a mental footnote referring to further, as yet implicit models of the false-antecedent cases. As long as the models of the false-antecedent cases remain implicit, people tend to regard these cases as irrelevant in a truth-table evaluation task. If we accept this interpretation of the TFII pattern, what should we predict for the inferences from "if" to "or" and vice versa? As long as people don't flesh out the implicit models in their representations of conditionals, they would not notice that conditionals and corresponding disjunctions have matching sets of mental models, so we should still expect predominantly rejection of the inferences. It could be, however, that people who produced the TFII pattern in the truth-table task fleshed out the implicit models when working on the inference task, generating either a material conditional or a biconditional representation. In that case, they could notice the correspondence between the full set of models for the conditional and the set of models for the inclusive or the exclusive disjunction, respectively. This might explain why most of the participants who produced the TFII pattern still endorsed the inference linking a conditional and a corresponding disjunction. This interpretation, however, would still leave unexplained why people tended to endorse these inferences even when they interpreted the conditional as biconditional and the disjunction as inclusive (see the second row in Table 6.5).

What underlies the inferences from "or" to "if" and from "if" to "or"? There seems to be not much reasoning behind endorsement of these inferences at all. The factor that most strongly affects whether people endorsed the inferences seems to be whether or not they understand both statements. Put simply, when the disjunction bears a negation, people become confused and reject the inference; otherwise they accept it. Experiment 3 showed that people often accepted even the inferences that are invalid by any normative theory, barely less frequently than those that are valid according to the propositional calculus. At least part of the latter (i.e., those from conditionals to disjunctions) are also valid according to the probabilistic view. Thus, people hardly distinguish between valid and invalid inferences.

Based on these findings, we propose the following tentative explanation of the inference data. When confronted with an inference from a disjunction to a conditional, or from a conditional to a disjunction, people try to construct a single set of mental models that is compatible with both statements. For the corresponding pair "if not A then C" and "A or C", that would be the two models

$$\neg A \quad C$$
$$A \quad \neg C$$

When this pair of models is successfully constructed and is judged to be compatible with both statements, the inference is accepted. That is, people don't construct separate sets of mental models for the two statements and compare them with each other. This assumption can be justified in two ways, depending on one's theoretical inclination. Proponents of mental model theory could argue that constructing separate sets of mental models for both statements and comparing them simply places a too high burden on working memory. Proponents of a probabilistic view could argue that there are even more principled reasons for not constructing separate sets of mental models. Although the probabilistic view is difficult to reconcile with the mental models theory (Evans et al., 2005), efforts have been made towards a reconciliation (Barrouillet, Gauffroy, & Lecas, 2008; Geiger & Oberauer, 2010). Our own view, elaborated in Geiger and Oberauer (2010), is that the probability conditional is not itself represented by a set of mental models, because its meaning cannot be captured by a set of models, but that it provides constraints for models that represent other statements. Thus, people could construct a set of mental models representing the meaning of the disjunction, and check whether it is compatible with the conditional. For instance, when asked whether "A or C" follows from "If not A then C", or the other way round, people could construct the two mental models sketched above to represent the meaning of the disjunction, and check whether the conditional is consistent with it. The probability conditional imposes the constraint that every model of the antecedent should be accompanied by a model of the consequent; this is the case in the two models above. Based on this reasoning, people could conclude that the direct inference from one to the other is valid. Incidentally, this line of argument can explain the slight advantage for making inferences from "or" to "if", because the construction of mental models must start from the disjunctive statement.

To conclude, we propose that people evaluate direct inferences by trying to construct a set of mental models that is compatible with both statements. With this reasoning strategy, people don't investigate whether one statement is stronger (i.e., excludes more possibilities) than the other. For instance, when the conditional is interpreted as biconditional, but the disjunction is interpreted as inclusive, people would still be strongly inclined to infer "if not A then C" from "A or C", without noticing that "A or C" is compatible with the A and C conjunction, whereas the biconditional is not. People do not construct the mental model of the A and C conjunction. The full set of models for the inclusive disjunction is never constructed in this task because people start right away constructing only those models that are compatible with both statements.

Acknowledgements

This research was supported by Deutsche Forschungsgemeinschaft (DFG, grant FOR 375 1–1). We thank Annekatrin Hudjetz and Moritz Ischebeck for programming the experiments. We are especially indebted to Mirko Wendland for posting Experiments 1 and 2 on his W-Lab server, http://w-lab.de, and to Ulf Reips for broadly advertising them through his web page: http://www.psychologie.unizh.ch/sowi/Ulf/Lab/WebExpPsyLabD.html.

References

Adams, E. W. (1975). *The logic of conditionals*. Dordrecht, Germany: Reidel.

Barrouillet, P., Gauffroy, C., & Lecas, J. F. (2008). Mental models and the suppositional account of conditionals. *Psychological Review*, *115*, 773–778.

Barrouillet, P., Grosset, N., & Lecas, J. F. (2000). Conditional reasoning by mental models: Chronometric and developmental evidence. *Cognition*, *75*, 237–266.

Barrouillet, P., & Lecas, J. F. (1999). Mental models in conditional reasoning and working memory. *Thinking & Reasoning*, *5*, 289–302.

Bennett, J. (2003). *A philosophical guide to conditionals*. Oxford: Oxford University Press.

Edgington, D. (1995). On conditionals. *Mind*, *104*, 235–329.

Evans, J. St B. T. (1972). Interpretation and matching bias in a reasoning task. *Quarterly Journal of Experimental Psychology*, *24*, 193–199.

Evans, J. St B. T., Newstead, S. E., & Byrne, R. M. J. (1993). *Human reasoning: The psychology of deduction*. Hove, UK: Lawrence Erlbaum Associates Ltd.

Evans, J. St B. T., & Over, D. E. (2004). *If*. Oxford: Oxford University Press.

Evans, J. St B. T., Over, D. E., & Handley, S. (2005). Suppositions, extensionality, and conditionals: A critique of the mental-models theory of Johnson-Laird and Byrne (2002). *Psychological Review*, *112*, 1040–1052.

Geiger, S. M., & Oberauer, K. (2010). Toward a reconciliation of mental model theory and probabilistic theories. In M. Oaksford & N. Chater (Eds.), *Cognition and conditionals: Probability and logic in human thinking*. Oxford: Oxford University Press.

Johnson-Laird, P. N., & Byrne, R. M. J. (1991). *Deduction*. Hillsdale, NJ: Lawrence Erlbaum Associates, Inc.

Johnson-Laird, P. N., & Byrne, R. M. J. (2002). Conditionals: A theory of meaning, pragmatics, and inference. *Psychological Review*, *109*, 646–678.

Johnson-Laird, P. N., & Tagart, J. (1969). How implication is understood. *American Journal of Psychology*, *82*, 367–373.

Oaksford, M., & Chater, N. (2001). The probabilistic approach to human reasoning. *Trends in Cognitive Sciences*, *5*, 349–357.

Oberauer, K., Geiger, S. M., Fischer, K., & Weidenfeld, A. (2007). Two meanings of "if"? Individual differences in the interpretation of conditionals. *Quarterly Journal of Experimental Psychology*, *60*, 790–819.

Oberauer, K., & Wilhelm, O. (2003). The meaning(s) of conditionals – Conditional probabilities, mental models, and personal utilities. *Journal of Experimental Psychology: Learning, Memory & Cognition, 29*, 680–693.

Ormerod, T. C., & Richardson, J. (2003). On the generation and evaluation of inferences from single premises. *Memory & Cognition, 31*, 467–478.

Over, D. E., Evans, J. St B. T., & Elqayam, S. (2010). Conditionals and non-constructive reasoning. In M. Oaksford & N. Chater (Eds.), *Cognition and conditionals: Probability and logic in human thinking*. Oxford: Oxford University Press.

7   The truth about conditionals

Philip N. Johnson-Laird

Princeton University

No one has done more for the psychology of reasoning than Jonathan Evans, and so it is a pleasure to have this opportunity of honouring him. He has carried out many studies of conditionals, and he and his colleagues have been flattering enough to criticize my ideas about them on several occasions (e.g., Evans, 1993; Evans, Over, & Handley, 2005; Over, Evans, & Elqayam, 2010). Hence, it seemed like a good idea to return the favour. My original plan was to contradict every one of his claims, so that you would know that on each point one of us was right and one of us was wrong. Alas, that goal was impossible because we agree on too much, and so instead this article defends a theory of conditionals that Ruth Byrne and I based on mental models (Johnson-Laird & Byrne, 2002). It aims to set the record straight where Jonathan and Co. may have bent the theory towards their preconceptions, or overlooked some of its principles. And at times, as you will see, the theory does succeed in contradicting Jonathan's "suppositional" account of conditionals.

In essence, the suppositional account, which Jonathan developed with David Over, can be summarized as follows: *if* is a verbal cue to consider hypothetical possibilities (Evans, 2007; Evans and Over, 2004). The account is based in part on mental model theory, but crucially on an idea due to the polymath Frank Ramsey (1929/1990). He took the meaning of a conditional to be *material implication* – a simple interpretation in logic that I will explain presently. But, in a footnote, he wrote:

> If two people are arguing "If p will q?" and both are in doubt as to p, they are adding p hypothetically to their stock of knowledge and arguing on that basis about q; so that in a sense "If p, q" and "If p, not q" are contradictories. We can say they are fixing their degrees of belief in q given p. If p turns out to be false, these degrees of belief are rendered void.
>
> (Ramsey, 1929/1990, p. 247)

Stalnaker (1968) turned this idea about beliefs in conditionals into a theory of the *meaning* of conditionals based on "possible worlds", and Evans and

Over are sympathetic to his account. They write: "our view of 'if' is that of a linguistic device the purpose of which is to trigger a process of hypothetical thinking and reasoning" (Evans & Over, 2004, p. 153). In what follows, the present chapter outlines the contrasting theory of mental models, step by step, in terms of its separate components. And, from time to time, it contrasts this theory with the suppositional account. Finally, it draws a general conclusion about theories of conditionals.

The principles of the model theory

The intuition lying behind the model theory is that perception yields models of the world (Marr, 1982), but individuals can also experience the world by proxy when someone describes it to them (Johnson-Laird, 1983). They can use such descriptions to simulate the world in mental models, and they can use these models to make all sorts of inferences, including valid deductions, which underlie science, mathematics, and sometimes the solutions to problems in daily life.

Validity is easy to define in logic: "A valid inference is one whose conclusion is true in every case in which all its premises are true" (Jeffrey, 1981, p. 1). A logical calculus has formal rules of inference that can be used to prove that inferences are valid in virtue of their logical form – that is, in terms of the formal structure of their premises and conclusion and without regard to their meaning. This method is feasible, because logic deals with the implications of *sentences* in a formal language in which logical form is transparent. But, matters are very different for natural language, because validity in daily life concerns *propositions* expressed by sentences, not sentences themselves. And the proposition expressed by a sentence, such as: "If she drank alcohol then she didn't drink *that*" depends on the meanings of its clauses, the identity of the person referred to as "she", and what the speaker points to on saying "that". No existing algorithm can recover the logical form of all propositions expressible in natural language. Hence, modern logicians confronted with natural language have eschewed logical form. As the late Jon Barwise (1989, p. 4) wrote: ". . . I was trying not to resort to the notion of 'logical form' since I find the notion unilluminating. Within the model-theoretic tradition, valid entailments are valid not in virtue of form, but in virtue of content". The model-theoretic tradition to which he refers relies on abstract models, such as truth tables, to specify the meanings of logical terms and to determine the validity of inferences that hinge on them.

The psychological theory of reasoning based on *mental* models is analogous to model theory in logic. It postulates that human reasoning depends, not on logical forms, but on mental models. Individuals use the meaning of sentences and their knowledge to envisage what is possible given the propositions expressed in the premises, and they represent these possibilities in mental models. A conclusion is valid provided it holds in every possibility in which the premises hold, and it is invalid if there is a counterexample, that is, a possibility in which the premises hold but the conclusion does not hold (e.g., Johnson-Laird & Byrne, 1991). Mental models differ from other proposed sorts of mental representation, because models are as iconic as possible: their structures correspond to the structure of what they represent. They can likewise unfold in time kinematically to simulate sequences of events (Johnson-Laird, 1983, Ch. 15). But, they can also contain symbols that are not iconic, such as a symbol for negation (see Peirce, 1931–1958, Vol. 4, for an account of icons and symbols). The model theory provides an explanation of how individuals make deductions, inductions, explanatory abductions, probabilistic inferences, and inferences to default conclusions that hold in the absence of evidence to the contrary (Johnson-Laird, 2006).

Basic conditionals and their meaning

Conditionals have many sorts of meaning, and one aim of the model theory is to explain this diversity as a result of interactions among a set of simple components (Johnson-Laird & Byrne, 2002). The theory postulates a single underlying meaning for conditionals, but it also describes a mechanism of *modulation* that can transform this meaning into an indefinite number of different sorts of interpretation. Modulation can have an impact on the inferences that individuals draw, and the present chapter illustrates this phenomenon.

A *basic* conditional is one for which general knowledge, the meaning or reference of its clauses, or knowledge of its context, has no effect on the interpretation of the relation between its if-clause and its then-clause. You can understand the following assertion, for instance, without such factors affecting your interpretation of the conditional relation:

If there is a circle then there is a triangle.

The model theory postulates that the core meaning of such a conditional refers to three possibilities, which are represented in the following diagram on separate rows:

$$
\begin{array}{ll}
\bigcirc & \triangle \\
\text{not-}\bigcirc & \triangle \\
\text{not-}\bigcirc & \text{not-}\triangle
\end{array}
$$

where "not" denotes a symbol for negation. The one case that is impossible given the truth of the conditional is:

$$
\bigcirc \quad \text{not-}\triangle
$$

This meaning corresponds to that of material implication in logic, which is defined in terms of a function from truth values to truth values. That is, a material implication is true in any case except when its if-clause is true (there is a circle) and its then-clause is false (there is not a triangle). It can therefore be expressed unambiguously as: If there is a circle then there is a triangle, and if there isn't a circle then there is, or isn't, a triangle.

A moment's thought should convince you that this assertion corresponds to the three possibilities above.

Pierre Barrouillet and his colleagues have shown that children develop the ability to list the three possibilities for conditionals (e.g., Barrouillet, Grosset, & Lecas, 2000). But, when individuals understand a conditional, such as, "if there is a circle then there is a triangle", they do not normally represent explicitly all three possibilities. That would be too demanding on working memory. The model theory accordingly gives a "dual-process" account of reasoning – an approach that Evans pioneered (see for example, Evans, 2003, 2007). Such theories distinguish between rapid intuitive responses and slower more deliberative inferences. And the model theory postulates that intuitive processes make no use of working memory and so they operate on just a single mental model (see Johnson-Laird, 1983, Ch. 6). In the case of a conditional, the single model is the one in which both its clauses hold:

○   △

Individuals realize that there are other possibilities, in which the if-clause is false, but they represent them with a model that is a place holder rather than an explicit representation of these possibilities. When individuals think more deliberatively, however, they can flesh out their *mental* models of conditionals into *fully explicit* models representing all the possibilities to which the conditionals refer.

Mental models suffice for a deduction of the sort known as modus ponens:

If there is a circle then there is a triangle.
There is a circle.
Therefore, there is a triangle.

But, they do not suffice for a deduction of the sort known as modus tollens:

If there is a circle then there is a triangle.
There isn't a triangle.
Therefore, there isn't a circle.

One way in which the inference can be made is to flesh out the mental models into fully explicit models, and so the inference is harder than modus ponens. Klaus Oberauer (2006) compared four theories of conditionals with the frequencies of the acceptance or rejection of such inferences. He examined the suppositional theory (Evans & Over, 2004), a probabilistic theory of reasoning (Oaksford, Chater, & Larkin, 2000), and two versions of the model theory – a dual-process version (formulated by Schroyens & Schaeken, 2003, and Verschueren, Schaeken, & d'Ydewalle, 2005), and a modified version of the original model theory, which took the directionality of inferences into account; that is, whether they proceeded from the if-clause to the then-clause or vice versa (see Evans, 1993, for this suggestion). He concluded that the two versions of the model theory provided a better account of his data than either the suppositional theory or the probabilistic theory.

The modulation of meaning

In the conditionals of daily life, the meaning of their clauses and co-referential relations between them can modulate the core meaning described in the previous section: a process of *semantic* modulation. Likewise, knowledge about the context and the topic of the conditional can modulate the core meaning: a process of *pragmatic* modulation. The effects of the two sorts of modulation are similar. One effect is to block the construction of models of possibilities. Consider the conditional:

If she drank alcohol then she didn't drink wine

and compare it with one of the same grammatical form:

If she drank alcohol then she didn't drink water.

The first conditional holds in only two possibilities:

She drank alcohol and she didn't drink wine.
She didn't drink alcohol and she didn't drink wine.

Your knowledge that wine is alcoholic blocks the construction of the possibility:

She didn't drink alcohol and she drank wine.

Hence, the conditional alone yields the valid inference:

Therefore, she didn't drink wine.

But, the second conditional does not yield the analogous inference that she didn't drink water, because it holds in the possibility that she didn't drink alcohol but did drink water. Likewise, individuals make the following modus tollens inference:

If she drank alcohol then she didn't drink water.

> In fact, she did drink water.
> Therefore, she didn't drink alcohol.

But, they balk at this inference:

> If she drank alcohol then she didn't drink wine.
> In fact, she did drink wine.
> Therefore, she didn't drink alcohol.

They do not draw the conclusion, because they know that wine is alcoholic.

An alternative way to try to cope with these phenomena is to argue that the conditionals about wine and water do have the same logical form, but that the knowledge that wine is alcoholic yields a missing premise – the second premise in the inference:

> If she drank alcohol then she didn't drink wine.
> If she drank wine then she drank alcohol.
> In fact, she did drink wine.
> Therefore, she didn't drink alcohol.

But, this stratagem fails to block the inference: the premises are self-contradictory, and in logic any conclusion whatsoever, including the one above, follows from a contradiction. In other words, logic is *monotonic*: the addition of a further premise merely adds to the number of valid conclusions, and never calls for the withdrawal of a prior valid inference.

The model theory, and its computer implementations, make use of grammatical form, but not logical form, and self-contradictions yield the null model – akin to an empty model – whose conjunction with other models yields only the null model again. This consequence is just one of the ways in which reasoning from models is not monotonic. The conditionals about wine and water have the same grammatical form, but modulation yields different possibilities for them. Overall, it yields 10 distinct interpretations of conditionals depending solely on which possibilities it blocks (Johnson-Laird & Byrne, 2002). But, as you will see, these 10 interpretations do not exhaust the possible interpretations of conditionals. A corollary is that no grammatical form of inference, such as: *if A then C; not C;* therefore, *not-A*, is guaranteed to yield a valid deduction regardless of its contents. The validity of inferences can be decided only on a case-by-case basis: valid entailments are valid not in virtue of form, but in virtue of content.

My colleagues Cristina Quelhas and Csongor Juhos have carried out numerous experiments showing that modulation occurs, both in terms of the different sets of possibilities that individuals list, and the conclusions that they draw (Quelhas, Juhos, & Johnson-Laird, 2010). Consider these two conditionals (translated from the Portuguese):

If the dish is kidney beans then its basis is beans.
If the dish is made of meat then it can be Portuguese stew.

At first sight, few of us are likely to notice the subtle difference in our interpretations of them. Yet, the experimental results showed that the meanings of their constituent clauses, and general knowledge, modulate their interpretation. In particular, when individuals evaluate various cases in relation to the first conditional, they judge that it is possible that the dish isn't kidney beans but its basis is beans (*not-A and C*), but that it is not possible that the dish is kidney beans and its basis isn't beans (*A and not-C*). In contrast, the participants made the opposite evaluations for the second conditional: it is impossible that the dish isn't made of meat and is Portuguese stew (*not-A and C*), but it is possible that that dish is made of meat and is not Portuguese stew (*A and not-C*). These interpretations, and those of other sorts of conditional, led to quite different patterns of inference.

Models can represent spatial and temporal information (Byrne & Johnson-Laird, 1989; Schaeken, Johnson-Laird, & d'Ydewalle, 1996). And another effect of modulation, which was overlooked by Evans et al. (2005), is to *add* such information to the models of conditionals. For instance, "if she put a book on the shelf then it fell off", elicits the temporal relation that the event in the if-clause occurred before the event in the then-clause, and the spatial relation that the book ended up below the shelf (Johnson-Laird & Byrne, 2002). The effects of temporal modulation were borne out in a study in which individuals drew conclusions corroborating the predicted temporal relations, which in some cases were that the event in the if-clause occurred before the one in the then-clause, and in other cases were that the events occurred in the opposite order (Quelhas et al., in press).

The model theory predicts that models can *simulate* a temporal sequence of events (Johnson-Laird, 1983, Ch. 15). My former colleague Geoffrey Goodwin, now of the University of Pennsylvania, has corroborated this prediction in a series of experiments on conditional reasoning (Goodwin and Johnson-Laird, 2009). The participants tackled problems of the following sort:

> Pat forgot to lock his door.
> If Pat forgot to lock his door then Viv entered his apartment and burgled it.
> Did Viv gain entry to Pat's apartment through the unlocked door?

For some problems, as in this case, a "yes" answer called for an inference about an event early in the temporal sequence. But, on other trials in the experiment, the question called for an inference about an event in the middle of a sequence, for example:

> Did Viv walk around at least one room in Pat's apartment?

On still other trials, the question was about an event towards the end of the sequence, for example:

Did Viv leave Pat's apartment with some of his possessions?

There were six different scenarios, and each of them occurred with questions on separate trials about events at the start, in the middle, or at the end of a temporal sequence. Each presentation of a scenario concerned different protagonists. In three experiments, which differed in procedure one from the other, the latencies of the correct answers to the "yes" questions increased as the relevant events occurred later in the temporal sequence. The increase, however, was not attributable to any reliable difference in the participants' confidence in their inferences. The participants were simulating the sequences of events in order to answer the questions. However, the inferences were not logically valid. For example, it is possible, though unlikely, that Viv did not leave the apartment with some of Pat's possessions. She could instead have passed them through the window to an accomplice. The conclusions therefore hold by default, that is, they hold as long as there is no evidence to the contrary (see for example, Johnson-Laird, 2006, p. 343). Theories based on formal logic cannot yield default conclusions in a straightforward way. In contrast, they occur as a spontaneous side effect of the use of knowledge to construct models.

There are indefinitely many interpretations of conditionals because modulation can add indefinitely many relations between the situations referred to in the if-clause and the then-clause. In logic, as we've seen, the connective of material implication corresponds to the interpretation of a basic conditional, but material implication has a "truth-functional" meaning: it takes as input merely the truth values of the two clauses. Such an interpretation cannot work for natural language. One reason is that interpretation normally concerns, not truth values, but possibilities. That is, when you understand an assertion, you envisage the possibilities in which it holds rather than evaluate whether it is true or false. Another reason is that modulation can always eliminate a possibility or add new relations between the if-clause and the then-clause. For example, a conditional for which modulation yields a temporal order, such as: "If she passed the exam then she studied hard", may not be true even if its if-clause and then-clause are individually true. The conditional implies that if she passed the exam, she studied hard beforehand, and the conditional would be false in case the two events occurred in the opposite temporal order. The interpretative process therefore needs access to the meaning and reference of the clauses in conditionals in case they, or the knowledge that they elicit, modulate the core interpretation. A corollary is that "conditionals are not truth functional" (Johnson-Laird & Byrne, 2002, p. 673; *pace* Evans & Over, 2004, p. 21; Evans et al., 2005; and Over et al., 2010).

Still another effect of modulation is to increase the likelihood that individuals flesh out their mental models of conditionals into fully explicit models of all the possibilities. For instance, given the conditional, "If Bill is in Rio de Janeiro then he is in Brazil", individuals are likely to use their knowledge to make explicit the possibility that Bill is not in Brazil and so not in Rio. As a consequence, they should be more likely to make the modus tollens inference:

> If Bill is in Rio de Janeiro then he is in Brazil
> Bill is not in Brazil.
> Therefore, he is not in Rio de Janeiro.

Indeed, individuals make this sort of inference more often than its analogues from basic conditionals (Johnson-Laird & Byrne, 2002, Experiment 4).

The paradoxes of material implication

An argument against the core interpretation of basic conditionals is that, like material implication, it yields "paradoxical" inferences (Evans & Over, 2004, p. 19). Here are examples of two such inferences, which are valid according to the core interpretation:

> There isn't a circle.
> Therefore, if there is a circle then there is a triangle.

and:

> There is a triangle.
> Therefore, if there is a circle then there is a triangle.

In fact, the model theory implies that the paradoxes are valid for some but not all interpretations of conditionals, it explains their counterintuitive nature, and it predicts that they should be acceptable in some cases (Johnson-Laird & Byrne, 2002, p. 651–652).

The paradoxes are counterintuitive in part because they throw away semantic information by adding a disjunctive alternative to the possibilities in which their premises hold. The premises of a modus ponens inference, such as:

> If there is a circle then there is triangle.
> There is a circle.

hold in just one possibility:

> ○   △

The conclusion of the inference, "there is a triangle", holds in this possibility. But, in the case of a paradoxical inference, such as:

There is a triangle.
Therefore, if there is a circle then there is a triangle.

the premise holds in a single model:

△

The conclusion, however, holds in the three possibilities shown earlier:

○	△
not-○	△
not-○	not-△

Granted the premise, the conclusion must hold too, but the conclusion does throw away semantic information by adding disjunctive alternatives, including one in which the premise fails to hold. The same is true of this inference yielding a disjunctive conclusion rather than a conditional:

There is a triangle.
Therefore, there is a circle or there is a triangle, or both.

And individuals also balk at this inference. Hence, the oddity of the "paradoxes" of material implication is attributable in part to this fact: the inferences throw information away.

In what cases, should individuals accept a "paradox" without balking? The model theory answers with a clear prediction: when the conclusion does not add a disjunctive alternative in which the premise fails to hold. Here is an example:

Viv didn't play soccer.
Therefore, if she played a game then she didn't play soccer.

The inference does not seem absurd; and its premise holds in both the models of its conclusion:

She played a game.	She didn't play soccer.
She didn't play a game.	She didn't play soccer.

Negation and the preference for small arguments

A recent development in the model theory concerns sentential operators, such as:

Surprisingly . . .
It is true that . . .

What is the probability that . . .?
It is not that . . .

These operators can take as their arguments an entire sentence, as in:

Surprisingly, if there is a circle then there is a triangle.

The model theory, however, postulates that individuals try to reduce the arguments of these operators from sentences to clauses, and sometimes to even smaller units (see Johnson-Laird, Byrne, & Girotto, 2009; Khemlani, Orenes, & Johnson-Laird, 2009). The reason for this principle of "small arguments" is transparent: operators are easier to understand when their arguments are small than when they are large. And, in some cases, smaller arguments result in a smaller number of models.

To understand how the small-argument principle applies to a conditional, you need to appreciate that its if-clause is, grammatically speaking, subordinate to its main clause (the then-clause). In general, a subordinate clause can contain a pronoun that refers forwards to the same entity that is referred to in the main clause. In both the following examples, "she" can refer to the same individual as "Pat" in the main clause:

Before she ate, Pat drank.
If she ate, Pat drank.

Such "cataphoric" or forward anaphoras are impossible for pronouns in main clauses. The principle of small arguments predicts that individuals should tend to interpret sentential operators as applying only to the main clauses of sentences containing subordinate clauses. These two assertions:

Surprisingly, before she ate, Pat drank.
Surprisingly, if she ate, then Pat drank.

should therefore tend to be interpreted as though they meant:

Before she ate, surprisingly Pat drank.
If she ate, then surprisingly Pat drank.

The two versions of each sentence do appear to be synonymous.

Where matters go wrong is in the case of certain other operators. Negation is a good example. The small-argument principle predicts that individuals should tend to deny a conditional, such as:

If she ate, then Pat drank

by negating only its main clause:

If she ate, then Pat did not drink.

Indirect evidence suggests that individuals do sometimes make such negations (Handley, Evans, & Thompson, 2006). They also occur when participants have to deny conditionals explicitly (Khemlani et al., 2009). Handley et al. (p. 566) write: "So what does a negated conditional mean? In our view, it does not mean that a determinate p, not-q state of affairs holds in the world. Instead, people understand negated conditionals as indicating that q does not hold under the supposition of p; otherwise stated, they understand it to mean 'if p then not-q'."

This view violates a principle going back to Aristotle and one that is maintained by modern logicians and linguists (e.g., Horn, 2001): a negation should *contradict* the proposition that it negates rather than merely be *contrary* to it. In a contradictory relation, one proposition is true and the other is a false. In a contrary relation, the two propositions cannot both be true but they can both be false. Hence, "Pat is tall" and "Pat is not tall" are contradictories, whereas "Pat is tall" and "Pat is short" are merely contraries, because both are false if Pat is of medium height. The pair of conditionals:

If she ate, then Pat drank.
If she ate, then Pat did not drink.

do not contradict one another, because both are compatible with the possibility that Pat did not eat. The error is transparent in the case of an assertion, such as:

If men are rich then they are conservative.

and its putative negation:

If men are rich then they are not conservative.

Like the previous pair of conditionals, these two assertions are contraries. Indeed, they are both false, and their correct negations are respectively:

Some rich men are not conservative.
Some rich men are conservative.

And the correct negation of the earlier conditional is:

Pat ate *and* she did not drink.

because it contradicts the conditional. It also fits Barrouillet's findings, described earlier, about the cases that individuals list as possible given the truth of a conditional. They list the preceding case as *impossible*. In general, the correct negation of any conditional, whether it is basic or not, should correspond to those cases that are impossible given the conditional.

So, what happens if experimenters ask individuals to negate a conditional? The short answer is: they don't understand the task, and often proceed to negate any or every clause in the assertion. But, they do understand the task if it is framed in terms of denying a conditional that is false. As my colleagues observed, some individuals follow the small-scope principle, but some do produce correct negations (Khemlani et al., 2009).

You might suppose that it doesn't much matter whether negations are contradictories or contraries. But, if an assertion, *A*, and its negation, *not-A*, are merely contraries, then their disjunction: *A or not-A*, is not necessarily true, because both propositions could be false. Hence, the negation of this disjunction: *not (A or not-A)* is not necessarily false, either.

This consequence affects inferences of a sort known as *reductio ad absurdum*: if an assumption for the sake of argument leads to contradiction then one is entitled to infer the negation of the assumption. Some logicians, especially those of the Intuitionist school (e.g., Heyting, 1971), reject the principle that *A or not-A* is necessarily true (see Evans, 2007, p. 51, for a similar scepticism). But, a consequence of this rejection is that a *reductio ad absurdum* cannot be used to prove affirmative conclusions from the assumption of their negations.

Most psychological theories of reasoning, however, allow that individuals make reductios (see for example, Rips, 1994; Braine & O'Brien, 1998; Johnson-Laird & Byrne, 1991), and Jonathan himself pioneered their study, both as an undergraduate and as a postgraduate (see Evans & Over, 2004, p. 46).

The truth of conditionals

A long-standing puzzle in the study of conditionals is the contrast between the sets of possibilities that individuals list for conditionals (as in Barrouillet's studies described earlier) and their judgements of the truth or falsity of conditionals in the light of various observed cases. In general, individuals evaluate a basic conditional, such as our earlier example:

If there is a circle then there is a triangle

as true given that there is a circle and a triangle, and as false given that there is a circle without a triangle. But, they judge cases in which there is no circle as irrelevant to the truth or falsity of a conditional (Johnson-Laird & Tagart, 1969). Following Quine (1974), these authors suggested a "defective truth table" in which conditionals have no truth value when their if-clauses are false. Evans and Over (2004) have also defended this idea. But, there's an alternative possibility. The small-argument principle implies that individuals interpret the task of evaluating the truth of the conditional as one in which they should take the if-clause for granted, and assess the truth of the then-clause alone. It is as though they interpret the following question:

> Given this contingency, is it true that if there is a circle then there is a triangle?

to mean:

> If there is a circle then, given this contingency, is it true that there is a triangle?

The result is that they judge that the cases in which there isn't a circle as irrelevant. But, of course, they are not really evaluating the truth of the conditional, but rather the truth of its then-clause *given* the truth of its if-clause.

Consider what would complete the following conditional in order to make it true, not probably true, but *definitely* true:

> If God exists then _____.

One such completion is:

> atheists are wrong.

This conditional is definitely true, and so the defective truth table yields the following valid inference:

> If God exists then atheists are wrong.
> Therefore, God exists.

The inference is valid because the only way in which a conditional can be true, according to the defective truth table, is when its if-clause is true. The premise is true, the inference is valid, and so the conclusion is true too. This proof for the existence of God is absurd: the fact that a conditional is true does not imply that its if-clause is true. It follows that conditionals do *not* have defective truth tables.

The probability of conditionals

One final consequence of the small-argument principle concerns the probability of conditionals. Probabilities can be assessed in two distinct ways. The *extensional* way depends on the fact that the probability of an event equals the sum of the probabilities of the different ways in which the event can occur. The *nonextensional* way relies on some relevant heuristic, index, or evidence, as, for example, when reasoners infer that because an exemplar is typical of a category, it has a high probability of being a member of the category (see, for example, Tversky & Kahneman, 1983). Psychologists have investigated both ways of estimating the probabilities of conditionals, but the model theory has so far been applied mainly to extensional probabilities (see, for example, Johnson-Laird, Legrenzi, Girotto, Legrenzi, & Caverni, 1999). It postulates that individuals construct models of the prior possibilities, and assume that they are equiprobable unless there is evidence to the contrary. They estimate the probability of an event as the proportion of these possibilities in which the event holds. Almost always, however, they do not know at first how to carry out the task for conditionals. They devise a *strategy* for coping, and different individuals devise different strategies, just as they do in deductive reasoning (see below).

The model theory postulates three main strategies that individuals are likely to adopt to infer the probabilities of a basic conditional (Girotto & Johnson-Laird 2004). First, the *equiprobable* strategy contrasts the one explicit mental model of a conditional with the alternative in which the if-clause of the conditional is false, and assigns them equal probabilities. For example, where two coins are tossed, individuals using this strategy infer a probability of a half for the following conditional:

If the nickel is heads then the dime is heads

They make this estimate because they assume that each of these mental models is equiprobable:

Nickel	*Dime*
heads	heads
. . .	

where the ellipsis denotes a model that is a place holder for the cases in which the if-clause is false. This strategy yields the same answer as the conditional probability that, given that the nickel is heads, the dime is heads. Second, the *conjunctive* strategy treats the conditional as though it were a conjunction – a tendency that has been observed independently (Johnson-Laird et al., 1999) – and assesses it in relation to all the possibilities. For example, where two coins are tossed, individuals using this strategy infer that the probability of the conditional: if the nickel is heads then the dime is heads, is a quarter, because the probability that both the coins are heads occurs in one of out of the four possible outcomes. Third, the *complete* strategy contrasts all the possibilities in which a conditional holds with the possibilities in which it does not hold. It yields a probability of three quarters for the preceding conditional, because there is only one possible outcome – where the nickel is heads and the dime is tails – in which the conditional does not hold. This strategy is equivalent to treating a basic conditional as though it were a material implication. We have corroborated the occurrence of the three strategies in studies of the extensional inferences that participants make, and the results provided more support for these strategies than for the suppositional account (Girotto & Johnson-Laird, 2004).

The suppositional account postulates that individuals should estimate the probability of a conditional by using a variant of Ramsey's test. They make a supposition of the proposition in the if-clause, and then assess the probability of the then-clause in these circumstances (Evans, Handley, & Over, 2003; Evans, Handley, Neilens, & Over, 2007; Oberauer & Wilhelm, 2003; Over, Hadjichristidis, Evans, Handley, & Sloman, 2007). Hence, the probability of the conditional is the conditional probability that the then-clause holds given that the if-clause holds, that is, the probability of *if A then C* equals the conditional probability of *C* given *A*. There is an overlap between this account and the model theory. The equiprobable strategy yields the same result as the suppositional account, at least for simple conditionals.

The suppositional account also comes into play if individuals follow the small-argument principle. When the participants thought aloud as they tackled the problems in Girotto and Johnson-Laird (2004), their protocols showed that they often transformed:

What is the probability of if A then C?

into:

If A then what is the probability of C?

One view is that this transformation in itself corroborates the suppositional account (Evans et al., 2005). Individuals certainly do follow the small-argument principle, but, as you have seen, it leads to erroneous negations of conditionals, and the following argument implies that it is erroneous for extensional probabilities, too.

Consider the following pair of assertions about two coins that come down either heads or tails with equal probabilities:

The nickel came down heads or the dime came down heads, or both did.
If the nickel didn't come down heads then the dime did come down heads.

If the disjunction is true, then the conditional is true too, because it holds in the same possibilities:

Nickel	Dime
Heads	Tails
Tails	Heads
Heads	Heads

According to the model theory, the inference from the disjunction to the conditional is valid, but I shall avoid the introduction of validity into this analysis, because not everyone accepts that validity is a matter of content, not form.

What is the probability of the disjunction above? That is, what is the probability that the nickel came down heads or the dime came down heads, or both did? Granted that the tosses are fair, each possible outcome is equiprobable. Hence, the answer is: three quarters, because the disjunction holds for three out of the four possible outcomes. And what is the following conditional probability:

> Given that the nickel did not come down heads, the dime did come down heads?

Equally plainly, this conditional probability is a half, because the second coin either comes down heads or tails with equal probabilities. The suppositional theory postulates that this conditional probability is the probability of the conditional. But, if so, there is an egregious error, because the disjunction is more probable (3/4) than the conditional (1/2). Such a relation is impossible, because whenever the disjunction is true the conditional is true too. And so the probability of the first assertion cannot be greater than the probability of the second assertion, because in every case in which the first assertion holds the second assertion also holds. A case in which the first assertion is true, but the second assertion isn't, would be a counterexample showing that the second assertion can be false even though the first assertion is true. But, no such counterexample exists. Hence, the probability of the conditional is not the conditional probability of its then-clause given its if-clause. The same problem arises with many other cases in which probabilities are computed extensionally. For example, in the case of a fair die, if this assertion is true:

> Either the die didn't come up even or else it came up 2

then so too is:

> If the die came up even then it came up 2.

But, the probability of the premise is 2/3, whereas the conditional probability corresponding to the conclusion is only 1/3. In summary, the suppositional account is violated in many extensional cases in which conditionals of the grammatical form, *if not-A then B* hold in all the cases in which disjunctions of the grammatical form, *A or B*, hold.

Other phenomena support the model theory of the probability of conditionals. Schroyens, Schaeken, and Dieussaert (2008) have shown that when a prior task increased the relevance of the possibilities in which the if-clause was false, there was a reliable increase in *complete* estimates of the probability of a conditional. Similarly, Sonya Geiger in some unpublished studies has shown that when individuals paraphrase a disjunction with a conditional, they are also more likely to make a complete estimate of the probability of the conditional. The model theory predicts both of these phenomena, but they are not easy to reconcile with the suppositional account.

Auxiliary verbs, deontic interpretations, and counterfactual conditionals

The interpretation of conditionals depends on the tense, mood, aspect, and the modality of their clauses. Certain conditionals are "deontic" in that they concern what is permissible or obligatory; that is, what is deontically possible or necessary. One clue to them is the use of certain modal auxiliary verbs, such as: "If you promised then you *must* go." The model theory postulates that such assertions are represented in terms of factual possibilities for their if-clauses and deontic possibilities for their then-clauses:

Factual possibilities	*Deontic possibilities*
You promised.	You go.
You didn't promise.	You go.
You didn't promise.	You don't go.

The case in which you promised and didn't go is factually possible – people do break promises, but it is not possible deontically; that is, you must not do it. Once again, individuals are unlikely to represent all three deontic possibilities, but they usually do represent what is salient. For example, in the domain of prudential obligations, such as, "If the nurse cleans up the blood then she should wear rubber gloves" (Manktelow & Over, 1990), they are likely to represent the salient deontic possibility, the nurse cleaned up blood and wore gloves, and the deontic impossibility that she cleaned up blood and did not wear gloves (Byrne, 2005; Quelhas & Byrne, 2003). The evidence shows that deontic assertions make what is impossible more salient than factual assertions do (Bucciarelli & Johnson-Laird, 2005).

Another effect of auxiliary verbs is to yield conditional sentences that are subjunctive in mood, for example:

If there had been any pudding then Pat would have eaten it.

Such conditionals can express a proposition that leaves open whether or not there was any pudding. But, they can also express a *counterfactual* proposition. For example, the assertion:

If the nickel hadn't landed heads then the dime would have landed heads

elicits a model of the facts:

Nickel	*Dime*
Heads	Tails

and a model of the counterfactual possibility:

Nickel	*Dime*
Tails	Heads

Individuals tend to balk at the following sort of inference (Over et al., 2010):

> The nickel landed heads.
> Either the nickel landed heads or the dime landed heads, or both.
> Therefore, if the nickel didn't land heads then the dime landed heads.

According to the model theory, the first premise rules out the following model of the disjunction:

Nickel	*Dime*
Tails	Heads

But, this model is the same as the explicit mental model of the conditional conclusion. The theory accordingly predicts that individuals should accept the inference when the conditional conclusion is counterfactual:

> Therefore, if the nickel hadn't landed heads the dime would have.

Isabel Orenes has corroborated this prediction in an unpublished study. Counterfactuals give rise to many other phenomena, and Byrne (2005) gives a comprehensive account of the model theory's application to them.

Suppositions and strategies

The model theory postulates that individuals can make suppositions, that is, they can make assumptions for the sake of argument, such as: suppose that there's a recession, what then? You use general knowledge to infer various consequences, for example, your pension plan will lose value. When you make a supposition, your conclusion should embody it. You should conclude: if there's a recession, then my pension plan will lose value. But, sometimes, your conclusion may feed back to show that your supposition itself is false: you make a *reductio ad absurdum*. Here is an example that Jonathan studied many years ago. You want to go to a movie but you also need some exercise. You think to yourself:

> If I go to a movie tonight then I'll go for a walk tomorrow.

But, you're very busy, and so you think:

> Either I'll go to a movie tonight, or else I'll go for a walk tomorrow.

You may then reason as follows: "Suppose I go to a movie tonight". It then follows from your mental models of the conditional premise that you'll go for a walk tomorrow. But, this conclusion and your mental models of the disjunctive premise yield the conclusion that you will *not* go to a movie tonight. So, your reasoning has led you to a negation of your supposition; that is, if I go to a movie tonight then I will *not* go to a movie tonight. If you flesh out the models of this conditional into fully explicit models, they yield the negation of your supposition: I will not go to a movie tonight. And this conclusion, taken in conjunction with your second premise yields the conclusion: I'll go for a walk tomorrow.

Individuals make suppositions in straightforward deductions. Van der Henst, Yang, and I (2002, p. 427) carried out a study in which we gave participants such problems as:

> There is a white pill in the box if and only if there is a green pill.
> Either there is a green pill in the box or else there is a red pill, but not both.
> There is a red pill in the box if and only if there is a blue pill.
> Does it follow that:
> If there isn't a white pill in the box then there is a blue pill in the box?

The inferences were very easy – indeed, this study of reasoning may be the only one in which every participant got every inference right (Van der Henst, Yang, & Johnson-Laird, 2002). The premises of each problem were compatible with just two possibilities, and half of the problems asked about a valid conclusion, as above, and half of them asked about an invalid conclusion. The point of the study, however, was to determine what reasoning strategies the participants developed during the course of the experiment. We gave the participants pencil and paper so they could write down anything they wanted to, but they also had to think aloud as they tackled the inferences. We video-recorded what they wrote, drew, and said. Their protocols made excellent sense. I wrote a computer program that parsed a subset of them, carried out the same operations that the participants described, and thereby made the same evaluations as they did. When the participants started out, they were not quite sure how to proceed. In due course, they spontaneously developed a strategy for coping with the inferences.

Different individuals developed different strategies. The most frequent strategy was to draw a diagram that integrated all the possibilities in which the premises hold – a fully explicit set of models. But, some participants made use of suppositions. Their actual strategy was to follow up step by step the consequences of a single possibility. If a problem included a premise that made a categorical assertion, then they followed up its consequences. Otherwise, they made a supposition to start the strategy rolling, one suggested by either a premise or the given conclusion. For the problem above, one protocol was:

> Suppose that there isn't a white pill in the box. It follows from the first premise that the box does not contain a green pill, either. It then follows from the second premise that there *is* a red pill in the box. And it follows from the third premise that there is a blue pill too. So, if there isn't a white pill in the box, then it follows that there is a blue pill in the box. The conclusion is correct.
>
> (Van der Henst, Yang, & Johnson-Laird, 2002, p. 427)

A characteristic sign of reasoning from a supposition is that it starts with a phrase, such as, "Suppose", or "Assuming we have . . .". Another sign is the integration of the supposition into the final conditional conclusion.

The participants in Van der Henst's experiments used suppositions in a variety of ways, not all of which were logically correct or in accordance with the suppositional theory. For example, they made suppositions corresponding to the then-clause of conditional conclusions. Likewise, they didn't realize that a proof of a biconditional conclusion, *A if and only if C*, calls for two suppositions, for example, one to show that the supposition of *A* yields the consequent, *C*, and one to show that the supposition of *C* yields the antecedent, *A*. In general, naïve reasoners are not fastidious about the suppositions they make – given, that is, that they are prepared to make suppositions. Some reasoners never made any suppositions, not even to prove a conditional conclusion. Suppositions may be a strategy in reasoning, not a universal principle.

Conclusions

If, as a prudent reader, you are reading this section first without having read the preceding parts of the article, you're probably wondering why conditionals – *if-then* assertions – merit a chapter to themselves. You may be reminded of the spoof headline in *The Times* of London years ago, announcing the discovery of a new meaning for *and*. So, why have Jonathan Evans and many others, including the present author, spent so much time on "if"? The fact is that conditionals have troubled theorists for two millennia. No consensus has ever existed about them. So, in the slight hope of a move towards a consensus, let me summarize the argument of this article, and draw to a general conclusion.

What do conditionals mean? One view is that they are material implications. The phenomenon of modulation shows that this view cannot be right. It may be true that Viv fell off her bike, and it may be true that she broke her leg, but the following conditional would be false if the two events occurred in the opposite order to the one it conveys:

If Viv fell off her bike then she broke her leg.

Another view is that conditionals are an invitation to make a supposition and to think hypothetically. This account implies that conditionals have a defective truth table: they are true when the if-clause and then-clause are both true, false when the if-clause is true but the then-clause is false, and lack a truth value when the if-clause is false. But, this account is refuted by the unacceptable proof for the existence of God from the true conditional: if God exists then atheists are wrong. This inference is valid according to the defective truth table, because the conditional is true, and, according to the defective truth table, the only way in which a conditional can be true is if its if-clause is true.

Still another view is that conditionals in daily life have a meaning that is weaker than material implication. As Pfeifer and Kleiter (2005) wrote: "In everyday contexts it seems to be more plausible to interpret conditionals not by material implications, but by much weaker conditional probabilities." In other words, the meaning of a conditional, *if A then C*, is that given *A* there is a reasonable probability that *C* holds. This view is refuted by several phenomena. For example, children develop the ability to list the possibilities for *basic* conditionals (Barrouillet et al., 2000). Likewise, as Isabel Orenes has shown, individuals accept the following sort of inference:

The nickel came down heads or the dime came down heads, or both did.
Therefore, if the nickel didn't come down heads then the dime did.

When the disjunction is true, then so is the conditional, and so the conditional cannot be less probable than the disjunction. The probability of the disjunction, granted the equiprobability of the four possible outcomes, is 3/4, whereas the conditional probability that the second coin came down heads, given that the first coin didn't, is only 1/2. It follows that the probability of conditionals in such cases cannot be the conditional probability.

Finally, what would show that the model theory of conditionals is false? The answer is: any of three following main phenomena.

(1) A conclusive argument that conditionals have only a single meaning, or logical form, which somehow predicts all the phenomena reviewed in this chapter.
(2) A robust demonstration of a hiatus between the possibilities that individuals list for a class of conditionals and the pattern of inferences that they make from these conditionals.
(3) An irremediable inability to overcome an erroneous application of the small-scope principle, so that individuals never make, say, correct negations of certain conditionals or correct assessments of their probabilities.

Until such phenomena are forthcoming, the model theory offers a viable account of conditionals. It predicts at least the possibilities in which they hold, their modulation, the patterns of inference from them, the principal interpretations of their negations, the main estimates of their extensional probabilities, and their use in temporal simulations. Hence, if it is wrong about some other facets of conditionals, then it at least predicts these phenomena.[1]

Note

1 Did you notice that this final inference corresponds to one of the paradoxes of material implication? According to Evans and Over (2004, p. 19), such inferences are absurd.

References

Barrouillet, P., Grosset, N., & Lecas, J. F. (2000). Conditional reasoning by mental models: Chronometric and developmental evidence. *Cognition, 75*, 237–266.

Barwise, J. (1989). *The situation in logic*. Stanford, CA: Center for the Study of Language and Information.

Braine, M. D. S., & O'Brien, D. P. (Eds.). (1998). *Mental logic*. Mahwah, NJ: Lawrence Erlbaum Associates, Inc.

Bucciarelli, M., & Johnson-Laird, P. N. (2005). Naïve deontics: A theory of meaning, representation, and reasoning. *Cognitive Psychology, 50*, 159–193.

Byrne, R. M. J. (2005). *The rational imagination: How people create alternatives to reality*. Cambridge, MA: MIT.

Byrne, R. M. J., & Johnson-Laird, P. N. (1989). Spatial reasoning. *Journal of Memory and Language, 28*, 564–575.

Evans, J. St B. T. (1993). The mental model theory of conditional reasoning: Critical appraisal and revision. *Cognition, 48*, 1–20.

Evans, J. St B. T. (2003). In two minds: Dual-process accounts of reasoning. *Trends in Cognitive Science, 7*, 454–459.

Evans, J. St B. T. (2007). *Hypothetical thinking: Dual processes in reasoning and judgement*. Hove, UK: Psychology Press.

Evans, J. St B. T., Handley, S. J., Neilens, H., & Over, D. E. (2007). Thinking about conditionals: A study of individual differences. *Memory & Cognition, 35*, 1759–1771.

Evans, J. St B. T., Handley, S. J., & Over, D. E. (2003). Conditionals and conditional probability. *Journal of Experimental Psychology: Learning, Memory and Cognition, 29*, 321–355.

Evans, J. St B. T., & Over, D. E. (2004). *If*. Oxford: Oxford University Press.

Evans, J. St B. T., Over, D. E., and Handley, S. J. (2005). Supposition, extensionality and conditionals: A critique of the mental model theory of Johnson-Laird and Byrne (2002). *Psychological Review, 112*, 1040–1052.

Girotto, V., & Johnson-Laird, P. N. (2004). The probability of conditionals. *Psychologia, 47*, 207–225.

Goodwin, G. P., & Johnson-Laird, P. N. (2009). Reasoning as simulation. Manuscript submitted for publication.

Handley, S. J., Evans, J. St B. T., & Thompson, S. C. (2006). The negated conditional: A litmus test for the suppositional conditional? *Journal of Experimental Psychology: Language, Memory, and Cognition, 32*, 559–569.

Heyting, A. (1971). *Intuitionism: An introduction* (3rd ed.). Amsterdam, The Netherlands: North-Holland.

Horn, L. R. (2001). *A natural history of negation* (Rev. ed.). Stanford, CA: CSLI Publications.

Jeffrey, R. (1981). *Formal logic: Its scope and limits.* New York: McGraw-Hill.

Johnson-Laird, P. N. (1983). *Mental models.* Cambridge: Cambridge University Press.

Johnson-Laird, P. N. (2006). *How we reason.* Oxford: Oxford University Press.

Johnson-Laird, P. N., & Byrne, R. M. J. (1991). *Deduction.* Hove, UK: Psychology Press.

Johnson-Laird, P. N., & Byrne, R. M. J. (2002). Conditionals: A theory of meaning, pragmatics, and inference. *Psychological Review, 109,* 646–678.

Johnson-Laird, P. N., Byrne, R. M. J., & Girotto, V. (2009). The mental model theory of conditionals: A reply to Guy Politzer. *Topoi, 28,* 75–80.

Johnson-Laird, P. N., Legrenzi, P., Girotto, V., Legrenzi, M., & Caverni, J.-P. (1999). Naive probability: A mental model theory of extensional reasoning. *Psychological Review, 106,* 62–88.

Johnson-Laird, P. N., & Tagart, J. (1969). How implication is understood. *American Journal of Psychology, 82,* 367–373.

Khemlani, S., Orenes, I., & Johnson-Laird, P. N. (2009). Negation: A theory of its meaning, interpretation, and verification. Manuscript submitted for publication.

Manktelow, K. I., and Over, D. E. (1990). Deontic thought and the selection task. In K. J. Gilhooly, M. T. G. Keane, R. H. Logie, & G. Erdos (Eds.), *Lines of thinking: Reflections on the psychology of thought* (Vol. 1). Chichester, UK: John Wiley.

Marr, D. (1982). *Vision.* San Francisco: W. H. Freeman.

Oaksford, M., Chater, N., & Larkin, J. (2000). Probabilities and polarity biases in conditional inference. *Journal of Experimental Psychology: Learning, Memory, and Cognition, 26,* 883–899.

Oberauer, K. (2006). Reasoning with conditionals: A test of formal models of four theories. *Cognitive Psychology, 53,* 238–283.

Oberauer, K., & Wilhelm, O. (2003). The meaning(s) of conditionals: Conditional probabilities, mental models and personal utilities. *Journal of Experimental Psychology: Learning, Memory and Cognition, 29,* 688–693.

Over, D. E., Evans, J. St B. T., & Elqayam, S. (2010). Conditionals and non-constructive reasoning. In M. Oaksford & N. Chater (Eds.), *Cognition and conditionals: Probability and logic in human thinking.* Oxford: Oxford University Press.

Over, D. E., Hadjichristidis, C., Evans, J. St B. T., Handley, S. J., & Sloman, S. A. (2007). The probability of causal conditionals. *Cognitive Psychology, 54,* 62–97.

Peirce, C. S. (1931–1958). *Collected papers of Charles Sanders Peirce* (8 vols, Eds. C. Hartshorne, P. Weiss, & A. Burks). Cambridge, MA: Harvard University Press.

Pfeifer, N., & Kleiter, G. D. (2005). Towards a mental probability logic. *Psychologica Belgica, 45,* 71–99.

Quelhas, C., & Byrne, R. M. J. (2003). Reasoning with deontic and counterfactual conditionals. *Thinking & Reasoning, 9,* 43–66.

Quelhas, A. C., Juhos, C., & Johnson-Laird, P. N. (2010). The modulation of conditional assertions and its effects on reasoning. *Quarterly Journal of Experimental Psychology, 63,* 1–24.

Quine, W. V. O. (1974). *Methods of logic* (3rd ed.). London: Routledge & Kegan Paul.

Ramsey, F. P. (1990). In D. H. Mellor (Ed.), *Foundations: Essays in philosophy, logic, mathematics and economics*. London: Humanities Press. (Originally published in 1929)

Rips, L. J. (1994). *The psychology of proof*. Cambridge, MA: MIT Press.

Schaeken, W. S., Johnson-Laird, P. N., & d'Ydewalle, G. (1996). Mental models and temporal reasoning. *Cognition, 60*, 205–234.

Schroyens, W., & Schaeken, W. (2003). A critique of Oaksford, Chater, and Larkin's (2000) conditional probability model of conditional reasoning. *Journal of Experimental Psychology: Learning, Memory, and Cognition, 29*, 140–149.

Schroyens, W., Schaeken, W., & Dieussaert, K. (2008). "The" interpretation(s) of conditionals. *Experimental Psychology, 58*, 173–181.

Stalnaker, R. C. (1968). A theory of conditionals. In N. Rescher (Ed.), *Studies in logical theory* (American Philosophical Quarterly Monograph No. 2) (pp. 98–122). Oxford: Blackwell.

Tversky, A., & Kahneman, D. (1983). Extensional versus intuitive reasoning: The conjunction fallacy in probability judgment. *Psychological Review, 90*, 293–315.

Van der Henst, J.-B., Yang, Y., & Johnson-Laird, P. N. (2002). Strategies in sentential reasoning. *Cognitive Science, 26*, 425–468.

Verschueren, N., Schaeken, W., & d'Ydewalle, G. (2005). A dual-process specification of causal conditional reasoning. *Thinking & Reasoning, 11*, 278–293.

8 Uncertain deductive reasoning

Niki Pfeifer and Gernot D. Kleiter

University of Salzburg

Probabilistic models have started to replace classical logic as the standard reference paradigm in human deductive reasoning. Mental probability logic emphasizes general principles where human reasoning deviates from classical logic, but agrees with a probabilistic approach (like nonmonotonicity or the conditional event interpretation of conditionals).

This contribution consists of two parts. In the first part we discuss general features of reasoning systems including consequence relations, how uncertainty may enter argument forms, probability intervals, and probabilistic informativeness. These concepts are of central importance for the psychological task analysis. In the second part we report new experimental data on the paradoxes of the material conditional, the probabilistic modus ponens, the complement task, and data on the probabilistic truth-table task. The results of the experiments provide evidence for the hypothesis that people represent indicative conditionals by conditional probability assertions.

Introduction

The title of this contribution appears paradoxical. Deduction is truth preserving and not uncertain. The alleged paradox is clarified in the following sections. A descriptive theory of human reasoning needs a normative theory in the background. The normative background provides rationality norms and specifies the correct answer to a reasoning task relative to these norms. It serves to provide the language and the inference rules to solve the problem. Moreover, it stimulates psychological hypotheses and guides the construction of experimental tasks. The shift from classical logic to alternative normative systems leads to new experimental paradigms. The choice of an appropriate normative framework is a fundamental problem and needs careful consideration before running psychological experiments. If the normative framework is ignored in the process of psychological model building, then one runs into the danger of not knowing what one investigates: in the worst case, the resulting experimental data become uninterpretable.

The research on human reasoning is a process that proceeds by asking questions and setting goals, by designing experiments and selecting experimental tasks, and by interpreting the results within a theoretical framework. All these steps are related to a normative paradigm. For many years it was taken for granted that classical logic is the appropriate normative paradigm for research on human reasoning. Modern logic and mathematical computer science, however, have developed many systems to describe reasoning tasks, properties of knowledge representation, and inference. Today there are many systems of "rational" reasoning. It is reasonable to consider some of these logical systems while asking questions and setting goals, while designing experiments and selecting experimental tasks, and while interpreting the results within a theoretical framework. Probability logics provide one class of such systems. The present contribution argues that the coherence-based probability logic is a fruitful normative frame for investigating human reasoning. Before we illustrate the application of probability logic to psychology, we discuss some theoretical notions that are important for human reasoning research.

Where do classical logic and probability logic differ and where not? First, what is common to both.

- Propositions (or events) are true or false. They have Boolean truth values.
- Inferences from premises to conclusions are deductive. Probability logic investigates argument forms like modus ponens and modus tollens, or various kinds of syllogisms in an analogous way as in classical logic.

Major differences concern the following points:

- In probability logic propositions are assigned degrees of belief. The degrees of belief are subjective probabilities. Subjective probabilities are coherent descriptions of partial knowledge states.
- Probability assessments should be coherent. A probability assessment is coherent if it cannot lead to bets with sure loss. There are different kinds of coherence.
- Probabilistic inference transmits probabilities from the premises to the conclusions. The inference itself is deductive and not probabilistic. It follows the rules of mathematics, like solving systems of linear equations or linear programming.
- There are a number of rather general properties in which both systems differ. Classical logic is monotonic, probability logic is defeasible and nonmonotonic. Classical logic is truth functional, a property that does not apply to probability logic. Systems with such meta-properties are investigated in artificial intelligence to mimic human reasoning. They are of special interest for psychological modelling.

In recent years several probabilistic models of human reasoning have been proposed (Oaksford & Chater, 1998, 2007; Evans & Over, 2004). These models do of course have many features in common with the present approach. One common feature is that the probabilities of conditionals, P(If A, then B), are interpreted as conditional probabilities, P(B|A), as opposed to the probability of material conditionals, P(A ⊃ B). Table 8.1 presents three prominent psychological interpretations of the indicative "if__, then__". The interpretation as a conditional event received compelling empirical support (e.g., Liu, Lo, & Wu, 1996; Evans, Handley, & Over, 2003; Over & Evans, 2003; Oberauer & Wilhelm, 2003). The dominant experimental paradigm for investigating the understanding of uncertain indicative conditionals is the probabilistic truth-table task. We proposed an alternative experimental paradigm by studying probabilistic argument forms. Our own approach is called "mental probability logic" (Pfeifer & Kleiter, 2005a, 2005b, 2009, 2010) and differs from other probabilistic approaches with respect to the following points:

- Our commitment to subjective probability and coherence is in the tradition of de Finetti (Coletti & Scozzafava, 2002). In combination with recent developments in computer science (like description logics; Baader, Calvanese, McGuinness, Nardi, & Patel-Schneider, 2007), the coherence approach leads to powerful systems of knowledge representation and inference (Gilio, 2002; Biazzo, Gilio, Lukasiewicz, & Sanfilippo, 2005; Lukasiewicz, 2005, 2008).
- In our approach it often occurs that the conclusions of an argument obtain lower and upper probabilities and not point probabilities. We investigate interval probabilities.
- In our approach the consequence relation itself is deductive and not probabilistic.

General features of reasoning systems

Human thinking and reasoning may lead to outstanding and fascinating achievements. Take as an example the proof of Fermat's Last Theorem. It took more than 350 years to come up with a proof (Wiles, 1995) of the famous conjecture that Euler or Poincaré could not solve. We think that any

Table 8.1 Truth tables of three prominent psychological interpretations of the indicative "if__, then__"

	State of the world		Material conditional	Conjunction	Conditional event
	A	B	A ⊃ B	A∧B	B|A
s1	true	true	true	true	true
s2	true	false	false	false	false
s3	false	true	true	false	undetermined
s4	false	false	true	false	undetermined

Note
Only rows s3 and s4 distinguish between the three interpretations.

reasonable theory of human reasoning should strive to explain how we solve difficult problems. Solving difficult problems requires a minimum of systematicity. Considering various normative background systems one should be careful to choose a system that does not exclude smart solutions right from the beginning. While evaluating formal systems for their appropriateness for psychological modelling, one should look out for "competent" and rich systems. Description logic is one such family of systems (Baader et al., 2007). It has replaced semantic networks for knowledge representation, it has many extensions (probabilistic, possibilistic, autoepistemic, etc.); so it is a rich system. There is software for real-world applications to build ontologies.[1] In our view it is important to look at principles developed in such fields to learn more also about features and constraints of human reasoning.

Features that cannot be expressed in classical logic include procedural mechanisms, defaults, closed-world reasoning, assumptions about missing information, nontruth functionality, nonmonotonicity, defeasible reasoning (in a wide sense), uncertainty, probability, vagueness, and fuzziness.

Several disciplines investigate knowledge representation and reasoning. Psychology is only one of them. During the last 50 years logicians and computer scientists have developed a large repertoire of logics and formal systems of reasoning (Van Harmelen, Lifschitz, & Porter, 2008), recently especially in connection with the semantic web projects. Usually these systems are "nonclassical", that is they are extensions of classical logic or they explicitly violate principles of classical logic. A typical example is nonmonotonic reasoning.

During the last few years these nonclassical systems have had a strong influence on which questions and experimental tasks are investigated. Extensions of classical logic include causal reasoning, autoepistemic reasoning, epistemic logic, dynamic logic, deontic logic, temporal logic, fuzzy logic, possibilistic logic, and – last but not least – probability logic.

Deduction and uncertainty

One of the basic concepts of classical logic is validity ("cl-validity" for short). Cl-validity guarantees that the truth of the premises propagates to the conclusion. As an example of an argument that is valid according to classical logic, consider the following instance of modus ponens:

𝔓1   If shape X is a triangle, then shape X is blue.
𝔓2   Shape X is a triangle.
_____cl-valid
ℭ   Shape X is blue.

𝔓1 and 𝔓2 denote the premises and ℭ denotes the conclusion. The horizontal line denotes the consequence relation. If the conditional in 𝔓1 (If A, then B) is formalized as a material conditional, $A \supset B$, then this argument is cl-valid, since $\mathfrak{C}$ is true under *all* interpretations that assign *true* to both $\mathfrak{P}1$ and $\mathfrak{P}2$.

Cl-validity is a meta-property of arguments, and not of the conclusion of arguments. However, if all premises are true *and* if an argument is cl-valid, then the conclusion must be true. If at least one premise is false, then classical logic *does not* tell us whether the conclusion is true or false. This distinction between the two questions – (1) is an argument cl-valid?; and (2) is the conclusion true if all premises are true? – leads to two classes of experimental tasks.

The first class of experimental tasks requires the judgement of cl-validity. These tasks require a choice between two options: the argument is (1) cl-valid; or (2) not cl-valid. Cl-validity is a meta-property of the (form of the) whole argument.

The second class of experimental tasks requires a judgement concerning the conclusion of an argument. In such tasks the participants are instructed to assume that each premise is true and to decide whether the *conclusion* is (1) true; (2) false; or (3) whether one cannot decide whether the conclusion is true or false. This task requires a choice between three options. Option (3) is of central importance but unfortunately not always made available for the participants (especially in the "possibilities" form of the truth-table tasks, which is often used by proponents of the mental model theory). Normatively, if the argument is not cl-valid, then the truth value of the conclusion is undetermined (for example denying the antecedent) or necessarily false (if, for example, the conclusion of modus ponens is negated). The normative relationships between both classes of tasks are explained in Table 8.2.

Cl-validity is a complex and abstract concept. It is a *meta-property* of arguments. To judge whether an argument is cl-valid is a rather artificial task that is hardly ever performed in everyday life. People usually do not

Table 8.2 Modus ponens, denying the antecedent, and their respective affirmative and negated versions

	Modus ponens		Denying the antecedent	
	affirmative	negated	affirmative	negated
$\mathfrak{P}1$:	$A \supset B$	$A \supset B$	$A \supset B$	$A \supset B$
$\mathfrak{P}2$:	A	A	$\neg A$	$\neg A$
$\mathfrak{C}$	B	$\neg B$	$\neg B$	B
cl-valid:	yes	no	no	no
$V(\mathfrak{C})$	true	false	undetermined	undetermined

Notes
$\mathfrak{P}1$: and $\mathfrak{P}2$: denote the premises and $\mathfrak{C}$ denotes the conclusion. A and B denote propositions. $\supset$ and $\neg$ denote the material conditional and negation, respectively, and are defined as usual. cl-valid denotes classical logical validity. V denotes the logical valuation – function V under all interpretations that assign *true* to each premise. If the antecedent, A, of the conditional premise is false, then the truth value of the conclusion is not determined. (Adapted from Pfeifer & Kleiter, 2007, p. 347.)

evaluate abstract meta-properties of arguments. Rather, people focus on the conclusion. This does not mean that we think that people are always prone to *belief biases*.[2] Rather, people are typically concerned with the problem of evaluating a concrete conclusion in the light of the given evidence. People try to infer the conclusion deductively from the premises. Moreover we assume that everyday life arguments are almost always uncertain and defeasible. Conclusions are often retracted in the light of new evidence, and uncertainty is at least implicitly present in almost all common-sense arguments. How does this uncertainty enter the normative models of everyday life arguments?

We discuss two different ways of introducing uncertainty to argument forms. The first option is to introduce an uncertain consequence relation between the premises and the conclusion. The second option is to attach probabilities to the premises and to keep the consequence relation deductive. Oaksford, Chater, and Larkin (2000) opted for the first option in their analysis of the four conditional syllogisms (modus ponens, modus tollens, affirming the consequent, and denying the antecedent). They represent a conditional syllogism by the conditional probability of the conclusion given the categorical premise, P(conclusion | categorical premise). This makes the consequence relation uncertain. As an example consider the modus ponens,

$\mathfrak{P}1$ If shape X is a triangle, then shape X is blue.
$\mathfrak{P}2$ Shape X is a triangle.

——————————————————————————uncertain

$\mathfrak{C}$ Shape X is blue.

Oaksford et al. (2000) interpret this argument as the conditional probability of $\mathfrak{C}$ given $\mathfrak{P}2$, P(Shape X is blue. | Shape X is a triangle.). The conditional premise ($\mathfrak{P}1$) does not enter the model. This analysis does not preserve the original propositional structures of the arguments. Liu (2003) and Oaksford and Chater (2007) modified this model such that the conclusion is conditionalized on the conditional ($\mathfrak{P}1$) and on the categorical premise ($\mathfrak{P}2$).

The normative treatment of the uncertain consequence relation beyond the four popular conditional syllogisms, however, is challenging. Adams' *p*-validity (Adams, 1975) is an example of *qualitatively* uncertain consequence relations. Systems of nonmonotonic reasoning provide other examples (Antoniou, 1997). The definition of satisfactory consequence relations that are *quantitatively* uncertain is an open problem.

We next turn to our approach. Because of its normative frame (probability logic based on coherence) we call it "mental probability logic" (Pfeifer & Kleiter, 2005b, 2009, 2010). In our approach the consequence relation is deductive and the conclusion is uncertain. As an example consider the probabilistic modus ponens:

℞1 P(Shape X is blue. | Shape X is a triangle.) = x
℞2 P(Shape X is a triangle.) = y
_____deductively valid
℞ $xy \leqslant P$(Shape X is blue.) $\leqslant xy + 1 - y$

The argumennt form contains two binary variables. A complete probabilistic assessment requires three probabilities, say x, y, and z of three logically independent events. The premises of the probabilistic modus ponens specify only two probability values, x and y. The coherent probability of the conclusion is imprecise. It is constrained by a lower and an upper bound. In ℞1 the conditional is interpreted as a conditional event, "Shape X is blue. | Shape X is a triangle.". If the conditional in ℞1 is interpreted as a material conditional, "Shape X is a triangle. ⊃ Shape X is blue.", then the probability propagation rule is different:

℞1′ P(Shape X is a triangle. ⊃ Shape X is blue.) = x
℞2 P(Shape X is a triangle.) = y
_____deductively valid
℞   max $\{0, x + y - 1\} \leqslant P$(Shape X is blue.) $\leqslant x$

The difference between the material conditional and the conditional event is that the truth value of the conditional event is undetermined if the antecedent of the conditional is false (see Table 8.1). This affects, of course, the probability propagation rules. Probability logic provides the language to represent and reason from different interpretations of the premises.

How people interpret conditionals is debated in the literature. We discuss two prominent positions. The first position favours the material conditional interpretation. The second position favours the conditional event interpretation. Mental model theory takes the first position (Johnson-Laird & Byrne, 2002). The theory postulates that people represent indicative conditionals either as implicit mental models or as explicit mental models. To be precise, this is postulated only for those conditionals that are as independent as possible from context or background knowledge. According to the mental model theory, the truth conditions of the implicit mental model coincide with the truth conditions of the conjunction, ∧. The truth conditions of the explicit mental model coincide with the truth conditions of the material conditional, ⊃. For the truth conditions see Table 8.1. Explicit mental models have a higher working memory demand and are harder to process than implicit mental models. Therefore, the theory predicts that people usually form more implicit mental models than explicit ones.

Barrouillet and Lecas (1999) instructed participants to list possible truth-table cases that are consistent with an indicative "if__, then__". The results are consistent with the material conditional interpretation, and are treated as strong evidence for the mental model theory. However, these results are *ambiguous* since they are consistent with the conditional event interpretation as well. Normatively, both interpretations differ only in the truth-table cases s3 and s4, where the material conditional is true but the conditional event is *undetermined* (see Table 8.1). The truth-table cases that are "possible" are consistent with both the truth-table cases that are *true* and those that are *undetermined*. Therefore, this version of a truth-table task cannot differentiate among the material conditional and the conditional event interpretation of the indicative "if__, then__".

The second position postulates that people interpret indicative conditionals as a conditional event. A specialty of our approach is, that the conditional event, B|A, is *basic* in mental probability logic. Probabilities are assigned *directly* to the conditional event. This is psychologically plausible and reduces the working memory demand: one does not need to process the joint ($P(A \wedge B)$) and the marginal ($P(A)$) probabilities.

Many empirical studies support the conditional event interpretation of conditionals (Evans et al., 2003; Over & Evans, 2003; Oberauer & Wilhelm, 2003). These studies use an experimental paradigm that investigates *complete* probabilistic knowledge. Probabilistic truth-table tasks present (or ask for) the probabilities of all truth-table cases. One version of the probabilistic truth-table task presents the probabilities of A∧B, A∧¬B, ¬A∧B, and of ¬A∧¬B to the participants. The participants infer the probability of a conditional. Since complete probabilistic knowledge is provided, the probabilities of conjunctions, material conditionals, and conditional events are *point values*. Another version of the probabilistic truth-table task provides the point probability of a conditional and the participants rate the probabilities of all four truth-table cases. Again, this results in a task that consists of inferences about complete probabilistic knowledge.

Our approach uses an alternative experimental paradigm. We investigate selected argument forms and present *incomplete* probabilistic knowledge in the premises. In our modus ponens tasks, for example, we present only two probabilities to the participants: $P(B|A)$ and $P(A)$. As explained above, the probability of the conclusion, $P(B)$, is an *interval probability* and not a point probability. If $P(B|\neg A)$ were also given, then the probability of the conclusion would be a point value. $P(B|\neg A)$, however, would be an additional premise and the resulting task would not map the modus ponens any more. Therefore, we investigate incomplete probabilistic knowledge. We observed good agreement between the responses and the coherent probability intervals of the probabilistic modus ponens (Pfeifer & Kleiter, 2007, 2009). How the participants understand conditionals can be inferred from the inferences they draw.

An important problem of probabilistic argument forms is whether the coherent probability of the conclusion is constrained by the premises. If the coherent probability of the conclusion of an argument form is not necessarily equal to the unit interval, [0, 1], then we call this argument form "*probabilistically informative*". We call an argument form "*probabilistically noninformative*" if the assignment of the unit interval to its conclusion is coherent for all probability assessments of the premises (Pfeifer & Kleiter, 2009). If an argument is probabilistically noninformative, then one cannot infer anything about the probability of the conclusion (except that it is between zero and one). Whether an argument is probabilistically informative can depend upon how the conditional is interpreted. We discuss this fact by two of the so-called "paradoxes of the material conditional":

Paradox 1: from B infer A ⊃ B.

Paradox 2: from ¬A infer A ⊃ B .

Both Paradox 1 and Paradox 2 are cl-valid. There is nothing paradoxical about this. However, the paradoxes arise if indicative natural language conditionals are interpreted as material conditionals. Consider, for example, the following instances:

Instance of Paradox 1:

From It is raining. infer If I'm happy, then it is raining.

Instance of Paradox 2:

From I'm not happy. infer If I'm happy, then it is raining. .

Such examples are well known in the history of logic (Lewis, 1918). Obviously both inferences are odd, but cl-valid if the conclusion is interpreted as a material conditional. Table 8.3 presents the paradoxes, and three probability logical interpretations of the "if__, then__". The probability of the conclusion is constrained under the material conditional interpretation and under the conjunction interpretation. Under the conditional event interpretation, however, the unit interval, [0, 1], is coherent for all probability assessments of the premise. Thus, the paradoxes are probabilistically noninformative if the conditional is interpreted as a conditional event. If the conditional is interpreted as a material conditional or as a conjunction, then the paradoxes are probabilistically informative (Pfeifer & Kleiter, 2006). Under the conditional event interpretation, however, the paradoxical nature of these argument forms disappears.

If the antecedent of the conditional in the respective conclusion is negated, we call the resulting argument forms the "negated versions" of the paradoxes (see Table 8.3). Both paradoxes and their negated versions provide different probability logical predictions on the three popular interpretations of the natural language "if__, then__". According to the mental model theory most participants will make inferences that correspond to the predictions of the conjunction interpretation (implicit mental model) or to the material conditional interpretation (explicit mental model) of the "if__, then__" (Johnson-Laird & Byrne, 2002). Mental probability logic predicts that

Table 8.3 Two paradoxes of the material conditional (P1 and P2) and their respective negated versions (NP1 and NP2)

		Premise		Conclusion			Probabilistically informative
P1:	(a)	B	$\models$		$A \supset B$		
	(b)	$P(B) = x$	$\models$	$x \leq$	$P(A \supset B)$	≤ 1	yes
	(c)	$P(B) = x$	$\models$	$0 \leq$	$P(A \wedge B)$	$\leq x$	yes
	(d)	$P(B) = x$	$\models$	$0 \leq$	$P(B \mid A)$	≤ 1	no
P2:	(a)	$\neg A$	$\models$		$A \supset B$		
	(b)	$P(\neg A) = x$	$\models$	$x \leq$	$P(A \supset B)$	≤ 1	yes
	(c)	$P(\neg A) = x$	$\models$	$0 \leq$	$P(A \wedge B)$	$\leq 1 - x$	yes
	(d)	$P(\neg A) = x$	$\models$	$0 \leq$	$P(B \mid A)$	≤ 1	no
NP1:	(a)	B	$\not\models$		$A \supset \neg B$		
	(b)	$P(B) = x$	$\models$	$1 - x \leq$	$P(A \supset \neg B)$	≤ 1	yes
	(c)	$P(B) = x$	$\models$	$0 \leq$	$P(A \wedge \neg B)$	$\leq 1 - x$	yes
	(d)	$P(B) = x$	$\models$	$0 \leq$	$P(\neg B \mid A)$	≤ 1	no
NP2:	(a)	$\neg A$	$\models$		$A \supset \neg B$		
	(b)	$P(\neg A) = x$	$\models$	$x \leq$	$P(A \supset \neg B)$	≤ 1	yes
	(c)	$P(\neg A) = x$	$\models$	$0 \leq$	$P(A \wedge \neg B)$	$\leq 1 - x$	yes
	(d)	$P(\neg A) = x$	$\models$	$0 \leq$	$P(\neg B \mid A)$	≤ 1	no

Notes
For each paradox four interpretations are given: (a) classical logic, and the three probability logical interpretations of the "if__, then__", (b) as a material conditional, (c) as a conjunction, and (d) as a conditional event. "$\models$" denotes deductive validity, "$\not\models$" denotes "not deductively valid". Only under the conditional event interpretation (d) are the paradoxes probabilistically noninformative, and therefore *not* paradoxical.

most participants make inferences that correspond to the predictions of the conditional event interpretation of the "if__, then__". We investigate these predictions in the following sections.

Experiment 1: Two paradoxes of the material conditional

Introduction and method

Experiment 1 investigates Paradox 1 and Paradox 2, and their respective negated versions, see Table 8.3. Between each paradox task we presented modus ponens tasks. The respective negated versions of these argument forms were presented in the second half of the experiment.

Participants

Thirty-two students of the University of Salzburg were paid 5 euros each for their participation in the experiment (mean age: 23 years, 21 female, 11 male participants). Psychology students, mathematics students, and students with a background in logic were not included in the sample. To ensure an atmosphere for thinking and reasoning, each participant was tested individually in an experimental room in the department of psychology. The participants were instructed to take their time and to think carefully about each problem.

Materials

Paradox 1 (From ⬜B⬜ infer ⬜If A, then B⬜) and Paradox 2 (From ⬜¬A⬜ infer ⬜If A, then B⬜ ; see Table 8.3) were translated into cover stories. As an example consider the following problem, which contains an instance of Paradox 1:

> Simon works in a factory that produces playing cards. He is responsible for what is printed on the cards.
> On each card, there is a *shape* (triangle, square, . . .) of a certain *colour* (green, blue, . . .), like:
>
> * green triangle, green square, green circle, . . .
> * blue triangle, blue square, . . .
> * red triangle, . . .
>
> Imagine that a card got stuck in the printing machine. Simon cannot see what is printed on this card. Since Simon observed the card production during the whole day, he is:
>
> ⬜A⬜ 90% certain: There is a *square* on this card.
>
> *Considering* ⬜A⬜, *how certain can Simon be that the following sentence is true?*
>
> **If** there is a *red* shape on this card, **then** there is a *square* on this card.

The premise is to the right of " ⬜A⬜ " and the box contains the conditional in the conclusion. We were careful to ensure that the conditionals were as independent as possible from background knowledge. According to the mental model theory, the truth conditions of such conditionals coincide either with those of the conjunction or with those of the material conditional (Johnson-Laird & Byrne, 2002).

First the participants decided whether the inference was probabilistically informative or not. If they judged it not to be, then they continued to the next problem. If the argument was identified as probabilistically informative, then the participants rated their degree of belief in the conclusion. This two-step procedure was phrased as follows:

> Considering ⬜A⬜, can Simon infer – at all – *how certain he can be* that the sentence in the box is true?
> ☐ NO, Simon cannot infer his certainty, since anything between 0% and 100% is possible.
> ☐ YES, Simon can infer his certainty.

In case you ticked **YES**, *please fill in*
Simon can be certain *from* at least ____% *to* at
most ____% that the sentence in the box is true.

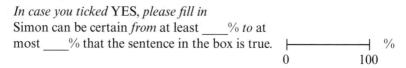

The thirty-two participants were randomly assigned to two conditions. In the first condition we presented five instances of Paradox 1 ($n_1 = 16$) and in the second condition we presented five instances of Paradox 2 ($n_2 = 15$, one participant was excluded from the data analysis because of misunderstandings of the instructions). The versions differed in the uncertainties attached to the premises. The uncertainties were: "60%", "70%", "90%", "pretty sure" (German original: ziemlich sicher), and "absolutely certain" (absolut sicher). Between each paradox we presented a modus ponens task. The uncertainty of the categorical premise *(P(A))* of the modus ponens tasks was kept constant at 100%. The uncertainties of the conditional premise *(P(if A, then B))* were: "90%", "70%", "80%", "pretty sure", and "absolutely certain". After the 10 tasks just described, we presented the same tasks in the same order again, with the difference that the *B* term in the conclusions was negated. In the negated modus ponens tasks the conclusion had the form ¬*B* (rather than *B*), and in both versions of the negated paradoxes the conditional had the form *If A, then* ¬*B* (rather than *If A, then B*).

Results

Averaging across subjects and items, more than 80% of the responses identified the modus ponens correctly as probabilistically informative (see Table 8.4). Of all those participants who inferred correctly that the modus ponens is

Table 8.4 Percentages of probabilistic noninformativeness responses in the paradox (P) tasks, and of probabilistic informativeness responses in the modus ponens (MP) tasks

	Affirmative argument forms									
	P_{60}	P_{70}	P_{90}	P_{ps}	P_{ac}	MP_{90}	MP_{70}	MP_{80}	MP_{ps}	MP_{ac}
P1	63	81	69	69	69	63	88	81	75	94
P2	73	73	73	80	67	73	73	87	80	93
	Negated argument forms									
P1	75	69	63	75	44	81	88	88	69	88
P2	87	87	87	67	67	80	87	73	93	93

Notes
P1: Paradox 1 ($n_1 = 16$), P2: Paradox 2 ($n_2 = 15$). The indices denote the percentages presented in the premises, "ac" denotes "absolutely certain", "ps" denotes "pretty sure". The indices of the modus ponens tasks denote the percentages presented in the conditional premise.

probabilistically informative, all participants – except one – inferred correctly that it is "absolutely certain"/"pretty sure" that the conclusion is true. In the negated modus ponens tasks, all participants – except two – inferred correctly that it is "absolutely certain"/"pretty sure" that the conclusion is not true. In these tasks most participants understood that complementary probabilities should add up to one. The good performance in our modus ponens tasks corresponds to the high endorsement rates of the nonprobabilistic modus ponens tasks reported in the literature (Evans, Newstead, & Byrne, 1993).

The majority of the participants (more than 70% on the average) inferred that all versions of the paradoxes are not probabilistically informative (see Table 8.4). This speaks for the conditional event interpretation of the conditional. According to the mental model theory, most participants should make probabilistically informative inferences. Their inferences should conform to the conjunction (implicit mental model) or to the material conditional interpretation (explicit mental model). These predictions are not confirmed by the data.

To our knowledge, this is the first experiment on these two paradoxes of the material conditional. The high percentage of probabilistically non-informative responses is remarkable from a pragmatic point of view: they are obviously not influenced by conversational implicatures that would call for informative inferences. Rather, the participants seem to interpret the conditional as a conditional event and therefore understand that one cannot infer anything.

In another experiment we investigated the following argument form, which is called "monotonicity" or "premise strengthening": From $\boxed{\text{If A, then B}}$ infer $\boxed{\text{If A and C, then B}}$. This argument form is another well-known paradox of the material conditional. The results are in line with the present data: we observed wide and practically noninformative interval responses (Pfeifer & Kleiter, 2003).

Experiment 2

Introduction and method

In the following sections we report selected parts of a study that consisted of 37 different tasks. One main purpose of Experiment 2 was to attempt to replicate the results on the paradoxes of Experiment 1. We report these tasks and focus on other tasks that investigate the representation of conditionals as well. Moreover, we present new data on the probabilistic truth-table task.

Participants

Forty students of the University of Salzburg were paid 5 euros each. They were divided into two groups of 20 participants each. Most tasks of group I investigated affirmative arguments and most tasks of group II included negations. The participants were tested individually in an experimental room. One participant was not included in the data analysis because he misunderstood the instructions. As in Experiment 1, the participants were instructed to take their time and to think carefully about each problem.

Materials and results

In Experiment 2 we investigated the two paradoxes of the material conditional (see Table 8.3). The thematic content of all tasks and the response modalities were the same as in Experiment 1. The uncertainty in each premise was formulated verbally as "pretty sure" (ziemlich sicher).

The 19 participants of group I solved Paradox 1 twice and the negated version of Paradox 1 twice (see Table 8.5). Between each paradox task, we presented tasks that investigate different argument forms. Table 8.5 presents the response frequencies of the affirmative and of the negated Paradox 1 tasks.

The majority (63–79%) of the participants understand that Paradox 1 and the negated version of Paradox 1 are probabilistically noninformative. This speaks for the conditional probability interpretation of the "if__, then__". The data replicate the findings of Experiment 1.

The participants of group II ($n_4 = 20$) solved Paradox 2 twice and the negated version of Paradox 2 twice (see Table 8.6). Between each paradox task, we presented again other tasks. Table 8.6 presents the response frequencies of the affirmative and of the negated Paradox 2 tasks.

Almost all participants (75–90%) understand that Paradox 2 and the negated version of Paradox 2 are probabilistically noninformative. This speaks for the conditional probability interpretation of the "if__, then__". The data replicate the findings of Experiment 1.

Table 8.5 Response frequencies of the two affirmative Paradox 1 tasks (P1) and the two negated Paradox 1 tasks (NP1) of Experiment 2 ($n_3 = 19$)

Response	First P1	Second P1	First NP1	Second NP1
Noninformative	13	15	13	12
Conclusion is true	3	2	0	1
Conclusion is false	3	2	6	6

Table 8.6 Response frequencies of the two affirmative Paradox 2 tasks (P2) and the two negated Paradox 2 tasks (NP2) of Experiment 2 ($n_4 = 20$)

Response	First P2	Second P2	First NP2	Second NP2
Noninformative	15	18	18	18
Conclusion is true	1	1	0	1
Conclusion is false	4	1	2	1

The complement tasks

The paradoxes are probabilistically noninformative, if the conditional is interpreted as a conditional event. They are probabilistically informative under the material conditional interpretation. There are argument forms in which the role of the probabilistic informativeness of the different interpretations is interchanged. In the following argument form, the conditional event interpretation is probabilistically informative but the material conditional interpretation is practically noninformative (a wide interval between a value close to zero and one).

From $\boxed{\text{If A, then B}}$ infer $\boxed{\text{If A, then } \neg\text{B}}$.

Let us call this argument form "complement". If the uncertain "if__ then__" of the complement is interpreted as a conditional event, then the resulting argument form is probabilistically informative:

From $\boxed{P(B|A) = x}$ infer $\boxed{(\neg B|A) = 1 - x}$.

If, however, the conditional is interpreted as a material conditional, then the complement is formalized as:

From $\boxed{P(A \supset B) = x}$ infer $\boxed{1 - x \leqslant P(A \supset \neg B) \leqslant 1}$.

Thus, if the conditional is interpreted as a material conditional and if the probability of the premise is sufficiently high, then the conclusion is practically noninformative, since the probability of the conclusion is anywhere between a very low value and one.[3]

If the conditional of the complement is interpreted as a conjunction, then it is formalized as:

From $\boxed{P(A \wedge B) = x}$ infer $\boxed{0 \leqslant P(A \wedge \neg B) \leqslant 1 - x}$.

If the conditional is interpreted as a conjunction (implicit mental model) and if the probability of the premise is sufficiently high, then the probability of the conclusion is close to zero.

The predictions concerning the complement task are straightforward. If the participants interpret the conditional as a material conditional, they should give a probabilistically noninformative response. The presented complement task does not distinguish between the conditional event interpretation and the conjunction interpretation. (If the probability of the premise would have been lower, then it could differentiate among all three interpretations.)

In Experiment 2, we presented the complement as the first task to all participants ($n_3 + n_4 = 39$). Twenty-eight participants responded by ticking the box "pretty sure" that the conclusion is false. This corresponds to the conditional event interpretation and to the conjunction interpretation. Nine participants opted for the probabilistic noninformativeness, which corresponds to the material conditional interpretation.

We included also a task that investigates the negated complement. The negated version of the complement corresponds to the trivial inference: from $\boxed{if\ A,\ then\ B}$ infer $\boxed{if\ A,\ then\ B}$ (the double negation is eliminated). All participants responded correctly that they are pretty certain that the conclusion is true.

The probabilistic truth-table tasks

All participants of Experiment 2 ($n_3 + n_4 = 39$) solved four probabilistic truth-table tasks. This task serves to investigate the representation of uncertain conditionals. The difference from the other tasks is that the probabilistic truth-table task investigates reasoning about complete probabilistic knowledge. We adapted the tasks from Evans et al. (2003). The participants were instructed to imagine a pack of 120 cards. They were informed that the cards are either red or blue and have either a circle or a square printed on them. They were asked to assume that in total there are:

40 red and circle,
40 red and square,
20 blue and circle, and
20 blue and square cards.

The participants were instructed to imagine that the pack is shuffled and that a card is drawn randomly. This makes the random process explicit. Then, they rated the following four assertions about the randomly drawn card.

(1) **If** the card is blue, **then** there is a circle on it.
(2) **If** there is a square on the card, **then** it is red.
(3) **If** the card is **not** red, **then** there is **not** a square on it.
(4) **If** there is a **not** a circle on the card, **then** it is **not** blue.

For the ratings we provided scales with the labels "absolutely certain not the case" (German original: stimmt absolut sicher nicht) and "absolutely certain the case" (stimmt absolut sicher).

The most important qualitative predictions are as follows. (1) and (3) are equivalent, as are (2) and (4). If the participants interpret the "if__then__" as a material conditional, all four assertions should obtain the same rating. If the participants interpret the "if__then__" as a conditional event or as a conjunction, then (1) and (3) should obtain a lower rating than (2) and (4), respectively. For differentiating between the conditional event and the conjunction interpretation, the ratings must be compared with the normative values. The quantitative predictions are summarized in Table 8.7. The

Table 8.7 Predicted probabilities and mean observed values in the four probabilistic truth-table tasks of Experiment 2 (*n* = 39)

Conditional	Predictions			Responses	
	$P(\cdot \supset \cdot)$	$P(\cdot \wedge \cdot)$	$P(\cdot \mid \cdot)$	*Mean*	*(SD)*
If blue, then circle	0.83	0.17	0.50	0.46	(0.18)
If square, then red	0.83	0.33	0.67	0.71	(0.15)
If not red, then not square	0.83	0.17	0.50	0.44	(0.22)
If not circle, then not blue	0.83	0.33	0.67	0.66	(0.23)

Notes
The predicted probabilities are the normative probabilities according to the material conditional ($\cdot \supset \cdot$), conjunction ($\cdot \wedge \cdot$), and according to the conditional event ($\cdot \mid \cdot$) interpretation of uncertain indicative conditionals.

predictions according to the conditional event interpretation are higher than the predictions according to the conjunction interpretation.

We counted the ratings as equal if they remained in a 15% interval. Only two of the 39 participants responded with equal ratings for all four assertions. This is clear evidence against the material conditional interpretation of indicative conditionals. Thirty participants rate the assertions (2) and (4) uniformly higher than both assertions (1) and (3). This pattern is predicted by both the conjunction interpretation and the conditional event interpretation. Twenty-five participants responded by giving both equal ratings between the assertions (1) and (3); and equal ratings between the assertions (2) and (4) (within a 15% interval). This shows that most participants really understood that the respective assertions are equivalent.

We divided the distance between the left pole of the rating scale ("absolutely certain **not** the case") and the participants' markings by the total length (63 mm) of the response scale. This procedure scales the response values from zero to one. Table 8.7 presents the mean response values and the normative probabilities of the material conditional, conjunction, and conditional event interpretation of the "if__, then__". Boxplots of the data are given in Figure 8.1. The mean and the median of the responses are close to the predictions of the conditional event interpretation. Therefore, conditional probability is the best predictor of the empirical values. We observed fewer responses that are consistent with the conjunction interpretation than reported in the literature (see for example, Evans et al., 2003; Oberauer & Wilhelm, 2003). A reason could be that we maximized the distances between the three predictions, and the coherent value of the conjunction interpretation is quite far away from the coherent value of the conditional event interpretation.

Moreover, we measured the distances between each response and each of the three normative predictions. The least distances provide another way of comparing the quality of the three predictions. A prediction "wins" if it has the least distance to the response value compared with the other

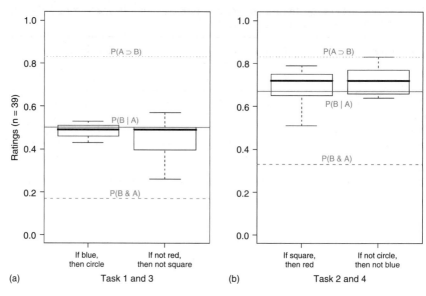

Figure 8.1 Boxplots of the probabilistic truth-table tasks: (a) tasks 1 and 3; (b) tasks 2 and 4. The boxes contain 50% of the responses and the median (thick line). The whiskers indicate 1.5 × the interquartile range. The three normative predictions are in grey. Conditional probability is the best predictor.

Table 8.8 Frequencies of least distances to the normative predictors ("winning predictor"; $n_3 + n_4 = 39$)

Conditional	Winning predictor			Ties
	$P(\cdot \supset \cdot)$	$P(\cdot \wedge \cdot)$	$P(\cdot \mid \cdot)$	
If blue, then circle	2	7	30	0
If square, then red	9	4	22	4
If not red, then not square	3	9	27	0
If not circle, then not blue	12	8	18	1

Notes
"Ties" denotes the number of participates that responded by values that lie exactly between two predictors. Ties were observed only between $P(\cdot \supset \cdot)$ and $P(\cdot \mid \cdot)$.

predictions. Table 8.8 presents the frequencies of the "winning" predictors. The conditional event interpretation received the highest frequencies. Again, the conditional event is the best predictor of the empirical values.

Discussion

The paradoxes of the material conditional are often used as one of the principal arguments for why one should not interpret indicative conditionals, "if

A, then B", as material conditionals, A ⊃ B. However, to our knowledge the paradoxes have not been investigated empirically yet. This contribution reports two first experiments on the paradoxes of the material conditional. One main result is that the great majority of participants do not endorse the paradoxes. We proposed *coherence-based probability logic* as a normative framework for the psychology of reasoning. Within this framework we formulated three psychologically prominent interpretations of the "if__, then__", and explained why most people do not endorse the paradoxes: most people interpret the "if__, then__" as a conditional event and they seem to understand that the paradoxes are *probabilistically noninformative*. Pragmatic reasons may play important roles in human reasoning in general, but for the paradoxes probabilistic noninformativeness fully explains why most people do not endorse these argument forms. We provided further empirical support for the conditional event interpretation by the results of the probabilistic truth-table task, which endorses Jonathan Evans' support of the conditional probability interpretation of uncertain conditionals (Evans & Over, 2004; Evans, 2007). We explained why all this evidence rejects central predictions of the mental model theory.

We started from a strong assumption, namely that there is just one logical system that fits all subjects, all tasks, all situations and, moreover, all their combinatorial interactions. This assumption is too strong. There are, for example, two subjects who give exactly equal ratings to all four truth-table tasks. This is what the material conditional of classical logic predicts. Most subjects, though, follow the predictions of probability logic. It is plausible to assume that there are not only systematic individual differences but that even one and the same subject has access to several different "logics" of reasoning. Human thinking can be excellent in switching strategies, in simplifying constraints, or in re-representing a problem structure. We have tried to identify and discuss one dominating system, probability logic.

Finding moderator variables that tell us who in which situation is using which kind of "logic" to make which inference is difficult. The large number of variables, the small effect sizes, and the realization of appropriate experimental conditions for motivated "real" thinking (and not just giving the next best guess answers) make empirical research difficult and require considerable efforts.

Is our position not a kind of logicism? Do we not say that to come up with a theory of human reasoning, we need to identify the formal system that best fits human performance? Logic and mathematical computer science provide the best theories on reasoning, not about human reasoning, of course. But they provide languages, properties, and systems to describe tasks, knowledge and belief, and inferences that the psychology of reasoning cannot ignore.

Ignoring modern logics leads to the use of a common-sense amateur logic. There is no way out, either: (1) explicitly exploiting the modern pluralistic approaches to logic; or (2) relying on classical logic; or (3) implicitly using self-baked logic. For about one 100 years parts of classical logic served as the favourite reference system to select experimental tasks and to build models. Typical examples are syllogisms, the Wason's card selection task, or the modus ponens, modus tollens, affirming the consequent, and the denying the antecedent tasks. The research questions had been centred around the logic of syllogisms (a highly specific subset of predicate logic going back to Aristotle and the Middle Ages), a special form of the conditional (the so-called material conditional), and just four forms of conditional syllogisms with two premises. Only recently systems that differ from classical logic were considered for psychological modelling (and for a re-analysis of the classical tasks). We are not saying that cognitive representations and processes are unimportant. Quite the contrary, cognitive representations and processes are of course central to psychological theory building. We have severe doubts, however, that it is a good research strategy to attempt to describe representations and processes on the background of an old-fashioned amateur logic. Moreover – and again – logic and mathematical computer science offer a rich repertoire of knowledge representation languages and systems. Several well-known representational systems in psychology were imported from computer science. Semantic networks, neural networks, production systems, or more recently, Bayesian networks are typical examples.

Notes

1 For example protégé, see http://protege.stanford.edu/.
2 "Belief bias" denotes the tendency to evaluate an argument just by the believability of the conclusion and to ignore the premises (Evans, Barston, & Pollard, 1983).
3 This argument form is strictly speaking probabilistically informative, since it is not the case that for all probability assignments of the premise, the coherent probability of the conclusion is necessarily between zero and one. Therefore we say that this argument form is "practically noninformative".

Acknowledgements

This work is supported by the LogICCC project "*The Logic of Causal and Probabilistic Reasoning in Uncertain Environments*" (European Science Foundation/Austrian Research Fonds) and by the FWF project "*Mental probability logic*" (Austrian Research Fonds). The authors thank Leonhard Kratzer for collecting the data, and David Over and Andy Fugard for helpful comments.

References

Adams, E. W. (1975). *The logic of conditionals*. Dordrecht, Germany: Reidel.
Antoniou, G. (1997). *Nonmonotonic reasoning*. Cambridge, MA: MIT Press.
Baader, F., Calvanese, D., McGuinness, D. L., Nardi, D., & Patel-Schneider, P. F. (Eds.). (2007). *The description logic hand book: Theory, implementation, and applications*. Cambridge: Cambridge University Press.

Barrouillet, P., & Lecas, J.-F. (1999). Mental models in conditional reasoning and working memory. *Thinking and Reasoning*, 5, 289–302.

Biazzo, V., Gilio, A., Lukasiewicz, T., & Sanfilippo, G. (2005). Probabilistic logic under coherence: Complexity and algorithms. *Annals of Mathematics and Artificial Intelligence*, 45, 35–81.

Coletti, G., & Scozzafava, R. (2002). *Probabilistic logic in a coherent setting*. Dordrecht, The Netherlands: Kluwer.

Evans, J. St B. T. (2007). *Hypothetical thinking: Dual processes in reasoning and judgement*. Hove, UK: Psychology Press.

Evans, J. St B. T., Barston, J. L., & Pollard, P. (1983). On the conflict between logic and belief in syllogistic reasoning. *Memory and Cognition*, 11, 295–306.

Evans, J. St B. T., Handley, S. J., & Over, D. E. (2003). Conditionals and conditional probability. *Journal of Experimental Psychology: Learning, Memory, and Cognition*, 29, 321–355.

Evans, J. St B. T., Newstead, S. E., & Byrne, R. M. J. (1993). *Human reasoning*. Hove, UK: Lawrence Erlbaum Associates Ltd.

Evans, J. St B. T., & Over, D. E. (2004). *If*. Oxford: Oxford University Press.

Gilio, A. (2002). Probabilistic reasoning under coherence in System P. *Annals of Mathematics and Artificial Intelligence*, 34, 5–34.

Johnson-Laird, P. N., & Byrne, R. M. J. (2002). Conditionals: A theory of meaning, pragmatics, and inference. *Psychological Review*, 109, 646–678.

Lewis, C. I. (1918). *A survey of symbolic logic*. Berkeley: University of California Press.

Liu, I.-M. (2003). Conditional reasoning and conditionalization. *Journal of Experimental Psychology: Learning, Memory, and Cognition*, 29, 694–709.

Liu, I.-M., Lo, K.-C., & Wu, J.-T. (1996). A probabilistic interpretation of 'If – Then'. *The Quarterly Journal of Experimental Psychology*, 49(A), 828–844.

Lukasiewicz, T. (2005). Weak nonmonotonic probabilistic logics. *Artificial Intelligence*, 168, 119–161.

Lukasiewicz, T. (2008). Expressive probabilistic description logics. *Artificial Intelligence*, 172, 852–883.

Oaksford, M., & Chater, N. (Eds.). (1998). *Rational models of cognition*. Oxford: Oxford University Press.

Oaksford, M., & Chater, N. (2007). *Bayesian rationality: The probabilistic approach to human reasoning*. Oxford: Oxford University Press.

Oaksford, M., Chater, N., & Larkin, J. (2000). Probabilities and polarity biases in conditional inference. *Journal of Experimental Psychology: Learning, Memory, and Cognition*, 26, 883–899.

Oberauer, K., & Wilhelm, O. (2003). The meaning(s) of conditionals: Conditional probabilities, mental models and personal utilities. *Journal of Experimental Psychology: Learning, Memory, and Cognition*, 29, 680–693.

Over, D. E., & Evans, J. St B. T. (2003). The probability of conditionals: The psychological evidence. *Mind & Language*, 18, 340–358.

Pfeifer, N., & Kleiter, G. D. (2003). Nonmonotonicity and human probabilistic reasoning. In *Proceedings of the 6th workshop on uncertainty processing* (pp. 221–234). Hejnice, Czech Republic: Oeconomic Publishers.

Pfeifer, N., & Kleiter, G. D. (2005a). Coherence and nonmonotonicity in human reasoning. *Synthese*, 146, 93–109.

Pfeifer, N., & Kleiter, G. D. (2005b). Towards a mental probability logic. *Psychologica Belgica*, 45, 71–99.

Pfeifer, N., & Kleiter, G. D. (2006). Inference in conditional probability logic. *Kybernetika, 42*, 391–404.

Pfeifer, N., & Kleiter, G. D. (2007). Human reasoning with imprecise probabilities: Modus ponens and denying the antecedent. In G. De Cooman, J. Vejnarov'a, & M. Zaffalon (Eds.), *5th international symposium on imprecise probability: Theories and applications* (pp. 347–356). Prague, Czech Republic: Action M agency for SIPTA.

Pfeifer, N., & Kleiter, G. D. (2009). Framing human inference by coherence based probability logic. *Journal of Applied Logics, 7*, 206–217.

Pfeifer, N., & Kleiter, G. D. (2010). The conditional in mental probability logic. In M. Oaksford & N. Chater (Eds.), *Cognition and conditionals: Probability and logic in human thinking* (pp. 153–173). Oxford: Oxford University Press.

Van Harmelen, F., Lifschitz, V., & Porter, B. (Eds.). (2008). *Handbook of knowledge representation*. Amsterdam, The Netherlands: Elsevier.

Wiles, A. (1995). Modular elliptic curves and Fermat's Last Theorem. *Annals of Mathematics, 142*, 443–551.

9 Thinking before you decide on the selection task

Matching bias requires analytic reasoning

Simon J. Handley, Stephen E. Newstead, and Helen Neilens

University of Plymouth

The three authors of this chapter have known Jonathan Evans for many years and have published a large number of joint papers with him. It has been and continues to be a pleasure working alongside him and we have all learnt much through this collaboration, not least the importance of objectivity, open-mindedness and integrity in research, characteristics that Jonathan shares with some of the very best scientists of his generation. During this time we have agreed on, or come to agreement on, many things and this has resulted in significant progress on a number of issues in the psychology of reasoning. To illustrate, in the case of the first author, this has included the development of a new theory of conditionals (Evans, Handley, & Over, 2003a; Evans, Over, & Handley, 2005; Handley, Evans, & Thompson, 2006), the empirical work that led to hypothetical thinking theory (Evans, 2007; Evans, Over, & Handley, 2003b; Handley & Evans, 2000; Evans, Handley, Harper, & Johnson-Laird, 1999), the selective-processing model of belief bias (Evans, Handley, & Harper, 2001; Morley, Evans, & Handley, 2004), and most recently the integration of a dual-process framework with the suppositional account of conditionals (Evans, Handley, Neilens, & Over, 2007, 2008). However, as with any productive collaboration, we also disagree on a number of things, and it is one of these areas of disagreement that is the focus of this chapter.

The task that we will discuss is Wason's selection task (Wason, 1966, to be described in detail later) and the issue of concern is the extent to which the selection of matching cards on this task really reflects the operation of heuristic processes. We will argue, based upon experimental evidence, individual differences research, and some new empirical data, that matching selections often reflect effortful processing and question the idea that it is possible to equate the type of response generated with a specific mechanism of thought as is the case in standard two-system analyses of the task. We will begin by providing some background to dual-process accounts, introduce the selection task as a prototypical example of two systems at work, and then consider the strength of the experimental and individual differences evidence claimed as support for the dual-process account of the task. We will then go on to present some new data which shows, contrary to previous work, that matching choices are generated by participants of the highest ability among a specific participant population. Finally the implications of these findings and the preceding discussion for our understanding of responses on the selection task will be discussed.

Dual-process accounts of thinking and reasoning

The idea that human thinking is influenced by the operation of two systems of thought is now a widely accepted view across many subdisciplines of psychology. According to this view judgements are often guided by rapid, unconscious associative processes, an idea that has been accepted in a whole range of domains of research, including memory, reasoning, and social judgement (Evans, 2008). However, it is also recognized that many processes are slow, conscious, and deliberative, drawing on the resources of working memory and executive functions (Evans, 2003). This has led many theorists to argue that responses to reasoning and decision-making tasks arise from the operation of two distinct cognitive systems. System 1 processes (using the terminology of Stanovich, 1999) are rapid, automatic, preconscious, and relatively undemanding of computational capacity. System 2 processes are controlled, conscious, analytic, and related to individual differences in working memory capacity and general intelligence. Under such accounts, logical performance on reasoning or judgement tasks is attributed to System 2's analytic reasoning processes and intuitive responses reflect System 1's heuristic processes.

In the reasoning literature researchers often like to categorize the responses that their participants generate into these two kinds, variously termed analytic or heuristic, deliberative or automatic, rational or intuitive, rule-based or associative. Such categorizations assume a fairly direct correspondence between a response and its underlying process. Consider, for example, an argument of the following kind (Sá, West, & Stanovich, 1999):

All plants need water
Roses need water
Therefore roses are plants

The endorsement of the conclusion as logically valid is assumed to reflect the operation of heuristic, associative or System 1 processes, whereas the appropriate rejection of the conclusion is assumed to reflect more deliberative, analytic or System 2 processes (Evans, 2009). A key question concerns the way in which these processes interact with one another. One of the most widely held accounts is the default-interventionist view (Evans, 2007), according to which System 1 processes cue a default response that must be resisted in favour of more deliberate processing. However, given that the initial answer is often compelling (Thompson, 2009) and generating the alternative requires cognitive effort (Stanovich, 2009), the initial answer is often accepted.

Wason's selection task and the heuristic–analytic theory

The default-interventionist version of dual-process theory has its origins in the heuristic–analytic theory (Evans, 1989), a dual-process model of reasoning developed primarily on the basis of observed performance on Wason's selection task (Evans, 1984). In its abstract form the task involves presenting participants with a representation of four cards, two of which have a letter on the upward facing side (e.g., A and L), and two of which have numbers (e.g., 3 and 7). Accompanying these cards is an indicative conditional rule such as:

If there is an A on one side of the card then there is a 3 on the other side

Participants are told that the rule may or may not govern what is on each side of the cards. Participants are asked which cards they would need to turn over in order to test whether the rule is true or false. The logically correct solution is the selection of the true antecedent (TA) or the A card and the false consequent (FC) or the 7 card. The letter A should be chosen, because the presence of a number other than a 3 on the other side falsifies the rule, and the number 7 (a number that is **not** a 3) because the presence of the letter A on the other side would also falsify the rule. This selection combination is made, on average, by only 10% of participants (see Evans, Newstead, & Byrne, 1993) and typically only by those participants of highest cognitive ability (Stanovich & West, 1998). The most common patterns of selection are the A card alone, or the A card and the 3 card (true consequent (TC)).

One of the most interesting aspects of this task is that the introduction of negations into the rule results in dramatically different selection patterns (Evans & Lynch, 1973). For example, if participants are presented with the rule, "If there is an A on one side of the card then there is NOT a 3 on the other side", the A and 3 combination remains the dominant choice, but is now the logically correct combination of true antecedent and false consequent cards. This phenomenon has been termed "matching bias" because it reflects a tendency to select cards which match the lexical content of the rule.

The heuristic–analytic theory was developed to account for selection task data from studies using the negations paradigm, in which negated components are introduced into the antecedent, consequent or both components of the conditional rule. There are two key findings using this paradigm: (1) a tendency for participants to select cards that match the lexical content of the rule more often than cards that do not, irrespective of their logical status; and (2) a preference for selecting true antecedent cards (the A card in the example above) more often than false antecedent cards (or the L card).

The dual-process or heuristic–analytic account of the abstract selection task proposes that choices are dominated by heuristic processes. These processes focus attention on those cards that are perceived as relevant, with relevance being determined by the combination of two heuristic mechanisms. The "if" heuristic makes cases where the antecedent is true appear to be more relevant than cases where the antecedent is false. The "matching" heuristic focuses attention on the relevance of cases that are denied; that is when participants are presented with a rule containing negations, such as "if A then not-3", the negation focuses attention on the number 3, rather than on a number that is not-3. Evans (2007) has argued that the selection of these cards reflects the operation of "the fundamental heuristic bias" whereby people focus selectively on information that is pre-consciously cued as relevant. Under this account there is little involvement of analytic processing; the cards that are pre-consciously cued are the cards that are subsequently chosen.

Analytic processes in the selection task: The experimental evidence

The heuristic–analytic account of the selection task suggests that the performance of a modal participant on abstract versions of the task can be explained purely through heuristic processing. Heuristics focus participants' attention on cards that are perceived as relevant and these cards are subsequently chosen. According to Evans (2007; see also, Evans & Over, 2004) analytic processes are engaged on the task, but they make little difference to the selection patterns observed.

There are two sources of evidence that have been cited in support of this claim: verbal reports and card inspection studies (Evans, 2007). The verbal report data show that participants do refer to the hidden sides of the cards that they choose in justifying their choices. However, the justifications produced consistently refer to the verification of the rule, suggesting that participants accept the rule as true and set out to describe how they would confirm this through their card selections (Wason & Evans, 1975). Evans and Over (2004) argue that the analytic processes apparently engaged and reported through concurrent protocols, simply reflect the rationalization of choices that have been pre-consciously cued. So on this account, people do reason, but they only reason about information that has been selectively cued as relevant to the task and ordinarily this reasoning has no impact on the choices made.

Card inspection studies also suggest that analytic processes are engaged on the task. These studies show that participants look disproportionately longer at those cards that they go on to select (up to eight times as long as non-selected cards). According to Evans (1995, 2007) this suggests that although analytic processing is occurring, as reflected by longer inspection times, this processing does not moderate card choices. That is, whatever analytic processes are occurring, they do not lead to a decision to reject the selection of a heuristically cued card. Similar findings have been reported using eye-tracking, an arguably more reliable method for tracking the focus of attention (Lucas and Ball, 2005).

The general conclusion that has been drawn from these findings is that analytic processing occurs, but has no functional role in determining card choices. Evans (2007) refers to this as an example of the "fundamental analytic bias", or the tendency for the analytic system to settle for a response based upon the first representation or model cued by the heuristic system. Such satisficing may occur because of limitations in cognitive motivation or available cognitive resources. Stanovich (2009) similarly refers to reasoning based upon a single-focal model, without any consideration of alternative models, as "serial associative cognition with a focal bias", reflecting the idea that the analytic system can be engaged in a very superficial manner that does not lead to logical responses.

Having outlined the experimental evidence and the theoretical arguments concerning the role of analytic processes in the selection task, we now turn to evidence that suggests that analytic processes can and do moderate card selections. One way of demonstrating that explicit reasoning is involved in the selection task is to demonstrate that manipulations that are known to influence other reasoning tasks have the same impact on the selection task. One such manipulation involves the presentation of a second conditional with an alternative antecedent, for example:

First conditional: If there is an A then there is a 3
Second conditional: If there is an L then there is a 3

This manipulation substantially reduces affirmation of the consequent (AC – there is a 3, therefore there is an A) and denial of the antecedent (DA – there is not an A, therefore there is not a 3) inferences on the conditional-arguments task (Rumain, Connell, & Braine, 1983). In a series of studies it has been shown that this manipulation also significantly reduces the selection of the TC (the "3") card and sometimes the FA (the not-A) card, which correspond to the inferences suppressed on the conditional-arguments task (Feeney & Handley, 2000; Handley, Feeney, & Harper, 2002). Importantly it appears that this effect has nothing to do with the impact the manipulation has in changing the probabilistic structure of the task (Feeney, Handley, & Kentridge, 2003).

This is a clear case where analytic reasoning results in the rejection of a card choice: Participants consider the "3" card and reason that it can tell them nothing about the truth or falsity of the rule because there may or may not be an A on the other side. Could this just be a case where the analytic post hoc justification for a heuristically cued choice fails, thus leading to the rejection of that card (Evans & Over, 2004)? We think not – in fact the basic motivation for the manipulation was to show that people *do* engage in analytic reasoning on this task in the same way as on the conditional-inference task. On the abstract conditional-arguments task participants draw the AC inference at very high rates (often upwards of 80% – see, for example, Evans & Handley, 1999). This has led a number of theorists, including ourselves, to argue that abstract conditionals readily cue an invited converse inference, if q then p. The suppositional account of conditionals makes the distinction between the converse, if q then p, and the inverse, if not-p then not-q, which are not equivalent under a defective truth table (Evans et al., 2003b). Consequently, the higher rates of AC with abstract conditionals can be explained on the basis of the differential availability of the converse inference with abstract conditionals. On affirmative versions of the selection task the q card is selected because participants infer, by combining this with the converse conditional, that there should be a "p" on the other side. Importantly, in our view, this is an analytic process of inference, which is suppressed by the presence of a second conditional.

Assuming that people are reasoning on the selection task, albeit reasoning that is often based upon invited inferences, why is it that so few people select the logically correct card choices? After all, typically on inference tasks participants draw modus tollens (MT – If A then 3, not-3, therefore not-A) at much higher rates (65–70%) than they select the not-q card on the selection task (typically less than 10%) and denial of the antecedent (If A then 3, not-A, therefore not-3) at much higher rates than they select the not-p card. In our view the answer to this question, and ultimately the explanation for the phenomenon of matching bias, lies in the use of implicit negation on the selection task. Consider, for example, the affirmative rule, "If A then 3". In the standard version of the task this is accompanied by the cards, A, 3, 7 and B, where "7" represents the not-3 case and "B" represents the "not-A" case. In order to make the modus tollens inference, that a "7" card should not have an A on the other side, participants must represent the 7 card as "not a 3". In contrast, on the conditional-inference task, the minor premise is almost always presented as an explicit negation. Could it be the case that selection task performance simply reflects the relative propensity to draw different conditional inferences when these are expressed using implicit negation? The evidence seems to be consistent with this position. In studies that have examined conditional inference using implicit negation in the minor premise (see, for example, Evans & Handley, 1999) there is a large and significant drop in endorsement rates across all four conditional inferences when implicit negation is used. This is consistent with an account of matching bias that has little to do with pre-conscious cueing of relevance for cards named in the rule, but more to do with the difficulty of encoding implicitly negated cards in order to draw inferences from them.

Assuming that selection task performance is simply a reflection of conditional inference *plus* implicit negation, then one might expect card selection patterns to mirror the inferences drawn on a conditional-arguments task if explicit negations are used. Evans, Clibbens, and Rood (1995) examined the impact of explicit negation on the selection task and in their Experiment 3, which most closely resembled a standard selection task, the pattern of selections broadly confirms this prediction. Explicit negation eliminated matching bias and was replaced by a dominant verification pattern involving the selection of TA and TC cases across all linguistic forms of the rule. These card choices correspond to the modus ponens (MP) and AC inferences that are the most common inferences on the conditional-arguments task and, as we have argued above, are those inferences supported by the conditional *plus* the converse.

Table 9.1 shows card selection rates under explicit negation and implicit negation (from Evans, et al., 1995) alongside (in parentheses) inference production rates under both conditions (from Evans & Handley, 1999). The data from the conditional-arguments task are based upon inference production rates (rather than endorsement rates), because this is equivalent to the requirement of making an inference about an unseen side of a card. Under implicit negation the matching cases are shown in italic and with explicit negation the verification pattern is shown in italic. What is striking about the data in Table 9.1 is the similarity between the selection patterns and the inference patterns under each type of negation. The preference for matching cases over mismatching cases with implicit negation on the selection task exactly mirrors the proclivity to produce an inference in each case when the minor premise is an implicit negation. Although the absolute selection rates and inference rates are not in all cases exactly the same, they are nevertheless highly correlated ($r(16) = .79$, $p < .01$) and there is no difference between the proportion of the four cards selected under implicit negation ($r = .42$) and the proportion of inferences drawn across all four argument forms ($r = .44$, $t(15) = 0.41$, n.s.). Similarly, under explicit negation, the dominant verification

Table 9.1 The percentage of selections for each card and the equivalent inference rates (in parentheses) under explicit and implicit negation[a]

	TA (MP)	FA (DA)	TC (AC)	FC (MT)
		Implicit negatives[b]		
If p then q	*73 (100)*	13 (11)	*60 (72)*	13 (17)
If p then not-q	*77 (72)*	7 (17)	27 (6)	*57 (56)*
If not-p then q	50 (72)	*23 (39)*	*77 (61)*	13 (33)
If not-p then not-q	60 (44)	*30 (39)*	47 (11)	*50 (61)*
		Explicit negatives[c]		
If p then q	*72 (100)*	19 (39)	69 (89)	25 (39)
If p then not-q	*59 (89)*	19 (28)	*59 (61)*	34 (61)
If not-p then q	*75 (89)*	22 (39)	*53 (89)*	25 (44)
If not-p then not-q	*78 (89)*	22 (50)	*56 (61)*	25 (39)

Notes

TA = true antecedent; MP = modus ponens; FA = false antecedent; DA = denial of the antecedent; TC = true consequent; AC = affirmation of the consequent; FC = false consequent; MT = modus tollens.

a From Evans et al. (1995, Experiment 3) and Evans and Handley (1999, Experiment 3).

b Matching cases shown in italic.

c Verification pattern shown in italic.

pattern (italic in Table 9.1) is reflected in card selections and mirrors the higher rates of MP and AC on the inference task. As with implicit negation there is a high correlation between inference production rates and card selections ($r(16) = .92, p < .01$), but in this case more inferences are produced than cards selected ($r = .62$ vs. $.45, t(15) = 7.7, p < .01$), presumably because there is some element of competition between cards that has an overall impact on the total number of cards selected (Oaksford & Chater, 1994).

Contrary to what is typically claimed in the literature, the data suggest that patterns of card choice on the selection task are driven by an explicit process of reasoning. Participants spend more time considering the cards they go on to choose, not because they are rationalizing pre-consciously cued choices, but because they are making inferences about the hidden sides of those cards that they are able to readily make inferences from. The parallel between data from the conditional-arguments task and the selection task under equivalent conditions, strongly suggests that a broadly equivalent process underlies performance on each task. Consequently if one is inclined to argue that people reason when given conditional arguments to consider (albeit sometimes quite badly) then one would have to concede that analytic processes are also driving selections on Wason's task.

Analytic processes in the selection task: Individual differences in cognitive ability

Thus far we have argued that performance on the abstract selection task can be explained by analytic reasoning. The typical pattern of p and q selections on the abstract task occurs because the converse, "if q then p" is readily available (Evans & Over, 2004) and this supports an inference that there should be a p on the back of the q card. This also explains the tendency for higher rates of MP and AC on the conditional-arguments task, the verification pattern on the selection task with explicit negation, and the reduction in the selection of the q card in the presence of a second conditional with an alternative antecedent. Matching bias occurs not because attention is pre-consciously directed to matching, but simply because people find it difficult to make inferences from implicitly negated premises.

The observation that most participants fail to get the problem right does not mean that analytic processing, or explicit inference, is absent. However, what of the 10% of participants who select the logically appropriate cards? According to default-interventionist dual-process accounts these participants are able to successfully overcome a powerful attentional bias to matching cards. In Stanovich's (1999) terms they must use the computational resources of System 2 to inhibit the automatically activated System 1 response. Consequently one would expect participants of higher cognitive capacity to be more likely to give the correct response. Stanovich and West (1998) report data from a large-scale study that bears this out; on a selection task with an affirmative rule, participants who select the p and not-q cards are of significantly higher cognitive capacity than those that give the p and q response. In contrast, on deontic versions of the task, where the context provides strong pragmatic cues to the logical response (Griggs & Cox, 1982; see Box 9.1 for a typical example), there is no relationship between responses and ability. In this case, presumably, System 1 and System 2 cue the same response so there is no requirement to draw on cognitive capacity to inhibit the intuitive response.

The individual differences data are persuasive, but there are a number of reasons why they are not decisive. First, the presence of a difference in ability between participants generating different responses cannot demonstrate that these responses are generated by different cognitive systems. It may simply be the case that certain responses are more resource demanding than others, for example some responses require more difficult thinking than other types of responses. Similarly the absence of a relationship between response type and cognitive ability, which is shown on the deontic task, cannot show that System 2 does not play a functional role in response generation. It may be that the degree of System 2 involvement among a particular participant group does not overly extend the maximal resources available within the population studied.

Box 9.1: A typical example of a deontic selection task based upon the "drinking age" rule

Drinking age
Imagine that you are a police officer on duty, walking through a local bar. It is your job to ensure that the drinking laws are in effect in this bar. When you see a person engaging in certain activities, the laws specify that certain conditions must first be met.

One such law is: "If a person is drinking beer then that person must be over 18 years of age."
Each of the boxes below represents a card lying on a table. There are two pieces of information about a person on each card. Whether or not the person is drinking beer is on one side of the card and the person's age is on the other side. For two of the people, you can see their age, but you cannot see what they are drinking. For the other two people, you can see what they are drinking, but you cannot see their age. Your task is to decide whether or not this law is being broken. You may select any of the cards.

Cards: | Age: 19 | | Age: 16 | | Drink: Beer | | Drink: Coke |

If these conjectures are right then we might expect to observe different patterns of relationship between ability and response type from study to study depending upon the characteristics of the participant population. This is exactly what has been reported. For example, in a recent study, we examined the relationship between intelligence and performance on a wide range of abstract and deontic selection tasks (Newstead, Handley, Harley, Wright, & Farrelly, 2004). Contrary to Stanovich and West's earlier findings, there was no relationship between cognitive ability and logical performance on the abstract selection task. However, high-ability participants did show a different pattern of selections when compared with low-ability participants. Higher ability participants were more likely to produce logically equivalent selection patterns across the four different versions of the abstract task that were administered, but these patterns, although consistent, were not logically correct.

An example of one of the tasks used is shown in Box 9.2, a task which we labelled the "menu" selection task. The problem includes a short scenario together with a rule describing an imaginary combination of foods on a restaurant menu. Although the problem is fairly arbitrary it may nevertheless cue related knowledge concerning food choices and combinations, restaurants, menus, and so on. Research has shown that subtle changes in the scenario accompanying a problem can result in quite dramatic changes in the selection choices made (see, for example, Sperber, Cara, & Girotto, 1995; Sperber & Girotto, 2002), although these choices are often not any more logical in a normative sense than the choices made on standard versions of the task (Evans, 1995). The presence of consistent responding among higher ability participants suggests that they were able to recognize that each abstract selection task had the same underlying logical structure and consequently demanded the same response. Inconsistent responders, on the other hand,

---

Box 9.2: An example of the "menu" selection task used in Newstead et al. (2004)

Each of the boxes below represents a menu. Each menu has a food on one side and a drink on the other side.

The rule is: "If the menu has 'fish' on its food side, then 'gin' is on its drink side."

As you can see, two of the menus are food-side up, and two of the menus are drink-side up. Your task is to decide which menu or menus must be turned over in order to find out whether the rule is true or false.

Cards: | Fish | | Steak | | Gin | | Whisky |

presumably treated each problem as a unique case being influenced by subtle pragmatic cues contained within the problem scenario and content. The most common consistent response was to select the p and q cards across all of the abstract problems, which further suggests that this selection pattern is not driven by heuristic pre-conscious processing, but relies on an explicit process of reasoning, which higher ability participants are able to generalize across logically equivalent problem forms.

Three other aspects of Newstead et al.'s data stand out. First, there was a positive association between correct responding on the deontic task and cognitive ability: higher ability participants generated more correct responses, a pattern absent in Stanovich and West's data. This shows, at least among the population studied, that deontic reasoning can depend upon effortful processing. This conclusion is consistent with more recent findings that demonstrate that reasoning on the deontic selection task is disrupted by the presence of a secondary task designed to load working memory (McKinnon & Moscowitch, 2007). The participants we sampled were below the norms for university students on the cognitive ability measure employed, which could explain the discrepancy in findings. However, the sample was nevertheless well above the norms for the general population, which suggests that the pattern observed may well be stronger amongst nonstudent participants. This illustrates an important point: the danger of generalizing findings and building theoretical arguments on individual differences data drawn from high-ability subgroups. It also illustrates the problems inherent in making inferences based upon the absence of a correlation.

A second finding was the observation in Experiment 3 (where we fortuitously sampled a higher ability group) that selecting the p card alone was associated with higher scores on the intelligence measure. There was no difference in ability between those participants selecting p alone compared with the logically correct p and not-q selection pattern (see also Stanovich & West, 1998). This demonstrates that selection of the not-q card is unrelated to measures of cognitive capacity, a finding that mirrors the absence of a relationship between MT rates and ability on the conditional-arguments task (Evans et al., 2007; Newstead et al., 2004). What this suggests is that the key insight on the abstract selection task, as we have argued above, is to understand that a conditional "if p then q" does not logically imply its converse "if q then p", and ability seems to be predicting the extent to which people are able to inhibit this inference and resist the selection of the q card, rather than inhibit heuristically cued choices.

A final finding provides some support for this analysis. In Experiment 3 we also administered a conditional-inference task, on the basis of which an index was calculated (derived from AC and DA endorsements) that reflected the tendency to make invited inferences. Scores on the index were significantly correlated with the logic index on the selection task, once again showing a strong relationship between performance on the two types of task, reflecting the common requirement to inhibit invited inferences across both tasks.

In our view matching responses on the selection task arise through an explicit process of inference. Although it has been argued that correlations between the selection task and cognitive capacity are diagnostic of the processing system involved in generating a response, we think that this argument is flawed. The evidence shows that, dependent upon the participant population sampled, there may or may not be a relationship between accuracy on the abstract task and cognitive ability. When a relationship is observed this relationship holds as strongly for non-normative (only p) selections as it does for logically correct combinations. As we have seen, among some populations cognitive ability is unrelated to correct responding but instead related to consistent responding (often involving the selection of the p and q cards). Although these responses are nonlogical, consistency nevertheless reflects an explicit understanding that the underlying logical structure of the rule is the same across multiple presentations. Finally, we have evidence that deontic selection task performance may or may not be related to cognitive capacity depending upon the population studied, once again suggesting that individual differences should not be seen as diagnostic of the underlying processes involved in the task.

The experiment

In the next section of this chapter we present the findings of an individual differences study in which we examined selection task performance among a large group of adolescent participants. Our main objective was to replicate the consistency of the findings described above in a different population. However, adolescents are an interesting group in their own right because although there is good evidence that they are more able to construct decontextualized task representations than younger children (Moshman, 1999), they do not have complete control over the ability to shift between predominantly intuitive processing to predominantly analytic or logical processing or vice versa (Klaczynski, 2004). There is increasing evidence in the literature that the development of thinking is characterized by an increasing ability to selectively inhibit inappropriate knowledge while remaining sensitive to information that may be useful to the task at hand. For example, Simoneau and Markovits (2003) have shown that among 12- and 16-year-old children, completing a task that requires the inhibition of background knowledge leads to poorer performance on subsequent tasks that require access to different knowledge. This suggests that adolescents, while often being able to reason from decontextualized representations, will have difficulty selectively making use of context or knowledge when it is helpful to the task at hand.

In the present study a large sample of 16- to 17-year-olds was presented with a range of both abstract and deontic selection tasks, together with two measures of cognitive ability. The tasks were presented in a fixed order with a set of abstract tasks presented prior to a set of deontic tasks (see Appendix to this chapter, p. 186, for an example of the tasks used). Our principal aim was to examine the extent to which decontextualization on abstract tasks (as reflected in consistent responding) would generalize to deontic tasks. We predicted that consistent responding on abstract tasks would be associated with higher ability than inconsistent responding, but may also lead to poorer performance on deontic tasks where resisting the influence of context removes an important cue to the correct solution.

Method

Participants

Participants were 126 adolescents aged between 16 and 18 years (mean age = 16 years 8 months) recruited from two local secondary schools in the Plymouth area.

Materials

As a measure of cognitive ability we used the AH4 Parts 1 and 2 (Heim, 1967). This is a commonly used general test of adult intelligence consisting of 65 items in two parts, with the first part designed to assess verbal and numerical ability, the second part visuospatial ability. We also administered a second measure of intellectual ability, Raven's Progressive Matrices, which is a highly reliable measure of fluid intelligence.

Eight selection tasks were used, four abstract and four deontic (see Appendix). The abstract problems were the letter–number task, a destination version, and the menu and grades tasks used by Stanovich and West (1998). The instructions asked participants to indicate which of the four cards (e.g., A, K, 8, and 5 in the first example) needed to be turned over to test whether the rule was true or false. The four deontic tasks were an anglicized version of the Sears problem in which Sears became Debenhams, the drinking age problem, the postage rule, and the cassava problem. Two of the deontic problems (the Sears and the postage rule) were assumed to invoke obligation schemas and two (the drinking age and the cassava problem) were designed to invoke a permission schema (Cheng & Holyoak, 1985). The scenario asked participants to choose the cards they thought needed to be turned over in order to test whether the rule was being violated. The four cards they had to choose from were in each case instances of the *p*, *not-p*, *q*, and *not-q* cards. The conditional rules and the scenarios that accompanied them for each problem are shown in full in the Appendix.

Procedure

Participants were run in groups of varying sizes. The order of presentation was: AH4; Raven's Matrices; selection tasks. The selection tasks were presented in the following fixed order for each participant: letter–number, destination, menu, grades, Sears, drinking age, cassava, and postage.

Results

In all of the analyses that follow we generated a composite measure of intellectual ability based upon the scores on the AH4 and the Raven's Matrices. This was calculated by combining *z*-scores on each of the measures. In all of the remaining analyses we report statistics with respect to this composite measure.

Overall performance on both the abstract and the deontic tasks was lower than the rates that are generally reported among adult participants (see, for example, Newstead et al., 2004). Nevertheless the usual facilitation of deontic tasks (16% correct) over abstract tasks (2% correct) was observed ($t(126) = 6.35, p < .001$).

A second analysis examined the composite ability scores of those who made the same selection pattern on all four of the abstract selection tasks compared with those who gave different responses. Recall that a consistent pattern reflects an understanding on the part of the participant that the tasks have a common underlying structure. The consistent responders were significantly higher in ability ($n = 77, z = 0.19$) than the inconsistent responders ($n = 49, z = -0.30, t(124) = 3.59, p < .001$). While the majority of consistent responders selected p and q throughout ($n = 58$), these participants did not significantly differ in ability from those who gave consistent responses of another kind ($n = 17, t(75) = 0.59, p = .55$).

Next, we examined accuracy on the deontic tasks as a function of consistent responding to the abstract tasks, to determine if resistance to contextual effects on the abstract tasks generalized to the deontic tasks, where the context provides cues to the solution. As predicted, the consistent responders gave significantly fewer correct responses to the deontic tasks (10% correct) than the inconsistent responders (25% correct, $t(124) = 3.59, p < .001$). This pattern was independently significant for the Sears problem (3% vs. 14%, $t(124) = 2.53, p < .025$) and the drinking age problem (23% vs. 51%, $t(124) = 3.3, p < .005$), and was marginally significant for both the cassava problem (5% vs. 14%, $t(124) = 1.77, p < .08$) and the postage problem (9% vs. 20%, $t(124) = 1.82, p < .07$).

The ability composite *z*-scores of participants giving different card choices on the selection tasks are presented in Table 9.2. We have included the three most common patterns of response here, the selection of p and q, the selection of p and not-q, and the selection of the p-card alone, together with a category that includes all other selection patterns. As Table 9.2 clearly shows, on deontic and abstract tasks, those participants who select the p and the q cards are of higher than average ability (*z*-scores above 0). In order to establish whether this effect was significant we compared the composite ability scores of those participants who selected p and q with those who selected

Table 9.2 The composite ability *z*-scores for selecting the most common card combinations for each selection task in our experiment

	Letter–number	Destination	Menu	Grades	Sears	Drinking age	Cassava	Postage
p, q	0.11 (69)	0.19 (67)	0.09 (82)	0.15 (74)	0.25 (55)	0.26 (41)	0.14 (63)	0.18 (60)
p, not-q	−0.42 (5)	0.11 (5)	–	0.91 (1)	0.18 (9)	−0.04 (43)	−0.02 (11)	−0.17 (17)
p	−0.27 (9)	−0.20 (11)	−0.34 (5)	0.2 (9)	−0.08 (11)	0.13 (4)	0.27 (10)	0.07 (5)
other	−0.07 (43)	−0.26 (43)	−0.15 (39)	−0.33 (42)	−0.28 (51)	−0.23 (38)	−0.26 (42)	−0.19 (44)

Note
The number of participants making each selection is shown in parentheses.

Table 9.3 Statistical comparison of ability *z*-scores of those participants selecting p and q compared with other selections for each task in our experiment

	p and q	*Other*	*t-value*	*p-value*
Letter–number	0.11	−0.13	1.78	< .08
Destination	0.20	−0.22	3.02	< .005
Menu	0.10	−0.17	1.84	< .07
Grades	0.15	−0.22	2.62	< .01
Sears	0.25	−0.19	3.18	< .01
Drinking age	0.26	−0.12	2.61	< .01
Cassava	0.14	−0.14	1.99	< .05
Postage	0.18	−0.16	2.51	< .025

a different combination on each of the tasks. Table 9.3 shows the mean ability score for each group together with the *t*-values and the significance level for each comparison. In every case the difference is significant at least at the $p < .1$ level for a two-tailed test.

Discussion

The main objective of this experiment was to evaluate whether the relationship between cognitive ability and consistency of responding observed in earlier work extended to another sample population. The pattern of findings was quite clear. Higher ability participants do not show facilitation on abstract tasks, but do show systematic patterns in their responses as shown by consistent selections from one task to the next. The majority of consistent responses involved selecting the p and q cards, the response that is generally viewed as resulting from heuristic processing. This finding suggests that our consistent responders are able to extract the underlying logical form of the rules across different problems but are then unable to resist the invited inference that supports this selection. What is striking about this aspect of the data, and undermines any argument which equates the matching response with heuristic processes, is the evidence that across all four abstract tasks, participants who produced matching responses were of *higher* cognitive ability than those participants who did not.

The consistency finding replicates one aspect of Newstead et al. (2004) who showed that consistent responding on abstract tasks was associated with higher ability. In Newstead et al.'s study consistent responders were more likely to give correct responses on deontic tasks. Seemingly they were more able to respond to contextual cues on the deontic tasks, while resisting them on the abstract task. In contrast the consistent responders in this study were *less* likely to give correct responses on the deontic task. Of course, on the deontic tasks the scenario itself can provide important cues to the correct solution. For example, the drinking age scenario cues one to think about underage drinkers, and, as research has shown, simple manipulations of scenarios to make counter-examples explicit have been shown to have a substantial effect on performance (see, for example, Sperber et al., 1995). The simple fact is that among this adolescent sample, those participants who decontextualize the rule from the scenario are discarding an aspect of the problem that provides a powerful cue to the correct solution. The discrepancy between these findings and Newstead et al. (2004) may indicate that adolescent reasoners are less able than adult reasoners to ascertain when context is useful.

In contrast the inconsistent responders are giving responses that are cued by the context of the problem. On abstract tasks the scenario does not provide a cue to the solution, while on deontic tasks it often does (Sperber & Girotto, 2002). Hence the inconsistent responders outperform the consistent responders on the deontic tasks, although they still perform at a relatively low level. This analysis suggests that differences on deontic tasks between these two groups may depend upon the contextual richness of the scenario accompanying the rule. There is some evidence in our data that indicates that this may indeed be the case. The biggest difference between the two groups was on the drinking age rule, in which the scenario is both familiar and contextually rich. This was followed by the Sears problem, which is also accompanied by an arguably familiar and detailed scenario. There were only marginal differences, however, on the cassava and postage problems, where the scenarios are unfamiliar and relatively arbitrary.

The findings presented here are important for a number of reasons. First, they are consistent with a number of recent claims that adolescents' thinking is characterized by an increasing ability to resist the influence of System 1 processes, while being less adept at recognizing when pragmatic or knowledge-based cues should or should not be used to best effect. The data presented here provide a compelling illustration of the impact that this can have on tasks where context provides the pragmatic cues to solution. Second, they demonstrate that the relationship between ability and performance on reasoning tasks is not always reflective of a higher number of normative responses among participants with higher ability. While the ability to reason normatively may often depend upon identifying the underlying structure of a problem and stripping back the context in which it is embedded, the opposite may often hold. That is, in many cases the context provides the crucial information that we need to make a normative response.

Summary and conclusions

The selection task is one of the most widely studied and hotly debated tasks in the literature on human thinking and the influence of research using this paradigm has been widespread, extending well beyond the psychology of reasoning. It has been used as a testing ground for evolutionary theories of human thinking (Cosmides, 1989) and driven the development of alternative normative accounts of reasoning grounded in Bayesian statistics and rational analysis (Oaksford & Chater, 1994). Some researchers have argued that the task tells us little about deductive reasoning but has much more to do with interpreting a communicative exchange (Sperber et al., 1995), the development of schemas for dealing with content specific rules (Cheng & Holyoak, 1985), or evaluating probabilities and utilities within a decision-making framework (Manktelow & Over, 1991). Interestingly all of these developments post-date the first publication of the heuristic–analytic theory of the selection task (Evans, 1984), and this account remains as relevant and as widely cited as any of the alternative accounts above. This is a real testament to the originality, clarity, and enduring nature of the idea, which was far ahead of its time.

However, although it is undoubtedly the case that much of our thinking is a product of the interaction between intuitive and more deliberative processing, the evidence to support the heuristic–analytic account of the selection task is weak. In this chapter we have reviewed experimental evidence that shows that when appropriate comparisons are made, performance on the selection task is very similar to patterns of inference on the conditional-arguments task. Manipulations that influence the arguments task, such as the presence of alternative rules, have the same impact on the selection task. This suggests that the processes involved in making explicit inferences from conditional arguments (albeit sometimes fallacious inferences) are the same processes underlying card selections, a view which is inconsistent with the idea that matching selections are pre-attentively cued by nonlogical heuristics.

The second issue that we considered is the extent to which individual differences analyses provide support for the claim that matching responses are generated by System 1 processes. The data presented here and elsewhere suggests that they do not. In fact, based upon the findings of our study, the evidence shows that matching responses are more often given by higher ability participants, suggesting that these responses are produced through System 2. Although the tendency to draw invited inferences may well be driven by automatic pragmatic processes, the inferences that people subsequently make are conscious and reflective. The positive conclusion to be drawn is that our participants are cleverer than we may have previously thought and perhaps we have failed to give them sufficient credit: people do think before they decide on the selection task.

References

Cheng, P. W., & Holyoak, K. J. (1985). Pragmatic reasoning schemas. *Cognitive Psychology, 17*, 391–416.

Cosmides, L. (1989). The logic of social exchange: Has natural selection shaped how humans reason? Studies with the Wason selection task. *Cognition, 31*, 187–276.

Evans, J. St B. T. (1984). Heuristic and analytic processes in reasoning. *British Journal of Psychology, 75*, 451–468.

Evans, J. St B. T. (1989). *Bias in human reasoning: Causes and consequences.* Hove, UK: Lawrence Erlbaum Associates Ltd.

Evans, J. St B. T. (1995). Relevance and reasoning. In S. E. Newstead & J. St B. T. Evans (Eds.), *Perspectives on thinking and reasoning: Essays in honour of Peter Wason* (pp. 147–171). Hove, UK: Lawrence Erlbaum Associates Ltd.

Evans, J. St B. T. (2003). In two minds: Dual process accounts of reasoning. *Trends in Cognitive Sciences, 7*, 454–459.

Evans, J. St B. T. (2007). *Hypothetical thinking: Dual processes in reasoning and judgement.* Hove, UK: Psychology Press.

Evans, J. St B. T. (2008). Dual-processing accounts of reasoning, judgment and social cognition. *Annual Review of Psychology, 59*, 255–278.

Evans, J. St B. T. (2009). How many dual processes do we need? One, two or many? In J. Evans & K. Frankish (Eds.), *In two minds: Dual processes and beyond.* Oxford: Oxford University Press.

Evans, J. St B. T., Clibbens, J., & Rood, B. (1995). Bias in conditional inference: Implications for mental models and mental logic. *Quarterly Journal of Experimental Psychology, 48A*, 644–670.

Evans, J. St B. T., & Handley, S. J. (1999). The role of negation in conditional inference. *Quarterly Journal of Experimental Psychology, 52A*, 739–769.

Evans, J. St B. T., Handley, S. J., & Harper, C. (2001). Necessity, possibility and belief: A study of syllogistic reasoning. *Quarterly Journal of Experimental Psychology, 54A*, 935–958.

Evans, J. St B. T., Handley, S. J., Harper, C., & Johnson-Laird, P. N. (1999). Reasoning about necessity and possibility: A test of the mental model theory of deduction. *Journal of Experimental Psychology: Learning Memory and Cognition, 25*, 1495–1513.

Evans, J. St B. T., Handley, S. J., Neilens, H., & Over, D. (2007). Thinking about conditionals: A study of individual differences. *Memory and Cognition, 35*, 1772–1784.

Evans, J. St B. T., Handley, S. J., Neilens, H., & Over, D. (2008). Understanding causal conditionals: A study of individual differences. *Quarterly Journal of Experimental Psychology, 61*, 1291–1297.

Evans, J. St B. T., Handley, S. J., & Over, D. E. (2003a). Conditionals and conditional probability. *Journal of Experimental Psychology: Learning, Memory and Cognition, 29*, 321–355.

Evans, J. St B. T., & Lynch, J. S. (1973). Matching bias in the selection task. *British Journal of Psychology, 64*, 391–397.

Evans, J. St B. T., Newstead, S. N., & Byrne, R. M. J. (1993). *Human reasoning.* Hove, UK: Lawrence Erlbaum Associates Ltd.

Evans, J. St B. T., & Over, D. E. (2004). *If.* Oxford: Oxford University Press.

Evans, J. St B. T., Over, D. E., & Handley, S. J. (2003b). A theory of hypothetical thinking. In D. Hardman & L. Macchi (Eds.), *The psychology of reasoning and decision making*. Chichester, UK: Wiley.

Evans, J. St B. T., Over, D. E., & Handley, S. J. (2005). Suppositions, extensionality and conditionals: A critique of the model theory of Johnson-Laird & Byrne (2002). *Psychological Review, 112*, 1040–1052.

Feeney, A., & Handley, S. J. (2000). The suppression of "q" card selections: Evidence for deductive inference in Wason's selection task. *Quarterly Journal of Experimental Psychology, 53A*, 1224–1243.

Feeney, A., Handley, S. J., & Kentridge, R. W. (2003). Deciding between accounts of the selection task: A reply to Oaksford. *Quarterly Journal of Experimental Psychology, 56A*, 1079–1088.

Griggs, R. A., & Cox, J. R. (1982). The elusive thematic materials effect in the Wason selection task. *British Journal of Psychology, 72*, 407–420.

Handley, S. J., & Evans, J. St B. T. (2000). Supposition and representation in human reasoning. *Thinking and Reasoning, 6*, 273–312.

Handley, S. J., Evans, J. St B. T., & Thompson, V. A. (2006). The negated conditional. *Journal of Experimental Psychology: Learning, Memory and Cognition, 32*, 559–569.

Handley, S. J., Feeney, A., & Harper, C. (2002). Alternative antecedents, probabilities and the suppression of fallacies in Wason's selection task. *Quarterly Journal of Experimental Psychology, 55A*, 799–818.

Heim, A. W. (1967). *AH4 group test of intelligence. Manual.* London: National Foundation for Educational Research.

Klaczynski, P. A. (2004). A dual process model of adolescent development: Implications for decision making, reasoning and identity. In R.V. Kail (Ed.), *Advances in child development and behavior* (Vol. 32, pp. 73–123). San Diego, CA: Academic Press.

Lucas, E. J., & Ball, L. J. (2005). Think-aloud protocols and the selection task: Evidence for relevance effects and rationalization processes. *Thinking and Reasoning, 11*, 35–66.

Manktelow, K. I., & Over, D. E. (1991). Social rules and utilities in reasoning with deontic conditionals. *Cognition, 39*, 85–105.

McKinnon, M. C., & Moscovitch, M. (2007). Domain general contributions to social reasoning: Theory of mind and deontic reasoning re-explored. *Cognition, 102*, 179–218.

Morley, N. J., Evans, J. St B. T., & Handley, S. J. (2004). Belief bias and figural bias in syllogistic reasoning. *Quarterly Journal of Experimental Psychology, 57*, 666–692.

Moshman, D. (1999). *Adolescent psychological development*. Mahwah, NJ: Lawrence Erlbaum Associates, Inc.

Newstead, S. E., Handley, S. J., Harley, C., Wright, H., & Farrelly, D. (2004). Individual differences in deductive reasoning. *Quarterly Journal of Experimental Psychology, 57A*, 33–60.

Oaksford, M., & Chater, N. (1994). A rational analysis of the selection task as optimal data selection. *Psychological Review, 101*, 608–631.

Rumain, B., Connell, J., & Braine, M. D. S. (1983). Conversational processes are responsible for reasoning fallacies in children as well as adults: If is not the biconditional. *Developmental Psychology, 19*, 471–481.

Sá, W. C., West, R. F., & Stanovich, K. E. (1999). The domain specificity and generality of belief bias: Searching for a generalizable critical thinking skill. *Journal of
Educational Psychology, 91*, 497–510.

Simoneau, M., & Markovits, H. (2003). Reasoning with premises that are not
empirically true: Evidence for the role of inhibition and retrieval. *Developmental
Psychology, 39*, 964–975.

Sperber, D., Cara, F., & Girotto, V. (1995). Relevance theory explains the selection
task. *Cognition, 57*, 31–95.

Sperber, D., & Girotto, V. (2002). Use or misuse of the selection task? Rejoinder to
Fiddick, Cosmides & Tooby. *Cognition, 85*, 277–290.

Stanovich, K. E. (1999). *Who is rational?* Mahwah, NJ: Lawrence Erlbaum
Associates, Inc.

Stanovich, K. E. (2009). Distinguishing the reflective, algorithmic, and autonomous
minds: Is it time for a tri-process theory? In J. Evans & K. Frankish (Eds.), *In
two minds: Dual processes and beyond*. Oxford: Oxford University Press.

Stanovich, K. E., & West, R. F. (1998). Cognitive ability and variation in selection
task performance. *Thinking and Reasoning, 4*, 193–230.

Thompson, V. A. (2009). Dual process theories: A metacognitive perspective. In
J. Evans & K. Frankish (Eds.), *In two minds: Dual processes and beyond*. Oxford:
Oxford University Press.

Wason, P. C. (1966). Reasoning. In B. Foss (Ed.), *New horizons in psychology* (Vol 1.)
Harmondsworth, UK: Penguin.

Wason, P. C., & Evans, J. St B. T. (1975). Dual processes in reasoning? *Cognition,
3*, 141–154.

Appendix

The scenario and rules associated with each selection task used in the
experiment.

Abstract tasks

Letter–number

Each of the boxes below represents a card lying on a table. Each one of the
cards has a letter on one side and a number on the other side.

> The rule is: "If a card has an A on its letter side, then it has an 8 on its
> number side."

As you can see, two of the cards are letter-side up, and two of the cards are
number-side up. Your task is to decide which card or cards must be turned
over in order to find out whether the rule is true or false.

Cards: K   A   8   5

Destination

Each of the tickets below has a destination on one side and a mode of travel on the other side.

The rule is: "If 'Glasgow' is on one side of the ticket, then 'train' is on the other side of the ticket."

As you can see, two of the tickets are destination-side up, and two of the tickets are mode of travel-side up. Your task is to decide which ticket or tickets you would need to turn over in order to find out whether the rule is true or false.

Cards: | Glasgow | | Edinburgh | | Coach | | Train |

Menu

Each of the boxes below represents a menu. Each menu has a food on one side and a drink on the other side.

The rule is: "If the menu has 'fish' on its food side, then 'gin' is on its drink side."

As you can see, two of the menus are food-side up, and two of the menus are drink-side up. Your task is to decide which menu or menus must be turned over in order to find out whether the rule is true or false.

Cards: | Fish | | Steak | | Gin | | Whisky |

Grades

Each of the boxes below represents a school report card lying on a table. Each one of the report cards has a grade on one side and a year on the other side.

The rule is: "If a report card has an 'A' on its grade side, then it has 'year 3' on its comment side."

As you can see, two of the report cards are grade-side up, and two of the cards are year-side up. Your task is to decide which report cards must be turned over in order to find out whether the rule is true or false.

Cards: | E | | Year 3 | | A | | Year 5 |

Deontic tasks

Sears

Suppose that you are the assistant manager at Debenhams, and it is your job to check sales receipts to make sure they are properly filled out according to a rule.

> The rule is: "Any sale over £30 must be approved by the section manager, Mr. Jones."

The amount of the sale is on one side of each receipt, and the space for the approval signature is on the other side. Which of the sales receipts shown below would you need to turn over in order to find out whether or not the rule is being violated?

Cards: | £70 | | £22 | | Approval: Mr. Jones | | Approval: ____ |

Drinking age

Imagine that you are a police officer on duty, walking through a local bar. It is your job to ensure that the drinking laws are in effect in this bar. When you see a person engaging in certain activities, the laws specify that certain conditions must first be met.

> One such law is: "If a person is drinking beer then that person must be over 18 years of age."

Each of the boxes below represents a card lying on a table. There are two pieces of information about a person on each card. Whether or not the person is drinking beer is on one side of the card and the person's age is on the other side. For two of the people, you can see their age, but you cannot see what they are drinking. For the other two people, you can see what they are drinking, but you cannot see their age. Your task is to decide whether or not this law is being broken. You may select any of the cards.

Cards: | Age: 19 | | Age: 16 | | Drink: Beer | | Drink: Coke |

Cassava

You are a Kaluame, a member of a Polynesian culture found only on Maku island in the Pacific. The Kaluame have many strict laws which must be enforced, and the elders have entrusted you with enforcing them. The elders have made rules governing what people eat.

The rule is: "If a man eats cassava root, then he must have a tattoo on his face."

The cards below have information about four young Kaluame men sitting in a temporary camp; there are no elders around. A tray filled with cassava root and molo nuts has just been left for them. Each card represents one man. One side of a card tells which food a man is eating, and the other side of the card tells whether or not a man has a facial tattoo. Your job is to catch men who break the law. If any get past you, you and your family will be disgraced. Indicate only those cards you definitely need to turn over to see if any of these Kaluame men are breaking the law.

Cards: | Eats molo nuts | | Tattoo | | No tattoo | | Eats cassava root |

Postage

Imagine that you are a post office worker in a foreign country. Part of your job is to check letters for postage. The country's postal regulations are strict.

The rule is: "If a letter is sealed then it must have a 20 cent stamp on it."

The rationale for the regulation is to increase profit from personal mail, which is nearly always sealed. Sealed letters are defined as personal and must therefore carry more postage than unsealed letters. Which of the letters below would you need to turn over in order to find out whether or not the rule is being violated?

Cards: | Sealed | | Unsealed | | 20 cents | | 10 cents |

10 Dual processes in the development of the understanding of conditionals

Pierre Barrouillet and
Caroline Gauffroy
Geneva University

In their prominent book entitled *If*, Evans and Over (2004) noted that this word is one of the most important and interesting words in language, because it conveys the hypothetical thinking by which humans go beyond the actual states of the world, imagining alternative possibilities, testing predictions in scientific experimental settings, and finally creating novelty. *If* is certainly one of the most important and interesting words in human language, but also one of the most complex. Indeed, developmental studies have revealed that its meaning is not mastered until late adolescence (see for example Barrouillet & Lecas, 1998; Daniel & Klaczynski, 2006), and even educated adults often experience surprising difficulties when reasoning from *If* sentences, as studies of the famous Wason's selection task or conditional syllogisms have demonstrated. Such complexity in so short a word has motivated a variety of theoretical proposals to account for the way humans understand conditionals and reason from them (Braine & O'Brien, 1991; Evans & Over, 2004; Evans, Over, & Handley, 2005; Johnson-Laird & Byrne, 2002; Johnson-Laird, Byrne, & Schaeken, 1992).

One of the most heuristic and comprehensive accounts of conditionals is probably the mental model theory proposed by Johnson-Laird and Byrne (1991, 2002). Based on the idea that reasoning relies on general processes also involved in language comprehension, the theory assumes that people reason from conditional assertions by representing the states of affairs that are possible given the truth of these assertions. Because this theory gives a precise account of the nature of both the representations involved and the processes acting on them, it was possible to derive a mental model account of the development of conditional reasoning (Markovits & Barrrouillet, 2002). However, Johnson-Laird and Byrne's (2002) mental model theory was the object of several criticisms from authors who privilege alternative conceptions based on suppositional and probabilistic approaches to the conditional (Evans & Over, 2004; Evans et al., 2005; Oaksford & Chater, 2003; Oberauer & Wilhelm, 2003). Although being mainly addressed to the standard theory of mental models, these criticisms undermine the foundations of any of its variants by denying the plausibility of reasoning by mental models representing a set of possibilities, thus weakening not only the standard, but all the modified theories of mental models, including its developmental application proposed by Markovits and Barrouillet (2002).

In this chapter, we present a revised version of this latter theory that integrates the dual-process approach proposed by Evans (2006, 2008) with the mental model framework. We argue that the contrast between heuristic and analytic processes and the ensuing differences in the representations created by the two systems permit us to reconcile the suppositional view of conditionals (Evans & Over, 2004) with the mental model account. The new theory accounts then for the phenomena usually considered as being at odds with Johnson-Laird and Byrne's conception. Moreover, it predicts new phenomena and developmental trends that we tested in several experiments. In the following, we will first recall the mental model account of conditionals and its developmental application, and present the main criticisms and rebuttals that have been recently raised. We then show how the introduction of the distinction between heuristic and analytic processes is sufficient to make a mental model theory able to account for facts previously considered as absolutely incompatible with the mental model approach. Finally, we propose a developmental theory of conditional reasoning by mental models that predicts new findings about how individuals evaluate the truth and the probability of conditionals, which are the domains that have always been presented as the main weaknesses of the standard mental model theory. Finally, we propose some considerations about the need for a developmental approach when trying to understand such complex human behaviour as reasoning.

The mental models theory of conditionals and its developmental application

The mental models theory assumes that individuals understand an *If p then q* conditional sentence by representing its meaning (its intension), from which they construct a representation of what it refers to, that is its extension (Johnson-Laird & Byrne, 1991, 2002; Johnson-Laird et al., 1992; Johnson-Laird, Legrenzi, Girotto, Legrenzi, & Caverni, 1999). Within this theoretical framework, a mental model of an assertion represents a possibility given the truth of this assertion (Johnson-Laird & Byrne, 2002). When a sentence refers to different possible states of affairs, such as *If p then q*, a complete understanding requires the construction of several mental models. Because these models are maintained in a limited-capacity working memory, subjects would tend to reduce the cognitive load resulting from constructing and coordinating models by making implicit some part of the information to be represented. They would then construct simplified models, called initial models. As far as *If p then q* is concerned, the initial model would have the following form:

p   q
. . .

The first line refers to a state of affairs in which the antecedent *p* and the consequent *q* are true. The other possibilities, in which the antecedent is false, would not be represented explicitly but implicitly (the ellipsis above). This implicit model includes a mental footnote indicating that the other possibilities refer to states of affairs in which *p* is false (Johnson-Laird et al., 1999). Mental footnotes are usually soon forgotten, but if they are retained, the reasoner can flesh out the implicit model to make the other possibilities explicit, resulting in either a biconditional:

$$p \qquad q$$
$$\neg p \qquad \neg q$$

or a conditional:

$$p \qquad q$$
$$\neg p \qquad \neg q$$
$$\neg p \qquad q$$

interpretation of the *If p then q* statement. In these fully explicit models, $\neg$ refers to a propositional-like tag for negation. It is worth noting that the process of fleshing out initial models would be demanding, time consuming, and prone to errors (Johnson-Laird & Byrne, 1991; Schroyens, Schaeken, & Handley, 2003).

The specific predictions issuing from this theory have been verified in several studies. It was demonstrated that when the number of models to be held is reduced by appropriately manipulating the order of the premises, reasoning improves in a conditional syllogisms task (Girotto, Mazzoco, & Tasso, 1997). It was established that the time course of conditional inferences is better predicted by the mental model theory than by alternative accounts (Barrouillet, Grosset, & Lecas, 2000). The theory predicts compelling but illusory conditional inferences that were observed (Johnson-Laird & Savary, 1999). Finally, at least two large-scale meta-analyses of conditional inferences established that the mental model theory with additional assumptions concerning the directionality of the models provides a better account of the data than, for example, probabilistic accounts of conditionals (Oberauer, 2006; Schroyens & Schaeken, 2003).

According to Johnson-Laird and Byrne (2002), the most compelling corroboration of the hypothesis that individuals represent *If p then q* statements by constructing a three-model representation by fleshing out an implicit initial representation comes from developmental studies. In several studies, we asked children and adolescents to identify those cases that falsify conditional statements or to produce all the cases compatible with them (Barrouillet, 1997; Barrouillet & Lecas, 1998, 1999, 2002; Lecas & Barrouillet, 1999). All the results converge towards a clear developmental trend. At the first developmental level, children adopt an interpretation limited to the initial model constructed by adults, but seem unable to construct additional models through fleshing out. Thus, they exhibit a conjunctive interpretation based on the sole *p q* model. At this level, *p q* cases are the sole cases considered as compatible with the conditional, the other possibilities (i.e., $\neg p \ q$, $\neg p \ \neg q$, and $p \ \neg q$) being considered as incompatible. A second level, usually reached in early adolescence, consists in constructing a two-model representation by adding a $\neg p$ $\neg q$ model. This results in a biconditional interpretation in which both *p q* and $\neg p \ \neg q$ cases are compatible with conditional statements whereas $\neg p \ q$ and $p \ \neg q$ cases are seen as falsifying. Finally, older adolescents and adults mainly adopt a conditional interpretation resulting from the complete fleshing out of the initial representation in which all the cases except $p \ \neg q$ are compatible with *If p then q*. Thus, these studies revealed a developmental trend by which the representation constructed when interpreting conditional sentences is progressively enriched by additional models as cognitive capacities increase with age. Accordingly, the level of interpretation and the number of models constructed proved to be correlated with working memory capacities, a relation that is still significant even when the effect of age is partialled out (Barrouillet & Lecas, 1999). The developmental trend in the number of models constructed also predicts the age-related evolution of conditional inference production from childhood to adulthood (Barrouillet et al., 2000). In summary, the mental model framework provides a fairly good account of how humans understand and reason from conditional sentences from childhood to adulthood.

Criticisms and rebuttals

Despite its remarkable capacity to account for and predict conditional reasoning, the mental model theory has recently been the object of strong criticism. These criticisms are based on the assumption that, within the mental model theory, the psychological meaning of a basic conditional[1] is the truth function of the material implication (Evans et al., 2005; Oberauer & Wilhelm, 2003). However, two types of findings, both related to the way individuals evaluate conditionals, contradict this view. First, when evaluating the truth value of basic *If p then q* conditionals in truth-table tasks, adult participants often produce a response pattern known as the defective conditional table wherein the *p q* case is considered as making the conditional true, the $p \ \neg q$ case as making it false, whereas the *not p* cases (i.e., $\neg p \ q$ and $\neg p \ \neg q$) are considered as irrelevant for the truth of the sentence. This departs from the truth function of the material implication for which *not p* cases are not irrelevant, but make the conditional true exactly in the same way as the *p q* case does. Second, when asked to evaluate the probability of conditional statements, people rarely produce evaluations compatible with the material implication interpretation, but rather adopt a suppositional interpretation. This was demonstrated by Evans, Handley, and Over (2003) who presented participants with frequency information about the cases *p q*, $p \ \neg q$, $\neg p \ q$, and $\neg p$ $\neg q$ in a pack containing cards that were either yellow or red and had either a circle or a diamond printed on them (for example 1 yellow circle, 4 yellow diamonds, 16 red circles, and 16 red diamonds). Participants were asked to evaluate the probability that the claim "If the card is yellow then it has a circle printed on it" is true for a card drawn at random from the pack. A material implication (MI) account, and thus, according to Evans et al. (2003), the mental model theory, would predict a probability p (MI) = p (*p q*) + p ($\neg p$ *q*) + p ($\neg p$ $\neg q$) because the material conditional is true in each of these three cases. However, this kind of response was practically never observed. Rather, participants mainly evaluated the probability of the conditional as the conditional probability p (*q/p*) = p (*p q*) / [p (*p q*) + p (*p* $\neg q$)], basing their judgement solely on the *p* cases. Surprisingly, a substantial part of the adult sample gave the conjunctive probability p (*p q*). Oberauer and Wilhelm (2003) observed the same phenomena in a similar but independent study.

It is worth noting that these findings are at odds with the mental model theory only if it is agreed that the meaning of a basic conditional for this theory is the truth function of the material implication. This is a complex problem because Johnson-Laird and Byrne (2002) have explicitly rejected this idea, assuming that conditionals are not truth functional. Nonetheless, two points in Johnson-Laird and Byrne's (2002) theory of conditionals blur this asser-tion. The first point concerns the inferences known as the paradoxes of material implication: for material implication, given *not p*, it validly follows for the ordinary conditional that *if p then q*, and given *q*, it validly follows that *if p then q*. Though they are often considered as offending common sense, Johnson-Laird and Byrne (2002) argue that these inferences are valid. Because the paradoxes are valid for a conditional if and only if the conditional is truth functional, Evans et al. (2005) argued that this confirms the truth functional meaning of basic conditionals within the mental model theory. The second and most important point concerns the defective truth-table. Johnson-Laird and Byrne (2002) consider that the defective truth table account of the conditional defended by Quine (1952), Wason and Johnson-Laird (1972), and more recently by Evans and Over (2004) is plausible at first sight, but founders on the case of biconditionals. They argue that the biconditional *If and only if p then q*, which is synonymous with the conjunction *If p then q, and if not p then not q*, has a complete truth table (true for *p q* and *not p not q* and false in the other cases). They wonder how the conjunction of two conditionals having defective truth tables could result in the complete truth table of the biconditional.

Of course, Johnson-Laird and Byrne are perfectly aware that the defective conditional pattern is very frequent in truth-table tasks. They account for this response by noting that the *not p* cases are not explicitly represented within the initial representation of the conditional, which is deemed neither true nor false for these cases that are thus irrelevant. As we recently argued (Barrouillet, Gauffroy, & Lecas, 2008a), this line of reasoning only holds when the initial representation has not yet been fleshed out, but what is the truth value of the conditional for *not p* cases when fleshing out occurs? A careful analysis of recent articles such as Girotto and Johnson-Laird (2004) lets us conclude that the standard mental model theory would consider that the conditional is true for *not p* cases.

The defective truth table and the way adults evaluate the probability of conditionals led Evans to propose that the psychological meaning of the conditional is not material implication, but rather is suppositional (Evans & Over, 2004; Evans et al., 2005). When understanding an *If p then q* conditional statement, people would hypothetically add *p* to their stock of knowledge and evaluate their degree of belief in *q* given *p*, a procedure known as the Ramsey test. This procedure leads one to disregard *not p* cases as irrelevant for the truth of the conditional, hence the defective pattern in truth-table tasks and the evaluation of the probability of the conditional as the conditional probability. It should be noted that this account departs only in a subtle way from the mental model conception. According to the mental model theory, understanding a conditional consists in representing the set of possibilities that can occur given its truth. Within this framework, the antecedent is the description of a possibility, and "the consequent is interpreted as though it were an isolated main clause in a context that satisfies the antecedent" (Johnson-Laird & Byrne, 2002, p. 649). This is very akin to the suppositional account. However, a complete understanding would also involve representing those cases in which the antecedent is not satisfied, and more precisely understanding that a basic conditional does not constrain these cases. Thus, according to Johnson-Laird and Byrne, the possibilities corresponding to a conditional are described by the conjunction of two conditionals: *If p then q, and If not p then either q or not q*. If this is the case, why do individuals so often produce the conditional probability when evaluating the probability of a conditional? According to Johnson-Laird and Byrne, it is because naïve individuals base their answer not on the actual possibilities but on mental models from them, and "if individuals rely on mental models, then they will think only of the case in which the antecedent is true as satisfying the conditional" (Johnson-Laird & Byrne, 2002, p. 651). The idea that naïve individuals rely on mental models rather than on actual possibilities to solve the problem is convincing, but it is not sufficient to account for the conditional probability response. Indeed, if individuals thought only of the case in which the antecedent is true as satisfying the conditional, they would produce a conjunctive probability response, dividing the number of *p q* cases by the total number of cases. Of course, we have seen that this response was reported by Evans et al. (2003), but it is not predominant. What Johnson-Laird and Byrne's account fails to explain is why individuals restrict their evaluation to *p* cases.

Thus, even if the mental model and the suppositional theories are very akin, it is not so simple to account for the main facts observed in the truth table and the evaluation of conditional tasks within the standard mental model theory. Does this mean that the mental model theory is not only inaccurate, but fundamentally mistaken and should be abandoned, as Evans has suggested (Evans et al., 2005)? We do not think so. In the following, we argue that minor changes in the mental model approach could account for the main facts at odds with the standard theory. These changes are theoretically grounded on the distinction made by Evans between heuristic and analytic processes and lead to a modified mental model theory of conditional understanding and its development. A series of predictions can be drawn from this new theory that we recently tested and verified.

Mental models and the suppositional account of conditionals

As we have seen, the data issuing from the truth table and the probability tasks are at odds with the standard mental model theory only because, among the three possibilities compatible with a basic conditional and constitutive of its core meaning (i.e., $p\ q$, $\neg p\ \neg q$, $\neg p\ q$), individuals deem the conditional true for the sole $p\ q$ case, while *not p* cases are considered as irrelevant. However, we recently noted that this is not a priori incompatible with the standard mental model theory because the three models are not psychologically equivalent (Barrouillet et al., 2008a). The mental model theory distinguishes between $p\ q$, which is part of the initial model and systematically leads to an explicit representation, and *not p* possibilities ($\neg p\ q$ and $\neg p\ \neg q$), which remain initially implicit and require the fleshing out process to be explicitly represented. Originally, the principle of implicit models was coined as a principle of cognitive economy: because constructing and maintaining transient representations in working memory is demanding, individuals would leave a large part of the information implicit (Johnson-Laird & Byrne, 1991). By contrast, we have suggested that the distinction between initial and fleshed out models is epistemic in nature: the initial model would represent those possibilities that make the assertion true, the other compatible possibilities necessitating a fleshing out process to be made explicit. We noted that introducing this new distinction only necessitated slightly modifying the principle of truth of the mental model theory, which states that: "Each mental model of a set of assertions represents a possibility given the truth of the assertions, and each mental model represents a clause in these assertions only when it is true in that possibility" (Johnson-Laird & Byrne, 2002, p. 653) by adding "The possibilities that make the assertions true give rise to explicit mental models whereas the others lead to models that remain initially implicit."

The *not p* cases are not explicitly represented within the initial model because they do not make the conditional true. However, they do not make it false either, because they can occur given its truth and are consistent with it. As a consequence, and as Evans and others have observed, the truth value of the conditional should be neither true nor false but remain indeterminate for *not p* cases. Those cases that are not part of the possibilities compatible with the conditional and that are not represented either explicitly or implicitly would falsify the conditional (i.e., $p\ \neg q$ in adults).

As noted by Barrouillet et al. (2008a), this proposal accounts perfectly for the phenomena observed in the truth-table task and also in the probability task. When asked to evaluate the probability that a conditional is true or false, individuals would focus on those cases for which the conditional can be readily evaluated, that is *p* cases. This leads to evaluating this probability as the conditional probability by considering the ratio between favourable cases (*p q*) and relevant (i.e. *p*) cases. A failure of this process would lead to the conjunctive probability often observed, individuals basing their computation on the entire set of cases (Evans et al., 2003; Girotto & Johnson-Laird, 2004). It is also worth noting that the proposed theory inherits most of the characteristics of the suppositional account. For example, Evans et al. (2005) noted that, though *if p then q* and *not p or q* elicit the same set of possibilities within the mental model theory (i.e., *p q*, $\neg p \; q$, and $\neg p \; \neg q$), the probability of the conditional is never judged to be equal to *not p or q*. According to our proposal, the disjunction *not p or q* is true only for those cases that are part of the initial model, that is *not p* on the one hand and *q* on the other, something clearly different from the case that makes *if p then q* true, which is *p q*. In the same way, though both *if p then q* and *if not q then not p* have the same set of possibilities, their probability should not be judged as equivalent and they should not elicit the same response pattern in truth-table tasks because their initial models differ (*p q* for *if p then q*, but $\neg q \; \neg p$ for *if not q then not p*).

Thus, the mental model theory and the suppositional account put forward by Evans are not so different. A mere extension of one of the principles of the mental model theory based on the fundamental distinction between initial and fleshed out models proved to be sufficient to account for phenomena usually considered as totally at odds with the theory. However, why are the cases explicitly represented in the initial model considered as making the conditional true, whereas those matching the models constructed through fleshing out are considered as leaving the truth value of the conditional indeterminate? The answer to this question is to be found in the nature of the cognitive processes responsible for constructing the initial model on the one hand, and for fleshing out this initial representation on the other. As we will see, Evans' heuristic–analytic theory provides the appropriate framework to understand why conditional statements are represented by a set of mental models that differ in their epistemic status.

Heuristic and analytic processes in mental models construction

Within the realm of the psychology of reasoning, a recent general account known as the dual-process theory has gained considerable credit. Dual-process theories assume that two reasoning systems coexist in the human mind (Evans, 1989; Evans & Over, 1996; Sloman, 1996; Stanovich, 1999). The first, often called System 1, is based on fast, automatic, and unconscious processes. Deeply contextualized and rooted in associative processes and implicit learning, it is often assumed to achieve adaptive rationality. By contrast, the second system, called System 2, would involve explicit, controlled, and conscious processes. Slow, sequential, and cognitively demanding, the operations of System 2 underpin deliberate inferences and are the basis of human logical rationality. In reviewing the dual-process theories of reasoning, judgement, and social cognition, Evans (2008) noted that although a distinction between two systems of reasoning is not explicitly discussed by mental model theorists, this distinction is implicitly present. Indeed, Evans (2008) stresses that the mental model theory describes the formation of the initial model as a relatively automatic and effortless process. The fleshing out of this initial representation is, by contrast, described as cognitively demanding, error prone, and constrained by working memory capacities. The differences between these two kinds of processes echo the distinction between System 1 and System 2, and more precisely between the heuristic and analytic systems described by Evans (2006) in his revised heuristic–analytic theory of reasoning.

Heuristic processes that are described as fast, tacit, unconscious, context- and knowledge-sensitive would correspond to the processes responsible for the construction of the initial model. Following the so-called relevance principle of the heuristic–analytic theory (Evans, 2006), when interpreting a conditional statement, this heuristic system would produce an epistemic model that is the most plausible and believable with reference to prior knowledge elicited by context and the current goals. This default mental model implies default responses, inferences, or decisions. This is exactly what the mental model theory considers as the initial model.

Interestingly, in the same way as the mental theory describes fleshing out as an optional process, Evans (2006) assumes that once the heuristic system has produced an initial model, the analytic system may or may not intervene, depending on instructional set, time available, and general intelligence. This system is controlled rather than automatic, slow, and sequential in nature. Its role is to replace or revise default mental models exactly as fleshing out adds additional models to the initial representation of a conditional. Thus, the analytic system inhibits default heuristic responding in the same way as the additional models block the fallacious inferences supported by the initial model such as affirmation of the consequent (Grosset, Barrouillet, & Markovits, 2005). As suggested by Evans (2008), the analytic system perfectly corresponds to the fleshing out process.

Barrouillet, Gauffroy, and Lecas (2008b) assumed that this contrast in the processes responsible for the construction of either the initial or the additional models has a direct impact on the epistemic status of these models. The fast and effortless heuristic system provides individuals with default models that come automatically to mind: they are what people are spontaneously thinking about when understanding a sentence. As a consequence, individuals consider these default models as capturing the psychological meaning of the sentence. It is thus natural that the states of affairs matching this representation are considered as making this sentence true when they occur. By contrast, the analytic processes are slow, conscious, and cognitively demanding. Accordingly, the intervention of the analytic system is optional in nature, and most of the time does not occur at all. However, within an adaptive language processing system, it cannot be imagined that the mechanisms of comprehension rely on a slow and cognitively demanding analytic system. It is for this reason that the analytic system adds interpretations to the default mental models that do not pertain to the core meaning[2] of the sentence, but that are only compatible with it. As a consequence, the cases that match mental models added through fleshing out would make the conditional neither true nor false, but leave its truth value indeterminate.

According to this view, *not p* cases are not irrelevant because the meaning of the conditional is suppositional in nature, leading individuals to concentrate on *p* cases, but instead because they are not part of the initial model. Thus, the suppositional nature of the conditional in situations of evaluation is not the cause of the irrelevance of *not p* cases, but its consequence. Because *not p* cases are not part of the initial model, they are irrelevant for the truth value of the conditional, and its evaluation concentrates on those cases that are relevant for its truth or falsity, that is the *p* cases. As we will see, this conception is corroborated by developmental phenomena.

A developmental prediction

According to Barrrouillet et al. (2008a), the hypothesis that the cases represented in the initial model make the conditional true whereas those that are represented in fleshed out models are irrelevant could be easily tested by taking advantage of the developmental changes affecting the fleshing out process. Because the number of models that can be constructed through fleshing out progressively increases with age, a correlative age-related increase in the rate of indeterminate responses should be observed in truth-table tasks. More precisely, children who construct only the *p q* model and adopt a conjunctive interpretation should judge the conditional true for *p q* cases, but false for all the other possibilities. These children should not produce "irrelevant" responses in truth-table tasks because they do not flesh out their initial representation. What would be the response pattern of adolescents who endorse a biconditional reading? According to the mental model approach, this interpretation results from an incomplete fleshing out of the initial representation and the construction of only one additional model of the form $\neg p$ $\neg q$. Thus, those adolescents should deem the conditional true for *p q* cases as younger children do, but should consider its truth value as indeterminate for the $\neg p$ $\neg q$ cases that match the model they construct through fleshing out. Finally, they should consider the conditional as false for the other cases $\neg p$ q and p $\neg q$, thus resulting in a pattern described by Evans and Over (2004) as a defective biconditional reading. Older adolescents and adults often adopt a conditional interpretation by achieving a complete fleshing out of the initial model and the construction of two additional models: $\neg p$ $\neg q$ and $\neg p$ q. Following our hypothesis, the cases matching the initial model *p q* should make the conditional true, those matching the fleshed out models (i.e., $\neg p$ $\neg q$ and $\neg p$ q) should leave its truth value indeterminate, whereas the cases that do not match any model (i.e., p $\neg q$) should make the conditional false, resulting in a defective conditional pattern. To summarize, a developmental pattern should emerge in truth-table tasks from a conjunctive to a defective biconditional and then a defective conditional pattern.

Barrrouillet et al. (2008a) tested these hypotheses using a task in which third, sixth, and ninth graders as well as adults were shown a conditional sentence of the form "If the circle is red, then the star is black" along with a picture representing a box with a circle and a star inside. The match between the colours of the circle and the star displayed in the box and those involved in the conditional sentence was manipulated to obtain four trials in each of the four possible logical cases $p\ q$, $\neg p\ q$, $p\ \neg q$, and $\neg p\ \neg q$. For example, a $\neg p$ $\neg q$ case was created by presenting a blue circle and a green star. Participants were asked to evaluate the truth value of the sentence from the content of the box by choosing between three possible responses: "true", "one cannot know", and "false". The results confirmed our predictions. Third graders mainly exhibited a conjunctive pattern of responses that disappeared progressively with age to leave room for the expected defective biconditional pattern in adolescence, whereas adults favoured a defective conditional pattern (Figure 10.1). Two other patterns were of interest in these results. The first,

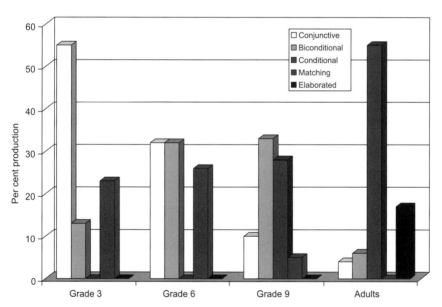

Figure 10.1 Distribution of response pattern in the truth-table task as a function of groups. For the $p\ q$, $\neg p\ \neg q$, $\neg p\ q$, and $p\ \neg q$ cases respectively, the conjunctive pattern refers to consistent T F F F the biconditional pattern to T I F F and the conditional pattern to T I I F responses. The matching pattern corresponds to T F I I and the elaborate pattern to I I I F responses (T = true; I = indeterminate; F = false). Data from Barrouillet et al. (2008). Adapted with permission. Copyright © (2008) by the American Psychological Association.

mainly produced by younger participants, consisted of choosing the "true" response for the *p q* case, "one cannot know" for the ¬*p q* and the *p* ¬*q* cases and "false" for the ¬*p* ¬*q* case. We considered this pattern as reflecting a matching response: Those cases that perfectly match the content of the rule are considered as making it true, a partial matching leading to the "one cannot know" response whereas a complete mismatch made the rule false. Revealing a deep misunderstanding of the conditional nature of *If* sentences, this pattern was restricted to the younger groups. By contrast, the other pattern was observed only in some adults and is probably highly elaborated. It consisted of responding "false" for the *p* ¬*q* case and "one cannot know" for all the other possibilities, including *p q*. These responses could result from a capacity to resist the inductive fallacy and to realize that a unique favourable case like *p q* is not sufficient to make true a universal statement such as *If p then q*.

This study lent strong support to our hypothesis that the mental models of the conditional differ in their epistemic status. Because the construction of *not p* models requires the intervention of an optional, slow, and demanding analytic system, they are not part of the core meaning of the basic conditional. As a consequence, the cases that match these models are compatible with the conditional, but they are not considered as making it "true" when they occur. Rather, they leave its truth value indeterminate: one cannot know if the conditional is either true or false when they occur in isolation. By contrast, the models constructed by the heuristic system come easily to mind and constitute the core meaning of the conditional. The cases that match this initial representation are considered as making the conditional true. Thus, the modified mental models theory proposed by Barrouillet et al. (2008a and 2008b) not only accounted for the main facts considered as being at odds with the standard mental model theory, but predicted how the evaluation of basic conditionals develops from childhood to adulthood. Moreover, integrating the dual-process approach within the mental model account of conditionals led us to modify our conception of the development of conditional reasoning.

A revised developmental theory of conditionals

Markovits and Barrouillet (2002) proposed a developmental theory assuming that conditional reasoning relies both on general processes implemented in existing cognitive architecture and on domain specific knowledge. When reasoning from *If p then q* sentences, reasoners would retrieve relevant knowledge from long-term memory related to the content of the conditional in order to construct transient mental models in working memory. Development would not only result from an age-related increase in the capacity of working memory permitting the construction of an increasing number of models with age, as suggested by Barrouillet and Lecas (1998), but also from changes in the amount and structure of available knowledge and from better access to this knowledge. However, although Markovits and Barrouillet (2002) integrated into their theory the idea of experience-based knowledge automatically activated, they did not use the distinction between deliberative and conscious processes on the one hand, and automatic, implicit, and unconscious mechanisms on the other. Nonetheless, we have seen that this distinction is especially appropriate within the mental model framework and allows new developmental predictions issuing from differences in the developmental course of the two systems.

The age-related increase in working memory capacities is now well documented (Barrouillet, Gavens, Vergauwe, Gaillard, & Camos, 2009; Case, Kurland, & Goldberg, 1982; Towse & Hitch, 1995). Thus, it can be expected that any process relying on working memory capacities should exhibit a developmental increase in efficiency. This is the case in analytic processes, described by Evans (2006) as slow, controlled, and demanding. Accordingly, several authors have described the analytic system as developing until late adolescence (Daniel & Klaczynski, 2006; Kokis, MacPherson, Toplak, West, & Stanovich, 2002). Concerning conditional reasoning, Barrouillet and Lecas (1998) observed that the number of models that children and adolescents can construct is a function of their working memory span, this relation being still significant even when the effect of age was partialled out. Thus, it can be assumed that the analytic processes responsible for the fleshing out of the initial representation increase in efficiency with age, from an initial state in childhood in which no fleshing out occurs to a final developmental state, reached at the end of adolescence, that permits reasoners to envision all the possibilities compatible with a conditional statement. By contrast, the heuristic system is based on unconscious and implicit processes known to remain immune to individual and developmental differences (Vinter & Perruchet, 2000). Accordingly it has been described as independent of general intelligence and age (Reber, 1993; Stanovich, 1999), and Klaczynski (2001) noted that heuristic processes are loosely consolidated by early adolescence and may not further consolidate with age.

The different developmental courses of the two systems along with their different roles in mental model construction lead to two predictions concerning the way children and adolescents understand conditional sentences. We have assumed that heuristic processes are responsible for the construction of the initial representation, which captures the core meaning of the conditional sentence and represents those cases that make it true when they occur. A direct consequence of these assumptions is that the initial model for conditionals and consequently the cases considered as making the conditional true should not evolve with age. It is worthy of note, as we will see, that this does not mean that the initial representation will be restricted to the single $p\ q$ model for all the conditionals at any age. Some conditionals elicit complex initial representations combining several mental models, but even in this case, this initial representation should not evolve with age. By contrast, the cases that leave indeterminate the truth value of the conditionals should evolve with age with the analytic processes that construct the corresponding mental models through fleshing out. Consequently, a correlative development should be observed in the cases considered as falsifying the conditional, their number decreasing with age.

Though the age-related changes in the efficiency of the analytic system should have a determinant impact on the way individuals understand conditionals, this cannot be the sole factor. Evans (2006) stresses that, even when the analytic system intervenes, its outcome is still influenced by the heuristic system because the construction of additional models by the analytic system often relies on the retrieval of knowledge from long-term memory, and both the mechanisms of memory retrieval and the structure of the accessed knowledge are under the influence of the heuristic system. Indeed, the associative nature of long-term memory involves automatic and uncontrolled retrievals through spreading activation phenomena (Anderson, 1983), and the structure of knowledge bases reflects the tacit and implicit learning mechanisms that capture the statistical regularities of the environment (Perruchet & Vinter, 2002). Thus, even if the development of reasoning is under the influence of the analytic system and should thus strongly evolve with age, the heuristic system could modulate this influence and modify developmental trajectories in specific and predictable ways. We tested these predictions in a recent study (Gauffroy & Barrouillet, 2009).

Predicting developmental trajectories in understanding conditional sentences

The preceding predictions were tested by studying the development of the understanding of several types of conditionals, such as basic and causal conditionals, but also inducements such as promises and threats. Interestingly, the mental model theory makes precise predictions concerning the representation of causal conditionals. Causal conditionals are conditionals in which the antecedent refers to a cause and the consequent to its effect, such as *If a piece of metal is heated, then it expands*. There is a great deal of evidence indicating that the way individuals interpret this kind of sentence is strongly influenced by the structure of knowledge related to the causal relation involved. Causal relations for whom people do not have access to potential alternative causes (i.e., strong causations) tend to elicit a biconditional reading, whereas weak causations for which alternative causes easily come to mind result in more frequent conditional interpretations (Barrouillet, Markovits, & Quinn, 2001; Cummins, 1995: Cummins, Lubart, Alksnis, & Rist, 1991; Markovits, 1984; Quinn & Markovits, 1998). Nonetheless, according to the mental model theory, both weak and strong causations involve the same initial model in which the cause and the effect occur. Johnson-Laird (2006; Goldvarg & Johnson-Laird, 2001) assumes that both weak and strong causations are represented using the following mental model:

p   q
. . .

with the ellipsis representing implicit possibilities in which the antecedent does not hold. Thus, the strength of the causal relation should not have any impact on the heuristic system and the initial representation it produces. As a consequence, our theory predicts that both weak and strong causal relations should be considered as true for the sole $p\ q$ cases by children, adolescents, and adults.

Markovits and Barrouillet (2002) assumed that the fleshing out process could lead to the retrieval of several classes of objects or events from long-term memory. The first concerns cases in which the objects or events are complementary to those specified in the conditional. This class would be composed of related events such as "*If a piece of metal is not heated, then it does not expand*" and leads to the construction of a model of the form $\neg p\ \neg q$. The second class concerns events that share the same relation to q as p does but that differ from p. These alternative causes lead to the construction of models of the form $\neg p\ q$. Thus, the retrieval of alternative causes through fleshing out leads to the construction of a complete representation with the $p\ q$, $\neg p\ \neg q$, and $\neg p\ q$ models, whereas, when no alternative cause is retrieved, this representation is restricted to the two models $p\ q$ and $\neg p\ \neg q$. According to our theory, those cases matching the $\neg p\ \neg q$ and $\neg p\ q$ models should leave indeterminate the truth value of the causal conditionals because these models are constructed through fleshing out by the analytic system. Thus, the biconditional interpretation induced by strong causal relations should not be a biconditional, but a defective biconditional interpretation, which should only appear in adolescence with the capacity to flesh out the initial representation. By contrast, weak causal relations should elicit the same developmental pattern as observed by Barrouillet et al. (2008a) with basic conditionals, with a succession of conjunctive, defective biconditional and defective conditional interpretations from childhood to adulthood.

These predictions were tested by Gauffroy and Barrouillet (2009) in third, sixth, ninth graders and adults, who were presented with a truth table task involving strong ("If button 3 is pressed then the blackboard's lights are switched on") and weak ("If the icon F5 is touched then the computer screen becomes black") causal relations. The rationale and method of the task were the same as in Barrouillet et al. (2008a). Participants were presented with a causal conditional sentence along with a drawing depicting either a $p\ q$, a $\neg p\ q$, a $p\ \neg q$, or a $\neg p\ \neg q$ situation, and were asked to say if this situation made the conditional either true, false, or one cannot know. The results confirmed our expectations (Figure 10.2). The strength of the causal relation did not affect younger children who rarely fleshed out their initial representation, producing a predominant conjunctive pattern and some matching patterns testifying to the difficulty of this task at this age. A dramatic change occurred in sixth graders, who produced a predominant defective biconditional pattern for both the weak and strong causal relations. However, while this pattern remained predominant until adulthood for strong relations, it was progressively replaced by a defective conditional

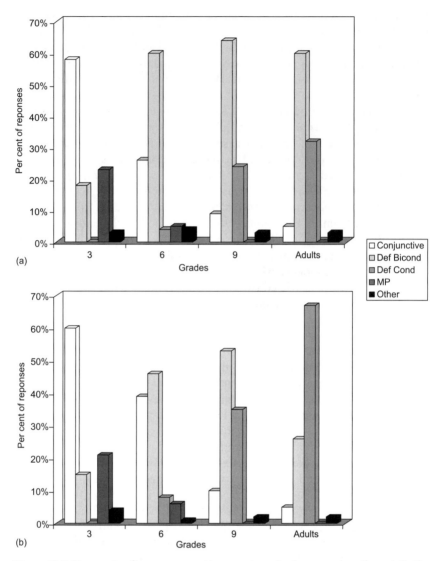

Figure 10.2 Per cent of response patterns categorized as conjunctive, defective
biconditional (Def Bicond), defective conditional (Def Cond), matching
(MP), and others as a function of grades for (a) strong and (b) weak
causal conditionals. From Gauffroy and Barrouillet (2009). Copyright ©
(2009), with permission from Elsevier.

pattern for weak causal relations that allow the retrieval of alternative
causes.

The same effect of the structure of semantic memory and the same developmental predictions were tested by taking advantage of a phenomenon
reported by Barrouillet and Lecas (1998, 2002) who observed that basic con-

ditionals involving binary terms as antecedent and consequent elicit a bicon-ditional interpretation. For example, a sentence like "If the bird is a female then it has light plumage" involves a biconditional interpretation in adoles-cents as well as in adults who reject both $p \neg q$ and $\neg p \, q$ cases as incompatible with the rule and produce a pattern of conditional inferences based on only two models, $p \, q$ and $\neg p \neg q$ (endorsement of the two logically correct infer-ences, modus ponens and modus tollens, but also of the two fallacies affirm-ation of the consequent and denial of the antecedent: Barrouillet & Lecas, 1998, 2002; Barrouillet et al., 2000). However, what remained indeterminate in these studies was the exact nature of this biconditional interpretation. On the one hand, it could be assumed that binary terms involve the pragmatic inverse implicature, which would be added to the initial representation by the heuristic system ("If the bird is a female then it has light plumage, hence if it is a male then it has dark plumage"). In this case, the resulting meaning would correspond to an equivalence, *If p then q* taking the meaning of *If and only if p then q*. On the other hand, as suggested by Barrouillet and Lecas (1998), the structure of semantic memory could constrain the fleshing out process. Because both "female" and "light" allow only one alternative, the first step of the fleshing out (i.e., the production of a $\neg p \neg q$ model) would lead to a complete representation in which each value of the antecedent is associated with a corresponding value of the consequent (*female light* and *male dark*). This would result in a one-to-one correspondence (*p* associated with q and $\neg p$ with $\neg q$) that blocks any further fleshing out and the produc-tion of the $\neg p \, q$ model. Although these two accounts could not be dis-entangled by the tasks used by Barrouillet and Lecas (1998) or by conditional inference tasks, our theory predicts different response patterns in a truth-table task. Namely, if the biconditional reading is due to a pragmatic implicature affecting the heuristic processes and the structure of the initial representa-tion, conditionals with binary terms should induce an equivalence reading and be considered as true for both $p \, q$ and $\neg p \neg q$ cases, and false for the other cases. By contrast, if binary terms affect the analytic system by constraining the fleshing out process that only constructs a $\neg p \neg q$ model, then $\neg p \neg q$ cases would leave indeterminate the truth value of these conditionals. Using the same task and the same age groups as previously described, Gauffroy and Barrouillet (2009) verified that the conditionals with binary terms (BB) elicited the same developmental pattern as the strong causal relations, with a conjunctive interpretation in the younger children followed by a predominant defective biconditional reading in all the older groups (Figure 10.3), whereas the conditionals with no binary terms (NN) elicited the developmental pat-tern already observed for basic and weak causal conditionals.

The case of complex initial representations

One of the main assumptions of our theory is that initial representations remain stable across age because they are constructed by heuristic processes.

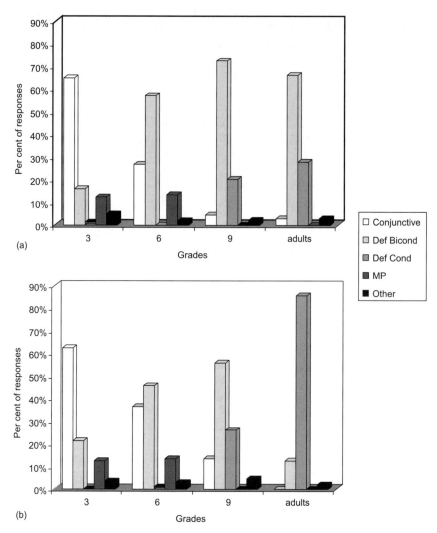

Figure 10.3 Per cent of response patterns categorized as conjunctive, defective
biconditional (Def Bicond), defective conditional (Def Cond), matching
(MP) and others as a function of grades for conditionals involving
(a) binary (BB) or (b) no binary (NN) terms. From Gauffroy and Barrouillet (2009). Copyright © (2009), with permission from Elsevier.

Although we have now reported developmental patterns in which the initial
representation is restricted to the sole *p q* model, this should not be the
case for all kinds of conditionals. Indeed, Evans (2006) stressed that the
default model could be enriched by pragmatic implicatures produced by
the heuristic system. If our theory is correct, those cases matching the
models resulting from these implicatures should be considered as making

the conditionals true. This seems to be the case for inducements such as promises and threats. When studying the way adults interpret conditionals with realistic materials, Newstead, Ellis, Evans, and Dennis (1997) observed that they mainly adopted an equivalence reading for promises and threats that were deemed as true for both $p\ q$ and $\neg p\ \neg q$ cases and false for $\neg p\ q$ and $p\ \neg q$ cases, a pattern never observed in the studies reported above. According to our theory, this would mean that promises and threats elicit a two-model initial representation with both $p\ q$ and $\neg p\ \neg q$ represented right from the start. As suggested by Evans (2006), the heuristic system would add to the promise "if you mow the lawn, then I'll give you five euros" the pragmatic implicature "if you don't, I'll give you nothing" resulting in the following initial representation

| Lawn mown | 5 euros |
| Lawn not mown | nothing |

This initial model would block any further fleshing out, the pragmatic implicature dismissing the possibility of having the 5 euros without mowing the lawn (i.e., the ¬p q model). If our developmental theory is correct and if the outcome of the heuristic processes is immune to age-related changes, the equivalence pattern observed by Newstead et al. (1997) should be also observed in adolescents and even in children. This prediction was tested and verified by Gauffroy and Barrouillet (2009) by presenting the same age groups with promises and threats using the same method as in the experiments previously reported. The results were particularly clear: in all age groups, a predominant equivalence pattern emerged for both types of inducements (Figure 10.4), providing strong support for our hypothesis. Incidentally, these results confirmed that the biconditional interpretations produced by adolescents when interpreting basic or causal conditionals in laboratory experiments do not result from applying real-world reasoning to artificial tasks or from an incapacity to inhibit pragmatic implicatures. The two types of biconditional readings differ in their nature and evolution: the defective biconditional interpretation observed with basic (NN) and weak causal conditionals is transitory in nature, resulting from immature analytic processes leading to an incomplete fleshing out of the initial representation, whereas the equivalence interpretation observed with inducements probably results from heuristic processes and consequently does not evolve with age.

What do developmental studies tell us about theories of reasoning?

The studies reported in this chapter illustrate the importance of studying development for understanding human cognition in general, and reasoning in particular. Most of the modern theories of conditional reasoning have been

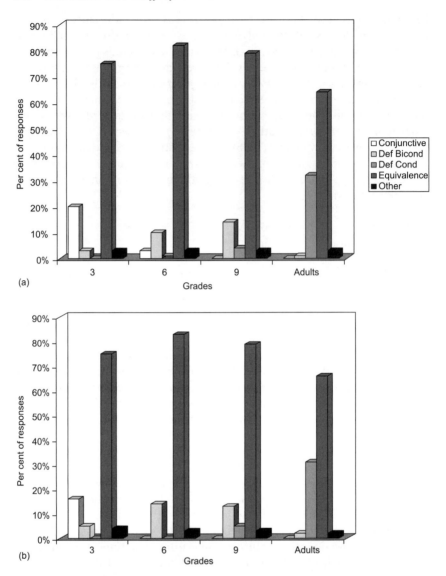

Figure 10.4 Per cent of response patterns categorized as conjunctive, defective biconditional (Def Bicond), defective conditional (Def Cond), equivalence, and others as a function of grades for (a) threats and (b) promises. From Gauffroy and Barrouillet (2009). Copyright © (2009), with permission from Elsevier.

elaborated by speculating on adult performance from a selected set of tasks without directly addressing the developmental origins of the cognitive mechanisms and structures underpinning this performance (Braine & O'Brien, 1991; Evans & Over, 2004; Johnson-Laird & Byrne, 1991; Oaksford & Chater,

2003). At the same time, many developmental theories of reasoning have been put forward, describing how competence and performance develop (Overton, 1990), the succession and nature of levels or stages in this development (Moshman, 1990, 2004; Halford, Wilson, & Phillips, 1998), but without strong connections with theories of adult reasoning. Nonetheless, following a tradition instigated by Piaget (Inhelder & Piaget, 1958), we assume that adult reasoning cannot be fully understood without a precise analysis of its genesis, and that theories of reasoning must account for developmental phenomena and explain how and why children's and adults' reasoning are related.

Among the different theories of conditional reasoning, the mental model theory has proved to be the most heuristic and appropriate in accounting for development. Many studies demonstrated how development converges towards the final state described by Johnson-Laird through a series of levels characterized by the number of models that can be constructed (Barrouillet & Lecas, 1998, 2002), and Markovits and Barrouillet (2002) designed a variant of the mental model theory that explains much of the developmental data. The proposals of the present chapter can be seen as a step further in the same direction. As Barrouillet et al. (2008a) noted, the mental model theory is mainly concerned with the way individuals represent sentences deemed as true and reason from these representations, whereas the judgement of the truth or falsity of assertions containing connectives is seen by Johnson-Laird and Byrne (2002) as a meta-ability that has been less studied. Accordingly, Barrouillet et al. (2008a) pointed out that all the facts at odds with the standard mental model theory issue from tasks that require evaluation of the truth or falsity of conditionals (truth table and probability tasks). However, we have seen that these facts are easy to accommodate with the mental model approach. Interestingly, Jonathan Evans has provided both the most convincing criticisms of the mental model theory of conditionals (Evans et al., 2005) and the heuristic–analytic theory (Evans, 2006) that offers the possibility of integrating the mental model theory with his suppositional approach. Following Klaczynski (2004; Klaczynski & Cottrell, 2004) who had already stressed the usefulness of applying a dual-process theoretical framework to developmental phenomena, we have proposed that Evans' heuristic–analytic theory sheds light on one of the main processes described by the mental model theory, the fleshing out of initial representations, and permits new developmental predictions concerning the construction of models. We have seen that these predictions are verified.

What developmental studies tell us is that the current theories of conditional reasoning are actually not so different from each other, their disparities being often overstated and their similarities overlooked. As we have seen, they are even fairly compatible. A comprehensive approach not only accounts for most of the data, but reveals a surprising variety of developmental trajectories in understanding sentences beginning with this short, but so complex word, *If*.

Notes

1 According to Johnson-Laird and Byrne (2002), basic conditionals are conditionals in which the antecedent and the consequent have no semantic or referential relations, or relations based on knowledge.
2 Following the standard mental model theory (Johnson-Laird & Byrne, 2002), the core meaning of a basic conditional contains three models (p q, ¬p ¬q, and ¬p q). We suggest here that the core meaning is restricted to the initial representation.

References

Anderson, J. R. (1983). *The architecture of cognition*. Cambridge, MA: Harvard University Press.

Barrouillet, P. (1997). Modifying the representation of if . . . then sentences in adolescents by inducing a structure mapping strategy. *Current Psychology of Cognition*, *16*, 609–637.

Barrouillet, P., Gauffroy, C., & Lecas, J. F. (2008a). Mental models and the suppositional account of conditionals. *Psychological Review*, *115*, 760–771.

Barrouillet, P., Gauffroy, C., & Lecas, J. F. (2008b). Postscript: A good psychological theory of reasoning must predict behavior and explain the data. *Psychological Review*, *115*, 771–772.

Barrouillet, P., Gavens, N., Vergauwe, E., Gaillard, V., & Camos, V. (2009). Working memory span development: A time-based resource-sharing model account. *Developmental Psychology*, *45*, 477–490.

Barrouillet, P., Grosset, N., & Lecas, J. F. (2000). Conditional reasoning by mental models: Chronometric and developmental evidence. *Cognition*, *75*, 237–266.

Barrouillet, P., & Lecas, J. F. (1998). How can mental models account for content effects in conditional reasoning? A developmental perspective. *Cognition*, *67*, 209–253.

Barrouillet, P., & Lecas, J. F. (1999). Mental models in conditional reasoning and working memory. *Thinking and Reasoning*, *5*, 289–302.

Barrouillet, P., & Lecas, J. F. (2002). Content and context effects in children's and adults' conditional reasoning. *Quarterly Journal of Experimental Psychology*, *55*, 839–854.

Barrouillet, P., Markovits, H., & Quinn, S. (2001). Developmental and content effects in reasoning with causal conditionals. *Journal of Experimental Child Psychology*, *81*, 235–248.

Braine, M. D. S., & O'Brien, D. P. (1991). A theory of If: A lexical entry, reasoning program, and pragmatic principles. *Psychological Review*, *98*, 182–203.

Case, R., Kurland, D. M., & Goldberg, J. (1982). Operational efficiency and the growth of short-term-memory span. *Journal of Experimental Child Psychology*, *33*, 386–404.

Cummins, D. D. (1995). Naïve theories and causal deduction. *Memory & Cognition*, *23*, 646–658.

Cummins, D. D., Lubart, T., Alksnis, O., & Rist., R. (1991). Conditional reasoning and causation. *Memory & Cognition*, *19*, 274–282.

Daniel, D. B., & Klaczynski, P. A. (2006). Developmental and individual differences in conditional reasoning: Effects of logic instructions and alternative antecedents. *Child Development*, *77*, 339–354.

Evans, J. St B. T. (1989). *Bias in human reasoning: Causes and consequences*. Hove, UK: Lawrence Erlbaum Associates Ltd.

Evans, J. St B. T. (2006). The heuristic–analytic theory of reasoning: Extension and evaluation. *Psychonomic Bulletin & Review, 13*, 378–395.

Evans, J. St B. T. (2008). Dual processing accounts of reasoning, judgment and social cognition. *Annual Review of Psychology, 59*, 255–278.

Evans, J. St B. T., Handley, S. J., & Over, D. E. (2003). Conditionals and conditional probability. *Journal of Experimental Psychology: Learning, Memory, and Cognition, 29*, 321–355.

Evans, J. St B. T., & Over, D. E. (1996). *Rationality and reasoning*. Hove, UK: Psychology Press.

Evans, J. St B. T., & Over, D. E. (2004). *If*. Oxford: Oxford University Press.

Evans, J. St B. T., Over, D. E., & Handley, S. J. (2005). Suppositions, extensionality and conditionals: A critique of the mental model theory of Johnson-Laird and Byrne (2002). *Psychological Review, 112*, 1040–1052.

Gauffroy, C., & Barrouillet, P. (2009). Heuristic and analytic processes in mental models for conditionals: An integrative developmental theory. *Developmental Review, 29*, 249–282.

Girotto, V., & Johnson-Laird, P. N. (2004). The probability of conditionals. *Psychologia, 47*, 207–225.

Girotto, V., Mazzocco, A., & Tasso, A. (1997). The effect of premise order in conditional reasoning: A test of the mental model theory. *Cognition, 63*, 1–28.

Goldvarg, E., & Johnson-Laird, P. N. (2001). Naïve causality: A mental model theory of causal meaning and reasoning. *Cognitive Science, 25*, 565–610.

Grosset, N., Barrouillet, P., & Markovits, H. (2005). Chronometric evidence for memory retrieval in causal conditional reasoning: The case of the association strength effect. *Memory & Cognition, 33*, 734–741.

Halford, G. S., Wilson, W. H., & Phillips, S. (1998). Processing capacity defined by relational complexity: Implications for comparative, developmental, and cognitive psychology. *Behavioral and Brain Sciences, 21*, 803–864.

Inhelder, B., & Piaget, J. (1958). *The growth of logical thinking from childhood to adolescence*. New York: Basic Books.

Johnson-Laird, P. N. (2006). *How we reason*. Oxford: Oxford University Press.

Johnson-Laird, P. N., & Byrne, R. M. J. (1991). *Deduction*. Hillsdale, NJ: Lawrence Erlbaum Associates, Inc.

Johnson-Laird, P. N., & Byrne, R. M. J. (2002). Conditionals: A theory of meaning, pragmatics, and inference. *Psychological Review, 109*, 646–678.

Johnson-Laird, P. N., Byrne, R. M. J., & Schaeken, W. (1992). Propositional reasoning by model. *Psychological Review, 99*, 418–439.

Johnson-Laird, P. N., Legrenzi, P., Girotto, V., Legrenzi, M. S., & Caverni, P. (1999). Naive probability: A mental model theory of extensional reasoning. *Psychological Review, 106*, 62–88.

Johnson-Laird, P. N., & Savary, F. (1999). Illusory inferences: A novel class of erroneous deductions. *Cognition, 71*, 191–229.

Klaczynski, P. A. (2001). Analytic and heuristic processing influences on adolescent reasoning and decision making. *Child Development, 72*, 844–861.

Klaczynski, P. A. (2004). A dual-process model of adolescent development: Implications for decision making, reasoning, and identity. In R. V. Kail (Ed.),

Advances in child development and behavior (Vol. 31, pp. 73–123). San Diego, CA: Academic Press.

Klaczynski, P. A., & Cottrell, J. M. (2004). A dual-process approach to cognitive development: The case of children's understanding of sunk cost decisions. *Thinking and Reasoning, 10*, 147–174.

Kokis, J. V., MacPherson, R., Toplak, M. E., West, R. F., & Stanovich, K. E. (2002). Heuristic and analytic processing: Age trends and associations with cognitive ability and cognitive styles. *Journal of Experimental Child Psychology, 83*, 26–52.

Lecas, J. F., & Barrouillet, P. (1999). Understanding of conditional rules in childhood and adolescence: A mental models approach. *Current Psychology of Cognition, 18*, 363–396.

Markovits, H. (1984). Awareness of the "possible" as a mediator of formal thinking in conditional reasoning problems. *British Journal of Psychology, 75*, 367–377.

Markovits, H., & Barrouillet, P. (2002). The development of conditional reasoning: A mental model account. *Developmental Review, 22*, 5–36.

Moshman, D. (1990). The development of metalogical understanding. In W. F. Overton (Ed.), *Reasoning, necessity, and logic: Developmental perspectives* (pp. 205–226). Hillsdale, NJ: Lawrence Erlbaum Associates, Inc.

Moshman, D. (2004). From inference to reasoning: The construction of rationality. *Thinking and Reasoning, 10*, 221–239.

Newstead, H. E., Ellis, M. C., Evans, J. St B. T., & Dennis, I. (1997). Conditional reasoning with realistic material. *Thinking and Reasoning, 3*, 49–76.

Oaksford, M., & Chater, N. (2003). Conditional probability and the cognitive science of conditional reasoning. *Mind and Language, 18*, 359–379.

Oberauer, K. (2006). Reasoning with conditionals: A test of formal models of four theories. *Cognitive Psychology, 53*, 238–283.

Oberauer, K., & Wilhelm, O. (2003). The meaning(s) of conditionals: Conditional probabilities, mental models, and personal utilities. *Journal of Experimental Psychology: Learning, Memory, and Cognition, 29*, 680–693.

Overton, W. F. (1990). Competence and procedures: Constraints on the development of logical reasoning. In W. F. Overton (Ed.), *Reasoning, necessity, and logic: Developmental perspectives* (pp. 1–32). Hillsdale, NJ: Lawrence Erlbaum Associates, Inc.

Perruchet, P., & Vinter, A. (2002). A self organized consciousness. *Behavioral and Brain Sciences, 25*, 297–388.

Quine, W. V. O. (1952). *Methods of logic*. London: Routledge.

Quinn, S., & Markovits, H. (1998). Conditional reasoning, causality, and the structure of semantic memory: Strength of association as a predictive factor for content effects. *Cognition, 68*, 93–101.

Reber, A. S. (1993). *Implicit learning and tacit knowledge*. Oxford: Oxford University Press.

Schroyens, W., & Schaeken, W. (2003). A critique of Oaksford, Chater and Larkin's (2000) conditional probability model of conditional reasoning. *Journal of Experimental Psychology: Learning, Memory, and Cognition, 29*, 140–149.

Schroyens, W., Schaeken, W., & Handley, S. (2003). In search of counterexamples: Deductive rationality in human reasoning. *Quarterly Journal of Experimental Psychology, 56 A*, 1129–1145.

Sloman, S. A. (1996). The empirical case for two systems of reasoning. *Psychological Bulletin, 119*, 3–22

Stanovich, K. E. (1999). *Who is rational? Studies of individual differences in reasoning.* Mahwah, NJ: Lawrence Erlbaum Associates, Inc.

Towse, J. N., & Hitch, G. J. (1995). Is there a relationship between task demand and storage space in tests of working memory capacity? *The Quarterly Journal of Experimental Psychology, 48A,* 108–124.

Vinter, A., & Perruchet, P. (2000). Implicit learning in children is not related to age: Evidence from drawing behavior. *Child Development, 71,* 1223–1240.

Wason, P. C., & Johnson-Laird, P. N. (1972). *Psychology of reasoning: Structure and content.* London: Batsford.

Part III

Dual processes and beyond

11 Dual-process theories of thinking

Paolo Legrenzi
University Iuav of Venice

Introduction

The hypothesis that human intelligence does not constitute a unitary system dates back to the origins of psychology. In William James's manifesto, *A Plea for Psychology as a "Natural Science"*, published in 1892, James argues that the foundation of psychology as a natural science is based on an intertwining between the notion of adaptation and the notion concerning the levels of consciousness. This functionalist concept – for which the content of thought flow (another concept coined by James) comes into awareness only when "there is need for it" – is taken up again in a recent book and article by Jonathan Evans (2007a, 2007b). Evans develops this intuition by breaking it down into specific hypotheses, and appeals to it for interpreting many experimental data in the field of judgement, reasoning, and decision making. This chapter is dedicated to the two systems of human intelligence in Evans's model.

Evans re-examines a concept of thought articulation in parallel and serial processes that had previously been advanced by Neisser. Evans analyses how the two systems of human intelligence function in their adaptation to the environment and in solving the problems that such adaptation presents. System 1 is unconscious, automatic, and rapid, whereas System 2 is slow, sequential, and linked to working memory and general intelligence. Neisser hypothesized something similar in *The Multiplicity of Thought* (1963), where he begins with a sort of review of the main dichotomies in the history of studies on human intelligence: productive and nonproductive thinking, creative and noncreative thinking, autistic and realistic, conscious and unconscious, intuitive and analytic. This last dichotomy was introduced by Bruner:

> The peculiar characteristic of analytic thinking is that it proceeds one step at a time. Each step is identifiable and the thinker can communicate it to another person in an adequate manner. The thought process takes place with an almost complete mastery of the information and operations involved. It may be founded on accurate deductive reasoning; often it makes use of logical and mathematical instruments and appeals

to explicit plans of action [. . .] whereas the essential feature of intuitive thinking does not involve reasoning based on a pre-organized and precise plan [. . .] the thinker arrives at her answer – whether correct or incorrect – despite the fact that she is completely, or almost, in the dark as to the processes which led her to the solution.

(Bruner, 1960/1964, pp. 57–58)

Neisser begins with this distinction of Bruner's in order to sustain the theory that human thought is an activity of multiple processes that can take place and interact in various ways. Alongside this explicit and conscious principal sequence, parallel reasoning may occur that is unconscious yet interfering with the reasoning of the principal sequence. In other words, people think in different ways, and they think about more than one thing at a time. But how do they do this? Neisser claims that it is possible provided that: (1) the two mental activities do not result in the same answer; (2) neither of the two activities is complex; (3) at least one is automatic enough to be performed outside the conscious.

The experimental paradigm adopted by Neisser (1963) for controlling these three assumptions is based on the visual exploration of a list of words. Participants in the experiment are asked to examine a list of words and to indicate which words contain a certain crucial feature, for example the letter Z. If we compare the time employed for identifying a letter, or for finding two letters (for example, Z and Q, or one letter among ten), we discover that there are no great differences. According to Neisser, this result demonstrates that multiple processes can exist; that is, mental operations carried out in parallel.

Neisser's approach has been articulated, elaborated, and refined thanks to the fantastic development of the experimental psychology of thinking, which is synthesized by Evans (2007a). The British scholar developed the hypothesis of two systems in intelligent adaptation to the environment by examining the functions of numerous cognitive activities, processes that are more complex than simply recognizing letters from a list.

In general terms, Evans follows Stanovich (1999) in distinguishing between two methods of thinking, System 1 (S1) and System 2 (S2). Approximately, the dimensions differentiating the two systems are as follows:

- (S1) automatic, unconscious / (S2) conscious and linked to language;
- (S1) rapid, parallel / (S2) slow, sequential;
- (S1) associative / (S2) linked to working memory and general intelligence;
- (S1) pragmatic (prior knowledge) / (S2) abstract and hypothetical thinking;
- (S1) low effort / (S2) high effort.

Evans (2007a) makes an accurate and close examination of all recent theories of cognitive processes. His conclusion is that System 2 – conscious, explicit, and slow – constitutes a unitary system, while System 1 is a combination of many different types of implicit, cognitive, and unconscious processes (see Stanovich, 2004). The criterion used here for discriminating between S1 and S2 is the presence of analogical transfer to explain facilitation in different versions of the same task; that is, the capacity to comprehend and transfer the solution of a problem in different, but structurally invariant, versions of the same problem.

Let us now apply the distinction made by Evans between S1 and S2 to several tasks in the psychology of reasoning. It involves determining whether it is possible to tackle these tasks in S1 and S2 environments, and what the results may be. To this aim, two classical hypothetical-deductive reasoning tasks will be analysed (the selection task and the THOG problem) and a more recent task about the naïve evaluation of probabilities.

The selection task

Wason (1966) introduced a reasoning task that became "one of the most studied in the literature" (Evans, 2007a, p. 39). The name "selection task" was chosen by Wason because it involves "selecting", from among a group of cards, those cards which constitute the correct response. Four cards are shown (on a table, or computer screen, etc. . . .). The cards, all of which have a letter on one side and a number on the other, are shown face up to display the following sequence: A, D, 3, 7. The task is to decide which cards would logically need to be turned over in order to verify whether the following stated rule is true or false: "If there is an A on one side of the card, then there is a 3 on the other side of the card".

The majority of participants choose the card showing the A, or the card showing the A and the card showing the 3. In order to solve this problem correctly, one must take into consideration that:

- the rule would be false if an A were paired with a number other than 3;
- it is logically necessary to turn over any card that could reveal such a falsifying condition.

Therefore, the correct answer is to turn over A and 7, leaving aside D and 3.

Many versions and advanced explanations of this same task have been proposed over the past 40 years. Evans concludes that essentially the standard version is "unnatural" (see Evans, 2007a). As Oaksford and Chater (2007, Ch. 6) emphasize, it is not spontaneous to resort to a conditional rule in this context. Try presenting the four cards in question by displaying each of their sides and by emphasizing that only one of the four violates the rule (the card with A on one side and 7 on the other). People do not spontaneously resort to the conditional for describing this state of things. It is more natural to say, "If there is an A on one side, then there shouldn't be a 7 on the other side" or "There can't be an A and a 7", using explicit negations (Legrenzi, 1971).

Mark Singley and John Anderson (1989, pp. 235–237) also discuss the selection task in an extensive essay dedicated to transfer in cognitive activities. They use data from previous research (Johnson-Laird, Legrenzi, & Legrenzi, 1972) where a "realistic" version is introduced that makes the solution to the problem transparent. The problem was formally equivalent to the card selection task but involved a rule pertaining to sealed letters and postage. This rule actually described British postal system practices and was well known in Britain at the time of the study. It involved four envelopes (one sealed, one open, one with a 3p stamp on it, and one with a 5p stamp on it) and stated that "if a letter is sealed, then it has a five-pence stamp on it". Singley and Anderson point out the following.

- There is no transfer from the realistic version (postal system) to the solution of the other logically equivalent problem (abstract). Having resolved the "realistic" version does not make finding the solution to the standard version, i.e., the "abstract" version, any easier, even if the two tasks are presented in sequence, as in the research conducted in 1972.
- The lack of transfer shows how difficult it is to "abstract" the common structure in the two versions, standard and realistic: a necessary condition for transferring the solution from one version to another.
- When we are taught the disciplines of logic, mathematics, statistics and, more generally, disciplines requiring System 2, we must keep in mind the difficulty, in many cases, of ridding ourselves of System 1.

Singley and Anderson allude to dual processes in thinking and to constraints that hinder transfer from happening. Evans and Lynch (1973) arrived at the same conclusion, although via a different route. They show the tendency to focalize (or perceive as relevant) the cases mentioned in the rule (A and 3) and, therefore, to choose the corresponding cards. These two English scholars named this misleading tendency "matching bias". Their experiment cleverly included the negation inside the rule. The simplistic tendency to select the cases mentioned in the rule is not limited to the selection task and to conditional expressions of the sort "if . . ., then . . .", but is a general tendency of S1 that manifests under the form of "matching bias" (see Evans, Legrenzi, & Girotto, 1999). These data as a whole show the nature of S1, characterized by a fast, simple, and economic (which here results as misleading) strategy with respect to S2, which leads to solving the problem. The abstraction of the logical structure (inasmuch as there are invariants among the different versions), a precondition for transfer, is difficult because the negation of 3 is implicit in the standard version of the selection task (it is not expressed as "not-3" but as "7"), while in the other cases it is explicit for both its context, which requires previous knowledge, and for the actual use of the word "not". A version in which the negation was explicit made it easier to find the solution (Legrenzi, 1970), given the focus on A and not-3 (the combination which, indeed, falsifies the rule). However, did the subjects in Legrenzi's studies (1970) truly understand the logical structure of the problem (if by "truly understand" we mean they were able to grasp and transfer the invariant structure, expressible in logical terms, to all the problems in which it was involved)? Certainly not. They simply provided the correct answers according to "matching bias" and did not, thus, "advance" from S1 to S2. This passage was made more difficult by the fact that when you pass to S2 – as Evans observed (2007a, p. 46) – that is, to a form of analytical reasoning, the logical solution may escape you in that S2 is used for rationalizing the "intuitive" choice of the cards that S1 points out as relevant (A and 3).

In conclusion, the various experiments on the different versions of the same selection task have constituted the first testing ground for controlling, effectively and in detail, the theory of dual-process thinking.

The THOG problem

According to Evans (2007a, p. 68), the THOG problem is one of the most difficult reasoning problems to solve. It too was developed by Wason and its name refers to a fictitious mythological character from British lore (Wason & Brooks, 1979). In the standard version of the problem participants are shown four figures: a black diamond, a white diamond, a black circle, and a white circle. Participants are told that the experimenter has written down one shape (triangle or circle) and one colour (white or black). They are then given the following rule: "In the designs there is a particular shape and a particular colour, such that any of the designs that has one, and only one, of these features is called a THOG". One of the figures (e.g., the black triangle) is identified as a THOG, and the participants are instructed to decide whether or not each of the other three figures is a THOG.

In order to solve this difficult task, participants must first determine which colour and shape combinations the experimenter might have written down. If the black triangle is a THOG, the experimenter could not have written down "black/triangle" because the THOG example would contain both of these characteristics (and it must contain *only* one!). Likewise, the experimenter could not have written down "white/circle" because the THOG example indicated would not contain any of the characteristics (and it must contain one!). Therefore, the experimenter had to have written down either the "black/circle" or the "white/triangle". No matter which of these two combinations the experimenter has written down, the other THOG must be the white circle because it shares one of the two characteristics written down by the experimenter.

Many subsequent investigations, using different experimental designs, have determined that the requirements for solving the task, as difficult as it is, are not beyond the reasoning capabilities of most participants. The majority of participants understand the rule (Wason & Brooks, 1979), are able to generate hypotheses for the two possible combinations (Girotto and Legrenzi, 1989), and can test the figures against the hypotheses (Wason & Brooks, 1979). The difficulty of the problem lies in the need to carry out all three of these tasks together.

Girotto and Legrenzi (1989) underlined the difficulty participants have in separating the features of the exemplar ("black/triangle") from the features that the experimenter may have written down ("black/circle" or "white/triangle"). There are two things that can be done in order to make the separating easier: create a sensible and well-thought out scenario that takes place over time, so as to label the two components of the problem in different ways; or, and more simply, give different names to the two components. Newstead and Griggs (1992) elaborated this explanation of cognitive impediments to the solution and called it "confusion theory". Specifically, when generating hypotheses for the possible combinations written down by the experimenter, starting with the exemplar indicated as the THOG, the working memory capacity of participants may be overwhelmed. Consequently, participants simplify the task by assuming that the features of the exemplar are the same features that have been written down by the experimenter (a variation of the erroneous tendency of *matching bias* described by Evans). This "unauthorized" simplification on the part of participants might explain the common mistake in indicating the "black/circle" and the "white/triangle" as the other THOGS, apart from the exemplar ("black/triangle") initially indicated by the experimenter. Actually, the only other possible THOG is the "white circle".

To verify the "confusion theory", Girotto and Legrenzi used the "trick" of giving the name SARS to the combinations written down, in order to distinguish their features from the features of the THOG already indicated. Griggs, Platt, Newstead, and Jackson (1998) confirmed the facilitation derived by this "trick"; however, they attributed this not to a true understanding of the task's structure (S2!), but to the fact that the linguistic formulation (i.e., naming the combinations) draws attention to the correct answer (S1!). Koenig, Platt, and Griggs (2007) suggested that transfer is the criterion for deciding whether the source of the solution was S1 or S2. They used the standard version, the version by Girotto and Legrenzi (1989), and a new version that visually, but not lexically, separates the two levels (the level of the indicated THOG exemplar and the level of the hypotheses on the possible combinations written down by the experimenter). Their conclusion is as follows: "The results of the studies replicate the facilitation obtained and proposed by Girotto and Legrenzi (1989), but the ability to indicate the correct solution does not rely on what Evans refers to as System 2 [. . .] but on System 1, which confirms the intuition made by Griggs et al. (1998)" (Koenig et al., 2007, p. 499).

This tradition of research shows how the transfer of the solution, made possible by the ability to isolate the invariant element in different versions of the same problem, or the nontransfer of the solution, is a good stratagem for probing the dual nature of thinking processes. But not only that. This technique also allows us to discriminate the eventual solutions obtained via S1 with respect to those obtained via S2, the latter not being superior in itself but rather capable of allowing for a true understanding of the problem's logical nature.

The Monty Hall problem

The *Monty Hall* problem takes its name from a game show on American television which, for the first time, revealed the problem to the public at large. In 1990 Marylin vos Savant presented the problem again in a column she wrote for *Parade* magazine. What followed was a heated debate revealing how even experts in the field of statistics were unable "to see" the correct solution (Krauss & Wang, 2003). The standard version of the problem is as follows.

> Suppose you're on a game show and you're given the choice of three doors. Behind one door is a car; behind the others, goats. You pick a door, say Number 1, and the host, who knows what's behind the doors, opens another door, say Number 3, which has a goat. He then says to you, "Do you want to switch to Door Number 2?" Is it to your advantage to switch your choice?
>
> Marylin vos Savant attempted to convince readers that "Yes, you should switch. The first door has a one-third chance of winning, but the second door has a two-thirds chance."

I myself presented this problem to 200 bank consultants and only a small minority of them indicated the exact solution, while hardly any of them were able to explain why. The problem was not a new one (Selvin, 1975), yet only in recent years has it been included in psychological literature (for an exhaustive review, see Krauss & Wang, 2003). Krauss and Wang show a table containing the three possible combinations (C1, C2, C3) for the car and for the two goats.

The structure in Table 11.1 demonstrates why it is advantageous to switch: in this way you have the chance of winning two out of three times. In the standard version this "advantage" is not transparent. One has to be able to block the following erroneous representations of the problem:

> Initially there are three doors. Behind one there is nothing. Therefore, two doors remain and my initial choice now has a 50 per cent chance of

Table 11.1 Given the three possible arrangements of two goats and one car (the prize), the table shows, in two out of three arrangements, that you win by switching

	Door 1	Door 2	Door 3	
C1	Goat (first choice)	Goat (open door)	Car	In C1 you win: by SWITCHING!
C2	Goat (first choice)	Car	Goat (open door)	In C2 you win: by SWITCHING!
C3	Car (first choice)	Goat	Goat	In C3 you win: by NOT SWITCHING no matter what the host does

winning given that there remain two possibilities. There is no reason for me to switch doors!

According to Krauss and Wang, in order to design a version that "obstructs" this blinding representation, it is necessary to bear in mind the following points.

(1) Rather than reasoning with probabilities, one has to count and compare frequencies, as in Table 11.1.
(2) These frequencies correspond to possible arrangements of goats and cars behind the doors. One has to compare the number of arrangements in which the contestant would win the car by switching to the number in which she would win by staying.
(3) One has to consider the possible arrangements as they would appear from behind the doors.
(4) One has to ignore the last piece of information provided in the standard version (Monty Hall opens Door 3).

If we construct a version that puts into effect the four suggestions above, each of whose theoretical bases is discussed at length by Krauss and Wang, the structure of Table 11.1 becomes less difficult.

The following is a version prepared by Krauss and Wang (2003), shown here in order to illustrate their objectives in creating a "facilitated" version of the problem. It should be read carefully, keeping in mind that the parts in block letters are not seen by participants.

Rules of the game

Rules

The contestant of this game can choose one of three doors. Behind one, and only one, of the doors there is a prize: a car. Behind each of the other two doors there is a goat. After the contestant chooses a door, that door remains closed for the entire duration of the game. According to the game rules, the game show host, Monty Hall, who knows what is behind each door, now has to *open one of the two remaining doors not chosen by the contestant, and the door he opens must have a goat behind it*. After Monty Hall has opened the door with a goat, he will ask the contestant whether she wants to stay with her first choice or switch to the other door.

CHANGE OF PERSPECTIVE BY TAKING MONTY HALL'S VIEWPOINT

Task

Imagine you are Monty Hall, the game show host, and that you know which door has the car behind it.

EMPHASIZING THE FIRST CHOICE
The contestant chooses one door, say, Door Number 1.

NOT SPECIFYING THE NUMBER OF THE DOOR OPENED BY MONTY HALL BUT SHOWN IN FIGURE 11.1
According to the rules of the game, you must now open another door which has a goat behind it. You must then ask the contestant if she wants to stay with her first choice (Door 1) or switch to the last remaining door.

INDUCE THE CONSTRUCTION OF CORRECT MENTAL MODELS SHOWN IN FIGURE 11.1
The car could be behind any of the *three doors*.

QUESTION BASED ON FREQUENCIES
In how many of the three possible arrangements would the contestant win the car after opening the "goat door":

- if she stays with her first choice (Door 1)? In __ out of 3 cases.
- if she switches to the last remaining door? In __ out of 3 cases.

The contestant should therefore:

__ stay with her initial choice   __ switch

Put an X next to the answer you choose.

GIVE JUSTIFICATIONS FOR YOUR ANSWER
Please also write down what went on in your head when you made your decision. You may use sketches, etc., to explain your answer.

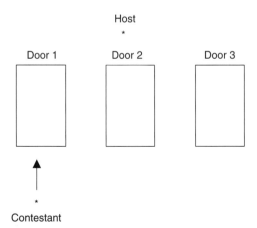

Figure 11.1 Diagram of the three doors.

The justifications in block letters indicate the reason for any changes with respect to the standard version of the problem. What are the results obtained with this version that should facilitate the correct construction of mental models corresponding to the three arrangements in Table 11.1 and that should not provide misleading information? Krauss and Wang obtained 59 per cent of switch choices from the initial choice with 38 per cent correct justifications. In other words, slightly more than one-third of the 34 participants provided a correct justification for their switch in choice, thus demonstrating to have actually reasoned at a System 2 level. Although the cognitive block remains very strong, it does indeed show itself to be penetrable. The most interesting result, from our point of view, comes from a final experiment conducted by Krauss and Wang in which they draw on an indication made by Johnson-Laird, Legrenzi, Girotto, Legrenzi, and Caverni (1999) and attempt to see whether a pedagogy of reasoning is possible. In other words, they observe whether training based on explanations triggers the solution of the task. Without any training, none of the 110 Berlin students interviewed were able to solve the problem, while one-third of them arrived at a "full" understanding, worthy of S2 reasoning, after receiving training based on the mental models involved (confirming the insight made by Johnson-Laird et al., 1999, pp. 82–83).

Pedagogy of reasoning and the passage from S1 to S2

A long and well-established tradition of logicism, reinforced by Piaget's theories at the origins of experimental psychology of thinking, tends to favour S2 over S1. It stands that S2 is the realm of scientific and logical rationality, appropriated by man with difficulty. System 1 is ruled by intuition, by rough estimation and approximation. The latter is a more ordinary, milder, and more thoughtless realm that allows us to make rapid decisions without much mental effort, but where the short cuts are also sources of blindness and error. If this were indeed the case, the duty of every teacher, educator, and consultant would be to ferry their students from S1 to S2 as much as possible. Many dual-process thinking theorists today no longer believe this is so.

We have seen how Neisser had already outlined the features of dual processes, in the sense that the automatization of a process allowed another process to be carried out in parallel, "outside" consciousness, leaving room in working memory. In fact, if the solution to a problem is found, thanks to the use of S1, why bother with S2? Put in these terms, the question remains vague. I will now discuss the following example in order to clarify the question in operative terms. Let us consider the Monty Hall problem in a more manageable version, one easy to present in the classroom. All that is needed are three ordinary, nontransparent, plastic cups. Two hundred bank consultants, in 20 classrooms of 10 consultants each, were systematically interviewed by using various versions of this problem. The standard version is seemingly simple, even if tricky like the classic Monty Hall problem. The problem was presented as follows:

There are three cups in front of you.

I have placed a prize in only one of the cups. The other two are empty.

I know which cup holds the prize.

ADDRESSING ONE PERSON IN THE ROOM, I ASK HER TO:

Please choose a cup.

THE PERSON INDICATED CHOOSES A CUP.

In your opinion, what's the chance that the prize is in the cup you have chosen?

ANSWER (WITH WHICH EVERYONE AGREES):

One-third

Considering that I know where the prize is, I am going to show you that this cup (indicating one of the two cups not chosen by the person) is empty.

THE EXPERIMENTER TURNS OVER THE CUP AND REVEALS THAT IT IS EMPTY.

THEN HE ASKS:

Do you wish to switch your choice?

ANSWER GIVEN BY THE MAJORITY OF PERSONS:

I see no reason to. Now each of the two remaining cups has a 50% chance of containing the prize.

This standard version was presented in 20 classrooms. Even in the cases where one of the 10 people is doubtful or perplexed, the majority easily convince her that it is useless to switch cups. Almost everyone shares this misleading intuition. Very few are doubtful, and those who are do not usually know how to justify their perplexity. The following "facilitated" version was then presented:

There are three cups in front of you.

I have placed a prize in only one of the cups. The other two are empty.

I know which cup contains the prize.

ADDRESSING ONE PERSON, I ASK HER TO:

Please choose a cup.

THE PERSON INDICATED CHOOSES A CUP:

In your opinion, what's the chance that the prize is in the cup you have chosen?

ANSWER (WITH WHICH EVERYONE AGREES):

One-third

UP TO THIS POINT THIS VERSION IS IDENTICAL TO THE STANDARD VERSION.

HOWEVER, IT DIFFERS FROM HERE ONWARDS.

AT THIS POINT EACH OF THE CUPS REMAINING AFTER THE PERSON HAS MADE HER CHOICE ARE INDICATED.

I ASK THE CLASS WHAT THE CHANCES ARE THAT THE PRIZE IS IN EACH OF THE CUPS.

EVERYONE RESPONDS:

*One out of three for the cup that they have chosen, one out of three for one
of the other cups, and one out of three for the last remaining cup.*
EVERYONE AGREES WITH THIS OBVIOUS ANSWER.
WITH ONE HAND I NOW LIFT UP THE TWO CUPS NOT
CHOSEN AND ASK:
What is the chance that the prize is in the two cups I am holding in my
hand?
EVERYONE RESPONDS:
Two-thirds.
STILL HOLDING THE TWO CUPS IN MY HAND, I NOW PUT
THEM IN A BAG AND ASK:
What is the chance that the prize is in the bag?
EVERYONE RESPONDS, SURPRISED BY HOW EASY THE
QUESTION IS:
Two-thirds, as before!
AT THIS POINT I ASK WITH EMPHASIS:
Is there at least one empty cup in the bag?
EVERYONE RESPONDS:
Yes, of course, because only one cup contains the prize.
I NOW SLOWLY TAKE OUT THE EMPTY CUP FROM THE BAG
AND SHOW IT TO THE CLASS BY HOLDING IT UPSIDE DOWN
OVER THE BAG. AT THE SAME TIME I ASK THE FOLLOWING
CRUCIAL QUESTION:
I know where the prize is. If I take out the cup that I know is empty and I
show you that it is empty – in your opinion, does the two-thirds chance
that the bag holds the prize change?

To this final and crucial question, circa 80% of participants state that the
chances of the bag containing the prize do not change if the empty cup remains
inside the bag or if it is taken out and shown to them. The chances remain at
two-thirds. Whoever comprehends this point also realizes that it is better to
change their initial choice, given that their chances pass from one-third to two-
thirds. I explain, to those people who are uncertain, that I did nothing more
than show them the empty cup that was already empty in the bag.

With this easier and more fluent version, I obtain the same situation indicated in Table 11.1 by Krauss and Wang. The difference with my version is
that the two cases, corresponding to two-thirds, are not shown in drawings,
but are placed inside a bag, which groups them into a single lump!

The most interesting fact is not that this version often produces the correct
answer, but the absence of transfer which takes place between the correct
answer given for this version and the correct answer given for the standard
version presented previously. On average only 10% transfer is obtained
because the invariance between the two scenarios is not understood. The
absence of transfer characterizes both the standard-facilitated order of
presentation, as well as the opposite order of facilitated-standard. This result

demonstrates that the correct answer is often given without truly understanding the problem's logical structure, or at least without having understood the common structure in all of these versions, as should theoretically happen at the S2 level.

In conclusion, the task is made easier when the two cups not chosen are grouped together ($p = 2/3$), with a modification similar to that of Krauss and Wang's. Yet, unlike that which Krauss and Wang obtain with complex instructions, procedures, and training, I was unable to reach, with the two versions presented above, a significant percentage of transfer. This case constitutes further evidence for the usefulness of transfer as a criterion for distinguishing S1 and S2. This does not imply that the solutions given to the problems thanks to S2 are in any way "superior". On the contrary, having at one's disposal only one of the two systems, instead of a dual-thinking process, would translate not to stronger and more consistent reasoning, but to weaker reasoning.

> Heuristic processes [or System 1] set up *default* responses that will occur unless the analytic system [or System 2] intervenes to alter them. [. . . S1's] function is to deliver relevant content into consciousness on a continuous basis. What is relevant depends upon the attentional characteristics of the problem presented, the current goals that are being pursued and the relevant prior knowledge evoked by the context. The analytic system, or System 2, [. . .] adds a capacity for strategic and abstract thinking that is not possible at the heuristic [or S1] level. It [S2] is sequential and constrained by working memory capacity.
>
> (Evans, 2007a, pp. 19–20)

These theoretical conclusions made by Evans coincide with the three types of strategies used for making easier and more manageable those problems of reasoning psychology which, in their standard version, tend to be difficult:

- *fragmentation technique*: the problems, disjointed in their steps, are diluted over time in such a way that the questions posed by the experimenter (with respect to the standard version) allow us to underline the logical structure a bit at a time, without taxing the working memory. Examples: Monty Hall (Krauss & Wang, 2003), selection task (Legrenzi & Murino, 1974), THOG (Girotto & Legrenzi, 1989);
- *previous knowledge* used in various forms (e.g., prescriptive scenarios of the selection task: Johnson-Laird et al., 1972, realistic content in THOG, see Koenig et al., 2007);
- *change in the concentration of people's attention on the relevant aspects, crucial for obtaining the solution, through the elimination of any interference:* the facilitated versions of the Monty Hall problem presented here, the selection task (Sperber & Girotto, 2003), and many other cases presented by Evans (2007a).

It should also not be thought that dual thinking works in such a way that S1 always leads us astray, while S2 always provides correct answers (see Evans, 2007a, p. 22). Gerd Gigerenzer (2007), in his recent essay, aims to uphold exactly the opposite thesis! The fact is, more simply, that both systems are useful in different scenarios and contexts. In addition, if both S1 and S2 can derail us, the source of error is a different one:

- misleading tendency of S1: To selectively concentrate on information, codified at a preconscious level, as relevant;
- misleading tendency of S2: To remain focused on already activated mental models, with insufficient consideration of alternative possibilities.

As Evans points out, "Both of these are biases only in the sense of the disposition of our cognitive systems to operate in particular ways, rather than in a pejorative sense implying irrationality" (Evans, 2007a, p. 22).

Conclusions

These reflections on the functions of the dual-process system of human thinking, developed in relation to the results of the psychology of reasoning and in line with those put forward by Evans in his recent essay (2007a), could seem an exclusive exercise for a small number of specialists in the field. However, I believe that the questions do not concern only specialists. The more general theoretical connection is, first, with a currently popular debate triggered by evolutionary psychology. One cannot but agree with Dan Sperber and Vittorio Girotto (2003, p. 197) when they claim that the work undergone up to now in this field, for example, regarding sexual customs – as interesting as the subject is – only skims the higher cognitive processes (see also Badcock, 2000). The only exception involves the task of selection, which has come into fashion again in its "cost–benefit" versions (if you pay for an expensive stamp, you are allowed to seal the letter). Yet, as Sperber and Girotto show, this presumed exception is not supported by a detailed analysis of experimental data. The hypothesis, which is extremely "inflated", is that recent experimental work on the variations of the selection task demonstrate just how essential it is, from an evolutionistic viewpoint, to identify and punish those who violate the rules (Sperber & Girotto, 2003, pp. 222–223). Nevertheless, we cannot but hypothesize that the human mind has adapted to the multi-millennial events of our past as hunters and gatherers. That was our world for at least 85,000 years, until the birth, just a few thousand years ago, of sedentary agriculture, which happened almost independently in six different areas across the globe.

Let us suppose, as recent studies show, that findings do not support the idea that our millennial past was an arcadia "à la Rousseau" but, to the contrary, a Hobbesism as that of *bellum omnium contra omnes*. This dangerous lifestyle maintained an equilibrium, for at least 100,000 years, between land utilized for procuring food (in a world without agriculture) and the population quantity. In hostile scenarios, in which survival took place in small groups thanks to simple and shared mental models and to rapid decision making, the thinking strategies of S1 were more functional than those of S2. In fact, not only Gigerenzer's essay (2007), but also the brilliant bestseller by Malcolm Gladwell (2005), shows how important it is still today, even if probably less than in the past, to be provided with a system that allows for quick decision making, triggered by little crucial information, and carried out almost as if in automatic mode (Gigerenzer shows how often *less is more*).

Finally, it is important to mention a tradition of research that strives to connect the thinking style, acquired in the environment of a given culture, to the differences between S1 and S2 strategies of thinking, in the sense that a certain education in "rationality" may place emphasis on S2. More specifically, Nisbett, Peng, Choi, and Norenzayan (2001) maintained that Western education tends to diffuse an analytical style similar to the one that Evans described as S2. Naturally, the multi-millennial times of biology and, at best, the secular ones of culture, are put on two temporal scales whose orders of greatness are completely different. However, if we imagine a "pedagogy of reasoning" to be possible, it is also plausible to suppose that a massive education in one direction has its own effects. Recent attempts have been made to conciliate these two temporal scales, without denying the different concepts of "adaptation" implicit in them both (see for example, the exhaustive review by Yama, Nishioka, Horishita, Kawasaki, & Taniguchi, 2007).

Can we then limit ourselves to celebrating the richness of the human mind, capable of passing to S2 when S1 proves insufficient? There is no doubt that only thanks to S2 have we been able to consciously construct science, technology and the whole arena of knowledge that makes up our contemporary world. Yet history is not only this. The picture is complex with respect to this idyllic and self-celebratory synthesis. Perhaps, although we will never know for certain, the integration of S1 and S2 functioned well until some centuries ago. What we are sure of today is that S1 often leads us off track, and at times in a systematic way.

Consider the choices for material survival. When we were hunters and gatherers, a value function, which propelled us to take large risks when in adverse situations and to remain prudent when in satisfactory ones, was plausibly "adaptive". Today, however, we can go "below zero", in the sense that an asset can have a negative psychological value (if it is worth less now than when we purchased it). The value function, which was once *always* functional (today only in certain contexts), pushes us, for example, to hold onto the financial entities on which we have made a loss, to sell those on which we have made a profit, and to enter and exit the financial markets with systematically incorrect *timing*.

Another example is the usefulness of fragmenting complex problems into subproblems so that they may be tackled one at a time (not just a technique for making the problems invented by psychologists of reasoning easier, see above). If we fragment complex problems, decentralizing the tasks, we find ourselves faced with a *trade-off* between the decomposition of the problem itself and the efficient solutions (see Marengo, Dosi, Legrenzi, & Pasquali, 2000). This result of Marengo et al. (2000) was obtained by resorting to "artificial experiments". Perhaps it would be possible to try to equip agents with different systems of thinking, such as systems S1 and S2, and even with certain possible intermediate variants.

In more general terms, it should be observed that economists would appreciate if experimental psychologists provided them with a unitary and simple model of human rationality and its limits, similar to the one they themselves hypothesize in theory. If psychologists could indeed do this, some economists would be ready to correct their own assumptions (see Fudenberg, 2006; Wilkinson, 2008). However, what they find, according to them, is a muddle, precisely because, as Evans clearly demonstrates (2007a), S1 is not a unitary system but a diversified network of heuristics. This makes a simple correction of classical assumptions very difficult and we are obliged to fall back on the less elegant "behavioural finance" which presents itself like a *bricolage*. For precisely this reason it is plausible that in the future the methodology of artificial experiments in this field of research will be enlarged so as to integrate laboratory experiments. Let us try to imagine an artificial experiment in which man, the product of a slow natural evolution, can be artificially readjusted by a thoughtful divinity concerned with our future. Probably, in environments like those of today, S2 would have a more relevant role than S1. Yet, in today's technological world, scenarios have survived in which we must make instant decisions, by ourselves or with a few other people, as once used to happen in the times of our hunter–gatherer ancestors. Unfortunately, we find that the present-day world has become too complicated at times for our S1 system, formatted in different contexts and assigned to rapid and intuitive decisions. This type of decision making was once applied in simple scenarios and not in complex ones like those of today, where S1 leads us off track and generates, among other things, car accidents, airplane, and military accidents (Klein, 1998). If S1 finds itself in difficulty, the same S2 system does not always do well either: it contents itself with what S1 passes it and ends up getting stuck by the "framework" of the problems and neglecting interesting alternatives (Legrenzi, Girotto, & Johnson-Laird, 1993).

In conclusion, a dual-process system would be an invaluable treasure, a great skill of the human mind, if it weren't for the fact that S1 and S2 find themselves immersed in the often complex worlds of today, to the point of preventing good coordination between the two systems and the surrounding environment. Understanding how the systems work is, thus, indispensible for proceeding, step by step, towards an efficient pedagogy of reasoning.

References

Badcock, C. (2000). *Evolutionary psychology*. Cambridge, UK: Polity.

Bruner, J. S. (1964). *The process of education*. Harvard, MA: Harvard University Press. (Original work published 1960)

Evans, J. St B. T. (2007a). *Hypothetical thinking. Dual processes in reasoning and judgment*. Hove, UK: Psychology Press.

Evans, J. St B. T. (2007b). On the resolution of conflict in dual process theories of reasoning, *Thinking & Reasoning*, *13*, 321–339.

Evans, J. St B. T., Legrenzi, P., & Girotto, V. (1999). The influence of linguistic form on reasoning: The case of matching bias, *Quarterly Journal of Experimental Psychology*, *52A*, 185–216.

Evans, J. St B. T., & Lynch, J. S. (1973). Matching bias in the selection task. *British Journal of Psychology*, *64*, 391–397.

Fudenberg, D. (2006). Advancing beyond advances in behavioral economics. *Journal of Economic Literature*, *14*, 694–711.

Gigerenzer, G. (2007). *Gut feelings*. London: Viking.

Girotto, V., & Legrenzi, P. (1989). Mental representation and hypothetico-deductive reasoning: The case of the THOG problem. *Psychological Research*, *51*, 129–135.

Gladwell, M. (2005). *Blink. The power of thinking without thinking*. London: Allen Lane.

Griggs, R. A., Platt, R. D., Newstead, S. E., & Jackson, S. L. (1998). Attentional factors in a disjunctive reasoning task. *Thinking & Reasoning*, *4*, 1–14.

James, W. (1892). A plea for psychology as a "Nature Science". *Philosophical Review*, *1*, 146–153.

Johnson-Laird, P. N., Legrenzi, P., Girotto, V., Legrenzi, M., & Caverni, J. P. (1999). Naive probability: A mental model theory of extensional reasoning. *Psychological Review*, *106*, 62–88.

Johnson-Laird, P. N., Legrenzi, P., & Legrenzi, M. (1972). Reasoning and a sense of reality. *British Journal of Psychology*, *63*, 395–400.

Klein, G. (1998). *Sources of power*. Cambridge, MA: MIT Press.

Koenig, C. S., Platt, R. D., & Griggs, R. A. (2007). Using dual-process theory and analogical transfer to explain facilitation on a hypothetico-deductive reasoning task. *Psychological Research*, *71*, 495–502.

Krauss, S., & Wang, X. T. (2003). The psychology of the Monty Hall problem: Discovering psychological mechanisms for solving a tenacious brain teaser. *Journal of Experimental Psychology: General*, *132*, 3–22.

Legrenzi, P. (1970). *Relations between language and reasoning about deductive rule*. In G. B. Flores D'Arcais & W. J. Levelt (Eds.), *Advances in psycholinguistics*. Amsterdam: North Holland.

Legrenzi, P. (1971). Discovery as a means to understanding. *Quarterly Journal of Experimental Psychology*, *23*, 417–422.

Legrenzi, P., Girotto, V., & Johnson-Laird, P. N. (1993). Focusing in reasoning and decision making. *Cognition*, *49*, 37–66.

Legrenzi, P., & Murino, M. (1974). Falsification at the pre-operational level. *Italian Journal of Psychology*, *3*, 363–368.

Marengo, L., Dosi, G., Legrenzi, P., & Pasquali, C. (2000). The structure of problem-solving knowledge and the structure of organizations. *Industrial and Corporate Change*, *9*, 757–788.

Neisser, U. (1963). Decision-time without reaction-time: Experiments in visual scanning. *American Journal of Psychology*, *76*, 336–385.

Newstead, S. E., & Griggs, R. A. (1992). Thinking about THOG: Sources of error in a deductive reasoning problem. *Psychological Research*, *54*, 299–305.

Nisbett, R., Peng, K., Choi, I., & Norenzayan, A. (2001). Culture and system of thought: Holistic versus analytic cognition. *Psychological Review*, *108*, 291–310.

Oaksford, M., & Chater, N. (2007). *Bayesian rationality*. Oxford: Oxford University Press.

Selvin, S. (1975). A problem in probability. *American Statistician*, *29*, 67.

Singley, M. K., & Anderson, J. R. (1989). *The transfer of cognitive skill*. Cambridge, MA: Harvard University Press.

Sperber, D., & Girotto, V. (2003). Does the selection task detect cheater-detection. In K. Sterelny & J. Fitness (Ed.), *From mating to mentality. Evaluating evolutionary psychology*. Hove, UK: Psychology Press.

Stanovich, K. E. (1999). *Who is rational? Studies of individual differences in reasoning*. Mahwah, NJ: Lawrence Erlbaum Associates, Inc.

Stanovich, K. E. (2004). *The robot's rebellion: Finding meaning in the age of Darwin*. Chicago: Chicago University Press.

vos Savant, M. (1990). Ask Marilyn. *Parade Magazine*, 9 September, p. 15.

Wason, P. C. (1966). *Reasoning*. In B. M. Foss (Ed.), *New horizons in psychology I* (pp. 106–137). Harmondsworth, UK: Penguin.

Wason, P. C., & Brooks, P. G. (1979). THOG: The anatomy of a problem. *Psychological Research*, *41*, 79–90.

Wilkinson, N. (2008), *An introduction to behavioral economics*. New York: Palgrave Macmillan.

Yama, H., Nishioka, M., Horishita, T., Kawasaki, Y., & Taniguchi, J. (2007). A dual process model for cultural differences in thought. *Mind & Society*, *6*, 143–172.

12 A conjunction of fallacies

What different types of causal conjunction error reveal about dual processes for thinking

Aidan Feeney and Aimée Crisp

University of Durham

As well as inventing or popularizing some of the most important paradigms in our field, Jonathan Evans has also investigated paradigms devised by other researchers. For example, Jonathan and his colleagues have made important empirical and theoretical contributions to our understanding of base rate neglect, one of the phenomena first demonstrated by Kahneman and Tversky (see Evans, Handley, Over, & Perham, 2002; Evans, Handley, Perham, Over, & Thompson, 2000). With one of the authors of this chapter he has investigated the related phenomenon of pseudodiagnosticity (see Evans, Venn, & Feeney, 2002; Feeney, Evans, & Clibbens, 2000; Feeney, Evans, & Venn, 2008), first demonstrated by Doherty and colleagues (see Doherty, Mynatt, Tweney, & Schiavo, 1979). Our subject here will be the conjunction fallacy, another phenomenon explored by Kahneman and Tversky (see Tversky & Kahneman, 1983). Given its notoriety it is somewhat surprising that Jonathan has not worked on the conjunction fallacy, although he has recently given a dual-process account of people's tendency to violate the law of conjunction (see Evans, 2007a, pp. 139–141). It is lucky that Jonathan has not been able to study everything, as this has left work for the rest of us to do, and conjunction fallacies have been studied experimentally by others working with the dual-process framework (see Sloman, Over, Slovak, & Stibel, 2003; Stanovich & West, 1998; De Neys, 2006a). In this chapter we will describe our own recent work on a variety of conjunction fallacies.

We have had two aims in our work on conjunction fallacies. First, we wished to examine causal versions of the fallacy. Many experiments have been carried out on the fallacy, but relatively few of them have investigated the causal variant that Tversky and Kahneman described in their seminal paper (Tversky & Kahneman, 1983). Second, we wished to use the causal conjunction fallacy to extend our understanding of the dual-process account of thinking. In particular, we wished to consider the challenge for that account posed by the effects of causal knowledge on reasoning. For all the attention that causality has received recently in the literature, there have been few attempts to give a dual process specification of causal thinking (for an important exception see Fugelsang & Thompson, 2003). Yet recent findings challenge the conventionally accepted dichotomy between contextualized heuristic processes and abstract analytical processes, suggesting that the latter can no longer be considered strictly decontextualized. We suggest that causal knowledge can interact with both reasoning processes. As demonstrated by our first set of studies on the causal conjunction fallacy, at the heuristic end of the reasoning spectrum, causal knowledge can bias the strength of the initial reasoning output. In contrast, our second set of studies on a different causal variant of the fallacy suggests that causal knowledge can also serve as input to contextualized analytical reasoning. Thus, it appears that some aspects of causal knowledge result in a heuristic response, whereas other aspects are dealt with via an analytical process. Prompted by these results, we will offer some very basic speculations as to how dual-process theories might capture the different effects of causal knowledge on reasoning.

The conjunction fallacy

Tversky and Kahneman described two versions of the conjunction fallacy in their seminal paper. The most famous of these is the M→A variant where participants are presented with a pen picture of an individual and a series of statements that they must place in rank order of probability. The target statement A is unrepresentative of the stereotype evoked by the pen picture, but an additional feature B is representative. Thus, people rank the conjunction of A & B as more probable than the target statement A. The most famous version of this variant of the fallacy consists of a description of Linda who is ". . . 31 years old, single, outspoken, and very bright. At university, she studied philosophy. As a student, she was deeply concerned with issues of discrimination and social justice, and she participated in anti-nuclear demonstrations." Participants are then asked to rank order a number of statements in terms of their probability. These include the statements (A) "Linda is a bank teller", (B) "Linda is a feminist", and (A&B) "Linda is a feminist and a bank teller". In between and within participant designs, Tversky and Kahneman observed that people ranked the conjunction of features as being more probable than the single feature (A). They interpreted this as a fallacy because $p(a\&b)$ can never be greater than $p(a)$ or $p(b)$.

The large literature on the conjunction fallacy primarily concerns the M→A variant. The size of that literature has been caused, to some degree at least, by disagreements about the status of the conjunction fallacy. Many authors have sought to reinterpret the tendency to rank the conjunction as more probable than the single feature A as being due to the pragmatics of the task (e.g., Dulany & Hilton, 1991; Hertwig, Benz, & Krauss, 2008; Macchi, 1995). Under such a reading, the effects described in the literature are not evidence of irrationality, but of sensible reasoning given everyday, conversational interpretations of experimental instructions and natural language connectives. On the other side are researchers who, convinced that the conjunction fallacy is real, argue that it can be used to help us make inferences about human rationality (see Crupi, Fitelson, & Tentori, 2008; Sides, Osherson, Bonini, & Viale, 2002; Stanovich, 1999). As we do not wish to make claims about the nature of rationality on the basis of our experiments, we will have little to say about this debate. Instead, we will focus on what conjunction fallacies can tell us about the processes involved in thinking.

Our interest throughout will be in the causal conjunction fallacy, the second variant described by Tversky and Kahneman. This version of the fallacy consists of a target event B that is made more likely by the addition of a causal event A, so that people consider the conjunction of A&B to be more probable than B on its own. For example, Tversky and Kahneman showed that people thought that Mr F., a participant selected by chance to be included in a representative sample of males from British Columbia of all ages and occupations, was more likely to have had one or more heart attacks and be over 55 than to have had one or more heart attacks. The causal conjunction fallacy has received far less attention than the M→A variant, and the results that have appeared in the literature are mixed. For example, Thüring and Jungerman (1990) found that manipulating the presence or absence of a causal link between A and B had no effect on rates of the fallacy. Fisk and Pidgeon (1998) on the other hand did find that the presence of a conditional relationship between A and B increased rates of the fallacy, but did not find a correlation between the strength of the conditional relationship and rates of the fallacy. However, Fabre, Caverni, and Jungermann (1995) contrasted pairs of events where a causal relationship was perceived to be "frequent" with pairs where the relationship was only "possible", and observed significantly greater rates of the fallacy in the first case. Our initial interest in the causal conjunction fallacy was to examine whether the strength of the causal relationship perceived to exist between the conjuncts would predict the rate at which participants committed the conjunction fallacy. To see why this prediction falls out of the dual process account of the fallacy (see De Neys 2006a; Stanovich & West, 1998), we must briefly review the dual-process framework.

Dual processes for thinking and the conjunction fallacy

There are now many dual-process accounts of thinking, in a variety of domains, and each different theory makes slightly different claims about the characteristics of the two processes that are supposed to enable our thoughts (for a recent review see Evans, 2008). Common to most accounts are the claims that Type 1 or heuristic processes are fast, parallel, and independent of general cognitive resources such as memory and IQ, whereas Type 2 or analytic processes are slow, sequential, symbol manipulating, and dependent on general cognitive resources. In addition, until very recently, just about everyone in the field of reasoning appeared to agree with Stanovich (1999) that if there are two processes for reasoning then one of them is sensitive to context whereas the other operates on decontextualized representations of reasoning problems.

A difficult problem currently faced by dual-process researchers is specifying how these two processes relate to one another. Evans (2007b) has outlined three possible relationships: the systems operate in parallel; the default heuristic system is intervened upon by the analytic system; or a decision is made at the start of the reasoning process about which type of process to engage. On the basis of their work on base rate neglect, De Neys and Glumicic (2008) have suggested that when the processes give rise to different responses, reasoners are aware of the conflict, regardless of whether they respond heuristically or analytically. This supports a parallel competitive account of the relationship between the processes. Recent fMRI evidence (De Neys, Vartanian, & Goel, 2008) suggests that participants who neglect the base rate have less activation in prefrontal areas associated with inhibitory control than do participants who take the base rate into account. Thus, the systems may operate in parallel, but in order for analytic processes to dominate, a response based on heuristic processing must be inhibited.

The conjunction fallacy can easily be explained in terms of failure to inhibit a heuristic response based on an assessment of the similarity between each of the descriptions in the task and, in the case of the Linda problem, the stereotype evoked by the pen-picture, or in the causal variant, the participant's causal model of the world. Such an explanation is compatible with both the parallel competitive and the default interventionist accounts outlined by Evans. This account is also compatible with findings that people higher in general cognitive resources are less susceptible to the fallacy (Stanovich & West, 1998), and that compromising people's analytic resources by limiting their response time or burdening their working memory (De Neys, 2006a) increases rates of the fallacy.

The prediction that for the causal variant of the task, the strength of the causal relationship between the conjoined events should determine the rate at which people commit the fallacy, falls nicely out of this inhibition account. The strength of the causal relationship between the conjuncts is likely to determine the strength of the heuristic response, and the ability of the analytical system to successfully inhibit or intervene upon that response will decline as the strength of the output from heuristic processes increases.

Causal knowledge causes problems for the dual-process account

Although finding that rates of the conjunction fallacy increase linearly with the strength of the perceived causal relationship between the conjuncts would support a dual-process account of thinking, such a finding could also be explained by other accounts. The dual-process account would be that strong causal relations lead to strong heuristic responses which are more difficult to inhibit. However, there is evidence that analytic processes may also reason about causal content. For example, Nestler, Blank, and von Collani (2008) have argued that the hindsight bias is caused by causal reasoning processes that make the outcome, once revealed to participants, seem more likely because of potential causes of that outcome present in the description of the problem. They show that the hindsight bias is reduced when participants are given a concurrent secondary task. Clearly, the hindsight bias is normatively inappropriate, yet the fact that it may be reduced under conditions designed to compromise analytic processes, suggests that those analytic processes, via causal reasoning, are responsible for its occurrence.

A conceptually similar finding has been reported by Verscheuren, Schaeken, and d'Ydewalle (2005) who showed that different measures predict inferences from causal conditionals depending on whether participants have sufficient time in which to reason. Thus, probabilistic assessments of the conditional relationship predict inferences drawn under time pressure, whereas people's ability to generate alternative causes and disabling conditions predicts nonspeeded reasoning. Importantly, the rate of logically valid inferences may be increased or decreased by a consideration of alternative causes and disablers. Here again is a case of non-normative reasoning due to output of the analytic system operating on contextualized, causal content rather than on a decontextualized representation of problem structure. Broadly similar findings have also been reported by De Neys, Schaeken, and d'Ydewalle (2005).

The evidence we have just described leads to an alternative prediction about why beliefs about the strength of the causal relationship between the conjuncts might predict rates of the conjunction fallacy: it is possible that people use analytic rather than heuristic processes to evaluate the strength of the causal relationship. Such a possibility would also be consistent with the recent claim by Hertwig and colleagues (2008) that the *and* in the A→B variant is understood as communicating a causal relation between A and B that leads some participants to estimate $P(B/A)$ rather than $P(A\&B)$ (but see Tversky & Kahneman, 1983, pp 308–309). Hertwig et al. show that participants who do not commit the fallacy overwhelmingly prefer a logical interpretation of the connective whereas those who commit the fallacy tend to give a causal reading of *and*. They argue that their findings mean that no conclusions can be drawn about rationality on the basis of causal conjunction fallacies. Our concern here is with the possibility that a pragmatically enriched interpretation of *and* might lead people to use their analytic resources to give estimates of $P(B/A)$. Based on this explanation one can also predict a correlation between the strength of the causal relationship between the conjuncts and susceptibility to the conjunction fallacy. As perceptions of causal strength increase so too will estimates of $P(B/A)$ and hence the likelihood that $P(B/A)$ will be judged to be greater than $P(B)$. This alternative explanation was addressed by an experiment in which we manipulated concurrent load.

Two experiments on the A→B paradigm

In the first experiment in this series (for a complete description, see Crisp and Feeney, 2009) 51 participants rated the probability of nine A→B conjunctions, each of which was presented alongside the single event B. Three of the conjunctions possessed a strong causal link, three were weakly related and three were unrelated. For example, 1, 2, and 3 below are strongly, weakly, and unrelated conjunctions based on the same scenario.

> The percentage of British households with a computer will increase by at least 25% and World Wide Web usage will double within the next year.   (1)
> The income of British households will rise more than average and World Wide Web usage will double within the next year.   (2)
> The percentage of British households with three cars will decrease slightly next year and World Wide Web usage will double within the next year.   (3)

Although strength was manipulated within participants, participants saw only one conjunction from each scenario. The experimental materials were interspersed with nine distracter problems and all problems were presented in one of three different random orders. The order in which participants read about the conjunction and the single event was counterbalanced and for each description participants produced a percentage likelihood judgement.

The difference in perceived causal strength between the strongly and weakly related conjunctions was validated in the pretest for an earlier experiment in which a separate group of 20 participants rated the strength of the causal link between all of the weak and strong causes and their corresponding effects on a 9-point scale. As for the main experiment, no participant saw both the strongly and weakly related conjunctions from the same scenario. The mean rating of causal strength for strongly related conjunctions (mean = 6.1) was significantly greater than the mean for weakly related conjunctions (mean = 4.5). Because we did not pretest perceptions of causal strength for the unrelated conjunctions used in the main experiment, we asked the participants in that experiment, once they had provided all of their probability ratings, to assess the strength of the causal relationship between the conjunctions. The results of this post-test confirmed our manipulation of causal strength with weakly related conjunctions (mean rating = 5.4) rated to have a stronger causal link than unrelated conjunctions (mean = 3). Strongly related conjunctions were rated as possessing a stronger causal link (mean = 6.4) than both of the other types of conjunction. The main effect of causal strength was significant, $F(1.79, 89.23) = 62.48, p = .0005$, as were all of the post hoc comparisons between means.

The results of the main experiment revealed, as we had predicted, that conjunction fallacies increased when the causal relation between the conjoined events was perceived to be strong. For strongly related conjunctions A&B was rated more probable than the single event B on 51% of trials. For weakly related conjunctions the fallacy rate was 35%, and 24% for the unrelated conjunctions. The main effect of strength was significant, $F(1.72, 82.4) = 11.46, p < .001$, as were all of the post hoc comparisons between mean proportions.

Because of the way we had operationalized the causal strength variable, our design contained 27 individual conjunctions (nine scenarios with three conjunctions each). To examine the relationship between causal strength and susceptibility to the fallacy we computed the correlation between ratings of causal strength from the post-test and the number of participants who succumbed to the fallacy on each problem. The correlation was highly significant, $r(27) = .67, p < .001$. That is, 45% of the variation in the number of participants susceptible to the fallacy on each problem was accounted for by perceptions of the strength of the causal relationship between the constituent events.

The perceived strength of the causal relationship between the conjoined events predicts the rate at which individual conjunctions lead to the causal conjunction fallacy. This finding is consistent with a dual-process account where in order to prevent a fallacious response, analytic processes must inhibit the response generated by heuristic processes. In other words, as the heuristic response becomes more compelling with increases in the strength of the causal relation between the conjuncts, so analytic processes become less likely to successfully inhibit it.

An alternative account of these results is that participants use analytic processes to estimate either $P(A\&B)$ or $P(B/A)$. If participants are estimating $P(B/A)$ then we would expect to observe the correlation that was found in our first experiment, but participants' responses need not be judged fallacious (see Hertwig et al., 2008). However, if participants turn out to be committing a conjunction fallacy because they estimate $P(A\&B)$ using analytic processes, then such a finding might be difficult for certain variants of the dual-process theory (e.g., Stanovich, 1999) to explain. That is because certain versions of dual-process theory suppose that analytic processes operate on decontextualized representations of problem structure, leading to normatively correct responding. As we have seen earlier, other biases in thinking (see Nestler et al., 2008) appear to rely on effortful processes in reasoning about causal relations. Perhaps this is also the case for the causal conjunction fallacy. To rule out both of these possibilities we carried out a second experiment where we manipulated the presence or absence of a secondary task.

Our dual-process account of the causal conjunction fallacy predicts interactive effects of manipulations of secondary tasks and causal strength. We have argued that rates of the causal conjunction fallacy increase with the perceived strength of the causal link between the conjuncts. We have suggested that this is because analytic processes are less able to control the more compelling heuristic output that results from conjunctions containing a strong causal link. If we burden analytic processes by the imposition of a secondary task load (for earlier use of this method in a dual-process framework, see De Neys, 2006a, 2006b) then this account predicts that analytic processes should be even less able to control compelling heuristic output and we might expect to see an increase in rates of the conjunction fallacy. However, the effect of secondary load should be bigger for conjunctions where the causal link is strong rather than weak. As fewer analytic resources are required to control heuristic output in the weak case, then the imposition of a secondary load should have smaller effects here.

It is difficult to see how an account of the findings from our first experiment that claim that people use analytic processes to estimate $P(A\&B)$ or $P(B/A)$ would predict an interaction here. Instead, if the conjunction fallacy is produced by analytic processes, then we might expect to observe fewer fallacies once those processes are burdened by a secondary task.

To test these competing predictions we asked 40 participants to rate the likelihood of eight A→B conjunctions and of B alone. For half of these conjunctions the events described had a strong perceived causal link while the remainder had a weak causal link. The materials were identical to those used in the first experiment, but we did not include unrelated conjunctions. Participants in this experiment saw only one conjunction from each scenario, and the problems, which were presented via PowerPoint, were interspersed with an equal number of distracter problems. To manipulate secondary load, we asked half of our participants to memorise a 4 × 4 dot matrix pattern presented for 1000 ms before they rated the conjunction and the corresponding single event.

As before we found a significant main effect of causal strength, $F(1, 36) = 24.89$, $p < .001$, so that the proportion of fallacious responses was higher when the conjuncts had a strong causal link than when the causal link was weak. The interaction between secondary load and causal strength about which we had made predictions was also significant, $F(1, 36) = 4.08$, $p < .05$. Post hoc tests on this interaction revealed that a secondary load led to increased rates of the fallacy for strongly related conjuncts (loaded mean = 0.64; unloaded mean = 0.43) but not for weakly related conjuncts (loaded mean = 0.34; unloaded mean = 0.30).

Finally, we collected post-test ratings of causal strength in this experiment that verified our manipulation of causal strength. Across all 16 individual problems (two different conjunctions from each of eight scenarios), the correlation between the number of people susceptible to the fallacy and the strength of the perceived causal link between the conjuncts was significant, $r(16) = .58$, $p < .02$.

The results of the second experiment replicated the effects of causal strength observed in our first experiment and confirmed a prediction, derived from a dual-process account of those effects, about the effects of secondary load. The effects of load are greater for conjunctions whose constituents are perceived to have a strong causal link than for those perceived to have a weak causal link. Because the heuristic output is more compelling in the strong case, the imposition of a secondary load makes it even less likely that the analytic system will be able to inhibit a heuristic response. Importantly, this interaction is not predicted by an account claiming that people are reasoning analytically about the causal relation between the conjuncts. It is also difficult to see how a conditional probability justification of the conjunction fallacy (see Hertwig et al., 2008) would account for these results. To sum up, this first set of studies suggests that causal knowledge can determine the strength of the heuristic response and thus the ease with which an analytical process might intervene upon or inhibit this response.

A different kind of conjunction fallacy

Since Tversky and Kahneman's original paper, causal conjunction fallacies have been discovered in a range of reasoning tasks. For example, Legrenzi and Johnson-Laird (2005) have shown that when explaining a contradiction between an inference from a conditional and a fact they have learned about the world, people think an explanation for the contradiction that specifies a cause and effect is more probable than explanations specifying only the cause or only the effect. With our goal of examining the implications of causality for the dual-process framework, we have investigated yet another causal conjunction fallacy. As we shall see, in sharp contrast with the results of our experiments on the A→B fallacy, the interesting effects of causal knowledge on this variant of the fallacy appear to be mediated by analytic rather than heuristic processes.

Medin, Coley, Storms, and Hayes (2003) have described evidence for two category-based conjunction fallacies. In a category-based argument, participants learn that members of one or more categories possess some property and are asked how likely it is that members of some other category (or categories) possess the same property (for reviews of the literature on category-based induction, see Feeney & Heit, 2007). In earlier work, we have considered whether several of the phenomena of category-based induction may be explained in terms of dual-process theory (see Feeney 2007a, 2007b; Feeney, Crisp, & Wilburn, 2008). Here we will argue that category-based conjunction fallacies may also be considered in dual process terms.

To demonstrate a category-based conjunction fallacy by property reinforcement, Medin et al. (2003) presented their participants with arguments such as 1, 2, and 3 in Table 12.1. Medin et al. observed that the average strength rating assigned to the arguments with just one category in the conclusion (1 and 2) was significantly less than the average rating assigned to the conjunctive arguments (3). This, of course, is a conjunction fallacy, which Medin et al. explained by virtue of the extra category making more salient the common superordinate to which all of the categories in the argument belong. Medin et al. demonstrated a category-based causal conjunction fallacy using arguments like 4, 5, and 6 presented in Table 12.1. Once

Table 12.1 Example arguments, similar to those used by Medin et al. (2003) to demonstrate category reinforcement and causal conjunction fallacies in category-based induction

Set 1: Category reinforcement		

(1) Chickens have property X1
    Therefore, cows have
    property X1
	(2) Chickens have property X1
	    Therefore, pigs have
	    property X1
		(3) Chickens have property X1
		    Therefore, cows and pigs
		    have property X1

Set 2: Causal		

(4) Single Distant
    Lead has property X3
    Therefore, plumbers have
    property X3
	(5) Single Near
	    Lead has property X3
	    Therefore, pipes have
	    property X3
		(6) Conjunction
		    Lead has property X3
		    Therefore, pipes and
		    plumbers have property X3

again, the average strength rating for arguments with two categories in the conclusion was significantly higher than for arguments with only one conclusion category. Medin et al. attributed this finding to the presence of an extra category making more salient the causal mechanism by which the property might be transmitted from the premise category to the conclusion categories.

Medin et al. compared strength ratings for conjunctive arguments to the average of the strength ratings for the two single conclusion category arguments. Feeney, Shafto, and Dunning (2007) showed that if the strength ratings assigned to the single conclusion category arguments are disaggregated, then the fallacy by category reinforcement may be seen to differ from the causal fallacy. Whereas in the category reinforcement case, both (1) and (2) differ significantly from (3), only the comparison between (4) and (6) was significant in the causal case. We termed arguments such as (4) as distant because the causal mechanism that might underlie projection of a property from lead to plumbers requires that participants infer the involvement of pipes. We termed arguments such as (5) near because there is a more direct causal relationship between lead and pipes. We observed a conjunction fallacy over 50% of the time when we compared strength ratings for distant arguments such as (4) with ratings for conjunctive arguments, and only 19% of the time when near arguments like (5) were compared with conjunctive arguments.

There is an obvious dual-process account of these findings. For category reinforcement problems, there is always a conflict between the heuristic and analytic responses, with the non-normative heuristic response being strengthened by the addition of a third category from the same superordinate as the other two. However, some individuals manage to inhibit a response based on heuristic output and give instead an analytic response, based on the law of conjunction. In the causal near case we observe very low rates of the fallacy because there is no conflict between the output of the two processes. Heuristic processes favour arguments like (5) over arguments like (6) because the causal mechanism is more straightforward in the first case than in the second.

Analytic processes, on the other hand, also favour arguments like (5), but on the basis of the law of conjunction. In the distant case, there is a conflict. Heuristic processes favour arguments like (6) over arguments like (4) because the causal mechanism is more salient in the former case. This preference conflicts with the output of the analytic system that prefers argument (4) over argument (6) on the basis of the law of conjunction. Many participants in Feeney et al.'s study either did not detect this conflict, or failed to resolve it (see De Neys & Glumicic, 2008; De Neys et al., 2008) and hence succumbed to the fallacy on 50% of trials.

We tested the standard dual-process account of category-based conjunction fallacies in the first two experiments in this series. Each experiment used a different method to compromise analytic processing. We reasoned that compromising analytic processes should always lead to an increase in rates of the conjunction fallacy except when the two processes are said not to be in conflict. Thus, we expected conjunction fallacies to be more frequent in every case except when ratings for causal near arguments are compared with ratings for the corresponding conjunctive arguments. We have argued that the low rates of the fallacy observed in this case are as a result of an absence of conflict between the outputs from the two processes. In the absence of a conflict, analytic processes are not required to inhibit heuristic output, and so compromising analytic processes should not result in an increased rate of the fallacy.

Before we briefly describe these experiments, it is worth considering an alternative dual-process account of the category-based conjunction fallacy. As we have just seen, that variant of the fallacy entails participants judging arguments like those from lead to pipes and plumbers as stronger than those from lead to plumbers. Under the standard dual-process account of this finding, people avoid the fallacy because they inhibit a heuristic response based on a compelling causal mechanism, in favour of an analytic response based on the logical structure of the problem. This account is consistent with versions of dual-process theory; which equate analytic processing over decontextualized or abstracted representations with normatively correct responding (e.g., Epstein, Donovan, & Denes-Raj, 1999; Stanovich, 1999). As we have seen however, there is evidence that non-normative responses can result from effortful processes reasoning about the causal structure of the problem (see De Neys et al., 2005; Nestler et al., 2008; Verschueren et al., 2005). This has prompted Evans (2007a) to argue that analytic processes can take contextualized representations as input. An alternative dual-process account of the causal conjunction fallacy observed in the distant case is that people who avoid this variant of the fallacy do so by using effortful reasoning processes to complete the causal mechanism that links grass and humans; that is, by inferring the involvement of cows. Once they have done this, arguments such as (4) are as strong as conjunctive arguments such as (6) and the fallacy is avoided. The third experiment in the series arbitrated between standard and alternative dual-process accounts of the category-based causal conjunction fallacy.

Testing the standard dual-process account of category-based conjunction fallacies

We tested a standard dual-process account of category-based conjunction fallacies by examining the effect of concurrent memory load and speeded responding on rates of the fallacy. Both the standard and our alternative dual-process accounts predict that these manipulations should increase fallacious responding when the outputs of the two systems are in conflict. Thus, we should find increased fallacious responding in every case except for causal near arguments.

In the first experiment in this series, 36 inductive arguments were presented in random order to 56 participants (for a full description of these experiments, see Crisp, Feeney, & Shafto, 2009). Half of the participants were encouraged to respond after 1 s and half could not respond until 15 s after the argument had appeared on the screen (analysis of reaction times showed that mean reaction times were no greater than 5 s for any of the speeded conditions in this experiment). Eighteen of the arguments tested for the fallacy by category reinforcement and 18 for the causal fallacy. Each group of 18 comprised six scenarios, each of which was used to produce three arguments. For example, arguments (1)–(3) in Table 12.1 were generated from a categorical reinforcement scenario and arguments (4)–(6) from a causal scenario. Each set of three arguments consisted of two single conclusion arguments and one conjunctive argument. In the causal case one of these single arguments was distant (e.g., lead to plumbers) and one was near (e.g., lead to pipes). There was no corresponding difference, due to distance or any other variable, between the two single conclusion arguments formed from each categorical reinforcement scenario. Nevertheless, to give the categorical reinforcement materials the greatest chance of behaving like the causal materials, we designated single arguments as *strong* or *weak* depending on which received the highest average strength rating. Participants rated the strength of all arguments on a 9-point scale (by pressing a button on a 9-button button-box) and the dependent variable was the proportion of trials (out of six) in which participants committed a conjunction fallacy.

The fallacy rates for causal distant, causal near, categorical strong and categorical weak problems presented under speeded and delayed conditions, are to be seen in Figure 12.1. Separate 2×2 mixed design ANOVAS on causal and categorical materials confirmed the predictions we made at the outset. Thus, for the categorical materials where we predicted that heuristic and analytic processes would be in conflict, there was a significant main effect of time, $F(1, 54) = 8.372$, $p = .005$, so that participants committed the conjunction fallacy more often under speeded conditions. Neither the main effect of strength, nor its interaction with time, was significant.

For the causal materials on the other hand we observed a significant main effect of distance, $F(1, 54) = 70.69$, $p < .001$, due to much higher rates of fallacious responding in the distant than in the near condition. There was

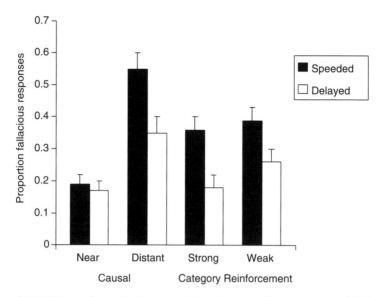

Figure 12.1 Effects of speeded versus delayed responding on rates of fallacious responding observed with causal and category reinforcement variants of the category-based conjunction fallacy.

also a significant main effect of time, $F(1, 54) = 4.65$, $p < .05$, which was qualified by a significant interaction between time and distance, $F(1, 54) = 8.22, p < .01$. Post hoc tests on the means involved in the interaction showed that the effect of time was significant for distant arguments but not for near arguments. That is, as we had predicted, in the distant case, where the systems were predicted to be in conflict, we observed that participants committed the conjunction fallacy more often under speeded conditions. In the near condition, which was the only case where we predicted the output of heuristic and analytic systems would not be in conflict, people committed as few fallacies under speeded conditions as under delayed conditions.

In the second experiment in this series, we attempted a conceptual replication of the results of the earlier experiment by using a secondary task to compromise analytic processes. Forty participants rated the arguments used in the earlier experiment, under conditions of load or conditions of no load. The problems were presented in one of four different orders. To load analytic processes we required participants to temporarily store four bisyllabic nonsense words. Rates of the fallacy observed in this experiment, broken down by fallacy variant and condition, may be seen in Figure 12.2. The ANOVAs and post hoc tests on significant interactions revealed the same results as for the earlier experiment: there was a significant main effect of load, $F(1, 38) = 4.50$, $p < .05$, for the categorical materials, and a significant interaction between load and distance, $F(1, 38) = 7.56$, p < .01, for the causal materials. The significant interaction was as a result of the differential effects of load on

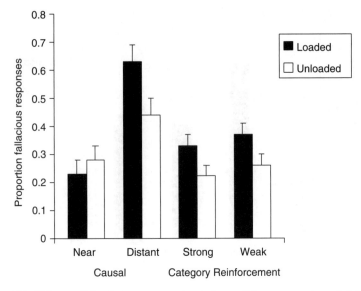

Figure 12.2 Effects of loaded versus unloaded conditions on rates of fallacious responding observed with causal and category reinforcement variants of the category-based conjunction fallacy.

fallacy rates for distant and near problems. The effect was significant for distant, but not for near, arguments.

The results of two experiments using different methods revealed that when analytic resources are compromised and the output of analytic and heuristic processes is predicted to be in conflict, rates of the category-based conjunction fallacy increase. On the other hand, when the processes are predicted not to be in conflict, manipulations designed to affect analytic processing have no effect on fallacy rates. These findings are consistent with a standard dual-process account of thinking that claims that when heuristic and analytic responses are in conflict, in order for normatively correct responses to dominate, the heuristic response must be inhibited. Manipulations that compromise the ability of analytic responses to perform this inhibitory function lead to an increase in heuristic responding, and hence in the rate of logical errors.

Deciding between standard and nonstandard dual-process accounts

Although the standard dual-process account of category-based conjunction fallacies is plausible, as we saw earlier there is an alternative account of the causal variant. This alternative account is similar to the standard account because it also holds that analytic processes prevent the conjunction fallacy, which is observed in the causal distant case (e.g., reasoning from grass to humans). Whereas the standard account is that analytic responses must inhibit a heuristic response based on the causal mechanism in favour of a response based on the logical structure of the problem, the alternative account is that the analytic system, by inferring the missing link in the distant causal relationship, judges the single distant argument to be as strong as the conjunctive argument. This alternative account is nonstandard because it holds that analytic processes can produce normatively correct responding by operating over contextualized representations (see also De Neys et al., 2005; Verscheuren et al., 2005).

To arbitrate between these accounts, in the final experiment in this series we examined the causal variant only. We presented 20 participants with five sets of five arguments. Each set of five included a causal distant (e.g., lead/plumbers) and causal near (lead/pipes) argument. It also included two conjunctive arguments. The complete conjunctive arguments contained all of the categories from the distant and near arguments (lead/pipes and plumbers), and thus specified a complete mechanism of transmission from members of the premise category, via members of the near conclusion category, to members of the distant conclusion category. The other conjunctive argument specified an incomplete transmission mechanism (e.g., lead/pipes and ropes). That is, there was no route from the premise category to the second conclusion category via the near conclusion category. Finally, we presented participants with single conclusion arguments whose conclusion category was the second conclusion category in the incomplete conjunctive arguments (e.g., lead/ropes). We will refer to these as single incomplete arguments.

Based on participants' strength ratings for these arguments we were able to work out, as before, the proportion of fallacious responses in the near and distant cases. Because both are derived from a comparison with the complete conjunctive argument, we will refer to these as the *complete* near and distant conditions. In addition we could calculate how often people committed a fallacy when ratings for the single near argument were compared with ratings for the incomplete conjunctive argument. We will refer to this as the *incomplete* near condition, and to the remaining condition, where fallacy rates were calculated by comparing ratings for single incomplete arguments to ratings for conjunctive incomplete arguments, as the *incomplete* distant condition.

The two types of dual-process account outlined above make very different predictions about the different rates of the fallacy that will be observed in the four conditions we have just described. According to the standard account, people give the analytic response on the basis of a consideration of the logical structure of the problem. People fail to give an analytic response when there is an alternative and compelling heuristic response. Under this account, we should observe fewer fallacies in the incomplete conditions than in the complete conditions, because the heuristic response based on the incomplete causal mechanism should be less compelling than the heuristic response produced by the complete mechanism. However, according to our nonstandard account, people are using their knowledge of the causal mechanism to avoid the conjunction fallacy in the causal distant case. Hence, when there is no causal mechanism available, people should commit the fallacy more often. That is, we should observe the fallacy significantly less often in the complete distant case than in the incomplete distant case.

The results of this experiment are presented in Figure 12.3 where it may be seen that, as predicted by our nonstandard account, participants committed a fallacy significantly more often in the incomplete distant condition than in the complete distant condition. A 2×2 within participants ANOVA revealed a significant interaction between distance and completeness, $F(1, 19) = 15.97$, $p = .001$. Post hoc tests on the means involved in this interaction showed that in the distant case, there were fewer fallacious responses for arguments where there was a complete transmission mechanism. In near cases however, the reverse was true, with significantly more fallacious responses when there was a complete mechanism. These findings strongly support our nonstandard account of the category-based causal conjunction fallacy. This account holds that analytic processes result in normative responding, not because they are sensitive to the logical structure of the problem, but because they operate on a contextualized representation of the causal relations between the categories in the argument. In other words, people infer a causal mechanism that might cause plumbers to share a property with lead.

Implications for dual-process theories

At this point the reader may feel that we have become a little task focused or that we have concentrated on conjunction fallacies more than is healthy for any one research group. In order to attempt to allay such fears, we will now draw out some of the implications of our results for dual-process theory. In particular, in the first series of experiments described here we observed

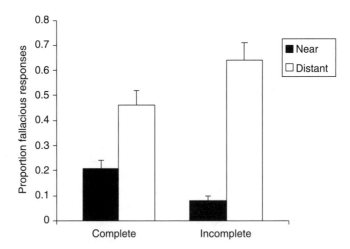

Figure 12.3 Rates of the causal conjunction fallacy for complete and incomplete causal chains, broken down by distance.

biasing effects of causal knowledge: the stronger the causal link between the conjuncts, the stronger the tendency for participants to commit the conjunction fallacy. The interaction between secondary load and causal strength observed in the second experiment in that series strongly suggests that the biasing effects of causal strength are mediated by heuristic processes whose output analytic processes often fail to inhibit. However, in our second series of experiments we have demonstrated that participants may sometimes avoid a conjunction fallacy not because of an analysis of the logical structure of the problem, but because they use analytic processes to reason (abductively) about the causal mechanism linking the categories in the argument.

There are a number of interesting consequences of this pattern of results. First, they underscore the point made by other researchers (De Neys et al., 2005; Evans, 2007a; Verscheuren et al., 2005) that both heuristic and analytic processes may operate over contextualized representations. However, once dual-process theorists make this concession, perhaps they leave themselves open to accusations that if both processes operate over contextualized representations, and both processes can result in reasoning errors (see Nestler et al., 2008), then perhaps they are not so different after all. This is a potentially serious criticism. In addition, if causal knowledge, for example, can be input to either process, then how does one predict in advance which process will dominate in any given task? As all of the exceptions to the standard dual-process account of analytic processes described here (our own experiments included) have involved causal content, perhaps dual-process theorists should consider in greater detail the effects of causal knowledge on reasoning.

Although much experimental work in the dual-process tradition has relied on paradigms that create conflicting knowledge- and logic-based responses, the precise effects of knowledge on reasoning have not been the focus of study. Instead, dual-process theorists have been interested in the dichotomy between heuristic and analytic processes and hence, in the way that knowledge biases reasoning (Evans, Barston, & Pollard, 1983), and in the biasing role played by heuristic processes (Goel & Dolan, 2003; Sloman, 1996; Stanovich, 1999). This emphasis can lead to all effects of knowledge and belief being treated similarly, that is, as something to be avoided in favour of decontextualized analytic reasoning. To be sure, there are many cases where causal beliefs are likely to result in erroneous responses based on heuristic processing. Our first series of experiments provides but one example. However, there also appear to be cases, such as the one considered in our second set of studies (see also Verschueren et al., 2005), where the effects of causal knowledge are mediated by Type 2 processes. It is plausible that other effects in the literature (e.g., Krynski & Tenenbaum, 2007; Lagnado & Sloman, 2004) depend on much more abstract knowledge about causal structure, whose effects are mediated by very effortful Type 2 processing. It may be possible to place effects of causal knowledge on a continuum where some, because they are mediated almost wholly by heuristic processes, are unaffected by experimental manipulations of analytic resources, and are uncorrelated with cognitive ability; some require contextualized Type 2 processing and so are affected by experimental manipulations but are uncorrelated with ability (for a recent discussion of when correlations will be observed with ability, see Stanovich & West, 2008); and some require decontextualized consideration of causal structure and alternative causes, and thus are affected by experimental manipulations and in addition, tend to be correlated with ability.

Of course, for a dual-process specification of the effects of causal knowledge on reasoning to be persuasive, we must be able to say when the effect of causal knowledge will be mediated by heuristic processes and when it will be mediated by analytic processes. One obvious answer is that the mediating process may depend on the form of the causal knowledge evoked by the task (see also Fugelsang & Thompson, 2003). Knowledge about relations between causes and effects that takes the form of associations may be handled by heuristic processes, whereas effects of knowledge about causal structure, particularly knowledge about alternative causes, may often require the involvement of analytic processes. Thus, in the first series of experiments described here we may simply have manipulated the strength of the association between cause and effect, thus determining the strength of the output from heuristic processes. In the second series of experiments, on the other hand, we manipulated how much information about causal structure was explicitly presented. In order to reason about causal mechanism, including enabling and disabling conditions (see Verscheuren et al., 2005), perhaps analytic processes are often required.

A slightly different claim has been made by Fugelsang and Thompson (2003) who argued that heuristic processes driven by knowledge about mechanisms may bias the more analytic evaluation of covariation data. In support of this claim they have shown that people are more aware of the effects of covariation information on their causal beliefs than they are of the effects of knowledge about mechanisms. In contrast, we have claimed above that reasoning about causal mechanisms may require the involvement of analytic processes. If it is indeed the case that the effects on reasoning of knowledge about causal mechanisms can be mediated by heuristic or analytic processes, then this would make it difficult to provide a satisfying account of how causal knowledge fits into the dual-process framework. However, Fugelsang and Thompson's manipulation of the plausibility of causal mechanisms appears quite similar to the manipulations of causal strength that we employed in our first set of studies. Certainly their participants were not required to reason in detail about aspects of causal structure such as alternative causes, or enabling conditions. Thus, we are optimistic that their effects are compatible with our own findings and our explanations for those findings.

Conclusions

In this chapter we have surveyed at least five different types of conjunction fallacy: the M→A and A→B variants (Tversky & Kahneman, 1983), the preference for cause and effect explanations for contradictions in reasoning (Legrenzi & Johnson-Laird, 2005), the category-based version produced by category reinforcement, and the category-based causal variant (Medin et al., 2003). This prompts us to wonder whether there is now a need for the adoption of a collective noun for conjunction fallacies. Apart from the, frankly rather obvious, *conjunction* of conjunction fallacies implied in our title, a *school*, a *covey*, or a *flock* are our current favourites. In the meantime, the effects of causal knowledge in the different causal conjunction fallacies that we have considered here appear to be mediated by different reasoning processes. Accounting for the varied effects of causal knowledge on thinking will be a significant challenge for dual-process theorists.

References

Crisp, A. K., & Feeney, A. (2009). Causal conjunction fallacies: The roles of causal strength and mental resources. *Quarterly Journal of Experimental Psychology, 62*, 2320–2337.

Crisp, A. K., Feeney, A., & Shafto, P. (2009). Testing dual process accounts of the category-based conjunction fallacy: When is decontextualised reasoning necessary for logical responding? Manuscript submitted for publication

Crupi, V., Fitelson, B., & Tentori, K. (2008). Probability, confirmation and the conjunction fallacy. *Thinking & Reasoning, 14*, 182–199.

De Neys, W. (2006a). Automatic-heuristic and executive-analytic processing during reasoning: Chronometric and dual-task considerations. *Quarterly Journal of Experimental Psychology, 59*, 1070–1100.

De Neys, W. (2006b). Dual processing in reasoning: Two systems but one reasoner. *Psychological Science, 17*, 428–433.

De Neys, W., & Glumicic, T. (2008). Conflict monitoring in dual process theories of thinking. *Cognition, 106*, 1245–1299.

De Neys, W., Schaeken, W., & d'Ydewalle, G. (2005). Working memory and counter-example retrieval for causal conditionals. *Thinking & Reasoning, 11*, 123–150.

De Neys, W., Vartanian, O., & Goel, V. (2008). Smarter than we think: When our brains detect that we are biased. *Psychological Science, 19*, 483–489.

Doherty, M. E., Mynatt C. R., Tweney, R. D., & Schiavo, M. D. (1979). Pseudodiagnosticity. *Acta Psychologica, 43*, 111–121.

Dulany, D. E., & Hilton, D. J. (1991). Conversational implicature, conscious representation and the conjunction fallacy. *Social Cognition, 9*, 85–110.

Epstein, S., Donovan, S., & Denes-Raj, V. (1999). The missing link in the paradox of the Linda conjunction problem: Beyond knowing and thinking of the conjunction rule, the intrinsic appeal of heuristic processing. *Personality and Social Psychology Bulletin, 25*, 204–214.

Evans, J. St B. T. (2007a). *Hypothetical thinking*. Hove, UK: Psychology Press.

Evans, J. St B. T. (2007b). On the resolution of conflict in dual process theories of reasoning. *Thinking & Reasoning, 13*, 21–339.

Evans, J. St B. T. (2008). Dual-processing accounts of reasoning, judgement and social cognition. *Annual Review of Psychology, 59*, 255–278.

Evans, J. St B. T., Barston, J. L., & Pollard, P. (1983). On the conflict between logic and belief in syllogistic reasoning. *Memory & Cognition, 11*, 295–306.

Evans, J. St B. T., Handley, S. J., Over, D. E., & Perham, N. (2002). Background beliefs in Bayesian reasoning. *Memory & Cognition, 30*, 179–190.

Evans, J. St B. T., Handley, S. J., Perham, N., Over, D. E., & Thompson, V. A. (2000). Frequency versus probability formats in statistical word problems. *Cognition, 77*, 197–213.

Evans, J. St B.T., Venn, S., & Feeney, A. (2002). Implicit and explicit processes in a hypothesis testing task. *British Journal of Psychology, 93*, 31–46.

Fabre, J. M., Caverni, J. P., & Jungermann, H. (1995). Causality does influence conjunctive probability judgements if context and design allow for it. *Organizational Behavior and Human Decision Processes, 63*, 1–5.

Feeney, A. (2007a). How many processes underlie category-based induction? Effects of conclusion specificity and cognitive ability. *Memory & Cognition, 35*, 1830–1839.

Feeney, A. (2007b). Individual differences, dual processes, and induction. In A. Feeney & E. Heit (Eds.), *Inductive reasoning* (pp. 302–327). Cambridge: Cambridge University Press.

Feeney, A., Crisp, A. K., & Wilburn, C. J. (2008). Inductive reasoning and semantic cognition: More than just different names for the same thing? *Behavioral and Brain Sciences, 31*, 715–716.

Feeney, A., Evans, J. St B. T., & Clibbens, J. (2000). Background beliefs and evidence interpretation. *Thinking & Reasoning, 6*, 97–124.

Feeney, A., Evans, J. St B. T., & Venn, S. (2008). Rarity, pseudodiagnosticity and Bayesian reasoning. *Thinking & Reasoning, 14*, 209–230.

Feeney, A., & Heit, E. (Eds.). (2007). *Inductive reasoning.* Cambridge: Cambridge University Press.

Feeney, A., Shafto, P., & Dunning, D. (2007). Who is susceptible to conjunction fallacies in category-based induction? *Psychonomic Bulletin & Review, 14*, 884–889.

Fisk, J. E., & Pidgeon, N. (1998). Conditional dependence, potential surprise and the conjunction fallacy. *Quarterly Journal of Experimental Psychology: A, 51*, 655–681.

Fugelsang, J. A., & Thompson, V. A. (2003). A dual-process model of belief and evidence interactions in causal reasoning. *Memory & Cognition, 31*, 800–815.

Goel, V., & Dolan, R. (2003). Explaining modulation of reasoning by belief. *Cognition, 87*, B11–B22.

Hertwig, R., Benz, B., & Krauss, S. (2008). The conjunction fallacy and the many meanings of "and". *Cognition, 108*, 740–753.

Krynski, T. R., & Tenenbaum, J. B. (2007). The role of causality in judgment under uncertainty. *Journal of Experimental Psychology: General, 136*, 430–450.

Lagnado, D., & Sloman, S. A. (2004). The advantage of timely intervention. *Journal of Experimental Psychology: Learning, Memory, and Cognition, 30*, 856–876.

Legrenzi, P., & Johnson-Laird, P. N. (2005). The evaluation of diagnostic explanations for inconsistencies. *Psychologia Belgica, 45*, 19–28.

Macchi, L. (1995). Pragmatic aspects of the base-rate fallacy. *Quarterly Journal of Experimental Psychology, 48*, 188–207.

Medin, D., Coley, J. D., Storms, G., & Hayes, B. (2003). A relevance theory of induction. *Psychonomic Bulletin and Review, 10*, 517–532.

Nestler, S., Blank, H., & von Collani, G. (2008). Hindsight bias doesn't always come easy: Causal models, cognitive effort, and creeping determinism. *Journal of Experimental Psychology: Learning, Memory, and Cognition, 34*, 1043–1054.

Sides, A., Osherson, D., Bonini, N., & Viale, R. (2002) On the reality of the conjunction fallacy. *Memory & Cognition, 30*, 191–198.

Sloman, S. A. (1996). The empirical case for two systems of reasoning. *Psychological Bulletin, 119*, 3–22.

Sloman, S. A., Over, D. E., Slovak, L., & Stibel, J. M. (2003). Frequency illusions and other fallacies. *Organisational Behaviour and Human Decision Processes, 91*, 296–309.

Stanovich, K. E. (1999). *Who is rational: Studies of individual differences in reasoning.* Mahwah, NJ: Lawrence Erlbaum Associates, Inc.

Stanovich, K. E., and West, R. F. (1998). Individual differences in framing and conjunction effects. *Thinking & Reasoning, 4*, 289–317.

Stanovich, K. E., & West. R. F. (2008). On the relative independence of thinking biases and cognitive ability. *Journal of Personality and Social Psychology, 94*, 672–695.

Thüring, M., & Jungermann, H. (1990). The conjunction fallacy: Causality vs. event probability. *Journal of Behavioral Decision Making, 3*, 61–73.

Tversky, A., & Kahneman, D. (1983). Extensional versus intuitive reasoning: The conjunction fallacy in probability judgement. *Psychological Review, 90*, 293–315.

Verschueren, N., Schaeken, W., & d'Ydewalle, G. (2005). A dual-process specification of causal conditional reasoning. *Thinking & Reasoning, 11*, 239–278.

13 Scalar implicature
Inference, convention, and dual processes

Keith Frankish

The Open University

Maria Kasmirli

University of Sheffield

Introduction

An utterance is said to generate an *implicature* if it conveys something that goes beyond what is literally said – if hearers form a pragmatic interpretation of the utterance that differs from the literal one. Common examples are *scalar* implicatures, where a weaker claim is interpreted as the denial of a stronger one on the same scale. For example "Some politicians take bribes" pragmatically implies "Not all politicians take bribes", even though "some" means *at least one* and is logically compatible with "all".

The first major analysis of implicature was by the philosopher Paul Grice, who coined the term "implicature" (see his "Logic and conversation" reprinted in Grice, 1989). Philosophers of language have continued to analyse the phenomenon, and linguists have theorized in detail about the pragmatic processes involved in implicature recovery and their relation to semantic processes. However, implicature has received less attention from psychologists. Until recently there has been little or no experimental work on implicature, and the topic has not figured prominently in the reasoning literature. This is changing now, however, and the past decade has seen a flurry of experimental work on the psychological basis of implicature, focusing in particular on the questions of whether implicature processing is automatic or effortful and whether pragmatic interpretations develop before or after literal, logical ones. This experimental work is still at a relatively early stage, but some clear findings have emerged, although their significance remains open to interpretation.

In this chapter we review this work, assess its significance, and set it within a wider theoretical context. There are two aspects to this last aim. First, we shall draw attention to a theoretical option largely ignored in the experimental literature. Most experimental work on implicature has been conducted within a broadly Gricean paradigm, according to which implicatures can be calculated and explained using general psychosocial principles. However, there is an alternative, anti-Gricean strand in contemporary philosophy of language, according to which many implicatures, including scalar ones, depend on convention rather than inference. We have no brief for this view, but we think it should not be ruled out and deserves experimental testing. Second, we shall make connections with the literature on dual-process theories of reasoning, as developed by Jonathan Evans and others. Superficially at least, implicature seems made for a dual-process analysis, involving as it does a contrast of pragmatic and logical responses, and we shall consider if this is correct. We shall close the chapter with some recommendations for future experimental work. Throughout we shall concentrate on scalar implicature, which has been the primary focus for experimenters.

Theories of implicature

This section briefly introduces the major theories of implicature. We begin with Grice's account, which provides the context for much subsequent work. Grice held that implicatures are derived by a process of inference, drawing on general principles of human communication, together with the literal meaning of the words uttered, contextual information, and background knowledge. According to Grice, communication is a cooperative enterprise, and hearers assume that speakers will adhere to certain maxims, to the effect that utterances should be: (1) as informative as required (the maxim of quantity); (2) true (the maxim of quality); (3) relevant (the maxim of relevance); and (4) perspicuously phrased (the maxim of manner). Grice proposed that hearers posit implicatures in order to preserve the assumption that speakers are following these maxims. For example, suppose Al asks Bea for her assessment of a student, and Bea replies "He is very punctual". This reply violates the maxim of quantity, and Al can preserve the assumption that Bea is being cooperative only by supposing that she wishes to convey something else – that the student is academically weak – which she does not wish to say directly. Al assumes that Bea thought he could work this out, and concludes that she is implicating that the student is weak.

This is an example of what Grice called a *particularized* implicature – that is, it is one that is heavily dependent on the context of utterance (in other contexts Bea's utterance would not generate the implicature mentioned). Grice held that other implicatures were *generalized*; that is, unless explicitly cancelled, the words would generate the same implicature in most contexts. Scalar implicatures are usually regarded as examples of this, and they, too, can be explained in Gricean terms. The speaker chooses a weak term in preference to a stronger one on the same scale – "some" rather than "all", for example. But if they had known that the stronger term was applicable, then in not using it they would have been failing to be as informative as required, violating the maxim of quantity. The hearer therefore infers that the speaker did not know that the stronger term was applicable, or, more strongly, that they knew it was not. In this way, Griceans argue, saying that some politicians take bribes can generate the implicature that not all do.

As a cognitive theory, Grice's account has serious limitations. However, it has provided the basis for later theories that aim to give a more cognitively oriented account of implicature derivation. Levinson's work is a particularly detailed example of this so-called *neo-Gricean* tradition (see also e.g., Gazdar, 1979; Horn, 1984, 1989). Levinson focuses on generalized implicatures, which are relatively independent of context. (He acknowledges that particularized implicatures require a different treatment.) Generalized implicatures, he argues, are *default inferences* – normal or preferred interpretations – which are the product of heuristics, applied at an early stage in language processing, interleaved with the processes of semantic decoding. The inferences are default and go through automatically unless implicitly or explicitly cancelled. This creates an extra level of meaning ("utterance type meaning"), which enriches the content of our utterances in reliable ways, thereby improving the efficiency of human communication.[1]

Levinson identifies three core heuristics, descendants of Grice's maxims. These are:

> The Q-heuristic: What isn't said isn't [the case].
> The I-heuristic: What is expressed simply is stereotypically exemplified.
> The M-heuristic: What's said in an abnormal way isn't normal.
>
> (Levinson, 2000, pp. 35–38)

We shall concentrate on the Q-heuristic, which is the one that is invoked to explain scalar implicatures. Speakers are presumed to make the strongest statement they legitimately can, with the result that the assertion of a weak claim implies the denial of a salient stronger one. Thus if a speaker chooses a weaker member of a contrast scale in preference to a stronger one, the Q-heuristic generates the inference that the stronger one does not apply. Hence "Some politicians take bribes" implicates "Not all politicians take bribes". The same applies for other scales, such as <*or, and*>, <*possibly, necessarily*>, <*occasionally, often, always*>, and so on. Levinson argues that this view explains a wide variety of linguistic phenomena, including certain facts about lexicalization. For example, we do not have a word meaning *some but not all*, since that meaning attaches by a default inference to the word "some".

An alternative approach is *relevance theory* (e.g., Carston, 2002; Sperber & Wilson, 1995; Wilson & Sperber, 2004). Relevance theorists agree with Grice that hearers have expectations of speakers, which motivate the search for implicatures. However, they do away with the apparatus of maxims and heuristics, and replace them with a simple expectation of relevance. On this view, human cognition is automatically geared to maximize the relevance of the inputs it processes, where the relevance of an input is a measure of the positive cognitive effects generated by processing it, set against the effort required to derive them (the "cognitive principle of relevance"). (A key measure of these positive effects is the number of *contextual implications* an input generates – roughly, how much you can learn from it.) Thus, since speakers want hearers to attend to what they say, utterances carry a presumption of *optimal relevance*, where an optimally relevant stimulus is one that is sufficiently relevant to be worth the hearer's attention and the most relevant the speaker is able and willing to provide. This presumption (the "communicative principle of relevance") then guides the hearer's comprehension processes.

Relevance theorists hold that language comprehension is an inferential process; the hearer seeks to infer (rather than decode) the speaker's meaning from their words and the context of utterance. This involves both fleshing out the speaker's literal meaning by resolving ambiguities, identifying references, and so on (a process called "explicature"), and the search for distinct implicated meanings. The process follows a path of least effort. The hearer forms hypotheses as to what the hearer is seeking to communicate, starting with the most accessible interpretation and progressing to more complex ones, until their expectations of relevance are met or they abandon the search. Implicatures are derived when the literal meaning fails to meet these expectations. For example (and simplifying considerably), suppose Cy asks Dee "Do all, or at least some, politicians take bribes?" and Dee replies "Some do". Since it would clearly be relevant to Cy to know whether all politicians take bribes, in answering thus Dee indicates that she is not in a position to assert that they all do, because (let us assume) she knows it is not true. This further information would increase the relevance of her utterance, so, in line with the principle of relevance, Cy interprets Dee as communicating that some but not all politicians take bribes (see Sperber & Wilson, 1995, pp. 277–278).

This example is a scalar implicature. It should be noted, however, that relevance theorists hold that many so-called scalar implicatures are not implicatures at all, properly speaking, but explicatures (e.g., Noveck & Sperber, 2007). In many contexts, they hold, the meaning of "some" is narrowed down (to, say, *a substantial proportion*) so that it entails *not all*, without generating a distinct *not all* implicature. "Some" genuinely implicates *not all*, on this view, only where there is an explicit or tacit question as to whether "all" is applicable, as in the example above. In both cases, however, the same process is at work – a search for an interpretation which meets the hearer's expectations of relevance.

In treating implicatures as derived from psychosocial principles, relevance theory is broadly Gricean (in effect, it assigns all the work to the maxim of relevance). However, there are important differences between it and the neo-Gricean approach, as developed by Levinson (2000). Most importantly, the theories differ in the *order* in which literal and pragmatic interpretations are derived and the processing effort required to derive them. In Levinson's view, the maxims that generate implicatures are applied automatically at an early stage in language comprehension, and pragmatic interpretations are the default ones. Literal interpretations, if they are derived, will require undoing or overriding the default pragmatic inferences. In relevance theory, the opposite is the case. Interpretations are derived in order of accessibility, and in most cases the literal interpretation will be processed first, and a pragmatic interpretation derived only if the literal one fails to meet the hearer's expectations of relevance. A second, related, difference is that relevance theory sees implicature derivation as *context-driven* (Breheny, Katsos, & Williams, 2006). Expectations of relevance vary with context, and the same utterance may generate an implicature in one context but not in another, where the hearer's expectations of relevance are different. Thus, from a cognitive perspective, relevance theory makes no distinction between generalized and particularized implicatures; in effect, it treats them all as particularized.

In the experimental literature on implicature the neo-Gricean view and relevance theory are typically the only theories considered. They are certainly the two best worked-out ones from a cognitive perspective. However, there is an important alternative strand in philosophical work on implicature, which rejects the Gricean view that implicatures are derived from the application of general principles. The most detailed development of this anti-Gricean approach is in the work of Wayne Davis (Davis, 1998; see also Morgan, 1978).

Davis treats particularized and generalized implicatures differently. In his view, particularized implicatures (he calls them "speaker implicatures") exist simply in virtue of the speaker's intentions. For a speaker to mean something beyond the literal meaning of their words is for them to intend to convey that further meaning. Hearers detect particularized implicatures by detecting these intentions, using any of the methods by which mental states can be inferred from behaviour. Generalized implicatures ("sentence implicatures"), on the other hand, depend on semantic *conventions*, according to Davis. It is a convention that sentences of the form "Some F are G" are used to implicate that not all F are G. Like other conventions, these implicature conventions are to some extent arbitrary. Davis accepts that there will usually be a connection between the literal meaning of a sentence and the implicature it carries that makes the implicature seem fitting. However, he argues that a measure of arbitrariness remains, and that particular implicature conventions cannot be inferred from general principles.

One important argument for Davis's view is that Gricean approaches overgenerate implicatures. For example "Some politicians take bribes" is a weaker claim than all of the following, which can be thought of as occupying higher points on relevant scales: "At least 50% of politicians take bribes", "Some politicians take bribes regularly", "Some politicians and financiers take bribes" (adapted from Davis, 2008). Yet "Some politicians take bribes" does not imply the denial of any of those claims. Davis concludes that which denials it implicates is a matter of convention, not inference. Davis also cites evidence that many generalized implicatures are language specific, drawing on Wierzbicka's work (1985, 1987). For example, in English "An X is an X" carries the implication that one X is as good as another, but the French translation does not, and the Polish translation implicates that there is something uniquely good about an X (Davis, 1998, p. 144, 2008).

Although Davis holds that implicatures are conventional, he does not claim that they are part of the meaning of the sentences that carry them. He distinguishes *first-order* and *second-order* semantic conventions. The former are conventions for the direct expression of thoughts in language; they assign literal meaning to sentences. The latter are conventions for the indirect expression of thoughts by the direct linguistic expression of other thoughts; they assign implicatures to sentences (or rather, to sentence forms; the conventions have some generality). According to Davis, a language is defined by its first-order rules, not its second-order ones, and implicature conventions are inessential to a language. (He compares them to other conventions of language use, such as that of greeting someone by saying "How are you?".) In what follows we shall refer to Davis's view of generalized implicature as *convention theory*.[2]

Note that convention theory cuts across the divisions between the other two approaches. Like relevance theory, it treats the logical meaning of scalar terms as the more basic one. Grasp of logical meanings requires mastery of first-order conventions only, whereas grasp of pragmatic meanings requires mastery of second-order conventions as well. However, like neo-Gricean theory, convention theory treats scalar implicatures as generalized, rather than particularized; once implicature conventions have been mastered they will be applied by default, unless contextually cancelled.

There is a large and complex literature surrounding these theories, drawing on pragmatic intuitions, detailed linguistic analysis, and theoretical considerations about communication and language comprehension. Until recently, however, there was little or no relevant experimental evidence on the topic. As we noted, this is changing, and we expect experimental work to play an increasingly important role in this area. (For useful discussion of the methodology of experimental pragmatics, see Noveck & Sperber, 2007.) The work is still at a relatively early stage, but we feel it is a good time to review the key findings and examine their bearing on the theories mentioned. We turn to this now.

Experimental evidence: Development

Experimental work on implicature has focused on scalar implicature, and its main aims have been to establish the reality of the phenomenon and to understand its development. It has been known for some time that children often overlook pragmatic readings of logical terms (e.g., Braine & Rumain, 1981; Smith, 1980). However, it is only recently that specific studies of this effect have been made. The first of these was by Ira Noveck, who argued that children are, in a sense, *more logical than adults* (Noveck, 2001). In one experiment (conducted in French) Noveck tested children's and adults' interpretation of sentences of the form "Some F are G" where it is known that in fact all F are G (e.g., "Some giraffes have long necks"). Such statements are *underinformative*, since they assert less than is commonly known to be the case, and they are true on a logical reading but false on a pragmatic one (they are *pragmatically infelicitous*). Noveck used a sentence verification task, presenting participants with samples of underinformative sentences and control sentences and asking whether or not they agreed with them. A total of 30 sentences were used, all of the general form "Some/All Fs are/have/do G". A sixth were underinformative, the rest were controls that were unambiguously true or false (e.g., "All chairs tell time", "Some birds live in cages"). Noveck found that most children accepted the underinformative sentences, even though they correctly evaluated the control sentences. The majority of adults, on the other hand, rejected them (89% of 8-year-olds and 85% of 10-year-olds accepted the pragmatically infelicitous sentences, whereas only 41% of adults did). Similar results were obtained with the scalar terms "Might" and "Must". Noveck concluded that a logical interpretation of scalar terms develops before a pragmatic one.

Other studies have replicated Noveck's findings (e.g., Guasti, Chierchia, Crain, Foppolo, Gualmini, & Meroni, 2005, Experiment 1; Papafragou & Musolino, 2003, Experiment 1; Pouscoulous, Noveck, Politzer, & Bastide, 2007, Experiment 1). However, the picture is not simple. At least one attempted replication (Feeney, Scrafton, Duckworth, & Handley, 2004, Experiment 1) has failed, with 7- to 8-year-old children and adults adopting logical interpretations at the same, high, rate (66% and 65%).[3] Moreover, several studies have found that by adjusting the experimental conditions, children's ability to detect implicatures can be much improved. Papafragou and Musolino (2003) made two modifications. First, children were given training to make them more aware of the possibility of pragmatic infelicity (saying "silly things"), as distinct from outright falsity. For example, they were alerted to the infelicity of describing a dog as "a little animal with four legs". Second, the task was adjusted to highlight the informational inadequacy of the underinformative statements. The experiment used stories involving a contest of some kind, where the focus was on the main character's performance – for example, whether he succeeded in putting *all* his hoops around a pole. The result was that the proportion of 5-year-olds rejecting pragmatically infelicitous statements rose dramatically. On some/all tasks, 52.5% rejected the underinformative statements in the modified condition as opposed to only 12.5% in the sentence verification condition. Moreover, like adults, these children justified their answers by invoking statements using the stronger term on the scale ("It was wrong to say some did, since *all* did"). In another study, Papafragou and Tantalou (2004) demonstrated that in naturalistic settings where informational expectations are clear, 4- to 5-year-olds derive scalar implicatures at high levels (70–90%).

Interestingly, this extended to *particularized* implicatures, dependent on ad hoc, context-dependent scales. For example, a cow was instructed to wrap two gifts, a toy parrot and a doll, which it took out of sight of the participants. On its return, it was asked if it had wrapped the gifts and responded that it had wrapped the parrot. Here the context creates a nonce action scale <*wrapped the parrot, wrapped the parrot and the doll*> and the cow's utterance implicates that it had not performed the stronger action. In Papafragou and Tantalou's tests children detected such ad hoc implicatures 90% of the time.

Guasti et al. (2005) obtained similar results (Experiment 4). They speculated that children might be accepting underinformative statements such as *Some giraffes have long necks*, not because they were failing to draw the scalar inference from *some* to *not all*, but because they were not sure that it was untrue that the statement was false under the pragmatic reading (e.g., that it was untrue that not all giraffes have long necks). To control for this, they used a truth-value judgement task (Crain & Thornton, 1998). They asked 7-year-old children to assess descriptions of scenarios (acted by toys and puppets) in which all the relevant information was readily available. For example, they showed children a video in which five soldiers debated whether to ride motorbikes or horses before all deciding to ride horses. They then asked the children whether a puppet was right or wrong to describe the scenario as one in which *some soldiers are riding a horse*. Their main finding was that children's rejection rate for underinformative statements rose virtually to adult levels (75% for children, 83% for adults). (Adult performance on this task also rose, in comparison to that on a simple sentence evaluation task, where only 50% of adults rejected the underinformative statements.) Guasti et al. conclude that 7-year-olds have the ability to derive scalar implicatures, but that it is masked in some experimental settings. In particular, 7-year-olds derive scalar implicatures at adult levels in naturalistic settings where all the relevant information is easily accessible.[4] Guasti et al. note, however, that the same does not go for younger children. Five-year-olds were much less sensitive to scalar implicature than adults, even when tested using a truth-value judgement task, with only 50% rejecting underinformative statements (Chierchia, Crain, Guasti, Gualmini, & Meroni, 2001; Papafragou & Musolino, 2003). At this age, it seems, at least some children simply lack the cognitive resources to derive implicatures.

Researchers have also begun to investigate other factors that help or hinder implicature derivation in children. Pouscoulous et al. (2007) suggest that implicature derivation is demanding of cognitive resources, and that it can be facilitated by removing distracting factors. To test this, they modified the standard task, by (1) reducing the number of distractors (no unnecessary control questions were used); (2) making the required response an action rather than a metalinguistic judgement (children were asked to adjust the contents of boxes in response to requests from a puppet that all, some, or none should contain items); and (3) using simpler (French) scalar terms ("quelques" was used rather than the more complex "certains"). The result was an increase in pragmatic responding across the board (at ages 4, 5, 7, and adult), with a developmental progression in performance (logical response rates were 32%, 27%, 17%, and 14% for the four age groups, respectively). In a separate experiment, Pouscoulous et al. confirmed that use of "quelques" rather than "certains" increases implicature production in 9-year-olds (logical response rates were 0% and 42%, respectively).

Let us sum up these results. The picture is complex, but the general outline is clear enough: Logical interpretations of scalar terms are more accessible to children than pragmatic ones, and the tendency to adopt pragmatic interpretations (that is, to derive scalar implicatures) increases steadily with age. However, when conditions are right, even relatively young children can derive scalar implicatures, and the process is facilitated in naturalistic settings where informational expectations are clear and all relevant information readily available. Reducing processing demands also helps. The finding that the logical sense of "some" is developmentally primary is, perhaps, surprising; as Bott and Noveck (2004, p. 440) remark, many people have an intuition that the pragmatic interpretation is more natural. Nevertheless, it is well established and theorists must take account of it. We consider now how these findings bear on the theories of implicature introduced earlier.

First, the data are compatible with relevance theory, and indeed are what the theory would predict. As we noted, on a relevance-theoretic view, interpretations are processed in order of accessibility, starting with the literal meaning, and implicatures are derived only if they are contextually required to satisfy the hearer's expectations of relevance. Thus, on this view, we should expect children to derive implicatures less often than adults, both because they are less sensitive to cues that would raise their expectations of relevance (e.g., about the informational value of possible alternative utterances), and because their cognitive resources are more limited, making implicatures harder to process and so diminishing their relevance (in line with the cognitive principle of relevance). For the same reason, we should expect that pragmatic interpretations would be facilitated by manipulations that serve to highlight the informational gains of alternative interpretations or to reduce computational demands – which is what seems to happen.

The neo-Gricean approach is less easy to reconcile with the data, since it predicts the opposite pattern, with the pragmatic reading of scalar terms being the default one, generated by automatic application of the Q-heuristic. Some explanation will be needed as to why this is not the case for children. Neo-Griceans might appeal to Guasti et al.'s data, arguing that older children at least (7 and upwards) do adopt pragmatic readings by default, and that when they fail to give the corresponding pragmatic *response*, it is because they fail to evaluate the statement correctly under that reading. On this view, the contextual adjustments that facilitate pragmatic responding do so by assisting evaluation rather than derivation. It is unlikely, however, that this explanation can account for all of the effect observed, and it certainly cannot explain the data from younger children. In response neo-Griceans might argue that it takes time for the heuristics to become automatized, and that, until they do, they have to be applied in a slow, effortful fashion. This would also explain why increasing the salience of stronger alternatives and reducing processing demands facilitates inference. We think this neo-Gricean position is a coherent one, although it may be in some tension with Levinson's view that pragmatic processes are closely interleaved with semantic ones (2000, Ch. 3). In the view just proposed, the semantic mechanisms would need to be in place first, with the pragmatic ones added later, and it is not clear how this developmental sequence could result in the interleaving Levinson describes – at least not without temporary disruption to the pre-existing semantic abilities.

What of the third alternative we introduced, the convention theory? This is less easy to assess, given that the theory is not developed from a cognitive perspective. However, prima facie it fits the data well. First, like relevance theory, it correctly predicts the developmental sequence. It will be necessary to master the first-order conventions governing the direct (literal) uses of sentences containing scalar terms before mastering the second-order ones governing their indirect use. (As Davis, 1998, p. 159, stresses, second-order conventions are inessential to language proper, and a person could master English without mastering its implicature conventions.) Thus the theory predicts that logical interpretations will precede pragmatic ones developmentally. (We should stress that this prediction is not made by Davis himself, though it follows naturally from his views.) Children who have not mastered the relevant implicature conventions might still be able to derive scalar implicatures, but only by using the methods for recovering particularized, context-dependent implicatures – which, in Davis's view, involve detecting the speaker's intentions. Again, establishing a naturalistic setting with clear conversational goals might be expected to facilitate this process, as the experimental data confirm. Finally, like the neo-Gricean, the convention theorist might argue that children who have mastered the implicature conventions sometimes fail to give appropriate responses because they misevaluate the implicated propositions, appealing again to Guasti et al.'s data.

The convention view also casts new light on data concerning the effect of word choice on implicature derivation. As noted, Pouscoulous et al. (2007) found that French 9-year-olds derive scalar implicatures more readily when "quelques" is used rather than "certains", even though both words mean the same (in the sentences used) and should support the same inferences. Pouscoulous et al. explain this effect by arguing that "certains" is a rarer and semantically more complex word, which soaks up processing resources that could otherwise have been devoted to implicature derivation. However, the effect might also be explained by reference to the second-order conventions associated with the two words. The implicature conventions governing "certains" might be harder to master than those associated with "quelques", perhaps because the word is rarer and has more uses. Or the conventions themselves might be more complex. There might even be no settled scalar implicature convention associated with "certains", with the consequence that any implicatures involving it are particularized. In order to assess such convention-based explanations, systematic study will be needed of the effects of word choice on implicature derivation, both within and across languages.

We conclude that the developmental data reviewed do not conclusively support one theory of implicature over another, though they harmonize better with relevance theory and the convention view. We turn now to other studies, which look at implicature processing in adults.

Experimental evidence: Reaction times

A central issue dividing Levinson's neo-Gricean approach and relevance theory is whether logical or pragmatic interpretations are the default ones, and this is something on which reaction time studies should shed light. In Levinson's view logical interpretations require the cancelling or overriding of the default pragmatic interpretations and should therefore, other things being equal, take longer to compute. Relevance theory takes the opposite view and predicts that pragmatic interpretations should take longer.

Bott and Noveck (2004) have carried out important work here, building on earlier findings by Rips (1975) obtained in the course of studies of categorization. Bott and Noveck ran several experiments to test adult subjects' response times to underinformative sentences. The first experiment used a sentence verification task. Participants saw 54 sentences of the form "Some/All F are G", half using "Some", half using "All". There were six types of sentence: an underinformative "some" sentence (e.g., "Some elephants are mammals"), a straightforwardly true "some" sentence (e.g., "Some mammals are elephants"), a straightforwardly false "some" sentence (e.g., "Some elephants are insects"), and three "all" sentences generated by replacing "Some" with "All" in the three types of "some" sentence. Bott and Noveck ran the task twice, in one session instructing participants to treat "some" logically, as meaning *some and possibly all*, and in the other instructing them to treat it pragmatically, as meaning *some but not all*. They reasoned that if underinformative sentences generate scalar inferences by default, as neo-Griceans claim, then responses to them should take longer in the logical condition than in the pragmatic one, since the initial pragmatic inference would have to be overridden. In fact, the opposite was the case. Correct responses to underinformative sentences took nearly 1400 ms in the pragmatic condition, as opposed to around 800 ms in the logical one. (Responses to control sentences also took longer in the pragmatic condition, but the effect was most marked for the underinformative ones.) Participants also made more mistakes when required to judge underinformative sentences in the pragmatic condition (accuracy rates of 60% as opposed to 90% for the logical condition).

A possible objection to this experiment is that underinformative sentences called for different responses in the logical and pragmatic conditions ("True" and "False", respectively), and that there might be a response bias in favour of positive answers. To control for this, Bott and Noveck ran a second experiment in which participants were asked to agree or disagree with a second sentence expressing a verdict on the original target sentence ("Mary says the following sentence is true/false . . ."). The polarity of the verdict was varied with the condition, so that underinformative sentences called for the same response in both conditions. The pattern of results was in line with those from the first experiment.

In a third experiment, Bott and Noveck conducted the test without instructions, allowing participants to adopt whatever interpretation of "some" they preferred. Again, those who adopted the logical interpretation (classifying underinformative sentences as true) responded more quickly than those who adopted the pragmatic one (2700 ms and 3300 ms respectively). (This finding was replicated in another study, by Noveck & Posada, 2003, where an even more striking difference was found, with pragmatic responders taking nearly twice as long to respond as logical responders.) In a fourth experiment, Bott and Noveck varied the time allowed for responses. In a short-lag condition participants were allowed 900 ms to respond to a presented sentence; in a long-lag condition they were allowed 3000 ms. Rates of logical responses to underinformative sentences fell from 72% in the short-lag condition to 56% in the long-lag one, suggesting that reducing available cognitive resources reduces the likelihood that the scalar inference will be drawn.

These findings suggest that the default reading of "some" is not *some but not all* and that the derivation of scalar implicatures is effortful and time consuming, and Bott and Noveck conclude that their studies provide evidence against a default inference account of the kind Levinson proposes. They also note that their experiments provide support for relevance theory – especially the final experiment, which indicates that the likelihood of deriving a scalar implicature varies with the availability of cognitive resources, as relevance theory predicts.

We do not deny that these findings offer support for relevance theory, but we wish to strike a note of caution. We have four points to make. First, Bott and Noveck's data may look different when viewed through the lens of dual-process theory. It may be that different tasks activate different *types* of reasoning process, and this needs to be taken into account in interpreting the resulting response times. We shall discuss dual-process theories in the next section.

Second, at most, the reaction-time data show that pragmatic readings are not derived *before* logical interpretations. They do not show that they are not derived by the application of the Q-heuristic. The heuristic might be applied *after* a logical interpretation has been derived and its application might be relatively effortful. Of course, the claim that the pragmatic reading is the initial one is central to Levinson's account, but a weaker neo-Gricean position might modify or drop it. Such an account might continue to hold that neo-Gricean heuristics are applied *by* default, in the sense that they are applied routinely unless contextually cancelled, even though the pragmatic reading is not itself the initial ("default") one.

Third, the data are broadly compatible with convention theory, as well as with relevance theory. Like relevance theory, convention theory holds that the logical reading of scalar terms is the more basic one, and it predicts that the derivation of pragmatic interpretations will be more effortful. Deriving a logical reading involves applying first-order conventions only, whereas deriving a pragmatic one involves applying both first-order and second-order conventions. Of course, without some account of the cognitive processes involved, it is difficult to make predictions from this, but, prima facie, one would expect the latter process to take longer. Like the neo-Gricean, the convention theorist might still hold that implicature conventions, once mastered, are applied by default, unless contextually cancelled.

Fourth, there is a possible alternative explanation for the delayed response times to underinformative sentences in the pragmatic condition, which does not attribute it to the cost of deriving the pragmatic interpretation. The response time to a sentence is the sum of two components: the time taken to derive the preferred interpretation and the time taken to evaluate it, and (as Bott & Noveck themselves acknowledge), it is possible that the delay in responding to underinformative sentences on the pragmatic condition is attributable to the latter component rather than the former. In these cases, the inferred proposition is of the form *Some but not all F are G*, where the hearer in fact knows that all F are G (e.g., *Some but not all elephants are mammals*). If evaluating this proposition involves a search for a (non-existent) counter-example (e.g., an elephant that is not a mammal), then this may well be the source of much of the delay in responding. (It might explain the high error rate, too.) On the logical condition, by contrast, the proposition to be evaluated is of the form *At least one F is G* (e.g., *At least one elephant is a mammal*), which is easily verified by finding a single confirming instance.

There is some support for this explanation. One interesting feature of the data from Bott and Noveck's Experiment 1 is that response times for under-informative *some* statements on the pragmatic condition were longer, not only than corresponding responses on the logical condition, but also (by around 400 ms) than responses to control *some* statements *on the same, pragmatic, condition*. It is implausible to attribute this delay to the time taken to derive the pragmatic interpretation, since participants were under instructions to adopt that interpretation for all sentences on this condition. It is more likely that it is as a result of the additional time required to evaluate the proposition derived in the underinformative cases. Bott and Noveck assume that the scalar inference is unique to underinformative (pragmatically infelicitous) statements – the "T1" statements in their materials (see e.g., 2004, p. 451). We do not understand this, however. Why wouldn't the control *some* statements (e.g., "Some mammals are elephants", "Some elephants are insects") prompt the inference as well? At any rate, they should on neo-Gricean or convention-based accounts, and it would be begging the question against those accounts to suppose otherwise. Moreover, it would be absurd to suggest that in real life situations, people only use "some" to imply *not all* if they know that the *not all* statement is false![5]

It may be objected that this explanation cannot account for the data from Bott and Noveck's fourth experiment, where time pressure produced a majority of logical responses to underinformative sentences. If participants derive the pragmatic interpretation in the short-lag condition but lack time to evaluate it, then we should expect their responses to be at chance, rather than showing a bias towards the logical answer. We acknowledge the power of this consideration but still feel that caution is necessary. For example, it is possible that under pressure participants defaulted to processing an association (elephant → mammal) or that the pressure induced a bias towards positive answers, which was not present in the other conditions (the logical response here was "True"). We conclude that although Bott and Noveck's data offer some support for relevance theory, the other theoretical options remain live, in particular convention theory.[6]

A dual-process perspective

The studies reviewed so far have been conducted largely in isolation from work on reasoning, and few connections have been made with the large body of work on "dual-process" theory – a field in which Jonathan Evans has been a pioneer. This work may be highly relevant, however, and we turn to it now. We begin with a brief introduction to dual-process theories. We should stress that this is highly simplified. In particular, many dual-process theorists are now recognizing that the neat binary divisions that have been proposed are too crude and require refinement and qualification (see the papers in Evans & Frankish, 2009). For present purposes, however, the following characterization will be sufficient.

There is abundant evidence for the existence of two separate but interacting types of processing in human reasoning, decision making, and social cognition, which may deliver different and sometimes conflicting results (for reviews, see Evans, 2003, 2008; Frankish & Evans, 2009). One type of processing (referred to as "implicit", "tacit", "heuristic", "experiential", or simply "Type 1") is fast, effortless, automatic, nonconscious, inflexible, and contextualized. The other ("explicit", "analytic", "Type 2") is slow, effortful, controlled, conscious, flexible, and decontextualized. Type 1 processes are often characterized as parallel and as either associative or based on "fast and frugal" heuristics, whereas Type 2 processes are usually described as serial and rule based. In the field of reasoning, dual-process theories were originally devised to explain evidence from deductive reasoning tasks, where subjects' responses often reveal a conflict between logical processes and nonlogical biases. The paradigm case of this is *belief bias*: a nonlogical preference for believable over unbelievable conclusions, which interferes with the goal of selecting valid over invalid conclusions (Evans, Barston, & Pollard, 1983). In the dual-process framework, belief bias is regarded as a Type 1 process, whereas logical responses are ascribed to Type 2 processing. Thus, our capacity for Type 2 reasoning is seen as the source of our ability to decontextualize problems and respond in accordance with logical norms.

Some researchers have gone on to develop dual-*system* theories of mental architecture, which integrate work on reasoning, decision making, and learning. These theories ascribe the two types of processing to distinct cognitive systems, usually known as *System 1* and *System 2*, which have different functions, processing styles, and evolutionary origins (Evans & Over, 1996; Sloman, 1996, 2002; Stanovich, 1999, 2004). One important claim is that individual differences in general intelligence and working memory are differences in the capacity of System 2, not System 1 – a claim defended at length in Stanovich's work (1999, 2004; Stanovich & West, 1998, 2001). For example, Stanovich and West (1998) showed that the ability to solve decontextualized versions of the Wason selection task, which require analytic processing, correlates with high IQ, whereas performance on heavily contextualized versions, which can be solved by nonconscious heuristics, is unrelated to IQ.

How does implicature processing fit into this framework? Since implicatures are pragmatic interpretations, a natural view would be to see them as the product of Type 1 processes, and to regard logical interpretations as the result of Type 2 reasoning – at least in adults, in whom such reasoning is well developed. There is some reason for thinking this may be the case. Although adults are sensitive to scalar implicatures, it is notable that, on all studies, they make some logical responses as well – sometimes at a high rate. They might be simply failing to derive the implicature, of course, perhaps because their expectations of relevance are met by the logical reading. But dual-process theory offers an alternative explanation: that they are deriving the implicature but inhibiting the response it dictates and responding in line with a logical interpretation generated by Type 2 processes. This is not implausible. It would not be surprising if underinformative scalar statements often provoke explicit, Type 2 reasoning, at least when presented without a natural conversational background. For the implicatures these statements generate are by definition known to be false, and in conversation one would use such statements only when one wanted to, as it were, *lie by implicature*. As Guasti et al. note (2005, pp. 690–692), this may cause some adult participants to depart from standard conversational norms, and either infer that the experimenter is using scalar terms in a technical, strictly logical sense, or search for counterexamples that would render the implicature true (in the latter case, the "logical" response would in fact manifest a pragmatic reading). Although Guasti et al. do not make a connection with dual-process theories, this process might well involve explicit, Type 2 reasoning.

The hypothesis that logical adult responders are inhibiting pragmatic responses has been tested by Feeney and collaborators (2004). Using a computerized sentence verification task, they measured the responses and reaction times of 50 adults to underinformative statements and controls (the materials used were similar to those in Noveck's original experiments).

They found that logical responses to infelicitous (i.e., underinformative) *some* statements took significantly longer than logical responses to felicitous ones (i.e., ones that are true under a pragmatic reading, such as "Some cars are red"). This suggests that the former responses are preceded by additional processing, which, Feeney et al. propose, involves the drawing and inhibiting of a pragmatic inference. Support for this, they argue, comes from a secondary finding that the tendency to respond logically to infelicitous *some* statements is positively correlated with cognitive capacity, as measured by a counting-span task – although they note that this result should be treated with caution owing to the small sample size. Again, this suggests that extra processing is involved in generating the logical responses, and Feeney et al. make an explicit link with dual-process theory. Feeney et al. also propose that their findings offer support for neo-Gricean theory, since they suggest that it is the undoing rather than the derivation of a scalar implicature that is effortful.[7]

We find these results suggestive but also puzzling. As noted earlier, we fail to see why felicitous *some* statements would not also prompt scalar implicatures, and if they do, then the time difference in logical responses to felicitous and infelicitous *some* statements cannot be attributed to the presence or absence of a pragmatic inference. However, this is not incompatible with Feeney et al.'s suggestion that the difference reflects the costs involved in inhibiting a pragmatic response. For in the infelicitous case, the pragmatic and logical interpretations dictate different responses, and if a subject switches from a pragmatic to a logical reading they will need to inhibit their initial disposition to answer "False". In the felicitous case, by contrast, the pragmatic interpretation dictates the same response ("True") as the logical one. Thus, even if a participant makes the same switch of readings, they should still respond more quickly, since they will not need to inhibit their initial, pragmatically driven, disposition to answer "True". (And, of course, if they do not make the switch, their response should be quicker still.) We feel this explanation – which is consistent with Feeney at al.'s overall conclusion – is the more plausible one.

In another study, Scrafton and Feeney (2006) used a dual-process framework to investigate the development of scalar implicature. They point out that there is evidence that Type 1 processes develop before Type 2 ones, with the former being well developed by age 10, but the latter continuing to mature up to age 15 (Handley, Capon, Beveridge, Dennis, & Evans, 2004; Klaczynski, 2001).[8] If scalar implicatures are generated by Type 1 processes, and logical responses (in adults) by Type 2 ones, then, Scrafton and Feeney argue, certain age-related effects should be evident. First, in children, when Type 1 processes are still developing, implicature detection should be patchy but facilitated by contextual cues. Second, in young adolescents pragmatic responding should be dominant regardless of context, since Type 1 processes are then well-developed but Type 2 ones still maturing. Third, logical responding should re-emerge in adulthood, as Type 2 processes become fully developed.

Scrafton and Feeney tested these predictions by comparing sensitivity to scalar implicature among five groups, of age 6, 9, 12, 15, and adult, using both contextually impoverished materials (sentences based on those used by Noveck, 2001) and contextually enriched materials (storyboards in which, for example, a girl was shown eating all the sweets on the table and then telling her mother that she had eaten *some* of them). The results confirmed the predictions. The 6-year-olds detected implicatures only in the enriched condition. The 9-year-olds detected implicatures in both conditions, but detected more in the enriched one. The 12-year-olds detected implicatures in both conditions at near ceiling. Finally, among the 15-year-olds and adults the rate of logical responses increased again and context had little effect, suggesting that the logical responders were decontextualizing the task. These developmental data thus fits well with a dual-process framework. Of course, as Scrafton and Feeney note, it is highly unlikely that young children's logical responses are due to Type 2 processes. When they respond logically, it is likely that they are doing so because they have not yet developed the Type 1 processes needed to derive the pragmatic reading, rather than because they possess the Type 2 processes needed to inhibit it.

How does this dual-process framework fit with the theories of implicature reviewed earlier? We think it is broadly compatible with all of them. The framework involves no commitment as to the nature of the Type 1 processes involved in implicature derivation, except that they should fit the general Type 1 profile – fast, nonconscious, effortless, etc. They might involve application of neo-Gricean heuristics, relevance-based processes, or second-order conventions. It might be objected that relevance theory should be excluded, since it treats implicature derivation as effortful and logical interpretation as effortless. However, it is important to distinguish two senses of "effortful". One is simply "computationally costly", and in this sense we can certainly speak of Type 1 processes as being more or less effortful. In the dual-process literature, by contrast, "effortful" is used to refer to processes that load on working memory, and in this sense effortful reasoning is, virtually by definition, a Type 2 process. Now, we assume that in discussions of relevance theory the term is used in the first sense. Relevance theorists think of pragmatic processes as spontaneous and nonconscious, rather than conscious and reflective (e.g., Sperber & Wilson, 1995, Ch. 2; Wilson & Sperber, 2004). Thus we do not see a conflict here between dual-process theory and relevance theory. The same goes for relevance theory's claim that logical interpretations are effortless. We need to distinguish between those logical interpretations that result from a failure to derive an implicature and those that result from inhibiting one. It is the former that relevance theory treats as effortless (first sense), and the latter that dual-process theory treats as effortful (second sense).

However, although we think that relevance theory is formally compatible with dual-process theory, there is one aspect of Scrafton and Feeney's work that does offer selective support for neo-Gricean theory or convention theory.

This is the finding that by early adolescence context ceases to have any effect on implicature derivation. That is, implicature derivation moves from being a context-driven process to being a largely default one, albeit one that can be overridden. This finding is hard to reconcile with relevance theory, according to which implicature derivation is always context-driven, and it harmonizes better with neo-Gricean or convention-based accounts, on which the process involves mastering general principles or conventions.

So far, we have assumed that implicature derivation is a Type 1 process, but can it also be a Type 2 process (effortful in the second sense)? De Neys and Schaeken (2007) have argued that it can. They used a dual-task methodology to see if cognitive load on working memory interfered with pragmatic processing. Subjects undertook a sentence verification task while performing a dot-pattern memorization task, once with a simple control pattern, once with a complex load pattern. De Neys and Schaeken found that there was a modest though significant decrease in the rate of pragmatic interpretations under the complex load (76% vs. 70%), but no decrease in the rate of correct responses to the control sentences. They also found that pragmatic responses took significantly longer under load (by about 700 ms), whereas responses to control sentences were not affected. De Neys and Schaeken conclude that their findings contradict the neo-Gricean account and support relevance theory, indicating that implicature derivation is effortful, not automatic, and that people are more logical under cognitive load. They also conclude that, since the pattern memorization task loaded on working memory (that is, was effortful in the second sense), implicature derivation also draws on working memory.

We have three points to make here. First, the fact that a task draws on working memory is not sufficient to show that it involves Type 2 reasoning. There are many processes that involve attention, and hence working memory, but which do not involve explicit, Type 2 thought processes (see Barrett, Tugade, & Engle, 2004, for a long list of processes associated with working memory capacity).[9] And it is plausible that additional attentional resources are needed for responding pragmatically to underinformative sentences (for one thing, as noted earlier, their evaluation is not simple). Second, even if Type 2 reasoning were involved in implicature derivation, this would not fit well with relevance theory. On a relevance-theoretic view, language comprehension is a complex process of nondemonstrative inference, involving the parallel forming and testing of hypotheses about explicit content, implicated premises, and implicated conclusions, and drawing on expectations about specific cognitive effects as well as a general assumption of relevance. This process is not one that could feasibly be performed by a slow, conscious, decontextualized, serial reasoning system. If implicature derivation were a Type 2 process, it is more likely that it would involve the application of simple heuristics. Thus De Neys and Schaeken's conclusion, were it sound, would actually favour a form of neo-Gricean view, albeit one which allows that heuristics can be applied effortfully as well as automatically. Third, although we think it implausible that implicature derivation is typically a Type 2 process, we do not exclude the possibility that it may sometimes be. In particular, utterances that are hard to interpret would be likely to provoke explicit, conscious reasoning, perhaps involving the application of general conversational principles such as those Grice proposed, or beliefs about the rules governing scalar terms.[10] Effortful (second sense) implicature derivation may occur in some experimental settings, too. For example, in Bott and Noveck's (2004) Experiment 1, where participants were instructed to interpret "some" pragmatically, it is likely that executing this instruction would involve Type 2 activity. (Responsiveness to verbal instruction is often regarded as a distinctive mark of Type 2 processing; e.g., Evans and Over, 1996.) It is important to recognize this possibility, and to control for it.

Dual-process approaches to implicature are still in their infancy, and it is too soon to draw firm conclusions. The findings reviewed are tantalizing but need replication, and they are also partially at odds with some of the work discussed earlier. In particular, the claim that adults' logical readings of underinformative sentences are often the product of Type 2 reasoning fits ill with the data from reaction-time studies. Here we can merely highlight the need for further work. Dual-task methodologies and searches for correlations between performance and measures of working memory capacity should be useful. It will also be important to consider the nonconscious control processes responsible for initiating Type 2 reasoning and resolving conflicts between the two systems – processes which Jonathan Evans has dubbed *Type 3* (Evans, 2009).

Conclusions

Our conclusions are modest. The experimental work reviewed establishes the psychological reality of scalar implicature and is highly relevant to the evaluation of competing theories of implicature processing. However, the data are not wholly consistent, and they are compatible with all three major accounts. There is some support for relevance theory over the neo-Gricean approach, particularly from reaction-time studies, but it is not decisive. The current experimental findings are also consistent with convention theory, which has an attractive economy and fits the developmental data well, combining the view that logical interpretations are basic with the view that pragmatic interpretations follow a developmental progression from context-driven to default. We shall conclude with some suggestions emerging from our discussion.

First, psychologists should give consideration to convention theory, developing cognitive models of convention-based processes and subjecting them to experimental testing. Studies of the effect of word choice on implicature derivation should be particularly useful here, since the theory predicts that implicatures will be specific to particular linguistic constructions. Cross-linguistic data should also be highly relevant. Second, it is important to devise methods of assessing the relative contribution of different types of process to the generation of responses to scalar statements, including deviation processes, evaluation processes, and inhibitory processes. Different computational paths may lead to similar overt responses and reaction times, and it is important to find ways of distinguishing them. Third, there is need for caution in the experimental use of underinformative statements. Although handy as touchstones, such statements are anomalous, in that the implicatures they generate are always false, and this may distort responses and reaction times. It is also important to remember that felicitous *some* statements generate scalar implicatures, too. Finally, we believe that work on scalar implicature will benefit from closer integration with the reasoning literature and in particular with dual-process theories. There is evidence that Type 2 reasoning is responsible for logical interpretations of scalar terms in adults, and it could play a role in generating pragmatic interpretations, too. In moving to a dual-process framework, theories of implicature will need to become more complex, allowing for a plurality of processes and methods, and taking account of the factors that trigger them.

Notes

1 For a related view, see Chierchia (2004), who argues that generalized implicatures are computed by default in the course of grammar processing.
2 Grice himself recognized the existence of a class of conventional implicatures (1989, pp. 25–26). However, he limited this class to those implicatures that are intrinsic to the meaning of the words used, and did not regard the generalized implicatures we are considering as conventional. In Davis's terms, Grice's conventional implicatures are first-order conventions rather than second-order ones (Davis, 1998, p. 157).
3 Feeney et al. (2004) speculate that this may be due to the fact that their experiment was conducted in English rather than French, and that their results reflect differences in the scope of the French quantifier "certains" and the English "some".
4 Guasti et al. (2005) also tested the effects of training to avoid pragmatic infelicity. They found that although this did improve children's performance, the effects of the training did not persist beyond the session.
5 We wonder if the term "underinformative" fosters some confusion. On a Gricean view, scalar implicatures arise when a less informative term is chosen in preference to a more informative one. In a sense, then, scalar implicatures arise from underinformative statements. But this sense of "underinformative" is different from the one used in the experimental literature, where a *some* statement is said to be underinformative if the corresponding *all* statement is commonly known to be true. Underinformativeness in this sense is not a prerequisite for scalar implicature on any account.
6 Another group of reaction-time studies, by Breheny et al. (2006), which used more naturalistic materials, escapes our third objection at least. In one experiment, Breheny et al. presented scalar sentences at the end of short vignettes, one creating a *lower-bound* context, in which the scalar implicature was not appropriate, the other an *upper-bound* context, in which it was. They found that participants took longer to read the scalar sentences in the upper-bound contexts than in the lower-bound ones, suggesting that scalar implicatures are not generated by default, but only where contextually needed.

7 Feeney et al.'s (2004) results were notable for the high rates of logical responding to underinformative *some* statements found among adults (77%, with half the participants giving logical responses only). We speculate that the abstract nature of the sentence verification task fostered an analytic approach in participants.

8 Scrafton and Feeney (2006) use the terms "heuristic" and "analytic" rather than "Type 1" and "Type 2", but we shall continue to use the latter, which are less loaded.

9 Thanks to Jonathan Evans for this point.

10 De Neys and Schaeken (2007) suggest that standard dual-process theory cannot allow that implicature derivation is a Type 2 process, since it attributes pragmatic biases to the automatic system and normatively correct responses to the effortful one. However, it is now widely accepted that Type 2 reasoning can generate non-normative responses, and that it can involve other procedures besides the application of logical rules. See the papers in Evans and Frankish, 2009.

Acknowledgements

The authors wish to thank Shira Elqayam and Jonathan Evans for helpful discussions about implicature and dual processes.

References

Barrett, L. F., Tugade, M. M., & Engle, R. W. (2004). Individual differences in working memory capacity and dual-process theories of the mind. *Psychological Bulletin, 130*, 553–573.

Bott, L., & Noveck, I. A. (2004). Some utterances are underinformative: The onset and time course of scalar inferences. *Journal of Memory and Language, 51*, 437–457.

Braine, M., & Rumain, B. (1981). Children's comprehension of "or": Evidence for a sequence of competencies. *Journal of Experimental Child Psychology, 31*, 46–70.

Breheny, R., Katsos, N., & Williams, J. (2006). Are generalised scalar implicatures generated by default? An on-line investigation into the role of context in generating pragmatic inferences. *Cognition, 100*, 434–463.

Carston, R. (2002). *Thoughts and utterances*. Oxford: Blackwell.

Chierchia, G. (2004). Scalar implicatures, polarity phenomena, and the syntax/pragmatics interface. In A. Belletti (Ed.), *Structures and beyond: The cartography of syntactic structures* (Vol. 3, pp. 39–103). New York: Oxford University Press.

Chierchia, G., Crain, S., Guasti, M. T., Gualmini, A., & Meroni, L. (2001). The acquisition of disjunction: Evidence for a grammatical view of scalar implicatures. In A. H. Do, L. Domínguez, & A. Johansen (Eds.), *Proceedings of the 25th annual Boston University conference on language development* (pp. 157–168). Sommerville, MA: Cascadilla Press.

Crain, S., & Thornton, R. (1998). *Investigations in universal grammar*. Cambridge, MA: MIT Press.

Davis, W. A. (1998). *Implicature: Intention, convention, and principle in the failure of Gricean theory*. Cambridge: Cambridge University Press.

Davis, W. A. (2008). Implicature. In E. N. Zalta (Ed.), *The Stanford encyclopedia of philosophy* (Winter 2008 edition). Retrieved April 7, 2009, from http://plato.stanford.edu/entries/implicature/.

De Neys, W., & Schaeken, W. (2007). When people are more logical under cognitive load: Dual task impact on scalar implicature. *Experimental Psychology, 54,* 128–133.

Evans, J. St B. T. (2003). In two minds: Dual-process accounts of reasoning. *Trends in Cognitive Sciences, 7,* 454–459.

Evans, J. St B. T. (2008). Dual-processing accounts of reasoning, judgment, and social cognition. *Annual Review of Psychology, 59,* 255–278.

Evans, J. St B. T. (2009). How many dual-process theories do we need? One, two, or many? In J. St B. T. Evans & K. Frankish (Eds.), *In two minds: Dual processes and beyond* (pp. 33–54). Oxford: Oxford University Press.

Evans, J. St B. T., Barston, J. L., & Pollard, P. (1983). On the conflict between logic and belief in syllogistic reasoning. *Memory and Cognition, 11,* 295–306.

Evans, J. St B. T., & Frankish, K. (2009). *In two minds: Dual processes and beyond.* Oxford: Oxford University Press.

Evans, J. St B. T., & Over, D. E. (1996). *Rationality and reasoning.* Hove, UK: Psychology Press.

Feeney, A., Scrafton, S., Duckworth, A., & Handley, S. J. (2004). The story of some: Everyday pragmatic inference by children and adults. *Canadian Journal of Experimental Psychology, 58,* 121–132.

Frankish, K., & Evans, J. St B. T. (2009). The duality of mind: An historical perspective. In J. St B. T. Evans & K. Frankish (Eds.), *In two minds: Dual processes and beyond* (pp. 1–29). Oxford: Oxford University Press.

Gazdar, G. (1979). *Pragmatics: Implicature, presupposition and logical form.* New York: Academic Press.

Grice, P. (1989). *Studies in the way of words.* Cambridge, MA: Harvard University Press.

Guasti, M. T., Chierchia, G., Crain, S., Foppolo, F., Gualmini, A., & Meroni, L. (2005). Why children and adults sometimes (but not always) compute implicatures. *Language and Cognitive Processes, 20,* 667–696.

Handley, S. J., Capon, A., Beveridge, M., Dennis, I., & Evans, J. St B. T. (2004). Working memory, inhibitory control and the development of children's reasoning. *Thinking and Reasoning, 10,* 175–195.

Horn, L. R. (1984). Toward a new taxonomy for pragmatic inference: Q-based and R-based implicature. In D. Schiffrin (Ed.), *Meaning, form, and use in context* (pp. 11–42). Washington, DC: Georgetown University Press.

Horn, L. R. (1989). *A natural history of negation.* Chicago: University of Chicago Press.

Klaczynski, P. A. (2001). Analytic and heuristic processing influences on adolescent reasoning and decision-making. *Child Development, 72,* 844–861.

Levinson, S. C. (2000). *Presumptive meanings: The theory of generalized conversational implicature.* Cambridge, MA: MIT Press.

Morgan, J. L. (1978). Two types of convention in indirect speech acts. In P. Cole (Ed.), *Syntax and semantics, Volume 9: Pragmatics* (pp. 261–280). New York: Academic Press.

Noveck, I. A. (2001). When children are more logical than adults: Experimental investigations of scalar implicature. *Cognition, 78,* 165–188.

Noveck, I. A., & Posada, A. (2003). Characterizing the time course of an implicature: An evoked potentials study. *Brain and Language, 85,* 203–210.

Noveck, I. A., & Sperber, D. (2007). The why and how of experimental pragmatics: The case of "scalar inferences". In N. Burton-Roberts (Ed.), *Pragmatics* (pp. 184–212). Basingstoke: Palgrave Macmillan.

Papafragou, A., & Musolino, J. (2003). Scalar implicatures: Experiments at the semantics–pragmatics interface. *Cognition, 86*, 253–282.

Papafragou, A., & Tantalou, N. (2004). Children's computation of implicatures. *Language Acquisition, 12*, 71–82.

Pouscoulous, N., Noveck, I. A., Politzer, G., & Bastide, A. (2007). A developmental investigation of processing costs in implicature production. *Language Acquisition, 14*, 347–375.

Rips, L. J. (1975). Quantification and semantic memory. *Cognitive Psychology, 7*, 307–340.

Scrafton, S., & Feeney, A. (2006). Dual processes, development, and scalar implicature. In R. Sun & N. Miyake (Eds.), *Proceedings of the 28th annual conference of the Cognitive Science Society* (pp. 774–779). Austin, TX: Cognitive Science Society.

Sloman, S. A. (1996). The empirical case for two systems of reasoning. *Psychological Bulletin, 119*, 3–22.

Sloman, S. A. (2002). Two systems of reasoning. In T. Gilovich, D. Griffin, & D. Kahneman (Eds.), *Heuristics and biases: The psychology of intuitive judgement* (pp. 379–396). Cambridge: Cambridge University Press.

Smith, C. L. (1980). Quantifiers and question answering in young children. *Journal of Experimental Child Psychology, 30*, 191–205.

Sperber, D., & Wilson, D. (1995). *Relevance: Communication and cognition* (2nd ed.). Oxford: Blackwell.

Stanovich, K. E. (1999). *Who is rational?: Studies of individual differences in reasoning.* Mahwah, NJ: Lawrence Erlbaum Associates, Inc.

Stanovich, K. E. (2004). *The robot's rebellion: Finding meaning in the age of Darwin.* Chicago: University of Chicago Press.

Stanovich, K. E., & West, R. F. (1998). Cognitive ability and variation in selection task performance. *Thinking and Reasoning, 4*, 193–230.

Stanovich, K. E., & West, R. F. (2001). Individual differences in reasoning: Implications for the rationality debate? *Behavioral and Brain Sciences, 23*, 645–665.

Wierzbicka, A. (1985). Different cultures, different languages, different speech acts. *Journal of Pragmatics, 9*, 145–178.

Wierzbicka, A. (1987). Boys will be boys: "Radical semantics" vs. "radical pragmatics". *Language, 63*, 95–114.

Wilson, D., & Sperber, D. (2004). Relevance theory. In L. R. Horn & G. L. Ward (Eds.), *The handbook of pragmatics* (pp. 607–632). Oxford: Blackwell.

14 The dynamics of reasoning

Chronometric analysis and dual-process theories

Linden J. Ball

Lancaster University

Dual-process theories dominate contemporary research on human reasoning (e.g., Evans, 2007a; Sloman, 2002; Stanovich, 2004) and embody the notion that reasoning reflects a sophisticated interplay between processes that are fast, automatic, low effort, and high capacity on the one hand, and processes that are slow, controlled, high effort and resource limited on the other hand. The first mention of dual processes in the reasoning literature seems to be traceable to Jonathan Evans' paper with Peter Wason, published in the mid-1970s, that focused on the famous four-card selection task (see Wason & Evans, 1975). There is little doubt that many fundamental concepts that form a part of dual-process theorizing have derived from Evans' major programme of research on this topic over the 30 years or so following the publication of this paper. Indeed, a core motivation behind the present chapter is to pay tribute to the multiplicity of valuable dual-process ideas that Evans has contributed to the reasoning domain over the past three decades and to which he is still actively contributing (e.g., see Evans, Chapter 19, this volume).

Wason and Evans' (1975) paper was simply entitled "Dual Processes in Reasoning?", with the question mark perhaps presaging some of the challenges that would surround the development of dual-process theories over the ensuing years and that still persist to this day (see Evans & Frankish, 2009, for a recent collection of papers addressing both established and emerging issues in this area). Although a few contemporary researchers still doubt whether dual-process concepts are necessary to provide an integrated account of reasoning phenomena (e.g., Osman, 2004), the majority appear to have embraced dual-process ideas. The present chapter, too, is predicated on the assumption that dual-process notions are critical for developing a comprehensive account of reasoning. Within this context, a key aim of the chapter is to examine the idea that *chronometric* data (i.e., time-based measures of performance in terms of processing latencies and problem inspection times) can provide valuable information that can inform dual-process accounts of reasoning. Indeed, I contend that chronometric data may well prove to be one of the most important sources of evidence not only for establishing support for dual-process predictions, but also for shaping the development of dual-process theories in the future (e.g., by clarifying dynamic aspects of reasoning such as the flow of control between dual processes over the time-course of reasoning, from problem presentation to response production).

To defend these claims I aim to review a range of time-based analyses that have focused on two of the most well-researched reasoning paradigms: Wason's four-card selection task, and syllogistic inference with belief-oriented problem contents. What will emerge from this review is an intriguing paradox. First, in the case of the selection task – where relevance-based effects such as "matching bias" appear to dominate responding (e.g., Evans 1998) – it appears that chronometric data are most readily interpreted as reflecting a *sequential* flow of processing. According to this sequential model, rapid, low-effort processes provide default responses that are then subjected to more effortful analytic processing that may serve either to accept or overturn default decisions. Second, in the case of belief-oriented categorical syllogisms, it seems that the best way to interpret time-based data that are associated with the emergence of so-called "belief-bias" effects is in terms of *parallel* processing streams. According to a parallel, dual-process model fast, low-effort processes and slow, high-effort processes compete in determining responding in situations where the logic of a presented conclusion conflicts with its believability.

The idea that we need one dual-process architecture to account for reasoning on the selection task and a radically different dual-process architecture to capture reasoning with belief-oriented syllogisms is not just paradoxical but highly questionable in terms of psychological and evolutionary plausibility. What I will attempt to show in this chapter is that a neat resolution to this paradox (and the conceptual problems it entails) may be afforded by recent dual-process theorizing, most notably the view that reasoning may arise from an integrated "hybrid" architecture involving both sequential and parallel processing components (Evans, 2009; see also Evans, this volume).

Hybrid dual-process theories have, in fact, been around in the reasoning literature for some time, with examples in the area of belief bias including Klauer, Musch, and Naumer's (2000) *multinomial model*, and Evans, Handley, and Harper's (2001) similar (though independently developed) *selective processing model* (see also Evans, 2000). Despite the existence of such hybrid accounts, however, many reasoning researchers (the present author included) have tended to make simplifying assumptions when interpreting reasoning data, often leading to an overly narrow focus on either the sequential or parallel components of such models. The argument that will be developed in this chapter is that it is only by embracing a fully hybrid, dual-process architecture that real headway can be made in grappling with the subtleties and complexities associated with the dynamics of human reasoning.

Dual processes in the Wason selection task: Historical perspectives

As noted above, the selection task was the focus of the first mention in the literature of the possible existence of dual processes in reasoning (Wason &

Evans, 1975). In their study Wason and Evans used two forms of selection task, one which involved an abstract, affirmative conditional rule such as *If there is a B on one side of a card then there is a 3 on the other side*, and the other which involved an abstract conditional rule with a negated consequent such as *If there is a B on one side of a card then there is not a 3 on the other side*. In conjunction with each task participants were also shown four cards (e.g., displaying the visible sides B, G, 3 and 2), and it was explained that each card had a letter on one side and a single digit number on the other side. Participants were asked to establish the truth value of the conditional for each task by selecting for inspection the necessary and sufficient cards from the set presented. The logically correct selections for the affirmative conditional (*If p then q*) are the B (*p*) and the 2 (*not-q*) cards, as only these cards could potentially reveal a letter–number combination that would be a counterexample to the rule (i.e., a B coupled with a number other than 3). On this task, however, the majority of participants selected the B (*p*) card alone, or else the B (*p*) and 3 (*q*) cards. On the negated-consequent conditional (*If p then not q*) the logically correct selections are the B (*p*) and the 3 (*not-q*) cards, since, again, these are the cards that could reveal a counterexample to the presented rule. Intriguingly, on this version of the task participants tended to choose the same cards as on the affirmative rule (i.e., the B and the 3), although this time the selections were logically appropriate.

The selection patterns observed by Wason and Evans (1975) on the affirmative and negative versions of the selection task appeared to arise from a tendency for people simply to choose cards mentioned in the rule irrespective of the presence of negations – a phenomenon that had previously been identified on this task by Evans and Lynch (1973) which they referred to as "matching bias" (see Evans, 1998, for a detailed review of this bias). Wason and Evans' (1975) study, however, did more than just replicate the presence of matching bias on the selection task; it also led to the observation that when requested to explain their selections participants would tend to justify choices on the negated rule in terms of their potential to provide counterexamples to the rule, while they would tend to justify choices on the affirmative rule in terms of their potential to verify the rule. Wason and Evans argued that it was implausible that participants would switch from apparent "insight" to "noninsight" on these task variants, and instead proposed that people's verbal explanations for their card selections were post hoc *rationalizations* of unconsciously determined choices. Thus emerged the original dual-process theory of reasoning: Type 1 processes such as matching unconsciously bias reasoning, while Type 2 processes serve to construct justifications for behaviour that are consistent with one's knowledge of the situation. In a follow-up study, Evans and Wason (1976) validated the rationalization capacity of Type 2 processes, showing that participants were not only happy to endorse just about any experimenter-generated "correct" selections, but, moreover, were readily willing to offer justifications for these selections.

Wason and Evans' (1975) initial dual-process proposals seemed to lean more toward a parallel rather than a sequential architecture. For example, they suggested that a staged account of nonconscious Type 1 processes followed by conscious Type 2 processes might be an "oversimplification", instead suggesting that "A weaker (but more plausible) assumption is that there is a dialectical relation between them: A process of rapid continuous feedback between tendencies to respond and consciousness rather than two temporally distinct phases" (Wason & Evans, 1975, p. 150). In the 1980s, however, Evans began to make a firmer commitment to a staged processing architecture; which eventually manifested itself in his proposals for a heuristic–analytic (H–A) theory of reasoning (e.g., Evans, 1984, 1989). In the H–A theory, heuristics are preconscious and function to focus attention selectively on information that appears to be *relevant* to the task at hand. The idea is that heuristics serve both to represent aspects of the information presented and also to retrieve pertinent prior knowledge from memory to augment this information. People subsequently reason on the basis of these individualized representations using analytic processes which allow for the generation of an inference or judgement. According to the H–A theory, biases in reasoning are viewed as arising primarily because either logically relevant information is excluded at the heuristic stage or logically irrelevant information is included.

This original H–A theory proved influential in accounting for many reasoning phenomena (Evans, 1989), although it did require some additional assumptions in order to capture the full range of phenomena associated with the abstract selection task. In particular, Evans (1989, 1995) argued that the abstract selection task was unique in that analytic processes played no role in card selections, which were based purely on heuristically cued considerations of relevance. Evans (1989) emphasized the operation of two key linguistically based heuristics in determining card choices. First, he described the "not-heuristic" (subsequently referred to by Evans, 1998, as the "matching heuristic"), which reflects the use of negation in natural language, which is to deny suppositions rather than to assert new information. The idea here is that a negative statement is a comment that does not alter the topic of an assertion (e.g., the topic of a statement such as "There is not a 3" is still about the number 3). Second, Evans (1989) described the "if-heuristic", which induces a preference for the true antecedent (TA) card rather than the false antecedent (FA) card irrespective of whether the presented conditional rule contains a positive antecedent term or a negated antecedent term. Evans suggests that the word "if" provokes hypothetical thinking about the state of affairs in which the antecedent holds true.

In summary, Evans' (1989) H–A theory viewed card choices on the abstract selection task as being driven entirely by the matching- and if-heuristics in the majority of individuals. Moreover, any analytic processing arising on the task was considered merely to rationalize choices in the manner observed by Wason and Evans (1975) and Evans and Wason (1976). In this way the selection task contrasted with other reasoning problems where it was claimed that analytic processes played a functional role in determining responses.

Evans (1989, 1995) further suggested that the special status of the selection task in obviating the involvement of analytic processes in card selections may arise from an instructional demand characteristic, since people are simply asked to choose cards that need to be turned over, a request which seems only to require an assessment of item relevance.

Dual processes in the Wason selection task: Current perspectives

The essential characteristics of the original H–A account of reasoning are still embodied in the recent instantiation of the theory presented by Evans (2006) and depicted schematically in Figure 14.1. The revised theory retains the sequential feel of the original account, while also emphasizing how heuristic processes can control behaviour directly unless analytic processes intervene. In other words, heuristic processes are claimed to provide "default" responses that may or may not be inhibited by analytic intervention (what Evans refers to as a *default-interventionist* framework). A major advantage of ascribing an interventionist function to analytic processes is that this provides a mechanism whereby a range of factors that are known to have a facilitatory role on reasoning can have an influence (e.g., see Stanovich & West, 2000), including instructions to think more abstractly or logically, personal dispositions to think critically, and increased available working-memory capacity in certain individuals. In addition, there are various studies in the literature demonstrating that default heuristics will control behaviour whenever participants are asked to respond rapidly to reasoning problems. For example, under speeded response requirements, matching bias is accentuated in the Wason selection task (Roberts & Newton, 2001) and belief bias is accentuated in syllogistic reasoning (Evans & Curtis-Holmes, 2005).

An important aspect of the revised H–A theory is that it allows for reasoning

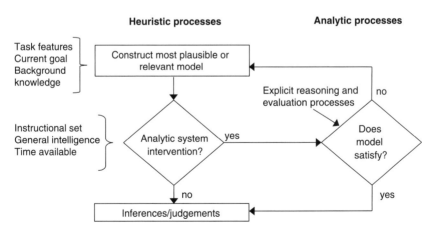

Figure 14.1 A schematic depiction of Evans' (2006) revised heuristic–analytic theory.

biases to arise at the analytic processing stage rather than just at the heuristic stage, as emphasized in the original account. As Figure 14.1 shows, analytic processing is viewed by Evans (2006) as being inherently "satisficing" in nature. This means that analytic processing is geared toward finding solutions to reasoning problems that are "good enough" in terms of satisfying task goals, rather than towards finding optimal solutions (see Simon, 1982). Such satisficing tendencies can explain many of the logical errors observed in human deduction, such as the endorsement of fallacious inferences that occurs in conditional and syllogistic reasoning. Satisficing that arises during analytic processing may also play a crucial role in the emergence of belief-bias effects in syllogistic reasoning, as will be discussed later in the chapter.

Evans' (2006) revised H–A theory continues to account for people's behaviour on the abstract, indicative selection task in essentially the same way as the original H–A theory (e.g., Evans, 1989). Thus, card selections are claimed to be determined through the operation of the if-heuristic and the matching-heuristic, while analytic processing serves to rationalize selections via a satisficing principle. This principle provides a neat account of why the analytic system typically fails to override heuristically cued selections: people's analytic systems will typically accept heuristically cued choices whenever a justification for selecting a card based on either verification or falsification can be found. This means that heuristically cued cards on the selection task will nearly always be accepted, except in a few individuals of much higher cognitive ability who seem to be able to inhibit heuristic cues in order to pay closer attention to all available response options (see Stanovich & West, 1998).

Evans' (2006) general H–A theory is also able to provide a compelling account of reasoning phenomena associated with a wide range of selection tasks that involve *deontic* rather than indicative conditional rules. Unlike indicative conditionals, which express factual, scientific, or common-sense knowledge, deontic conditionals specify social regulations, laws and moral norms, typically in the form of rules that describe permissions or obligations. Johnson-Laird, Legrenzi, and Legrenzi (1972) were the first researchers to study a deontic selection task, using the rule *If a letter is sealed then it has a 50 lire stamp on it*. Participants played the role of postal workers, sorting mail and checking for rule violations. Presented "cards" were real envelopes: a sealed letter (*p*), an unsealed letter (*not-p*), a letter with a 50 lire stamp (*q*), and one with a 40 lire stamp (*not-q*). The violating *p* and *not-q* instance for the specified postal rule would be a sealed letter with a lower-value stamp on it. In Johnson-Laird et al.'s study 21 out of 24 participants selected cards that could reveal this combination compared with 2 out of 24 in the standard, indicative version of the task.

Although this apparently logical performance on this deontic-selection task was originally dubbed the "thematic facilitation effect" it is now known that the influence of thematic content on this task is rather more subtle than merely to provide a catalyst for logical responding. There are two main reasons for this subtlety (Evans, 1996). First, it is not the case that thematic content always alters selection frequencies. When materials are "arbitrarily realistic" participants seem to succumb to the same matching bias as observed with indicative rules (e.g., see Manktelow & Evans', 1979, study using rules such as *Every time I eat haddock then I drink gin*). Second, even when thematic content does change card-selection patterns it does not always produce increases in logical choices. For example, studies using certain kinds of social contract rule have shown that a *not-p* and *q* pattern can be induced instead of a *p* and *not-q* pattern (e.g., Cosmides & Tooby, 1989; Gigerenzer & Hug, 1992; Manktelow & Over, 1991). In the study reported by Manktelow and Over (1991) the rule that was used was described as being one given by a mother to a son: *If you tidy your room then you may go out to play*. The four cards represented different days, which showed on one side whether the room was tidied and on the other whether the son played outside. When participants adopted the role of the son checking whether the rule had been followed they selected logically correct "Room tidied" (*p*) and "Did not go out to play" (*not-q*) cards. However, when asked to check the rule from the perspective of the mother, the typical response was to select "Room not tidied" (*not-p*) and "Went out to play" (*q*).

Manktelow and Over (1991) proposed that people may be selecting cards on deontic variants of the selection task because of pragmatic influences (e.g., striving to satisfy personal goals such as detecting whether cheating is arising in a social-contact situation), rather than because they are reasoning logically. How, though, might the H–A theory accommodate the selection patterns observed on deontic versions of the selection task? Evans and Over (1996) concur with Manktelow and Over's proposals and argue that heuristically cued relevance on deontic-selection tasks is related to the current goal that the participant is pursuing. Thus, any card that could reveal an outcome costing the participant something (e.g., extra money for a sealed letter or prevention from playing outside) will have high "goal relevance", thereby becoming the focus of attention and determining card selection. Instructional and scenario changes can, of course, alter what the participant will see as costly outcomes for a task. Thus, perspective effects can readily be accommodated within this extended notion of heuristically cued relevance. As for analytic processing in deontic selection tasks, such processing would, once again, serve a pure rationalization function, being employed to justify choices in an equivalent manner to that which arises in the indicative paradigm (see Evans, 1996).

Converging evidence for dual processes in the Wason selection task

Over the past two decades the production of empirical evidence in support of the H–A theory of the selection task in both its indicative and deontic versions has moved beyond patterns of card selections and has focused on measures of card decision orders, indices of card inspection times, and data derived from the deployment of process-tracing techniques such as requests for people to generate concurrent think-aloud protocols. For example, in the first piece of collaborative research that I conducted with Jonathan Evans as an undergraduate student (Evans, Ball, & Brooks, 1987) we examined card decision orders using computer-presented versions of the indicative selection task, where participants were required to make yes/no decisions about all four cards. As predicted by the H–A account, people made decisions about matching cards before nonmatching cards, and there was a correlation between the frequency of choice of a card and the tendency to decide about it earlier rather than later. These decision-order effects are suggestive of attentional biases impacting upon selection behaviour, although Evans, Newstead, and Byrne (1993) noted that such effects may simply indicate a response bias for people to register "yes" decisions before "no" decisions.

Stronger evidence for the H–A account was provided by Evans (1996) in research involving the acquisition of chronometric data. Evans reported two studies that adopted a mouse-pointing technique to record people's card inspection times. This technique involved participants tackling computer-presented selection tasks (some involving indicative rules and some involving deontic rules) while simultaneously using a mouse pointer to denote the card they were considering. A card could be selected by clicking the mouse while the pointer was touching it, while no action was required for nonselected cards. The cumulative time that the pointer hovered over a card provided a measure of its inspection time, which was assumed to reflect the duration that the individual spent thinking about that card.

In order to understand Evans' (1996) inspection-time predictions, it is useful to recapitulate the two fundamental tenets of the H–A theory: first, card selections are assumed to be determined purely by heuristic processes; second, analytic processing that occurs is assumed not to affect choices, instead being aimed at rationalizing heuristically cued decisions. The consequence of these assumptions is that participants should think more about selected cards than rejected ones. More specifically, Evans specified the following predictions: cards associated with higher selection rates will be associated with longer inspection times; and for any given card, participants who choose it will have longer inspection times than those who do not. Evans' (1996) studies provided good support for both predictions. For example, there were large and reliable differences in mean inspection times between selected and nonselected cards, with the former generally being greater than 4 s and the latter typically being less than 2 s.

Despite the seemingly compelling evidence for the H–A account of selection-task performance deriving from Evans' (1996) study, Roberts (1998) expressed a need for caution in interpreting inspection-time findings. He argued that there are potential sources of bias inherent in the inspection-time paradigm that could induce artefactual evidence for the view that people are spending time rationalizing choices that have been cued by relevance-determining heuristics. For example, Roberts notes that people may have a tendency to pause the mouse pointer over a card before making an active "select" decision (by clicking on it). Since in Evans' (1996) studies active responses were only required for selected cards, such momentary hesitations would add additional time to the total inspection-time values for selected versus rejected items. As another example of a task-format bias, Roberts refers to the possibility for "sensory leakage", whereby cards may be looked at and even rejected before the mouse pointer has had a chance to reach them, which would also tend to add additional time to selected cards, which we know are decided about earlier (see Evans et al., 1987) rather than rejected cards, which are decided about later. Roberts (1998) manipulated the presence of such task-format biases across a series of ingenious experiments, and demonstrated that the magnitude of the inspection-time effect was closely related to the number of sources of bias present.

Overall, the key issue that appears to have been highlighted by Roberts' (1998) critique of the inspection-time paradigm is that the mouse-pointing technique may lack sufficient sensitivity for monitoring the second-by-second attentional processing of cards in a way that could inform H–A predictions. Such insensitivity appears to derive from the indirect measure of attentional processing that mouse pointing provides, in that participants have actively to self-monitor their attentional focus and move the mouse pointer to whatever card they are thinking about. To overcome the problems associated with the mouse-pointing methodology my colleagues and I (e.g., Ball, Lucas, Miles, & Gale, 2003) advocated the use of eye-gaze tracking as a more precise approach for measuring the moment-by-moment attentional shifts that are typically associated with cognitive performance with highly display-based problems like the selection task. The validity of the gaze-tracking method relies on the so-called "eye–mind" assumption, which claims that a close association exists between the location of eye fixations and the locus of attention. The validity of this assumption has been supported in some wide-ranging reviews of eye-movement research (e.g., Rayner, 1998), and an increasing number of researchers have started to capitalize on the gaze-tracking methodology to examine fundamental processes in thinking and problem solving (e.g., Grant & Spivey, 2003; Jones, 2003; Knoblich, Ohlsson, & Raney, 2001).

Ball et al. (2003) reported three experiments using abstract, indicative versions of the selection task that systematically eradicated the sources of artefact discussed by Roberts (1998) by combining careful task constructions with eye-movement tracking to measure directly on line processing. All three experiments produced good evidence for the robustness of the inspection-time effect, so supporting the predictions of Evans' H–A account. For example, in Ball et al.'s most unbiased experiment (Experiment 3, which enforced a "yes/no" decision for all presented cards), the mean time difference for selected versus rejected cards was 0.36 s, revealing a small but highly reliable inspection-time effect. The size of the inspection-time effect concurs with the 0.3 s effect observed by Roberts and Newton (2001) in a mouse-pointing study using both indicative and deontic-selection tasks that deployed a methodological innovation to eradicate task-format artefacts. In more recent research using eye-gaze measures, the inspection-time effect has been generalized to deontic selection tasks (Ball, Lucas, & Phillips, 2005), with the size of the observed effect again being small (0.48 s) but highly reliable.

At first sight, however, the small magnitude of the gaze-based inspection-time effect seems rather curious when considered in terms of the H–A theory. Recall that the inspection-time effect is assumed to arise because analytic processes are applied to *rationalize* the selection of relevant cards, whereas cards that are deemed irrelevant are not subjected to further analytic thought. But surely analytic rationalization processes should take more than 300–500 ms to be applied? One explanation for the small magnitude of the inspection-time effect is that some level of rationalization actually occurs when participants *re-inspect* presented rules – perhaps to reflect on the consequences of card selection for the conditional – rather than arising only when cards are being attended to. Such rule re-inspection appeared to arise frequently in Ball et al.'s (2003) study. However, a recent gaze-tracking experiment by Lucas and Ball (2008) provides data that run counter to this explanation. In their study, Lucas and Ball employed selection tasks in which the presentation of each rule was separated from the presentation of the four associated cards (i.e., people had to memorize the rule prior to making card selections). This minor task change meant that participants were *unable* to spend time thinking about selections while re-inspecting the conditional rule, yet Lucas and Ball's data showed that the inspection-time effect remained identical in size to that seen in research with the standard presentation format.

An alternative account of the small magnitude of the inspection-time effect is simply that analytic rationalization processes take place very rapidly in the selection task. Perhaps, for example, the explicit consideration of what may be on the reverse sides of to-be-selected cards is itself cued by heuristic processes. Both Evans (1995) and Lucas and Ball (2005) present think-aloud data from protocol-analysis studies that support this proposal. Lucas and Ball (2005) uncovered striking evidence in people's concurrent verbal reports that *secondary matching heuristics* guide the consideration of hidden card values during the justification of selections (see Evans & Wason, 1976). Such secondary matching heuristics are presumably very rapid in nature, hence accounting for the rapidity of the analytic rationalization that arises in the task.

A final piece of eye-gaze research that I have recently conducted with colleagues at Lancaster (Ball, Towse, & Phillips, 2008) seems also worthy of mention, since it again re-affirms the role of sequential dual-reasoning processes in the selection task. Our study was inspired by a method pioneered by Roberts and Newton (2001, Experiments 2 and 3), which they refer to as the "rapid-response selection task". In this task Roberts and Newton used typical indicative and deontic-selection tasks, but required participants to respond within 2 s of each card presentation. A control group made selections under no time pressure. Unlike Roberts and Newton's rapid response paradigm, which entailed sequential presentation of the cards associated with each task (with a select/reject decision required for each one), our study involved the standard, simultaneous presentation of cards. In addition, select/reject responses were required for all of four cards within a 10 s time limit, with participants being presented with a series of warning sounds to alert them to the impending cut-off time. Our predictions, which we derived from the H–A theory, were as follows:

(1) we assumed that the standard inspection-time effect would be replicated in the free-time paradigm, since time would be available for participants to rationalize card selections;
(2) in the rapid-response paradigm we predicted that a reduced or absent inspection-time effect would be observed, since there would be insufficient time available for participants to pursue rationalizations of heuristically cued selections; and
(3) since heuristics would largely be determining choices in both the rapid-response and free-time paradigms, we expected little change in actual selection patterns across the two paradigms.

As Figure 14.2 indicates, Ball et al.'s (2008) inspection-time predictions were supported: The rapid-response paradigm all but eradicated the standard inspection-time effect that was present in the free-time paradigm. As for the predictions relating to response patterns, these were, again, largely corroborated. Figure 14.3 shows the card selection frequencies in the rapid-response and free-time paradigms for the conditions involving the affirmative rule (*If p then q*) and the negated consequent rule (*If p then not q*). The selection patterns appear to be very similar across both paradigms, although there is

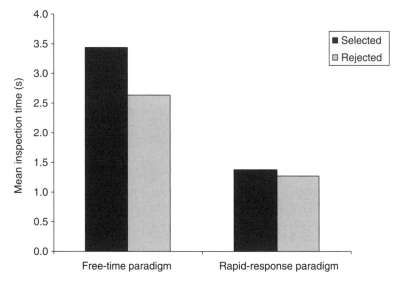

Figure 14.2 Card inspection times in free-time versus rapid-response paradigms (Ball et al., 2008).

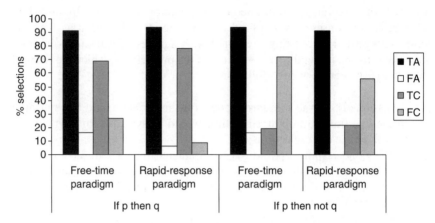

Figure 14.3 Card selection frequencies in free-time versus rapid-response paradigms (Ball et al., 2008). FA = false antecedent; FC = false consequent; TA = true antecedent; TC = true consequent.

some evidence for fewer logically correct false consequent selections across these two rules under speeded decision requirements (see also Roberts and Newton, 2001, for evidence of increased matching responses in the rapid-response paradigm, though not necessarily with reduced logical selections). We wonder whether the slight reduction in false consequent selections seen in our rapid-response tasks may reflect the behaviour of a small subgroup of high-ability individuals who under free-time requirements are able to use analytic processes to determine the value of the false consequent card, but who are less able to conduct such an analysis when the decision time is severely limited. We have yet to conduct the detailed analyses to support this proposal, but it would appear to provide a plausible account of the slight alteration in selection frequencies for false consequent items across rapid-response and free-time response modes. Suffice it to say for now that the rapid-response paradigm, when combined with time-based measures of the locus of people's attention, seems a fruitful way to explore further the nature of heuristic and analytic processes in the selection task.

Interim summary

Overall, then, I would suggest that a number of lines of converging evidence point to the viability of Evans' H–A theory of performance with both indicative and deontic versions of the selection task. Card selections would appear to be largely determined by relevance-based heuristics, with analytic processes pursuing satisficing-oriented justifications of heuristically cued decisions. At an architectural level, moreover, the dual-reasoning processes that are associated with the H–A theory appear to be highly sequential in their operation, with heuristics providing default responses that have the potential to be overturned through the intervention of analytic processes, but where such analytic effort is often biased itself in the majority of individuals because of an inherent tendency to stick with satisficing solutions to reasoning problems (Evans, 2006). It has also been demonstrated how chronometric data arising in the card inspection-time paradigm have played an important role in recent years in corroborating a sequential, dual-process view of reasoning behaviour with the selection task. In the next section the focus shifts to another reasoning paradigm: syllogistic inference with belief-oriented problem contents.

Dual processes and belief-bias effects in syllogistic reasoning

Categorical syllogisms are deductive-reasoning problems that involve two premises and a conclusion, each of which features a standard logical quantifier (i.e., *all*, *no*, *some*, or *some . . . are not*). A classic example of a categorical syllogism based around abstract problem content is "Some artists are bee-keepers; No beekeepers are carpenters; *Therefore*, some artists are not carpenters". A logically valid conclusion describes the relationship between the quantified terms appearing in the premises in a way that is necessarily true. In other words, conclusions that are consistent with the premises but not necessitated by them are invalid. In studies of syllogistic reasoning participants are asked either to generate a logical conclusion in response to given premises or to evaluate the validity of a presented conclusion. To simplify the following discussion I focus exclusively on conclusion-evaluation tasks (see Stupple & Ball, 2007, for a recent study examining various reasoning biases associated with abstract syllogisms in this paradigm). Of course, it must be acknowledged that a comprehensive theoretical account of syllogistic inference should also be able to accommodate evidence deriving from conclusion-production tasks.

The concern in the present chapter is not so much with how people reason with syllogisms containing the kinds of abstract or arbitrary problem contents shown in the previous example, but rather how they deal with syllogisms where the contents relate to real-world knowledge and beliefs (see Table 14.1 for examples). What has emerged from many studies of syllogistic inference with belief-oriented problems is robust evidence for a so-called "belief-bias" effect, which is a nonlogical tendency for people to accept conclusions that are compatible with their beliefs more frequently than conclusions that contradict their beliefs (Table 14.1). This bias is more pronounced on invalid than valid problems, giving rise to a logic by belief interaction in conclusion-acceptance rates that has been researched extensively since it was established by Evans, Barston, and Pollard (1983) in a study that applied the various methodological controls that had been lacking in previous belief-bias research.

Both historical and contemporary explanations of belief bias are couched within a dual-process framework, which again characterizes the phenomenon as arising from the interplay between belief-driven heuristic processes that are

Table 14.1 Examples of the four types of belief-oriented syllogisms used by Ball et al. (2006) together with conclusion acceptance rates from the same study

Belief-oriented syllogisms	%
Valid–believable	
Some metals are soft	
No soft things are steel	
Therefore, some metals are not steel	75
Valid–unbelievable	
Some cats are ornaments	
No ornaments are animals	
Therefore, some cats are not animals	63
Invalid–believable	
No men are boys	
Some boys are kings	
Therefore, some men are not kings	53
Invalid–unbelievable	
No tulips are blue	
Some blue things are flowers	
Therefore, some tulips are not flowers	6

rapid, associative, and implicit, and rule-based analytic processes that are slow, resource constrained, and explicit. The belief-bias effect suggests that heuristic processes may often dominate over analytic processes in determining responses, much like what was observed in the case of the selection task. Dual-process theories of belief bias have continued to gain support over the past few decades from a wide range of sources. For example, Gilinsky and Judd (1994) have shown that the capacity to find a logical solution to belief-oriented syllogisms declines with age, which suggests a diminution in analytic processing in older participants. Likewise, individual difference studies (e.g., Stanovich & West, 1997) have demonstrated how people who are lower in measures of general intelligence are less able to resist belief bias. More recently too, neuroimaging research (e.g., Goel & Dolan, 2003) has suggested that logic-based and belief-based responding on syllogistic problems may be neurologically differentiated.

Despite such support for a general dual-process account of belief bias, there appears to be little consensus in the literature as to which specific form of dual-process theory is best able to explain the full range of available findings concerning the phenomenon. Indeed, all extant theories find some level of support, yet differ considerably in their assumptions about the sequencing of heuristic and analytic operations. Evans et al.'s (1983) original account of belief-bias effects mirrors the original Wason and Evans (1975) account of the selection task as involving a dialectical relation between logical and non-logical processes. Thus Evans et al. described belief bias as emerging from a within-participant "conflict" between belief-oriented processes and logic-oriented processes. Their analysis of the verbal protocols that had been produced by participants concurrent to task performance supported this notion of an intra-individual conflict, since it appeared that participants could show more conclusion-centred reasoning on some problems (with such behaviour being associated with increased belief bias) and more premise-centred reasoning on other problems (with such behaviour this time being associated with increased logical responding). As such, Evans et al.'s (1983) original account emphasized the probabilistic nature of resolving belief–logic competition in favour of either a belief-based or logic-based response.

Stupple and Ball (2008) suggest that an examination of belief-bias theories that have been proposed over the past few decades reveals that they fall into three distinct classes, which they refer to as "belief-first", "reasoning-first", and "parallel-process" models. Belief-first models come in two distinct flavours, referred to by Evans (2007b) as *pre-emptive conflict resolution* and *default-interventionist* models. An example of a pre-emptive conflict resolution model of belief bias is the *selective scrutiny model* described by Evans et al. (1983). This assumes that believable problems are dealt with purely heuristically and are simply accepted, whereas unbelievable conclusions motivate analytic processing aimed at determining the validity of the conclusion. This model can account for the increased effect of logic typically observed on unbelievable conclusions relative to believable ones as arising from the increased analytic scrutiny that the former are subjected to.

Like pre-emptive conflict-resolution models, default-interventionist models also assume that beliefs exercise an early influence on reasoning. Such models view heuristically cued "default" responses as being either supported or inhibited by subsequent analytic processing in cases where such analytic processing is invoked by the reasoner (note that this general type of model was discussed above in the context of the revised H–A theory of the selection task; see Figure 14.1). A good example of a default-interventionist model of belief bias is that presented by Evans (2000; see also Evans, Handley, & Harper, 2001), which is referred to as the *selective-processing model*. According to this account, the default, heuristic response in reasoning with belief-oriented syllogisms is to endorse believable conclusions and to reject unbelievable conclusions. This basic heuristic effect explains why an element of belief bias is typically observed on *both* valid and invalid problems, as shown for the conclusion-acceptance data presented in Table 14.1. The selective-processing model further suggests, however, that analytic processes will often intervene on default responses, with the assumption being that such analysis will aim to construct only a single "mental model" of the premises. Furthermore, in line with the satisficing nature of analytic processing, it is proposed that this analytic component of reasoning is itself biased by conclusion believability, such that a search will be initiated for a *confirming* model when conclusions are believable and for a *disconfirming* model when conclusions are unbelievable (see Klauer et al., 2000). These various assumptions can explain the increased belief bias seen on responses to invalid syllogisms since both confirming and disconfirming models exist. This belief-first, selective-processing theory also readily explains the increased levels of belief bias and the decreased levels of logical performance that arise under rapid-response instructions (Evans & Curtis-Holmes, 2005), since such effects are a predictable consequence of elevations in default, heuristic responding that would occur in speeded decision making.

The next class of belief-bias theories to be considered encompasses reasoning-first models. According to such models, people are claimed to strive to reason analytically from the outset, only falling back on heuristic responding when analytic processing is unsuccessful in determining a definitive response. Such accounts have been referred to as "computational escape hatch" models (Ball & Quayle, 2000; Stanovich & West, 2000). An example is Quayle and Ball's (2000) *metacognitive uncertainty theory*, which they proposed as a refinement of the *misinterpreted necessity model* discussed by Evans et al. (1983). Both accounts emphasize uncertainty as a key determinant of belief bias, with people generating a belief-based response to syllogisms when a conclusion is possible but not necessitated by the premises (i.e., when conclusions are indeterminate in nature, as arises for the typical invalid problem forms used in belief-bias studies). The difference between the metacognitive uncertainty theory and the misinterpreted necessity model primarily relates to the importance attributed to constraints on available working-memory capacity as a determinant of uncertainty.

The final way in which heuristic and analytic processes may operate in engendering belief-bias effects is as parallel streams of processing. The best contemporary example of a generic parallel-process account of reasoning is arguably Sloman's (1996, 2002) theory, which posits parallel "associative" (i.e., heuristic) and "rule-based" (i.e., analytic) systems. Sloman suggests that both systems will normally try to generate a response when a reasoning task is presented, and that the rule-based system has some capacity to suppress the output of the associative system, although the associative system "always has its opinion heard" (Sloman, 2002, p. 391) and can defuse a rule-based response because of its speed and efficiency.

In the context of belief-oriented problems, such a parallel-process model would lead to response conflicts whenever belief-based (associative/heuristic) and logical (rule-based/analytic) processes cue different outputs. For such problems the reasoner would essentially be "in two minds" (Evans, 2003), with people believing two contradictory responses simultaneously. Of course, such internal conflicts would need to be resolved, perhaps according to some mechanism favouring logic with a certain probability. Evans (2007b) has presented a mathematical account of such a mechanism that is capable of capturing standard belief-bias effects on response rates.

Using chronometric evidence to inform dual-processes models of belief bias

In recent years belief-bias researchers have started to employ chronometric analysis as a way to examine the assumptions of the belief-bias theories summarized above. While these chronometric studies are relatively few in number they have, nevertheless, provided interesting sources of evidence that afford novel insights into the viability of alternative theories. Two pioneering belief-bias studies that have used response-time measures are those reported by Thompson, Striemer, Reikoff, Gunter, and Campbell (2003) and Ball, Phillips, Wade, and Quayle (2006). Thompson et al.'s experiment involved a straightforward decision latency measure that simply recorded the overall time that people took to register a conclusion evaluation subsequent to problem presentation. Ball et al.'s study, on the other hand, used eye-movement tracking to capture a richer set of chronometric data relating to the time people spent attending to individual premise and conclusion components of presented syllogisms.

The studies of Thompson et al. (2003) and Ball et al. (2006) revealed some relatively minor mutual inconsistencies in the time-based data obtained, which may have arisen as a consequence of differences between the measurement techniques employed. At the same time there were some striking commonalities in the studies' core findings. In particular, people were observed to spend more time processing syllogisms with believable conclusions than with unbelievable conclusions. Such a finding is in the *opposite* direction to that predicted by some belief-first theories such as the selective scrutiny model described by Evans et al. (1983). The selective-scrutiny model assumes that it is *unbelievable* conclusions that are subjected to increased analytic scrutiny, with believable conclusions being accepted rapidly as a result of heuristic processing. As such, it is unbelievable conclusions – not believable ones – which should be associated with longer processing times. Ball et al.'s experiment also revealed the presence of a highly reliable cross-over interaction between logic and belief in the global measure of total syllogism processing time as well as in the local measure of inspection times for premises alone. This interaction indicated that people spent longer processing the "conflict" syllogisms, where logic and belief are in competition (i.e., those with invalid–believable conclusions and valid–unbelievable conclusions) relative to the "nonconflict" syllogisms, where logic and belief concur (i.e., those with valid–believable and invalid–unbelievable conclusions).

The latter interaction effect has recently been replicated in an experiment by Stupple and Ball (2008). Rather than using eye-movement tracking to monitor processing times, Stupple and Ball instead used a technique whereby people had to click a mouse pointer over masked premises and conclusions so as to reveal the underlying statements. As soon as the mouse pointer moved away from the area that it was hovering over the mask re-appeared. Participants could revisit masked areas as often as they wished before registering a "yes" or "no" decision as to the conclusion's necessity. In this way the computer was able to log the cumulative inspection times associated with syllogistic premises and conclusions. Premise processing data from this study are depicted in Figure 14.4 for the two problem forms that were used, labelled Figure AB-CB and Figure BA-CB (the term "figure" refers to the order in which the quantified terms appeared in the premises). For both problem forms it is readily apparent that premise processing times are elevated for the conflict problems (where logic and belief collide) relative to the nonconflict problems.

The interaction between logic and belief on syllogism processing times identified by Ball et al. (2006) and replicated by Stupple and Ball (2008) is intriguing, not least because it suggests that in some sense participants are aware that the logic of the conclusion and its belief status are in conflict, such that they have to put extra processing effort into resolving this conflict so as to be able to register a response. The one theory that places a central emphasis on the emergence and resolution of heuristic–analytic conflicts in reasoning is Sloman's (1996, 2002) parallel-process model. Stupple and Ball (2008) reached the conclusion that the capacity of this model to explain a majority of their findings may well make it the strongest contender for a comprehensive account of belief-bias phenomena. They also noted an additional strength of the model, which is its sheer parsimony; other models embody a large number of assumptions to enable them to accommodate conclusion-endorsement findings, yet such accounts still seem to struggle to interpret response-time data.

The trouble with accepting the viability of a *parallel* dual-process account of belief-bias effects, however, is that this leads to a rather awkward paradox when considered alongside the compelling evidence discussed earlier for a *sequential* dual-process account of the selection task: how can it be that two radically different dual-process architectures are needed to capture the nature of human reasoning? And how plausible is it that these contrasting processing

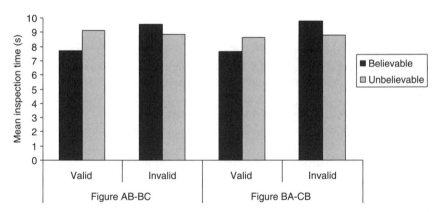

Figure 14.4 Premise inspection times for belief-oriented syllogisms in the Figures AB-BC and BA-CB (Stupple & Ball, 2008).

architectures can co-exist in the same reasoner such that sequential heuristic and analytic processes are invoked in response to selection tasks involving indicative and deontic conditionals while parallel-competitive heuristic and analytic processes are cued by belief-oriented syllogisms? In the next section I examine a possible resolution to this paradox that derives from Evans' most recent theorizing about dual processes in reasoning (e.g., Evans, 2009).

Resolving the parallel/sequential paradox in dual-process theorizing

In his most recent discussions of dual-process theories of reasoning Evans (2009) has grappled with similar concerns to those mentioned in the present chapter – and many other complex, related issues besides. He, too, has reached the striking conclusion that both sequential and parallel dual-process theories seem be needed to capture the full range of findings that have been established in the reasoning literature. His way of dealing with the conceptual problems entailed by such a conclusion is to suggest a "hybrid" dual-process model that combines elements of both types of theory within a single architecture. This is an intriguing notion that seems to have much strength in terms of explanatory breadth, while also retaining evolutionary and psychological plausibility.

The essential features of Evans' (2009) hybrid dual-process model are three-fold. First, an associative processing stream that is driven by *implicit* knowledge and beliefs can provide a direct route to behaviour without the need for any level of conscious control. Second, operating in parallel to this associative-processing stream is a rule-based processing stream that is driven by the *explicit* retrieval of knowledge and beliefs, with such retrieval being heavily influenced by pragmatic factors that contextualize problem information. Moreover, this rule-based processing, being explicit in nature, is proposed to be heavily dependent on available working-memory resources. A further interesting aspect of the rule-based processing stream is that it effectively embodies the H–A account of reasoning, with explicit knowledge retrieval reflecting the heuristic stage of default problem representation, and with working-memory constrained rule-based processing reflecting a satisficing-oriented analytic stage of reasoning. The third aspect of the model is a decision-making and conflict-resolution process that monitors the outputs of the associative and rule-based systems in order to deliver a judgement or inference – or to bring into play further rule-based processing, if this is deemed necessary.

The importance of Evans' hybrid model in terms of understanding reasoning with the selection task and with belief-oriented syllogisms should now be readily apparent. Since the proposed hybrid architecture embodies both a sequential H–A component and a parallel-competitive component it has the potential to account for the paradoxical chronometric evidence that I have presented above for sequential dual processes arising in the selection task and for parallel dual processes arising in belief-oriented syllogistic inference. Rather than needing two distinct cognitive architectures to capture such evidence, a single, hybrid architecture can instead function in an integrated manner that has the potential to account for many of the nuances of reasoning across a wide range of paradigms.

While I could profitably stop at this point, there remains an issue that has been troubling me for a while and which has recently led me to wonder whether the suggested resolution to the paradoxical chronometric data I have discussed is as neat as it might appear at first sight. The issue in question follows on from adopting a pure parallel-process explanation of the increased processing times for belief-logic conflict syllogisms relative to nonconflict syllogisms, and can be stated as follows. If a parallel-process view of reasoning is correct then this means that on conflict syllogisms people are able to reason through the logic of the problem in an *optimal* manner – otherwise there would be no logical output from the rule-based system that could conflict with the belief-based output from the associative system. But this assumption of effective logical processing taking place via the rule-based system is surely implausible, and is certainly contrary to a wide range of evidence for suboptimal and biased analytic processing arising in many reasoning situations (Evans, 2006, 2007a and 2007b).

These latter concerns have led me to entertain the possibility that a fully-fledged parallel-process account of belief-bias phenomena as embraced by Stupple and Ball (2008) may not be correct, and that the selective-processing model espoused by Evans and colleagues may, in fact, provide the best way forward in explaining the chromomeric data that I have discussed. As noted previously, the selective-processing model is highly default-interventionist in nature, and it can therefore be embodied within the rule-based processing stream that forms part of Evans' hybrid dual-process account. The selective-processing model also allows for an element of pure response bias to affect performance, whereby people have a general tendency to prefer believable rather than unbelievable conclusions (see Evans et al., 2001; Klauer et al., 2000). This response bias could also be accommodated in the hybrid model through the operation of the parallel, associative-processing stream. But how, exactly, might the critical observation of increased processing times on belief–logic conflict problems be explained using the selective-processing model?

My latest thinking on the matter has been fuelled by a valuable suggestion from Jonathan Evans, who noted that it might be informative to examine more closely the contrasting chronometric data for those conflict trials where people respond with logic versus where they respond with belief. The specific motivation behind this focused analysis is simply to determine whether on conflict problems logic responses are associated with *longer* processing times relative to belief responses – since to respond in line with logic people must generally have devoted considerable processing effort to resisting the default response. If such an effect could be established then it would suggest that these longer processing times for logic responses might actually be producing the overall inflation in processing times for the conflict syllogisms, as observed in the studies reported by Ball et al. (2006) and Stupple and Ball (2008). With these latter questions in mind, Ed Stupple and I have recently re-examined the chronometric datasets for the conflict problems from the Ball et al. (2006) and Stupple and Ball (2008) studies. Re-analysis of the data for both studies showed the predicted trend for increased processing times for logic responders on conflict problems, but with the effect being more apparent on invalid–believable problems than on valid–unbelievable problems.

To obtain more convincing evidence on these issues, Ed Stupple and I have recently collected a new chronometric dataset with considerably increased test power relative to our previous studies. We also adopted an individual-differences approach, and split reasoners into two separate groups: those who were of relatively high logical ability (i.e., individuals who generally responded logically on the presented syllogisms) and those who were of relatively low logical ability (i.e., individuals who generally responded in a belief-based manner). Our preliminary analyses of these new processing-time data seem conclusive, and corroborate the trends that we identified previously. First, the data show that on both invalid–believable and valid–unbelievable conflict problems the low-logic group have equivalent and relatively rapid processing times, whilst the high-logic group have reliably longer processing times on these conflict trials. Second, this separation in processing times for low-logic versus high-logic groups is more marked for the invalid–believable problems than the valid–unbelievable problems (i.e., there is a highly reliable group by problem type interaction).

I would suggest that this latter pattern of chronometric data seems most readily explained using the hybrid dual-process model together with selective-processing concepts. A sketch of a possible account might go as follows. The low-logic group will be inclined to respond heuristically for both types of conflict problems and will tend to do so via the direct associative route (i.e., reasoning in an essentially response-biased manner). Such rapid, heuristic responding explains the equivalent levels of relatively rapid conclusion evaluation by this group for unbelievable–valid and believable–invalid problems. When the high-logic group deal with valid–unbelievable problems they can successfully identify the logical solution via the rule-based route, since the selective search for a falsifying model will reveal that no such counterexample is possible. This process, being rule-based, will take longer than a purely heuristic response, hence explaining the increased processing time for these valid–unbelievable problems by this group compared with the low-logic group.

What, however, about this high-logic group's processing of syllogisms with invalid–believable conclusions? Something very interesting must arise for these syllogisms with this group in order for these problems to be associated with the longest processing times of all. Note that according to the selective-processing model, these conclusions should be endorsed via a satisficing-oriented rule-based process, since a model can be found that supports the conclusion. To avoid belief bias on these problems the high-logic reasoners must have been able to overcome the tendency to stick with a satisficing solution and instead have searched assiduously for a counterexample model – hence explaining their long response latencies for these syllogisms. It is possible, too, that an "intermediate" ability group who show a mixture of logic-based and belief-based responding may adopt a purely satisficing-based analysis of invalid–believable conclusions, perhaps showing intermediate processing times for these; we have yet to conduct the relevant analyses to determine whether there is any support for this proposal.

Conclusions

In this chapter I have reviewed a range of chronometric data arising from reasoning studies based around the Wason selection task and belief-oriented syllogisms. Such data not only offer good converging evidence in support of dual-process assumptions concerning the involvement of both heuristic/associative and analytic/rule-based processes in reasoning, but they also seem to provide evidence to inform an understanding of the intricate way in which dual-reasoning processes may operate on different reasoning tasks. One upshot of the evidence presented is that both sequential *and* parallel dual-process streams seem to be needed to accommodate data from different paradigms, and even from within the same paradigm. For example, belief-bias effects seem to require an architecture that involves both a sequential heuristic–analytic stream that operates on explicit problem representations, and an implicit stream that operates at a more implicit level.

To accommodate the various nuances arising from the operation of dual processes in reasoning I have argued that the recently proposed hybrid model of Evans (2009; see also Evans, this volume) may provide a neat way forward. The hybrid model, being based around a single, integrated cognitive architecture, overcomes concerns with the implausibility of having two separate cognitive architectures within the same individual – one sequential and the other parallel. At the same time, the hybrid model has the richness and sophistication to capture many factors that are known to impact on reasoning responses and processing times, such as problem complexity, available time, instructional manipulations and individual differences relating to cognitive ability and thinking dispositions. Evans (2009) has developed this hybrid model in a variety of important ways that go well beyond many extant dual-process accounts in terms of the levels of explanatory detail it provides concerning the nature and organization of its processing components. Suffice it to say that the hybrid model seems to represent one of the most important recent advances in dual-process theorizing and, as such, has the potential to fuel a great deal of valuable research over the next few years aimed at examining the dynamics of human reasoning.

Acknowledgements

I am grateful to my following colleagues for many helpful conversations regarding dual processes in reasoning: Maggie Gale, Erica Lucas, Tom

Ormerod, Melanie Pitchford, Jeremy Quayle, Ed Stupple, Andrea Towse, Caroline Wade, and Meredith Wilkinson. Most of all my gratitude goes to Jonathan Evans for his many years of mentorship and friendship.

References

Ball, L. J., Lucas, E. J., Miles, J. N. V., & Gale, A. G. (2003). Inspection times and the selection task: What do eye-movements reveal about relevance effects? *Quarterly Journal of Experimental Psychology, 56A*, 1053–1077.

Ball, L. J., Lucas, E. J., & Phillips, P. (2005). Eye movements and reasoning: Evidence for relevance effects and rationalisation processes in deontic selection tasks. In B. G. Bara, L. Barsalou, & M. Bucciarelli (Eds.), *Proceedings of the twenty-seventh annual conference of the Cognitive Science Society* (pp. 196–201). Alpha, NJ: Sheridan Printing.

Ball, L. J., Phillips, P., Wade, C. N., & Quayle, J. D. (2006). Effects of belief and logic on syllogistic reasoning: Eye-movement evidence for selective processing models. *Experimental Psychology, 53*, 77–86.

Ball, L. J., & Quayle, J. D. (2000). Alternative task construals, computational escape hatches, and dual-system theories of reasoning. *Behavioral & Brain Sciences, 23*, 667.

Ball, L. J., Towse, A. S., & Phillips, P. (2008). *Relevance effects in reasoning: Eye-movement evidence using a rapid-response paradigm*. Unpublished manuscript, Lancaster University, UK.

Cosmides, L., & Tooby, J. (1989). The logic of social exchange: Has natural selection shaped how humans reason? Studies with the Wason selection task. *Cognition, 31*, 187–276.

Evans, J. St B. T. (1984). Heuristic and analytic processes in reasoning. *British Journal of Psychology, 75*, 451–468.

Evans, J. St B. T. (1989). *Bias in human reasoning: Causes and consequences*. Hove, UK: Lawrence Erlbaum Associates Ltd.

Evans, J. St B. T. (1995). Relevance and reasoning. In S. E. Newstead and J. St B. T. Evans (Eds.), *Perspectives on thinking and reasoning* (pp. 147–172). Hove, UK: Psychology Press.

Evans, J. St B. T. (1996). Deciding before you think: Relevance and reasoning in the selection task. *British Journal of Psychology, 87*, 223–240.

Evans, J. St B. T. (1998). Matching bias in conditional reasoning: Do we understand it after 25 years? *Thinking & Reasoning, 4*, 45–82.

Evans, J. St B. T. (2000). Thinking and believing. In J. Garcia-Madruga, N. Carriedo, & M. J. González-Labra (Eds.), *Mental models in reasoning* (pp. 41–56). Madrid: UNED.

Evans, J. St B. T. (2003). In two minds: Dual-process accounts of reasoning. *Trends in Cognitive Sciences, 7*, 454–459.

Evans, J. St B. T. (2006). The heuristic–analytic theory of reasoning: Extension and evaluation. *Psychonomic Bulletin & Review, 13*, 378–395.

Evans, J. St B. T. (2007a). *Hypothetical thinking: Dual processes in reasoning and judgement*. Hove, UK: Psychology Press.

Evans, J. St B. T. (2007b). On the resolution of conflict in dual process theories of reasoning. *Thinking & Reasoning, 13*, 378–395.

Evans, J. St B. T. (2009). How many dual process theories do we need: One, two or many? In J. St B. T. Evans & K. Frankish (Eds.), *In two minds: Dual processes and beyond*. Oxford: Oxford University Press.

Evans, J. St B. T., Ball, L. J., & Brooks, P. G. (1987). Attentional bias and decision order in a reasoning task. *British Journal of Psychology*, *78*, 385–394.

Evans, J. St B. T., Barston, J. L., & Pollard, P. (1983). On the conflict between logic and belief in syllogistic reasoning. *Memory & Cognition*, *11*, 295–306.

Evans, J. St B. T., & Curtis-Holmes, J. (2005). Rapid responding increases belief bias: Evidence for the dual-process theory of reasoning. *Thinking & Reasoning*, *11*, 382–389.

Evans, J. St B. T., & Frankish, K. (Eds.). (2009). *In two minds: Dual processes and beyond*. Oxford: Oxford University Press.

Evans, J. St B. T., Handley, S. J., & Harper, C. (2001). Necessity, possibility and belief: A study of syllogistic reasoning. *Quarterly Journal of Experimental Psychology*, *54A*, 935–958.

Evans, J. St B. T., & Lynch, J. S. (1973). Matching bias in the selection task. *British Journal of Psychology*, *64*, 391–397.

Evans, J., St B. T., Newstead, S. E., & Byrne, R. M. J. (1993). *Human reasoning: The psychology of deduction*. Hove, UK: Lawrence Erlbaum Associates Ltd.

Evans, J. St B. T., & Over, D. E. (1996). *Rationality and reasoning*. Hove, UK: Psychology Press.

Evans, J. St B. T., & Wason, P. W. (1976). Rationalization in a reasoning task. *British Journal of Psychology*, *67*, 479–486.

Gigerenzer, G., & Hug, K. (1992). Domain-specific reasoning: Social contracts, cheating and perspective change. *Cognition*, *31*, 127–171.

Gilinsky, A. S., & Judd, B. B. (1994). Working memory and bias in reasoning across the life span. *Psychology & Aging*, *9*, 356–371.

Goel, V., & Dolan, R. J. (2003). Explaining modulation of reasoning by belief. *Cognition*, *87*, B11–B22.

Grant, E. R., & Spivey, M. J. (2003). Eye movements and problem solving: Guiding attention guides thought. *Psychological Science*, *14*, 462–466.

Johnson-Laird, P. N., Legrenzi, P., & Legrenzi, M. S. (1972). Reasoning and a sense of reality. *British Journal of Psychology*, *63*, 395–400.

Jones, G. (2003). Testing two cognitive theories of insight. *Journal of Experimental Psychology: Learning, Memory, & Cognition*, *29*, 1017–1027.

Klauer, K. C., Musch, J., & Naumer, B. (2000). On belief bias in syllogistic reasoning. *Psychological Review*, *107*, 852–884.

Knoblich, G., Ohlsson, S., & Raney, G. E. (2001). An eye movement study of insight problem solving. *Memory & Cognition*, *29*, 1000–1009.

Lucas, E. J., & Ball, L. J. (2005). Think-aloud protocols and the selection task: Evidence for relevance effects and rationalization processes. *Thinking & Reasoning*, *11*, 35–66.

Lucas, E. J., & Ball, L. J. (2008). *Gaze tracking evidence for heuristic and analytic processes in a reasoning problem*. Unpublished manuscript, Lancaster University, UK.

Manktelow, K. I., & Evans, J. St B. T. (1979). Facilitation of reasoning by realism: Effect or non-effect? *British Journal of Psychology*, *70*, 477–488.

Manktelow, K. I., & Over, D. E. (1991). Social roles and utilities in reasoning with deontic conditionals. *Cognition*, *39*, 85–105.

Osman, M. (2004). An evaluation of dual-process theories of reasoning. *Psychonomic Bulletin & Review*, *11*, 988–1010.

Quayle, J. D., & Ball, L. J. (2000). Working memory, metacognitive uncertainty, and belief bias in syllogistic reasoning. *Quarterly Journal of Experimental Psychology*, *53A*, 1202–1223.

Rayner, K. (1998). Eye movements in reading and information processing: 20 years of research. *Psychological Bulletin*, *124*, 372–422.

Roberts, M. J. (1998). Inspection times and the selection task: Are they relevant? *Quarterly Journal of Experimental Psychology*, *51A*, 781–810.

Roberts, M. J., & Newton, E. J. (2001). Inspection times, the change task, and the rapid response selection task. *Quarterly Journal of Experimental Psychology*, *54A*, 1031–1048.

Simon, H. A. (1982). *Models of bounded rationality*. Cambridge, MA: MIT Press.

Sloman, S. A. (1996). The empirical case for two systems of reasoning. *Psychological Bulletin*, *119*, 3–22.

Sloman, S. A. (2002). Two systems of reasoning. In T. Gilovich, D. Griffin, & D. Kahneman (Eds.), *Heuristics and biases: The psychology of intuitive judgment* (pp. 379–398). Cambridge: Cambridge University Press.

Stanovich, K. E. (2004). *The robot's rebellion: Finding meaning in the age of Darwin*. Chicago: University of Chicago Press.

Stanovich, K. E., & West, R. F. (1997). Reasoning independently of prior belief and individual differences in actively open-minded thinking. *Journal of Educational Psychology*, *89*, 342–357.

Stanovich, K. E., & West, R. F. (1998). Cognitive ability and variation in selection task performance. *Thinking & Reasoning*, *4*, 193–230.

Stanovich, K. E., & West, R. F. (2000). Individual differences in reasoning: Implications for the rationality debate. *Behavioral and Brain Sciences*, *23*, 645–726.

Stupple, E. J. N., & Ball, L. J. (2007). Figural effects in a syllogistic evaluation paradigm: An inspection-time analysis. *Experimental Psychology*, *54*, 120–127.

Stupple, E. J. N., & Ball, L. J. (2008). Belief–logic conflict resolution in syllogistic reasoning: Inspection-time evidence for a parallel-process model. *Thinking & Reasoning*, *14*, 168–181.

Thompson, V. A., Striemer, C. L., Reikoff, R., Gunter, R. W., & Campbell, J. D. (2003). Syllogistic reasoning time: Disconfirmation disconfirmed. *Psychonomic Bulletin & Review*, *10*, 184–189.

Wason, P. C., & Evans, J. St B. T. (1975). Dual processes in reasoning? *Cognition*, *3*, 141–154.

15 Methodological and theoretical issues in belief bias

Implications for dual-process theories

Valerie A. Thompson

University of Saskatchewan

Stephen E. Newstead

University of Plymouth

Nicola J. Morley

Unilever Research & Development

Introduction

Dual-process theories are ubiquitous in many domains of psychology. Although the various instantiations of dual-process theories differ somewhat in terms of their architectural assumptions, they all posit that cognitive functions are mediated by two types of processes: fast, automatic processes that require little cognitive capacity (Type 1) and slow, deliberate processes that draw heavily on working memory capacity (Type 2).

In the reasoning domain, dual-process theories (see Evans & Frankish, 2009 for a recent overview) have been particularly successful because they can account not only for the raft of reasoning biases reported in the literature, but also for the normative reasoning competence that is achieved by at least some participants on many tasks. By allowing the potential for rule-based, Type 2 processes, dual-process theory can account for the possibility of normative thinking. However, because a number of factors restrict the probability of meaningful Type 2 analyses, reasoners are prone to relying on Type 1 outputs. Specifically, it is assumed that many so-called biases can be attributed to the dominance of Type 1 processes, which suggest a compelling, if normatively erroneous, response to a problem before Type 2 processes are fully engaged. In order to generate an alternative, Type 2 processes must undertake the working-memory demanding task of inhibiting the Type 1 output and produce an alternative representation of the premises.

One common reasoning phenomenon that has been explained in such a manner is belief bias. Belief bias is ubiquitous, and refers to the tendency to endorse conclusions on the basis of believability rather than validity, even when instructed to set aside beliefs and draw only logically necessary inferences. Researchers have attempted (with modest success) to ameliorate belief bias by use of instructions (e.g., Evans, Newstead, Allen, & Pollard, 1994), under the assumption that this will cue the reasoner to the need to engage Type 2 thinking. Belief bias is more likely when reasoning under time pressure (Evans & Curtis-Holmes, 2005), suggesting that reasoners are forced to make decisions on the basis of the faster Type 1 output without recourse to the slower Type 2 output. There is also some indication that belief bias is stronger when reasoning from one's own perspective as opposed to that of a third party (Greenhoot, Semb, Colombo, & Schreiber, 2004), consistent with the hypothesis that belief bias results from a tendency to contextualize input. Finally, there is some evidence that belief bias is more common among reasoners of lower cognitive capacity (e.g., De Neys, 2006; Newstead, Handley, Harley, Wright, & Farrelly, 2004; Stanovich & West, 1997) suggesting that those who lack the resources to reformulate and maintain an alternative representation in working memory are more likely to rely on the output of Type 1 processes. All of the aforementioned findings support dual-process theories, and indeed the need to give an adequate account of belief bias was a driving force behind the development of dual-process theories of reasoning.

The first empirical demonstration of the belief-bias effect in syllogistic reasoning was that of Wilkins (1928) and the finding has been replicated many times. A number of the early studies had methodological confounds, but in a now classic study, Evans, Barston, and Pollard (1983) controlled for these factors and still replicated the effect. In fact their study produced three main findings, which have themselves been replicated numerous times and which have stimulated an enormous amount of subsequent work (the original paper has been cited well over 100 times). First, there is the main effect of belief, with believable conclusions more likely to be accepted than unbelievable ones. Second, there is a main effect of validity, with valid conclusions more readily accepted than invalid ones. Finally, there is an interaction between these two variables, such that validity has a larger effect on unbelievable than on believable conclusions (or, viewed from a different perspective, belief has a much larger effect on invalid than on valid conclusions). Virtually every study has found these effects, although sometimes one (but seldom more than one) of the effects has failed to reach statistical significance.

It was this robust interaction that suggested the need to posit the interaction of two types of processes. Main effects of either variable were relatively easy to explain: A main effect of belief implies a response bias (a Type 1 process) favouring believable conclusions that occurred either after or in lieu of a reasoning process (e.g., Klauer, Musch, & Naumer, 2000), while a main effect of validity would imply the ability of at least some reasoners to apply the principles of logical necessity (i.e., Type 2 processing). The fact that these variables interact, however, demanded an explanation in terms of interdependent processes. Over the years, many explanations of belief bias were developed and the ability to predict the interaction between validity and belief has become a key factor in discriminating among the competing explanations (Newstead, Pollard, Evans, & Allen, 1992).

All of these theories of belief bias can be phrased in dual-process terms, but they differ in terms of the sequence in which the two processes operate and how they interact. From the present perspective, a key factor is that virtually all the theories predict that unbelievable conclusions will trigger additional processing.

One group of theories posits that believable conclusions receive relatively little processing, whereas reasoners engage in an active effort to discredit unbelievable conclusions. Several different variants of this hypothesis have been proposed over the years, starting with the selective scrutiny model (Evans et al., 1983). A more sophisticated version of this is Evans' (1989) two-process model, which is framed in terms of his heuristic–analytic model. In this model, heuristic processes identify aspects of the problem as relevant and form a representation and the analytic stage then acts on the aspects of the problem identified as relevant. Beliefs act as heuristic processes, such that only unbelievable items are selected for analytic thinking. Evans (1989) argued that this is an efficacious strategy for a cognitive system, given that there is little to be gained by scrutinizing information that accords with information already known to be true. It is reasonable, on the other hand, to question information that is inconsistent with known facts.

There are a number of recent variants of this basic model, for example in the default-interventionist approach of Evans (2006) and Kahneman (2003). This suggests that Type 1 processes act quickly and automatically to suggest an answer. Whether or not this answer is questioned depends on its suitability to the reasoner's goals. Unbelievable conclusions are more likely to be deemed unsuitable, and therefore more likely to evoke Type 2 processes.

The mental models theory (Oakhill, Johnson-Laird, & Garnham, 1989; Newstead et al., 1992) also assumes additional processing for unbelievable conclusions. On this view, people build up a mental model consistent with the premises and conclusion. If the conclusion is believable, they may search no further, but if the conclusion is unbelievable they will be more inclined to check for falsifying models.

Recently, two sets of researchers (Evans, Handley, & Harper, 2001; Klauer et al., 2000) have proposed a rather different explanation for the belief by validity interaction. Both Evans et al.'s (2001) selective processing account (we adopt the terminology coined by Ball, Phillips, Wade, & Quayle, 2006) and Klauer et al.'s (2000) multinomial account posit that reasoners attempt to formulate only a single model of the premise information. The nature of the model differs, however, according to the believability of the conclusion. When the conclusion is believable, reasoners attempt to construct a model that is consistent with the conclusion. If successful, the conclusion is accepted; otherwise, the conclusion is rejected.

The two accounts diverge somewhat in terms of their assumptions for unbelievable conclusions. The selective-processing view assumes that reasoners attempt to formulate a model that is inconsistent with the conclusion. If they are successful, the conclusion is rejected; if not, the conclusion is accepted. The multinomial view posits a much more demanding process in that reasoners first construct the logical negation of the conclusion (e.g., given Some A are not C they would construct All A are C). They then look for a model that is consistent with this negated conclusion.

All of the aforementioned theories assume that unbelievable conclusions trigger additional processing. What is more, researchers in the social psychology tradition (Ditto & Lopez, 1992; Edwards & Smith, 1996; Kunda, 1990; Lord, Ross, & Lepper, 1979) have developed similar explanations for reasoning with belief-threatening material called the disconfirmation hypothesis (Thompson, Striemer, Reikoff, Gunter, & Campbell, 2003). Specifically, they proposed that when presented with evidence that is consistent with one's belief system, it is accepted uncritically; however, reasoners are motivated to discredit evidence that threatens one's belief system. Thus, one is more likely to detect flaws in arguments (Stanovich & West, 1997), apply statistical principles such as the law of large numbers (Klaczynski & Robinson, 2000) and generally spend more time reasoning about belief-challenging information (Edwards & Smith, 1996).

One theory that does not predict additional processing for unbelievable items is the misinterpreted necessity model (Evans et al., 1983). If the problem is unambiguously either valid or invalid, then people respond accordingly. If, however, the problem is ambiguous in that the conclusion is true in some interpretations of the premises but not in others, people inspect the conclusion for believability and respond accordingly. Thus this theory does not posit additional processing for unbelievable conclusions. A modern successor to this view is the metacognitive uncertainty explanation offered by Quayle and Ball (2000). This view elaborates on the earlier one by suggesting that the cause of uncertainty for indeterminately invalid conclusions can be attributed to working memory limitations. That is, whereas a correct answer to a valid syllogism can be generated on the basis of a single model (all models of a valid syllogism are consistent with its conclusion), invalid syllogisms require testing of multiple models before a conclusion can be refuted (Ball et al., 2006; Thompson et al., 2003). Thus, on this account, invalid syllogisms require additional analytic processing relative to valid ones (Ball et al., 2006).

A second class of theories that do not predict additional processing for unbelievable problems is what Evans (2007) terms "parallel competitive" theories (e.g., De Neys & Glumicic, 2008; Sloman, 1996, 2002). According to this view, Type 1 and Type 2 processes are engaged simultaneously, but may produce different outcomes. In such cases, the reasoner must resolve the conflict between the two outcomes in order to generate a response. On this view, therefore, the problems that receive the most processing are those in which Type 1 and Type 2 potentially generate conflicting outputs (Stupple & Ball,

2008). In the case of syllogistic reasoning, conflict arises when an answer based on the believability of the conclusion conflicts with the answer generated from a logical analysis (i.e., believable–invalid and unbelievable–valid problems). When the two cues point to the same response, processing should be easier as no resolution is required. Thus according to these theories the conflict problems (i.e., valid–unbelievable and unbelievable–valid) are the ones which demand most processing effort.

Testing the theories

All of the theories make predictions as to the processing effort required, with most of them predicting unequivocally that unbelievable conclusions require additional processing. This means that measuring solution times for different problems is an obvious way to test between them.

It is perhaps surprising then, that solution times have been looked at only infrequently in the belief-bias literature and the available data are somewhat contradictory. The first published study of which we are aware is that of Thompson et al. (2003). Contrary to the predictions made by most of the above theories, believable conclusions took *longer* to evaluate than unbelievable ones, an effect which was especially marked on invalid items. Even the misinterpreted necessity, metacognitive uncertainty, and parallel competitive theories would predict no difference between believable and unbelievable items, rather than a significant difference in the direction obtained. Thus none of the theories described above can offer a straightforward explanation of this finding, and it is in exactly the opposite direction to that predicted by most of them.

In addition to the main effect of believability, Thompson et al. (2003) found a main effect of validity, with valid conclusions taking less time than invalid ones. There was also an interaction between belief and validity, where believable conclusions took longer than unbelievable ones but only for invalid problems. Although the fact that one of the conflict problems (invalid–believable) required a lot of analysis is consistent with the parallel competitive model, the fact that response times for the other conflict problems (valid–unbelievable) were not reliably longer than the nonconflict problems is problematic for the theory. Similarly, the fact that the invalid conclusions took longer than the valid ones is consistent with the metacognitive uncertainty hypothesis, but the fact that this difference was only observed for believable conclusions is not.

Thompson et al. (2003) provided a post hoc explanation of their findings that combines the assumption of Polk and Newell's (1995) verbal response theory and Klauer et al.'s (2000) multinomial theory. Specifically, Thompson et al. (2003) assumed that reasoners attempt to construct a model that integrates the premises and conclusions, and that when such a model is discovered, reasoners accept the conclusion. Finding such a model is more likely for valid than invalid conclusions, because all models of the premises are consistent with valid conclusions, whereas only some such models are consistent with invalid ones.

Less clear is the explanation for the effects of belief and the interaction. Thompson et al. (2003) speculated that participants try harder to discover an integrated model for believable than unbelievable conclusions, because believable conclusions ". . . are more palatable than unbelievable ones, and reasoners may try harder to justify acceptance of these conclusions on logical grounds" (p. 188). In other words, they assumed that reasoners are not inclined to spend a lot of time making sense out of a conclusion that is otherwise dubious (i.e., unbelievable); when the conclusion is believable, in contrast, they argued that reasoners are motivated to discover grounds to accept it, and devote extra effort to solving it. The effect of this motivation was posited to be more likely to emerge for the more difficult, invalid problems.

Regardless of whether one is prepared to accept Thompson et al.'s (2003) explanation, the finding itself is of considerable importance, and, if replicated, will have major implications for theories of belief bias. It is not too extreme to suggest that it can potentially undermine all existing theories because the data clearly show that unbelievable conclusions are not processed more extensively than believable ones and that conflict problems do not require more processing than nonconflict ones. In terms of dual-process theory explanations, there is no a priori reason to expect that believable conclusions are more likely than unbelievable conclusions to evoke Type 2 analysis.

To date, we know of only one study that has attempted a replication (Ball et al., 2006). These researchers used an eye-tracking device to measure the time required to process premises (both before and after reading the conclusion), conclusion, and total solution time. All of the measures, with the exception of the pre-conclusion premise times, showed an interaction between validity and belief. These authors concluded that their data were most consistent with the parallel competitive view in that processing times were longer for the conflict than the nonconflict problems. Closer examination of their data, however, reveals that this claim is not well-substantiated and that the data instead provide a very clean replication of Thompson et al.'s (2003) data. Their data are summarized in Table 15.1.

The problem is that the authors did not provide any post hoc contrasts of their data. An eyeball inspection reveals that for two of the three measures (post-conclusion viewing of the premises and overall solution times), the time required for the conflict problems was numerically greater than for the other two. However, the difference between the valid–unbelievable problems and the two nonconflict problems was numerically small and in the case of conclusion-inspection times, it was even smaller than the valid–believable times (conclusion viewing times were the only measures not analysed in the paper). Moreover, the pattern is very similar to the one reported by Thompson et al. (2003): For every measure save the pre-conclusion premise inspection times, invalid–believable conclusions took substantially longer to process than any of the others.

Table 15.1 Mean inspection times (in seconds) as a function of conclusion validity and believability as reported by Ball et al. (2006, p. 83)

Validity	Conclusion believability	
	Believable	*Unbelievable*
Pre-conclusion premises		
Valid	4.27	4.12
Invalid	4.27	4.03
Post-conclusion premises		
Valid	6.36	7.21
Invalid	9.71	5.56
Premises: total		
Valid	10.62	11.33
Invalid	13.97	9.57
Conclusion		
Valid	4.37	4.00
Invalid	6.14	3.97
Overall		
Valid	14.99	15.32
Invalid	20.11	13.54

Although the authors did not report post hoc tests, pair-wise *t*-tests can be computed using the MorePower calculator (Campbell & Thompson, 2002; available as freeware at http://homepage.usask.ca/~jic956/work/MorePower.html) using the mean squared error (MSE) from the interaction as the error term (Masson & Loftus, 2003) and the difference between means as the numerator. For the three ANOVAs reported in their paper, inspection times for invalid–believable syllogisms were greater than for all the others ($t > 1.68$, $p \leq .05$, with the exception of the valid–unbelievable post-conclusion viewing times). None of the other comparisons approached significance. Thus, the data are clearly consistent with the pattern reported by Thompson et al. (2003) and not with the pattern expected from the parallel-competitive models. Given the potential importance of Thompson et al.'s (2003) findings, it is essential to establish the reliability of the response time effects. In this chapter we will do so with two new sets of data. The primary goal is to test Thompson et al.'s (2003) basic assumption that the interaction between validity and belief on solution times is driven by Type 2 processes. Consequently, it should come and go with manipulations that encourage or discourage analytic thinking.

There are three strands to this chapter. First, we present the findings of an experiment in which we attempt to manipulate the probability of Type 2 processing being engaged by manipulating testing conditions. For the second strand, we present the results of two large datasets gathered for different purposes and previously unreported. One dataset was collected under conditions

316 Thompson, Newstead, Morley

similar to those that were used in the first experiment to promote Type 2 thinking; the other was collected under conditions similar to our control condition. Finally, for the third strand, we present a meta-analysis of all three studies in which we analysed the response time data as a function of reasoning ability. This allowed a third test of the hypothesis that the interaction between validity and belief on response times will be observed in conditions characterized by high levels of Type 2 thinking, in this case, by the more able reasoners.

Experiment 1

The purpose of Experiment 1 was to provide a direct test of the hypothesis that the interaction observed by Thompson et al. (2003) arises under circumstances designed to promote Type 2 reasoning. We used two groups. Participants in the first group were tested individually, with encouragement to take their time, and with a practice trial (individual testing). There was an experimenter in the room with the participant observing their responses. The second group was tested in groups of varying sizes in an impersonal computer laboratory where the experimenter could not see how they were responding (group testing). In addition, there was no practice trial and no exhortation to spend as much time as necessary. For the sake of convenience, we will continue to use the labels "group" and "individual" testing to refer to these conditions, even though they differed on a number of different variables designed to foster Type 2 thinking. As a further test of our hypothesis that our manipulation affected reasoners' predisposition to engage System 2 thinking, half of the participants in each group were given a standard measure of thinking dispositions.

Under Thompson et al.'s (2003) hypothesis, interaction between validity and belief on response times should be present when Type 2 processes are engaged and absent when they are not. Thus, we expect the interaction to be present in the individual but not the group testing conditions. Because the remaining theories specify different conditions for the evocation of Type 2 processes, they make different predictions about the effect of interventions designed to increase Type 2 reasoning. Specifically, the heuristic–analytic, mental models, selective-processing and default-interventionist accounts all predict that the manipulation of Type 2 processes should have most effect on unbelievable conclusions, and this effect should be larger in the individual than the group condition. The parallel-competitive view predicts that fostering Type 2 processes should have the most effect on invalid–believable and valid–unbelievable problems, and the difference between conflict and non-conflict problems should be larger under individual than group testing. Finally, the metacognitive uncertainty account predicts that the difference between invalid and valid problems should increase under individual relative to group testing.

Method

Participants

Two groups of 64 participants were tested. The first group consisted of students at the University of Plymouth (mean age = 24.5 years; 39 female). Allocation to conditions was determined by availability: whenever three or more students could attend at the same time they were allocated to the group condition, otherwise they were tested individually. Participants were paid a small fee (£1.50) for participating. The second group consisted of introductory psychology students at the University of Saskatchewan (mean age = 19.5 years; 36 female). These students received a partial course credit for participating.

Materials

The materials consisted of eight three-term, multiple model syllogisms. For each problem, participants were presented with two premises, followed by a conclusion of the form "Some ____ are not __". The syntax of the problems was identical to that used by Evans et al. (1994; Experiment 1). These problems combined one premise of the type "No __ are ____" with one premise of the type "Some ____ are ____". The configuration of the premises was always "AB-CB". Valid and invalid versions of each problem were created; one-half of the problems led to conclusions of the form "Some of the C are not A", and one-half led to conclusions of the form "Some A are not C".

Content was assigned to the "A", "B", and "C" terms such that the "A" and "C" terms referred to familiar categories (e.g., "well-educated people" and "judges"), and the "B" term was a nonsense term (e.g., "Pennes"). This was done in order to avoid any effects that might be attributed to the believability of the premises (Thompson, 1996). Eight different "A", "B", and "C" terms were chosen for this study, and each set of "A", "B", and "C" terms could be accompanied by both a believable (e.g., Some of the well-educated people are not judges) or unbelievable conclusion (e.g., Some of the judges are not well-educated people). The believability of these conclusions was established in a rating study by Evans et al. (1983).

Design and procedure

Participants received one block of "Some A are not C" conclusions, and one block of "Some C are not A" conclusions, with order counterbalanced across participants. Each block consisted of one problem in each belief by validity cell; the order of these conditions was determined by a Latin Square, which was repeated every four participants. Content was assigned to problems such that no problem content was repeated during the eight problems, and each of the eight problem contents was assigned equally often to each of the experimental conditions.

Procedure

The materials were presented on a computer screen. The "1" key on the keyboard was labelled "yes" and the "3" key was labelled "no". Participants in the individual condition were tested in a small, sound-proofed room with a female experimenter being the only other person in the room. In Plymouth, testing was done on a laptop computer, the screen of which was in full view of both the participant and the experimenter. In Saskatchewan, testing was done on a desktop computer, the screen of which was in full view of both the participant and the experimenter. The instructions, which were presented on the computer screen, indicated that the task involved deciding whether the conclusion given followed logically from the information given. Participants were asked to assume that the information given was true. It was emphasized that they should respond "yes" only if the conclusion followed logically, and "no" if they thought it did not necessarily follow.

Participants were instructed to press the space bar after which a practice problem would appear, and informed that if they had any questions they should ask. The practice trial was the three model syllogism "Some of the doctors are sculptors; All of the sculptors are golfers; Therefore, some doctors are golfers." No feedback was given on the accuracy of the response, but any questions that were raised were answered. Following the practice trial, the eight test syllogisms were presented.

In the group condition, testing was carried out in a computer room containing seating for 12–15 people. The experimenter (who was the same person that did the individual testing) stayed in the room while the study was being done but could not see what individual participants were doing and made no attempt to do so or to walk around the room. The computers were all desktops, and the instructions were presented on the computer screen. There was no practice trial. The instructions were identical to those in the individual condition up to the point at which participants were instructed to press the space bar to receive the practice trial. In the group condition, participants were instructed simply to press the space bar to receive the first problem and to ask any questions before the session started. They were not instructed to think carefully, as was the case in the individual condition. After the instructions had been given the eight test syllogisms were presented. Group sizes ranged from 3 to 12.

Following testing, all of the Saskatchewan participants were given the Actively Open-minded Thinking scale. This is a 41-item questionnaire measuring willingness to engage in analytic thinking. Some examples are: "A person should always consider new possibilities", "Considering too many different opinions often leads to bad decisions", and "No one can talk me out of something I know is right". The full questionnaire is available online at http://falcon.jmu.edu/~westrf/stimuli/dispositions.html; Stanovich & West, 1997, 2007; Sá, West, & Stanovich, 1999.

Results

Acceptance data

Table 15.2 presents the findings on responses accepted. There was the usual main effect of belief, $F(1,126) = 37.00$, $MSE = 0.109$, $p < .001$, with believable conclusions more likely to be accepted than unbelievable ones, and the usual effect of validity, with valid conclusions more likely to be endorsed than invalid ones, $F(1,126) = 63.24$, $MSE = 0.137$, $p < .001$. The interaction between these two was not significant, $F(1,126) = 2.84$, $MSE = 0.091$, $p = .09$, although the three-way interaction with test condition was reliable, $F(1,126) = 6.58$, $MSE = 0.091$, $p = .011$.

Since we were interested in obtaining a more detailed picture of what was happening in the two conditions, we carried out separate analyses of variance on the two conditions. In the individual condition, both main effects and the interaction were significant $F(1,63) \leq 8.82$, $p \leq .004$. In the group condition, both main effects were reliable $F(1,63) \leq 16.67$, $p < .01$, but there was no hint of an interaction, $F < 1$. In other words, the typical interaction between belief and validity for conclusion acceptance only occurred in the individual testing condition. Analogous findings have been reported by Shynkaruk and Thompson (2006) with reasoning ability, such that the typical interaction was observed only for "good" reasoners. "Poor" reasoners either did not produce an interaction, or produced an atypical version of it. However, it should be borne in mind that the interaction has been found in the majority of studies, irrespective of testing method.

Response time data

The latency results are presented in Table 15.3. The top and bottom 2% of observations in each condition were removed as outliers; as a result, two

Table 15.2 Proportion of conclusions accepted as a function of conclusion believability and validity in Experiment 1; standard errors are in parentheses

Validity	Conclusion believability		
	Believable	Unbelievable	Mean
Individual condition			
Valid	.80 (.04)	.73 (.04)	.77 (.03)
Invalid	.61 (.05)	.32 (.05)	.47 (.04)
Mean	.70 (.03)	.53 (.03)	
Group condition			
Valid	.81 (.04)	.61 (.05)	.71 (.03)
Invalid	.57 (.04)	.41 (.05)	.49 (.03)
Mean	.69 (.03)	.51 (.04)	

Table 15.3 Response latencies (in seconds) as a function of conclusion believability and validity in Experiment 1; standard errors are in parentheses

| Validity | Conclusion believability | | |
	Believable	Unbelievable	Mean
Individual condition			
Valid	26.0 (1.8)	25.3 (1.6)	25.7 (1.5)
Invalid	37.0 (2.5)	28.8 (2.0)	32.9 (2.1)
Mean	31.5 (1.9)	27.1 (1.6)	
Group condition			
Valid	20.8 (1.7)	20.6 (1.7)	20.7 (1.5)
Invalid	25.3 (2.5)	23.2 (2.0)	24.2 (2.0)
Mean	23.0 (1.9)	21.9 (1.6)	

participants in the individual condition did not have response times in all cells and were thus excluded from the analysis. Save for the interaction between test condition and validity, $F(1,124) = 2.91$, $MSE = 151.04$, $p = .09$, all other main effects and interactions were significant $F(1,124) \leq 4.11$, $p < .05$, including the critical three-way interaction between test condition, belief, and validity $F(1,124) = 4.37$, $MSE = 55.97$, $p < .04$. Before analysing the predictions for the group and individual testing conditions, it is worth noting that response times in the individual condition ($M = 29.3$ s) were about 30% longer than those in the group condition ($M = 22.5$), indicating that the manipulation worked as intended.

Analyses carried out separately on each condition supported our hypothesis that the pattern of response times observed by Thompson et al. (2003) would be observed only for the individual condition. In the group condition, there was a main effect of validity such that invalid conclusions took longer to process than valid ones, $F(1,63) = 6.65$, $MSE = 119.18$, $p = .012$, but no other effects approached significance, $F \leq 1.46$, $MSE = 37.68$ and 72.34 for the interaction and effect of belief respectively, $p > .1$. In contrast, in the individual condition, there was a main effect of validity, $F(1,61) = 17.74$, $MSE = 183.95$, $p < .001$, a main effect of belief, $F(1,61) = 12.69$, $MSE = 96.52$, $p = .001$, and a significant interaction between these, $F(1,61) = 11.42$, $MSE = 74.87$, $p = .001$. The form of the interaction was almost identical to that observed by Thompson et al. (2003): Believable conclusions took longer to process than unbelievable conclusions when they were invalid ($t(61) = 4.60$, $p < .001$), but not when they were valid ($t < 1$). In the current study, invalid–unbelievable conclusions also took longer to process than valid–unbelievable ones, $t(61) = 2.16$, $p = .034$.

Analysis of the Thinking Dispositions Questionnaire

We hypothesized that individual testing would make people more motivated or inclined to engage System 2 reasoning. The data from the Saskatchewan sample, who were administered the Actively Open-minded Thinking scale, support our basic hypotheses: scores in the individual condition ($M = 174.22$, $SD = 13.08$) were less variable and higher than scores in the group condition ($M = 158.66$, $SD = 20.56$), $F(32,32) = 5.52$, $p = .022$ and $t(1, 53) = 3.61$, $p = .001$, *df* corrected for unequal variances). This is corroborating evidence that our manipulation did, indeed, change our participants' motivation to engage in analytic, open-minded thinking.

In turn, scores on the open-minded thinking scale were related to response times. Thinking dispositions correlated with response times for both of the invalid cells: $r = .32$ and $.31$, $p < .05$ for the believable and unbelievable conditions respectively; correlations for the valid cells were close to zero: $r = -.03$ and $.02$, respectively. Thus, response times to invalid, but not valid questions appeared to discriminate between those who showed more or less predisposition to engage in Type 2 reasoning. Another way to view these data is that the effect of validity (i.e., the difference in response time between invalid and valid problems) was positively correlated with the thinking dispositions scores, $r = .48$, $p < .001$. We interpret these data to mean that those who were inclined to engage Type 2 processes adopted a reasoning strategy that discriminated between valid and invalid conclusions. However, this strategy was not necessarily successful, given that parallel correlations with accuracy were nonsignificant, $r \leq .15$, $p > .1$.

Discussion

These data clearly confirm Thompson et al.'s (2003) hypothesis that the relationship between conclusion believability and response time arises because of a Type 2 process. Specifically, invalid–believable conclusions required longer to process than any other type, but only in circumstances designed to promote analytical, System 2 thinking. This finding is consistent with Thompson et al.'s (2003) speculation that reasoners try harder to make sense of believable than unbelievable conclusions. As outlined in our introduction, however, it is inconsistent with the assumption derived from many theoretical frameworks that suggest that such analytic processes are triggered by unbelievable conclusions. Reasoners took less time to reason about unbelievable than believable conditions, and there was no evidence to suggest that a difference in favour of unbelievable conditions emerged under conditions designed to promote Type 2 processing.

Overall, invalid problems took longer to process than valid ones; these data are consistent with Thompson et al.'s (2003) speculation that invalid problems were more difficult to solve than valid problems because it is harder to find a model that integrates the premises with the conclusion. For this reason, one might expect reasoners who made even a modest attempt at reasoning to show this validity effect, and indeed, this effect was present even under group testing conditions. However, reasoners who show a greater willingness to engage in analytic thought, as diagnosed by their scores on the Actively Open-minded Thinking scale, show an even larger effect of validity, supporting the conclusion that the observed response time differences reflect analytic processes.

The difference between invalid and valid conclusions is also consistent with the metacognitive uncertainty hypothesis. According to this view, indeterminately invalid problems require more resources to process than reasoners have capacity for. This creates a sense of uncertainty that is resolved by defaulting to a belief-based choice. To explain the correlation with the Actively Open-minded Thinking scale, one would have to assume that reasoners who are more inclined to engage Type 2 processes are more likely to discover the ambiguities entailed by the invalid problems and thus take longer to process them. However, the fact that only one of the invalid conclusion types (i.e., invalid–believable) required longer processing is not consistent with this view.

Finally, as in earlier studies (Ball et al., 2006; Thompson et al., 2003), there was a significant interaction between belief and validity. In these earlier studies, the form of the interaction was such that invalid–believable problems took longer than all problem types, which did not differ among themselves. In the current experiment, the interaction was observed only under conditions designed to foster Type 2 thinking, clearly implying that the engagement of analytic processes is a necessary component of the interaction. In addition, the form of the interaction was slightly different to that observed previously. While invalid–believable problems took longer than all other types, it was also the case that the invalid–unbelievable problems took longer than their believable counterparts. This is additional evidence that invalid problems are more difficult to process than valid ones, and that this difference results from analytic reasoning processes.

One might challenge these data because we did not examine processing times for the premises and conclusions separately (Stupple & Ball, 2008). However, in the one reported instance where that was undertaken (Ball et al., 2006), the basic effects were the same regardless of whether the individual components of the problems or the overall response times were analysed. Moreover, given that the process of model construction almost certainly begins with the reading of the premises and continues until an answer is generated, the total time required to produce an answer is clearly an appropriate measure of reasoning time.

In sum, these findings are challenging to explain in terms of existing theories. While the metacognitive uncertainty account can explain the relative difficulty of invalid problems, the interaction with belief is not interpretable from this framework. The parallel-competitive view suggests that invalid–believable problems (nonconflict) should take less time, not more, than the valid–unbelievable ones (conflict). Finally, as above, the remaining theories predict that unbelievable conclusions should take longer than believable ones, a prediction that has now been disconfirmed three times.

Experiment 2

In this experiment, we present data that attempt to replicate our findings that the response time pattern observed by Thompson et al. (2003) is driven by analytic engagement. To do so, we present the results of two large sets of unpublished data. One set was collected under conditions that were very similar to our individual group in Experiment 1; the other closely resembled the group condition.

The individual data were collected in Thompson's lab using an exact replication of her 2003 methodology, except that confidence ratings were collected after each problem (they will not be reported here). The group data were collected by Nicki Lambell (1998) in an unpublished PhD dissertation (Lambell is the maiden name of Nicki Morley, one of the co-authors of the present chapter). In all, Lambell reported nine studies, six of which looked directly at belief bias in syllogisms. The procedure for these studies is summarized in Table 15.4 The studies investigated a range of different aspects of belief bias, including the effect of delays between the premises and conclusion, the effect of presenting the conclusion before the premises (Lambell, Evans, & Handley, 1999), the effect of different kinds of material and middle terms, and the effects of the type of syllogism (number of models and syllogistic figure). For our purposes, the crucial aspect of her procedure was that participants were tested on computers in large groups, without close supervision by the experimenter, and were not given a practice problem. Thus, the testing conditions of the individual and group conditions are similar to those in Experiment 1.

In order to compare Lambell's (1998) studies to Thompson et al.'s (2003), we decided to combine the results from the different studies. We used the data from her Experiments 1, 3, 8, and 9. In choosing these, decisions had to be taken as to which studies could be sensibly combined. We decided to collapse across different syllogistic figures, different materials, delays (i.e., whether the premises and conclusion were presented simultaneously or not), and truth type (whether the conclusions were definitionally or empirically believable). However, we decided not to include those conditions in her Experiments 1 and 3 in which the conclusion was presented prior to the premises, because this is such an unusual technique and may lead to very different processing strategies. Nor did we include conditions using single-model syllogisms, since there is considerable debate about the existence of belief-bias effects in these (Newstead et al., 1992; Klauer et al., 2000); hence only three-model syllogisms were used in the analysis.

Our basic predictions were the same as in Experiment 1, namely that the pattern of response times observed by Thompson et al. (2003) would only be observed in circumstances that strongly encourage Type 2 processing.

Table 15.4 Summary of Lambell (1998) methods and materials

Lambell	Participants	Material	Presentation	Notes
Experiment 1	$n = 80$ University of Plymouth students in groups of 16	8 three-model syllogisms using EBP[a] material with neutral middle terms	Computerized. Half participants had premises first, half conclusion first; half had 3 s delay between premises and conclusion	Only data from premises-first condition used in analysis
Experiment 3	$n = 80$ University of Plymouth students run in groups of 6	32 syllogisms, half realistic, half abstract, half single model, half three model. Realistic content novel and definitionally true or false	Computerized, with delay between premises and conclusion. Half participants received conclusion first	Only three-model syllogisms with realistic content and premises presented first used in analysis
Experiment 6	$n = 26$ University of Plymouth students run in small groups	16 three-model syllogisms using novel content and nonsense middle terms	Computerized, premises and conclusion presented simultaneously	
Experiment 7	$n = 40$ University of Plymouth students run in groups of about 8	As in Expt 6	Computerized, premises and conclusion presented simultaneously	
Experiment 8	$n = 60$ University of Plymouth students run in groups of about 8	16 three-model syllogisms using EBP[a] material with neutral middle terms	Computerized, premises and conclusion presented simultaneously	
Experiment 9	$n = 60$ University of Plymouth students run in groups of about 8	8 three-model syllogisms some using EBP[a] material with nonsense middle terms, others using definitionally believable material	Computerized, premises and conclusion presented simultaneously	

Note
a. EBP = Evans, Barston, and Pollard (1983).

Consequently, we expected the interaction to be observed under the individual, but not the group testing conditions.

Method

Participants

There were 96 (78 women) participants in the individual condition; these were first-year undergraduate students from the University of Saskatchewan who participated in partial fulfilment of a course requirement; the mean age was 19.7 years. There were a total of 280 participants in the group condition. All of these were University of Plymouth undergraduate students who participated either for payment or for course credit. Participants were tested in groups ranging from 6 to 16.

Materials

For the group condition, three of Lambell's (1998) studies (1, 8, and 9) used the same material as used by Evans et al. (1983), and hence relied on the believability ratings derived from that study. Lambell's (1998) Experiment 3 used novel material that was definitionally true or false (e.g., Some spaniels are not dogs), and for which believability ratings were independently obtained prior to running the study. The materials used in the individual condition were identical to those used in Experiment 1 and were counterbalanced in the same way as in Experiment 1.

Procedure

For the group condition, the instructions varied slightly between experiments, but all emphasized the need to assume that the information given was true, and asked participants to decide whether the conclusion followed logically from the information given. Presentation was computer controlled and responses were given via keys labelled "yes" (left button) and "no" (right button). Participants were instructed to answer "yes" only if the conclusion followed logically from the premises; otherwise they should respond "no". The presentation order of the syllogisms was completely randomized.

For the individual condition, testing was nearly identical to that of the individual condition of Experiment 1, except that a paper and pencil test was used. Problems were presented one to a page. Following each problem were two options, "yes" and "no". Instructions, which were adapted from the "standard" instructions used by Evans et al. (1994), were stapled to the front of the booklet. The instructions emphasized that participants were to judge whether or not a conclusion followed logically from the premises. If they judged a conclusion followed logically, they were instructed to say "yes", but if the conclusion did not necessarily follow from the premises, they were to say "no". Participants were instructed not to make notes or diagrams while solving the problems, and not to return to previous problems after they had been completed.

Timing was done manually, using a stop watch accurate to 0.01 s. There was a blank sheet on the top of the test booklet. The experimenter, who was masked to the belief and validity status of the conclusions, gave a verbal signal to begin, and started the timer. The participant turned the page over; timing ended when the response was spoken aloud. After the participant's response was recorded, the experimenter gave the signal to begin the next trial.

Prior to starting the experimental trials, participants were given two practice trials, and were allowed to ask questions. Participants were tested individually and testing took about 10 minutes.

Results

In order to keep the numbers (n) roughly comparable, we have preserved each of Lambell's (1998) experiments as a separate condition in the analyses. Thus, for the purpose of the analyses, there are four group conditions (ns = 80, 80, 60, and 60) and one individual condition (n = 96). These data are presented in Table 15.5 (conclusion acceptance) and Table 15.6 (response time). For the response time analyses, the top and bottom 2% of the responses in each condition were removed as outliers. The data were analysed using a 5 (group) × 2 (validity) × 2 (belief) mixed ANOVA with group as a between-subjects factor.

The first analysis concerns the acceptance data in Table 15.5. With the exception of the interaction between validity and group, all main effects and interactions were significant, including the three-way interaction between validity, belief, and condition, $F(4,371) = 2.44$, $MSE = 0.098$, $p = .047$). As is clear in the table, the pattern revealed by this omnibus analysis exactly replicates the pattern expected: There were more believable (.75) than unbelievable (.47) conclusions accepted, there were more valid (.69) than invalid (.53) conclusions accepted, and the effect of validity was larger for the unbelievable (.26) than believable (.07) conclusions.

The most straightforward interpretation of the three-way interaction is that the belief × validity interaction is present in some of the groups (Lambell's, 1998, Experiments 1 and 8, and the individual group, $F ≤ 8.17$, $p ≤ .005$), but not others (Lambell's, 1998, Experiments 3 and 9, $F ≤ .145$, $p ≤ .1$). As mentioned in the introduction, although the belief × validity interaction is a robust effect, it is not always observed in every experiment.

More important are the response time data reported in Table 15.6. When the outlying observations were removed, three participants had to be excluded from the analysis because they did not have observations in all four cells. All of the main effects and interactions were significant (largest $p = .019$), including the critical three-way interaction between validity, belief, and group, $F(4,368) = 13.55$, $MSE = 89.30$, $p < .001$). We carried out two sets of analyses

Table 15.5 Proportion of conclusions accepted in the individual (Thompson et al., 2003) and group (Lambell, 1998) conditions in Experiment 2 as a function of conclusion believability and validity; standard errors are in parentheses

Validity	Conclusion believability		
	Believable	Unbelievable	Mean
Individual			
Valid	.88 (.03)	.64 (.04)	.76 (.03)
Invalid	.73 (.04)	.30 (.03)	.51 (.03)
Mean	.80 (.03)	.47 (.03)	
Group: Experiment 1			
Valid	.74 (.04)	.59 (.04)	.67 (.03)
Invalid	.70 (.04)	.29 (.04)	.49 (.03)
Mean	.72 (.03)	.44 (.03)	
Group: Experiment 3			
Valid	.78 (.04)	.71 (.04)	.75 (.03)
Invalid	.66 (.04)	.51 (.04)	.58 (.03)
Mean	.72 (.03)	.61 (.03)	
Group: Experiment 8			
Valid	.72 (.04)	.58 (.05)	.65 (.03)
Invalid	.77 (.05)	.27 (.05)	.52 (.03)
Mean	.74 (.03)	.42 (.04)	
Group: Experiment 9			
Valid	.80 (.04)	.49 (.05)	.65 (.03)
Invalid	.71 (.05)	.33 (.05)	.52 (.03)
Mean	.75 (.03)	.41 (.04)	
Overall			
Valid	.78 (.02)	.60 (.02)	.69 (.01)
Invalid	.71 (.02)	.34 (.02)	.53 (.01)
Mean	.75 (.01)	.47 (.01)	

Note
Table reports the mean for Lambell's (1998) Experiments 1, 3, 8, and 9.

to test the prediction that the pattern of response times observed by Thompson et al. (2003) is a product of Type 2 processing, and would thus be most marked under conditions that encourage analytic thinking (i.e., the individual condition).

First, we computed the interaction separately for each of the five conditions. The data from the individual condition replicated Thompson et al.'s (2003) findings that believable conclusions took longer to process than unbelievable ones, $F(1,95) = 9.23$, $MSE = 158.61$, $p = .003$; invalid conclusions took longer than valid ones, $F(1,95) = 17.40$, $MSE = 202.72$, $p < .001$; and these variables interacted, $F(1,95) = 15.02$, $MSE = 175.17$, $p < .001$. Post hoc t-tests confirmed that the form of the interaction was as expected: invalid believable problems took longer to solve than all others, $t(95) \leq 3.78$, $p < .001$, but none of the other groups differed, $t(95) \leq 1.52$, $p \leq .1$.

Table 15.6 Response times (in seconds) in the individual (Thompson et al., 2003) and group (Lambell, 1998) conditions in Experiment 2 as a function of conclusion believability and validity; standard errors are in parentheses

	Conclusion believability		
Validity	*Believable*	*Unbelievable*	*Mean*
Individual			
Valid	20.7 (1.0)	22.1 (1.1)	21.4 (0.9)
Invalid	32.0 (1.7)	22.9 (1.2)	27.4 (1.3)
Mean	26.4 (1.2)	22.5 (0.9)	
Group: Experiment 1			
Valid	20.0 (1.2)	18.2 (1.2)	19.3 (1.0)
Invalid	19.6 (1.9)	20.1 (1.3)	19.9 (1.4)
Mean	19.8 (1.3)	19.4 (1.0)	
Group: Experiment 3			
Valid	14.8 (1.2)	11.8 (1.2)	13.3 (1.0)
Invalid	11.8 (1.9)	15.7 (1.3)	13.7 (1.4)
Mean	13.3 (1.3)	13.8 (1.0)	
Group: Experiment 8			
Valid	22.8 (1.3)	17.7 (1.3)	20.2 (1.2)
Invalid	18.5 (2.2)	19.4 (1.5)	19.0 (1.6)
Mean	20.6 (1.6)	18.5 (1.1)	
Group: Experiment 8			
Valid	18.7 (1.3)	14.2 (1.3)	16.5 (1.2)
Invalid	16.5 (2.2)	19.3 (1.5)	17.9 (1.6)
Mean	17.6 (1.5)	16.7 (1.1)	
Overall			
Valid	19.40 (.54)	16.87 (.55)	18.13 (.47)
Invalid	19.67 (.89)	19.48 (.60)	19.58 (.65)
Mean	19.53 (.63)	18.12 (.46)	

Note
Table reports the mean for Lambell's (1998) Experiments 1, 3, 8, and 9

The pattern for the four group conditions was very different. With the exception of the main effect of belief in Lambell's (1998) Experiment 3, $F(1,58) = 5.89$, $MSE = 43.23$, $p = .02$, neither of the main effects of belief or validity was significant, $F \leq 2.72$, $p > .1$ in any of the studies. Although there was a significant belief by validity interaction for Lambell's (1998) Experiments 3, 8, and 9, $F \leq 11.93$, $p \leq .001$ (but not in her Experiment 1, $F < 1$), it is clear from Table 15.6 that the patterns are different from that reported for the individual condition. When pooled together, the pattern that emerges is for the nonconflict problems (valid–believable and invalid–unbelievable) to take *longer* than the conflict problems (invalid–believable and valid–unbelievable), $t(276) = 3.33$, $p \leq .001$, with no difference within the pairs $t(277) = 1.54$, $p > .1$. This pattern, while particularly problematic for the parallel competitive view, does not fit well with any of the theories, nor does it replicate the pattern for the group condition in the present Experiment 1.

Our second, and stronger, test of the prediction that the pattern of response times would differ between the individual and group conditions involved computing an interaction score ((valid–believable minus valid–unbelievable) minus (invalid–believable minus invalid–unbelivable)) for each participant. This "difference of difference" score was analysed in a univariate ANOVA with group as the between-subjects factor. Because the ANOVA computed in this fashion is exactly equivalent to the three-way interaction reported above, the omnibus F value was identical, $F(4,368) = 13.55$, $p < .001$. More importantly, however, we were able to compute post hoc tests to compare the interaction from the individual condition to each of the others. Newman–Keuls tests ($p = .05$) indicated that the interaction from the individual condition was different from the remaining four, which did not differ among themselves.

Together with the findings from Experiment 1, these data provide additional evidence that the interaction observed by Thompson et al. (2003) can be attributed to Type 2 processing. That is, the fact that invalid, believable conclusions took longer to process than the others can be attributed to actively engaged reasoning on behalf of the reasoners; under conditions that discouraged such reasoning, the pattern changed dramatically. Indeed, it would seem that the pattern under less encouraging conditions is highly variable, perhaps due to a variety of heuristic processes.

Combined analysis of Experiments 1 and 2: Response times as a function of response category and reasoning ability

Before we consider how the major theories could accommodate our findings, we present two meta-analyses of our two experiments. The purpose of these analyses was to eliminate two alternative explanations for the response time patterns reported in Experiments 1 and 2. The first alternative considered was that the response time differences among the four belief × validity cells could be caused by differences in the distribution of "yes" and "no" responses among the cells. The second alternative addressed was that the longer response times associated with invalid–believable responses were not causally linked to the generation of an answer.

With respect to the different distribution of "yes" and "no" responses among the belief × validity cells, for example, it is possible that the lengthy response times observed for the believable–invalid problems might be attributed to the fact that it takes an especially long time to reject conclusions in that cell, rather than to more general processing differences associated with processing believable–invalid problems. Given that the group and individual conditions were also characterized by different response patterns, a similar explanation could be applied to those differences as well.

To rule out that alternative, we pooled the data from Experiments 1 and 2

(n = 504) and we computed mean response times associated with "yes" and "no" observations in each of the four cells as a function of testing condition; these data are plotted in Figure 15.1. As is clear from Figure 15.1, in the individual testing condition, believable–invalid problems were associated with long response times regardless of whether the participant responded "yes" or "no"; the distribution of response times in the group testing condition was flat. Although it is not possible to conduct a statistical analysis of these data because each bar in the figure represents different numbers of observations (and because few participants made both "yes" and "no"

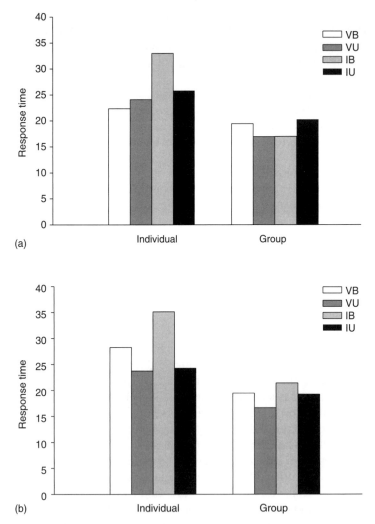

Figure 15.1 Response time distributions for (a) "yes" and (b) "no" responses as a function of conclusion believability, conclusion validity, and testing condition. B = believable; I = invalid; U = unbelievable; V = valid.

responses in each of the cells), the overall pattern is nonetheless clear. Consequently, neither the response time differences among the belief × validity cells nor the differences between group and individual testing, can be attributed to different distribution of "yes" and "no" responses among conditions.

The second goal was to provide additional evidence that the response time distribution observed by Thompson et al. (2003) and in the individual conditions of Experiments 1 and 2 was associated with Type 2 thinking. In particular, we hoped to address the concern that the extra time associated with invalid–believable responses was somehow epiphenomenal rather than being causally determined by the processes used to generate a response. At the extreme, too little time clearly affects accuracy (Evans & Curtis-Holmes, 2005); however, beyond that, it is not clear that additional time devoted to thinking about a problem contributes to the answer that is produced, or, instead, is part of a post hoc justification phase that contributes little to the outcome (e.g., Evans, 1996; Shynkaruk & Thompson, 2006). Even if differences in response time could be attributed to differences in the cognitive processes used to evaluate conclusions, there is no reason to assume that increased effort will necessarily lead to better answers. That is, effortful System 2 reasoning will fail if System 2 is utilizing a strategy that produces non-normative answers (Evans, 2006).

If response time is linked to answer production, then the probability of observing our response time effects should vary at an individual as well as at a group level. For this analysis, we again combined the data from Experiments 1 and 2, but this time split them into three groups. The first group consisted of those reasoners who performed at or below chance (i.e., correctly solved four or fewer of the eight problems). About 40% of the sample ($n = 220$) fell into this group. The remaining participants were divided into two approximately equal groups of 129 and 155 participants; the former solved exactly five problems correctly and the latter solved six or more. The participants from the individual and group testing conditions were not evenly divided among the three groups, $\chi^2(2) = 7.08$, $p = .029$. Consistent with our hypothesis that the participants in the group testing conditions took the task less seriously, a relatively high percentage (47%) of them solved four or fewer problems correctly, versus 36% for those tested individually.

Response times for the three levels of reasoning ability are reported in Table 15.7. These data were analysed using a 2 (validity) × 2 (belief) × 3 (group) mixed ANOVA. The interaction between validity and belief was not reliable, $F < 1$; however, all other main effects and interactions, including the critical three-way interaction between group, validity, and belief were significant, $F(2,496) = 6.06$, $MSE = 89.95$, $p = .003$. As is clear in Table 15.7, the belief × validity interaction shows a different pattern in each of the three reasoning groups. For the poor reasoners, the interaction was similar to that observed by Lambell (1998) in Experiment 2: Valid–believable and invalid–unbelievable conclusions took longer than the other types, $F(1,216) = 6.65$,

Table 15.7 Response times (in seconds) as a function of conclusion validity, believability, and overall accuracy in Experiments 1 and 2; standard errors are in parentheses

	Conclusion believability		
Validity	Believable	Unbelievable	Mean
Poor			
Valid	20.2 (.79)	18.1(.79)	19.1 (.71)
Invalid	19.0 (1.3)	19.6 (.89)	19.3 (.99)
Mean	19.6 (.93)	18.9 (.72)	
Medium			
Valid	19.6 (1.0)	18.2 (1.0)	18.9 (.92)
Invalid	23.4 (1.7)	21.9 (1.2)	22.7 (1.3)
Mean	21.5 (1.2)	20.1 (.94)	
Good			
Valid	21.2 (.94)	19.7 (.94)	20.5 (.84)
Invalid	28.7 (1.5)	23.0 (1.1)	25.9 (1.2)
Mean	25.0 (1.1)	21.4 (.86)	

$MSE = 58.41$, $p = .011$. For the medium group, there was no interaction, $F < 1$, although the effects of both validity, $F(1,127) = 12.01$, $MSE = 148.96$, $p = .001$, and belief, $F(1,127) = 4.22$, $MSE = 65.28$, $p = .042$, were reliable. For the good reasoners, the interaction was similar to that observed in the individual test conditions of Experiments 1 and 2, $F(1,153) = 5.91$, $MSE = 119.38$, $p = .016$: Responses to invalid–believable problems took longer than for any other type, $t(153) = 3.70$, $p < .001$. In addition, invalid–unbelievable syllogisms took longer than valid–unbelievable ones, $t(153) = 2.83$, $p = .005$. These data provide further support for the conclusion that the pattern of response times observed by Thompson et al. (2003) can be attributed to differences in the methodology that encouraged participants to engage in rational analysis.

These data also provide evidence that differences in response times indicate outcome-relevant aspects of cognitive processing. That is, reasoners who differed in terms of their success at the reasoning task showed different patterns of responses. As evidenced by the main effect of group, $F(2,496) = 5.36$, $MSE = 525.14$, $p = .005$, response times varied across groups: the good reasoners ($M = 23.2$) took longer than either the poor ($M = 19.2$) or medium ($M = 20.8$) reasoners, $t(373$ and $282) = 1.88$, $p = .06$. The latter two groups did not differ, $p > .1$. Moreover, as outlined above, both the medium and good reasoners took longer to process believable than unbelievable conclusions, and longer to process invalid than valid conclusions. Only the good reasoners, however, showed the interaction effect observed by Thompson et al. (2003).

General discussion

Thompson et al. (2003) obtained a counter-intuitive finding, namely that reasoners spend most time reasoning about invalid–believable problems. The explanation given for this apparently anomalous finding was clearly attributed to Type 2 processing. In other words, the longer response times for invalid–believable problems arose due to problem-specific characteristics that required additional processing from reasoners. The goal of the current studies was to test the claim that the pattern observed by Thompson et al. (2003) was, indeed, due to the engagement of analytic thinking strategies rather than heuristic or confabulatory ones. Consistent with this view, the response time pattern of Thompson et al. (2003) was replicated exactly under conditions designed to promote analytic thinking (such as individual testing), among reasoners inclined to engage analytic thinking (as measured by the Actively Open-minded Thinking scale), and among reasoners with demonstrated analytic ability (i.e., good reasoners). Under conditions that did not encourage analytic thinking and among reasoners lacking motivation and ability, there seemed to be no differences in response latencies or, perhaps more accurately, any differences that were found were inconsistent and highly variable.

These data are consistent with the broad tenets of dual-process theory, namely that the engagement of Type 2 thinking is, to some extent, under volitional control, such that the probability of analytic thinking strategies varies according to testing conditions and individual inclination. It is also clear that the quantity of analytic thinking engaged is causally relevant to the quality of the answers produced, at least as evaluated by a normative standard of logic: those who spent more time thinking about the problems were more likely to reach a logically valid conclusion. Beyond that, however, none of the current instantiations of dual-process theory can account for our data. Specifically, it appears that a consistent consequence of promoting Type 2 thinking is to increase time spent on invalid–believable problems relative to other types; a pattern that is not consistent with any previous theory of belief bias. Most current theories claim that unbelievable conclusions promote further analysis to check the validity of the conclusion. This additional analysis should take time and lead to unbelievable conclusions taking longer than believable ones – a pattern that was not observed in any of our analyses. It simply does not seem to be the case that people devote additional time to unbelievable conclusions as they search for disconfirming instances; if anything, exactly the opposite happens.

These data also challenge views that accord special status to the so-called conflict syllogisms (see Ball et al., 2006, for a review). For a variety of reasons, these problems are thought to be difficult to solve as they put System 1 and System 2 processes into conflict (e.g., Evans, 2003) or because they are especially difficult to construct representations for (e.g., Ball et al., 2006; Klauer et al., 2000). Although we observed that one type of conflict problem, namely the invalid–believable syllogisms, required additional processing, there was no evidence that reasoners required extra time to process the valid–unbelievable problems.

Instead, we argue that the only existing explanation for the present findings is that given by Thompson et al. (2003). They suggested that people try to integrate the premises and conclusion into a single model and that this process is more difficult for invalid than valid conclusions. They also proposed that reasoners try harder to find such a model for believable than unbelievable conclusions. In many ways, this turns current theories on their head, since it claims that people are motivated to find evidence to support a conclusion they believe rather than to disprove a conclusion they find unbelievable.

Indeed, these data might lead one to question the value of the dual-process theory framework, given that this framework was used to both generate predictions (i.e., that unbelievable or conflict problems would require additional Type 2 processing) and to explain the falsified prediction (i.e., that the extra processing time observed for invalid–believable processes could be accounted for in terms of Type 2 processing). There are, however, a variety of dual-process theory explanations for phenomena that differ in terms of how they "define . . . the nature of the interaction between the two processes and . . . assist the generation of experimental predictions about particular reasoning tasks" (Evans, 2006; p. 379). These more specific pairings of assumptions are, indeed, more readily falsified than the broader theory from which they derive, the utility of which can be evaluated in terms of its ability to account for normatively poor and normatively accurate performance on a wide range of tasks.

Regardless of the explanation that is proposed, there are clear lessons to be learned from our studies, for example, the danger entailed in interpreting patterns of conclusion acceptance in the absence of converging measures. Specifically, the fact that the canonical acceptance pattern is observed in situations where there is not a consistent pattern in response times casts doubt on its reliability as an indicator of analytic engagement. Consistent with this hypothesis, Shynkaruk and Thompson (2006) observed that the canonical pattern of conclusion acceptance was observed in as little as 10 seconds, which indicates that the pattern is produced after a minimum of logical analysis. Given that the data from our meta-analysis provided evidence that successful reasoners show different and longer patterns of response times than less successful ones, a reasonable hypothesis would be that much of the variance in conclusion acceptance may be driven by non-analytic, heuristic processing. For example, Chater and Oaksford (1999) showed that the pattern of conclusion acceptance for abstract syllogisms could be predicted by heuristic strategies that evaluate the informativeness of the premises and conclusions; adapting such a model to belief-based problems, may, therefore, prove worthwhile.

However, given the degree of variability in both response times and acceptance patterns that we have observed, it seems unlikely that a single process or strategy will be sufficient to explain our data. It is evident that participants' responding is highly strategic (Bucciarelli & Johnson-Laird, 1999; Ford, 1995;

Schaeken, De Vooght, Vandierendonck, & d'Ydewalle, 2000) and is sensitive to small changes in the testing environment, such that researchers need to be sensitive to this when planning, interpreting, and comparing experimental findings. Thus, reasoning theories need to specify how and when the various strategies come into play; for this, we will need to develop a variety of ways to measure performance, given that acceptance data appear relatively insensitive to differences in strategic choice. For example, although our response time data showed systematic variability in accuracy as a function of test condition and individual differences, the relative rates of acceptance among the problem types appears to be less sensitive to strategic variance than the pattern of response times.

A potentially useful direction to pursue would be to extend the Bayesian analysis of belief effects in conditional reasoning (e.g., Evans, Handley, & Over, 2003; Oaksford, Chater, & Larkin, 2001; Oberauer & Wilhelm, 2003) to the evaluation of syllogisms. That is, in most syllogistic reasoning experiments, beliefs are treated as a dichotomous variable: conclusions (and their premises) are classified as either believable or unbelievable and reasoners are asked to make a dichotomous evaluation: valid or invalid. Instead, however, it is clear that reasoners judge belief on a continuum and that the effect of variability in assessed degree of belief can be measured by allowing reasoners to express their evaluations along a continuum (George, 1997; Stevenson & Over, 1995).

Finally, our data have relevance for the broader literature on reasoning. Many current theories incorporate some version of a disconfirmation hypothesis into their assumptions (e.g., Edwards & Smith, 1996; Evans, 2003; Klaczynski & Robinson, 2000) and these theories extend beyond the parameters of the deductive paradigm. For example, for informal arguments, Edwards and Smith (1996) observed that belief-inconsistent conclusions were scrutinized longer than belief-consistent ones. Klaczynski and his colleagues have repeatedly observed that scientific reasoning is more likely to be invoked to discredit unbelievable conclusions than to support believable ones (Klaczynski & Fauth, 1997; Klaczynski & Gordon, 1996; Klaczynski & Robinson, 2000). Given the potential implications for our data, it is necessary to reconcile the evidence from the deductive and nondeductive paradigms. One possibility is that methodological differences can account for the observed differences. For example, in the studies cited above, the tendency is to compare believable and unbelievable conclusions without a concomitant variation in argument strength, making it difficult to compare to the standard (2 × 2) belief-bias paradigm in deduction. Alternatively, it may be the case that the findings for deduction are relatively self-contained and do not generalize to other types of reasoning tasks (Evans & Thompson, 2004). Finally, it is possible that carefully controlled experiments may reveal little evidence for a disconfirmation process per se, a finding that will have wide implications for dual-systems approaches to reasoning.

Acknowledgements

Funding for this project was provided by the Natural Sciences Engineering Research Council of Canada, the Department of Psychology at the University of Plymouth, and the Biotechnology and Biological Sciences Research Council, UK. We would like to acknowledge the assistance of Kealee Playford, Stephanie Bennet, Erin Beatty, and Nicole Roberts who collected the data for Experiments 1 and 2.

References

Ball, L. J., Phillips, P., Wade, C. N., & Quayle, J. D. (2006). Effects of belief and logic on syllogistic reasoning: Eye-movement evidence for selective processing models. *Experimental Psychology, 53*, 77–86.

Bucciarelli, M., & Johnson-Laird, P. N. (1999). Strategies in syllogistic reasoning. *Cognitive Science, 23*, 247–303.

Campbell, J. I. D., & Thompson, V. A. (2002). More power to you: Simple power calculations for treatment effects with one degree of freedom. *Behavior Research Methods, Instruments & Computers, 34*, 332–337.

Chater, N., & Oaksford, M. (1999). The probability heuristic model of syllogistic reasoning. *Cognitive Psychology, 38*, 191–258.

De Neys, W. (2006). Dual processing in reasoning: Two systems but one reasoner. *Psychological Science, 17*, 428–433.

De Neys, W., & Glumicic, T. (2008). Conflict monitoring in dual process theories of thinking. *Cognition, 106*, 1248–1299.

Ditto, P. H., & Lopez, D. F. (1992). Motivated skepticism: Use of differential decision criteria for preferred and nonpreferred conclusions. *Journal of Personality and Social Psychology, 63*, 568–584.

Edwards, K., & Smith, E. E. (1996). A disconfirmation bias in the evaluation of arguments. *Journal of Personality and Social Psychology, 71*, 5–24.

Evans, J. St B. T. (1989). *Bias in human reasoning*. Hove, UK: Lawrence Erlbaum Associates Ltd.

Evans, J. St B. T. (1996). Deciding before you think: Relevance and reasoning in the selection task. *British Journal of Psychology, 87*, 223–240.

Evans, J. St B. T. (2003). In two minds: Dual process accounts of reasoning. *Trends in Cognitive Science, 7*, 454–459.

Evans, J. St B. T. (2006). The heuristic–analytic theory of reasoning: Extension and evaluation. *Psychonomic Bulletin and Review, 13*, 378–395.

Evans, J. St B. T. (2007). On the resolution of conflict in dual-process theories of reasoning. *Thinking & Reasoning, 13*, 321–329.

Evans, J. St B. T., Barston, J. L., & Pollard, P. (1983). On the conflict between logic and belief in syllogistic reasoning. *Memory & Cognition, 11*, 295–306.

Evans, J. St B. T., & Curtis-Holmes, J. (2005). Rapid responding increases belief bias: Evidence for the dual process theory of reasoning. *Thinking & Reasoning, 11*, 382–389.

Evans, J. St B. T., & Frankish, K. (2009). *In two minds: Dual processes and beyond*. Oxford: Oxford University Press.

Evans, J. St B. T., Handley, S. H., & Harper, C. N. J. (2001). Necessity, possibility and belief: A study of syllogistic reasoning. *Quarterly Journal of Experimental Psychology: Human Experimental Psychology, 54A*, 935–958.

Evans, J. St B. T., Handley, S. H., & Over, D. (2003). Conditionals and conditional probability. *Journal of Experimental Psychology: Learning, Memory, & Cognition, 29*, 321–335.

Evans, J. St B. T., Newstead, S. E., Allen, J. L., & Pollard, P. (1994). Debiasing by instruction: The case of belief bias. *European Journal of Cognitive Psychology, 61*, 263–285.

Evans, J. St B. T., & Thompson, V. (2004). Informal reasoning: Theory and method. *Canadian Journal of Experimental Psychology, 58*, 69–74.

Ford, M. (1995). Two models of mental representation and problem solution in syllogistic reasoning. *Cognition, 54*, 1–71.

George, C. (1997). Reasoning with uncertain premises. *Thinking & Reasoning, 3*, 161–189.

Greenhoot, A. F., Semb, G., Colombo, J., & Schreiber, T. (2004). Prior beliefs and methodological concepts in scientific reasoning. *Applied Cognitive Psychology, 18*, 203–221.

Kahneman, D. (2003). A perspective on judgment and choice: Mapping bounded rationality. *American Psychologist, 58*, 697–720.

Klaczynski, P. A., & Fauth, J. (1997). Developmental differences in memory-based intrusions and self-serving statistical reasoning biases. *Merrill-Palmer Quarterly, 43*, 539–566.

Klaczynski, P. A., & Gordon, D. H. (1996). Everyday statistical reasoning during adolescence and young adulthood: Motivational, general ability, and developmental influences. *Child Development, 67*, 2873–2891.

Klaczynski, P. A., & Robinson, B. (2000). Personal theories, intellectual ability, and epistemological beliefs: Adult age differences in everyday reasoning biases. *Psychology and Aging, 15*, 400–416.

Klauer, K. C., Musch, J., & Naumer, B. (2000). On belief bias in syllogistic reasoning. *Psychological Review, 107*, 852–884.

Kunda, Z. (1990). The case for motivated reasoning. *Psychological Bulletin, 108*, 480–498.

Lambell, N. J. (1998). *The influence of belief bias on syllogistic reasoning*. Unpublished PhD thesis, University of Plymouth.

Lambell, N. J., Evans, J. St B. T., & Handley, S. J. (1999). Belief bias, logical reasoning and presentation order on the syllogistic evaluation task. In M. Hahn & S. C. Stoness (Eds.), *Proceedings of the twenty-first annual conference of the Cognitive Science Society* (pp. 282–288). Hillsdale, NJ: Lawrence Erlbaum Associates, Inc.

Lord, C. G., Ross, L., & Lepper, M. R. (1979). Biased assimilation and attitude polarization: The effects of prior theories on subsequently considered evidence. *Journal of Personality and Social Psychology, 37*, 2098–2109.

Masson, M. E. J., & Loftus, G. R. (2003). Using confidence intervals for graphically based data interpretation. *Canadian Journal of Experimental Psychology/Revue Canadienne De Psychologie Experimentale, 57*, 203–220.

Newstead, S. E., Handley, S. J., Harley, C., Wright, H., & Farelly, D. (2004). Individual differences in deductive reasoning. *The Quarterly Journal of Experimental Psychology A: Human Experimental Psychology, 57A*, 33–60.

Newstead, S. E., Pollard, P., Evans, J. St B. T., & Allen, J. (1992). The source of belief bias in syllogistic reasoning. *Cognition, 45*, 257–284.

Oakhill, J., Johnson-Laird, P. N., & Garnham, A. (1989). Believability and syllogistic reasoning. *Cognition, 31*, 117–140

Oaksford, M., Chater, N., & Larkin, J. (2001). Probabilities and polarity bias in conditional inference. *Journal of Experimental Psychology: Learning, Memory, and Cognition, 26*, 883–899.

Oberauer, K., & Wilhelm, O. (2003). The meaning(s) of conditionals: Conditional probabilities, mental models, and personal utilities. *Journal of Experimental Psychology: Learning, Memory, and Cognition, 29*, 680–693.

Polk, T. A., & Newell, A. (1995). Deduction as verbal reasoning. *Psychological Review, 102*, 533–566.

Quayle, J. D., & Ball, L. J. (2000). Working memory, metacognitive uncertainty, and belief bias in syllogistic reasoning. *Quarterly Journal of Experimental Psychology, 53A*, 1202–1223.

Sá, W. C., West, R. F., & Stanovich, K. E. (1999). The domain specificity and generality of belief bias: Searching for a generalizable critical thinking skill. *Journal of Educational Psychology, 91*, 497–510.

Schaeken, W., De Vooght, G., Vandierendonck, A., & d'Ydewalle, G. (2000). Strategies and tactics in deductive reasoning In W. Schaeken, G. De Vooght, A. Vandierendonck, & G. d'Ydewalle (Eds.), *Deductive reasoning and strategies* (pp. 301–309). Mahwah, NJ: Lawrence Erlbaum Associates, Inc.

Shynkaruk, J. M., & Thompson, V. A. (2006). Confidence and accuracy in deductive reasoning. *Memory & Cognition, 34*, 619–632.

Sloman, S. A. (1996). The empirical case for two systems of reasoning. *Psychological Bulletin, 119*, 3–22.

Sloman, S. A. (2002). Two systems of reasoning. In T. Gilovich, D. Griffin, & D. Kahneman (Eds.), *Heuristics and biases: The psychology of intuitive judgment* (pp. 379–396). New York: Cambridge University Press.

Stanovich, K. E., & West, R. F. (1997). Reasoning independently of prior belief and individual differences in actively open-minded thinking. *Journal of Educational Psychology, 89*, 342–357.

Stanovich, K. E., & West, R. F. (2007). Natural myside bias is independent of cognitive ability. *Thinking & Reasoning, 13*, 225–247.

Stevenson, R., & Over, D. (1995). Deduction from uncertain premises. *Quarterly Journal of Experimental Psychology, 48A*, 613–643.

Stupple, E. J. N., & Ball. L. J. (2008). Belief–logic conflict resolution in syllogistic reasoning: Inspection-time evidence for a parallel-process model. *Thinking & Reasoning, 14*, 168–181.

Thompson, V. A., (1996). Reasoning from false premises: The role of soundness in making logical deductions. *Canadian Journal of Experimental Psychology, 50*, 315–319.

Thompson, V. A., Striemer, C. L., Reikoff, R., Gunter, R. W., & Campbell, J. I. D. (2003). Syllogistic reasoning time: Disconfirmation disconfirmed. *Psychonomic Bulletin & Review, 10*, 184–189.

Wilkins, M. C. (1928). The effect of changed material on the ability to do formal syllogistic reasoning. *Archives of Psychology, 102*, 1–83.

16 Dual systems and dual processes but a single function

Mike Oaksford

Birkbeck College, University of London

Nick Chater

University College London

For 35 years now Jonathan Evans has been the leading proponent of the dual-process approach to human reasoning (Evans, 2003; Wason & Evans, 1975). We follow Evans (2003) and use Stanovich and West's (2000) terms for these systems: System 1 and System 2. Originally, these two systems were described using the terms *heuristic* (System 1) and *analytic* (System 2) (Evans, 1989). In his own words, Jonathan's current conception of each system is as follows:

> **System 1** processes are rapid, parallel and automatic in nature: only their final product is posted in consciousness ... The System 1 processes most often described are those that are formed by associative learning processes of the kind produced by neural networks.
>
> **System 2** thinking is slow and sequential in nature and makes use of the central working memory system ... System 2 permits abstract hypothetical thinking that cannot be achieved by System 1.
>
> Evans (2003, p. 454)

Dual-systems theory is frequently contrasted with single system/process theories (see Evans, 2003); in particular, our probabilistic approach (Oaksford & Chater, 2007, 2009a, 2009b). In this chapter we will argue that this contrast is not appropriate because dual-systems/process theory and the probabilistic approach address different levels of computational explanation. We explore the consequences of this fact and outline briefly why a dual system that implements different reasoning functions in System 1 and System 2 could lead to inferential chaos. We then briefly outline an account that shows that a probabilistic approach is compatible with dual-systems theory.

Dual processes, dual functions and Marr

Marr (1982) defined three levels of computational explanation. At the *computational* level *what* gets computed in performing some task is defined. For example, if we are designing a calculator we want to know that it computes arithmetic, so that, e.g., if you input "2", "+," and "2," the machine outputs "4." What goes on between input and output, i.e., *how* the calculator computes arithmetic, is specified at the *algorithmic* level. At this level the representations and algorithms that perform arithmetic are defined. So for example we may specify that the algorithm uses Arabic numerals and performs addition, say, by lining up columns, adding column wise, and then carrying. You can use many different algorithms to implement arithmetic, each having its own level of complexity. For example, another way of implementing addition would be to take 1 from the second number and add it to the first number until the second number is 0. Although this would take a lot longer than the first more familiar method, it still respects the rules of the computational level theory of arithmetic. Finally, at the *implementational* level, the physical structure of the device on which the algorithm runs is defined.

With respect to *reasoning*, standard logic and probability theory are computational-level theories of how people should reason. That is they provide at the very least the theory of what the cognitive system is trying to compute even if for a variety of reasons – to do with memory limitations or the particular representation/process pair implementing these theories – these systems occasionally or even systematically fail. Arguing that the hypothesized cognitive systems in dual-systems theory are involved in reasoning only makes sense on this assumption. Otherwise, these systems are simply responsible for whatever people do on psychologists' "reasoning" tasks. But this just puts the question one step back, because these tasks are only *reasoning* tasks if they require reasoning according to the laws of logic or probability to reach the *correct* answer; which is only definable within these functional theories.

The dual systems in dual-systems theory derive from theories of *cognitive architecture*, i.e., the basic structures and processes that underpin human cognition (Anderson, 1983). The definitions provided by Evans (2003) clearly implicate working memory (WM) as System 2 and long-term memory for world knowledge (LTM) as System 1. These two systems will invoke different processes because they perform different memorial functions. So to solve a problem, WM may trigger an interrogation of LTM but WM does not use the spreading activation processes used to retrieve information in LTM. Working memory and LTM are general systems, that is, they are invoked in many cognitive processes. As such, it would seem that both would have to be invoked by almost any theory of reasoning. For example, mental logic theory could rely on storing the rules of logic in LTM that are retrieved and deployed in WM during a passage of reasoning or language comprehension. Another possibility is that logic is *constitutive* of processes in WM or LTM. So, for example, WM processes may be inherently logical. Prima facie, this would seem consistent with the control function of the central executive component of WM if such functions are identified with the control statements, e.g., if_then_else, of a programming language. But as Kowalski's (1979) classic equation, "Algorithm = Logic + Control", reminds us, logic and control processes are not the same thing (see also, Anderson, 1983). We will not explore these possibilities further but note that the contrast between logic and control processes has recently prompted some dual-process theorists to propose a tri-process approach, i.e., including control processes, to explain human reasoning (for example, Stanovich, Evans).

Returning to the question of whether dual systems and the probabilistic approach are in genuine conflict, *it is an additional question as to whether these dual systems and processes respect different reasoning theories when engaged in reasoning*. It is perfectly coherent to hypothesize that the processes involved in WM and in LTM during a passage of reasoning all respect a single computational-level theory of reasoning, be it logic or probability theory. If this is the case, then there is no reason why dual-system/process theories need be viewed as in conflict with the probabilistic approach.

Is it equally coherent to suggest that one system respects one computational-level theory and the other system respects another? There are four possibilities for the reasoning theories WM and LTM processes might respect, only two of which, we will argue, need to be considered in the context of current dual-process theories. Working memory and LTM could both obey either logical or probabilistic principles. So a single-function theory would insist that when engaged in reasoning, the processes in WM and LTM respect either logic or probability theory. A dual-function theory would insist either that WM respects logic whereas LTM respects probability theory, or that it is the other way round. The two possibilities that we rule out in the context of the debate with Jonathan and other dual-process theorists are the cases where System 1 processes implement logical reasoning. However, this is not an incoherent position – indeed it is an assumption of classical cognitive architectures (Pylyshyn, 1984). However, neither Jonathan nor any other dual-process theorist countenances this position. In the next section, however, we show that our arguments against classical cognitive architectures (Oaksford & Chater, 1991) generalize to dual-function approaches.

This leaves the possibility in which during reasoning, WM processes respect logic and LTM processes respect probability theory, i.e., the now classical dual-"process" view, and the possibility that both WM and LTM processes respect probability theory, the view which we explicitly endorse here and elsewhere (Oaksford & Chater, 2010). Notice of course that both approaches are dual-system/process theories.

An argument against dual-function theories

The probabilistic approach argues that the processes in WM and LTM both respect (probably only to an approximation) the same underlying theory of reasoning. The probabilistic approach developed out of a critique of the classical logicist approach to cognitive architecture (Fodor, 1975), where cognitive architecture is defined as a specification of the cognitive systems and the representation/process pairs used in cognition (Anderson, 1983; Pylyhsyn, 1984).

According to the classical logicist approach, scientific psychology must reconstruct folk psychology in representationalist terms. Folk psychology concerns the propositional attitudes, i.e., believing, desiring, or whatever. Having a propositional attitude is to stand in a relation to a mental representation – the relation of believing, desiring, and so on. The contents of a propositional attitude are described in natural language and so the interpretation of the corresponding mental representations must be at the level of everyday objects and relations. This is the substance of Fodor's representational theory of mind (e.g., Fodor, 1987). Folk psychology explains behaviour in terms of inference over propositional attitudes.

Hence, a representationalist reconstruction of folk psychology must provide mechanisms for drawing inferences over the representations that capture the content of the propositional attitudes. In classical cognitive architectures, these mechanisms are taken to be formal operations over syntactically structured representations. That is, mental operations are taken to apply purely in virtue of the structural properties of the representations. These syntactic mental operations must be coherent with respect to the semantics of the representations being manipulated. This is the substance of Fodor's computational theory of mind (Fodor, 1987). Currently, the only way in which the semantic coherence of formal structural manipulation may be guaranteed is by showing that each manipulation of the representations corresponds to a sound proof-theoretic derivation in some appropriately interpreted formal language. In other words, the language of mental representation constitutes a *logic*, in which mental representations correspond to well-formed formulae, and manipulations over them correspond to sound logical inferences. According to this view, a central task of cognitive science is to characterize the logical language of mental representation, the proof-theoretic rules defined over it, and the content of the representations employed in the production of particular behaviours.

On this classical logicist view, the store of world knowledge in LTM consists of a consistent set of formulae in the language of thought that can be combined with given information in WM using inference rules to yield new information in a proof-theoretic derivation. Oaksford and Chater (1991) argued that the defeasiblity of human reasoning counted strongly against this logicist single-function view. Defeasible reasoning creates two problems for such systems. In standard logic, defeasible reasoning leads to contradictions. Suppose that *if x is a bird, then x flies* is part of your world knowledge in LTM, then when someone asserts that *Tweety is a bird*, you may validly infer that *Tweety can fly* and so add this to your world knowledge in LTM. But if you are then told that *Tweety is an ostrich* your belief that ostriches can't fly will lead you to add *Tweety cannot fly* to your world knowledge in LTM resulting in a contradiction, i.e., *Tweety can fly AND Tweety cannot fly*. One attempt to avoid this unacceptable conclusion is to propose a nonmonotonic logic (Reiter, 1985). However, as Oaksford and Chater (1991) argued based on critiques in artificial intelligence (McDermott, 1987), this leads to triviality – all that can be concluded is that *Tweety can fly OR Tweety cannot fly* (something you knew before drawing any inferences) – and to computational intractability (see Oaksford & Chater, 1991, 2007).

The now classical dual-process view embodies a dual-function perspective. In this respect, the dual-process view seems very close to proposing a hybrid connectionist/symbolic cognitive architecture (e.g., Sun, Slusarz, & Terry, 2005). Could such a hybrid approach resolve the problems of defeasible reasoning that we previously identified for classical logicist cognitive architectures? As we have recently argued (Oaksford & Chater, 2009b) we do not think that it can.

We argued that the fundamental problem with this dual-function view is that these two systems must interact – and if the systems obey fundamentally different principles, it is not clear how this is possible. Consider again the familiar example of inferring that *Tweety flies* from the general claim that *birds fly* and the fact that *Tweety is a bird*. In the dual-function view, this inference could be drawn logically from the premises given by System 2, from the assumption that *birds fly* is a true universal generalization; System 1, by contrast, might tentatively draw this conclusion by defeasible, associative processes, drawing on general knowledge. But a lack of synchrony between the two systems, presumed to operate by different rational standards, threatens to cause inferential chaos. Consider, for example, what happens if we consider the possibility that *Tweety is an ostrich*. If System 2 works according to logical principles, the clash of two rules threatens contradiction: we know that birds fly, but that ostriches do not. To escape contradiction, one of the premises must be rejected: most naturally, *birds fly* will be rejected as false. But we now have two unpalatable possibilities. On the one hand, suppose that this retraction is *not* transferred to general knowledge and hence is not assimilated by System 1. Then the two systems will have contradictory beliefs (moreover, if System 2 reasoning cannot modify general knowledge, its purpose seems unclear). On the other hand, if *birds fly* is retracted from world knowledge, along with other defeasible generalizations, then almost all of general knowledge will be stripped away (as generalizations outside mathematics are typically defeasible; Oaksford & Chater, 2007, 2009b), leading System 1 into inferential paralysis.

It seems that the best way to avoid these unpalatable conclusions and account for the defeasibility of human reasoning is to adopt a single-function view in which representing *birds fly* in WM amounts to the assumption that the probability that something flies given it is a bird is very close to 1 ($P(flies(x)|bird(x)) \sim 1$). In this case, rather than having to reject *birds fly* as false in System 2, the observation that *Tweety is an ostrich* simply provides a negative instance that leads to a reduction of $P(flies(x)|bird(x))$ in System 1.[1] That is, the two systems can properly communicate.

A single-function dual-process approach

We now show directly how the dual-process approach could be implemented preserving the ability to deal with the defeasibility of human reasoning with both WM and LTM respecting probability theory (see Oaksford & Chater, 2010). Figure 16.1 shows a possible implementation of dual-process theory (Evans & Over, 2004). The operations over LTM for world knowledge are the System 1 processes. In the System 1 box we show a simple system of two alternative dependencies, $p \rightarrow q$ and $r \rightarrow q$, which are context sensitive, that is, if the defeaters, *d1* or *d2*, are present q does not occur. Here we represent this knowledge as a constraint satisfaction neural network, i.e., an associationist mechanism of the kind Jonathan argues constitutes System 1. The connections with arrowheads are facilitatory connections and those with circular ends are inhibitory connections. Thus both p and r will activate the q unit, whereas *d1* and *d2* will inhibit it. We can think of the dependencies under the following translation: *p*: x is a bird, *q*: x flies, *r*: x is a fly, *d1*: x is an ostrich, *d2*: x is a penguin. This is the knowledge acquired by learning about things that fly. Notice that the weight between p and q is not 1, because people cannot know of all the exceptions, *d1*, *d2* . . . etc., that can defeat the conclusion that q.

People can interrogate this network and store the results as perhaps an annotated mental model in WM. So on encountering an modus ponens inference, they may clamp on the *p*-unit, corresponding to the categorical premise, e.g., *Tweety is a bird*. The network is allowed to settle into a new equilibrium

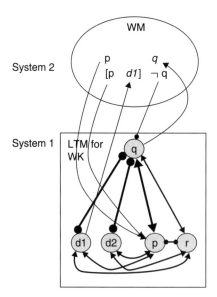

Figure 16.1 A dual-process implementation of the probabilistic model. LTM = long-term memory; WM = working memory; WK = world knowledge.

state and the activation of the *q*-unit is read off. We argue that this process in the model corresponds to performing a Ramsey test. The activation level of the *q*-unit corresponds to the probability of *q* given that *p* is true and our other prior beliefs, *B*, embodied in the connection weights in the network. The result of performing this Ramsey test can be stored in WM as an annotated mental model. In Figure 16.1, clamped units are represented as normal text in a mental model in WM. The target of the inference, *q*, is in italics. This model would be annotated with the probability of the target, i.e., $P(q|p,B)$.

People may also interrogate LTM to investigate different possibilities, e.g., they might want to explore the conditions under which the opposite of the conclusion is possible. This involves clamping the *p*-unit on and the *q*-unit off (in the second row of the mental model in WM both *p* and *q* are in normal text). In the model, because of the weak co-occurrence relation between *p* (being a bird) and the defeaters, one of *d1* or *d2* will become active because they are no longer inhibited by the *q*-unit. So *d1* is added to the mental model. The activation level of the activated (as opposed to clamped) unit is represented as an annotation to the model that relates to the unclamped unit represented in the mental model.

Figure 16.1 also shows that we can construe the model in terms of dual-process theory (Evans & Over, 2004). The operations over world knowledge in LTM are System 1 processes. These processes are heuristic, fast, automatic, and largely unconscious. Notice, however, this would not prevent these processes from being normatively justified if they can be seen to implement a probabilistic account of reasoning (even if only to an approximation). In contrast, the storage and manipulation in WM of the results of interrogating LTM about various possibilities can be considered a System 2 process. These processes are analytic, slow, controlled, and may be conscious.

This model suggests that mental models (or a similar representational format) are required to store the results of interrogating world knowledge in LTM about various possibilities. Consequently, the emergence of the ability to consider possibilities by interrogating LTM and working-memory capacity must be intimately linked. Moreover, the cognitive system would require this function to be performed regardless of whether there was a demand for explicit verbal reasoning with conditional sentences. That is, this ability is perhaps the pre-adaptation (Bickerton, 2000), that has allowed the development of our explicit reasoning abilities.

We now show that the processes in both LTM and in WM can be shown to respect probability theory, i.e., this model is a dual-system, dual-process but single-function model of human reasoning.

Probabilistic interpretation of System 1 and System 2

In discussing the way in which both systems are operating probabilistically, we observe that the consideration of different possibilities in WM is likely to lead to characteristic errors. This is because, for say the modus ponens inference MP – *if p then q, p, therefore, q* – interrogating LTM with *p* as the probe will provide the best estimate of $P(q|p,B)$. Considering other possibilities in WM such as p, $\neg q$, will prompt consideration of finer grained partitions of the probability space – ones in which *d1* or *d2* hold – that yield different estimates of the probability of *q* in these different conditions. When combined with other possibilities, errors are likely to result. We go into the details when we get to discussing System 2. However, this means that considering other possibilities is likely to lead to errors from a probabilistic point of view because it engages further world knowledge. In effect, this is the probabilistic equivalent of Stanovich and West's (2000) *fundamental computational bias*.

System 1

Oaksford and Chater (2010) argue that the probabilistic interpretation of the constraint satisfaction network making up System 1 relies on setting the weights and the bias terms into units of particular values (McClelland, 1998). Figure 16.2 shows the LTM component of the model including the bias terms that are represented as additional weights between each unit and a bias unit. We have also subdivided the units into *context* units, i.e., representations of the context, *C*, in which the antecedents of a conditional lead to their consequent. As we described above these correspond to the defeaters that if present could prevent the consequent from occurring.

The operations of System 1 can be interpreted as computing real posterior probabilities. There are three components to understanding how this is achieved (McClelland, 1998). First, the activation function must take the following logistic form:

$$a_i(t) = 1/(1 + e^{-G\Sigma w_{ij}a_i(t-1) - Bias})$$

(16.1)

(16.1) relates the activation level of unit *i* at time *t*, $a_i(t)$, to its activation level at time $t - 1$, $a_i(t - 1)$, the weights from units *j* into unit *i*, w_{ij}, the bias term, *Bias*, and a *gain* parameter, *G*. Second, the weights must be set to a quantity referred to as consistency:

$$w_{ij} = \ln((P(x_i, x_j) \, P(\neg x_i, \neg x_j))/(P(x_i, \neg x_j) \, P(\neg x_i, x_j)))$$

(16.2)

That is, the weights between unit x_i and unit x_j depend on their co-occurrence statistics. Finally, the bias term for unit x_i should be set to the log of the prior odds:

$$Bias(x_i) = \ln(P(x_i)/(1 - P(x_i)))$$

(16.3)

Setting the weights in this way has the consequence that the network will compute the real posterior probability given the values of the clamped nodes and other prior knowledge (McClelland, 1998). However, this is not strictly

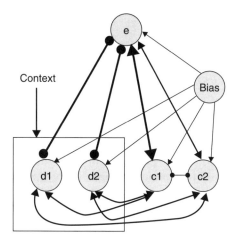

Figure 16.2 The long-term memory constraint satisfaction network showing the bias term and context units.

the case for the LTM component of the network presented in Figure 16.1. This is because one other condition that must be met is that in a feed-forward network, units at lower levels must be conditionally independent of the units they are connected to at the next level up. So formally, for example, $P(p|q,d1,B)$ = $P(p|q,B)$. However, the weak connections between $d1$ and p prevent this condition being properly met. Moreover, Oaksford and Chater (2010) allowed the network to operate in either direction, i.e., not just as a feed-forward network. Finally given the connectivity of the network used for the LTM component, it is not guaranteed to settle into a stable configuration. However, for now it is sufficient to comment that in using the network to model reasoning data, Oaksford and Chater (2010) encountered few problems.

System 2

To model the empirical data Oaksford and Chater (2010) argued that the representations in WM, along the lines of a mental model, are annotated with probabilities retrieved from LTM. In Figure 16.1, the first model in WM would be annotated with $P(q|p,B)$, say .8, as this, according to the probabilistic interpretation, is the value of the q-node after clamping on the p-node. Annotations are subject to simple averaging operations that respect probability theory, in so far as the possibilities are regarded as exhaustive. So if out of two possibilities someone considers, the probability of q is .8 in one and .6 in the other, participants compute the probability of q to be .7. This calculation involves assigning a second order probability of .5 (or more generally, 1/number of possibilities considered) that $P(q|B)$ takes the value in a possibility's annotation and then calculating the expected value of $P(q|B)$ given all the possibilities considered.

The annotated mental models in WM wear their probabilistic interpretation on their sleeves. Consequently, defeasible reasoning creates few problems. The subsequent discovery that *Tweety is an ostrich* involves simply considering a slightly different possibility, i.e., *p* and *d1*. Should *Tweety* turn out to be a nonflying bird, as our defeasible reasoner will be led to strongly suspect given her prior knowledge in System 1, then *Tweety* is identified as an exemplar from which the cognitive system can learn by adjusting the weights in the neural network making up LTM to incorporate this new knowledge.

The first model in Figure 16.1, which for the modus ponens inference results from clamping on the *p*-node, will result in the most accurate estimate of the probability of the conclusion, *q*. However, as more possibilities are considered, even though the calculations over annotations in WM are probabilistically pristine and simple, the information delivered up from LTM may lead to errors.

The second model in Figure 16.1 is the result of clamping on the *p*-node and clamping off the *q*-node in System 1. In System 2, this means considering the possibility that although *p* holds, *q* does not hold. In System 1, this allows the defeater nodes to become active, suggesting that Tweety is either an ostrich (*d1*) or a penguin (*d2*). The activation levels of the *d1* and *d2* correspond to $P(d1|p,\neg q,B)$ and $P(d2|p,\neg q,B)$. Having retrieved this information, a reasoner needs to explore how it affects the target of the modus ponens inference, i.e., *q*. This means computing the inverse probability, normally computed by Bayes' theorem, by probing LTM with the possibility *p*, *d1*, to provide an estimate of $P(q|p,d1,B)$. Oaksford and Chater (2010) suggested that participants do not take this extra step of using System 1 to compute this inverse probability by clamping on *p* and *d1*, but compute it directly by ignoring bases rates (or assuming that they are equal) so that, e.g., $P(\neg q|p,d1,B) = P(d1|p,\neg q,B)$ and therefore $P(q|p,d1,B) = 1 - P(d1|p,\neg q,B)$. They do the same for *d2* and take the average, i.e., $1 - ((P(d1|p,\neg q,B) + P(d2|p,\neg q,B))/2)$, which is then used as the annotation for the *p*, $\neg q$ possibility (Figure 16.1, line 2 in System 2). Oaksford and Chater (2010) go on to show that simple averaging over the annotations to the possibilities considered by System 2, provide good "eyeball" fits to a range of data on conditional inference.

These processes suggest that while considering these further possibilities is eminently reasonable – they allow people to retrieve information relevant to the inference at hand – it cannot improve on the initial estimate of the probability of the target of the inference provided by probing LTM only with the categorical premise of the inference. This suggests that the quickest and most simple-minded processing of the inference is likely to lead to the most probabilistically accurate results. More time and thought cannot improve on this initial estimate because it invites people to consider possibilities not determined by the premises. Nonetheless, combining the information in the annotations to the possibilities considered in WM can nonetheless follow probabilistic guidelines. However, due to the retrieval process these possibilities and their annotations won't necessarily respect the assumptions of probability theory to allow them to be combined in this way. In particular, the possibilities will not be exhaustive because when interrogating world knowledge the possibilities involved in a conditional inference go beyond the four defined by the antecedent, p, the consequent, q, and their negations.

Considering the p, $\neg q$ possibility reveals what can go wrong. Suppose the first row of the mental model in "WM" shown in Figure 16.1 is annotated with $P(q|p,B) = .8$. $P(q|p,d1,B)$ and $P(q|p,d2,B)$ must be close to zero, so averaging these annotations is going to provide a lower estimate of the conclusion probability. However, considering these other possibilities of $d1$ or $d2$, cued by considering the p and $\neg q$ possibility is bound to lead to errors. If all that is known is that p, i.e., what is stated in the categorical premise, then $P(q|p,B)$ is the desired result, i.e., the possibility of $d1$ and $d2$ is irrelevant.

The possibility of $d1$ and $d2$ is relevant to explaining suppression effects (Byrne, 1989; Cummins, 1995) where specific information about $d1$, $d2$, or r is provided explicitly (Byrne, 1989) or is highly salient in background knowledge B (Cummins, 1995). Moreover, we have argued that they are probably always considered for the other conditional inferences, modus tollens, and for the fallacies of denying the antecedent and affirming the consequent, although not for modus ponens (Oaksford & Chater, 2007). Oaksford and Chater (2010) also model suppression effects directly in this framework.

In sum, considering possibilities that go beyond what is stated in the categorical premise can lead to errors when combining the different probabilities for the target of the inference from possibilities that cue finer grained partitions of the probability space. Considering different suppositional possibilities allows reasoners to retrieve the conditions under which an inference may fail or alternative ways of getting to the conclusion. Once such a system is in place it is perhaps only a short step to proposing that people may learn to ignore the information these possibilities retrieve from System 1 and simply consider what arises from the possibilities considered exhaustively in their own right. It may be that the systems with which we are genetically endowed respect one set of principles, but using these systems over the course of development promotes the ability to use the systems in different ways. So for example, the more linguistically competent a child becomes the more able they are to abstract away from the noisy world in which they live and consider just the structural relations between symbols in WM. At this point some form of logical competence might be in evidence.

Conclusions

In this chapter we have argued that there is no dispute between dual-systems/process theories and the probabilistic approach with respect to the cognitive architecture underlying human reasoning. The dispute, if there is one, relates to the functions computed by System 1 (LTM) and System 2 (WM). We argued that to deal with the problems posed by defeasible reasoning for classical cognitive architectures (Oaksford & Chater, 1991), requires a dual-systems theory where both systems are concerned with probabilistic information and in computing probabilistic functions. For System 1, we showed that a constraint satisfaction neural network, i.e., the kind of process Jonathan identifies with this system, can be interpreted as computing real posterior probabilities (McClelland, 1998; Oaksford & Chater, 2010). Moreover, we argued that possibilities in System 2 must be annotated with probabilities relating to the probability of the target of an inference in that given possibility. These annotations can be combined in ways that respect probability theory under certain assumptions. However, these assumptions are not normally met because these possibilities acting as retrieval cues in System 1 trigger information about other factors that may affect the inference. So combining $P(q|p,B)$ and $P(q|p,d1,B)$ by averaging is an error that relates to the fundamental computational bias (Stanovich & West, 2000) whereby people automatically contextualize an inference by importing retrieved information not stated in the premises. However, other than the highly intelligent few who can learn to abstract away from world knowledge or others who are explicitly taught to do so, we argue that the cognitive architecture is largely attempting to compute probabilistic functions in both System 1 and System 2.

Note

1 Exactly this proposal has been made to account for the inferential asymmetries in conditional reasoning (Oaksford & Chater, 2008).

References

Anderson, J. R. (1983). *The architecture of cognition*. Hillsdale, NJ: Lawrence Erlbaum Associates, Inc.

Bickerton, D. (2000). Biomusicology and language evolution studies. In N. L. Wallin, B. Merker, & S. Brown (Eds.), *The origins of music* (pp. 153–164). Cambridge, MA: MIT Press.

Byrne, R. M. J. (1989). Suppressing valid inferences with conditionals. *Cognition*, *31*, 1–21.

Cummins, D. D. (1995). Naïve theories and causal deduction. *Memory & Cognition*, *23*, 646–658.

Evans, J. St B. T. (1989). *Bias in human reasoning: Causes and consequences*. Hillsdale, NJ: Lawrence Erlbaum Associates, Inc.

Evans, J. St B. T. (2003). In two minds: Dual processes account of reasoning. *Trends in Cognitive Sciences*, *7*, 454–459.

Evans, J.St B.T., & Over, D.E. (2004). *If*. Oxford: Oxford University Press.

Fodor, J. A. (1975). *The language of thought*. Cambridge, MA: Harvard University Press.

Fodor, J. A. (1987). *Psychosemantics*. Cambridge, MA: MIT Press.

Kowalski, R. (1979). Algorithm = Logic + Control. *Communications of the Association for Computing Machinery*, *22*, 424–436.

Marr, D. (1982). *Vision*. San Francisco: W. H. Freeman.

McClelland, J. L. (1998). Connectionist models and Bayesian inference. In M. Oaksford & N. Chater (Eds.), *Rational models of cognition* (pp. 21–53). Oxford: Oxford University Press.

McDermott, D. (1987). A critique of pure reason. *Computational Intelligence, 33*, 151–160.

Oaksford, M., & Chater, N. (1991). Against logicist cognitive science. *Mind and Language, 6*, 1–38.

Oaksford, M., & Chater, N. (2007). *Bayesian rationality*. Oxford: Oxford University Press.

Oaksford, M., & Chater, N. (2008). Probability logic and the Modus Ponens–Modus Tollens asymmetry in conditional inference. In N. Chater & M. Oaksford (Eds.), *The probabilistic mind: Prospects for Bayesian cognitive science* (pp. 97–120). Oxford: Oxford University Press.

Oaksford, M., & Chater, N. (2009a). Precis of "Bayesian rationality: The probabilistic approach to human reasoning". *Behavioral and Brain Sciences, 32*, 69–84.

Oaksford, M., & Chater, N. (2009b). The uncertain reasoner: Bayes, logic and rationality. *Behavioral and Brain Sciences, 32*, 105–120.

Oaksford, M., & Chater, N. (2010). Conditionals and constraint satisfaction: Reconciling mental models and the probabilistic approach? In M. Oaksford & N. Chater (Eds.), *Cognition and conditionals: Probability and logic in human thought*. Oxford: Oxford University Press.

Pylyshyn, Z. (1984). *Computation and cognition*. Cambridge, MA: MIT Press.

Reiter, R. (1985). On reasoning by default. In R. Brachman & H. Levesque (Eds.), *Readings in knowledge representation* (pp. 401–410). Los Altos, CA: Morgan Kaufman.

Stanovich, K. E., & West, R. F. (2000). Individual differences in reasoning: Implications for the rationality debate. *Behavioral and Brain Sciences, 23*, 645–726.

Sun, R., Slusarz, P., & Terry, C. (2005). The interaction of the explicit and the implicit in skill learning: A dual-process approach. *Psychological Review, 112*, 159–192.

Wason, P. C., & Evans, J. St B. T. (1975). Dual processes in reasoning. *Cognition, 3*, 141–154.

Part IV
Rationality and reasoning

17 Individual differences as essential components of heuristics and biases research

Keith E. Stanovich

University of Toronto

Richard F. West

James Madison University

Maggie E. Toplak

York University, Toronto

Introduction

We are honoured to contribute to this volume because Jonathan Evans' work has been a key inspiration to us since even before we began contributing to the thinking and reasoning literature. Richard and Keith had been admirers of the heuristics and biases tradition from its inception in the early 1970s. However, their first research contributions were in the psychology of reading and this occupied them for 15 years (see Stanovich, 2000; Stanovich, Cunningham, & West, 1998). By the late 1980s though, we had decided to make a contribution to the literature on thinking and reasoning that we had admired so much for so long. Keith set off to Cambridge in early 1991 on a sabbatical with reading colleague Usha Goswami, and Rich visited for an important brainstorming week. The sabbatical really ended up being about reasoning and rationality rather than reading, however, and there were two books that we took to England to study in detail: Stich's *The Fragmentation of Reason* (1990) and Jonathan's *Biases in Human Reasoning* (1989). The former was obviously to bone up on the philosophical issues surrounding the concept of rational thought. However, the latter really became our bible on that sabbatical. In an amazingly few pages Jonathan zeroed in on the key issues surrounding the important biases and also gave the relative novice an introduction to the central tasks in the literature. That book, his insights as one of the first dual-process theorists, and almost four decades of continuous creative work in the area have made Jonathan one of our most important intellectual guideposts throughout our careers in this field.

The Great Rationality Debate

Our initial contribution to the field was to argue for the potential usefulness of individual difference data in the disputes surrounding what has been termed the Great Rationality Debate in cognitive science. It concerns the interpretation of the voluminous data indicating that human behaviour deviates from optimal standards as determined by decision scientists. How to interpret these deviations is, however, a matter of contentious dispute. As Tetlock and Mellers (2002) point out, "the debate over human rationality is a high-stakes controversy that mixes primordial political and psychological prejudices in combustible combinations" (p. 97). The so-called Great Debate about human rationality is a "high-stakes controversy" because it involves nothing less than the models of human nature that underlie economics, moral philosophy, and the personal theories (folk theories) we use to understand the behaviour of other humans.

The root of the debate is the substantial research literature – one comprising literally hundreds of empirical studies conducted for more than three decades – showing that people's responses often deviate from the performance traditionally considered normative on many reasoning tasks. For example, people assess probabilities incorrectly; they display confirmation bias; they test hypotheses inefficiently; they violate the axioms of utility theory; they do not properly calibrate degrees of belief; they overproject their own opinions onto others; they allow prior belief to become implicated in their evaluation of evidence and arguments; and they display numerous other information processing biases (for summaries of the large literature, see Baron, 2008; Camerer, Loewenstein, & Rabin, 2004; Evans, 1989, 2007a; Gilovich, Griffin, & Kahneman, 2002; Johnson-Laird, 2006; Kahneman & Tversky, 2000; Koehler & Harvey, 2004; LeBoeuf & Shafir, 2005; Nickerson, 2008; Pohl, 2004; Stanovich, 1999, 2009). Indeed, demonstrating that descriptive accounts of human behaviour diverged from normative models was a main theme of the so-called heuristics and biases literature from its beginning in the 1970s and early 1980s (Dawes, 1976; Evans, 1984, 1989; Kahneman & Tversky, 1972, 1973; Kahneman, Slovic, & Tversky, 1982; Tversky & Kahneman, 1973, 1974; Wason & Evans, 1975).

The interpretation of the gap between descriptive models and normative models in the human reasoning and decision-making literature has been the subject of contentious debate for almost three decades now (Cohen, 1981, 1983; Evans & Over, 1996; Gigerenzer, 1996; Kahneman, 1981; Kahneman & Tversky, 1983, 1996; Koehler, 1996; Nickerson, 2008; Stanovich, 1999; Stein, 1996). The debate has arisen because some investigators wished to interpret the gap between the descriptive and the normative as indicating that human cognition was characterized by systematic irrationalities. Due to the emphasis that these theorists place on reforming human cognition, they were labelled the Meliorists by Stanovich (1999). Disputing this contention were numerous investigators (termed the Panglossians, see Stanovich, 1999) who argued that there were other reasons why reasoning might not accord with normative theory – reasons that prevent the ascription of irrationality to subjects. First, instances of reasoning might depart from normative standards due to performance errors – temporary lapses of attention, memory deactivation, and other sporadic information processing mishaps. Second, there may be stable and inherent computational limitations that prevent the normative response (Cherniak, 1986; Oaksford & Chater, 1993, 1995, 1998; Stich, 1990). Third, in interpreting performance, we might be applying the wrong normative model to the task (Koehler, 1996). Alternatively, we may be applying the correct normative model to the problem as set, but the subject might have construed the problem differently and be providing the normatively appropriate answer to a different problem (Adler, 1984, 1991; Berkeley & Humphreys, 1982; Broome, 1990; Hilton, 1995; Schwarz, 1996; Stanovich, 1999).

However, in referring to the various alternative explanations (other than systematic irrationality) for the normative/descriptive gap, Rips (1994) warns that "a determined skeptic can usually explain away any instance of what seems at first to be a logical mistake" (p. 393). In an earlier criticism of Henle's (1978) Panglossian position, Johnson-Laird (1983) made the same point: "There are no criteria independent of controversy by which to make a fair assessment of whether an error violates logic. It is not clear what would count as crucial evidence, since it is always possible to provide an alternative explanation for an error" (p. 26). The most humorous version of this argument was made by Kahneman (1981) in his dig at the Panglossians who seem to have only two categories of errors, "pardonable errors by subjects and unpardonable ones by psychologists" (p. 340). Referring to the four classes of alternative explanation discussed above – random performance errors, computational limitations, alternative problem construal, and incorrect norm application – Kahneman notes that Panglossians have "a handy kit of defenses that may be used if [subjects are] accused of errors: temporary insanity, a difficult childhood, entrapment, or judicial mistakes – one of them will surely work, and will restore the presumption of rationality" (p. 340).

These comments by Rips (1994), Johnson-Laird (1983), and Kahneman (1981) highlight the need for principled constraints on the alternative explanations of normative/descriptive discrepancies. We have tried to show that patterns of individual differences might help to provide just such principled constraints (Stanovich, 1999; Stanovich & West, 1998a, 1998b, 1998c, 1998d, 1999, 2000; West & Stanovich, 2003). For example, Panglossian theorists who argue that discrepancies between actual responses and those dictated by normative models are not indicative of human irrationality (e.g., Cohen, 1981) sometimes attribute the discrepancies to performance errors. Borrowing the idea of a competence/performance distinction from linguists (see Stein, 1996, pp. 8–9), these theorists view performance errors as the failure to apply a rule, strategy, or algorithm that is part of a person's competence because of a momentary and fairly random lapse in ancillary processes necessary to execute the strategy (lack of attention, temporary memory deactivation, distraction, etc.). Stein (1996) explains the idea of a performance error by referring to a "mere mistake" – a more colloquial notion that involves "a *momentary lapse*, a divergence from some typical behaviour. This is in contrast to attributing a divergence from norm to reasoning in accordance with principles that diverge from the normative principles of reasoning. Behaviour due to irrationality connotes a *systematic* divergence from the norm" (p. 8). Similarly, in the heuristics and biases literature, the term bias is reserved for systematic deviations from normative reasoning and does not refer to transitory processing errors ("a bias is a source of error which is systematic rather than random", Evans, 1984, p. 462). More technically, performance errors represent algorithmic-level problems that are transitory in nature. Nontransitory problems at the algorithmic level that would be expected to recur on a re-administration of the task should instead be viewed as computational limitations.

Another way to think of the performance error explanation is to conceive of it within the true score/measurement error framework of classical test theory. Mean or modal performance might be viewed as centred on the normative response – the response all people are trying to approximate. However, scores will vary around this central tendency due to random performance factors (error variance). In fact, a parallel argument has been made in economics where, as in reasoning, models of perfect market rationality are protected from refutation by positing the existence of local market mistakes of a transitory nature (temporary information deficiency, insufficient attention due to small stakes, distractions leading to missed arbitrage opportunities, etc.).

This notion of a performance error as a momentary attention, memory, or processing lapse that causes responses to appear non-normative even when competence is fully normative has implications for patterns of individual differences across reasoning tasks. For example, the strongest possible form of this view is that *all* discrepancies from normative responses are due to performance errors. This strong form of the hypothesis has the implication that there should be virtually no correlations among non-normative processing biases across tasks. If each departure from normative responding represents a momentary processing lapse due to distraction, carelessness, or temporary confusion, then there is no reason to expect covariance among biases across tasks (or covariance among items *within* tasks, for that matter) because error variances should be uncorrelated.

In contrast, positive manifold (uniformly positive bivariate associations in a correlation matrix) among disparate tasks in the heuristics and biases literature – and among items within tasks – would call into question the notion that all variability in responding can be attributable to performance errors. This was essentially Rips and Conrad's (1983) argument when they examined individual differences in deductive reasoning: "Subjects' absolute scores on the propositional tests correlated with their performance on certain other reasoning tests. . . . If the differences in propositional reasoning were merely due to interference from other performance factors, it would be difficult to explain why they correlate with these tests" (pp. 282–283).

In several studies, we have found very little evidence for the strong version of the performance error view. With virtually all of the tasks from the heuristics and biases literature that we have examined, there is considerable internal consistency. Further, at least for certain classes of task, there are significant cross-task correlations (Stanovich & West, 1998c, 2000; West, Toplak, & Stanovich, 2008). Our purpose here is not to review the results of these studies, but to illustrate how individual differences shed light on a major dispute in the great rationality debate – how to interpret the normative/ descriptive gap in empirical studies. As with performance errors, individual difference findings have implications for the argument that algorithmic limitations create discrepancies between descriptive and normative models. A strong correlation between measures of cognitive capacity and a rational thinking task suggests important algorithmic-level limitations that might make the normative response not prescriptive for those of lower cognitive capacity. In contrast, the absence of a correlation between the normative response and cognitive capacity suggests no computational limitation and thus no reason why the normative response should not be considered prescriptive. We have found that the computational limitations on most of the classic heuristics and biases tasks – at least as inferred from individual differences in cognitive ability – are not extreme.

More contentiously, however, we have argued that individual differences might be a piece of the puzzle in a very wide reflective equilibrium (Daniels, 1979, 1996; Elgin, 1996; Stich & Nisbett, 1980; Thagard, 1982; Thagard & Nisbett, 1983) regarding the wrong norm and alternative construal explanations of the normative/descriptive gap. Stanovich and West (2000) showed how Panglossian theorists use empirical data patterns to justify their critiques, but they rely exclusively on the modal response. An interesting aspect of some Panglossian positions is that because the descriptive is simply indexed to the normative, the latter can simply be "read off" from a competence model of the former (Cohen, 1982, terms this the norm extraction method). For example, Stein (1996) noted that this seems to follow from the Panglossian view because "whatever human reasoning competence turns out to be, the principles embodied in it are the normative principles of reasoning. . . . This argument sees the reasoning experiments as revealing human reasoning competence, and, thereby, as also revealing the norms. . . . The reasoning experiments just give us insight into what our reasoning abilities are; by knowing what these abilities are, we can determine what the normative principles of reasoning are" (pp. 231–232).

Stein (1996) terms this type of Panglossian position the no extra-human norms view because it "rejects the standard picture of rationality and takes the reasoning experiments as giving insight not just into human reasoning competence but also into the normative principles of reasoning. . . . The no extra-human norms argument says that the norms just are what we have in our reasoning competence; if the (actual) norms do not match our pre-conceived notion of what the norms should be, so much the worse for our preconceived notions" (pp. 233–234). Stein (1996, p. 239) terms an extreme form of this strategy – that of explaining away *all* normative/descriptive gaps in terms of incorrect norm application – the "reject-the-norm strategy". It is noteworthy that this strategy is used exclusively by the Panglossian camp in the rationality debate, although this connection is not a necessary one.

Specifically, the reject-the-norm strategy is exclusively used to *eliminate* gaps between descriptive models of performance and normative models. When this type of critique is employed, the normative model that is suggested as a substitute for the rejected normative model is one that coincides perfectly with the descriptive model of the subjects' performance – thus preserving a view of human rationality as ideal. It is rarely noted that the strategy could be used in just the opposite way – to *create* gaps between the normative and descriptive. Situations where the modal response coincides with the standard normative model could be critiqued, and alternative models (normative models) could be suggested that would result in a new normative/descriptive gap. But this is never done. The Panglossian camp, often highly critical of empirical psychologists ("Kahneman and Tversky ... and not their experimental subjects, commit the fallacies", Levi, 1983, p. 502), is never crit-ical of psychologists who design reasoning tasks in instances where the modal subject gives the response the experimenters deem correct. Ironically, in these cases, according to the Panglossians, the same psychologists seem never to err in their task designs and interpretations.

It is quite clear that Cohen's (1979, 1981, 1986) trenchant criticisms of experimental psychologists would never have been written had human performance coincided with the standard normative models that the psy-chologists were using. The fact that the use of the reject-the-norm stra-tegy is entirely contingent on the existence or nonexistence of a normative/descriptive gap suggests that the strategy is *empirically*, not conceptually, triggered (norms are never rejected for purely conceptual reasons when they coincide with the modal human response). What this means is that in an important sense the norms being endorsed by the Panglossian camp are conditioned (if not indexed entirely) by descriptive facts about human behaviour. Gigerenzer (1991) is clear about his adherence to an empirically d riven reject-the-norm strategy:

> Since its origins in the mid-seventeenth century. ... When there was a striking discrepancy between the judgment of reasonable men and what probability theory dictated – as with the famous St. Petersburg paradox – then the mathematicians went back to the blackboard and changed the equations (Daston, 1980). Those good old days have gone. ... If, in studies on social cognition, researchers find a dis-crepancy between human judgment and what probability theory seems

to dictate, the blame is now put on the human mind, not the statistical model.

(p. 109)

That Gigerenzer and Cohen concur here – even though they have somewhat different positions on normative justification – simply shows how widespread is the acceptance of the principle that descriptive facts about human behaviour condition our notions about the appropriateness of the normative models used to evaluate behaviour.

Interestingly, the descriptive component of performance around which Panglossian theorists almost always build their competence models (which index the normative in their view) is the central tendency of the responses (usually the mean or modal performance tendency). But if we are going to "read off" the normative from the descriptive in this way, why is this the only aspect of group performance that is relevant? Do the pattern of responses around the mode tell us anything? What about the rich covariance patterns that would be present in any multivariate experiment? Are these totally superfluous – all norm-relevant behavioural information residing in the mode? We have argued in several papers that if something about the normative must be inferred from the descriptive, then there is more information available than has traditionally been relied upon.

How should we interpret situations where the majority of individuals respond in ways that depart from the normative model applied to the problem by reasoning experts? Thagard (1982) calls the two different interpretations the populist strategy and the elitist strategy: "The populist strategy, favored by Cohen (1981), is to emphasize the reflective equilibrium of the average person. . . . The elitist strategy, favored by Stich and Nisbett (1980), is to emphasize the reflective equilibrium of experts" (p. 39). Thus, Thagard (1982) identifies the populist strategy with the Panglossian position and the elitist strategy with the Meliorist position.

But there are few controversial tasks in the heuristics and biases literature where all untutored laypersons disagree with the experts. There are always some who agree. Thus, the issue is not the untutored average person versus experts (as suggested by Thagard's formulation), but experts plus some laypersons versus other untutored individuals. Might the cognitive characteristics of those departing from expert opinion have implications for which normative model we deem appropriate? Larrick, Nisbett, and Morgan (1993) made just such an argument in their analysis of what justified the cost–benefit reasoning of microeconomics: "Intelligent people would be more likely to use cost–benefit reasoning. Because intelligence is generally regarded as being the set of psychological properties that makes for effectiveness across environments . . . intelligent people should be more likely to use the most effective reasoning strategies than should less intelligent people" (p. 333). Larrick et al. (1993) are alluding to the fact that we may want to condition our inferences about appropriate norms based not only on what response the majority of people make but also on what response the most cognitively competent subjects make.

Slovic and Tversky (1974) made essentially this argument years ago, although it was couched in very different terms in their paper and thus was hard to discern. Slovic and Tversky (1974) argued that descriptive facts about argument endorsement should condition the inductive inferences of experts regarding appropriate normative principles. In response to the argument that there is "no valid way to distinguish between outright rejection of the axiom and failure to understand it" (p. 372), Slovic and Tversky observed that "the deeper the understanding of the axiom, the greater the readiness to accept it" (pp. 372–373). Slovic and Tversky (1974) argued that this understanding/acceptance congruence suggested that the gap between the descriptive and normative was as a result of an initial failure to fully process and/or understand the task.

Slovic and Tversky's argument has been termed (see Stanovich & West, 1999) the understanding/acceptance assumption – that more reflective and engaged reasoners are more likely to affirm the appropriate normative model for a particular situation. From their understanding/acceptance principle, it follows that if greater understanding resulted in more acceptance of the axiom, then the initial gap between the normative and descriptive would be attributed to factors that prevented problem understanding (for example lack of ability or reflectiveness on the part of the subject). Such a finding would increase confidence in the normative appropriateness of the axioms and/or in their application to a particular problem. In contrast, if better understanding failed to result in greater acceptance of the axiom, then its normative status for that particular problem might be considered to be undermined. In short, the direction that performance moves in, in response to increased understanding, provides an empirical clue as to what is the proper normative model to be applied.

One might conceive of two generic strategies for applying the understanding/acceptance principle based on the fact that variation in understanding can be created or it can be studied by examining naturally occurring individual differences. Slovic and Tversky employed the former strategy by providing subjects with explicated arguments supporting the Allais or Savage normative interpretation, which we have also done with a variety of classic heuristic and biases tasks (Stanovich & West, 1999). Other methods of manipulating understanding have provided evidence in favour of some traditional normative principles. For example, it has been found that being forced to take more time or to provide a rationale for selections increases adherence to descriptive invariance (Miller & Fagley, 1991; Sieck & Yates, 1997; Takemura, 1992, 1993, 1994). Moshman and Geil (1998) found that group discussion facilitated performance on Wason's selection task.

As an alternative to the experimental manipulation of understanding, the understanding/acceptance principle can be transformed into an individual differences prediction. For example, the principle might be interpreted as indicating that more reflective, engaged, and intelligent reasoners are more likely to respond in accord with normative principles. Thus, it might be expected that those individuals with cognitive/personality characteristics more conducive to deeper understanding would be more accepting of the appropriate normative principles for a particular problem. This was the emphasis of Larrick et al. (1993) when they argued that more intelligent people should be more likely to use cost–benefit principles. Similarly, need for cognition – a dispositional variable reflecting the tendency toward thoughtful analysis and reflective thinking – has been associated with aspects of epistemic and practical rationality (Cacioppo, Petty, Feinstein, & Jarvis, 1996; Kardash & Scholes, 1996; Klaczynski, Gordon, & Fauth, 1997; LeBoeuf & Shafir, 2003; Smith & Levin, 1996; Verplanken, 1993).

The latter application of the understanding/acceptance principle derives from the assumption that a normative/descriptive gap that is disproportionately created by subjects with a superficial understanding of the problem provides no warrant for amending the application of standard normative models. It is the application (the individual differences application) that we have employed in most of our work. We have found that in most cases the traditionally used normative model was supported – but not always (Stanovich & West, 1998c, 2000, 2008b; West & Stanovich, 2003; West et al., 2008).

A framework for individual differences in heuristics and biases tasks

As we proceeded with our work in the 1990s – using individual differences to provide principled constraints on the interpretations of reasoning task responses – we began to focus on broader trends in our data. One was that the correlations between cognitive ability and performance on heuristics and biases tasks varied widely – from moderate to literally zero. What was obviously needed was a theoretical explanation that accounted for the variation in the magnitudes of the correlations.

One such attempt was made by Kahneman (2000) in his commentary on our summary of this work in *Behavioral and Brain Sciences*. He pointed out that many of the moderate correlations came from within-subjects designs that contain cues signalling the necessity of heuristic system override (Bartels, 2006; Fischhoff, Slovic, & Lichtenstein, 1979; Frisch, 1993; Kahneman & Tversky, 1982a; Shafir, 1998). Kahneman argued that between-subjects tests of the coherence of responses represents a much stricter criterion and perhaps a more appropriate one because "much of life resembles a between-subjects experiment" (Kahneman, 2000, p. 682). Shafir (1998) makes a similar argument when speculating about why people's behaviour is often at variance with their own normative intuitions. He argues that this discrepancy "mirrors a discrepancy between the nature of people's everyday experiences and the conditions that yield philosophical intuitions. In life, people typically experience and evaluate things one at a time, as in a between-subjects design, whereas many of the relevant intuitions result from concurrent, within-subject introspections" (p. 72).

That the mental factors operative in within-subjects designs might be different from those operative in between-subjects designs suggests that the individual difference factors associated with biased processing in the two different paradigms might also vary. LeBoeuf and Shafir (2003) have produced some data indicating that biases that are assessed within subjects display different relationships with individual difference variables compared with biases assessed between subjects. They found that various framing effects were associated with the need for cognition thinking disposition (see Cacioppo et al., 1996) when evaluated on a within-subjects basis but were independent of need for cognition when framing was assessed between subjects.

In a more systematic attempt to test Kahneman's conjecture, we found that correlations between cognitive ability and performance on heuristics and biases tasks tended to be low in between-subjects designs but not uniformly so (Stanovich & West, 2008b). On the left side of Table 17.1 is a list of heuristics and biases tasks that are dissociated from cognitive ability.[1] On the right side of Table 17.1 is a selection of heuristics and biases tasks that show significant correlations with cognitive ability. The between/within design structure of the tasks is a factor in explaining the nature of the relationship (associations tend to be lower in between-subjects tasks) but they are hardly the whole story. In a 2008 paper in the *Journal of Personality and Social Psychology* (Stanovich & West, 2008b), we attempted to develop a more comprehensive explanation.

We did begin, however, by building on Kahneman's insights. His argument begins with the distinction between coherence rationality and reasoning rationality. Reasoning rationality "requires an ability to reason correctly about the information currently at hand without demanding perfect consistency among beliefs that are not simultaneously evoked" (Kahneman & Frederick, 2005, p. 277). In contrast, "coherence is much stricter. . . . coherence requires choices and beliefs to be immune to variations of framing and context. This is a lot to ask for, but an inability to pass between-subjects tests of coherence is indeed a significant flaw" (Kahneman, 2000, p. 682). Kahneman and Frederick (2002; see Kahneman, 2000), utilizing a dual-process framework, argue that correlations with cognitive ability will occur only in the intermediate range of difficulty. There, they argue,

> intelligent people are more likely to possess the relevant logical rules and also to recognize the applicability of these rules in particular situations. In the terms of the present analysis, high-IQ respondents benefit from relatively efficient System 2 operations that enable them to overcome erroneous intuitions when adequate information is available. When a problem is too difficult for everyone, however, the correlation is likely to reverse.
>
> (Kahneman & Frederick, 2002, p. 68)

Table 17.1 Tasks that do and do not show associations with cognitive ability

Tasks/effects that fail to correlate with cognitive ability	Tasks/effects that correlate with cognitive ability
Noncausal base rate usage (Stanovich & West, 1998c, 1999, 2008b)	Causal base rate usage (Kokis et al., 2002; Stanovich & West, 1998c, 1998d)
Conjunction fallacy between-subjects (Stanovich & West, 2008b)	Outcome bias between- and within-subjects (Stanovich & West, 1998c, 2008b)
Framing between-subjects (Stanovich & West, 2008b)	Framing within-subjects (Bruine de Bruin et al., 2007; Frederick, 2005; Parker & Fischhoff, 2005; Stanovich & West, 1998b, 1999)
Anchoring effect (Stanovich & West, 2008b)	Denominator neglect (Kokis et al., 2002; Stanovich & West, 2008b)
Evaluability "Less is more" effect (Stanovich & West, 2008b)	Probability matching (West & Stanovich, 2003; Stanovich & West, 2008b)
Proportion dominance effect (Stanovich & West, 2008b)	Hindsight bias (Stanovich & West, 1998c)
Sunk cost effect (Stanovich & West, 2008b; Parker & Fischhoff, 2005)	Ignoring P(D/NH) (probability of the data given the negative hypothesis) (Stanovich & West, 1998d, 1999)
Risk/benefit confounding (Stanovich & West, 2008b)	Covariation detection (Sá, West, & Stanovich, 1999; Stanovich & West, 1998c, 1998d)
Omission bias (Stanovich & West, 2008b)	Belief bias in syllogistic reasoning (Macpherson & Stanovich, 2007; Stanovich & West, 1998c, 2008b)
One-side bias, within-subjects (Stanovich & West, 2008a)	Belief bias in modus ponens (Stanovich & West, 2008b)
Certainty effect (Stanovich & West, 2008b)	Informal argument evaluation (Stanovich & West, 1997, 2008b)
Willingness to pay/willingness to accept difference (Stanovich & West, 2008b)	Four-card selection task (Stanovich & West, 1998a, 2008b; Toplak & Stanovich, 2002; Valentine, 1975)
Myside bias – between- and within-subjects (Klaczynski & Lavallee, 2005; Klaczynski & Robinson, 2000; Sá, Kelley, Ho, & Stanovich, 2005; Stanovich & West, 2007, 2008a, 2008b; Toplak & Stanovich, 2003)	Expected value maximization in gambles (Benjamin & Shapiro, 2005; Frederick, 2005)
Newcomb's problem (Stanovich & West, 1999; Toplak & Stanovich, 2002)	Overconfidence effect (Bruine de Bruin et al., 2007; Stanovich & West, 1998c)

The phrase "possess the relevant logical rules and also to recognize the applicability of these rules in particular situations" suggests two conditions that have to be fulfilled for a heuristically based response to be overridden by analytic processing (Evans, 2003, 2006, 2007a, 2009; Kahneman & Frederick, 2002; Stanovich, 1999). These two conditions are actually the two sources of judgemental error that Kahneman and Tversky (1982a), two decades ago, labelled as: errors of application and errors of comprehension. The latter refers to errors that occur because people do not recognize the validity of a norm that they have violated because this knowledge has not been learned. The former occurs when the person fails to apply a rule they have learned.

In the remainder of this paper, we will use two slightly different terms for the loci of these problems. An error of comprehension we call a *mindware gap* (Stanovich, 2009; Stanovich, Toplak, & West, 2008). This is because in dual-process models, an important function of the analytic system is to take early representations triggered by the autonomous (heuristic) system offline and to substitute better responses. Mindware, a term coined by Perkins (1995; Clark, 2001, uses it in a slightly different way from Perkins' original coinage), refers to the rules, procedures, and strategies that can be retrieved by the analytic system and used to substitute for the heuristic response. However, if the mindware available to the analytic system for heuristic override has not been learned, then we have a case of a mindware gap.

In contrast, errors of application can only occur when the relevant mindware has been learned and is available for use in the override process. Errors of application occur when people fail to detect the situational cues indicating that the heuristically primed response needs to be overridden and an analytically derived response substituted. We give this requirement the label *override detection* (detecting the necessity for heuristic override). The above quote from Kahneman and Frederick (2002) suggests that cognitive ability differences only arise when the experimental task allows for variation in the presence of the relevant mindware and in the override detection process. It will be argued here that this analysis ignores a third potent source of non-normative responding that might be an even more important source of individual differences.

To understand our model of individual differences it is important to note that most of the tasks in the heuristics and biases literature were deliberately designed to pit a heuristically triggered response against a normative response. As Kahneman (2000) notes, "Tversky and I always thought of the heuristics and biases approach as a two-process theory" (p. 682). However, what this means is that even after the necessity for override has been detected and the relevant mindware is available, the conflict has to be resolved. Resolving the conflict in favour of the analytic response may require cognitive capacity, especially if cognitive decoupling (that is, inhibiting the heuristic response and simulating alternative responses) must take place for a considerable period of time while the analytic response is computed. Recent work on inhibition and executive functioning has indicated that such cognitive decoupling is very capacity demanding and that it is strongly related to individual differences in fluid intelligence (Duncan et al., 2008; Engle, 2002; Gray, Chabris, & Braver, 2003; Kane & Engle, 2002, 2003; Salthouse, Atkinson, & Berish, 2003; Unsworth & Engle, 2005, 2007).

It will be argued here that it is this third factor present in some heuristics and biases tasks – the necessity for sustained cognitive decoupling – that is the major source of the variability in the association between cognitive ability and task performance that is displayed in Table 17.1. Building on the conjectures of Kahneman (2000) and Kahneman and Frederick (2002), our framework for conceptualizing individual differences in heuristics and biases tasks is displayed in Figure 17.1. The question addressed in the first stage of the framework is whether, for a given task, the mindware is available to carry out override (whether the procedures and declarative knowledge are available to substitute an analytic response for a heuristic one). If the relevant mindware is not available, then the person must, of necessity, respond heuristically. It is immaterial whether the person detects the necessity for override or has the capacity to sustain override if the normatively appropriate

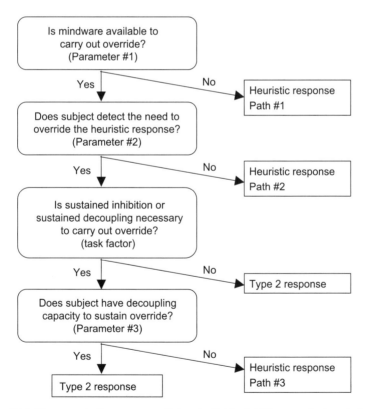

Figure 17.1 Framework for conceptualizing individual differences in heuristics and biases tasks.

response is simply not available. If the relevant mindware (probabilistic thinking skills, falsifiability tendencies, disposition to search for alternative explanations, sensitivity to contradiction, etc.) is not present, then participants will end up at what has been termed in Figure 17.1 path #1 to a heuristic response.

If the relevant mindware is in fact available, then the next question that becomes operative is whether or not the person detects the need to override the heuristic response. Even if the relevant mindware is present, if the participant does not detect any reason to override the heuristic response, then it will be emitted (this is path #2 to a heuristic response as labelled in Figure 17.1). Many heuristics and biases tasks lead people down this path. They do not detect the need to override the response that comes naturally (Kahneman, 2003) even though, in retrospect, they would endorse the norm that the heuristic response violated (Kahneman & Tversky, 1982a; Shafir, 1998; Shafir & Tversky, 1995; Thaler, 1987).

The next choice point in Figure 17.1 concerns the task rather than the participant. If the relevant mindware is present and if the need for override has been noted, the question then becomes whether or not the task requires sustained inhibition (cognitive decoupling) in order to carry out the override of the heuristic response. If not (or if the capacity required is low – this of course may not be an all or nothing issue), then the analytic response will be substituted for the heuristic response. In contrast, if the task requires sustained decoupling in order to carry out override, then we must ask whether the participant has the cognitive capacity that will be necessary. If so, then the analytic response will be given. If not, then the heuristic response will be given (path #3 to the heuristic response in Figure 17.1) – despite the availability of the relevant mindware and the recognition of the need to use it.

In order for cognitive ability to associate with a bias, there must be differences correlated with cognitive ability at some of the choice points in the framework – that is, in some of the person parameters that branch toward or away from heuristic paths. As Kahneman (2000) notes "a task will be too difficult if (1) System 1 favors an incorrect answer, and (2) System 2 is incapable of applying the correct rule, either because the rule is unknown [mindware gap] or because the cues that would evoke it are absent [no override detection]" (p. 682). Performance on such a task will be floored and will show no association with cognitive ability. Some of the tasks in Table 17.1 are no doubt of this type (between-subjects conjunction effects for example). However, several of the tasks in Table 17.1 without associations with cognitive ability cannot be viewed as displaying floor effects. For a cognitive ability difference to be observed, there must be differential cleaving by intelligence at some of the critical nodes in Figure 17.1 – that is, there must be a correlation between intelligence and at least one of the person parameters. Of course, the partitioning of cognitive ability groups at each of the nodes will vary from task to task. We will advance here a generic conjecture about the source of associations with cognitive ability. The conjecture is that the primary source of associations with cognitive ability in heuristics and biases tasks is the way that people are partitioned by person parameter #3 ("does the person have the decoupling capacity to sustain override").

Cognitive decoupling in heuristics and biases tasks

There is direct evidence in the literature that intelligence tests (especially tests of fluid intelligence, see Carroll, 1993; Horn & Cattell, 1967; Horn & Noll, 1997) directly tap the ability to sustain the decoupling of representations from the world so that cognitive simulations can be run which test the outcomes of imaginary actions (Currie & Ravenscroft, 2002; Dienes & Perner, 1999; Evans, 2007a; Evans & Over, 2004; Nichols & Stich, 2003). Thus, there is probably substantial variation in parameter #3 of the model because there is substantial variability in decoupling ability (Duncan, Emslie, Williams, Johnson, & Freer, 1996; Kane & Engle, 2002; Salthouse et al., 2003). In contrast, we conjecture that, for many tasks in the heuristics and biases literature, the other two person parameters show only modest differential partitioning based on cognitive ability.

Regarding person parameter #1, it is true that the rules, knowledge, and strategies available to the analytic system to use in heuristic-system overrides are in part the product of past learning experiences. One might expect that people with more cognitive ability would profit more from learning experiences. However, the relevant mindware for our present discussion is not just generic procedural knowledge, nor is it the hotchpotch of declarative knowledge that is often used to assess crystallized intelligence on ability tests. Instead, it is a very special subset of knowledge related to: how one views probability and chance; whether one has the tools to think scientifically and the propensity to do so; the tendency to exhaustively examine possibilities; the tendency to avoid myside thinking; knowledge of some rules of formal and informal reasoning; and good argument evaluation skills. At least among the university students typically tested in these studies, acquiring these sets of skills and knowledge bases might be, experientially, very haphazard.

Although it is true that more intelligent individuals learn more things than the less intelligent, many thinking dispositions relevant to rationality are acquired rather late in life and the explicit teaching of this mindware is very spotty and inconsistent. For example, the tendency to think of alternative explanations for a phenomenon leads to the ability to more accurately infer causal models of events. Such principles are taught very inconsistently (by either explicit or implicit means). Or take, for example, the conjunction rule of probability, the violation of which is illustrated in the Linda Problem. Kahneman and Tversky (1982a) report that tests of rule endorsement and argument endorsement conducted after participants had made the conjunction error revealed that statistically sophisticated psychology graduate students did endorse the rule they had violated (they possessed the relevant mindware but did not detect the necessity for override). However, a majority of statistically naïve undergraduate students failed to endorse the conjunction rule – they lacked the relevant mindware ("much to our surprise, naive subjects did not have a solid grasp of the conjunction rule", Kahneman & Tversky, 1982a, p. 127). The lack of uniform teaching and learning conditions for the acquisition of this mindware might attenuate any natural correlation with intelligence that there would be if it were taught under uniform conditions.

Override detection (person parameter #2), we would argue, is perhaps even more likely to display a low correlation with cognitive ability. First, it would seem to be more of a thinking disposition (related to constructs like need for cognition, for instance, see Cacioppo et al., 1996) than a cognitive capacity. Psychometricians have long distinguished typical performance situations from optimal (sometimes termed maximal) performance situations (Ackerman, 1994, 1996; Ackerman & Heggestad, 1997; Ackerman & Kanfer, 2004; Cronbach, 1949; Matthews, Zeidner, & Roberts, 2002). Typical performance situations are unconstrained in that no overt instructions to maximize performance are given, and the task interpretation is determined to some extent by the participant. In contrast, optimal performance situations are those where the task interpretation is determined externally (not left to the participant). The participant is instructed to maximize performance, and is told how to do so. All tests of intelligence or cognitive aptitude are optimal performance assessments, whereas measures of rational thinking dispositions (need for cognition, actively open-minded thinking, reflectivity/impulsivity) are often assessed under typical performance conditions.

Override detection, particularly in between-subjects designs, is exercised under typical rather than optimal conditions. It thus parses, in terms of the structure of cognitive abilities (Ackerman & Kanfer, 2004; Baron, 1985, 2008; Matthews et al., 2002; Sinatra & Pintrich, 2003; Sternberg, 1997) with thinking dispositions rather than cognitive capacity measures such as intelligence. For these theoretical reasons, we think that person parameter #2 in the framework is less the source of associations with cognitive ability than is person parameter #3.

There are two other ways that the influence of parameter #2, as a generator of individual differences, becomes attenuated – essentially by floor effects (as Kahneman, 2000, argues), but also by ceiling effects. Certain tasks in between-subjects designs (perhaps anchoring problems or the Linda Problem) give so few cues to the possibility of heuristic–analytic conflict that this parameter is probably floored for most subjects. Conversely, the instructions in other tasks (belief bias assessed with syllogisms for example), and some situations in real life ("the salesperson is trying to sell to you – don't forget") are so explicit in calling attention to heuristic–analytic conflict that this parameter is probably near ceiling.

The case of belief bias in syllogistic reasoning is probably a good illustration of our argument that it is person parameter #3 – the decoupling capacity parameter – that is the primary generator of associations with cognitive ability in rational thinking tasks[2] (see De Neys, 2006a, 2006b). The mindware available to reason logically on these simple categorical syllogisms (person parameter #1) is probably pretty uniformly present in the sample of university students studied here (and in most studies in the reasoning literature). The procedures needed to reason through the syllogisms used in these studies (for example, the invalid syllogism: all A are B, all C are B, therefore all C are A) are within the mindware of the vast majority of even the students who are classified as of low cognitive ability in our university sample. Additionally, as just mentioned, the instructions on this task probably ceiling out person parameter #2 – override detection. Recall that the instructions to the task sensitize the participants to potential conflict (between argument validity and the truth of argument components). Thus, person parameters #1 and #2 probably leave little room for any individual difference variable to associate with performance.

In contrast, the task does require sustained cognitive decoupling (De Neys, 2006b). In the "rose" syllogism for example (all flowers have petals; roses have petals; therefore, roses are flowers – which is invalid), participants must suppress the tendency to endorse a valid response because of the "naturalness" (see Kahneman, 2003) of the conclusion – roses are flowers. This response must be held in abeyance while reasoning procedures work through the partially overlapping set logic indicating that the conclusion does not necessarily follow and that the syllogism is thus invalid. The reasoning process may take several seconds of perhaps somewhat aversive concentration (see Botvinick, Cohen, & Carter, 2004; Glenberg, 1997; Kahneman, 1973; Navon, 1989) – seconds during which the tendency to foreclose the conflict by acceding to the natural tendency to affirm "roses are flowers" (by responding "valid") must be avoided. Such response suppression while reasoning is closely related to the inhibitory and conflict resolution processes being studied by investigators examining the construct of executive functioning (Baddeley, Chincotta, & Adlam, 2001; Botvinick et al., 2004; Kane, 2003; Salthouse et al., 2003). Individual differences in such inhibitory processes have been found to be strongly associated with individual differences in fluid intelligence.

We conjecture that many of the other tasks that do show associations with cognitive ability (second column of Table 17.1) are tasks that involve some type of inhibition and/or sustained cognitive decoupling. For example, in within-subjects tests of outcome bias (Stanovich & West, 1998c) the appearance of the second item gives a pretty clear signal to the participant that there is an issue of consistency in their responses to the two different forms – that is, the within-subjects design probably puts person parameter #2 at ceiling, thus insuring that it is not the source of any associations with cognitive ability that are obtained. Detecting the need for consistency is not the issue. Instead, the difficulty comes from the necessity of inhibiting the tendency to downgrade the decision in the negative outcome condition, despite its having a better rationale than the positive outcome decision. Even in the between-subjects version of this task, one group of participants – those getting the negative outcome version – is alerted to the potential conflict between the seemingly good reasons to have the operation and the shockingly bad outcome. Participants must suppress the desire to sanction the decision, decouple their knowledge of the outcome, and simulate (see Evans & Over, 1996, 2004; Nichols & Stich, 2003) what they would have thought had they not known the outcome. Indeed, this condition creates a situation similar to those of various "curse of knowledge" paradigms (see Birch, 2005; Camerer, Loewenstein, & Weber, 1989; Gilovich, Medvec, & Sativsky, 1998; Hinds, 1999; Keysar & Barr, 2002).

The "curse of knowledge" logic of the negative item in the outcome bias task is similar to that in hindsight bias paradigms (e.g., Christiansen-Szalanski & Williams, 1991; Fischhoff, 1975; Pohl, 2004) which have also shown associations with cognitive ability (Stanovich & West, 1998c). In hindsight paradigms, the marking of the correct response sensitizes every respondent to the potential conflict involved – between what you know now, versus what you would have known without the correct response being indicated. Thus again, parameter #2 must be at ceiling. However, there is a need for sustained decoupling in the task, so whatever association between bias and cognitive ability exists on the task (a modest one, see Stanovich & West, 1998c) is likely generated by individual differences in parameter #3.

Within-subjects framing paradigms probably have a similar logic. The appearance of the second problem surely signals that an issue of consistency is at stake (putting parameter #2 at ceiling) and virtually all of the university students in these studies have acquired the value of consistency (parameter #1 is also at ceiling). The modest cognitive ability associations that are generated by this task probably derive from lower cognitive ability participants who cannot suppress the attractiveness of an alternative response despite the threat to consistent responding that it represents – in short, from variation in parameter #3. In contrast, between-subjects framing situations probably drive parameter #2 to a very low value (few people recognize that there is a conflict to be resolved between a potentially different response to an alternative framing), thus eliminating associations with individual differences (in the manner suggested by Kahneman, 2000).

The logic of the Linda Problem is similar. Transparent, within-subjects versions are easier because they signal the conflict involved and the necessity for override. Such versions create at least modest associations with cognitive ability. In the between-subjects version, however, individual differences are eliminated entirely because this design obscures the heuristic–analytic conflict and puts parameter #2 at floor.

As a final example, consider the difference between causal and noncausal base rates[3] illustrated in Table 17.1. Noncausal base-rate problems trigger conflict detection in so few participants that parameter #2 is floored and hence cognitive ability differences are eliminated. In contrast, in a classic causal base-rate problem such as the Volvo versus Saab problem (see Note 3, p. 383), where aggregate information is pitted against indicant information, the aggregate information has a causal relationship to the criterion behaviour. Thus, the aggregate information in causal base-rate scenarios clearly signals that there are two pieces of information in conflict, parameter #2 is near ceiling, and individual differences are determined largely by parameter #3 (the sustained decoupling parameter) which is, we conjecture, linked to individual differences in cognitive ability. Thus, causal, but not noncausal, base-rate problems show cognitive ability differences.

It is important to note that this interpretation does not contradict the results of De Neys (De Neys & Glumicic, 2008; De Neys, Vartanian, & Goel, 2008) who demonstrated that various implicit measures of performance on noncausal base-rate problems (decision latencies, unannounced recall, brain activation in the anterior cingulate) indicated that conflict between base rate and indicant information was detected and that when indicant information was overridden that inhibition areas of the brain were activated (lateral prefrontal cortex). Unlike the classic 70/30 lawyer/engineer problem of Kahneman and Tversky (1973), very extreme base rates were used in the De Neys work, for example: "In a study 1000 people were tested. Among the participants there were 5 engineers and 995 lawyers". These extreme numbers serve to draw attention to the base rate and move parameter #2 to ceiling from its relatively low level in the traditional 70/30 version of the problem. The problem is turned from one where the pitfall is override detection to one where the central task is to inhibit the stereotype that is automatically triggered and replace it with reliance on the extreme base rate. Thus, individual differences in these extreme base-rate problems would be determined largely by parameter #3 (the sustained decoupling parameter), and it is thus to be expected that inhibition areas of the brain would be activated on trials where successful override is achieved. Likewise, because this version of the paradigm results in a moderate to high value of parameter #2, it is expected under our model that various implicit measures (including brain activation) would indicate that conflict between base rate and indicant information was detected.

Dual-process models and the reflective mind

We have used dual-process models to understand patterns of performance in heuristics and biases tasks. Our conjecture is that the reason why cognitive ability is dissociated from so many rational thinking tasks is that intelligence tests are very incomplete indices of Type 2 processing because they fail to assess a level of cognitive control that is critical to rational thought. In order to explicate what we mean by this statement, we will briefly sketch the dual-process conception that we work from – not a novel conception, but instead a synthesis of the literally dozens of such views now extant in the literature (see Evans, 2003, 2006, 2007a, 2008, 2009; Evans & Over, 1996; Kahneman & Frederick, 2002, 2005; Sloman, 1996; Stanovich, 1999, 2004).

Like many theorists, we distinguish Type 1 (heuristic) processing from Type 2 (analytic) processing. The defining feature of Type 1 processing is its autonomy. Other features often associated with Type 1 processing (speed, for example) are characteristic, but not defining of Type 1 processing. Type 1 processes are termed autonomous because: (1) their execution is mandatory when the triggering stimuli are encountered; (2) they do not put a heavy load on central processing capacity (i.e., they do not require conscious attention); (3) they are not dependent on input from high-level control systems; and (4) they can operate in parallel without interfering with themselves or with Type 2 processing.

Type 1 processing operations are multifarious. In a previous publication (Stanovich, 2004) they are referred to as TASS – the autonomous set of systems. Type 1 processing would include behavioural regulation by the emotions; the encapsulated modules for solving specific adaptive problems that have been posited by evolutionary psychologists; processes of implicit learning; and the automatic firing of overlearned associations. There has been extensive research on each of the different kinds of Type 1 processing (e.g., Atran, 1998; Buss, 2005; Evans, 2003; Fodor, 1983; Lieberman, 2000, 2003; Ohman & Mineka, 2001; Willingham, 1998, 1999). Type 1 processes conjoin the properties of automaticity, quasi-modularity, and heuristic processing as these constructs have been variously discussed in cognitive science (e.g., Bargh & Chartrand, 1999; Barrett & Kurzban, 2006; Carruthers, 2006; Coltheart, 1999; Evans, 1984, 2006, 2008, 2009; Samuels, 2005, 2009; Shiffrin & Schneider, 1977; Sperber, 1994).

Type 1 processing, because of its computational ease, is a common processing default. Type 1 processes are sometimes termed the adaptive unconscious (Wilson, 2002) in order to emphasize that Type 1 processes accomplish a host of useful things – face recognition, proprioception, language ambiguity resolution, depth perception, etc. – all of which are beyond our awareness. Heuristic processing is a term often used for Type 1 processing – to connote that it is fast, automatic, computationally inexpensive, and does not engage in extensive analysis of all the possibilities.

Type 2 processing is nonautonomous. It is relatively slow and computationally expensive. Many Type 1 processes can operate at once in parallel, but Type 2 processing is largely serial. Type 2 processing is often language based, but it is not necessarily so. One of the most critical functions of Type 2 processing is to override Type 1 processing. This is sometimes necessary because Type 1 processing is designed to get you into the right ballpark when solving a problem or making a decision, but it is not designed for the type of fine-grained analysis called for in situations of unusual importance (financial decisions, fairness judgements, employment decisions, legal judgments, etc.).

Heuristic processing depends on benign environments (see Stanovich, 2009, Ch. 6). In this context, a benign environment means one that contains useful cues that can be exploited by various heuristics (for example, affect-triggering cues, vivid and salient stimulus components, convenient anchors). Additionally, for an environment to be classified as benign, it also must contain no other individuals who will adjust their behaviour to exploit those relying only on heuristics. In contrast, a hostile environment for heuristics is one in which there are no cues that are usable by heuristic processes. Another way that an environment can turn hostile for a heuristic processor is if other agents discern the simple cues that are being used and the other agents start to arrange the cues for their own advantage (for example, advertisements, or the deliberate design of supermarket floorspace to maximize revenue).

All of the different kinds of Type 1 processing (processes of emotional regulation, Darwinian modules, associative and implicit learning processes) can produce responses that are irrational in a particular context if not overridden. For example, often humans act as cognitive misers (see Stanovich, 2009) by engaging in attribute substitution (Kahneman & Frederick, 2002) – the substitution of an easy-to-evaluate characteristic for a harder one even if the easier one is less accurate. For example, the cognitive miser will substitute the less effortful attributes of vividness or affect for the more effortful retrieval of relevant facts (Kahneman, 2003; Slovic & Peters, 2006; Wang, 2009). But when we are evaluating important risks – such as the risk of certain activities and environments for our children – we do not want to substitute vividness for careful thought about the situation. In such situations, we want to employ Type 2 override processing to block the attribute substitution of the cognitive miser.

In order to override Type 1 processing, Type 2 processing must display at least two related capabilities. One is the capability of interrupting Type 1 processing and suppressing its response tendencies. Type 2 processing thus involves inhibitory mechanisms of the type that have been the focus of recent work on executive functioning (Hasher, Lustig, & Zacks, 2007; Miyake, Friedman, Emerson, & Witzki, 2000; Zelazo, 2004). But the ability to suppress Type 1 processing gets the job only half done. Suppressing one response is not helpful unless there is a better response available to substitute for it. Where do these better responses come from? One answer is that they come from processes of hypothetical reasoning and cognitive simulation[4] that are a unique aspect of Type 2 processing. When we reason hypothetically, we create temporary models of the world and test out actions (or alternative causes) in that simulated world.

In order to reason hypothetically we must, however, have one critical cognitive capability – we must be able to prevent our representations of the real world from becoming confused with representations of imaginary situations. For example, when considering an alternative goal state different from the one we currently have, we must be able to represent our current goal and the alternative goal and to keep straight which is which. Likewise, we need to be able to differentiate the representation of an action about to be taken from representations of potential *alternative* actions we are trying out in cognitive simulations. But the latter must not infect the former while the mental simulation is being carried out. Otherwise, we would confuse the action about to be taken with alternatives that we were just simulating.

As many theorists have argued, a process of cognitive decoupling (see Stanovich, 2009) is necessary to ensure this. Through the process of cognitive decoupling, the analytic system is responsible for the ability to create temporary models of the world and test the outcomes of imaginary actions (Currie & Ravenscroft, 2002; Evans, 2007a; Evans & Over, 1996, 2004; Nichols & Stich, 2003; Sterelny, 2001). By taking early representations triggered by Type 1 processing offline and substituting better responses that have survived the cognitive selection process of simulation, the Type 2 processing exemplifies activities often labelled as executive or inhibitory control. Decoupling for the purpose of offline simulation is a cognitively demanding operation. The raw ability to sustain such simulations while keeping the relevant representations decoupled is one key aspect of the brain's computational power that is being assessed by measures of fluid intelligence. This is becoming clear from converging work on executive function and working memory that both display correlations with intelligence that are quite high. The high degree of overlap in individual differences on working memory and other executive functioning tasks and individual differences in intelligence is probably due to the necessity for sustained decoupling operations on all the tasks involved (Duncan et al., 2008; Gray et al., 2003; Kane, 2003; Kane & Engle, 2002, 2003; Kane, Hambrick, & Conway, 2005; Salthouse et al., 2003).

Our studies of individual differences have led us to the important conclusion that Type 2 processing needs to be understood in terms of two levels of processing – the algorithmic level and the reflective level. We can see this if we consider the logic of autonomous system override. Type 1 processing will determine the response unless overridden by the algorithmic mechanisms of the analytic system. But override itself is initiated by higher level control. That is, the algorithmic level of the analytic system is conceptualized as subordinate to higher level goal states and epistemic thinking dispositions, some of which have been studied empirically (e.g., Cacioppo et al., 1996; Stanovich & West, 1997, 2007). These goal states and epistemic dispositions exist at what might be termed the reflective level of processing – a level containing control states that regulate behaviour at a high level of generality. Such high-level goal states are common in the intelligent agents built by artificial intelligence researchers (Franklin, 1995; Pollock, 1995; Sloman, 1993; Sloman & Chrisley, 2003).

In Figure 17.2, we have presented the tripartite proposal in a simple form. In the spirit of Dennett's (1996) book *Kinds of Minds*, we have labelled the traditional source of Type 1 processing the autonomous mind. The distinction between the algorithmic and reflective mind derives from conceptual and empirical distinctions in the study of individual differences. At the algorithmic level the concern is information processing efficiency. The cognitive psychologist works largely at this level when they show that human performance can be explained by positing certain information processing mechanisms

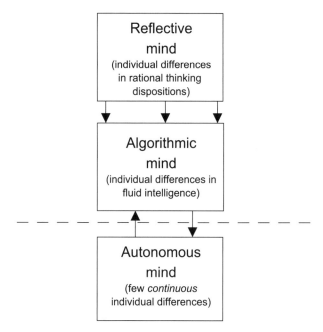

Figure 17.2 Individual differences in the tripartite structure.

in the brain (input coding mechanisms, perceptual registration mechanisms, short- and long-term memory storage systems, etc.). We turn to the level of the reflective mind where we ask questions about the *goals* of the system's computations (*what* the system is attempting to compute and *why*). In short, the reflective mind is concerned with the goals of the system, beliefs relevant to those goals, and the choice of action that is optimal given the system's goals and beliefs. It is only at the level of the reflective mind where issues of rationality come into play. Importantly, the algorithmic mind can be evaluated in terms of efficiency but not rationality.

This concern for the efficiency of information processing as opposed to its rationality is mirrored in the status of intelligence tests. For example, investigators have attempted to decompose intelligence into more basic operations such as perceptual speed, discrimination accuracy, working memory capacity, and the efficiency of the retrieval of information stored in long-term memory (Ackerman, Kyllonen, & Richards, 1999; Carpenter, Just, & Shell, 1990; Deary, 2000, 2001; Hunt, 1987, 1999; Kane & Engle, 2002; Lohman, 2000; Sternberg, 1985, 1997, 2003; Unsworth & Engle, 2005). Such measures are indices of efficiency of information processing but not rationality – a point made clear by considering the distinction discussed earlier, that between typical performance situations and optimal (sometimes termed maximal) performance situations. Typical performance measures are measures of the reflective mind – they assess in part goal prioritization and epistemic regulation. In contrast, optimal performance situations are those where the task interpretation is determined externally. The person performing the task is instructed to maximize performance and is told how to do so. Thus, optimal performance measures examine questions of efficiency of goal pursuit – they capture the processing efficiency of the algorithmic mind. All tests of intelligence or cognitive aptitude are optimal performance assessments, whereas measures of critical or rational thinking are often assessed under typical performance conditions.

The difference between the algorithmic mind and the reflective mind is captured in another well-established distinction in the measurement of individual differences – the distinction between cognitive ability and thinking dispositions. The former are, as just mentioned, measures of the efficiency of the algorithmic mind. The latter travel under a variety of names in psychology – thinking dispositions or cognitive styles being the two most popular. Many thinking dispositions concern beliefs, belief structure and, importantly, attitudes toward forming and changing beliefs. Other thinking dispositions that have been identified concern a person's goals and goal hierarchy. Examples of some thinking dispositions that have been investigated by psychologists are: actively open-minded thinking, need for cognition (the tendency to think a lot), consideration of future consequences, need for closure, superstitious thinking, and dogmatism (e.g., Ackerman & Heggestad, 1997; Baron, 1985, 2008; Cacioppo et al., 1996; Kruglanski & Webster, 1996; Perkins, 1995; Schommer, 1990; Sternberg, 2003; Sternberg & Grigorenko, 1997).

The literature on these types of thinking dispositions is vast and our purpose is not to review that literature here. It is only necessary to note that the types of cognitive propensities that these thinking disposition measures reflect are: the tendency to collect information before making up one's mind; the tendency to seek various points of view before coming to a conclusion; the disposition to think extensively about a problem before responding; the tendency to calibrate the degree of strength of one's opinion to the degree of evidence available; the tendency to think about future consequences before taking action; the tendency to explicitly weigh pluses and minuses of situations before making a decision; and the tendency to seek nuance and avoid absolutism. In short, individual differences in thinking dispositions are assessing variation in people's goal management, epistemic values, and epistemic self-regulation – differences in the operation of reflective mind. They are all psychological characteristics that underpin rational thought and action.

The cognitive abilities assessed on intelligence tests are not of this type. They are not about high-level personal goals and their regulation, or about the tendency to change beliefs in the face of contrary evidence, or about how knowledge acquisition is internally regulated when not externally directed. People have indeed come up with *definitions* of intelligence that encompass such things. Theorists often define intelligence in ways that encompass rational action and belief but, despite what these theorists argue, *the actual measures of intelligence in use assess only algorithmic-level cognitive capacity.* No current intelligence test that is even moderately used in practice assesses rational thought or behaviour.

Individual differences in the tripartite structure

We can use this structure to understand why measures of intelligence provide a very incomplete assessment of Type 2 functioning. The algorithmic/reflective distinction reflects the contrast mentioned previously between optimal performance situations and typical performance situations. The psychology of individual differences maps this distinction into the difference between measures of cognitive capacity (intelligence) and measures of thinking dispositions.

Cognitive psychologists have focused on optimal performance indicators when studying the type of algorithmic-level cognitive capacities that underlie traditional psychometric intelligence (rightly so, because intelligence is assessed under maximal performance conditions). Fluid g in the Horn–Cattell model (Carroll, 1993; Horn & Cattell, 1967) indexes primarily individual differences in cognitive capacity at the algorithmic level (as indicated in Figure 17.2). In contrast, thinking dispositions are measured with instructions emphasizing typical performance and are tapping the reflective mind. Many concern beliefs, belief structure and, importantly, attitudes toward forming and changing beliefs. Other cognitive styles concern a person's goals and goal hierarchy. Thinking disposition measures are telling us about the individual's goals and epistemic values – and they are indexing broad tendencies of pragmatic and epistemic self-regulation (Stanovich, 1999). They index individual differences in the reflective mind (as indicated in Figure 17.2). This is why such rational thinking dispositions will predict variance in performance on heuristics and biases tasks after the effects of general intelligence have been controlled (Bruine de Bruin et al., 2007; Klaczynski et al., 1997; Klaczynski & Lavallee, 2005; Klaczynski & Robinson, 2000; Kokis et al., 2002; Newstead, Handley, Harley, Wright, & Farrelly, 2004; Parker & Fischhoff, 2005; Sá & Stanovich, 2001; Stanovich & West, 1997, 1998c, 2000; Toplak, Liu, Macpherson, Toneatto, & Stanovich, 2007; Toplak & Stanovich, 2002; West et al., 2008).

Figure 17.2 provides a framework for understanding why intelligence sometimes dissociates from thinking biases related to rationality. The reason is that rationality is a more encompassing construct than intelligence. Rationality is an organismic-level concept. It concerns the actions of an entity in its environment that serve its goals. As long as variation in thinking dispositions is not perfectly correlated with intelligence, then there is the statistical possibility of dissociations between rationality and intelligence. Substantial empirical evidence indicates that individual differences in thinking dispositions and intelligence are far from perfectly correlated. Many different studies involving thousands of subjects have indicated that measures of intelligence display only moderate to weak correlations (usually less than

.30) with some thinking dispositions (e.g., actively open-minded thinking, need for cognition) and near zero correlations with others such as conscientiousness, curiosity, and diligence (Ackerman & Heggestad, 1997; Austin & Deary, 2002; Baron, 1982; Bates & Shieles, 2003; Cacioppo et al., 1996; Eysenck, 1994; Goff & Ackerman, 1992; Kanazawa, 2004; Kokis et al., 2002; Noftle & Robins, 2007; Reiss & Reiss, 2004; Zeidner & Matthews, 2000).

Integrative summary

In summary, what has been termed Type 2 processing in the dual-process literature (Evans, 2009) is composed of (at least) the distinct operations of the reflective and algorithmic minds, and only individual differences in the latter are strongly related to individual differences in intelligence. In terms of the framework illustrated in Figure 17.1, it is parameter #3 that relates strongly to the decoupling operation of the algorithmic mind and hence generates large individual differences based on cognitive ability. In contrast, it is conjectured that person parameter #1 is related more to the environmental/education history of the person that determines whether or not they have been exposed to the discrete packets of mindware that relate to rational thinking in the domains of cause, probability, choice tradeoffs, logic, and other specific domains. Finally, parameter #2 is posited to vary based upon individual differences in the reflective mind – specifically, whether the person has a tendency to default to heuristic responses or whether they are alert to cues indicating that heuristic override is necessary.

The framework illustrated in Figures 17.1 and 17.2 illustrates why rationality will not be uniformly related to intelligence. Instead, that relationship will depend upon the degree that rational responding requires sustained cognitive decoupling. When the heart of the task is recognizing the need for heuristic override but the override operation itself is easily accomplished, no sustained decoupling is necessary and rational thinking will depend more on the operations of the reflective mind than on the algorithmic mind. Thus, relationships with intelligence will be attenuated. Additionally, as Kahneman (2000) has argued, when detecting the necessity for override is very difficult (person parameter #2 is low), performance overall will be quite low and no relationships with cognitive ability will be evident.

Conversely however, highly intelligent people will display fewer reasoning biases when you tell them what the bias is and what they need to do to avoid it. That is, when parameters #1 and #2 are ceilinged and considerable cognitive capacity is needed to sustain decoupling while the correct response is computed, then highly intelligent people will do better in a rational thinking task. However, if there is no advance warning that biased processing must be avoided (as is the case in many between-subjects designs), then more intelligent individuals are not much more likely to perform any better on the task. Another way to phrase this is to say that, often, people of high cognitive ability are no more likely to recognize the *need* for a normative principle than are individuals of lower cognitive ability. When the former believe that nothing normative is at stake, they behave remarkably like other people (equally likely for example to be "anchored" into responding that redwoods are almost 1,000 feet tall! – as was the case in one of our experiments). If told, however, that they are in a situation of normative conflict and if resolving the conflict requires holding a prepotent response in abeyance, then the individual of high cognitive ability will show less of many different cognitive biases.

Under the view presented here, there turn out to be numerous circumstances in which rational thought will dissociate from cognitive ability. First, cues to the necessity for override might be missing, thus leading most individuals to respond heuristically regardless of cognitive ability. Second, cues to the need for override might be present, but the disposition to respond to such cues may not be correlated with algorithmic capacity. If this is the case, there will be no association with cognitive ability as long as there is no need for sustained decoupling. The disposition to spot a heuristic–analytic conflict is not necessarily related to the computational power needed (in some situations) to resolve the conflict in favour of the analytic response. Thinking dispositions that relate to override cue detection are not assessed on intelligence tests and are thus not part of the intelligence construct.[5]

An important caveat to the model presented in Figure 17.1 is that which rational thinking tasks yield a conflict between heuristic and analytic responses is not fixed, but instead is a function of the individual's history of mindware acquisition. Early in developmental history, the relevant mindware will not be present and the heuristic response will be inevitable – no conflict will even be detected. Someone with no training in thinking probabilistically – or, for that matter, logically in terms of subset and superset – may experience no conflict in the Linda Problem. As experience with statistical and probabilistic thinking grows, a person will begin to experience more of a conflict because relevant mindware is available for use in the Type 2 simulation of an alternative response. The final developmental stage in this sequence might well be that the mindware used in analytic simulation becomes so tightly compiled that it is triggered from the autonomous mind in the manner of a natural heuristic response. Some statistics instructors, for example, become unable to empathize with their students for whom the basic probability axioms are not transparent. The instructor can no longer remember when these axioms were not primary intuitions. This final stage of processing is perhaps captured by developmental models of heuristic versus analytic processing that trace a trajectory where fluent adult performance looks very heuristic (Brainerd & Reyna, 2001; Ericsson & Charness, 1994; Klein, 1998; Reyna, Lloyd, & Brainerd, 2003; Reyna, Adam, Poirier, LeCroy, & Brainerd, 2005).

Of course, with this discussion of what creates associations between biases and cognitive ability, we do not mean to draw attention away from one of our most salient outcomes – that a startlingly wide range of rational thinking tendencies appear to be somewhat independent of intelligence. Across many of the studies we have reported, we have found that many biases discussed in the heuristics and biases literature are surprisingly independent of cognitive ability. We say surprisingly because ever since Spearman (1904) first discovered positive manifold, intelligence indicators have correlated with a plethora of cognitive abilities and thinking skills that are almost too large to enumerate (e.g., Ackerman et al., 1999; Carroll, 1993; Deary, 2000, 2001; Deary, Whiteman, Starr, Whalley, & Fox, 2004; Lubinski, 2000, 2004; Lubinski & Humphreys, 1997). Nevertheless, as the left column of Table 17.1 indicates, the list of biases and effects that appear to be dissociated from intelligence is fairly long.

Of course, it is not true that all thinking biases are independent of cognitive ability. The right column of Table 17.1 lists some effects and biases from other studies where an association was found. Nevertheless, the correlations have tended to be modest: .35–.45 for belief bias in syllogistic reasoning, in the range of .25–.35 for various probabilistic reasoning tasks, in the range of .20–.25 for various covariation detection and hypothesis testing tasks, .25–.35 on informal reasoning tasks, .15–.20 with outcome bias measured within-subjects, .20–.40 with performance in the four-card selection task, .10–.20 with performance in various disjunctive reasoning tasks, .15–.25 with hindsight bias, .25–.30 with denominator neglect, and .05–.20 with various indices of Bayesian reasoning. All correlations were in the expected direction. Other investigators have found relationships of a similar effect size between cognitive ability and a variety of tasks in the heuristics and biases literature (Bruine de Bruin et al., 2007; DeShon, Smith, Chan, & Schmitt, 1998; Handley, Capon, Beveridge, Dennis, & Evans, 2004; Klaczynski & Lavallee, 2005; Newstead et al., 2004; Parker & Fischhoff, 2005; Perkins & Ritchhart, 2004; Valentine, 1975).

The overall modest correlational trends are what led us to claim that intelligence tests are radically incomplete as measures of cognitive functioning (Stanovich, 2009; West et al., 2008). It is important to stress the word *cognitive* in this conclusion. Critics of intelligence tests are eager to point out that the tests ignore important parts of mental life – many largely noncognitive domains such as socioemotional abilities, empathy, and interpersonal skills, for example. However, a tacit assumption in such critiques is that although intelligence tests miss certain key noncognitive areas, they do encompass most of what is important in the cognitive domain. It is just this unstated assumption that we have challenged in our work – where we have shown that intelligence tests represent only a small sample of the cognitive skills importantly related to human rationality.

Notes

1 One caveat concerning the associations that we observed in these studies relates to the restriction of range in our sample. Certainly, it is true that individuals with average and above average cognitive ability are overrepresented in samples

composed entirely of university students. Nevertheless, the actual range in cognitive ability found among college students in the USA is quite large. In the past 30 years, the percentage of 25- to 29-year-olds in the USA who have attended college increased by 50%. By 2002, 58% of these young adults had completed at least one or more years of college, and 29% had received at least a bachelor's degree (US Department of Health and Human Services, 2003). However, the restriction of range in cognitive ability is somewhat greater in our sample, because our participants attended a moderately selective state university. The SAT total means of our samples are roughly .60 of a standard deviation above the national mean of 1021 (College Board, 2006). The standard deviation of the distribution of scores in our sample is roughly .55–.70 of the standard deviation in the nationally representative sample.

2 Our conjecture here amounts to an endorsement of what Evans (2007b) calls the quality hypothesis regarding cognitive ability – that individuals higher in cognitive ability are more likely to compute the correct response *given* that they have engaged in Type 2 processing. The corresponding quantity hypothesis is that individuals higher in cognitive ability are more likely to engage in Type 2 processing.

3 Base rates that have a causal relationship to the criterion behaviour (Ajzen, 1977; Bar-Hillel, 1980, 1990; Tversky & Kahneman, 1979) are often distinguished from noncausal base rate problems – those involving base rates with no obvious causal relationship to the criterion behaviour. A famous noncausal problem is the well-known cab problem (see Bar-Hillel, 1980; Lyon & Slovic, 1976; Tversky & Kahneman, 1982):

> A cab was involved in a hit-and-run accident at night. Two cab companies, the Green and the Blue, operate in the city in which the accident occurred. You are given the following facts: 85 percent of the cabs in the city are Green and 15 percent are Blue. A witness identified the cab as Blue. The court tested the reliability of the witness under the same circumstances that existed on the night of the accident and concluded that the witness correctly identified each of the two colors 80 percent of the time. What is the probability that the cab involved in the accident was Blue?

(Amalgamating the base rate and the indicant according to Bayes' rule yields .41 as the posterior probability of the cab being blue.) The causal variant of the same problem substitutes for the first fact the phrase "Although the two companies are roughly equal in size, 85% of cab accidents in the city involve Green cabs and 15% involve Blue cabs" (Tversky & Kahneman, 1982, p. 157).

Another type of causal base rate problem is structured so that the participant has to make an inductive inference in a simulation of a real-life decision. The information relevant to the decision is conflicting and of two different types. One type of evidence is statistical: either probabilistic or aggregate base-rate information that favours one of the bipolar decisions. The other evidence is a concrete case or personal experience that points in the opposite direction. The classic Volvo versus Saab item (Fong, Krantz, & Nisbett, 1986, p. 285) provides an example. In this problem, a couple are deciding to buy one of two otherwise equal cars. Consumer surveys, statistics on repair records, and polls of experts favour the Volvo over the Saab. However, a friend reports experiencing a severe mechanical problem with the Volvo he owns. The participant is asked to provide advice to the couple. Preference for the Volvo indicates a tendency to rely on the large-sample information in spite of salient personal testimony. A preference for the Saab indicates reliance on the personal testimony over the opinion of experts and the large-sample information.

4 Hypothetical reasoning and cognitive simulation are central topics in cognitive science (see Barrett, Henzi, & Dunbar, 2003; Buckner & Carroll, 2007; Byrne, 2005;

Currie & Ravenscroft, 2002; Decety & Grezes, 2006; Dougherty, Gettys, & Thomas, 1997; Evans, 2007a; Evans & Over, 2004; Kahneman & Tversky, 1982b; Nichols & Stich, 2003; Oatley, 1999; Roese, 1997; Sterelny, 2001; Suddendorf & Corballis, 2007; Suddendorf & Whiten, 2001).

5 The Cognitive Reflection Test (CRT) developed by Frederick (2005) appears to be a combination index of the algorithmic mind and the reflective mind. It indexes both cognitive capacity and thinking dispositions, as exemplified by the tendency of the CRT to correlate with both intelligence indicators and thinking dispositions such as need for cognition and actively open-minded thinking, both in Frederick's (2005) own study and in unpublished work of our own.

Acknowledgements

This research was supported by grants from the Social Sciences and Humanities Research Council of Canada and the Canada Research Chairs program to Keith E. Stanovich; and also by a grant from the Social Sciences and Humanities Research Council of Canada to Maggie E. Toplak.

References

Ackerman, P. L. (1994). Intelligence, attention, and learning: Maximal and typical performance. In D. K. Detterman (Ed.), *Current topics in human intelligence* (Vol. 4, pp. 1–27). Norwood, NJ: Ablex.

Ackerman, P. L. (1996). A theory of adult development: Process, personality, interests, and knowledge. *Intelligence, 22,* 227–257.

Ackerman, P. L., & Heggestad, E. D. (1997). Intelligence, personality, and interests: Evidence for overlapping traits. *Psychological Bulletin, 121,* 219–245.

Ackerman, P. L., & Kanfer, R. (2004). Cognitive, affective, and conative aspects of adult intellect within a typical and maximal performance framework. In D. Y. Dai & R. J. Sternberg (Eds.), *Motivation, emotion, and cognition: Integrative perspectives on intellectual functioning and development* (pp. 119–141). Mahwah, NJ: Lawrence Erlbaum Associates, Inc.

Ackerman, P., Kyllonen, P., & Richards, R. (Eds.). (1999). *Learning and individual differences: Process, trait, and content determinants.* Washington, DC: American Psychological Association.

Adler, J. E. (1984). Abstraction is uncooperative. *Journal for the Theory of Social Behaviour, 14,* 165–181.

Adler, J. E. (1991). An optimist's pessimism: Conversation and conjunctions. In E. Eells & T. Maruszewski (Eds.), *Probability and rationality: Studies on L. Jonathan Cohen's philosophy of science* (pp. 251–282). Amsterdam, The Netherlands: Editions Rodopi.

Ajzen, I. (1977). Intuitive theories of events and the effects of base-rate information on prediction. *Journal of Personality and Social Psychology, 35,* 303–314.

Atran, S. (1998). Folk biology and the anthropology of science: Cognitive universals and cultural particulars. *Behavioral and Brain Sciences, 21,* 547–609.

Austin, E. J., & Deary, I. J. (2002). Personality dispositions. In R. J. Sternberg (Ed.), *Why smart people can be so stupid* (pp. 187–211). New Haven, CT: Yale University Press.

Baddeley, A., Chincotta, D., & Adlam, A. (2001). Working memory and the control of action: Evidence from task switching. *Journal of Experimental Psychology: General, 130*, 641–657.

Bargh, J. A., & Chartrand, T. L. (1999). The unbearable automaticity of being. *American Psychologist, 54*, 462–479.

Bar-Hillel, M. (1980). The base-rate fallacy in probability judgments. *Acta Psychologica, 44*, 211–233.

Bar-Hillel, M. (1990). Back to base rates. In R. M. Hogarth (Ed.), *Insights into decision making: A tribute to Hillel J. Einhorn* (pp. 200–216). Chicago: University of Chicago Press.

Baron, J. (1982). Personality and intelligence. In R. J. Sternberg (Ed.), *Handbook of human intelligence* (pp. 308–351). Cambridge: Cambridge University Press.

Baron, J. (1985). *Rationality and intelligence*. Cambridge: Cambridge University Press.

Baron, J. (2008). *Thinking and deciding* (4th ed.). Cambridge: Cambridge University Press.

Barrett, H. C., & Kurzban, R. (2006). Modularity in cognition: Framing the debate. *Psychological Review, 113*, 628–647.

Barrett, L., Henzi, P., & Dunbar, R. (2003). Primate cognition: From "what now?" to "what if?". *Trends in Cognitive Sciences, 7*, 494–497.

Bartels, D. M. (2006). Proportion dominance: The generality and variability of favoring relative savings over absolute savings. *Organizational Behavior and Human Decision Processes, 100*, 76–95.

Bates, T. C., & Shieles, A. (2003). Crystallized intelligence as a product of speed and drive for experience: The relationship of inspection time and openness to g and Gc. *Intelligence, 31*, 275–287.

Benjamin, D., & Shapiro, J. (2005, February 25). *Does cognitive ability reduce psychological bias?* JEL manuscript: J24, D14, C91.

Berkeley, D., & Humphreys, P. (1982). Structuring decision problems and the "bias heuristic". *Acta Psychologica, 50*, 201–252.

Birch, S. A. J. (2005). When knowledge is a curse: Children's and adult's reasoning about mental states. *Current Directions in Psychological Science, 14*, 25–29.

Botvinick, M., Cohen, J. D., & Carter, C. S. (2004). Conflict monitoring and anterior cingulate cortex: An update. *Trends in Cognitive Sciences, 8*, 539–546.

Brainerd, C. J., & Reyna, V. F. (2001). Fuzzy-trace theory: Dual processes in memory, reasoning, and cognitive neuroscience. In H. W. Reese & R. Kail (Eds.), *Advances in child development and behavior* (Vol. 28, pp. 41–100). San Diego, CA: Academic Press.

Broome, J. (1990). Should a rational agent maximize expected utility? In K. S. Cook & M. Levi (Eds.), *The limits of rationality* (pp. 132–145). Chicago: University of Chicago Press.

Bruine de Bruin, W., Parker, A. M., & Fischhoff, B. (2007). Individual differences in adult decision-making competence. *Journal of Personality and Social Psychology, 92*, 938–956.

Buckner, R. L., & Carroll, D. C. (2007). Self-projection and the brain. *Trends in Cognitive Sciences, 11*, 49–57.

Buss, D. M. (Ed.). (2005). *The handbook of evolutionary psychology*. Hoboken, NJ: John Wiley.

Byrne, R. M. J. (2005). *The rational imagination: How people create alternatives to reality*. Cambridge, MA: MIT Press.

Cacioppo, J. T., Petty, R. E., Feinstein, J., & Jarvis, W. (1996). Dispositional differences in cognitive motivation: The life and times of individuals varying in need for cognition. *Psychological Bulletin, 119*, 197–253.

Camerer, C., Loewenstein, G., & Rabin, M. (Eds.). (2004). *Advances in behavioral economics*. Princeton, NJ: Princeton University Press.

Camerer, C., Loewenstein, G., & Weber, M. (1989). The curse of knowledge in economic settings: An experimental analysis. *Journal of Political Economy, 97*, 1232–1254.

Carpenter, P. A., Just, M. A., & Shell, P. (1990). What one intelligence test measures: A theoretical account of the processing in the Raven Progressive Matrices Test. *Psychological Review, 97*, 404–431.

Carroll, J. B. (1993). *Human cognitive abilities: A survey of factor-analytic studies*. Cambridge: Cambridge University Press.

Carruthers, P. (2006). *The architecture of the mind*. New York: Oxford University Press.

Cherniak, C. (1986). *Minimal rationality*. Cambridge, MA: MIT Press.

Christiansen-Szalanski, J. J., & Williams, C. F. (1991). The hindsight bias: A meta-analysis. *Organizational Behavior and Human Decision Processes, 48*, 147–168.

Clark, A. (2001). *Mindware: An introduction to the philosophy of cognitive science*. New York: Oxford University Press.

Cohen, L. J. (1979). On the psychology of prediction: Whose is the fallacy? *Cognition, 7*, 385–407.

Cohen, L. J. (1981). Can human irrationality be experimentally demonstrated? *Behavioral and Brain Sciences, 4*, 317–370.

Cohen, L. J. (1982). Are people programmed to commit fallacies? Further thoughts about the interpretation of experimental data on probability judgment. *Journal for the Theory of Social Behavior, 12*, 251–274.

Cohen, L. J. (1983). The controversy about irrationality. *Behavioral and Brain Sciences, 6*, 510–517.

Cohen, L. J. (1986). *The dialogue of reason*. Oxford: Oxford University Press.

College Board (2006). College Board SAT: 2006 College-Bound Seniors: Total Group Profile Report. Retrieved February 26, 2010, from http://www.collegeboard.com/prod_downloads/about/news_info/cbsenior/yr2006/national-report.pdf

Coltheart, M. (1999). Modularity and cognition. *Trends in Cognitive Sciences, 3*, 115–120.

Cronbach, L. J. (1949). *Essentials of psychological testing*. New York: Harper.

Currie, G., & Ravenscroft, I. (2002*). Recreative minds: Imagination in philosophy and psychology*. Oxford: Clarendon Press.

Daniels, N. (1979). Wide reflective equilibrium and theory acceptance ethics. *The Journal of Philosophy, 76*, 256–282.

Daniels, N. (1996). *Justice and justification: Reflective equilibrium in theory and practice*. Cambridge: Cambridge University Press.

Daston, L. (1980). Probabilistic expectation and rationality in classical probability theory. *Historia Mathematica, 7*, 234–260.

Dawes, R. M. (1976). Shallow psychology. In J. S. Carroll & J. W. Payne (Eds.), *Cognition and social behavior* (pp. 3–11). Hillsdale, NJ: Lawrence Erlbaum Associates, Inc.

De Neys, W. (2006a). Automatic-heuristic and executive-analytic processing during reasoning: Chronometric and dual-task considerations. *Quarterly Journal of Experimental Psychology*, *59*, 1070–1100.

De Neys, W. (2006b). Dual processing in reasoning – Two systems but one reasoner. *Psychological Science*, *17*, 428–433.

De Neys, W., & Glumicic, T. (2008). Conflict monitoring in dual process theories of thinking. *Cognition*, *106*, 1248–1299.

De Neys, W., Vartanian, O., & Goel, V. (2008). Smarter than we think: When our brains detect that we are biased. *Psychological Science*, *19*, 483–489.

Deary, I. J. (2000). *Looking down on human intelligence: From psychometrics to the brain*. Oxford: Oxford University Press.

Deary, I. J. (2001). *Intelligence: A very short introduction*. Oxford: Oxford University Press.

Deary, I. J., Whiteman, M. C., Starr, J. M., Whalley, L. J., & Fox, H. C. (2004). The impact of childhood intelligence on later life: Following up the Scottish Mental Surveys of 1932 and 1947. *Journal of Personality and Social Psychology*, *86*, 130–147.

Decety, J., & Grezes, J. (2006). The power of simulation: Imagining one's own and other's behavior. *Brain Research*, *1079*, 4–14.

Dennett, D. C. (1997). *Kinds of minds: Toward an understanding of consciousness*. New York: Basic Books.

DeShon, R. P., Smith, M. R., Chan, D., & Schmitt, N. (1998). Can racial differences in cognitive test performance be reduced by presenting problems in a social context? *Journal of Applied Psychology*, *83*, 438–451.

Dienes, Z., & Perner, J. (1999). A theory of implicit and explicit knowledge. *Behavioral and Brain Sciences*, *22*, 735–808.

Dougherty, M. R. P., Gettys, C. F., & Thomas, R. P. (1997). The role of mental simulation in judgments of likelihood. *Organizational Behavior and Human Decision Processes*, *70*, 135–148.

Duncan, J., Emslie, H., Williams, P., Johnson, R., & Freer, C. (1996). Intelligence and the frontal lobe: The organization of goal-directed behavior. *Cognitive Psychology*, *30*, 257–303.

Duncan, J., Parr, A., Woolgar, A., Thompson, R., Bright, P., Cox, S., et al. (2008). Goal neglect and Spearman's g: Competing parts of a complex task. *Journal of Experimental Psychology: General*, *137*, 131–148.

Elgin, C. Z. (1996). *Considered judgment*. Princeton, NJ: Princeton University Press.

Engle, R. W. (2002). Working memory capacity as executive attention. *Current Directions in Psychological Science*, *11*, 19–23.

Ericsson, K. A., & Charness, N. (1994). Expert performance: Its structure and acquisition. *American Psychologist*, *49*, 725–747.

Evans, J. St B. T. (1984). Heuristic and analytic processes in reasoning. *British Journal of Psychology*, *75*, 451–468.

Evans, J. St B. T. (1989). *Bias in human reasoning: Causes and consequences*. Hove, UK: Lawrence Erlbaum Associates Ltd.

Evans, J. St B. T. (2003). In two minds: Dual process accounts of reasoning. *Trends in Cognitive Sciences*, *7*, 454–459.

Evans, J. St B. T. (2006). The heuristic–analytic theory of reasoning: Extension and evaluation. *Psychonomic Bulletin and Review*, *13*, 378–395.

Evans, J. St B. T. (2007a). *Hypothetical thinking: Dual processes in reasoning and judgement*. Hove, UK: Psychology Press.

Evans, J. St B. T. (2007b). On the resolution of conflict in dual process theories of reasoning. *Thinking and Reasoning, 13*, 321–339.

Evans, J. St B. T. (2008). Dual-processing accounts of reasoning, judgment, and social cognition. *Annual Review of Psychology, 59*, 255–278.

Evans, J. St B. T. (2009). How many dual-process theories do we need? One, two, or many? In J. St B. T. Evans & K. Frankish (Eds.), *In two minds: Dual processes and beyond* (pp. 33–54). Oxford: Oxford University Press.

Evans, J. St B. T., & Over, D. E. (1996). *Rationality and reasoning.* Hove, UK: Psychology Press.

Evans, J. St B. T., & Over, D. E. (2004). *If.* Oxford: Oxford University Press.

Eysenck, H. J. (1994). Personality and intelligence: Psychometric and experimental approaches. In R. J. Sternberg & P. Ruzgis (Eds.), *Personality and intelligence* (pp. 3–31). Cambridge: Cambridge University Press.

Fischhoff, B. (1975). Hindsight ≠ foresight: The effect of outcome knowledge on judgment under uncertainty. *Journal of Experimental Psychology: Human Perception and Performance, 1*, 288–299.

Fischhoff, B., Slovic, P., & Lichtenstein, S. (1979). Subjective sensitivity analysis. *Organizational Behavior and Human Performance, 23*, 339–359.

Fodor, J. (1983). *Modularity of mind.* Cambridge, MA: MIT Press.

Fong, G. T., Krantz, D. H., & Nisbett, R. E. (1986). The effects of statistical training on thinking about everyday problems. *Cognitive Psychology, 18*, 253–292.

Franklin, S. (1995). *Artificial minds.* Cambridge, MA: MIT Press.

Frederick, S. (2005). Cognitive reflection and decision making. *Journal of Economic Perspectives, 19*, 25–42.

Frisch, D. (1993). Reasons for framing effects. *Organizational Behavior and Human Decision Processes, 54*, 399–429.

Gigerenzer, G. (1991). How to make cognitive illusions disappear: Beyond "heuristics and biases". *European Review of Social Psychology, 2*, 83–115.

Gigerenzer, G. (1996). On narrow norms and vague heuristics: A reply to Kahneman and Tversky (1996). *Psychological Review, 103*, 592–596.

Gilovich, T., Griffin, D., & Kahneman, D. (Eds.). (2002). *Heuristics and biases: The psychology of intuitive judgment.* New York: Cambridge University Press.

Gilovich, T., Medvec, V. H., & Sativsky, K. (1998). The illusion of transparency: Biased assessment of others' ability to read one's emotional states. *Journal of Personality and Social Psychology, 75*, 332–346.

Glenberg, A. M. (1997). What memory is for. *Behavioral and Brain Sciences, 20*, 1–55.

Goff, M., & Ackerman, P. L. (1992). Personality–intelligence relations: Assessment of typical intellectual engagement. *Journal of Educational Psychology, 84*, 537–552.

Gray, J. R., Chabris, C. F., & Braver, T. S. (2003). Neural mechanisms of general fluid intelligence. *Nature Neuroscience, 6*, 316–322.

Handley, S. J., Capon, A., Beveridge, M., Dennis, I., & Evans, J. St B. T. (2004). Working memory, inhibitory control and the development of children's reasoning. *Thinking and Reasoning, 10*, 175–195.

Hasher, L., Lustig, C., & Zacks, R. (2007). Inhibitory mechanisms and the control of attention. In A. Conway, C. Jarrold, M. Kane, A. Miyake, & J. Towse (Eds.), *Variation in working memory* (pp. 227–249). New York: Oxford University Press.

Henle, M. (1978). Foreword. In R. Revlin & R. E. Mayer (Eds.), *Human reasoning.* Washington, DC: Winston.

Hilton, D. J. (1995). The social context of reasoning: Conversational inference and rational judgment. *Psychological Bulletin, 118*, 248–271.

Hinds, P. J. (1999). The curse of expertise: The effects of expertise and debiasing methods on predictions of novice performance. *Journal of Experimental Psychology: Applied, 5*, 205–221.

Horn, J. L., & Cattell, R. B. (1967). Age differences in fluid and crystallized intelligence. *Acta Psychologica, 26*, 1–23.

Horn, J. L., & Noll, J. (1997). Human cognitive capabilities: Gf-Gc theory. In D. Flanagan, J. Genshaft, & P. Harrison (Eds.), *Contemporary intellectual assessment: Theories, tests, and issues* (pp. 53–91). New York: Guilford Press.

Hunt, E. (1987). The next word on verbal ability. In P. A. Vernon (Ed.), *Speed of information-processing and intelligence* (pp. 347–392). Norwood, NJ: Ablex.

Hunt, E. (1999). Intelligence and human resources: Past, present, and future. In P. Ackerman & P. Kyllonen (Eds.), *The future of learning and individual differences research: Processes, traits, and content.* Washington, DC: American Psychological Association.

Johnson-Laird, P. N. (1983). *Mental models.* Cambridge, MA: Harvard University Press.

Johnson-Laird, P. N. (2006). *How we reason.* Oxford: Oxford University Press.

Kahneman, D. (1973). *Attention and effort.* Englewood Cliffs, NJ: Prentice Hall.

Kahneman, D. (1981). Who shall be the arbiter of our intuitions? *Behavioral and Brain Sciences, 4*, 339–340.

Kahneman, D. (2000). A psychological point of view: Violations of rational rules as a diagnostic of mental processes. *Behavioral and Brain Sciences, 23*, 681–683.

Kahneman, D. A. (2003). A perspective on judgment and choice: Mapping bounded rationality. *American Psychologist, 58*, 697–720.

Kahneman, D., & Frederick, S. (2002). Representativeness revisited: Attribute substitution in intuitive judgment. In T. Gilovich, D. Griffin, & D. Kahneman (Eds.), *Heuristics and biases: The psychology of intuitive judgment* (pp. 49–81). New York: Cambridge University Press.

Kahneman, D., & Frederick, S. (2005). A model of intuitive judgment. In K. J. Holyoak & R. G. Morrison (Eds.), *The Cambridge handbook of thinking and reasoning* (pp. 267–293). New York: Cambridge University Press.

Kahneman, D., Slovic, P., & Tversky, A. (Eds.). (1982). *Judgment under uncertainty: Heuristics and biases.* Cambridge: Cambridge University Press.

Kahneman, D., & Tversky, A. (1972). Subjective probability: A judgment of representativeness. *Cognitive Psychology, 3*, 430–454.

Kahneman, D., & Tversky, A. (1973). On the psychology of prediction. *Psychological Review, 80*, 237–251.

Kahneman, D., & Tversky, A. (1982a). On the study of statistical intuitions. *Cognition, 11*, 123–141.

Kahneman, D., & Tversky, A. (1982b). The simulation heuristic. In D. Kahneman, P. Slovic, & A. Tversky (Eds.), *Judgment under uncertainty: Heuristics and biases* (pp. 201–208). Cambridge: Cambridge University Press.

Kahneman, D., & Tversky, A. (1983). Can irrationality be intelligently discussed? *Behavioral and Brain Sciences, 6*, 509–510.

Kahneman, D., & Tversky, A. (1996). On the reality of cognitive illusions. *Psychological Review, 103*, 582–591.

Kahneman, D., & Tversky, A. (Eds.). (2000). *Choices, values and frames.* New York: Cambridge University Press.

Kanazawa, S. (2004). General intelligence as a domain-specific adaptation. *Psychological Review, 111*, 512–523.

Kane, M. J. (2003). The intelligent brain in conflict. *Trends in Cognitive Sciences, 7*, 375–377.

Kane, M. J., & Engle, R. W. (2002). The role of prefrontal cortex working-memory capacity, executive attention, and general fluid intelligence: An individual-differences perspective. *Psychonomic Bulletin and Review, 9*, 637–671.

Kane, M. J., & Engle, R. W. (2003). Working-memory capacity and the control of attention: The contributions of goal neglect, response competition, and task set to Stroop interference. *Journal of Experimental Psychology: General, 132*, 47–70.

Kane, M. J., Hambrick, D. Z., & Conway, A. R. A. (2005). Working memory capacity and fluid intelligence are strongly related constructs: Comment on Ackerman, Beier, and Boyle (2005). *Psychological Bulletin, 131*, 66–71.

Kardash, C. M., & Scholes, R. J. (1996). Effects of pre-existing beliefs, epistemological beliefs, and need for cognition on interpretation of controversial issues. *Journal of Educational Psychology, 88*, 260–271.

Keysar, B., & Barr, D. J. (2002). Self-anchoring in conversation: Why language users do not do what they "should". In T. Gilovich, D. Griffin, & D. Kahneman (Eds.), *Heuristics and biases: The psychology of intuitive judgment* (pp. 150–166). New York: Cambridge University Press.

Klaczynski, P. A., Gordon, D. H., & Fauth, J. (1997). Goal-oriented critical reasoning and individual differences in critical reasoning biases. *Journal of Educational Psychology, 89*, 470–485.

Klaczynski, P. A., & Lavallee, K. L. (2005). Domain-specific identity, epistemic regulation, and intellectual ability as predictors of belief-based reasoning: A dual-process perspective. *Journal of Experimental Child Psychology, 92*, 1–24.

Klaczynski, P. A., & Robinson, B. (2000). Personal theories, intellectual ability, and epistemological beliefs: Adult age differences in everyday reasoning tasks. *Psychology and Aging, 15*, 400–416.

Klein, G. (1998). *Sources of power: How people make decisions.* Cambridge, MA: MIT Press.

Koehler, D. J., & Harvey, N. (Eds.). (2004). Blackwell handbook of judgment and decision making. Oxford: Blackwell.

Koehler, J. J. (1996). The base rate fallacy reconsidered: Descriptive, normative and methodological challenges. *Behavioral and Brain Sciences, 19*, 1–53.

Kokis, J., Macpherson, R., Toplak, M., West, R. F., & Stanovich, K. E. (2002). Heuristic and analytic processing: Age trends and associations with cognitive ability and cognitive styles. *Journal of Experimental Child Psychology, 83*, 26–52.

Kruglanski, A. W., & Webster, D. M. (1996). Motivated closing of the mind: "Seizing" and "freezing". *Psychological Review, 103*, 263–283.

Larrick, R. P., Nisbett, R. E., & Morgan, J. N. (1993). Who uses the cost–benefit rules of choice? Implications for the normative status of microeconomic theory. *Organizational Behavior and Human Decision Processes, 56*, 331–347.

LeBoeuf, R. A., & Shafir, E. (2003). Deep thoughts and shallow frames: On the susceptibility to framing effects. *Journal of Behavioral Decision Making, 16*, 77–92.

LeBoeuf, R. A., & Shafir, E. (2005). Decision making. In K. J. Holyoak & R. G. Morrison (Eds.), *The Cambridge handbook of thinking and reasoning* (pp. 243–266). Cambridge: Cambridge University Press.

Levi, I. (1983). Who commits the base rate fallacy? *Behavioral and Brain Sciences, 6*, 502–506.

Lieberman, M. D. (2000). Intuiton: A social cognitive neuroscience approach. *Psychological Bulletin, 126*, 109–137.

Lieberman, M. D. (2003). Reflexive and reflective judgment processes: A social cognitive neuroscience approach. In J. P. Forgas, K. R. Williams, & W. von Hippel (Eds.), *Social judgments: Implicit and explicit processes* (pp. 44–67). New York: Cambridge University Press.

Lohman, D. F. (2000). Complex information processing and intelligence. In R. J. Sternberg (Ed.), *Handbook of intelligence* (pp. 285–340). Cambridge, MA: Cambridge University Press.

Lubinski, D. (2000). Scientific and social significance of assessing individual differences: "Sinking shafts at a few critical points". *Annual Review of Psychology, 51*, 405–444.

Lubinski, D. (2004). Introduction to the special section on cognitive abilities: 100 years after Spearman's (1904) "General Intelligence, Objectively Determined and Measured". *Journal of Personality and Social Psychology, 86*, 96–111.

Lubinski, D., & Humphreys, L. G. (1997). Incorporating general intelligence into epidemiology and the social sciences. *Intelligence, 24*, 159–201.

Lyon, D., & Slovic, P. (1976). Dominance of accuracy information and neglect of base rates in probability estimation. *Acta Psychologica, 40*, 287–298.

Macpherson, R., & Stanovich, K. E. (2007). Cognitive ability, thinking dispositions, and instructional set as predictors of critical thinking. *Learning and Individual Differences, 17*, 115–127.

Matthews, G., Zeidner, M., & Roberts, R. D. (2002). *Emotional intelligence: Science and myth*. Cambridge, MA: MIT Press.

Miller, P. M., & Fagley, N. S. (1991). The effects of framing, problem variations, and providing rationale on choice. *Personality and Social Psychology Bulletin, 17*, 517–522.

Miyake, A., Friedman, N., Emerson, M. J., & Witzki, A. H. (2000). The utility and diversity of executive functions and their contributions to complex "frontal lobe" tasks: A latent variable analysis. *Cognitive Psychology, 41*, 49–100.

Moshman, D., & Geil, M. (1998). Collaborative reasoning: Evidence for collective rationality. *Thinking and Reasoning, 4*, 231–248.

Navon, D. (1989). The importance of being visible: On the role of attention in a mind viewed as an anarchic intelligence system. *European Journal of Cognitive Psychology, 1*, 191–238.

Newstead, S. E., Handley, S. J., Harley, C., Wright, H., & Farrelly, D. (2004). Individual differences in deductive reasoning. *Quarterly Journal of Experimental Psychology, 57A*, 33–60.

Nichols, S., & Stich, S. (2003). *Mindreading: An integrated account of pretence, self-awareness and understanding other minds*. Oxford: Oxford University Press.

Nickerson, R. S. (2008). *Aspects of rationality*. New York: Psychology Press.

Noftle, E. E., & Robins, R. W. (2007). Personality predictors of academic outcomes: Big five correlates of GPA and SAT scores. *Journal of Personality and Social Psychology, 93*, 116–130.

Oaksford, M., & Chater, N. (1993). Reasoning theories and bounded rationality. In K. Manktelow & D. Over (Eds.), *Rationality: Psychological and philosophical perspectives* (pp. 31–60). London: Routledge.

Oaksford, M., & Chater, N. (1995). Theories of reasoning and the computational explanation of everyday inference. *Thinking and Reasoning, 1,* 121–152.

Oaksford, M., & Chater, N. (Eds.). (1998). *Rationality in an uncertain world.* Hove, UK: Psychology Press.

Oatley, K. (1999). Why fiction may be twice as true as fact: Fiction as cognitive and emotional simulation. *Review of General Psychology, 3,* 101–117.

Ohman, A., & Mineka, S. (2001). Fears, phobias, and preparedness: Toward an evolved module of fear and fear learning. *Psychological Review, 108,* 483–522.

Parker, A. M., & Fischhoff, B. (2005). Decision-making competence: External validation through an individual differences approach. *Journal of Behavioral Decision Making, 18,* 1–27.

Perkins, D. N. (1995). *Outsmarting IQ: The emerging science of learnable intelligence.* New York: Free Press.

Perkins, D., & Ritchhart, R. (2004). When is good thinking? In D. Y. Dai & R. J. Sternberg (Eds.), *Motivation, emotion, and cognition: Integrative perspectives on intellectual functioning and development* (pp. 351–384). Mahwah, NJ: Lawrence Erlbaum Associates, Inc.

Pohl, R. (2004). Hindsight bias. In R. Pohl (Ed.), *Cognitive illusions: A handbook on fallacies and biases in thinking, judgment and memory* (pp. 363–378). Hove, UK: Psychology Press.

Pollock, J. L. (1995). *Cognitive carpentry: A blueprint for how to build a person.* Cambridge, MA: MIT Press.

Reiss, S., & Reiss, M. M. (2004). Curiosity and mental retardation: Beyond IQ. *Mental Retardation, 42,* 77–81.

Reyna, V. F., Adam, M. B., Poirier, K., LeCroy, C., & Brainerd, C. J. (2005). Risky decision making in childhood and adolescence: A fuzzy-trace theory approach. In J. E. Jacobs & P. A. Klaczynski (Eds.), *The development of judgment and decision making in children and adolescents* (pp. 77–106). Mahwah, NJ: Lawrence Erlbaum Associates, Inc.

Reyna, V. F., Lloyd, F. J., & Brainerd, C. J. (2003). Memory, development, and rationality: An integrative theory of judgment and decision making. In S. L. Schneider & J. Shanteau (Eds.), *Emerging perspectives on judgment and decision research* (pp. 201–245). New York: Cambridge University Press.

Rips, L. J. (1994). *The logic of proof.* Cambridge, MA: MIT Press.

Rips, L. J., & Conrad, F. G. (1983). Individual differences in deduction. *Cognition and Brain Theory, 6,* 259–285.

Roese, N. (1997). Counterfactual thinking. *Psychological Bulletin, 121,* 131–148.

Sá, W., Kelley, C., Ho, C., & Stanovich, K. E. (2005). Thinking about personal theories: Individual differences in the coordination of theory and evidence. *Personality and Individual Differences, 38,* 1149–1161.

Sá, W., & Stanovich, K. E. (2001). The domain specificity and generality of mental contamination: Accuracy and projection in judgments of mental content. *British Journal of Psychology, 92,* 281–302.

Sá, W., West, R. F., & Stanovich, K. E. (1999). The domain specificity and generality of belief bias: Searching for a generalizable critical thinking skill. *Journal of Educational Psychology, 91,* 497–510.

Salthouse, T. A., Atkinson, T. M., & Berish, D. E. (2003). Executive functioning as a potential mediator of age-related cognitive decline in normal adults. *Journal of Experimental Psychology: General*, *132*, 566–594.

Samuels, R. (2005). The complexity of cognition: Tractability arguments for massive modularity. In P. Carruthers, S. Laurence, & S. Stich (Eds.), *The innate mind* (pp. 107–121). Oxford: Oxford University Press.

Samuels, R. (2009). The magical number two, plus or minus: Dual-process theory as a theory of cognitive kinds. In J. St B. T. Evans & K. Frankish (Eds.), *In two minds: Dual processes and beyond* (pp. 129–146). Oxford: Oxford University Press.

Schommer, M. (1990). Effects of beliefs about the nature of knowledge on comprehension. *Journal of Educational Psychology*, *82*, 498–504.

Schwarz, N. (1996). *Cognition and communication: Judgmental biases, research methods, and the logic of conversation*. Mahwah, NJ: Lawrence Erlbaum Associates, Inc.

Shafir, E. (1998). Philosophical intuitions and cognitive mechanisms. In M. R. DePaul & W. Ramsey (Eds.), *Rethinking intuition: The psychology of intuition and its role in philosophical inquiry* (pp. 59–83). Lanham, MD: Rowman & Littlefield Publishers, Inc.

Shafir, E., & Tversky, A. (1995). Decision making. In E. E. Smith & D. N. Osherson (Eds.), *Thinking* (Vol. 3, pp. 77–100). Cambridge, MA: MIT Press.

Shiffrin, R. M., & Schneider, W. (1977). Controlled and automatic human information processing: II. Perceptual learning, automatic attending, and a general theory. *Psychological Review*, *84*, 127–190.

Sieck, W., & Yates, J. F. (1997). Exposition effects on decision making: Choice and confidence in choice. *Organizational Behavior and Human Decision Processes*, *70*, 207–219.

Sinatra, G. M., & Pintrich, P. R. (Eds.). (2003). *Intentional conceptual change*. Mahwah, NJ: Lawrence Erlbaum Associates, Inc.

Sloman, A. (1993). The mind as a control system. In C. Hookway & D. Peterson (Eds.), *Philosophy and cognitive science* (pp. 69–110). Cambridge: Cambridge University Press.

Sloman, A., & Chrisley, R. (2003). Virtual machines and consciousness. *Journal of Consciousness Studies*, *10*, 133–172.

Sloman, S. A. (1996). The empirical case for two systems of reasoning. *Psychological Bulletin*, *119*, 3–22.

Slovic, P., & Peters, E. (2006). Risk perception and affect. *Current Directions in Psychological Science*, *15*, 322–325.

Slovic, P., & Tversky, A. (1974). Who accepts Savage's axiom? *Behavioral Science*, *19*, 368–373.

Smith, S. M., & Levin, I. P. (1996). Need for cognition and choice framing effects. *Journal of Behavioral Decision Making*, *9*, 283–290.

Spearman, C. (1904). General intelligence, objectively determined and measured. *American Journal of Psychology*, *15*, 201–293.

Sperber, D. (1994). The modularity of thought and the epidemiology of representations. In L. A. Hirschfeld & S. A. Gelman (Eds.), *Mapping the mind: Domain specificity in cognition and culture* (pp. 39–67). Cambridge: Cambridge University Press.

Stanovich, K. E. (1999). *Who is rational? Studies of individual differences in reasoning*. Mahwah, NJ: Lawrence Erlbaum Associates, Inc.

Stanovich, K. E. (2000). *Progress in understanding reading: Scientific foundations and new frontiers*. New York: Guilford Press.

Stanovich, K. E. (2004). *The robot's rebellion: Finding meaning in the age of Darwin*. Chicago: University of Chicago Press.

Stanovich, K. E. (2009). *What intelligence tests miss: The psychology of rational thought*. New Haven, CT: Yale University Press.

Stanovich, K. E., Cunningham, A. E., & West, R. F. (1998). Literacy experiences and the shaping of cognition. In S. Paris & H. Wellman (Eds.), *Global prospects for education: Development, culture, and schooling* (pp. 253–288). Washington, DC: American Psychological Association.

Stanovich, K. F., Toplak, M. E., & West, R. F. (2008). The development of rational thought: A taxonomy of heuristics and biases. *Advances in child development and behavior, 36*, 251–285.

Stanovich, K. E., & West, R. F. (1997). Reasoning independently of prior belief and individual differences in actively open-minded thinking. *Journal of Educational Psychology, 89*, 342–357.

Stanovich, K. E., & West, R. F. (1998a). Cognitive ability and variation in selection task performance. *Thinking and Reasoning, 4*, 193–230.

Stanovich, K. E., & West, R. F. (1998b). Individual differences in framing and conjunction effects. *Thinking and Reasoning, 4*, 289–317.

Stanovich, K. E., & West, R. F. (1998c). Individual differences in rational thought. *Journal of Experimental Psychology: General, 127*, 161–188.

Stanovich, K. E., & West, R. F. (1998d). Who uses base rates and P(D/~H)? An analysis of individual differences. *Memory & Cognition, 26*, 161–179.

Stanovich, K. E., & West, R. F. (1999). Discrepancies between normative and descriptive models of decision making and the understanding/acceptance principle. *Cognitive Psychology, 38*, 349–385.

Stanovich, K. E., & West, R. F. (2000). Individual differences in reasoning: Implications for the rationality debate? *Behavioral and Brain Sciences, 23*, 645–726.

Stanovich, K. E., & West, R. F. (2007). Natural myside bias is independent of cognitive ability. *Thinking & Reasoning, 13*, 225–247.

Stanovich, K. E., & West, R. F. (2008a). On the failure of intelligence to predict myside bias and one-sided bias. *Thinking and Reasoning, 14*, 129–167.

Stanovich, K. E., & West, R. F. (2008b). On the relative independence of thinking biases and cognitive ability. *Journal of Personality and Social Psychology, 94*, 672–695.

Stein, E. (1996). *Without good reason: The rationality debate in philosophy and cognitive science*. Oxford: Oxford University Press.

Sterelny, K. (2001). *The evolution of agency and other essays*. Cambridge: Cambridge University Press.

Sternberg, R. J. (1985). *Beyond IQ: A triarchic theory of human intelligence*. Cambridge: Cambridge University Press.

Sternberg, R. J. (1997). *Thinking styles*. Cambridge: Cambridge University Press.

Sternberg, R. J. (2003). *Wisdom, intelligence, and creativity synthesized*. Cambridge: Cambridge University Press.

Sternberg, R. J., & Grigorenko, E. L. (1997). Are cognitive styles still in style? *American Psychologist, 52*, 700–712.

Stich, S. P. (1990). *The fragmentation of reason*. Cambridge, MA: MIT Press.

Stich, S. P., & Nisbett, R. E. (1980). Justification and the psychology of human reasoning. *Philosophy of Science, 47*, 188–202.

Suddendorf, T., & Corballis, M. C. (2007). The evolution of foresight: What is mental time travel and is it unique to humans? *Behavioral and Brain Sciences, 30*, 299–351.

Suddendorf, T., & Whiten, A. (2001). Mental evolution and development: Evidence for secondary representation in children, great apes, and other animals. *Psychological Bulletin, 127*, 629–650.

Takemura, K. (1992). Effect of decision time on framing of decision: A case of risky choice behavior. *Psychologia, 35*, 180–185.

Takemura, K. (1993). The effect of decision frame and decision justification on risky choice. *Japanese Psychological Research, 35*, 36–40.

Takemura, K. (1994). Influence of elaboration on the framing of decision. *Journal of Psychology, 128*, 33–39.

Tetlock, P. E., & Mellers, B. A. (2002). The great rationality debate. *Psychological Science, 13*, 94–99.

Thagard, P. (1982). From the descriptive to the normative in philosophy and logic. *Philosophy of Science, 49*, 24–42.

Thagard, P., & Nisbett, R. E. (1983). Rationality and charity. *Philosophy of Science, 50*, 250–267.

Thaler, R. H. (1987). The psychology of choice and the assumptions of economics. In A. E. Roth (Ed.), *Laboratory experimentation in economics: Six points of view* (pp. 99–130). Cambridge: University of Cambridge Press.

Toplak, M., Liu, E., Macpherson, R., Toneatto, T., & Stanovich, K. E. (2007). The reasoning skills and thinking dispositions of problem gamblers: A dual-process taxonomy. *Journal of Behavioral Decision Making, 20*, 103–124.

Toplak, M., & Stanovich, K. E. (2002). The domain specificity and generality of disjunctive reasoning: Searching for a generalizable critical thinking skill. *Journal of Educational Psychology, 94*, 197–209.

Toplak, M. E. & Stanovich, K. E. (2003). Associations between myside bias on an informal reasoning task and amount of post-secondary education. *Applied Cognitive Psychology, 17*, 851–860.

Tversky, A., & Kahneman, D. (1973). Availability: A heuristic for judging frequency and probability. *Cognitive Psychology, 5*, 207–232.

Tversky, A., & Kahneman, D. (1974). Judgement under uncertainty: Heuristics and biases. *Science, 185*, 1124–1131.

Tversky, A., & Kahneman, D. (1979). Causal schemas in judgements under uncertainty. In M. Fishbein (Ed.), *Progress in social psychology*. Hillsdale, NJ: Lawrence Erlbaum Associates, Inc.

Tversky, A., & Kahneman, D. (1982). Judgments of and by representativeness. In D. Kahneman, P. Slovic, & A. Tversky (Eds.), *Judgment under uncertainty: Heuristics and biases* (pp. 84–98). Cambridge: Cambridge University Press.

Unsworth, N., & Engle, R. W. (2005). Working memory capacity and fluid abilities: Examining the correlation between Operation Span and Raven. *Intelligence, 33*, 67–81.

Unsworth, N., & Engle, R. W. (2007). The nature of individual differences in working memory capacity: Active maintenance in primary memory and controlled search from secondary memory. *Psychological Review, 114*, 104–132.

US Department of Health and Human Services (2003). *Trends in the well being of America's children & youth, 2003*. US Department of Health and Human Services Office of the Assistant Secretary for Planning and Evaluation, Retrieved February 26, 2010, from http://aspe.hhs.gov/hsp/ø3trends/

Valentine, E. R. (1975). Performance on two reasoning tasks in relation to intelligence, divergence and interference proneness: Content and context effects in reasoning. *British Journal of Educational Psychology, 45*, 198–205.

Verplanken, B. (1993). Need for cognition and external information search: Responses to time pressure during decision-making. *Journal of Research in Personality, 27*, 238–252.

Wang, L. (2009). Money and fame: Vividness effects in the National Basketball Association. *Journal of Behavioral Decision Making, 22*, 20–44.

Wason, P. C., & Evans, J. St B. T. (1975). Dual processes in reasoning? *Cognition, 3*, 141–154.

West, R. F., & Stanovich, K. E. (2003). Is probability matching smart? Associations between probabilistic choices and cognitive ability. *Memory & Cognition, 31*, 243–251.

West, R. F., Toplak, M. E., & Stanovich, K. E. (2008). Heuristics and biases as measures of critical thinking: Associations with cognitive ability and thinking dispositions. *Journal of Educational Psychology, 100*, 930–941.

Willingham, D. T. (1998). A neuropsychological theory of motor-skill learning. *Psychological Review, 105*, 558–584.

Willingham, D. T. (1999). The neural basis of motor-skill learning. *Current Directions in Psychological Science, 8*, 178–182.

Wilson, T. D. (2002). *Strangers to ourselves*. Cambridge, MA: Harvard University Press.

Zeidner, M., & Matthews, G. (2000). Intelligence and personality. In R. J. Sternberg (Ed.), *Handbook of intelligence* (pp. 581–610). New York: Cambridge University Press.

Zelazo, P. D. (2004). The development of conscious control in childhood. *Trends in Cognitive Sciences, 8*, 12–17.

18 Grounded rationality

A relativist framework for normative rationality

Shira Elqayam

De Montfort University

An old Jewish story tells about two litigants appearing before the town's rabbi. The first litigant having presented his case, the rabbi tells him: You are right. Then the second litigant presents his case, and the rabbi tells him, too: You are right. After the litigants had gone, the rabbi's wife reproaches him: How can they both be right? The rabbi listens to her attentively, and says: You know what? You are right, too!

Stories like this reflect the deep unease that some of us feel about relativism, the "you are right too" view, the idea that judgement should be done in context. How can everyone be right? And when rationality is the issue, relativism seems a particularly bad idea. It seems that one cannot be relatively rational: the question of rationality is an absolute one. As Stein (1996) memorably put it: "prima facie, relativism seems implausible with respect to reasoning. It seems crazy to say that reasoning in accordance with principles based on rules of logic is a good thing for some people but not for others" (Stein, 1996, p. 32; more on Stein's critique later). Oaksford and Chater recently voiced a similar objection, saying "there is a strong intuition [. . .] that there is some absolute sense in which some reasoning or decision-making is good, and other reasoning and decision-making is bad" (Oaksford & Chater, 2007, pp. 24–25).

In this chapter, I address the issue of relativism in rationality.[1] Rationality seems a suitable topic for a book in honour of Jonathan Evans's sixtieth birthday: Jonathan's contribution to the field of human rationality (much of it with David Over) has shaped the way many of us think about rationality. In their seminal *Rationality and Reasoning* (1996), Evans and Over famously defended a distinction between rationality$_1$, the pragmatic, instrumental sort of rationality involved in obtaining goals, and rationality$_2$, implied by explicit normative rule following. This distinction is pertinent to the present discussion: relativism has a different meaning in the context of instrumental rationality and normative rationality. In instrumental rationality, a relativist viewpoint means that goals are relative to the individual, or, even more strongly, that cognitive tools for obtaining these goals are relative too. This is the approach that Evans and Over take regarding instrumental rationality: rationality$_1$ is "personal and relative to the individual" (p. 4), focusing on "what our individual goals are, and whether we are reasoning or acting in a way that is generally reliable for achieving these" (p. 7). It is explicitly relative. Similarly, Oaksford and Chater have recently defended the goal relativity of rational analysis (Oaksford & Chater, 2009, p. 100).

In comparison, in the context of normative rationality, relativism means that normative systems are relative to an individual in a particular context and *should be judged in that context*. That is, if an individual explicitly follows her own relevant normative system and conforms to its rules, then from a relativist angle this is both necessary and sufficient to make her normatively rational (rational$_2$ in Evans and Over's terms). A relativist viewpoint means that the normative system followed does not have to be objectively justified or impersonal, although it does have to be subjectively and contextually justified. The issue seems orthogonal to the question of relativism in instrumental rationality: one can grant that goals are relative to the individual, that reliability of various cognitive tools for achieving them is relative, and yet leave open the issue whether normative systems are relative, or even opt for an absolutist view of the latter. While Evans and Over (1996) do not explicitly discuss the issue, they seem to adopt the latter view: rationality$_2$ is presented as "impersonal".

In this chapter, I will take one step further a view I have recently defended in collaboration with Jonathan (Elqayam & Evans, 2010), and will argue that, if psychologists wish to preserve a notion of normative rationality, this can best be done within a relativist framework. I will then examine a possible framework for such a relativist conception of normative rationality and defend it. I will argue that normative judgements in psychology run the risk of a problematic inference, whose solution requires a relativist viewpoint. I will also argue that the same principle that underlies bounded rationality, the "ought implies can" principle, means that normative judgement has to be taken in context. I will start by demonstrating how some of the arguments against normativism undermine an absolutist framework of normative rationality and that a relativist framework is a viable potential solution. Moving on to describing the relativist framework, I will start by sketching the way normative relativism changes the normative research question. The following section examines in some detail the way relativism would work for normative rationality. I will propose and defend a conception of *grounded rationality*, which is a relativist version of bounded rationality. Next examined is a major question that relativism and grounded rationality have to deal with, the role of universal constraints. Next, I examine the role of explicit processing. Finally, I will look in some detail at possible objections to the proposed relativist framework.

Relativism, normativism, and inferring the *ought* from the *is*

Notwithstanding what seems like the counterintuitive character of relativism in human thought, relativism does acquire greater plausibility in historical context. Plurality of formal systems is a matter of record in the history of science. Like any domain of knowledge, formal systems develop and change over time and space (see Olson & Torrance, 1996). Consider the history of logic, mathematics and statistics – the leading candidates for normative systems. The simple observation is that they keep changing. The logic of, say, twenty-first century textbooks, is hardly what medieval students learned in the *trivium*. The highly sophisticated methods that Chinese mathematicians, for example, used to obtain results comparable in accuracy to those of the Greek mathematicians, were entirely different, involving no use of axioms (Lloyd, 1996). Contemporary formal systems vary too – think about many-valued logics (Gottwald, 2001; Rescher, 1969), or non-Euclidean geometries (Greenberg, 2008).

Add to this the accumulating evidence for cultural and individual differences in the psychology of reasoning and judgement and decision making. Different people do seem to think differently, depending on cultural (Buchtel & Norenzayan, 2009; Nisbett, Peng, Choi, & Norenzayan, 2001) and individual differences in style (Epstein, 1994; Epstein, Pacini, Denes-Raj, & Heier, 1996), ability and cognitive motivation (Stanovich, 1999, 2004; Stanovich & West, 2000). Even what people count as knowledge seems to be culture sensitive (Weinberg, Nichols, & Stich, 2006; also see Nichols, 2004). The case for descriptive pluralism, then (in the term coined by Stich, 1990), seems beyond dispute. And from descriptive pluralism to normative relativism seems but one easy step.

So here is the paradox: On the one hand, this intuitive "prima facie implausibility" (in Stein's terms) of normative relativism; on the other – the historical, geographical, and psychological evidence for descriptive pluralism. Of course, a step from "is" to "ought" is never easy! One can accept the evidence for descriptive cultural pluralism and yet defend an absolutist normative view. However, this very gap between the is and the ought, the factual and the evaluative, provides us with a very good reason to embrace a relativist approach to human thought.

Recently, Elqayam and Evans (2010) identified and argued against normativism as a dominant paradigm in the psychology of human thinking. Normativism was defined as the view that (N1) human thinking reflects some kind of formal system S; and (N2) should be judged against S as a normative system. A major part of the argument was based on the descriptive pluralism of formal systems. Several authors (Evans, 1993; Stanovich, 1999) have pointed out a problem of arbitration (dubbed "the normative system problem" and "the inappropriate norm argument" respectively), when more than one normative system fits in with a particular empirical corpus. Elqayam and Evans (2010) pointed out that the problem of arbitration is particularly acute for normativism, because normative systems assume an "ought" component that is absent from computational (in Marr's terms) or competence (in Chomsky's terms) level theories (also see Elqayam, 2007; Evans, 2009a; Schroyens, 2009). Elqayam and Evans argued that, while supporting "is" theory with "is" evidence is fairly straightforward, supporting an "ought" theory with "is" evidence seems to invite an "is–ought" (Hume, 2000) or naturalistic (Moore, 1903) inference: where the premises are purely factual, inferring evaluative, deontic conclusions has been argued to be fallacious (Hudson, 1969; Schurz, 1997). A notorious example of the naturalistic fallacy – in fact, the one that prompted Moore's criticism – is Spencer's Social Darwinism (Hofstadter, 1955; although see Weinstein, 2002), which converts Darwinian adaptation mechanisms ("is") into a form of extreme capitalism captured by the catchphrase "survival of the fittest", and presented as a moral argument ("ought"). Since any empirical solution to the arbitration problem requires inferring an "ought" (normative system) from an "is" (empirical evidence), normativism is problematic for psychology; Elqayam and Evans concluded, therefore, with an outline of a descriptivist agenda in the psychological study of human thinking.

It is far from clear, however, that inferring the "ought" from the "is" is indeed a fallacy. A tradition in meta-ethics endeavours to clear "is–ought" inference: the core argument is that the separation of factual from evaluative is artificial, and that many acts of communication (concepts, speech acts) in ordinary language are both (e.g., Frankena, 1939; Searle, 1964; Williams, 1985). For example, if Jones promises to pay Smith £5, then Jones ought to pay Smith £5; no fallacy is involved, since promising as a deontic speech act already incorporates an "ought" (Searle, 1964). Elqayam and Evans acknowledge this; but, they argue, here is the rub: these amalgam concepts ("thick" concepts, to borrow a term from Williams, 1985) typically depend on social construction. It is social consensus that gives them the evaluative, deontic meaning, and social consensus is relative to the society. The amalgam solution seems to be a package deal: if we use it to support normative judgement, such judgement would have to be in context. To save normative rationality from the is–ought problem, then, one has to opt for a solution that depends on a type of relativism alien to normativism.

The amalgam solution, then, cannot save normativism, but it can and it does support relativism. Normative evaluation free from the is–ought problem is only possible within a relativistic framework. Stich (1990) has already mounted a comprehensive support of relativism in *instrumental* rationality, a view shared, as mentioned, by Evans and Over (1996) and to some extent by Oaksford and Chater (2009). However, the amalgam solution to the is–ought problem implies that relativism is mandatory in order to preserve some notion of *normative* rationality in psychology. The price of saving normative rationality, then, is giving up on comparison against an absolute evaluative norm. But this changes everything: many of the research questions in the rationality debate depend on the normativist paradigm and share its presupposition. In the following sections, I will pick up where Elqayam and Evans (2010) have stopped, and examine in some detail the way a relativist paradigm changes the face of research where normative rationality is concerned.

.

Relativism: The research question

Once the normativist paradigm is discarded, then the psychology of reasoning and judgement has two main options. The first one, advocated by Elqayam and Evans (2010), is a purely descriptivist agenda, giving up any normative considerations. However, it seems that relativism allows a second option: retain a modicum of normative judgement, provided this is done in relativist context. The relativist option, however, is not that far different from a purely descriptivist agenda. I will take this issue up again in the final section, but before that, I should examine in some detail what normative relativism means.

So how does relativism change the agenda of normative rationality? I will start with the basics: the research question is different. The typical normativist, absolutist research question is Q_{na}:

Q_{na}. *Is formal system S normative?*

With relativism, Q_{na} becomes too underspecified, and is no longer even meaningful; it would be replaced by Q_{nr}:

Q_{nr}. *Is formal system S normative for agent A in epistemic context E?*

Where epistemic context is both diachronic and synchronic, and sensitive to culture, society, geography, ecology, as well as the individual: anything that can have an effect on one's acceptance of a particular normative system. Thus, both personal and collective influences are taken into account in Q_{nr}. *Note that relativism obviates the arbitration problem or at least attenuates it considerably: Different normative systems, S_1 and S_2, can be normative at the same time, if applied to different agents A_1 or A_2, or different epistemic contexts E_1 or E_2, or both.*

I should also note that normative relativism is different from the instrumental or pragmatic sort, which acquired prominence in Stich's seminal defence of relativism (Stich, 1990), and which can be summarized as:

Q_{pr}. *Is [formal] system S useful (efficient, conducive to goal attainment) for agent A in epistemic context E?*

One of the main differences in epistemic context is the one between analytic, decontextualizing thinking style and holistic, contextualizing ones. There are cultures in which such contextual holistic thinking is the normative, trained response (Buchtel & Norenzayan, 2009; Choi, Koo, & Choi, 2007; Koo & Choi, 2005). The cultural differences literature tends to focus on the Eastern/Western dichotomy, but the differences seem to be a matter of training rather than geography: for example, responses of Korean students differed for Oriental medicine versus psychology majors, the latter responding similarly to Western students (Koo & Choi, 2005). I will therefore prefer the terms contextualizing versus decontextualizing cultures or epistemic contexts.

Just like normativism, relativism can vary, and seems to be a matter of degree rather than a dichotomy. Elqayam and Evans (2008) argued that both N1 (human thinking reflects normative system S) and N2 (S is the normative rational standard) are better conceived as vectors rather than dichotomies: N2, in particular, is sensitive to questions such as the a priori status of the normative system, whether conforming to it is considered both necessary and sufficient to normative rationality or only necessary, and whether the same normative system holds universally or only for each specific task. Relativism, as the mirror image of N2, is sensitive to the same factors. At its very extreme, each unique combination of individual in epistemic context should be tested for rational norms and conforming to them; the more one allows room for universal norms and behaviours, the weaker the relativism. In the next section, I will elaborate more on the role of universal and particular factors in a possible relativist framework.

Bounded rationality and grounded rationality:
A relativist framework

In the previous sections, I have defended a relativist conceptualization of normative rationality by, following Elqayam and Evans (2008), demonstrating it to be a viable solution to the is–ought dilemma. To some of the readers of this chapter, though, this defence may seem rather ad hoc, and relativism too high a price to pay for some quaint nicety. Now that we have examined the research question, however, we can see that there are theoretical benefits to be reaped by adopting a relativist position that go beyond solution to the arbitration problem. First, normativism in its absolutist form runs a substantial risk of "cultural blindness" (Norenzayan & Heine, 2005), or, in the more general term coined by Stich (1990), "epistemic chauvinism": the tendency to generalize individual intuitions to universal norms. While epistemic chauvinism is always a risk for normative rationality in any form, the risk is considerably lower with relativism. It may be impossible to take epistemic context fully into account: after all, each situation is a unique combination of individual, cultural and historical context. But overgeneralization is a higher risk if all this is completely ignored.

More importantly, relativism adds a significant dimension to the traditional concerns of bounded rationality. Simon's (1957, 1982, 1983) model of bounded rationality refers mainly to the way that human rationality is constrained by what Cherniak (1986) calls "the finitary predicament"; that is, physical and cognitive limitations on processing. The fact that humans do not live forever, that our brain capacity is finite, dictates that only tractable computations could count as rational. The underlying rationale is the age old "ought implies can" attributed to Kant (1932/1787).

In addition to bounded rationality, once epistemic context is taken into account, it also makes sense to talk about what I will term *grounded rationality*: that is, normative as well as instrumental rationality that is grounded in the individual's epistemic context and everything that goes into it: species specific cognition, personal ability and cognitive style, history, culture, society, and ecology.[2] Grounded rationality does not replace bounded rationality; they are conceptually distinct ideas, contextual versus universalist respectively, albeit based on a similar "ought implies can" principle. Note that bounded rationality itself is a relativist kind of constraint (Nickerson, 2008): it binds rationality to the relative context of human finitary considerations. However, from an angle of normative relativism, bounded rationality is just the beginning.

Accepting grounded rationality considerations means that the psychology of human thinking needs to consider seriously where contextual epistemic boundaries lie. Cultural differences are perhaps the prototypical (albeit not the only) source of epistemic context. They are certainly more accessible for psychological research: one can hardly time travel to the fourteenth century and study William of Ockham's contemporaries under controlled experimental conditions. Cross-cultural studies,[3] therefore, seem to be the best bet for analysing the effects of epistemic context. It is easy to forget that within-culture studies represent a biased sample of human behaviour – what Norenzayan and Heine (2005) call the "restricted database" of psychology. This oft-neglected truism has far-reaching implications for bounded rationality as a universalist concept: it is easy to mistake cultural constraints for universal cognitive limitations, when the sample is biased towards one culture. To avoid this error, we need to understand where bounded rationality ends and grounded rationality begins.

There is a precedent in cognitive science. Much of the ground I am trying to cover has already been covered in linguistics, where universalism has been a significant issue for many decades. In a way, cross-cultural studies of human thinking are now where linguistics was about half a century ago, perhaps because the easily accessible evidence is different in each case. In language, the empirical facts of linguistic diversity are blindingly obvious: different languages have different lexicons, different grammars. It took the Chomskyan revolution for linguistics to focus on language universals, to look for constraints on language that go beyond those imposed by particular languages (although see Harris, 1980, for a social constructionist critique of this approach; and Evans & Levinson, 2009, for a recent cognitive science critique).

In contrast, cross-cultural differences in thought may not be all that obvious or accessible, and it is only in the last two decades or so that psychologists have started to have some inkling of their extent, mainly thanks to the efforts of Nisbett, Norenzayan, and their collaborators (Norenzayan & Heine, 2005; Buchtel & Norenzayan, 2009; Nisbett et al., 2001). It is even more recently that authors have started comparing the role of universal and cultural constraints on thinking, in particular within a dual-process framework

(Buchtel & Norenzayan, 2009; Norenzayan & Heine, 2005; Yama, Nishioka, Horishita, Kawasaki, & Taniguchi, 2007). There is no guarantee that thinking is indeed analogous to language and that the role of universal and local constraints can be profitably transferred from the study of the latter to the study of the former; however, it seems a useful starting point, at least as a work postulate. The next section looks into this analogy in more detail.

Grounded rationality and the question of cognitive universals

The analogy between linguistic and thinking universals and their implications for bounded rationality is illustrated in Figure 18.1. The first part of the figure, 18.1(a), centres on the role of linguistic universals. To explain it, I will draw on a classic example of linguistic universals: the order in which each language prefers to arrange the subject (S), verb (V), and object (O) in a normal ("unmarked") sentence (Comrie, 1981; Greenberg, 1963; Hawkins, 1983). A brief consideration shows that with three components, potentially there can be six permutations of word order in any language: SVO, SOV, VSO, VOS, OVS, and OSV. The outermost of the concentric circles in Figure 18.1(a) represents this possibility. For word order, the possibilities embodied in all languages, natural as well as formal (i.e., logic), would include these six permutations. However, out of these six, only three are prevalent in known natural human languages: SOV (subject–object–verb), SVO, and VSO (in that order). The other orders are much rarer. This would be captured in the intermediate circle in 18.1(a), which represents linguistic universals in natural human languages. The classic explanation that goes back to Greenberg (1963) is that linguistic universals in general and word order universals in particular are a product of constraints on processing: in all the prevalent orders, subject precedes the object (also see Evans & Levinson, 2009). Lastly, particular languages, represented in the innermost circle, tend to adopt specific orders as the "unmarked", default word order: English is an SVO language, Arabic is a VSO language, and so on.

The potential possibilities space, then, is narrowed down by constraints on processing that determine language universals, and that is further narrowed down in particular languages. Note that in this case as in most cases, neither type of constraint is entirely rigid: other word orders exist in world languages even if they are far less common (although whether they all exist is moot); some languages do not have any preferred order; and in languages with preferred order, the constraints only apply to the unmarked, normal sentence structure. Different word order may be used, mainly for emphatic purposes. (Compare, for example, this pair of SVO and OSV English sentences: "The police detained the suspect. The witnesses, they released after questioning.") How far universality extends and what role linguistic diversity has is moot. Evans and Levinson (2009) have recently defended a strong diversity-based approach to universals, maintaining that diversity exceeds universality, and that whatever universals do exist reflect cognitive rather than

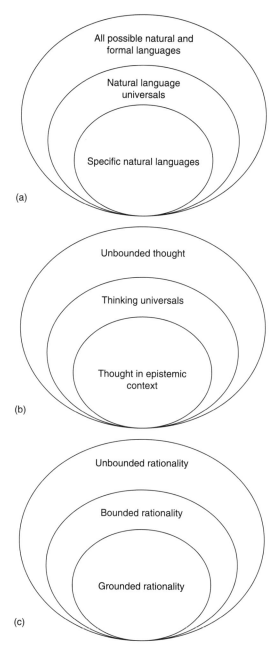

Figure 18.1 (a) Linguistic universals, (b) human thought, and (c) bounded and grounded rationality.

linguistic constraints. What is not moot, however, is that both universality and diversity play a role, and that at least some linguistic universals are a function of cognitive universals.

The analogy to human thought and rationality can be seen in Figures 18.1(b) and 18.1(c) respectively. The outermost circle of 18.1(b) depicts unbounded thought (perhaps something like a universal Turing machine), echoed in unbounded rationality in the outermost circle of 18.1(c) – both out of reach for humanity's finitary context. Bounded rationality, in contrast, acknowledges universal processing constraints on human thought, just as language universals give us access to processing constraints on human language. Bounded rationality in the intermediate circle of 18.1(c) acknowledges – an "ought implies can" sort of acknowledgement – that thinking universals, represented in the intermediate circle of 18.1(b), are shaped by finitary processing constraints.

Bounded rationality neglects, however, the innermost circle of Figure 18.1(b), that of the epistemic context, exemplified in cultural diversity and individual differences. This is acknowledged in grounded rationality, in the innermost circle of 18.1(c). As particular languages pick specific linguistic tools from this limited space (Jackendoff, 2002), so may particular epistemic contexts – combinations of cultures and individuals – pick out specific thinking tools. For example, decontextualizing cultures tend to pick object-based thinking, whereas holistic cultures tend to be, by definition, context based (Buchtel & Norenzayan, 2009). Here, too, constraints often seem to be "soft", making leading authors refer to thinking styles (Nisbett et al., 2001; Norenzayan, Smith, Kim, & Nisbett, 2002) rather than differences in cognitive architecture (Buchtel & Norenzayan, 2009; Evans, 2008, 2009b).

Note that empirical evidence will always be gathered at the innermost of the concentric circles, and generalized by comparing the space taken up by different languages or different epistemic contexts. To borrow a distinction from Harris (1980), we have no access to Language (with a capital L), only to languages. With just one language, or one type of epistemic context (such as culture) to draw on, overgeneralization is a clear hazard. Without cross-linguistic studies, it is easy to mistake particular language constraints for universal constraints, a sin typically committed by traditional grammar. Similarly, with no cross-cultural comparison, evidence from a specific culture can easily be mistaken for thinking universals (see Norenzayan & Heine, 2005, for a similar argument). The point is that both linguistic universals and thinking universals are a result of second-order theorizing. We only have access to human cognition in particular epistemic contexts. Unlike bounded rationality, grounded rationality takes this into account.[4]

Bounded and grounded rationality considerations alike are constraints rather than positive theories. Neither can dictate what the content of rationality norms *is*; they can only determine what it *cannot* be: norms can be neither computationally intractable nor contextually alien, respectively. The question therefore remains what the content of relativist, epistemic-context sensitive norms would actually be. A theory of the content of rational norms – that is, what different cultures consider to be norms of rational thinking – would have to be accessed descriptively. This is part of the task that the cross-cultural approach undertook in recent years (e.g., Buchtel & Norenzayan, 2009; Choi et al., 2007; Koo & Choi, 2005; Nisbett et al., 2001).

If there is an answer, it has to be found in some level of abstraction, an approach dominant in mainstream linguistics (Chomsky, 1965, pp. 27–30; Jackendoff, 2002, pp. 74–78) and voiced in psychology, for example, by Norenzayan and Heine (2005). This is a "hard-core" approach to universals: the idea that at some level, there lurks a formalized or natural universal which is foundational to all particular manifestations. Such a hard core may constitute, in Cherniak's (1986) terms, an element of "minimal rationality" (see also Saunders & Over, 2009). For psychological universals in general, the evidence does seem to support a universal hard core. It is not obvious, however, that such strong psychological universals, common to all epistemic contexts, can also be found in the domain of rational norms. The evidence that Norenzayan and Heine review only supports the existence of a hard core of psychological tools; it does not conclusively support that rational norms, specifically, are among these hard-core universal tools. If there is a universal, perhaps it is only the existence of norms *simpliciter*, as Carruthers (2006) recently suggested – not necessarily *rational* norms. An alternative relativist view would be that such a universal hard core for rational norms will never be found. Perhaps rational norms belong to the relativist part of the psychological toolbox. Or perhaps normative universals are like Wittgensteinian families, with partially overlapping features but no universal hard core, whatever the level of abstraction (for a similar proposal see Stich, 1990, p. 88). For example, perhaps there is a family of cognitive systems that shares noncontradiction as a rule, and another cognitive family that depends on dialectics; while both families share, say, a correspondence conception of truth. Note that this Wittgensteinian option is a possible alternative to any claim of universalism, but would be rather difficult to determine empirically. A limited survey of cognitive systems may come up with a feature that seems universal, but may not be shared by another cognitive family, left out of the survey.

Universal constraints on rationality, then, still allow a wide margin for local factors, both because finitary boundaries are somewhat elastic, and because the question of specific solutions remains open. As pointed out earlier, however, the link from "is" to "ought" is a particularly tenuous one. That cognition varies in epistemic context does not necessarily mean that normative rationality should take this into account. In other words, it is perfectly possible to acknowledge the innermost circle in Figure 18.1(b), and yet reject its analogue in 18.1(c), acknowledging only the universal constraints in the middle circle. The most extreme form of relativism would focus on grounded rationality, the particular component, to the exclusion of bounded rationality, the universal component. I doubt, however, that such a position is viable. It seems beyond dispute that the intermediate, universal circle should be acknowledged, and indeed bounded rationality considerations seem to be a consensus in the rationality debate regardless of position. However, it is certainly possible to adopt a universalist position, ignoring grounded rationality altogether. The question, then, is if grounded rationality constraints should be taken into account at all, given their particular and local nature. The next section examines this issue.

Weak versus strong normative relativism: The question of universals

Given bounded rationality as a departure point, one can still accept grounded rationality as an additional relativist set of constraints, or reject it. Weak relativism would accept bounded rationality constraints but reject grounded rationality, whereas strong relativism would acknowledge both types of constraints. To reiterate, the question is not whether bounded rationality, the intermediate circle of Figure 18.1(c), should be accepted as a relevant set of constraints on what accounts as normative: that much goes without saying. Indeed in this weak sense, all contributors to the rationality debate can be said to hold a relativist position. The question is whether grounded rationality, or constraints sensitive to epistemic context, should be ignored, while bounded rationality, or more generally universal constraints on normative rationality, should be given a privileged status. Nozick (1993), for example, argues that if norms are particular to epistemic context – place, time, or individual – then they are just accidental generalizations. It is only "nomic universals" – scientific lawlike statements – that can provide viable norms.

In this section I will compare these weak and strong approaches to normative relativism. On the face of it, the idea that cognitive universals should have a special place in our normative considerations, over and above that of contextual systems, seems an appealing and sensible position to take. Weak normative relativism acknowledges relative constraints – recall that bounded rationality itself is relativist to some degree – while avoiding the potentially unsettling implications of strong normative relativism. It even seems to deflect the criticism of epistemic chauvinism, since only universals are taken into account. Suppose, for example, that a principle of noncontradiction is a cognitive rational universal (as suggested by, e.g., Over, 2004). If all humans have access to this principle, and some individuals violate it, no one can accuse us of being epistemic chauvinists if we condemn them as irrational. Weak normative relativism is also congruent with the amalgam solution to the is–ought fallacy presented above. Even if different cultures construct different factual-evaluative compounds, the very fact that such compounds exist seems to be universal.

It seems, then, that weak normative relativism carries all of relativism's blessings and none of its hazards; that while we have to acknowledge bounded rationality, we can safely ignore grounded rationality. However, there are still good reasons to adopt grounded rationality in addition to the bounded sort – that is, good reasons to prefer strong relativism to the weak version, as the next section proposes.

How normative universals vary

The most basic argument in favour of strong relativism, the one examined in the beginning of this section, is the "ought implies can" principle. If there are local constraints on cognitive mechanisms, then they have to be taken into account when setting rational norms, alongside universal constraints: one can hardly be accused of being irrational if one does not use cognitive tools that one cannot access. It makes little difference if a particular cognitive tool cannot be accessed because it is computationally intractable, and therefore inaccessible to all humans, or just not part of the cognitive repertoire of a particular epistemic context, and accessible to some individuals but not others. Can't is can't.

A possible objection here is that "ought implies can" may be a good reason for bounded rationality, but not for grounded rationality, because the intermediate circle reflects genuine processing constraints, whereas the innermost circle reflects mere optional constraints. In other words, there is a qualitative difference between bounded rationality constraints and grounded rationality constraints: the former makes a much more powerful "can't" than the latter. Training, for example, can transcend cultural constraints (Koo & Choi, 2005). Hence, if the rationale is that processing limitations have to be taken into account, and if these limitations are much less severe for epistemic context, then "ought implies can" can be used to justify bounded but not grounded rationality.

However, as pointed out earlier in this section, constraints of bounded rationality, too, may be less rigid than they seem. Recall that in natural language universals there may be exceptions to the rules at least in some cases. In our example of word orders, despite the processing difficulty, some examples of each of the six possible word orders do exist in the world languages. Granted some are very rare, one cannot defend a "cannot" thesis in any absolute sense here. Even finitary boundaries vary across individuals. True, no one lives for ever; nevertheless, finitary limits on computation are not the same for everyone. There are always outliers with exceptional abilities, such as Luria's famous mnemonic genius S (Luria, 2002), whose memory for long lists remained intact decades after memorizing them.

The point is that cognitive universals come in various shapes and degrees. Norenzayan and Heine (2005), for example, distinguish between accessibility universals, functional universals, and existential universals. By their typology, all universals share cognitive tools, but only accessibility universals use the same cognitive tool for the same function and with the same degree of accessibility for all cultures (or, in the terminology suggested here, for all epistemic contexts). Functional universals use the same cognitive tools for the same cognitive function but with varying degrees of accessibility, and existential universals, the weakest type of universals, use the same cognitive tools for different functions.

Even within bounded rationality, then, constraints are graded rather than absolute. If a qualitative line is to be drawn, it might be easier to defend within bounded rationality, than between bounded and grounded rationality. For example, one may claim that only access universals are genuine cognitive constraints that need to be taken into account in bounded rationality. The risk of this approach is that one may be left with an empty set, a theoretical notion that has intension but no extension. As Norenzayan and Heine point out, robust empirical support for such hard-core universals can be rather difficult to come by. There is always the possibility that some culture, some language, some individual, would prove an exception by function or access. The only viable alternative is to give up "ought implies can" altogether, which seems radical and difficult to justify. To maintain "ought implies can", then, grounded rationality should be acknowledged.

The observation that normative constraints vary reflects on another argument in favour of weak relativism, the epistemic chauvinism argument. Recall that weak relativism seems to be no less successful than the strong sort in deflecting such accusations. However, since cognitive constraints vary in their accessibility, epistemic chauvinism is still a non-negligible risk with weak relativism. For example, decontextualizing tools seem to be existential rather than access universals: they are universal in that they are shared by all humans, but some individuals and cultures can access them more easily then others. If we take decontextualization for a normative universal, we still risk epistemic chauvinism towards individuals and cultures that prefer contextualization.

In conclusion, I see little reason to prefer universal norms to culturally sensitive ones. Both need to be acknowledged. This means that all rational norms potentially take part in the normative game. For each individual in each specific epistemic context, the relevant norms would include the ones dictated by that epistemic context relevant to that individual, as well as any universal norms. Normative rationality would still have to be strongly relativistic, even while incorporating universal elements.

Grounded rationality, Panglossianism, and dual processing

With grounded rationality defined, we can now get back to the big rationality debate. Are humans, then, rational? With this question in mind, grounded rationality still seems a rather risky business. One particular pitfall is the Panglossian (or "anything goes") risk; the second and related one is loss of relevance to cognitive architecture. The term "Panglossian" was coined by Gould and Lewontin (1979), after Voltaire's ever-optimistic protagonist Dr Pangloss, and later on adopted by Stanovich (1999) in the context of the rationality debate. (Ironically perhaps for our context, the name "Pangloss" means "all languages".) The Panglossian view maintains that humans are a priori rational, a view introduced into the rationality arena by Cohen (1981), and taken up by such diverse psychological programmes as rational analysis (Oaksford & Chater, 1998, 2007) and the "fast and frugal" approach (Gigerenzer & Selten, 2001; Gigerenzer & Todd, 1999).

The problem with grounded rationality seems to be, first, that it invites a "you are right too" type of Panglossianism; and, even worse, that it seems to invite a particularly unattractive version it. The argument goes like this: surely everyone follows some sort of normative rules, however harebrained. Thus, if we allow room for relativism of this kind, then not only does everyone becomes rational, it is an uninteresting and trivial sort of rationality. Stich (1990) calls this the "anything goes" argument: evaluation is no longer possible because it is entirely subjugated to the particular. Oaksford and Chater (2007) seem to have this type of the "anything goes" argument in mind, when they argue that one can always claim rationality "by cooking up a bizarre set of assumptions about a problem that a person thinks they are solving" (Oaksford & Chater, 2007, p. 31). It seems, then, that if everyone is rational in some context, this obviates the need for a good psychological theory of rationality: the link between rationality and cognition is lost. The challenge, then, is to create a framework for normative relativism that avoids the "anything goes" pitfall. This is what the present section attempts to achieve.

On its own, grounded rationality does not necessarily imply any specific cognitive architecture. However, it is potentially compatible with a dual-processing framework, and with this added set of constraints, the "anything goes" argument loses much of its force. Dual-processing theories vary (for a recent review see Evans, 2008), but they all share a distinction between one family of processes, variably described as rapid, automatic, unconscious, high capacity, and parallel, and another family of processes described as slow, controlled, explicit, high effort, sequential, and correlated with general ability (e.g., Evans, 2006, 2007; Evans & Over, 1996; Sloman, 1996; Stanovich, 1999, 2004; Stanovich & West, 2000). Labels vary too, so here I will adopt the neutral labels "Type 1" and "Type 2" respectively (Evans, 2009b; Frankish & Evans, 2009).

Dual-process theorists tend to conceptualize normative rationality as linked to Type 2 processing, although again, theories vary in the particulars of this connection. While no theory seems to support a one-to-one parallel, what they do share is the idea that Type 2 processes are necessary (though not sufficient) for normative rationality. Thus, according to Evans and Over (1996), one is rational$_2$ when one explicitly conforms to a normative theory: "To possess rationality$_2$, people need to have good reasons for what they are doing, which must be part of an explanation of their action. They have to follow rules sanctioned by a normative theory: this is what makes the reasons 'good' ones" (p. 9). The crucial aspect here is the existence of explicit (hence Type 2) normative rationale; "good", which seems evaluative, means no more and no less than "normative". Stanovich's early conception of normative

rationality is broader, emphasizing individuals and goals rather than processes (Stanovich, 1999, 2004), but he too, champions the crucial role of Type
2 processes in overriding the evolutionary goals that Type 1 processes are
adapted to. Later writings, both sets of authors emphasize that Type 2 processes can fail – for example, Evans (2007) refers to a "fundamental analytic
bias", which Stanovich (2009) calls "serial associative cognition" – but their
earlier approaches viewed them as necessary for normative rationality (as
opposed to mere normative responding).

Of these two approaches, Stanovich's seems to be difficult to reconcile with
grounded rationality, since his approach is explicitly broad – that is, it
encompasses critique of beliefs and desires (Stanovich, 2004). In contrast,
although Evans and Over's (1996) rationality$_2$ is silent on the issue of culture-
sensitive norms, there seems to be nothing to preclude conformity to such
norms from being rational$_2$, so long as this conformity is made explicit. The
advantage of this approach is that it manages to avoid both Panglossian and
epistemic chauvinism concerns at the same time. Let me examine what this
proposal entails. In a chapter for Jonathan's Festschrift book, you just can't
do without an Arsenal example. So here is one:

> Joe and Tom, an engineer and accountant respectively, and ardent
> Arsenal fans both, discuss the latest successful match. The outcome was
> a surprise: Arsenal has won despite the absence of a key player due to
> injury the week before. "I knew all along they would win," says Joe. Tom
> agrees: "They just had to, they have been on a winning streak since the
> season started," he adds.

> Thousands of miles away, Haneul and Chul, students of Oriental
> medicine in a prestigious Korean university (Koo & Choi, 2005) and avid
> followers of English football, discuss the same match: why has Bendtner
> seemed out of form? Chul feels that there must be many complex reasons.
> Haneul agrees. "The wise man does not judge or divide," she quotes from
> the *Tao Te Ching* (Lao Tzu, 2001, p. 102).

All four people contextualize, but they vary in explicit conformity to cultural
norms. Haneul and Chul both conform to holistic cultural norms by weighing complex contextual causes to performance.[5] However, only Haneul has an
explicit reason for her judgement. By explicitly following Taoism, Haneul
conforms to a system that is normative for her particular epistemic context.
This context includes her holistic culture as well as her training in Oriental
medicine (recall that responses of psychology students in a comparably pres-
tigious Korean university were indistinguishable from those of Western participants; Koo & Choi, 2005). By this view, then, Haneul is rational$_2$, but Chul,
who follows the same rules implicitly and with no apparent reflection, is not.
Haneul is no less rational$_2$ than, say, a participant from a decontextualizing
culture taking part in a conjunction fallacy (Tversky & Kahneman, 1983)

experiment, who estimates that Linda is more likely to be a banker than a feminist banker, and gives an explicit probabilistic explanation.

Now compare Haneul and Chul with Joe and Tom. The latter two fall prey to hindsight ("I knew it all along") bias, which falls outside the decontextualizing rational norms of their professions. However, Joe does so implicitly, whereas Tom has an explicit rationale. The rationale, however, is not "good": a version of the "hot hand fallacy", it does not conform to a culturally relevant expert norm. Explicit but non-normative, Tom's explanation falls into the category of what Stanovich recently called "contaminated mindware" (Stanovich, 2009). This means that neither Joe nor Tom is rational$_2$.

In an open peer commentary discussion of *Rationality and Reasoning* (Evans & Over, 1997; Over & Evans, 1997), Evans and Over clarified that they considered rationality$_1$ as basic: rationality$_2$ is justified by providing good means of achieving goals (Over & Evans, 1997, pp. 255–256). Prima facie, it seems that for Haneul, this is indeed the case: by explicitly conforming to the principles of the *Tao Te Ching*, she can achieve everyday goals, such as success in her chosen profession and esteem of her peers. She can even achieve her epistemic goals; spiritual harmony, for example.

Evans and Over's suggestion, that normative rationality has to include explicit normative reasons, is rather attractive, and as we just saw, perfectly compatible with a relativist solution, so long as we include sensitivity to epistemic context as a caveat. The main attraction is that it allows us to distinguish between Haneul, who is rational$_2$, and, say, a tree, which may be in perfect spiritual harmony with the universe but cannot be said to be normatively rational. This is an extension of the original suggestion, which distinguished between the rational$_1$ behaviour of a bumble-bee and consequentialist, rational$_2$ decision making (Evans & Over, 1996, p. 148). Implicit rule conformity does not make one rational$_2$, and this applies to spiritual harmony just as it applies to consequential decision making. Explicit rule following does so, and again this applies just as well to spiritual harmony. The fact that some of us may strongly reject spiritual harmony as an epistemic goal is entirely beside the point, if we opt for normative relativism.

Note that this solution obviates Panglossianism worries. One can fail to be normatively rational by failing to conform explicitly to a normative system; the addition is that this normative system has to be relevant to the individual within her or his epistemic context (in our example, this is a combination of professional and geographical context). Thus, Haneul and Tom both respond contextually and explicitly, but only Haneul is normatively rational, since only she conforms to an epistemically relevant system.

Two caveats are in order. One is that normative responses should not be taken as indication for explicit processing – what Elqayam and Evans dubbed "ought–is fallacy". This is still true for the relativist version of normative rationality. The second, and perhaps more interesting caveat, is that what falls under the heading of explicit processing can vary considerably: it would be analytic for decontextualizing epistemic contexts, but it may well be holistic for contextualizing cultures and individuals (Buchtel & Norenzayan, 2009). This is a strength of grounded rationality. Consider the case of fundamental attribution error (correspondence bias), the tendency to attribute other people's behaviours to their disposition and personality, discounting the effects of context. People in decontextualizing cultures are much more likely to commit this particular error, since they focus on the object rather than its environment (e.g., Choi, Nisbett, & Norenzayan, 1999). Decontextualization in itself, then, does not guarantee inoculation against bias, in the conventional absolutist sense used by psychologists.

In conclusion, a dual-processing framework of rationality does not necessarily acknowledge grounded rationality concerns; indeed, the broad version advocated by Stanovich seems to contradict it. However, processing-based versions such as Evans and Over's seem to be potentially compatible. From a grounded rationality point of view, the advantage in adopting a dual-processing framework seems to be a more rounded and psychologically relevant perspective, and avoiding the unpalatable "anything goes" version of the Panglossian position, that humans are necessarily and unfailingly rational.

Grounded rationality and the descriptive agenda

Before I wind up this discussion, there is one last thing that needs to be examined, and that is the relationship between the grounded rationality framework presented in this chapter, and the descriptivist agenda defended by Elqayam and Evans (2010). A possible objection to grounded rationality is that it has an implicit descriptivist agenda: that it pulls the carpet from underneath normative rationality. With a relativist framework, what constitutes normative rationality is no longer an ought question. It becomes a purely descriptive question: the question of which normative system holds for a particular agent in a particular epistemic context, and to what extent they satisfy it. Ultimately, then, there is no such thing as *normative* relativism. The ought is replaced with an is.

There are two possible answers here. One is that, even with a relativist framework, evaluation is still possible. As we saw in the previous section, even with a grounded rationality framework, people can still fail to be normatively rational in a variety of nontrivial ways. Stich (1990) defended a similar argument, proposing that agents can still fail to be rational within a relativist context, if they fail to adhere to their own standards. Hence, even with a relativist framework of the sort inherent in grounded rationality, normative evaluation is still attainable to those who want it.

The other answer, however, is precisely the opposite, and that is the answer that I tend to favour, at least as far as the empirical study of human thought is concerned. I do not deny that relativism does weaken the ought in normative rationality, and ultimately replaces it with an is question. However, such an outcome, far from being a detriment, is actually quite desirable for psychology. Elqayam and Evans (2010) conclude with an outline a descriptivist agenda for the psychology of reasoning and judgement and decision making. Such a framework, they argue, proved beneficial to the development of linguistics as a mature science, and may carry similar benefits for psychology. The same observation is still relevant here.

In conclusion, while grounded rationality is an anathema to the absolutist concerns of normativism, it still allows some scope for normative research questions. Within empirical psychological science, grounded rationality sits particularly well with a descriptivist agenda for the psychology of human thought. By now, I hope I have convinced you at least that normative relativism, in the form of grounded rationality, should be taken seriously, and that it can provide an interesting and productive framework for normative rationality and the associated empirical paradigms of human thought. Perhaps not everyone is right, but what is right and what is wrong cannot be taken out of context.

Notes

1 I will not address the related though separable issue of moral relativism (for a recent review see Gowans, 2008), although I will draw on it occasionally.
2 The term is inspired by (rather than directly draws on) Barsalou's (2008) notion of grounded cognition.
3 By cross-cultural I mean any study that systematically compares two cultures or more. This covers what Norenzayan and Heine (2005) call two-culture and three-culture or triangulation studies, as well as their genuine cross-cultural studies which cover multiple cultures.
4 Some readers may be wondering where the linguistic equivalent of Figure 18.1(c) has disappeared to. That is, if 18.1(b) is descriptive of human thought, and 18.1(c) is prescriptive, why does Figure 18.1 include no representation of normative linguistic considerations, only the descriptive ones represented in 18.1(a)? The answer is simple: Modern linguistic theory is concerned very little with normative considerations, a tradition that goes back as far as de Saussure (1959).
5 By doing so they avoid the fundamental attribution error. They have not, for example, maintained that Bendtner always underperforms when he is under pressure.

Acknowledgements

The research reported in this chapter was partially supported by research travel funding from De Montfort University to the author. A preliminary sketch of the arguments in this chapter was presented at the London Workshop on Reasoning in honour of Jonathan Evans's 60th birthday, held in Birkbeck College in August 2008. I thank Jonathan Evans for detailed comments on previous versions. Lastly, my heartfelt thanks, as always, go to Jonathan Evans, for inspiration, for mentorship, for friendship, for challenges and disputes; and for gallons of coffee.

References

Barsalou, L. W. (2008). Grounded cognition. *Annual Review of Psychology, 59,* 617–645.

Buchtel, E., & Norenzayan, A. (2009). Thinking across cultures: Implications for dual processes. In J. St B. T. Evans & K. Frankish (Eds.), *In two minds: Dual processes and beyond* (pp. 217–238). Oxford, UK: Oxford University Press.

Carruthers, P. (2006). *The architecture of the mind.* Oxford, UK: Oxford University Press.

Cherniak, C. (1986). *Minimal rationality.* Cambridge, MA: MIT Press.

Choi, I., Koo, M., & Choi, J. A. (2007). Individual differences in analytic versus holistic thinking. *Personality and Social Psychology Bulletin, 33,* 691–705.

Choi, I., Nisbett, R. E., & Norenzayan, A. (1999). Causal attribution across cultures: Variation and universality. *Psychological Bulletin, 125,* 47–63.

Chomsky, N. (1965). *Aspects of the theory of syntax.* Cambridge, MA: MIT Press.

Cohen, L. J. (1981). Can human irrationality be experimentally demonstrated? *Behavioral and Brain Sciences, 4,* 317–370.

Comrie, B. (1981). *Language universals and linguistic typology: Syntax and morphology.* Oxford, UK: Blackwell.

de Saussure, F. (1959). *Course in general linguistics.* New York: McGraw-Hill. (Original work published 1916)

Elqayam, S. (2007). Normative rationality and the is–ought fallacy. In S. Vosniadou, D. Kayser, & A. Protopapas (Eds.), *Proceedings of the second European cognitive science conference* (pp. 294–299). Hove, UK: Lawrence Erlbaum Associates Ltd.

Elqayam, S., & Evans, J. St B. T. (2010). Substracting 'ought' from 'is': Descriptivism versus normativism in the study of human thinking. *Unpublished manuscript, De Montfort University.*

Epstein, S. (1994). Integration of the cognitive and the psychodynamic unconscious. *American Psychologist, 49,* 709–724.

Epstein, S., Pacini, R., Denes-Raj, V., & Heier, H. (1996). Individual differences in intuitive-experiential and analytical-rational thinking styles. *Journal of Personality and Social Psychology, 71,* 390–405.

Evans, J. St B. T. (1993). Bias and rationality. In K. I. Manktelow & D. E. Over (Eds.), *Rationality: Psychological and philosophical perspectives* (pp. 6–30). London: Routledge.

Evans, J. St B. T. (2006). The heuristic–analytic theory of reasoning: Extension and evaluation. *Psychonomic Bulletin & Review, 13,* 378–395.

Evans, J. St B. T. (2007). *Hypothetical thinking: Dual processes in reasoning and judgement.* Hove, UK: Psychology Press.

Evans, J. St B. T. (2008). Dual-processing accounts of reasoning, judgment, and social cognition. *Annual Review of Psychology, 59,* 255–278.

Evans, J. St B. T. (2009a). Does rational analysis stand up to rational analysis? *Behavioral and Brain Sciences, 32,* 88–89.

Evans, J. St B. T. (2009b). How many dual process theories do we need: One, two or many? In J. St B. T. Evans & K. Frankish (Eds.), *In two minds: Dual processes and beyond* (pp. 33–54). Oxford, UK: Oxford University Press.

Evans, J. St B. T., & Over, D. E. (1996). *Rationality and reasoning.* Hove, UK: Psychology Press.

Evans, J. St B. T., & Over, D. E. (1997). Rationality in reasoning: The case of deductive competence. *Current Psychology of Cognition, 16,* 3–38.

Evans, N., & Levinson, S. (2009). The myth of language universals: Language diversity and its importance for cognitive science. *Behavioral and Brain Sciences*, *32*, 429–448.

Frankena, W. (1939). The naturalistic fallacy. *Mind*, *48*, 464–477.

Frankish, K., & Evans, J. St B. T. (2009). The duality of mind: A historical perspective. In J. St B. T. Evans & K. Frankish (Eds.), *In two minds: Dual processes and beyond*. Oxford, UK: Oxford University Press.

Gigerenzer, G., & Selten, R. (2001). *Bounded rationality: The adaptive toolbox*. Cambridge, MA: MIT Press.

Gigerenzer, G., & Todd, P. M. (1999). *Simple heuristics that make us smart*. Oxford, UK: Oxford University Press.

Gottwald, S. (2001). *A treatise on many-valued logics* (Studies in logic and computation, Vol. 9). Baldock, UK: Research Studies Press Ltd.

Gould, S. J., & Lewontin, R. C. (1979). The spandrels of San Marco and the Panglossian paradigm: A critique of the adaptationist programme. *Proceedings of the Royal Society of London, Series B*, *205*, 581–598.

Gowans, C. (2008). Moral relativism. In E. N. Zalta (Ed.), *Stanford encyclopedia of philosophy* (Winter 2008 edition). Stanford, CA: Stanford University. Retrieved February 28, 2010, from http://plato.stanford.edu/entries/moral-relativism/

Greenberg, J. H. (1963). Some universals of grammar with particular reference to the order of meaningful elements. In J. H. Greenberg (Ed.), *Universals of language* (pp. 58–90). Cambridge, MA: MIT Press.

Greenberg, M. J. (2008). *Euclidean and non-Euclidean geometries* (4th ed.). New York: W. H. Freeman.

Harris, R. (1980). *The language-makers*. London: Duckworth.

Hawkins, J. A. (1983). *Word order universals*. New York: Academic Press.

Hofstadter, R. (1955). *Social Darwinism in American thought*. Boston, MA: Beacon Press.

Hudson, W. D. (1969). *The is–ought question: A collection of papers on the central problem in moral philosophy*. London: Macmillan.

Hume, D. (2000). *A treatise on human nature*. Oxford, UK: Clarendon Press. (Original work published 1739–1740)

Jackendoff, R. (2002). *Foundations of language: Brain, meaning, grammar, evolution*. Oxford, UK: Oxford University Press.

Kant, I. (1932). *Critique of pure reason*. London: Macmillan. (Original work published 1787)

Koo, M., & Choi, I. (2005). Becoming a holistic thinker: Training effect of oriental medicine on reasoning. *Personality and Social Psychology Bulletin*, *31*, 1264–1272.

Lao Tzu (2001). *The way of life: Dao de jing* (R. B. Blakney, trans.). New York: New American Library.

Lloyd, G. (1996). Science in antiquity: The Greek and Chinese cases and their relevance to the problems of culture and cognition. In D. R. Olson & N. Torrance (Eds.), *Modes of thought: Explorations in culture and cognition* (pp. 15–33). Cambridge, UK: Cambridge University Press.

Luria, A. R. (2002). *The mind of a mnemonist: A little book about a vast memory*. Cambridge, UK: Harvard University Press.

Moore, G. E. (1903). *Principia ethica*. New York: Cambridge University Press.

Nichols, S. (2004). Folk concepts and intuitions: From philosophy to cognitive science. *Trends in Cognitive Sciences*, *8*, 514–518.

Nickerson, R. S. (2008). *Aspects of rationality: Reflections on what it means to be rational and whether we are.* New York: Psychology Press.

Nisbett, R., Peng, K., Choi, I., & Norenzayan, A. (2001). Culture and systems of thought: Holistic vs analytic cognition. *Psychological Review, 108,* 291–310.

Norenzayan, A., & Heine, S. J. (2005). Psychological universals: What are they and how can we know? *Psychological Bulletin, 131,* 763–784.

Norenzayan, A., Smith, E. E., Kim, B. J., & Nisbett, R. E. (2002). Cultural preferences for formal versus intuitive reasoning. *Cognitive Science, 26,* 653–684.

Nozick, R. (1993). *The nature of rationality.* Princeton, NJ: Princeton University Press.

Oaksford, M., & Chater, N. (1998). *Rationality in an uncertain world.* Hove, UK: Psychology Press.

Oaksford, M., & Chater, N. (2007). *Bayesian rationality: The probabilistic approach to human reasoning.* Oxford, UK: Oxford University Press.

Oaksford, M., & Chater, N. (2009). The uncertain reasoner: Bayes, logic, and rationality. *Behavioral and Brain Sciences, 32,* 69–120.

Olson, D. R., & Torrance, N. (1996). *Modes of thought: Explorations in culture and cognition.* Cambridge, UK: Cambridge University Press.

Over, D. E. (2004). Rationality and the normative/descriptive distinction. In D. J. Koehler & N. Harvey (Eds.), *Blackwell handbook of judgment and decision making* (pp. 3–18). Oxford, UK: Blackwell.

Over, D. E., & Evans, J. St B. T. (1997). Two cheers for deductive competence. *Current Psychology of Cognition, 16,* 255–278.

Rescher, N. (1969). *Many-valued logics.* New York: McGraw-Hill.

Saunders, C. E., & Over, D. E. (2009). In two minds about rationality? In J. St B. T. Evans & K. Frankish (Eds.), *In two minds: Dual processes and beyond* (pp. 317–334). Oxford, UK: Oxford University Press.

Schroyens, W. (2009). On is and ought: Levels of analysis and the descriptive versus normative analysis of human reasoning. *Behavioral and Brain Sciences, 32,* 101–102.

Schurz, G. (1997). *The is–ought problem: An investigation in philosophical logic.* Dordrecht: Kluwer.

Searle, J. R. (1964). How to derive "ought" from "is". *Philosophical Review, 73,* 43–58.

Simon, H. A. (1957). *Models of man: Social and rational.* New York: Wiley.

Simon, H. A. (1982). *Models of bounded rationality.* Cambridge, MA: MIT Press.

Simon, H. A. (1983). *Reason in human affairs.* Stanford, CA: Stanford University Press.

Sloman, S. A. (1996). The empirical case for two systems of reasoning. *Psychological Bulletin, 119,* 3–22.

Stanovich, K. E. (1999). *Who is rational? Studies of individual differences in reasoning.* Mahwah, NJ: Lawrence Elrbaum Associates, Inc.

Stanovich, K. E. (2004). *The robot's rebellion: Finding meaning in the age of Darwin.* Chicago: Chicago University Press.

Stanovich, K. E. (2009). Distinguishing the reflective, algorithmic, and autonomous minds: Is it time for a tri-process theory? In J. St B. T. Evans & K. Frankish (Eds.), *In two minds: Dual processes and beyond.* Oxford, UK: Oxford University Press.

Stanovich, K. E., & West, R. F. (2000). Individual differences in reasoning: Implications for the rationality debate. *Behavioral and Brain Sciences, 23,* 645–726.

Stein, E. (1996). *Without good reason: The rationality debate in philosophy and cognitive science*. Oxford, UK: Oxford University Press.

Stich, S. P. (1990). *The fragmentation of reason: Preface to a pragmatic theory of cognitive evaluation*. Cambridge, MA: MIT Press.

Tversky, A., & Kahneman, D. (1983). Extensional vs intuitive reasoning: The conjunction fallacy in probability judgment. *Psychological Review*, *90*, 293–315.

Weinberg, J. M., Nichols, S., & Stich, S. P. (2006). Normativity and epistemic intuitions. In R.Viale, D. Andler, & L. A. Hirschfeld (Eds.), *Biological and cultural bases of human inference* (pp. 191–222). Mahwah, NJ: Lawrence Erlbaum Associates, Inc.

Weinstein, D. (2002). Herbert Spencer. In E. N. Zalta (Ed.), *Stanford encyclopedia of philosophy* (Winter 2002 edition). Stanford, CA: Stanford University. Retrieved February 28, 2010 from http://plato.stanford.edu/entries/spencer/

Williams, B. (1985). *Ethics and the limits of philosophy*. Cambridge, MA: Harvard University Press.

Yama, H., Nishioka, M., Horishita, T., Kawasaki, Y., & Taniguchi, J. (2007). A dual process model for cultural differences in thought. *Mind and Society*, *6*, 143–172.

Part V

Perspectives on thinking and reasoning

19 The psychology of reasoning

Reflections on four decades of research

Jonathan St B. T. Evans

University of Plymouth

In this chapter, I shall look back over the four decades in which I have been actively involved in research into the psychology of reasoning, from the 1970s onwards. This will be a rather informal history, as I try to plot the nature of the changes and development over this period, but also record the ways in which my own work and thinking about the subject developed. Young academics and those new to a field can only hope to know its history by reading back through the literature. It is a very different thing to have lived through the history as an active participant, reading the literature as it was published and interacting with the main protagonists. It is that unique perspective that I hope to convey here.

The pre-history: Psychology of reasoning prior to 1970

I actually entered the field as a PhD student in October 1969, working at University College London (UCL) with Peter Wason as my principal supervisor and with some additional support from Phil Johnson-Laird. During the period of my PhD studies the two of them completed their famous book, *Psychology of Reasoning: Structure and Content* (Wason & Johnson-Laird, 1972). Peter Wason had a particularly strong influence on the early development of my work, as I have recorded elsewhere (Evans, 2005) but of course he also shaped the foundations of the modern study of the psychology of reasoning, particularly with the work he published in the 1960s. But he did not actually invent the field, and it is worthwhile to note briefly some earlier historical influences. An excellent source for these – if you can still obtain it – is a book edited by Wason and Johnson-Laird (1968). Some account of this work can also be found in my first textbook on reasoning (Evans, 1982).

The first experimental papers on the psychology of reasoning of which I am aware were published before World War II and used categorical syllogisms (Sells, 1936; Wilkins, 1928; Woodworth & Sells, 1935). This started a tradition of work on syllogistic reasoning in the USA that continued steadily thereafter, including studies in the late 1950s and 1960s in a parallel with the work that Peter Wason developed on conditional reasoning in the same period (see Evans, 1982). What is interesting about the early papers is that they demonstrate cognitive biases in reasoning, similar to those that were to exercise authors greatly from the 1970s onwards. Wilkins (1928) was the first to demonstrate the belief-bias effect in syllogistic reasoning – something that led to a number of papers in the social psychological literature prior to the re-launch of the paradigm in cognitive psychology by Evans, Barston, and Pollard (1983), of which more later. Woodworth and Sells claimed evidence for an "atmosphere effect" in which participants supposedly endorsed conclusions with similar mood to the premises, regardless of their logical validity. This resonates with the phenomenon of matching bias that I first published in the 1970s and both proved controversial for the same reason: they appeared to portray people as simple minded and irrational.

By the time Peter Wason got his own research programme going on the psychology of reasoning, however, he was railing against the forces of rationalism. In particular, Wason objected strongly to the theory of Inhelder and Piaget (1958) that portrayed a developmental sequence in which adults became formal logical reasoners. Wason believed instead that people were illogical and irrational, and that his two famous reasoning problems provided clear evidence of this. These were, of course, the "2 4 6" problem (Wason, 1960) and the infamous four-card selection task (Wason, 1966). The rationalist camp was also highly influenced at that time by the writings of Mary Henle, whose famous paper (Henle, 1962) was included in the Wason and Johnson-Laird collection of papers published in 1968. Henle argued that people were invariably logical unless they "failed to accept the logical task". Otherwise, they erred only because they interpreted the reasoning problems differently from that intended by the experimenter: for example, by adding, subtracting or changing premises. The logicist positions of Piaget and Henle in a sense legitimized the deductive reasoning paradigm, because it seemed important to establish that people untrained in formal logic, could nevertheless reason logically (Evans, 2002).

During the 1960s, Wason ran a number of experiments with the "2 4 6" and especially the selection task, the results of which – he claimed – showed how deeply irrational most people are. Wason accepted logic as a normative theory of reasoning and endorsed Popper's (1959) logicist philosophy of science while demonstrating, apparently, that his participants were chronically disposed to verify rather than falsify their hypotheses. However, he did not have things all his own way. He was critiqued by one of his formal pupils (Wetherick, 1962, 1970) and found it difficult to publish in American journals, sending the bulk of his papers to the *British Journal of Psychology* and the *Quarterly Journal of Experimental Psychology*. The value of his work was never fully recognized by his own university either, as he ended his career with the rank of Reader, a British title that confers distinction in research but below the level of a full professor.

The 1970s: The rise of cognitive biases

The Wason and Johnson-Laird 1972 book, *Psychology of Reasoning*, was successful and widely read. It established certain "facts" about reasoning that became widely known beyond the immediate research field. One of these was that thematic content facilitates reasoning. This was first discovered when a research assistant of Peter Wason's, who was at UCL at the same time that I was a PhD student, tried a realistic version of the task. The usual format was to ask people to check the truth of a statement such as "If a card has a vowel on one side then it has an even number on the other side", with cards showing (say) E, T, 4, and 1. The answer that Wason always regarded as correct was to choose the E and the 1, because only a card with a vowel on one side and an odd number on the other could disprove the statement. These are the p and not-q cards for a statement of the form "if p then q". Diana Shapiro used a version that became known as the "towns and transport" materials. Each card represented a journey with a destination on one side and a means of transport on the other. For a rule "Every time I go to Manchester, I travel by car", the four cards showed Manchester, Leeds, car and train. The correct answer – Manchester and train (p and not-q) – was chosen significantly more often than on the abstract version (Wason & Shapiro, 1971). Wason was at first disconcerted by this result that appeared to contradict a series of papers he had recently published showing that the difficulty of the selection task was invariant across many procedural changes. However, he soon decided that the difference between abstract and thematic versions was of great psychological significance, as it was portrayed in the 1972 book.

The thematic facilitation effect did not rest on this study alone but was supported by another study run before the 1972 book was published (Johnson-Laird, Legrenzi, & Legrenzi, 1972). In this version, envelopes were substituted for cards and a postal rule used. Although Italian lire were used instead of pence as the stamp values, the rule was compatible with one then used in England: sealed envelopes required higher value postage than unsealed envelopes. Participants correctly turned over sealed envelopes and those with lower value stamps. With hindsight, it is ironic that these two studies formed the basis for one of the most famous claims in the 1972 book. The towns and transport materials of Wason and Shapiro were subsequently shown to have a weak effect, which often failed to replicate in later studies. The facilitation by the envelopes problem did turn out to be a reliable effect, but only for participants who had actually experienced the postal rule. Both problems were exposed in an excellent paper by Griggs and Cox (1982), following a failure to replicate thematic facilitation by Manktelow and Evans (1979) but the true nature of the facilitation effect on the Wason selection task was not understood until the 1990s.

The other major message of the 1972 book was that people were illogical and chronically biased in much of their reasoning. I have named this decade as the "rise of cognitive biases" because of the striking parallel between the message that Peter Wason was giving the world with that of Danny Kahneman and Amos Tversky. Like most researchers working in the deductive-reasoning tradition, I was very interested in their work on statistical reasoning and judgement, having previously seen little connection with the study of judgement and decision making. Their seminal papers on judgement by availability (Tversky & Kahneman, 1973) and representativeness (Kahneman & Tversky, 1972) were published in the early 1970s and the "heuristics and biases" research programme was launched. This work immediately caught my attention and inspired the first of an occasional series of papers on this topic (Evans & Dusoir, 1977) that I have published over my career. Just as Wason challenged the logicism of Piaget and Henle, so Kahneman and Tversky's work attacked the late 1960s consensus that "man" was a good intuitive statistician (Peterson & Beach, 1967). By the end of the decade, Kahneman and Tversky (1979) had revolutionized the field of economics as their new prospect theory permanently eclipsed the standard game theory account of risky decision making.

My own work in the 1970s was concerned mostly with demonstrating cognitive biases in conditional reasoning. In my PhD studies, I devised what has become known as the "negations paradigm", introducing negative components into either the antecedent or consequent of conditional statements. I cannot really recall why I did this now, but it led to discovery of two new biases: a double-negation effect with conditional inferences (Evans, 1972b) and "matching bias" on the truth-table task (Evans, 1972a), later extended to the selection task (Evans & Lynch, 1973). Research on both of these biases has featured in all the subsequent decades that this review covers. Matching bias was a striking result and an effect that could be used to facilitate performance on the abstract selection task. When given a statement such as "if there is an A one side of the card, then there is *not* a 3 on the other side", most people choose the A and 3, which is logically correct. However, it seemed that they did this only because these were the cards mentioned in the rule.

The 1970s also saw the first work on dual-process theories of reasoning, which have become so fashionable in the past 10 years. I collaborated briefly but productively with Peter Wason, leading to two papers. In the first of these, entitled "Dual processes in reasoning?" (Wason & Evans, 1975), we addressed the question of why participants apparently matched on the selection task, getting some problems right and others wrong as a result. Introspective reports were always consistent with the choices made, so that when matching bias facilitated the correct choice, they sounded very logical. People would say they were turning over cards to check if the rule was falsified. However, when matching produced the usual error, people said instead that they were looking for hidden sides that would *verify* the conditional statement. Wason and Evans concluded that the verbal reports were rationalizations – or confabulations as they are commonly called nowadays. (For a recent study that replicates the main findings of this paper, see Lucas & Ball, 2005.) Two years later, the highly influential critique of introspective reports by Nisbett and Wilson (1977) was published, with an essentially similar argument based on a much wider range of evidence in cognitive and social psychology. Like us, they believed that participants had no special or direct access to their cognitive processes, and when asked to explain their behaviour tended to theorize and self-interpret. I see no reason to change this view, now, as evidence has accumulated since to support this position (Carruthers, 2009; Wilson, 2002). However, while confabulation is an issue for the dual-process theory, it is not the main thrust of contemporary research. Other key elements of the story developed in the 1980s, as we shall see.

The 1980s: A decade of theoretical development

A great deal happened in the 1980s that provides the basis of much of the psychology of reasoning as we know the field today. The most influential single event, without doubt, was the publication of Phil Johnson-Laird's book *Mental Models* (Johnson-Laird, 1983). This was a work of cognitive science and dealt with issues in linguistics and logic as well as psychology. There was much discussion of language comprehension, the distinction between implicit and explicit models, imagery, consciousness, and so on. However, the most influential part from the viewpoint of the psychology of reasoning was the attack on mental logic and the alternative proposal of semantic mental models as the basis for deduction.

Martin Braine (1978) had earlier proposed that "natural logics", as philosophers call them, provided that basis for human deductive reasoning. Such logics are made up of a set of inference rules. Mental logics, as they became known, were supposedly sets of rules that people carried in their heads. When faced with the need to make deductions, they would strip away the content to reveal the abstract nature of the underlying propositions, reason by iterative application of relevant rules, and then finally restore the content to the conclusions drawn. This approach remained influential for many years to come (Braine & O'Brien, 1998) and was later given computational substance by the working computer programs of Lance Rips (1983, 1994). Johnson-Laird was even an advocate of this approach himself at one time. However, in his 1983 book, he attacked mental logic as a false doctrine and launched the soon to become massive research programme on mental model theory.

Like most good theories, it is simple in essence. Johnson-Laird's mental models are representations of states of the world. Hence, in general, they are truth verifiable, in that any given model is either true or false with respect to the world state it purports to represent. In my view, this is an essential feature for the semantic principle of deduction that Johnson-Laird proposed: *an argument is valid if there is no counterexample to it.*[1] The psychological account was fairly straightforward. Given some premises, people formulate a mental model to represent the state of affairs that they describe. Any nontrivial and novel proposition that emerges from this model is a potential conclusion. However, to prove its validity, people need to conduct a search for counterexamples. That is, they must look for alternative models of the premises that do not support the putative conclusion. If no such models (counterexamples) can be found, the conclusion is deemed to be valid. Unlike the mental logic theory that needed to bolt on explanations of error, bias, and content effects to a core competence theory of deduction, mental model theory envisaged the fallibility of human inference from the start. People had limited working-memory capacities and hence might fail to consider alternative models of the premises. Search for counterexamples might be weak or biased by prior belief. Models may be biased in the process of construction and not fully represent the world as intended, and so on. The scope of psychological theorizing was endless and the theory was rapidly applied to a wide range of reasoning tasks by Johnson-Laird, his main collaborator of the time, Ruth Byrne, and many others. By the time of the publication of his next book, *Deduction* (Johnson-Laird & Byrne, 1991), a large body of experimental evidence had been accrued to support a number of specific applications of the theory.

While hugely influential, model theory was not the only show in town. Work on the Wason selection task continued, with Wason publishing his last major paper on the task (Wason & Green, 1984). Richard Griggs (e.g., Griggs, 1983) pursued the thematic facilitation effect and other aspects of the selection task throughout the 1980s and beyond as well as working on Wason's less influential THOG problem (Wason & Brooks, 1979). Research at this time focused on the thematic facilitation effect and its exact causes. Did the rule need to be familiar or just realistic? Was a short context or scenario needed to obtain the effect? Did it matter whether instructions mentioned falsification or not? And so on. Johnson-Laird was not much interested in the selection task, and so this work mostly proceeded in parallel with the new paradigm. Eventually, he did publish a mental models account of the task (Johnson-Laird & Byrne, 1991), if only for completeness. The task also acquired brand new theories in this decade – that of pragmatic reasoning schemas (Cheng & Holyoak, 1985; Cheng, Holyoak, Nisbett, & Oliver, 1986) and the born to be controversial evolutionary account of Cosmides and Tooby (Cosmides, 1989). For the first time, reasoning researchers were exposed to the idea that reasoning might reflect domain specific cognitive modules that had evolved for the purpose of controlling our social exchanges. Extraordinarily, however, the key insight that realistic versions of the task shifted the problem to one framed in terms of deontic rather than indicative logic, was not to appear until the early 1990s (Manktelow & Over, 1991).

In 1982, I published my first book, which was essentially a high-level textbook on the psychology of deductive reasoning (Evans, 1982). However, it also contained a fair amount of theoretical argument, including the "two factor" theory which was one of the precursors of modern dual-process theory. This was more of a descriptive than a cognitive model at this stage. Essentially, I suggested that reasoning data reflected a combination of "logical" or "interpretational" factors on the one hand, and "response biases" on the other. None of these terms seem appropriate now. However, from a purely descriptive point of view, I was right to state that participants' responses to reasoning tasks partly reflect the logic of the task as instructed and partly reflect nonlogical processes and biases. I had formalized this as an additive statistical model (Evans, 1977; for a very recent and sophistocated development of this approach, see Klauer, Stahl, & Erdfelder, 2007). Perhaps the best known implementation of the idea, however, was the belief bias paper of Evans et al. (1983). While postulating parallel influences of logical and nonlogical processes, this well-cited paper also provided some development in the cognitive basis for dual-process theories.

Evans et al. (1983) is usually cited as the starting point for the modern literature on the belief-bias effect in the psychology of reasoning. In fact, this research was run as a response to the paper of Revlin, Leirer, Yopp, and Yopp (1980), now rarely cited. Revlin was an author who favoured a rationalist perspective on reasoning and appeared to dislike the idea of cognitive biases. In this paper, he and his colleagues actually did demonstrate belief bias, but tried strongly to play it down in the discussion. I became interested in the phenomenon and read the back literature on it, mostly published in social psychological journals. I decided that most of the studies were poorly designed (see Evans, 1982) and we made the topic the major focus for the PhD work of Julie Barston (later Allen). Evans et al. (1983) is well cited because we demonstrated a robust belief-bias effect with all relevant controls in place. In fact, the paper shows three findings, which since have proved highly reliable: (1) people endorse more valid than invalid arguments; (2) they endorse (as valid) more arguments with believable and unbelievable conclusions – the belief-bias effect; and (3) the two factors interact, such that belief bias is stronger for invalid arguments. We also analysed protocols and performed other analyses that showed that what we termed the conflict between logic and belief was *within* participants. This was very important in the later development of thought about dual-process theory. Participants giving a logical answer more often referred to the premises in their protocols, while those giving a belief-based response typically mentioned only the conclusion. But these were not two different kinds of people. The same participant would show one pattern on some trials, and a different pattern on others. Belief bias was soon given an account within the fashionable mental model theory (Oakhill, Johnson-Laird, & Garnham, 1989).

Up to this point my thinking about two factors was as parallel influences. For reasons I cannot entirely remember, I took the nascent dual-process theory in a different, sequential direction with the publication of the heuristic–analytic theory of reasoning (Evans, 1984, 1989). These were probably not the best terms to use, but they have stuck and are commonly used in the field to the present day. Heuristic processes were conceived of as fast and preconscious, delivering cognitive representations of "relevant" content for subsequent (slow, conscious, potentially logical) analytic processing. The general idea was that fast, preconscious processes automatically contextualized the task prompting default responses that often resulted in cognitive biases. These might or might not be overridden by subsequent slow and effortful reasoning. One of the accounts of belief bias proposed by Evans et al. (1983) – the *selective scrutiny* model – was also of this type. The 1984 journal publication of the theory provoked little interest, but it became well known following the publication of my 1989 book *Bias in Human Reasoning*.

On reflection, the 1980s was a decade of considerable advance in the psychology of reasoning. At the theoretical level it saw the launch of mental model theory, heuristic–analytic theory and evolutionary accounts of reasoning, as well as significant development of the mental logic approach. It was also a decade that marked considerable understanding of the dependence of reasoning processing upon content and context. There was much work on content effects in the Wason selection task and, as mentioned, the essential features of the belief-bias effect in syllogistic reasoning were also established. As if this were not enough, the decade also saw the launch of the great rationality debate, when the philosopher Jonathan Cohen published his major attack on bias research in the psychology of reasoning and decision making (Cohen, 1981). We were introduced to three major criticisms of the idea that such research showed people to be biased, and therefore irrational (see also Evans, 1993; Stanovich, 1999). Experiments might be unrepresentative of real-world situations, participants might interpret the task differently from the way in which the experimenter intended, and experimenters may be applying the wrong normative theory. As with other significant work in the 1980s, the rationality debate has continued to influence thinking about the topic to the current day.

The 1990s: A decade of transition

The 1990s started out with the mental model theory at its peak of popularity and dominance. Even I and my colleagues in the Plymouth reasoning group got drawn into the paradigm and wrote papers testing model theory accounts (e.g., Newstead, Pollard, Evans, & Allen, 1992). I was well aware that I had not specified a mechanism for deduction with the analytic component of heuristic–analytic theory, and thought that the model account might provide a more plausible candidate than rule-based mental logics. However, my interest in model theory also led me to identify weaknesses and problems with it and to publish an attempt to reformulate the theory of propositional inference. I call this a decade of transition, however, because by 2000 the look of the field had changed enormously. To be sure model theory was still a significant paradigm, but by now it had powerful competitors. The changes that occurred were in part due to the continuing debate about rationality and in part due to the beginning of a shift away from studying deductive reasoning and towards recognition of the pragmatic nature of human reasoning. It was also the decade in which dual-process theory finally came of age.

One major development was the launch of the rational analysis programme of Oaksford and Chater, in the early 1990s, which had a substantial impact following their publication of an alternative account of choices on Wason's selection task (Oaksford & Chater, 1994). There are several key elements to this programme (for a history of its later development see Oaksford & Chater, 1998, 2007). Rational analysis (see also Anderson, 1990), as I understand it, presumes that human behaviour – by some combination of evolution and learning – will be well adapted to its environment. Hence, by analysing the nature of that environment and what is required to succeed within it, we can derive many clues as to the nature of human thought. There are clear links here with Marr's (1982) computational level of analysis as well as to earlier ecological approaches to vision and cognition (Brunswik, 1955; Gibson, 1979). From this perspective, it makes little sense to discover a psychology of reasoning and decision making littered with evidence of error and bias. Hence, authors of this persuasion are drawn towards one of Cohen's (1981) arguments – psychologists are seeing errors because they are using the wrong normative system.

Oaksford and Chater (1991) attacked logicism as a normative framework and started their pursuit of alternative normative accounts of various reasoning phenomena, in terms of probabilistic concepts. Choices on Wason's selection task were described as making sense in terms of expected information gain, in their first major paper of this kind (Oaksford & Chater, 1994). This was to be followed by an account of syllogistic reasoning in terms of probability heuristics (Chater & Oaksford, 1999) and of conditional inference in terms of conditional probability (Oaksford, Chater, & Larkin, 2000) and so on. This work has elements in common with my own. I have also rejected logicism as a normative framework (e.g., Evans, 2002) and later developed, with David Over, an account of conditionals in terms of probability logic (Evans & Over, 2004). But there are significant differences as well – they do not share my interest in dual-process theory, for example. Nor am I as attached as they are to the importance of normative theories. The Oaksford and Chater programme has, however, contributed substantially to a new ways of thinking about reasoning and rationality, and continues to be a major influence to the current day (Oaksford & Chater, 2007).

A major event in the 1990s was the re-launch of dual-process theory in the psychology of reasoning, this time to have a much wider impact. Two works, developed in parallel and independently, were published in 1996. Sloman (1996) argued the case of two systems of reasoning, one associative and one rule based. This was an explicitly parallel theory, in which Sloman argued that both systems had their say. He suggested that people often became aware of the conflict between the two systems when they proposed alternative answers, and might make a conscious effort to resolve this conflict. As with all dual-process theories in cognitive and social psychology, Sloman's account contrasted fast, automatic, and intuitive processes (Type 1) with those that are slow, reflective, and conscious (Type 2). The theory was also influential in social psychology, as Smith and DeCoster (2000) were later to apply a very similar framework in an attempt to integrate the many dual-process accounts of social cognition that feature in the literature.

If I read Sloman correctly, however, his theory was just intended to describe two forms of reasoning and not the mind as a whole. He also refrained from making wider claims about such matters as evolution and the nature of consciousness. Such claims were included in the two-systems approach of other authors, which also had implications for the architecture of the mind as a whole. Evans and Over (1996) developed such a dual-system approach, building partly on the earlier work on dual processes in the psychology of reasoning and partly on the ideas of Arthur Reber (1993), developed from his extensive studies of implicit and explicit learning. This idea was then further developed by Stanovich (1999, 2004) who introduced the now famous terms, System 1 and System 2. A key idea was that fast, System 1 processes led to contextualized reasoning and were responsible for a number of the intuitive errors and cognitive biases observed in the literature. System 2 – slow, explicit, rule-based reasoning – was, however, required for effective abstract reasoning with novel problems, and could be applied to inhibit and replace default intuitive responses. What Stanovich and his colleague West added particularly to the dual-process research programme, however, was the study of individual differences. They argued that the effectiveness of System 2, but not System 1 reasoning was subject to cognitive ability and conducted many empirical studies to support this claim.

A common feature between the Oaksford and Chater work and the dual-process developments was a focus on the problem of rationality in human reasoning. The massive evidence of cognitive bias accumulated from the 1970s onwards presented a paradox that a number of authors tried to resolve. Given the obvious success and intelligence of the human species, how come we make so many errors when our reasoning and decision making are tested in the laboratory? Earlier, I mentioned the three lines of argument used by Cohen (1981). One of these was that people are using the wrong normative system to judge the correctness of their participants' reasoning. This was the one developed by Oaksford and Chater who effectively replaced logic with normative accounts based on probability theory. Evans and Over (1996) attempted to separate instrumental from normative rationality which we termed rationality$_1$ and rationality$_2$ respectively. We argued that explicitly following normative rules was difficult and effortful, but that goals could often be achieved by following innate programming or associative learning, which operated at an implicit level. This led us to propose the dual-system theory for which the book is best known. However, we were careful to explain that the two forms of rationality could not simply be mapped one to one with the two forms of cognitive processing. For example, we stated (p. 147) that "We obviously cannot make an equation between rationality$_1$, as we have defined it, and successful type 1 implicit processes, or between rationality$_2$, and correct by some normative definition, type 2 explicit processes." Our readers were not so careful, however, and the two dualities sometimes blended into one when the book was cited.

Stanovich (1999) devoted a substantial part of his influential book to the discussion of rationality. He attacked authors like Cohen who always had a rational account for human judgements, labelling them as "Panglossian".[2] He attacked the alternative norms argument on the grounds that participants of higher cognitive ability could often provide normatively correct solutions according to *standard* normative accounts, while cognitive biases were much more prevalent in those of lower ability. He also developed an intriguing distinction between evolutionary and individual rationality, developed further in a later book (Stanovich, 2004). Here he argued that what is adaptive for the genes is not necessarily in the interests of us as individual persons. System 2, he suggested, was on a "long-leash" from the genes whose programming we may be able to escape. He entitled his 2004 book, *The Robot's Rebellion*, with the analogy that our selfish genes had built a robot vehicle (us) so intelligent, that it could escape the genes and think for itself.

In summary, the 1990s started with the mental model paradigm in firm command of the field. By the end of the decade the field looked very different. Model theory was still there, but we now had alternative research programmes of very different orientation. Authors were starting to abandon logic as any kind of normative framework for the study of human reasoning. Dual-process ideas that had been lurking the background since the 1970s, now emerged in the foreground and became the focus of much interest and the driving force behind now experimental research studies. The debate about rationality profoundly influenced these developments. The age of logicism in the psychology of reasoning was drawing to a close, although all the implications of this had yet to be understood.

2000+ – the shifting paradigm

At the International Conference on Thinking, held at Durham University in 2000, I was invited to give a keynote address, giving me an opportunity to address a very large proportion of the international research community in the psychology of reasoning. I entitled this talk "*Why study deduction? History and future of the paradigm*", although my colleague Simon Handley quickly dubbed it my "Deduction is dead" talk. In this presentation I outlined an argument that was to be more fully developed in a *Psychological Bulletin* paper published two years later (Evans, 2002). The essence of the argument can be summarized quite briefly. I focused on the deduction paradigm – the method most commonly used to study human reasoning, at least in the main tradition in which I have worked. The paradigm involves giving people the premises of an argument and asking them whether a conclusion follows logically from them. There are also two key components in the instructions given: (1) participants are told to assume the truth of the premises; and (2) to draw only conclusions that are logically necessary.

The question I raised was this: why are we continuing to use this paradigm to study human reasoning? I pointed out that the paradigm was born in the era of strong logicism, when psychologists like Piaget and philosophers like Popper were in their pomp. In the 1960s, logic was not only unchallenged as a normative account of human reasoning, but taken quite seriously by many as a descriptive account also. Wason's work attacked the latter but not the former assumption. But from the 1980s onwards, interest in experimental studies focused heavily on the influence of content and context effects. Using the deduction paradigm to study these, with its requirement to assume the truth of the premises, meant that any such effects were by definition, cognitive biases. What if normal, everyday reasoning was just naturally belief based? As we have also seen, by the end of the 1990s logicism was all but dead (or at least severely wounded) as a normative system. So why, I asked, 40 years on, was it still important to use the deduction paradigm to study reasoning? If logic is no longer a central concern, why ask our participants to assume premises and draw necessary conclusions?

In fact, the paradigm has been progressively shifting since 2000. Deductive reasoning instructions are still used in some studies, but pragmatic reasoning is being studied more in its own right, and researchers are exploring alternative methods. In particular, participants are being asked to make probabilistic judgements about conditional statements and their underlying beliefs (Evans, Handley, & Over, 2003a; Oberauer, Weidenfeld, & Fischer, 2007; Oberauer & Wilhelm, 2003; Over, Hadjichristidis, Evans, Handley, & Sloman, 2007) and the role of probabilistic belief relations in conditional inference has come under intensive study (De Neys, Schaeken, & d'Ydewalle, 2003; Verschueren, Schaeken, & d'Ydewalle, 2005; Weidenfeld, Oberauer, & Hornig, 2005). In general, researchers are much more interested now in how beliefs influenced reasoning than they are in studying logical competence with abstract reasoning tasks.

This decade has been marked by a major argument about the nature of conditional statements in ordinary language. Johnson-Laird and Byrne (2002) published a revised version of their theory of conditionals in *Psychological Review*. The theory defined the core meaning of a "basic" conditional in extensional terms. The statement "if p then q" allowed three possibilities: pq, ¬pq and ¬p¬q and excluded one: p¬q. Only the pq possibility is represented explicitly unless there is reason to "flesh-out" implicit not-q cases. This much was familiar, but the theory also added the principles of semantic and pragmatic modulation, which could affect the permitted possibilities or introduce relations between p and q. Shortly after this theory was published, I started work on a new theory of conditionals in collaboration with David Over and Simon Handley. We were particularly influenced by work in philosophical logic on the nature of "ordinary" conditionals, that is those used in everyday language, especially the writing of Dorothy Edgington (e.g., 1995, 2003). Whereas psychologists had traditionally adopted propositional logic as their normative system, together with the material conditional, it appeared that many philosophers had rejected the idea that the ordinary conditional could be material. Without going into the detail here, the essential reason is that the material conditional means the same as "either not-p or q" and this leads to paradoxical and unacceptable inferences.

In 2004, David Over and I published a detailed review and discussion of both the philosophical and psychological literatures on conditionals in the same book – the first time this had been attempted (Evans & Over, 2004). We focused our own account on the Ramsey test: a psychological hypothesis that had hitherto been discussed mostly in the philosophical literature. It was actually introduced to psychologists by Rips and Marcus (1977), but without lasting impact at that time. The essential idea is that a conditional statement invites supposition of the antecedent. We believe a conditional, to the extent that we believe q in a mental simulation of p. Just as Edgington (2003) was developing the implications of this suppositional notion of a conditional in her philosophical work, so Evans and Over (2004) developed the psychological aspects of it. We also realized that the suppositional conditional was at odds with the material conditional and the extensional definition of core semantics offered by Johnson-Laird and Byrne (2002), putting our theory into direct conflict with theirs. This led us to publish a detailed critique of the model theory (Evans, Over, & Handley, 2005) as well as series of experimental papers supporting our new theoretical account (Evans, Handley, Neilens, & Over, 2007; Evans et al., 2003a; Handley, Evans, & Thompson, 2006; Over et al., 2007). Supporters of the mental model theory in some cases challenged our arguments (Johnson-Laird, 2005; Schroyens & Schaeken, 2004) and in others attempted to reconcile the suppositional conditional with the mental model theory (Barrouillet, Gauffroy, & Lecas, 2008; but see Oberauer & Oaksford, 2008).

Experimental work on conditionals in recent years has led to a number of interesting findings. For example, there is now evidence to suggest that beliefs influence causal conditional inference in two different ways (Verschueren et al., 2005; Weidenfeld et al., 2005) – one associative, graded, or probabilistic and the other an all-or-none explicit method of reasoning about counterexamples. This gives us cause to rethink the notion that dual-process theory should necessarily distinguish contextualized Type 1 thinking from decontextualized Type 2 thinking, as both can be influenced by belief. In fact, it is a mistake to think of Type 2 reasoning as abstract and logical (Evans, 2007a, 2008). Another recent line of research with conditionals that suggests the same conclusion has been concerned with individual differences in cognitive capacity. Some studies, for example (Evans et al., 2007; Newstead, Handley, Harley, Wright, & Farelly, 2004), have shown that higher ability participants are no better (the data actually suggests *worse*) at drawing the valid modus tollens inference than those of lower ability, against the general run of findings that high-ability participants produce more normative solutions (Stanovich, 1999). In fact, the general assumption of an association between high ability, Type 2 reasoning and correct responses has been somewhat undermined recently. Stanovich and West (2008) have shown that a number of cognitive biases are quite independent of cognitive ability. I have pointed out (Evans, 2007b) that the evidence does not necessarily support the claim that high-ability people engage in more Type 2 reasoning. It may be just that the *quality* of such reasoning is better – and more likely to deliver the correct answer – when it is engaged.

The most recent years for me have been spent exploring the wider aspects of dual-process theory. I was fortunate enough to obtain a personal research fellowship from the Economic and Social Research Council in 2005, which effectively freed me from other duties for a full-time theoretical research project spread over three academic years. This project enabled me both to develop the narrower focus on dual-processing accounts of reasoning and judgement as well as a much broader overview of the subject. With regard to the former, I have reformulated the heuristic–analytic theory to incorporate principles of hypothetical thinking developed with my collaborators (Evans, Over, & Handley, 2003b) leading to publication of a theoretical paper and a book (Evans, 2006b, 2007a) developing hypothetical-thinking theory. There are some significant changes in the new account, which also incorporates the suppositional theory of conditionals as a particular application. One major change is that cognitive biases are as often explained by analytic (Type 2) processes as by heuristic (Type 1) processes.

On the broader front, my remit was to examine dual-process theories across cognitive and social psychology that have previously been little connected, as well as to assess the foundations of "dual-system" theory – that is, the idea that Type 1 and 2 thinking results from operation of Systems 1 and 2, with distinct evolutionary origins. I quickly found some serious concerns with the dual-system approach (Evans, 2006a) some of which were mentioned in my later review paper, relating social and cognitive theories together (Evans, 2008). In the end, I questioned many of the received views about Systems 1 and 2, including (1) the idea that System 2 is uniquely human and more recently evolved than System 1; (2) the view that all dual-process theories could be mapped into the two systems; (3) the distinction between conscious and nonconscious processing; and (4) the association between System 1 and biases, and between System 2 and correct reasoning. One development was to classify dual-process theories into two kinds that I called *parallel-competitive* (Sloman, 1996; Smith & DeCoster, 2000) and *default-interventionist* (Evans, 2006b; Kahneman & Frederick, 2002; Stanovich, 1999) respectively. In a recent publication (Evans, 2009), I have proposed a hybrid model that can incorporate both kinds of theory, as well as proposing the need to investigate Type 3 processes!

Conclusions and final thoughts

This brief and somewhat egocentric history of the psychology of reasoning reflects both how the field has developed over the past four decades, as well as the way my own work has changed and (I hope) progressed. Back in the 1960s, the field was concerned mostly with logic and discovering whether people could reason logically. This defined the deduction paradigm as the main instrument of study, something that has persisted well after theoretical developments undermined its original basis. Only quite recently have researchers turned to alternative methods, and many studies continue to use this traditional method. However, the past 40 years have seen a wealth of important psychological findings accrued, as well as a number of major theoretical developments. I can honestly say that the psychology of reasoning is a much more interesting field of study now than the one I joined around 1970. The range and complexity of issues studied have developed enormously, to the point where theorizing about dual processes and systems now seems to take in pretty much the whole mind.

The evolution of the field is also a testament to the nature of empirical science and the people who research it. The assumption around 1960 that reasoning was a logical or quasi-logical process was very reasonable given the thinking at the time. The problem was that the experimental evidence was always suggesting other things. First, errors and biases – relative to standard logic – were encountered in almost every published study, even though population groups of high intelligence were sampled. If logical reasoning was the basis of intelligence and rationality, how could this be? Next, it became transparently obvious that reasoning performance was highly dependent upon content and context. Sometimes these effects seemed to make reasoning "better" (e.g., the thematic selection task) and sometimes "worse" (e.g., belief bias). These judgements, of course, depended on using logic as a normative framework, something which soon came under close scrutiny. Cohen's (1981) paper opened a debate on human rationality that has substantially influenced the field to the present day. Some researchers persist in rooting their theories of reasoning in some kind of logical system, some use alternatives like probability theory, and still others (me included) are not that interested in normative theory at all.

Something I have not yet mentioned in this chapter is the advent of neuroscience. Over the past 10–15 years, there have been great advances in methods that enable us to relate brain function to cognitive processes and this field has become highly fashionable and well funded. Although limited in comparison with studies of memory and lower cognitive processes, there has been increasing interest in neural imaging studies of reasoning, albeit with fairly confusing and inconclusive results (Goel, 2008). Social neuroscience has rapidly become a large field of study, and has been specifically applied to the case for dual-process accounts of social cognition (Lieberman, 2007). While I am somewhat sceptical about the value of these methods, this is one growth industry that is bound to have profound effects on the psychology of reasoning in years to come.

Where will the field go from here? It would have been almost impossible to predict the developments over the past four decades, so I guess it would be foolish to try to anticipate even the next 10 years. I am, however, fairly confident that the syntactic and semantic theories of reasoning that dominated most of the past 40 years will be progressively replaced with theories couched at the pragmatic level. Instead of thinking of reasoning as some abstract process that is influenced by or interfered with by belief and knowledge, we need to turn that around. Our reasoning systems developed to deal with the content, context, and uncertainty that the real world provides. Once this is granted, we may need to recognize that there is perhaps no singular (or even dual) system of reasoning to be found at all. Reasoning may just be the emergent property of various cognitive subsystems that differ from task to task, like ad hoc committees. Certainly, the attempt to isolate one or more reasoning systems in the brain by neuroscience methods is getting nowhere fast at present. Every task seems to involve lots of brain areas, and no two studies report the same set being involved (Goel, 2008). In any event, there seems to be no clear basis for mapping neurological into cognitive systems.

For myself, while I am far from certain where the dual-process story is leading, we are some way off discovering the final chapter. There are lines of further enquiry that are definitely worth pursuing. My current focus is on the cognitive control problem. Why does some behaviour seem to be controlled by Type 1 processes and others by Type 2? How does this get decided in the brain? Is the mechanism for this entirely preconscious, or partially conscious? Is conscious thinking an illusion anyway? Is there any such thing as a conscious mind, and if not, can dual-system theory stand on other robust foundations? These questions should keep me occupied for a while.

Notes

1 Phil Johnson-Laird and I have some difference of view on this issue. He insists that (his) mental models can include relations and other epistemic elements, so that they are not necessarily truth verifiable. I agree that mental model theorists do sometimes introduce such elements, but my view is that they undermine the semantic principle of deduction in the process, thereby compromising the main strength of the theory. From recent email exchanges, I can say that Phil does not seem to agree with me on this point.
2 Pangloss was a fictional philosopher, portrayed by Voltaire in his satirical novel *Candide*, who was wont to remark that "all is for the best in the best of all possible worlds". The use of the term Panglossian to refer to enthusiastic rationalism in the academic literature seems to have originated with Gould and Lewontin (1979).

Dedication

I have worked with many collaborators and students over the years and am grateful to them all. However, I would like to dedicate this chapter to the three colleagues with whom I have enjoyed the most extensive and productive collaborations over my career: Steve Newstead, David Over and Simon Handley.

References

Anderson, J. R. (1990). *The adaptive character of thought*. Hillsdale, NJ: Lawrence Erlbaum Associates, Inc.

Barrouillet, P., Gauffroy, C., & Lecas, J. F. (2008). Mental models and the suppositional account of conditionals. *Psychological Review, 115*, 760–772.

Braine, M. D. S. (1978). On the relation between the natural logic of reasoning and standard logic. *Psychological Review, 85*, 1–21.

Braine, M. D. S., & O'Brien, D. P. (Eds.). (1998). *Mental logic*. Mahwah, NJ: Lawrence Erlbaum Associates, Inc.

Brunswik, E. (1955). Representative design and probabilistic theory in a functional psychology. *Psychological Review, 62*, 193–217.

Carruthers, P. (2009). How we know our own minds: The relationship between mindreading and metacognition. *Behavioral and Brain Sciences, 32*, 121–138.

Chater, N., & Oaksford, M. (1999). The probability heuristics model of syllogistic reasoning. *Cognitive Psychology, 38*, 191–258.

Cheng, P. W., & Holyoak, K. J. (1985). Pragmatic reasoning schemas. *Cognitive Psychology, 17*, 391–416.

Cheng, P. W., Holyoak, K. J., Nisbett, R. E., & Oliver, L. M. (1986). Pragmatic versus syntactic approaches to training deductive reasoning. *Cognitive Psychology, 18*, 293–328.

Cohen, L. J. (1981). Can human irrationality be experimentally demonstrated? *Behavioral and Brain Sciences, 4*, 317–370.

Cosmides, L. (1989). The logic of social exchange: Has natural selection shaped how humans reason? *Cognition, 31*, 187–276.

De Neys, W., Schaeken, W., & d'Ydewalle, G. (2003). Causal conditional reasoning and semantic memory retrieval: A test of the semantic memory framework. *European Journal of Cognitive Psychology, 15*, 161–176.

Edgington, D. (1995). On conditionals. *Mind, 104*, 235–329.

Edgington, D. (2003). What if? Questions about conditionals. *Mind & Language, 18*, 380–401.

Evans, J. St B. T. (1972a). Interpretation and matching bias in a reasoning task. *Quarterly Journal of Experimental Psychology, 24*, 193–199.

Evans, J. St B. T. (1972b). Reasoning with negatives. *British Journal of Psychology, 63*, 213–219.

Evans, J. St B. T. (1977). Toward a statistical theory of reasoning. *Quarterly Journal of Experimental Psychology, 29*, 297–306.

Evans, J. St B. T. (1982). *The psychology of deductive reasoning*. London: Routledge.

Evans, J. St B. T. (1984). Heuristic and analytic processes in reasoning. *British Journal of Psychology, 75*, 451–468.

Evans, J. St B. T. (1989). *Bias in human reasoning: Causes and consequences*. Hove, UK: Lawrence Erlbaum Associates Ltd.

Evans, J. St B. T. (1993). Bias and rationality. In K. I. Manktelow & D. E. Over (Eds.), *Rationality: Psychological and philosophical perspectives* (pp. 6–30). London: Routledge.

Evans, J. St B. T. (2002). Logic and human reasoning: An assessment of the deduction paradigm. *Psychological Bulletin, 128*, 978–996.

Evans, J. St B. T. (2005). *How to do research: A psychologist's guide*. Hove, UK: Psychology Press.

Evans, J. St B. T. (2006a). Dual system theories of cognition: Some issues. *Proceedings of the 28th Annual Meeting of the Cognitive Science Society, Vancouver*. Retrieved March 1, 2010, from http://csjarchive.cogsci.rpi.edu/Proceedings/2006/docs/p202.pdf

Evans, J. St B. T. (2006b). The heuristic–analytic theory of reasoning: Extension and evaluation. *Psychonomic Bulletin and Review, 13*, 378–395.

Evans, J. St B. T. (2007a). *Hypothetical thinking: Dual processes in reasoning and judgement*. Hove, UK: Psychology Press.

Evans, J. St B. T. (2007b). On the resolution of conflict in dual-process theories of reasoning. *Thinking & Reasoning, 13*, 321–329.

Evans, J. St B. T. (2008). Dual-processing accounts of reasoning, judgment and social cognition. *Annual Review of Psychology, 59*, 255–278.

Evans, J. St B. T. (2009). How many dual-process theories do we need: One, two or many? In J. St B. T. Evans & K. Frankish (Eds.), *In two minds: Dual processes and beyond* (pp. 33–54). Oxford: Oxford University Press.

Evans, J. St B. T., Barston, J. L., & Pollard, P. (1983). On the conflict between logic and belief in syllogistic reasoning. *Memory & Cognition, 11*, 295–306.

Evans, J. St B. T., & Dusoir, A. E. (1977). Proportionality and sample size as factors in intuitive statistical judgement. *Acta Psychologica, 41*, 129–137.

Evans, J. St B. T., Handley, S., Neilens, H., & Over, D. E. (2007). Thinking about conditionals: A study of individual differences. *Memory & Cognition, 35*, 1772–1784.

Evans, J. St B. T., Handley, S. J., & Over, D. E. (2003a). Conditionals and conditional probability. *Journal of Experimental Psychology: Learning, Memory and Cognition, 29*, 321–355.

Evans, J. St B. T., & Lynch, J. S. (1973). Matching bias in the selection task. *British Journal of Psychology, 64*, 391–397.

Evans, J. St B. T., & Over, D. E. (1996). *Rationality and reasoning*. Hove, UK: Psychology Press.

Evans, J. St B. T., & Over, D. E. (2004). *If*. Oxford: Oxford University Press.

Evans, J. St B. T., Over, D. E., & Handley, S. J. (2003b). A theory of hypothetical thinking. In D. Hardman & L. Maachi (Eds.), *Thinking: Psychological perspectives on reasoning, judgement and decision making* (pp. 3–22). Chichester, UK: Wiley.

Evans, J. St B. T., Over, D. E., & Handley, S. J. (2005). Supposition, extensionality and conditionals: A critique of Johnson-Laird & Byrne (2002). *Psychological Review, 112*, 1040–1052.

Gibson, J. J. (1979). *The ecological approach to visual perception*. Boston: Houghton Mifflin.

Goel, V. (2008). Anatomy of deductive reasoning. *Trends in Cognitive Sciences, 11*, 435–441.

Gould, S. J., & Lewontin, R. C. (1979). Spandrels of San Marco and the Panglossian paradigm – a critique of the adaptationist programme. *Proceedings of the Royal Society of London Series B – Biological Sciences, 205*, 581–598.

Griggs, R. A. (1983). The role of problem content in the selection task and in the THOG problem. In J. St B. T. Evans (Ed.), *Thinking and reasoning: Psychological approaches* (pp. 16–43). London: Routledge.

Griggs, R. A., & Cox, J. R. (1982). The elusive thematic materials effect in the Wason selection task. *British Journal of Psychology*, *73*, 407–420.

Handley, S., Evans, J. St B. T., & Thompson, V. A. (2006). The negated conditional: A litmus test for the suppositional conditional? *Journal of Experimental Psychology. Learning, Memory, and Cognition*, *32*, 559–569.

Henle, M. (1962). On the relation between logic and thinking. *Psychological Review*, *69*, 366–378.

Inhelder, B., & Piaget, J. (1958). *The growth of logical thinking*. New York: Basic Books.

Johnson-Laird, P. N. (1983). *Mental models*. Cambridge: Cambridge University Press.

Johnson-Laird, P. N. (2005). If bears eat in the woods . . .? *Trends in Cognitive Sciences*, *9*, 43–44.

Johnson-Laird, P. N., & Byrne, R. M. J. (1991). *Deduction*. Hove, UK: Lawrence Erlbaum Associates Ltd.

Johnson-Laird, P. N., & Byrne, R. M. J. (2002). Conditionals: A theory of meaning, pragmatics and inference. *Psychological Review*, *109*, 646–678.

Johnson-Laird, P. N., Legrenzi, P., & Legrenzi, M. S. (1972). Reasoning and a sense of reality. *British Journal of Psychology*, *63*, 395–400.

Kahneman, D., & Frederick, S. (2002). Representativeness revisited: Attribute substitution in intuitive judgement. In T. Gilovich, D. Griffin, & D. Kahneman (Eds.), *Heuristics and biases: The psychology of intuitive judgment* (pp. 49–81). Cambridge: Cambridge University Press.

Kahneman, D., & Tversky, A. (1972). Subjective probability: A judgment of representativeness. *Cognitive Psychology*, *3*, 430–454.

Kahneman, D., & Tversky, A. (1979). Prospect theory: An analysis of decision under risk. *Econometrica*, *47*, 263–291.

Klauer, K. C., Stahl, C., & Erdfelder, E. (2007). The abstract selection task: New data and an almost comprehensive model. *Journal of Experimental Psychology: Learning, Memory and Cognition*, *33*, 680–703.

Lieberman, M. D. (2007). Social cognitive neuroscience: A review of core processes. *Annual Review of Psychology*, *58*, 259–289.

Lucas, E. J., & Ball, L. J. (2005). Think-aloud protocols and the selection task: Evidence for relevance effects and rationalisation processes. *Thinking & Reasoning*, *11*, 35–66.

Manktelow, K. I., & Evans, J. St B. T. (1979). Facilitation of reasoning by realism: Effect or non-effect? *British Journal of Psychology*, *70*, 477–488.

Manktelow, K. I., & Over, D. E. (1991). Social roles and utilities in reasoning with deontic conditionals. *Cognition*, *39*, 85–105.

Marr, D. (1982). *Vision: A computational investigation into the human representation and processing of visual information*. San Francisco: Freeman.

Newstead, S. E., Handley, S. J., Harley, C., Wright, H., & Farelly, D. (2004). Individual differences in deductive reasoning. *Quarterly Journal of Experimental Psychology*, *57A*, 33–60.

Newstead, S. E., Pollard, P., Evans, J. St B. T., & Allen, J. L. (1992). The source of belief bias effects in syllogistic reasoning. *Cognition*, *45*, 257–284.

Nisbett, R. E., & Wilson, T. D. (1977). Telling more than we can know: Verbal reports on mental processes. *Psychological Review*, *84*, 231–295.

Oakhill, J., Johnson-Laird, P. N., & Garnham, A. (1989). Believability and syllogistic reasoning. *Cognition*, *31*, 117–140.

Oaksford, M., & Chater, N. (1991). Against logicist cognitive science. *Mind & Language, 6*, 1–38.

Oaksford, M., & Chater, N. (1994). A rational analysis of the selection task as optimal data selection. *Psychological Review, 101*, 608–631.

Oaksford, M., & Chater, N. (1998). *Rationality in an uncertain world.* Hove, UK: Psychology Press.

Oaksford, M., & Chater, N. (2007). *Bayesian rationality.* Oxford: Oxford University Press.

Oaksford, M., Chater, N., & Larkin, J. (2000). Probabilities and polarity biases in conditional inference. *Journal of Experimental Psychology: Learning, Memory and Cognition, 26*, 883–889.

Oberauer, K., & Oaksford, M. (2008). What must a psychological theory of reasoning explain? Comment on Barrouillet, Gauffroy, and Lecas (2008). *Psychological Review, 115*, 773–778.

Oberauer, K., Weidenfeld, A., & Fischer, K. (2007). What makes us believe a conditional? The role of covariation and causality. *Thinking & Reasoning, 13*, 340–369.

Oberauer, K., & Wilhelm, O. (2003). The meaning(s) of conditionals: Conditional probabilities, mental models and personal utilities. *Journal of Experimental Psychology: Learning, Memory and Cognition, 29*, 680–693.

Over, D. E., Hadjichristidis, C., Evans, J. St B. T., Handley, S. J., & Sloman, S. A. (2007). The probability of causal conditionals. *Cognitive Psychology, 54*, 62–97.

Peterson, C. R., & Beach, L. R. (1967). Man as an intuitive statistician. *Psychological Bulletin, 68*, 29–46.

Popper, K. R. (1959). *The logic of scientific discovery.* London: Hutchinson.

Reber, A. S. (1993). *Implicit learning and tacit knowledge.* Oxford: Oxford University Press.

Revlin, R., Leirer, V., Yopp, H., & Yopp, R. (1980). The belief bias effect in formal reasoning: The influence of knowledge on logic. *Memory & Cognition, 8*, 584–592.

Rips, L. J. (1983). Cognitive processes in propositional reasoning. *Psychological Review, 90*, 38–71.

Rips, L. J. (1994). *The psychology of proof.* Cambridge, MA: MIT Press.

Rips, L. J., & Marcus, S. L. (1977). Suppositions and the analysis of conditional sentences. In M. A. Just & P. A. Carpenter (Eds.), *Cognitive processes in comprehension* (pp. 185–219). New York: Wiley.

Schroyens, W., & Schaeken, W. (2004). Guilt by association: On Iffy propositions and the proper treatment of mental models theory. *Current Psychology Letters, 12.* Retrieved March 1, 2010, from http://cpl.revues.org/index411.html

Sells, S. B. (1936). The atmosphere effect: An experimental study of reasoning. *Archives of Psychology,* No. 316.

Sloman, S. A. (1996). The empirical case for two systems of reasoning. *Psychological Bulletin, 119*, 3–22.

Smith, E. R., & DeCoster, J. (2000). Dual-process models in social and cognitive psychology: Conceptual integration and links to underlying memory systems. *Personality and Social Psychology Review, 4*, 108–131.

Stanovich, K. E. (1999). *Who is rational? Studies of individual differences in reasoning.* Mahwah, NJ: Lawrence Elrbaum Associates, Inc.

Stanovich, K. E. (2004). *The robot's rebellion: Finding meaning the age of Darwin.* Chicago: Chicago University Press.

Stanovich, K. E., & West, R. F. (2008). On the relative independence of thinking biases and cognitive ability. *Journal of Personality and Social Psychology, 94,* 672–695.

Tversky, A., & Kahneman, D. (1973). Availability: A heuristic for judging frequency and probability. *Cognitive Psychology, 5,* 207–232.

Verschueren, N., Schaeken, W., & d'Ydewalle, G. (2005). A dual-process specification of causal conditional reasoning. *Thinking & Reasoning, 11,* 239–278.

Wason, P. C. (1960). On the failure to eliminate hypotheses in a conceptual task. *Quarterly Journal of Experimental Psychology, 12*–40.

Wason, P. C. (1966). Reasoning. In B. M. Foss (Ed.), *New horizons in psychology I* (pp. 106–137). Harmondsworth, UK: Penguin.

Wason, P. C., & Brooks, P. G. (1979). THOG: The anatomy of a problem. *Psychological Research, 41,* 79–90.

Wason, P. C., & Evans, J. St B. T. (1975). Dual processes in reasoning? *Cognition, 3,* 141–154.

Wason, P. C., & Green, D. (1984). Reasoning and mental representation. *Quarterly Journal of Experimental Psychology, 36A,* 597–610.

Wason, P. C., & Johnson-Laird, P. N. (Eds.). (1968). *Thinking and reasoning.* Harmondsworth, UK: Penguin.

Wason, P. C., & Johnson-Laird, P. N. (1972). *Psychology of reasoning: Structure and content.* London: Batsford.

Wason, P. C., & Shapiro, D. (1971). Natural and contrived experience in a reasoning problem. *Quarterly Journal of Experimental Psychology, 23,* 63–71.

Weidenfeld, A., Oberauer, K., & Hornig, R. (2005). Causal and noncausal conditionals: An integrated model of interpretation and reasoning. *Quarterly Journal of Experimental Psychology, 58,* 1479–1513.

Wetherick, N. E. (1962). Eliminative and enumerative behaviour in a conceptual task. *Quarterly Journal of Experimental Psychology, 14,* 246–249.

Wetherick, N. E. (1970). On the representativeness of some experiments in cognition. *Bulletin of the British Psychological Society, 23,* 213–214.

Wilkins, M. C. (1928). The effect of changed material on the ability to do formal syllogistic reasoning. *Archives of Psychology, 16,* No. 102.

Wilson, T. D. (2002). *Strangers to ourselves.* Cambridge, MA: Belknap Press.

Woodworth, R. S., & Sells, S. B. (1935). An atmosphere effect in syllogistic reasoning. *Journal of Experimental Psychology, 18,* 451–460.

Author index

Strict alphabetical ordering is used, e.g. d'Ydewalle appears under D, not Y; van der Henst under V, not H, etc.

Subject index